The Rise and Fall of the Soviet Union

The Rise and Fall of the Soviet Union provides a comprehensive overview of Soviet history. This edited collection of sources, drawn from contemporary accounts, official documents and recently released archive material, places the Soviet experience in comparative and historical context.

The Rise and Fall of the Soviet Union examines the internal politics of the USSR, including the emergence of Marxism-Leninism, the revolutions of 1917, Stalinism and the Great Terror. It also gives thematic coverage of the Soviet Union's role as a world power, including such major topics as the Second World War, the Cold War and the *glasnost* era. Richard Sakwa concludes this volume with a reassessment of the coup of August 1991, which ended in the collapse of the USSR.

Richard Sakwa is Professor of Russian and European Politics in the Department of Politics and International Relations at the University of Kent at Canterbury.

ROUTLEDGE SOURCES IN HISTORY
Series Editor
David Welch, University of Kent

The Rise and Fall of the Soviet Union 1917–1991

Richard Sakwa

London and New York

First published 1999
by Routledge
11 New Fetter Lane, London EC4P 4EE

Simultaneously published in the USA and Canada
by Routledge
29 West 35th Street, New York, NY 10001

Routledge is an imprint of the Taylor & Francis Group

© 1999 Richard Sakwa

Typeset in Galliard and Gill by Keystroke, Jacaranda Lodge, Wolverhampton
Printed and bound in Great Britain by TJ International Ltd, Padstow, Cornwall

British Library Cataloguing in Publication Data
A catalogue record for this book is available from the British Library

Library of Congress Cataloging in Publication Data
Sakwa, Richard
     The rise and fall of the Soviet Union, 1917–1991 / Richard Sakwa.
         p. cm. – (Routledge Sources in history)
     Includes bibliographical references and index.
     1. Soviet Union–History–Sources. I. Title. II. Series.
   DK266.S28   1999
   947.084—dc21 98-51322
                        CIP

ISBN 0–415–12289–9 (hbk)
ISBN 0–415–12290–2 (pbk)

To the memory of the victims of the rise and fall

Marble crumbles, steel rots like a leaf,
Gold rusts. Everything's ready to die.
The most durable things on earth are grief
And a single word, majestically high.

1945

Source: Anna Akhmatova, 'Quatrain Sequence (Selections)', *Poems*, selected and translated by Lyn Coffin, Introduction by Joseph Brodsky (New York, W. W. Norton & Co., 1983), p. 88

Contents

Series editor's preface

Sources in History is a new series responding to the continued shift of emphasis in the teaching of history in schools and universities towards the use of primary sources and the testing of historical skills. By using documentary evidence, the series is intended to reflect the skills historians have to master when challenged by problems of evidence, interpretation and presentation.

A distinctive feature of *Sources in History* will be the manner in which the content, style and significance of documents is analysed. The commentary and the sources are not discrete, but rather merge to become part of a continuous and integrated narrative. After reading each volume a student should be well versed in the historiographical problems which sources present. In short, the series aims to provide texts which will allow students to achieve facility in 'thinking historically' and place them in a stronger position to test their historical skills. Wherever possible the intention has been to retain the integrity of a document and not simply to present a 'gobbet', which can be misleading. Documentary evidence thus forces the student to confront a series of questions with which professional historians also have to grapple. Such questions can be summarised as follows:

1 *What* type of source is the document?
- Is it a written source or an oral or visual source?
- What, in your estimation, is its importance?
- Did it, for example, have an effect on events or the decision-making process?
2 *Who* wrote the document?
- A person, a group or a government?
- If it was a person, what was their position?
- What basic attitudes might have affected the nature of the information and language used?
3 *When* was the document written?
- The date, and even the time, might be significant.
- You may need to understand when the document was written in order to understand its context.
- Are there any special problems in understanding the document as contemporaries would have understood it?
4 *Why* was the document written?
- For what purpose(s) did the document come into existence, and for whom was it intended?

- Was the document 'author-initiated' or was it commissioned for somebody? If the document was ordered by someone, the author could possibly have 'tailored' his piece.
5 *What* was written?
- This is the obvious question, but never be afraid to state the obvious.
- Remember, it may prove more revealing to ask the question: what was *not* written?
- That is, read between the lines. In order to do this you will need to ask what other references (to persons, events, other documents, etc.) need to be explained before the document can be fully understood.

Sources in History is intended to reflect the individual voice of the volume author(s) with the aim of bringing the central themes of specific topics into sharper focus. Each volume will consist of an authoritative introduction to the topic; chapters will discuss the historical significance of the sources, and the final chapter will provide an up-to-date synthesis of the historiographical debate. Authors will also provide an annotated bibliography and suggestions for further reading. These books will become contributions to the historical debate in their own right.

In *The Rise and Fall of the Soviet Union*, Richard Sakwa provides a panoramic survey of the origins, development and fall of communism in the Soviet Union. This volume makes available some of the more important sources charting the main stages in the extraordinary experiment that we call Soviet communism. Some of this material has been translated into English for the first time. It will also provide new perspectives on many of the key issues in the Soviet experience. Professor Sakwa draws on not only political sources, but also on literary and memoir literature. The author cites some of the great poetic works to stand as testimony to the grandeur and terror of the Soviet epoch. While Professor Sakwa provides detailed commentaries, placing each source in context, he has sought to allow the documents to speak for themselves. The book will thus provide a valuable source of reference for some of the major documents of the period.

The Rise and Fall of the Soviet Union is a work of extraordinary scope and intensity written by one of the leading political historians of the Soviet Union. Richard Sakwa's text will become an indispensable source for historians and political scientists interested in charting one of the most important social experiments in the history of the twentieth century.

David Welch

Canterbury 1999

Glossary of Russian terms and abbreviations

Ban on factions	the banning in March 1921 of all horizontal contacts in the CPSU
Banderite	supporter of the militant Ukrainian nationalist Stepan Bandera
Bolshevik	the name claimed by the radicals following the split at the Second Congress of the RSDLP in 1903
CC	Central Committee
CCC	Central Control Commission
Cheka	All-Russian Commission for the Struggle Against Counter-Revolution, Sabotage and Speculation
CIS	Commonwealth of Independent States
commune democracy	a participatory and self-managing society
CP	Communist Party
CPSU	Communist Party of the Soviet Union
dictatorship of the proletariat	the rule of the working class unrestrained by law
First Secretary	see 'General Secretary'
General Secretary	the post established in 1922 that came to designate the head of the CPSU, known as First Secretary in the 1950s and up to 1964
glasnost	openness
Gosplan	State Planning Committee
GPU	Main Political Directorate (secret police)
Gulag	the system of labour camps, from the abbreviation GULag (Main Administration for the Camps)
Kadet	Constitutional Democratic Party
KGB	Committee of State Security
Kolkhoz	collective form
krai	territory
Kulaks	rich peasants, but usually used indiscriminately as a term of abuse for any peasant who got in the way of Bolshevik plans.

LSR	Left Socialist Revolutionary (the SR party split in late 1917, with the left SRs going on to become a separate party before the whole lot were banned by the Bolsheviks)
Menshevik	the label given to the moderate wing of the RSDLP after the split at the Second Congress in 1903
MGB	Ministry of State Security
MVD	Ministry of Internal Affairs
NEP	New Economic Policy
NKVD	People's Commissariat of Internal Affairs
oblast	region
OGPU	United Main Political Directorate (secret police)
okrug	district
perestroika	restructuring
podmena	substitutionism
raion	district
reform	the periodic attempt by the USSR to remedy its problems
RKP(b)	Russian Communist Party (Bolsheviks)
RSDLP	Russian Social Democratic Labour Party, established in 1898
RSFSR	Russian Soviet Federated Socialist Republic
soviet	council, first established in 1905
Sovnarkom	Council of People's Commissars, the name of the government Lenin established on seizing power in October 1917
SR	Socialist Revolutionary, a radical agrarian party
TsIK	see '(V)TsIK'
UkSSR	Ukrainian Soviet Socialist Republic
USSR	Union of Soviet Socialist Republics
VKP(b)	All-Union Communist Party (Bolsheviks)
(V)TsIK	(All-Russian and from 1924 All-Union) Central Executive

Acknowledgements

As usual in producing a work of this sort my debts are many and various. Philip Boobbyer and Ronnie Kowalski helped point me in roughly the right direction, and were generous in sharing their time and knowledge. As series editor David Welch was invariably supportive throughout the tortuous process that gave rise to this book. Heather McCallum's patience at Routledge was probably tested beyond reasonable limits, and I only hope that her forbearance was worth it in the end. It is with pleasure that I acknowledge the help that I received from Anna Miller in the Library and the Secretariat in the Department of Politics and International Relations at the University of Kent. The generous support of the Nuffield Foundation contributed to the completion of this project, as with so many others.

Permissions

The publishers and I are particularly grateful to Vladimir Kandelaki for permission to reproduce a section of the triptych 'House of Cards' for the cover, as well as to Janet Koridze for her kind assistance in this matter. Every effort has been made to trace the owners of copyright material. If copyright has been infringed it has been done so unintentionally. My gratitude, and that of the publishers, are owed to the following for permission to reproduce copyright material: Allen & Unwin for extracts from Bertrand Russell, *The Practice and Theory of Bolshevism* (London, 1920); Allison & Busby for an extract from Christian Rakovsky, *Selected Writings on Opposition in the USSR* (London, 1980); Anchor Press/Doubleday for extracts from *Kontinent* (New York, 1976); Aspekt Press for extracts from *Khrestomatiya po istorii Rossii 1917–1940* (Moscow, 1995); Bantam for extracts from George F. Kennan, *Memoirs 1950–63* (New York, 1969); Calder & Boyars Ltd for 'Babii Yar' from *Yevgeny Yevtushenko: Early Poems*, translated by George Reavey (London, 1989); Cambridge University Press for extracts from Michael Bakunin, *Statism and Anarchy*, translated and edited by Marshall S. Shatz (Cambridge, 1990), and Catherine Andreyev, *Vlasov and the Russian Liberation Movement: Soviet Reality and Emigré Theories* (Cambridge, 1987); Cassell and The Reprint Society for an extract from Winston Churchill, *The Second World War: The Gathering Storm* (London, 1948); Collins/Harvill for extracts from Alexander Solzhenitsyn, *Letter to Soviet Leaders*, translated by Hilary Sternberg (London, 1974), and Mikhail Gorbachev, *Perestroika:*

New Thinking for our Country and the World (London, 1987); *Current Digest of the Soviet Press* for various extracts; André Deutsch for extracts from Vladimir Bukovsky, *To Build a Castle: My Life as a Dissenter*, translated by Michael Scammell (London, 1978); Editions du Seuil for extracts from Leonid Plyushch, *History's Carnival: A Dissident's Autobiography* (London, Collins and Harvill Press, 1979); Fontana/Collins for extracts from Alexander Solzhenitsyn (ed.), *From Under the Rubble* (London, 1974); Victor Gollancz for extracts from Leon Trotsky, *The History of the Russian Revolution* (London, 1934), Valentine Kataev, *Forward, Oh Time!*, translated by Charles Malamuth (London, 1934), and Joseph E. Davies, *Mission to Moscow* (London, 1942); Robert Hale and Charles Scribner Publishers for extracts from Victor Kravchenko, *I Chose Freedom: The Personal and Political Life of a Soviet Official* (London, 1947); Hamish Hamilton for extracts from Richard Crossman (ed.), *The God That Failed: Six Studies in Communism* (London, 1950); Harcourt Brace for extracts from Milovan Djilas, *The New Class* (New York, Praeger, 1957); Harper Colophon Books for extracts from Andrei Amalrik, *Will the Soviet Union Survive until 1984?*, edited by Hilary Sternberg, revised and expanded edition (London, 1981); Harvester Wheatsheaf for extracts from Zoë Zajdlerowa, *The Dark Side of the Moon*, edited by John Coutouvidis and Thomas Lane (London, 1989); The Harvill Press for extracts from Vasily Grossman, *Life and Fate* (London, 1995); The Hoover Institution for extracts from R. H. McNeal (ed.), I. V. Stalin, *Works*, vol. 3 (16) (Stanford, 1967); Houghton Mifflin for extracts from Winston Churchill, *The Second World War: Triumph and Tragedy* (Boston, 1953); Hutchinson for extracts from Generalissimo Stalin, *War Speeches* (London, n.d.); Kraus International Publications for an extract from Ronnie Kowalski (ed.), *Kommunist: A Weekly Journal of Economic, Political and Social Opinion* (Millwood, New York, 1990); Lawrence & Wishart for extracts from Lenin, *Selected Works* (London, 1969); Longman for extracts from Sidney and Beatrice Webb, *The Truth About Soviet Russia* (London, 1942), Martin McCauley, *The Origins of the Cold War* (London, 1983), and Dan J. Jacobs, *From Marx to Mao and Marchais* (London, 1979); Macmillan Press Ltd for extracts from Kevin McDermott and Jeremy Agnew, *The Comintern: A History of International Communism from Lenin to Stalin* (Basingstoke and London, 1996), E. H. Carr, *The Interregnum* (London, 1954); Merlin Press for extracts from Georg Lukács, *History and Class Consciousness* (London, 1971); University of Michigan Press for extracts from Rosa Luxemburg, *Leninism or Marxism?* (Ann Arbor, 1961), and Rosa Luxemburg, *The Russian Revolution* (Ann Arbor, 1961); Monad Press for extracts from Ivan Dzyuba, *Internationalism or Russification? A Study in the Soviet Nationalities Problem* (New York, 1974), and George Saunders (ed.), *Samizdat: Voices of the Soviet Opposition* (New York, 1974); New Park Publications for extracts from *Documents of the 1923 Opposition* (London, 1975), Leon Trotsky, *The New Course*, annotated and translated by Max Shachtman (London, 1956), Leon Trotsky, *The Revolution Betrayed* (London, 1973), Leon Trotsky, *Terrorism and Communism: A Reply to Karl Kautsky* (London, 1975); W. W. Norton & Co. for extracts from Anna Akhmatova, *Poems*, selected and translated by Lyn Coffin, Introduction by Joseph Brodsky (New York, 1983), and

Stephen F. Cohen (ed.), *An End to Silence: Uncensored Opinion in the Soviet Union* (New York, 1982); Oxford University Press for extracts from Karl Marx and Frederick Engels, *The Communist Manifesto*, edited by David McLellan (Oxford, 1992), and Isaac Deutscher, *The Unfinished Revolution: Russia 1917–1967* (Oxford, 1967); Penguin Books for extracts from N. Bukharin and E. Preobrazhensky, *The ABC of Communism*, introduction by E. H. Carr (Harmondsworth, 1969), John Reed, *Ten Days That Shook the World* (Harmondsworth, 1966), Nadezhda Mandelshtam, *Hope Abandoned*, translated by Max Hayward (Harmondsworth, 1974), Milovan Djilas, *Conversations With Stalin* (Harmondsworth, 1969), Alexander Solzhenitsyn, *One Day in the Life of Ivan Denisovich* (Harmondsworth, 1963); Pergamon Press for extracts from Yu. V. Andropov, *Speeches and Writings*, 2nd edn (Oxford, 1983); University of Pittsburgh Press for extracts from Marshall S. Shatz, *Jan Waclaw Machajski: A Radical Critic of the Russian Intelligentsia and Socialism* (Pittsburgh, 1989); Pluto Press for extracts from *The Bolsheviks and the October Revolution: Minutes of the Central Committee of the Russian Social-Democratic Labour Party (Bolsheviks), August 1917–February 1918*, translated by Ann Bone (London, 1974), Alexander Berkman, *The Bolshevik Myth* (London, 1989), and Evgeny B. Pashukanis, *Law and Marxism: A General Theory: Towards a Critique of the Fundamental Juridical Concepts* (London, 1989); Praeger Publishers for extracts from Boris Nicolaevsky, *Power and the Soviet Elite* (New York, 1965); Princeton University Press for extracts from Paul Avrich, *Kronstadt 1921* (Princeton 1970); Radio Free Europe/Radio Liberty for extracts from *RFE/RL Research Report*; Rosspen for extracts from *Istoriya sovetskoi politicheskoi tsenzury: dokumenty i kommentarii* (Moscow, 1997); Routledge for extracts from *Late Marx and the Russian Road: Marx and 'the Peripheries of Capitalism'*, edited by Teodor Shanin (London, 1983); Selwyn and Blount Ltd for extracts from John Brown, *I Saw for Myself* (London, n.d.); Sheed & Ward for extracts from Nicholas Berdyaev, *The Russian Revolution* (London, 1931); Sinclair-Stevenson for extracts from Eduard Shevardnadze, *The Future Belongs to Freedom* (London, 1991); Spokesman Books for extracts from Mihailo Markovic and Robert S. Cohen, *The Rise and Fall of Socialist Humanism* (Nottingham, 1975), and Roy A. Medvedev, *On Socialist Democracy*, translated and edited by Ellen de Kadt (Nottingham, 1977); Stanford University Press for extracts from Robert Paul Browder and Alexander F. Kerensky (eds), *The Russian Provisional Government 1917: Documents*, vol. III (Stanford 1961), and from James Bunyan and H. H. Fisher, *The Bolshevik Revolution, 1917–1918* (Stanford, 1934); The University of Toronto Press for extracts from Carter Elwood (ed.), and R. H. McNeal (ed.), *Resolutions and Decisions of the CPSU* (Toronto, 1974); *A Documentary History of Communism*, vol. 1, *Communism in Russia*, vol. 2, *Communism and the World*, 2nd edn, edited by Robert V. Daniels © 1985 by the Trustees of the University of Vermont, reprinted by permission of the University Press of New England; YMCA-Press for extracts from *Nezavisimoe rabochee dvizhenie v 1918 godu: dokumenty i materialy*, edited by M. S. Bernshtam (Paris, 1981), and Nicolas Berdyaev, *The Origin of Russian Communism* (Michigan, Ann Arbor Paperback, 1960); Westview Press for extracts from Yegor Ligachev, *Inside*

Gorbachev's Kremlin (Boulder, 1996); Williams and Norgate for extracts from Paul Dukes, *Red Dusk and the Morrow: Adventures and Investigations in Red Russia* (London, 1923).

Introduction

The rise to power of the Bolsheviks in October 1917 represented one of the most important turning points of the twentieth century, while the fall of the regime to which it gave birth in August 1991 was an equally important defining moment in the development of the post-communist era. Between these two dates the Bolshevik Party, renamed the Communist Party in March 1918, ruled the largest country in the world, covering one-sixth of the world's land surface. The ideological challenge of revolutionary socialism after 1945 took the form of a geopolitical challenge for world mastery that was formalised in the conventions of the Cold War. For seventy-four years the Soviet Union represented an alternative form of social development, focusing above all on the attempt to implement some of the main ideas of Karl Marx on the development of an economy without markets or private property in the means of production. This was one of the grandest and most devastating social experiments in the history of humanity.

The attempt to reflect the great sweep of the rise and fall of the Union of Soviet Socialist Republics (USSR) in just a few hundred pages proved more challenging than appeared to be the case when work began on the book. No sooner is one theme pursued, than a hundred others demand their place on the page. Where does one start in tracing the origins of the system, in Russia itself or in Western Marxism? Given the need for conciseness I have focused on some contributions of Marx and above all Lenin to help trace the emergence of what later became known as Marxism-Leninism. The forging of a distinctively Leninist version of Marxism in struggle with numerous tendencies within Russia was clearly crucial in the development of the Russian system, and this element has been given considerable space.

In analysing the development of the system one of the most difficult questions was where to place commentaries in relation to basic documents and statements of the regime itself. Fairly early on it became clear that these materials fitted in best, broadly speaking, in chronological sequence. Thus, for example, Milovan Djilas's notion of a 'new class' was first published in the 1950s, and although the points he makes are of relevance for the entire period, his thinking at the same time represented something of the period itself, the disillusionment of one of the leaders of Yugoslav communism, and therefore it appeared best to present the material in the relevant chapter. Collecting all this sort of commentary material in a separate overview chapter at the end would have precisely drawn attention to the distinction between primary and secondary historical sources that might well have reduced the wholeness of the overall picture of the rise and fall of the USSR.

The biggest question, of course, was what to include and what to leave out. A dozen volumes of this size would only begin to provide a comprehensive survey of the relevant materials. Faced by constraints of space, I have focused on representative samples that provide a snapshot of a particular issue, allowing us to glimpse the thinking of an individual, the development of a debate or the working out of a problem. The sources have been selected to provide information and analyses about the Soviet system through which a theoretical appraisal of its rise and fall can be made. Together the material is intended to provide an overview of the central concerns of a period. Rather than providing many small pieces that might have provoked a rather disjointed perception, the main material is quoted at some length where necessary to allow the reader to savour the flavour of the original. My commentary is intended to provide no more than the context for the material and has thus been kept relatively short. The sources should speak for themselves.

Historical evidence, however, is not passive and no interpretation emerges fully-blown from the materials, and we as readers choose, order and question the sources. In this sense, these are not mere 'sources' but part of the dialogue of the ages between the actors themselves, the writings of historians, and the developing patterns of historical change of which we are part. The writing of history is a political act and the past is as much (and as little) a discursive construction as the present. The aim of this book is to allow the reader to enter into dialogue with the sources, and, indeed, to allow the sources to interrogate each other. This book proposes no grand theoretical reformulation, but it will provide sources that question existing theories and ideas about the Russian revolution and its fate. The focus will be on the originality of the Bolshevik attempt to overcome the division between state and society and to establish a new type of human and political community.

This collection of sources tries to place the Soviet experience in historical and comparative context. The book begins by examining the reasons for the success of the Bolsheviks both in terms of their own ideas and ideology, and also in the context of the accumulating failures of the Russian state before 1917. Chapter 3 examines the Bolshevik consolidation of power, the role of the Cheka (the secret police), the aims of the White movement, debates within the party and the sailors' revolt against Bolshevism in 1921 in Kronstadt. We then examine the establishment of the USSR in 1922 and the constitution of 1924, the NEP compromise, and then the emergence of Stalin and 'Stalinism', the revolution from above, the purges and the 'heroic' aspects of building socialism in one country. The grandiose aims of the Bolshevik experiment will be juxtaposed to the harsh realities of Soviet-type power.

Chapter 6 examines the war, and in broader terms examines the foreign policy of the Soviet state both before and after the war, as well as the Nazi–Soviet pact, Katyn, the annexation of the Baltic republics and Bessarabia, and the final victory with the 'Red Flag over Berlin'. The supreme achievement and mythological representations of the Great Patriotic War will be discussed. Out of this victory sprang the ultimate failure of the regime. The factors that had allowed the regime victory in the war threatened to undermine it with the onset of peace. In response Stalin once again after 1945 imposed his brand of dogmatic authority on the country and the parts of Eastern Europe under his control, and this played no small part in provoking the onset of the Cold War.

With Stalin's death in 1953 the regime faced fundamentally new challenges, above all overcoming the legacy of Stalin's terror itself, together with the modernisation of the country's political and economic institutions. While partially successful in the first task, Stalin's successors signally failed to come to terms with the second and third. A so-called neo-Stalinist 'contract' emerged whereby the regime implicitly promised to respect a sphere of personal autonomy and to guarantee rising standards of living as long as individuals made no political demands of the system. This was a recipe for stagnation, and by the late 1970s the system had broken down as standards of living began to decline and tensions accumulated in society and the polity. It was left to Gorbachev in the late 1980s to try a new model of reviving socialism in the USSR. His failure reflected the larger failure of the system; by 1991 the political system had dissolved and by the end of the year the USSR itself had disintegrated.

This book has been composed with the aim of allowing the reader to glimpse at least some of the pathos of the Soviet experience. If it does this, then it will have succeeded in its purpose.

Richard Sakwa
Canterbury, March 1998

Russia and the rise of Bolshevism |

The roots of Soviet communism lie both in Russia itself and abroad, in particular the development of the Marxist brand of revolutionary socialism. The last decades of the nineteenth century were marked by accumulating pressure for change countered by ever-increasing resistance to reform by the tsarist authorities. The legacy of serfdom and the unresolved problem of redemption payments, the growing social contradictions as an immiserated working class came into existence, and the blockage on reforms from above, all conspired to undermine chances for an evolutionary outcome to Russia's social and political crisis. The critical figure in the synthesis of Western revolutionary theory with the realities of Russia was Vladimir Il'ich Ul'yanov (Lenin). His views on the role of the party and other issues were challenged at every step, yet they ultimately triumphed not so much because they were 'right' in any absolute sense, but because of his leadership skills, the failure of the alternatives to win adequate support and the depth of Russia's crisis exacerbated by war.

Marx and the Russian Road

The question exercising a generation of radicals in late nineteenth-century Russia was whether the country could avoid following the Western path and instead use its own traditions, above all the peasant rural commune (*mir*, also called the *obshchina*) to move straight from feudalism (however decayed) to socialism. The Populists believed that Russia could avoid the misery of the Western developmental path and move straight into communism from feudalism without an intervening stage of capitalist exploitation. Reflecting these concerns and hopes, Vera Zasulich, a Populist who would later become a Menshevik, wrote to Marx asking him his opinion of the question.

Document 1.1   Vera Zasulich's Letter to Marx

16 Feb. 1881,
Genève,
Rue de Lausanne, no. 49,
L'imprimerie polonaise.

Honoured Citizen,

You are not unaware that your *Capital* enjoys great popularity in Russia. Although the edition has been confiscated, the few remaining copies are read and re-read by the mass of more or less educated people in our country; serious men are studying it. What you probably do not realise is the role which your *Capital* plays in our discussions on the agrarian question in Russia and our rural commune. You know better than anyone how urgent this question is in Russia. You know what Chernyshevskii thought of it. Our progressive literature – *Otechestvennye Zapiski*, for example – continues to develop his ideas. But in my view, it is a life-and-death question above all for our socialist party. In one way or another, even the personal fate of our revolutionary socialists depends upon your answer to the question. For there are only two possibilities. Either the rural commune, freed of exorbitant tax demands, payment to the nobility and arbitrary administration, is capable of developing in a socialist direction, that is, gradually organising its production and distribution on a collectivist basis. In that case, the revolutionary socialist must devote all his strength to the liberation and development of the commune.

If, however, the commune is destined to perish, all that remains for the socialist, as such, is more or less ill-founded calculations as to how many decades it will take for the Russian peasant's land to pass into the hands of the bourgeoisie, and how many centuries it will take for capitalism in Russia to reach something like the level of development already attained in Western Europe. Their task will then be to conduct propaganda solely among the urban workers, while these workers will be continually drowned in the peasant mass which, following the dissolution of the commune, will be thrown on to the streets of the large towns in search of a wage.

Nowadays, we often hear it said that the rural commune is an archaic form condemned to perish by history, scientific socialism and, in short, everything above debate. Those who preach such a view call themselves your disciples *par excellence*: 'Marksists'. Their strongest argument is often: 'Marx said so.'

'But how do you derive that from *Capital*?' others object. 'He does not discuss the agrarian question, and says nothing about Russia.'

'He would have said as much if he had discussed our country,' your disciples retort with perhaps a little too much temerity. So you will understand, Citizen, how interested we are in Your opinion. You would be doing us a very great favour if you were to set forth Your ideas on the possible fate of our rural commune, and on the theory that it is historically necessary for every country in the world to pass through all the phases of capitalist production.

In the name of my friends, I take the liberty to ask You, Citizen, to do us this favour.

If time does not allow you to set forth Your ideas in a fairly detailed manner, then at least be so kind as to do this in the form of a letter that you would allow us to translate and publish in Russia.

> With respectful greetings,
> Vera Zassoulich

Source: Teodor Shanin (ed.), Late Marx and the Russian Road: Marx and 'the Peripheries of Capitalism' *(London, Routledge & Kegan Paul, 1983), pp. 98–9.*

Document 1.2   Marx's Reply to Zasulich

Marx took up the challenge and prepared his answer carefully, rejecting four drafts before daring to send his reply, fully aware of the momentous nature of the question. Marx had towards the end of his life, indeed, learnt Russian to allow him to pursue the study of the agrarian question in a country that increasingly exercised his imagination.

> 8 March 1881
> 41, Maitland Park Road, London N.W.

Dear Citizen,

A nervous complaint which has periodically affected me for the last ten years has prevented me from answering sooner your letter of 16 February. I regret that I am unable to give you a concise account for publication of the question which you did me the honour of raising. Some months ago, I already promised a text on the same subject to the St. Petersburg Committee [of the People's Will organisation]. Still, I hope that a few lines will suffice to leave you in no doubt about the way in which my so-called theory has been misunderstood.

In analysing the genesis of capitalist production, I said:

> At the heart of the capitalist system is a complete separation of . . . the producer from the means of production . . . *the expropriation of the agricultural producer* is the basis of the whole process. Only in England has it been accomplished in a radical manner . . . *But all the other countries of Western Europe* are following the same course.
> (*Capital*, French edition, p. 315.)

The 'historical inevitability' of this course is therefore *expressly* restricted to the *countries of Western Europe*. The reason for this restriction is indicated in Ch. XXXII: '*Private property*, founded upon **personal** labour . . . is supplanted by capitalist private property, which rests on exploitation of the labour of others, on wage-labour.' (*Loc. cit.*, p. 340.)

In the Western case, then, *one form of private property is transformed into another form of private property*. In the case of the Russian peasants, however, *their communal property* would have to be *transformed into private property*.

The analysis in *Capital* therefore provides no reasons either for or against the vitality of the Russian commune. But the special study I have made of it, including a search for original source material, has convinced me that the commune is the fulcrum for social regeneration in Russia. But in order that it might function as such, the harmful influences assailing it on all sides must first be eliminated, and it must then be assured the normal conditions for spontaneous development.

> I have the honour, dear Citizen, to remain
> Yours sincerely,
> Karl Marx

Source: Shanin (ed.), Late Marx and the Russian Road, *pp. 123–4.*

Document 1.3   Later Thoughts

Marx's extremely guarded response was repeated in his preface of 21 January 1882 to the Russian edition of the *Communist Manifesto*, also prepared by Zasulich.

The Communist Manifesto had as its object the proclamation of the inevitably impending dissolution of modern bourgeois property. But in Russia we find, face to face with the rapidly developing capitalist swindle and bourgeois landed property, just beginning to develop, more than half the land owned in common by the peasants. Now the question is: can the Russian *obshchina*, though greatly undermined, yet a form of the primeval common ownership of land, pass directly to the higher form of communist common ownership? Or on the contrary, must it first pass through the same process of dissolution as constitutes the historical evolution of the West?

The only answer to that possible today is this: If the Russian revolution should become the signal for a proletarian revolution in the West also, so that both complement each other, then the present Russian common ownership of land may serve as the starting point for a communist development.

Source: Karl Marx and Frederick Engels, 'Preface to the Russian Edition of 1882', in Karl Marx and Frederick Engels, The Communist Manifesto, *edited by David McLellan (Oxford, Oxford University Press, 1992), p. 43.*

Zasulich herself, as a member of the Land and Liberty Populist faction, in 1878 shot and wounded General F. F. Trepov, the governor of St Petersburg. Hailed as a martyr to the democratic cause, she was acquitted by a sympathetic jury. This wave of terror culminated in the assassination of Alexander II on 1 March 1881, when the seventh attempt on his life succeeded in blowing up his carriage as he was driving through St Petersburg.

The Emergence of Bolshevism

Marxism had been gaining strength in Russia, and was adopted by a group of so-called 'Legal Marxists' to support the view that capitalism should develop in Russia before there could be any talk of a socialist alternative. Marx's *Capital* itself was published in Russia in 1872, its first foreign publication, fifteen years after it came out in England. It was only on 1–3 March 1898, however, that a group of nine men met in a founding 'congress' in Minsk to establish the Russian Social-Democratic Workers' Party (RSDWP).

Document 1.4 Manifesto of the Russian Social-Democratic Workers' Party (RSDWP)

The manifesto was drawn up by Peter Struve, a Legal Marxist who not long after repudiated Marxism altogether. The manifesto adapted Marxism to Russian circumstances and stressed the role that the working class would have to play.

The working class everywhere becomes more demanding the more it is given, and the Russian proletariat will do the same. In the past it has obtained something only when it *made the demand*, and in the future it will get only what it *demands* as well.

And what does the Russian working class not need? It is totally deprived of that which its foreign comrades enjoy freely and peacefully: a share in the state administration, freedom of speech and the press, freedom of assembly and of association – in a word, all the instruments and means with which the western European and American proletariat improve their position and at the same time battle for their ultimate liberation, against private property and capitalism – for socialism. Political liberty is as necessary to the Russian proletariat as clean air is for healthy breathing. It is the basic condition of its free development and of success in the struggle for partial improvements and final liberation.

But only the Russian proletariat *itself* can win the political liberty which it needs.

The further east one goes in Europe, the more cowardly, mean, and politically weak is the bourgeoisie, and the greater are the cultural and political tasks confronting the proletariat. The Russian working class must and will bear on its own sturdy shoulders the cause of winning political freedom. This is an essential, but only an initial step in discharging the great historical mission of the proletariat – creating a social order in which there will be no exploitation of man by man. The Russian proletariat will throw off the yoke of autocracy, and thus with greater energy will continue the struggle against capitalism and the bourgeoisie for the complete victory of socialism.

Source: 'Manifesto of the Russian Social Democratic Labour Party' (RSDLP)',
in Ralph Carter Elwood (ed.), Resolutions and Decisions of the Communist
Party of the Soviet Union, *vol. 1,* The Russian Social Democratic Labour
Party 1898–October 1917 *(Toronto, University of Toronto Press, 1974),*
p. 35.

The position stated in this extract is essential for understanding the evolution of Lenin's thinking later. While the working-class movement in Western Europe and America had a range of instruments to pursue its interests, the Russian movement had still to fight for basic political freedoms. The argument that the Russian bourgeoisie was less able and less interested in achieving for itself those freedoms that its counterpart in the West had achieved meant that the Russian working class had to fight not only for its own freedom but for the middle class as well. If that was the case, then why give up part of its achievement to allow the bourgeoisie to consolidate its rule over the proletariat? Thus the origins of Leninism lie in this analysis. By 1902 Lenin was ready to draw out the organisational consequences.

Document 1.5   Lenin – *What is to be Done?*

While Marx had allowed that it might be possible for Russia to skip stages, Lenin, on the basis of his studies of the agrarian situation in the 1890s in his *The Development of Capitalism in Russia* (written in 1896–9) and many other works on the agrarian question, insisted that capitalism had already destroyed the old communal economy and thus, he argued, this short cut into the future no longer existed. Lenin went into exile in 1900, joining some of the older Marxists, including Georgii Plekhanov (the 'father' of Russian Social Democracy), in Geneva. While working here on the RSDWP paper *Iskra* (*The Spark*) Lenin formulated what were to become the organisational principles of Russian communism based on the idea of a tightly organised party of professional revolutionaries. These ideas were developed in his *What Is To Be Done?*, a polemic against the 'Economists', Marxists (like the Legal Marxists) who assumed that the revolution would emerge spontaneously out of the development of a polarised class society and therefore focused on the economic struggle of workers and not on the establishment of a separate revolutionary organisation.

Without a revolutionary theory there can be no revolutionary movement. This thought cannot be insisted upon too strongly at a time when the fashionable preaching of opportunism goes hand in hand with a support for the narrowest forms of practical activity . . . Our party is only in process of formation, its features are only just becoming discernible, and it is yet far from having dealt with other trends of revolutionary thought, which threaten to divert the movement from the correct path . . . The national tasks of Russian Social Democracy are such as have never confronted any other socialist party in the world . . . *The role of vanguard fighter can be fulfilled only by a party that is guided by the most advanced theory . . .*

We said that *there could not be* Social-Democratic consciousness among the workers [in the Russian strikes of the 1890s]. That consciousness could only be brought to them from outside. The history of all countries shows that the working class, exclusively by its own effort, is capable of developing only trade union consciousness, i.e. a realisation of the necessity of joining together in unions, fighting against the employers, striving for adoption by the government of necessary labour legislation, etc. The doctrines of socialism, however, grew out of the philosophical, historical and economic theories that were elaborated by the educated representatives of the propertied classes, the intelligentsia. The founders of contemporary scientific socialism, Marx and Engels, by their social status themselves belonged to the bourgeois intelligentsia. Similarly, in Russia, the theoretical doctrines of Social Democracy arose entirely independently of the spontaneous growth of the labour movement; they arose as a natural and inevitable outcome of the development of ideas within the revolutionary socialist intelligentsia.

Since there can be no talk of an independent ideology being developed by the masses of the workers themselves in the process of their movement the *only* choice is: either bourgeois or socialist ideology. There is no middle course (for humanity has not created a 'third' ideology, and, moreover, in a society torn by class antagonisms there can never be a non-class or above-class ideology). Hence, to belittle socialist ideology *in any way, to turn away from it to the slightest degree* means to strengthen bourgeois ideology. There is a lot of talk about *spontaneity*, but the spontaneous development of the working-class movement leads to its becoming subordinated to bourgeois ideology, leads to its developing according to the programme of the *Credo* [of the Economistic Marxists, 1899], for the spontaneous working-class movement is trade unionism, . . . and trade unionism means the ideological enslavement of the workers by the bourgeoisie. Hence, our task, the task of Social Democracy, is to *combat spontaneity*, to divert the working-class movement from this spontaneous, trade unionist striving to come under the wing of the bourgeoisie, and to bring it under the wing of revolutionary Social Democracy . . .

Class political consciousness can be brought to the workers *only from outside*, that is, only from outside of the economic struggle, from outside of the sphere of relations between workers and employers. The sphere from which alone it is possible to obtain this knowledge is the sphere of relationships between *all* the classes and strata and the state and the government, the sphere of the relations between *all* the classes . . .

And thus I affirm: (1) that no revolutionary movement can be firm without a solid and authoritative organisation of leaders; (2) that the wider the masses spontaneously drawn into the struggle, acting as the basis of the movement and participating in it, all the more urgent is the necessity of such an organisation and all the more solid should that organisation be (because it is all the easier for demagogues to influence the undeveloped section of the masses); (3) that such an organisation should consist primarily of people who are professional revolutionaries; (4) that in an autocracy, the more that we *restrict* the membership of such an organisation to those who are professional revolutionaries and who received professional training in the art of struggle against the political police, the harder it will be to 'draw out' such an organisation . . .

Source: V. I. Lenin, Chto delat'? (What Is To Be Done?), Polnoe sobranie sochinenii, *5th edn (henceforth* PSS), *(Moscow, 1975–9), vol. 6, pp. 24, 25, 30, 39–40, 79, 124.*

Lenin's thinking on the role of a tight conspiratorial organisation of professional revolutionaries drew on the ideas of Louis Auguste Blanqui, the leader of French Utopian communism, who rejected action by a revolutionary party in favour of action by a secret handful of conspirators. In contrast to Lenin, however, Blanquists failed to take into account the specific historical moment when a successful uprising could take place and despised contact with the masses. In Russia Blanquist ideas were popularised by Sergei Nechaev, whose views were held in high regard by Lenin; both were consumed by a hatred for the upper classes and sought revenge for the people's sufferings. Nechaev's *Revolutionary Catechism* of 1869 established the principles of revolutionary professionalism based on ruthless discipline and dedication, shorn of all morality and compassion. These ideas were given greater focus by Petr Tkachev in the 1870s when he argued that the revolutionary vanguard should seize power and through dictatorship begin the construction of socialism. Influenced by Tkachev's ideas, the People's Will (*Narodnaya Volya*) group split away from Land and Liberty to carry out acts of terrorism, including the murder of the tsar. Lenin combined this Jacobin strain in Russian Populism with the intellectual vigour of Marxism.

Document 1.6 Lenin – *One Step Forward, Two Steps Backwards*

Many in the Social Democratic party were reluctant to accept Lenin's ideas, and matters came to a head at the second congress of the RSDWP, which first met in summer 1903 in Brussels and then, harassed by the Belgian police, moved to London. Yulius Martov argued for a broader and more representative movement, whereas Lenin insisted on a tighter and more exclusive organisation. In voting for membership of *Iskra*'s editorial board Lenin found himself in a temporary majority and thus took the label 'Bolshevik' (from the Russian *bol'shinstvo*, majority), leaving the minority (*menshinstvo*) with the inglorious moniker of 'Mensheviks'. From this fateful split in Russian social democracy emerged the two trends of evolutionary and revolutionary socialism. Lenin justified his views on the need for a 'hard' organisation, especially when contrasted with the softness of the intellectuals on display at the congress. Leninism as a distinct brand of revolutionary socialism was forged in constant struggle with other socialists perhaps more than in the fight against the autocracy. The militaristic tone in Bolshevik thinking is clearly in evidence here.

One step forward, two steps backwards – It happens in the lives of individuals, and it happens in the history of nations and in the development of parties . . . In its struggle for power the proletariat has no other weapon but organisation. Disunited by the rule of anarchic competition in the bourgeois world, ground down by forced labour for capital, constantly thrust back to the 'lower depths' of utter destitution, savagery and degeneration, the proletariat can become, and inevitably will become, an invincible force only when its ideological unification by the principles of Marxism is con-solidated by the material unity of an organisation which will forge millions of toilers into an army of the working class. Neither the decrepit rule of Russian autocracy, nor the senile rule of international capital will be able to withstand this army. Its ranks will become more and more consolidated, in spite of all zigzags and backward steps, in spite of the opportunist phrase-mongering of the Girondists of present-day Social Democracy, in spite of the smug praise of the outdated circle spirit [*krugovshchiny*], and in spite of the tinsel and fuss of *intelligentsia* anarchism.

Source: Lenin, Shag vpered, dva shaga nazad: krizis v nashei partii (One Step Forward, Two Steps Backward), *May 1904,* PSS, *vol. 8, pp. 403–4.*

Early Critics of Leninism

The criticism of Lenin's views about 'the party of a new type' was not restricted to the Russian movement alone. Rosa Luxemburg (1870–1919), born of Jewish parents in Russian-occupied Poland, became the most effective advocate of idealistic revolutionism – i.e., the view that one could be no less revolutionary even without faith in organisational centralisation. Until 1917 Trotsky, too, criticised the dangers of centralism in Lenin's views on party organisation. Born Lev Davidovich Bronstein in 1881 and assassinated by a Stalinist agent in Mexico on 21 August 1940, Trotsky quickly rose to the first rank among the Russian Social Democrats, remaining with the Mensheviks until 1917. On joining the Bolsheviks his ultra-radicalism was overshadowed by his commitment to the consolidation of the Bolshevik victory, advocating now the harshest possible discipline and centralisation. Only when his position in the leadership was threatened from 1923 (see pp. 156–62) did he return to his earlier radicalism.

Document 1.7   Luxemburg – *Leninism or Marxism?*

With remarkable percipience, Luxemburg in 1904 identified the tendencies that would later allow Stalinism to flourish. She dismissed Lenin's view that the revolution-ary organisation had to mimic the methods of the autocracy itself. Luxemburg's name is associated with the revolutionary socialist alternative to Leninism – what Paul Mattick (1978) called 'anti-Bolshevik communism'.

The obstacles offered to the socialist movement by the absence of democratic liberties are of relatively secondary importance. Even in Russia, the people's movement has succeeded in overcoming the barriers set up by the state . . . The problem there is how to create a Social Democratic movement at a time when the state is not yet in the hands of the bourgeoisie. This circumstance has an influence on agitation, on the manner of transplanting socialist doctrine to Russian soil. It also bears in a peculiar and direct way on the question of *party organization*. Under ordinary conditions – that is, where the political domination of the bourgeoisie has preceded the socialist movement – the bourgeoisie itself instills in the working class the rudiments of political solidarity . . . In Russia, however, the Social Democracy must make up by its own efforts an entire historic period . . .

One Step Forward, Two Steps Backwards, written by Lenin, an outstanding member of the *Iskra* group, is a methodical exposition of the ideas of the ultra-centralist tendency in the Russian movement. The viewpoint presented with incomparable vigor and logic in this book, is that of pitiless centralism. Laid down as principles are: 1. The necessity of selecting, and constituting as a separate corps, all the active revolutionists, as distinguished from the unorganized, though revolutionary, mass surrounding this elite . . . The Central Committee would be the only thinking element in the party. All other groupings would be its executive limbs . . . Here we have the second peculiarity of conspiratorial centralism – the absolute and blind submission of the party sections to the will of the center, and the extension of this authority to all parts of the organization . . .

But what has been the experience of the Russian socialist movement up to now? The most important and most fruitful changes in its tactical policy during the last ten years have not been the inventions of several leaders and even less so of any central organizational organs. They have always been the spontaneous product of the movement in ferment . . . It is the product of a series of great creative acts of the often spontaneous class struggle seeking its way forward . . .

The ultra-centralism asked by Lenin is full of the sterile spirit of the overseer. It is not a positive and creative spirit. *Lenin's concern is not so much to make the activity of the party more fruitful as to control the party – to narrow the movement rather than to develop it, to bind rather than to unify it . . .*

If we assume the viewpoint claimed as his own by Lenin and we fear the influence of intellectuals in the proletarian movement, we can conceive of no greater danger to the Russian party than Lenin's plan of organization. *Nothing will more surely enslave a young labor movement to an intellectual elite hungry for power than this bureaucratic strait jacket, which will immobilize the movement and turn it into an automaton manipulated by a Central Committee.* On the other hand, there is no more effective guarantee against opportunist intrigue and personal ambition than the independent revolutionary action of the proletariat, as a result of which the workers acquire the sense of political responsiblity and self-reliance . . . In Lenin's overanxious desire to establish the guardianship of an omniscient and omnipotent Central Committee in order to protect so promising and vigorous a labor movement against any misstep, we recognize the symptoms of the same subjectivism that has already played more than one trick on socialist thinking in Russia . . .

Let us speak plainly. Historically, the errors committed by a truly revolutionary movement are infinitely more fruitful than the infallibility of the cleverest Central Committee.

Source: Rosa Luxemburg, Leninism or Marxism?, *published in German under the original title of 'Organizational Questions of the Russian Social Democracy' (Ann Arbor, University of Michigan Press, 1961), pp. 81, 82, 84, 85, 91, 92, 94, 102, 107, 108.*

Document 1.7   Trotsky – *Our Political Tasks*

Responding to Lenin's *What Is To Be Done?* and his *One Step Forwards, Two Steps Back*, Trotsky's critique of August 1904 was truly perceptive, above all for its formulation of the concept of substitutionism.

We wish that our comrades would not overlook the difference of principle between the two methods of work . . . This difference, if we reduce it to its basis of principle, has decisive significance in determining the character of all the work of our party. In the one case we have the contriving of ideas for the proletariat, the political *substitution* for the proletariat; in the other, political *education* of the proletariat, its political mobilisation . . .

Poorly or well (more poorly) we are revolutionising the masses, arousing in them the simplest political instincts. But to the extent that this involves complicated tasks – the transformation of these 'instincts' into the conscious striving for the political self-determination of the working class – we resort in the broadest way to abbreviated and simplified methods of 'contriving' and 'substitution'.

In the internal politics of the party these methods lead, as we shall yet see, to this: the party organisation is substituted for the party, the Central Committee is substituted for the party organisation, and finally a 'dictator' is substituted for the Central Committee . . .

According to Lenin's new philosophy . . . it is enough for the proletarian to pass through the 'school of the factory' to be able to give lessons in *political discipline* to the intelligentsia, which has hitherto been playing the leading role in the party. According to this new philosophy, anyone who does not consider the ideal party 'as a vast factory', who thinks on the contrary that such a picture is 'monstrous', anyone who does not believe in the unlimited power of a machine to achieve political education, 'immediately exhibits the psychology of the bourgeois intellectual' . . .

Without fear of exhibiting the 'psychology of the bourgeois intellectual', we affirm above all that the conditions which propel the proletariat to collectively agreed-upon methods of struggle lie not in the factory but in the general social conditions of the proletariat's existence; we affirm, moreover, that between these *objective conditions and conscious discipline* of political action lies a long path of struggles, mistakes, education – not 'the school of the factory', but the school of political life . . .

Source: Leon Trotsky, 'Nashi politicheskie zadachi', in L. D. Trotskii, K istorii russkoi revolyutsii (Moscow, Izd-vo politicheskoi literatury, 1990), pp. 72, 73, 74–5.

In 1905 Trotsky's belief in the spontaneous ability of the working class to advance its interests appeared vindicated by the creation of *soviets* (councils), first in Moscow and then in St Petersburg. Trotsky became chairman of the latter and played a prominent part in the 1905 revolution.

1905 and Beyond

The shooting of a demonstration led by Father Gapon on 9 January 1905 ('Bloody Sunday') heralded over a year of revolutionary upheaval. Regardless of the theo-retical debates over organisation and consciousness, in practice the revolutionary parties played only a marginal role in the disturbances; the 'spontaneity' of worker self-organisation triumphed, as in the creation of the soviets later that year. The dilemma for the Russian Social Democrats was to find a role for the workers' party in what traditional Marxists assumed to be the 'bourgeois-democratic' revolution. Lenin finessed the problem by insisting that the Russian bourgeoisie was so pusillanimous and cowardly that the Russian working class would have to push through the 'bourgeois' revolution, in alliance with the land-hungry peasantry, establish a 'revolutionary democratic dictatorship of the proletariat and peasantry', and only then begin the move towards socialism.

Document 1.8   Lenin on the 1905 Revolution

The central issue for Lenin was whether the working class was to assume the role of the leader of the popular revolt against the autocracy, or whether it should content itself with taking a subordinate part. Written in the heat of the revolution in July 1905, Lenin's analysis represented a landmark in the development of Bolshevism.

In the final analysis force alone settles the great problems of political liberty and the class struggle, and it is our business to prepare and organise this force and to employ it actively, not only for defence but also for attack. The long reign of political reaction in Europe, which has lasted almost uninterruptedly since the days of the Paris Commune [1871], has made us too greatly accustomed to the idea that action can only proceed 'from below', has too greatly inured us to seeing only defensive struggles. We have now undoubtedly entered a new era – a period of political upheavals and revolutions has begun . . .

Those who really understand the role of the peasantry in a victorious Russian revolution would not dream of saying that the sweep of the revolution will be diminished if the bourgeoisie recoils from it. For, in actual fact, the Russian revolution will really assume its real sweep, and will really assume the widest revolutionary sweep possible in the epoch of bourgeois-democratic revolution, only when the bourgeoisie recoils from it and when the masses of the peasantry come out as active revolutionaries side by side with the proletariat. To be consistently carried through to its conclusion, our democratic revolution must rely on forces capable of paralysing the inevitable inconsistency of the bourgeoisie . . .

The proletariat must carry the democratic revolution to completion, by allying to itself the mass of the peasantry to crush by force the resistance of the autocracy and to counter the instability of the bourgeoisie. The proletariat must accomplish the socialist revolution, by allying to itself the mass of the semiproletarian elements of the population to crush by force the resistance of the bourgeoisie and to counter the instability of the peasantry and the petty bourgeoisie . . .

The democratic revolution is bourgeois in nature. The slogan of a general redistribution, or 'land and freedom' – that most widespread slogan of the peasant masses, dowtrodden and ignorant, yet passionately yearning for light and happiness – is a bourgeois slogan. But we Marxists should know that there is not, nor can there be, any other path to real freedom for the proletariat and the peasantry, than the path of bourgeois freedom and bourgeois progress. We must not forget that there is not, nor can there be at the present time, any other means of bringing socialism nearer, than complete political liberty, than a democratic republic, than the revolutionary-democratic dictatorship of the proletariat and the peasantry . . .

Revolutions are the locomotives of history, said Marx. Revolutions are festivals of the oppressed and the exploited. At no other time are the mass of the people in a position to come forward so actively as creators of a new social order, as at a time of revolution. At such times the people are capable of performing miracles, if judged by the limited, philistine yardstick of gradualist progress. But it is essential that leaders of the revolutionary parties, too, should advance their aims more comprehensively and boldly at such a time, so that their slogans shall always be in advance of the revolutionary initiative of the masses, serve as a beacon, reveal to them our democratic and social ideal in all its magnitude and splendour, and show them the shortest and most direct route to complete, absolute, and decisive victory.

Source: Lenin, 'Two Tactics of Social Democracy in the Democratic Revolution', June–July 1905, V. I. Lenin, Selected Works (London, Lawrence & Wishart, 1969), pp. 61–2, 117, 125, 125–6.

Document 1.9   Trotsky and 'Permanent Revolution'

Analysing a situation where it appeared that the proletariat could find itself precariously in power, Trotsky in 1906 argued that workers' power in Russia could only be consolidated by the revolution becoming an international phenomenon. The world revolution would then rescue Russian socialism from its underdevelopment. This was the genesis of Trotsky's concept of the continuous or 'permanent' revolution, a way of combining Russia's apparent readiness for revolution with the country's relative backwardness.

The revolution in Russia was unexpected for all, except for Social Democrats. Marxism long foretold the inevitability of the Russian revolution, which would break out as a result of the conflict between the forces of capitalist development and those of a stagnant absolutism . . . The Russian revolution has a completely original character as a result of the peculiarities of our entire social-historical development and which, in turn, opens up entirely new perspectives . . .

The Russian working class of 1906 differs entirely from the Vienna working class of 1848. The best proof of it is the all-Russian practice of the Councils of Workmen's Deputies (Soviets). Those are no organisations of conspirators prepared beforehand to step forward in times of unrest and to seize command over the working class. They are organs consciously created by the masses themselves to coordinate their revolutionary struggle. The Soviets, elected by and responsible to the masses, are thoroughly democratic institutions following the most determined class policy in the spirit of revolutionary socialism . . . .

Two main aspects of proletarian policy will encounter resistance from its [peasant] allies: that is its *collectivism and internationalism* . . .

Once power is in the hands of the revolutionary government with a socialist majority, then immediately the distinction between the minimum and maximum programme loses any theoretical or practical meaning . . . Once the party of the proletariat takes power, it will fight to retain it to the end . . .

The political supremacy of the proletariat is incompatible with its economic slavery. Whatever the banner under which the proletariat will find itself in possession of power, it will be forced to take the path of socialism. It is the greatest Utopia to think that the proletariat, brought to state supremacy by the mechanics of a bourgeois revolution, would be able, even if it wanted, to limit its mission with the establishment of a republican-democratic situation for the social supremacy of the bourgeoisie. The political dominance of the proletariat, even if temporary, would extremely weaken the resistance of capital, which always requires state support, and would give grandiose opportunities for the economic struggle of the proletariat . . . The distinction between the minimum and the maximum programme is eliminated as soon as the proletariat takes power . . .

How far, however, can the socialist policy of the working class advance in Russia's economic environment? One thing we can say with confidence: it will encounter political obstacles long before it can be stymied by the technical backwardness of the country. *Without direct political support of the European proletariat the working class of Russia will not be able to retain power and convert its temporary supremacy into an enduring socialist dictatorship.* This cannot be doubted for a moment. On the other hand, there is no doubt that a *socialist revolution in the West would allow us to convert the temporary supremacy of the working class directly into a socialist dictatorship* . . .

The influence of the Russian revolution on the proletariat of Europe is immense. Not only does it destroy Petersburg absolutism, the main force of European reaction; it also creates the necessary revolutionary preconditions and consciousness in the European proletariat.

Source: Leon Trotsky, 'Results and Prospects', in Trotskii, K istorii russkoi revolyutsii, pp. 101, 102, 104, 105–6, 108–9.

Document 1.10 Lenin on Party-mindedness in Literature

Faced with the abolition of censorship and emergence from illegality, the question of the relationship between the party and non-party press rose to the fore. Lenin was well aware that his notion of literature as part of the 'cog and the screw' of a single Social Democratic organisation would be controversial, yet none of his protestations about the 'lameness' of the comparison between art and industry addressed the core of the problem of his conception of the relationship between politics and culture.

The revolution is not yet completed. While tsarism is *no longer* strong enough to defeat the revolution, the revolution is *not yet* strong enough to defeat tsarism . . . the half-way revolution compels all of us to set to work at once organising the whole thing on new lines. Today literature, even that published 'legally', can be nine-tenths party literature. It must become party literature . . .

What is this principle of party literature? It is not simply that, for the socialist proletariat, literature cannot be a means of enriching individuals or groups: it cannot, in fact, be an individual undertaking, independent of the common cause of the proletariat. Down with non-partisan writers! Down with literary supermen! Literature must become *part* of the common cause of the proletariat, 'a cog and a screw' of one single great Social-Democratic mechanism set in motion by the entire politically conscious vanguard of the entire working class. Literature must become a component of organised, planned and integrated Social-Democratic Party work.

'All comparisons are lame', says a German proverb. So is my comparison of literature with a cog, of a living movement with a mechanism. And I daresay there will be hysterical intellectuals to raise a howl about such a comparison, which degrades, deadens, 'bureaucratises' the free battle of ideas, freedom of criticism, freedom of literary creation, etc., etc. Such outcries, in point of fact, would be nothing more than an expression of bourgeois-intellectual individualism.

Source: Lenin, 'Party Organisation and Party Literature', November 1905, Selected Works, pp. 148, 149.

Document 1.11   Lenin on 'Democratic Centralism'

There were many attempts to reconcile the Bolshevik and Menshevik wings of the RSDWP following the 1905 revolution, but all fell foul of Lenin's fight to preserve the Bolsheviks as a separate and independent organisation. Condemned for indiscipline, Lenin responded with the concept of 'democratic centralism', defending the rights of minorities within the framework of organisational unity. After 1917 democratic centralism became the core principle of Bolshevik discipline, and from 1921 factional activity was proscribed in its entirety.

The principle of democratic centralism and autonomy of local institutions means precisely *freedom of criticism*, complete and everywhere, as long as this does not undermine the unity of *action already decided upon* – and the intolerability of *any* criticism disrupting or impeding the *unity* of action decided on by the party.

Source: Lenin, 'Svoboda kritiki i edinstvo deistvii' ('Freedom of Criticism and Unity of Action'), May 1906, PSS, vol. 13, p. 129.

The 1905 revolution ushered in a period of 'constitutional monarchy'. A Constitution (Basic Law) was adopted in 1906 that began at least to temper the autocracy's divine right to rule, and in that year a new parliamentary system was introduced. Elections to the first State Duma, however, produced an oppositional majority, and it was dissolved in June 1906. The second Duma fared little better, lasting barely three months (March–June 1907). Only after the prime minister, Peter

Stolypin, devised an ingeniously indirect system of elections did the tsar, Nicholas II, receive the Duma he wanted, and the third Duma lasted out its full term (1907–12), while the fourth was dissolved by the February revolution in 1917. This was a period of rapid economic development accompanied by unresolved political problems.

The Intelligentsia and Revolution

In his *What Is To Be Done?* Lenin had gone beyond the standard Marxist formulations of the relationship between the working class and the intelligentsia. No longer was it a straightforward matter of those privileged with education articulating for workers, in a scientific form, the need for socialism (as criticised by Bakunin below); socialism itself was now cast as a product of the consciousness of the intelligentsia, and it was the duty thereafter for the revolutionary intelligentsia to instil it in the working class who would otherwise fail to understand the necessity of the revolutionary destruction of the existing order and its replacement by socialism. Although Lenin went on to argue in favour of creating a party of workers as well as *intelligenty*, these were to be workers sharing the intelligentsia's concept of socialism. Lenin's arguments represented the ideological expropriation of the working class, and prepared the way for their later political expropriation by the communist authorities. This was certainly the argument of Jan Wacław Machajski. If Bakunin was the Nemesis of Marx, Machajski was Lenin's.

Bolshevism was the most radical fulfilment of Enlightenment ideas about the perfectibility of man. Following the 1905 revolution a group including Anatoly Lunacharsky, the future Bolshevik cultural commissar, and Alexander Bogdanov (1873–1928), one of Lenin's closest associates in the early years of Russian Social Democracy, sought to portray revolutionary socialism as a new secular religion – hence they became known as 'God-builders'. Considering their views dangerous to his vision of dedicated revolutionism, they were condemned in forthright (if not theoretically very sound) terms by Lenin. Their views were also condemned by the *Vekhi* (Landmarks or Signposts) group, who published a collection of essays in 1909 repudiating revolutionism as a method and its false religiosity as a principle. Later we shall return to the views of one of the contributors to the volume, Nikolai Berdyaev.

The notion of the 'intelligentsia' is a distinctively Russian category. Emerging in the nineteenth century, they were a group of educated people who took upon themselves concern for the country's future. Usually bitterly divided among themselves, they were nevertheless united in their common struggle against what they perceived to be reaction. The notion of the 'intelligentsia' was therefore as much an ethical category as a cultural one. It was also a political category in that the intelligentsia often saw themselves as fulfilling the role of the missing political opposition to tsarism.

Document 1.12   Bakunin – *Statism and Anarchy*

The irony of a working-class movement led by non-workers was not lost on anyone after the publication of *The Communist Manifesto* in 1848, where the relationship between the revolutionary leadership and the proletariat was at best ambiguous. In his *Statism and Anarchy* in 1873 Michael Bakunin (1814–76) had stated the problem succinctly. It was just prior to this (1870–2) that Bakunin collaborated with Nechaev and may have contributed to the gruesome 'Catechism of a Revolutionary'.

This means that no state, however democratic its forms, not even the *reddest* political republic – a people's republic only in the sense of the lie known as popular representation – is capable of giving the people what they need: the free organization of their own interests from below upward, without any interference, tutelage, or coercion from above. That is because no state, not even the most republican and democratic, not even the pseudo-popular state contemplated by Marx, in essence represents anything but government of the masses from above downward, by an educated and thereby privileged minority which supposedly understands the real interests of the people better than the people themselves.

Source: Michael Bakunin, Statism and Anarchy, *translated and edited by Marshall S. Shatz (Cambridge, Cambridge University Press, 1990), p. 24.*

Document 1.13   Machajski – The Intelligentsia and Socialism

The arguments of the unjustly neglected Jan Waclaw Machajski (1866–1926) pre-figured later thinking about the role of the revolutionary socialist intelligentsia and the emergence of a 'new class'. A corruption of his name was the basis of the creed of *Makhaevshchina*, particularly strong in the early Bolshevik years, denoting un-reasoning hostility to the intelligentsia and with it contempt for technical specialists. Machajski drew on the anarchist critique of Marxism (particularly Bakunin's) and drew some radical conclusions about the class nature and aspirations of the intelligentsia. His arguments gave form to the pervasive anti-intelligentsia sentiments in Russia that lasted well into the Soviet period. The heart of his theory, as his biographer puts it, was that 'the intelligentsia was a rising new class of 'intellectual workers' using socialism to pursue its own interests at the expense of the workers' (Shatz, 1989, p. 36). While the Populists had placed their hopes on the peasantry, the Russian Social Democrats understood that the working class would make a better instrument to free itself from tsarism. Thus Makhaevism insisted 'that socialism embodied the interests not of the laboring classes whom it claimed to defend, but of the intelligentsia which had created it and propagated it' (ibid., p. 68).

Anyone who rebels, like the socialists, only because the degenerate, idle masters are no longer capable of governing, demands only new, more capable masters; he blazes the trail for these new masters and thus does not weaken but strengthens oppression. This is what results from all the activity of the socialists. They force the crude, ignorant *kulaks*, the puffed-up magnates, and the untalented governors to call on the whole learned world of masters for help, to admit the intelligentsia, educated society, to power . . .

The rights of ownership of the means of production pass into the hands of the state. The latter, in the guise of 'replacing' the ever-growing 'social constant capital', takes from the working class all the fruits of the increasing productivity of labour and hands them over to all the ranks of the army of 'intellectual workers' as a reward for their 'special talents and abilities'.

Source: Jan Waclaw Machajski, Burzhuaznaia revolyutsiia i rabochee delo (The Bourgeois Revolution and the Workers' Cause) *(St Petersburg, 1906);* Umstvennyi rabochii (The Intellectual Worker) *(Geneva, 1904), p. 13, Marshall S. Shatz,* Jan Waclaw Machajski: A Radical Critic of the Russian Intelligentsia and Socialism *(Pittsburgh, University of Pittsburgh Press, 1989), pp. 85, 87.*

Document 1.14 Bogdanov on Truth

After 1905 Bogdanov became leader of a group of radical idealists who refused to compromise the purity of their views by making use of the new opportunies, like involvement in the Duma (the parliament established in 1906). Bogdanov was a true polymath, mastering the fields of medicine, economics, sociology and, above all, philosophy, as well as writing futuristic fiction. His romantic revolutionism was always grounded in real-life problems, above all the relationship of the movement (the working class) and the revolutionary party (the Bolsheviks). Essentially, Bogdanov and his associates argued that a cultural and psychological transformation was required to accompany the economic revolution that was at the centre of Marxist theory. This cultural revolution in their view should precede or at least occur at the same time as the economic change so that the enlightened proletariat would understand and support such a transformation. Bogdanov warned that a premature political revolution that lacked a cultural foundation would inevitably have to rely on coercion to ensure compliance. Thus he stressed the importance of worker initiative and self-organisation in the drive for socialism, arguing that proletarian self-consciousness could be the basis of the new economic system. As a result, culture emerged as an autonomous as opposed to a residual category, a view that was taken further during the Proletcult (proletarian culture) movement during the Civil War. His advocacy of a party led by workers and of a revolution from below undermined Lenin's notion of a vanguard party directing the masses. 'Empiriocriticism' was devised by the Prague physicist Ernst Mach and the Zurich philosopher Richard Avenarius in an attempt to reconcile the epistemological challenge of modern science with the classic materialist worldview, stressing the source of knowledge in sensation and observation. In the extract Bogdanov applies this philosophy to the problem of consciousness and organisation. His view that truth is conditioned by classes and class struggle infuriated Lenin, who responded by trying to impose much tighter ideological uniformity on the party. Whether his response was to the philosophical postulates of Bogdanovism or to the challenge it posed to his theory of organisation remains a moot point. The debate echoed on through the early years of the Soviet regime until Stalin 'resolved' the issue.

Truth is an ideological form – the organising form of human experience; and if we know this without doubt, and know that the material basis of ideology changes, that the content of experience expands – do we have any right whatsoever to assert that this given ideological form will never be transformed by the development of its social basis, that this given form of experience will not be burst apart by its growing contents? Consistent Marxism does not allow such dogmatic and static notions . . .

Marxist philosophy must above all be one of natural science. Of course, natural science is the *ideology of the productive forces of society*, because it serves as the basis for technical experience and the technical sciences; in concordance with the basic idea of historical materialism, the productive forces of society represent the base of its development in general. But it is so clear that Marxist philosophy must reflect the *social form* of the productive forces, relying obviously on the 'social' sciences proper . . .

Ideological forms are the *organisational adaptation of social life*, and in the last analysis (directly or indirectly), of the *technical process*. Therefore the development of ideology is determined by *necessities* in the organisational adaptations of the social process and by the *material present* for them.

Source: Alexander A. Bogdanov, Empiriomonism *(St Petersburg, 1905–6), in R. V. Daniels (ed.),* A Documentary History of Communism, *vol. 1,* Communism in Russia *(London, I. B. Tauris, 1987), p. 35.*

Document 1.15   Lenin on Eternal Verities

Lenin wrote a polemical reply to Bogdanov that sharply revealed his limitations as a philosopher. Lenin insisted on the unquestionable truth in the works of Marx and Engels, dogmatically asserting a simplistic positivistic materialistic view of the world. For Lenin, like most orthodox Marxists, self-consciousness reflected the social order and was conditioned by it. Thus, in their view, once the revolution had destroyed the economic dominance of the bourgeoisie there would inevitably occur a cultural and psychological transformation of the workers. With the means of production in the hands of the workers, cultural transformation would occur naturally. Out of these apparently arcane philosophical debates (explained in detail by Sochor, 1988) emerged an intolerant and philistine social ideology.

Materialism, in full agreement with natural science, takes matter as primary and regards consciousness, thought and sensation as secondary, because in its well-defined form sensation is associated only with higher forms of matter (organic matter), while 'in the foundation of the structure of matter' one can only surmise the existence of a faculty akin to sensation . . . Machism holds to the opposite, the idealist point of view, and at once lands into an absurdity: since, in the first place, sensation is taken as primary, in spite of the fact that it is associated only with definite processes in matter organised in a definite way; and, since, in the second place, the basic premise that bodies are complexes of sensations is violated by the assumption of the existence of other living beings in general, of other 'complexes' beside the given great I . . . Bogdanov's denial of objective truth is agnosticism and subjectivism . . .

Source: Lenin, Materialism and Empirio-Criticism – Critical Comments on a Reactionary Philosophy, *1908, in Daniels,* Communism in Russia, *pp. 38–9.*

Document 1.16   The *Vekhi* Response – Struve

We have already noted the virulent strain of anti-intelligentsia sentiment reflected in Machajski's thinking, but 'Makhaevism' was no more than an acute symptom of the intelligentsia's own doubts about its role, racked by guilt over its own material and intellectual privileges. The *Vekhi* collection of 1909 represented a landmark in the intelligentsia's thinking about itself – 'Makhaevists from above', as one wit put it at the time (cited by Shatz, 1989, p. 143) – and marked the point when revolutionism as a form of social action began to be repudiated: the Russian intelligentsia had at last matured. The contributors took a searching look at the Russian intelligentsia and did not like what they saw: a narrow sectarianism combined with the uncritical adoption of the West European Enlightenment tradition in its emaciated nineteenth-century positivistic and atheistic form, advancing various forms of materialism and 'scientific communism' that rejected traditional spiritual values. One of the earliest Legal Marxists in Russia, Petr Struve had repudiated Marxism and the whole theory of revolutionary socialism. His discussion of the role of the intelligentsia in Russian society indeed was a landmark in Russian intellectual development.

The intelligentsia is a totally distinctive factor in Russian political development. Its historical significance arises from its attitude to both the idea and the reality of the state. The intelligentsia, as a political category, appeared in Russian history only during the era of reforms [1860s], and it became fully apparent in the revolution of 1905–7. Its intellectual foundations, however, date back to the 'remarkable era' of the [18]40s.

   In considering the intelligentsia as an ideological and political force in Russian historical evolution we can distinguish between a constant element, the stable *form*, as it were, and a more changeable element, its transitory *content*. The Russian intelligentsia's ideological form is its *dissociation*, its alienation from the state and hostility to it. This alienation in the intelligentsia's spiritual history emerges in two forms, absolute and relative. The absolute type appears as anarchism, the denial of the state and of any social order *per se* (Bakunin and Prince Kropotkin). Relative alienation appears in various forms of Russian revolutionary radicalism, and I have in mind here mainly the varieties of Russian socialism . . . In the above sense, Marxism and its teaching about class struggle and the state was, as it were, only the intensification and completion of the intelligentsia's alienation from the state.

Our definition of the intelligentsia's essence would be incomplete, however, if we limited ourselves to just this one aspect of its dissociation. The intelligentsia's alienation is not merely anti-state but atheistic as well. The intelligentsia denies the state and struggles against it, but it rejects the mystique of the state not for the sake of some other mystical or religious principle, but in the name of a rational, empirical one. This is the most profound philosophical and psychological contradiction burdening the intelligentsia. It denies the world in the name of the world, and thereby serves neither the world nor God . . . West European eighteenth-century positivism and rationalism is not so alien to the religious idea as nineteenth-century Russian positivism and rationalism with which our intelligentsia is so intoxicated . . .

It is suggested that the Russian intelligentsia's anarchism and socialism are a form of religion, and that precisely this maximalism reveals the presence of a religious principle. It is argued that anarchism and socialism are only a distinctive form of individualism, and like it aspire to the utmost fullness and beauty of individual life, and therein lies their religious content. The concept of religion behind all these and similar assertions is entirely formal and intellectually empty . . .

Religion cannot exist without the idea of God and the idea of personal achievement. Religious alienation from the state is entirely possible – Tolstoy is an example. But precisely because Tolstoy is religious, he is ideologically hostile both to socialism and to atheistic anarchism, and he stands outside the Russian intelligentsia . . . The fundamental philosophy of any religion, predicated not on fear but on love and reverence, is 'The Kingdom of God is within you'. For the religious mind, therefore, nothing can be more valuable and important than a person's individual self-perfection, which socialism disregards on principle. As a purely economic doctrine socialism does not contradict any religion, but neither is it in any way a religion itself. A religious person cannot believe in socialism . . . any more than he can believe in railways, radio or proportional representation.

Source: Petr Struve, 'Intelligentsiya i revolyutsiya' ('The Intelligentsia and Revolution'), Vekhi: sbornik statei o russkoi intelligentsii *(Moscow, 1909), pp. 159–60, 160–1, 162.*

Nationalism, Imperialism and the Great War

The twentieth century was dominated by nationalism and the wars associated with it. The Second International at its Basle congress in 1912 had vowed that the working class of the various countries would not go to war with each other. Luxemburg exemplified this spirit to the full, condemning nationalism and espousing the internationalism of the working-class movement. In August 1914 this promise was spectacularly betrayed, with social democratic parties everywhere (with the exception of the Serbian and Russian) placing nation above class and voting for war credits so that French workers could slaughter German workers, and vice versa. The Second International never recovered from this blow. For Lenin, however, the central issue was not so much the abstract patriotism of the workers as the economic basis to war. First, however, he had to deal with the aspirations to self-affirmation of the nations of the Russian empire itself. The Russian empire was a multinational state, dubbed by Marx 'the prison-house of peoples', with a population of 170 million in which ethnic Russians (the Great Russians) comprised some 75 million.

Document 1.17   Lenin on National Self-determination

In the first half of 1914 Lenin discussed the question of national minorities in Russia. While conceding the principle of national self-determination to undermine the tsarist system, he was not wholly comfortable with nationalism. Like all Marxist socialists (and liberals), he considered nationalism retrograde in comparison with the benefits of internationalism, a view identified in particular with Rosa Luxemburg who unequivocally placed class interests above those of nations. Lenin took issue with this extreme view, but qualified the right of minorities to independence by advocating the higher principle of proletarian internationalism.

As far as the theory of Marxism is concerned, the question of the right of self-determination presents no difficulty. No one can seriously dispute the London resolution [of the Socialist International] of 1896, or the fact that self-determination implies only the right to secede, or that the formation of independent national states is the tendency in all bourgeois-democratic revolutions.

The difficulty is to some extent created by the fact that in Russia the proletariat of both the oppressed and oppressor nations are fighting, and must fight, side by side. The task is to preserve the unity of the proletariat's class struggle for socialism, and to resist all bourgeois and Black Hundred [extreme right-wing] nationalist influences. Where the oppressed nations are concerned, the separate organisation of the proletariat as an independent party sometimes leads to such a bitter struggle against local nationalism that the perspective becomes distorted and the nationalism of the oppressor nation is lost sight of . . .

Even now, and probably for a fairly long time to come, proletarian democracy must reckon with the nationalism of the Great Russian peasants (not with the object of making concessions to it, but in order to combat it). The awakening of nationalism among the oppressed nations, which became so pronounced after 1905 (let us recall, say, the group of 'Federalist-Autonomists' in the first Duma, the growth of the Ukrainian movement, of the Muslim movement, etc.), will inevitably lead to greater nationalism among the Great Russian petty bourgeoisie in town and country. The slower the democratisation of Russia, the more persistent, brutal and bitter will be the national persecution and bickering among the bourgeoisie of the various nations. The particularly reactionary nature of the Russian Purishkeviches [Purishkevich was a reactionary politician] will simultaneously give rise to (and strengthen) 'separatist' tendencies among the various oppressed nationalities, which sometimes enjoy far greater freedom in the neighbouring states.

In this situation, the proletariat of Russia is faced with a twofold or, rather, with a two-sided task: to combat nationalism of every kind, above all Great Russian nationalism; to recognise, not only fully equal rights for all nations in general, but also equality of rights as regards polity, i.e., the right of nations to self-determination, to secession. And at the same time, it is their task, in the interests of a successful struggle against all and every kind of nationalism among all nations, to preserve the unity of the proletarian struggle and the proletarian organisations, amalgamating these organisations into a close-knit international association, despite bourgeois strivings for national exclusiveness.

Complete equality of rights for all nations; the right of nations to self-determination; the amalgamation of the workers of all nations – such is the national programme that Marxism, the experience of the whole world, and the experience of Russia, teach the workers.

Source: Lenin, 'O prave natsii na samoopredelenie' ('The Right of Nations to Self-determination'), February–May 1914, PSS, vol. 25, pp. 316–17, 318–20.

Document 1.18   Lenin – Socialism and Self-determination

Lenin returned to the question in the middle of the war, spurred on by disputes over the fate of the oppressed nations of the Central European empires, above all Poland.

The right of nations to self-determination implies exclusively the right to independence in the political sense, the right to free political separation from the oppressor nation. Specifically, this demand for political democracy implies complete freedom to agitate for secession and for a referendum for secession by the seceding nation. This, demand, therefore, is not the equivalent of a demand for separation, fragmentation and the formation of small states. It implies only a consistent expression of struggle against all national oppression. The closer a democratic state system is to complete freedom to secede the less frequent and less ardent will the desire for separation be in practice, because big states afford indisputable advantages, both from the standpoint of economic progress and from that of the interests of the masses and, furthermore, these advantages increase with the growth of capitalism. Recognition of self-determination is not synonymous with recognition of federation as a principle . . .

The aim of socialism is not only to end the division of mankind into tiny states and the isolation of nations in any form, it is not only to bring nations closer together but to integrate them. And it is precisely in order to achieve this aim that we must, on the one hand, explain to the masses the reactionary nature of Renner and Otto Bauer's idea of so-called 'cultural and national autonomy' and, on the other, demand the liberation of oppressed nations . . . the socialists of the oppressed nations must, in particular, defend and implement the full and unconditional unity, of the workers of the oppressed nation and those of the oppressor nation . . . The bourgeoisie of the oppressed nations persistently utilise the slogans of national liberation to deceive the workers . . .

Source: Lenin, 'The Socialist Revolution and the Right of Nations to Self-determination', January–February 1916, Selected Works, pp. 159, 160, 161.

Document 1.19 But Self-determination Did Not Mean Secession

In the same spirit at this time Lenin stressed that self-determination did not mean secession.

The right of self-determination of nations . . . is in no way equivalent to a demand for secession, subdivision and the formation of small states . . . The closer we are to a democratic government and the full freedom of secession, all the rarer and weaker will be the aspiration for secession in practice . . . The goal of socialism is not only the destruction of the splintering of mankind into small states and the isolation of nations, not only the bringing of nations together but even their fusion.

[A later note was even more forceful:]

The freedom of separation is the best and only *political* means against the idiotic system of small states and national isolation, which, fortunately for mankind, are inevitably destroyed through the entire development of capitalism.

Source: Lenin, 'Sotsialisticheskaya revolyutsiya i pravo natsii na samoopredelenie (tezisy)', PSS, vol. 27, pp. 255–6; and 'Zametka k tezisam', PSS, vol. 27, p. 457.

Self-determination for Lenin did not mean federalism, and it would only be after coming to power in 1917 that the Bolsheviks were forced to accept the principle. For Lenin socialism meant the creation of larger units and not the fragmentation of the world into small states. The Austrian Social Democrats Karl Renner and Otto Bauer in the 1890s had argued that in any given country people of the same nationality, irrespective of where they lived, should join together in an autonomous national union with jurisdiction over schools and other aspects of cultural life. Thus, there would be separate schools for each nationality, allowing the free development of separate languages and national traditions, but undermining the unity – from the Leninist perspective – of the working class.

Document 1.20   Lenin and the 'United States of Europe'

In this article Lenin discussed the problem of relations between those countries that made the socialist revolution, and those that did not. Lenin dismissed the radical idea of an international socialist federation as premature as long as some countries remained capitalist, noting that war would be likely between socialist and capitalist countries. The genesis of Stalin's notion of 'socialism in one country' lay here.

But while the slogan of a republican United States of Europe – if accompanied by the revolutionary overthrow of the three most reactionary monarchies, headed by Russia – is quite invulnerable as a political slogan, there still remains the highly important question of its economic content and significance. From the standpoint of the economic conditions of imperialism – i.e., the export of capital and the division of the world by the 'advanced' and 'civilised' colonial powers – a United States of Europe, under capitalism, is either impossible or reactionary . . .

Capital has become international and monopolist . . . A United States of Europe under capitalism is tantamount to an agreement on the partition of colonies . . .

A United States of the World (not of Europe alone) is the state form of the unification and freedom of nations which we associate with socialism – until the time when the complete victory of communism brings about the total disappearance of the state, including the democratic state. As a separate slogan, however, the slogan of a United States of the World would hardly be a correct one, first, because it merges with socialism; second, because it may be wrongly interpreted to mean that the victory of socialism in a single country is impossible; and it may also create misconceptions as to the relations of such a country to the others.

Uneven economic and political development is the absolute law of capitalism. Hence, the victory of socialism is possible first in several or even in one capitalist country alone. After expropriating the capitalists and organising their own socialist production, the victorious proletariat of that country will arise *against* the rest of the world – the capitalist world – attracting to its cause the oppressed classes of other countries, raising revolts in those countries against the capitalists, and in the case of need using even armed force against the exploiting classes and their states. The political form of society in which the proletariat is victorious in overthrowing the bourgeoisie will be a democratic republic, which will more and more centralise the forces of the proletariat of the given nation, or nations, in the struggle against the states that have not yet gone over to socialism. The abolition of classes is impossible without the dictatorship of the oppressed class, the proletariat. A free union of nations in socialism is impossible without a more or less prolonged and stubborn struggle of the socialist republics against the backward states.

Source: Lenin, 'The United States of Europe Slogan', 23 August 1915, Selected Works, pp. 153–4, 154, 155–6.

Document 1.21   Lenin on Imperialism

This is one of Lenin's most important works. Drawing freely on the work of liberals like John A. Hobson, whose *Imperialism* (published in 1902) argued that the excessive accumulation of goods and capital sought the coercive conquest of new markets, and the Austrian Marxist Rudolf Hilferding, whose *Finance Capital* in 1910 advanced the notion of the interpenetration of industrial and banking capital, Lenin forged the explosive theory that 'imperialism' was far more than colonialism, and indeed the very essence of the most advanced state of capitalism: the search for markets and colonies made war inevitable between advanced capitalist states. Already in 1913 Rosa Luxemburg in *The Accumulation of Capital* had argued that the concentration of capital encouraged colonial expansion leading to ever more forceful contradictions and intra-imperial rivalries that would lead to world revolution. This 'imperialist' definition of the capitalist world remained the dominant one until modified by Gorbachev in the late 1980s.

Preface to the French and German Editions, 6 July 1920

. . . [T]he main purpose of the book was, and remains, to present, on the basis of summarised returns of irrefutable bourgeois statistics, and the admissions of bourgeois scholars of all countries, a *composite picture* of the world capitalist system in its international relationships at the beginning of the twentieth century – on the eve of the first world imperialist war . . .

It is proved in the pamphlet that the war of 1914–18 was imperialist (that is, an annexationist, predatory, war of plunder) on the part of both sides; it was a war for the division of the world, for the partition and repartition of colonies and spheres of influence of finance capital . . .

Private property based on the labour of the small proprietor, free competition, democracy, all the catchwords with which the capitalists and their press deceive the workers and the peasants – are things of the distant past. Capitalism has grown into a world system of colonial oppression and of the financial strangulation of the overwhelming majority of the population of the world by a handful of 'advanced' countries. And this 'booty' is shared between two or three powerful world plunderers armed to the teeth (America, Great Britain, Japan), who are drawing the whole world into their war over the division of *their* booty . . .

Obviously, out of such enormous *superprofits* (since they are obtained over and above the profits which capitalists squeeze out of the workers of their 'own' country) it is *possible to bribe* the labour leaders and the upper stratum of the labour aristocracy. And that is just what the capitalists of the 'advanced' countries are doing: they are bribing them in a thousand different ways, direct and indirect, overt and covert.

This stratum of workers turned bourgeois, or the labour aristocracy, who are quite philistine in their way of life, in the size of their earnings and in their entire outlook, is the principal prop of the Second International, and in our days, the principal *social* (not military) *prop of the bourgeoisie*. For they are the real *agents of the bourgeoisie in the working-class movement*, the labour lieutenants of the capitalist class, real vehicles of reformism and chauvinism . . .

Monopolies, oligarchy, the striving for domination and not for freedom, the exploitation of an increasing number of small or weak nations by a handful of the richest or most powerful nations – all these have given birth to those distinctive characteristics of imperialism which compel us to define it as parasitic or decaying capitalism. More and more prominently there emerges, as one of the tendencies of imperialism, the creation of the 'rentier state', the usurer state, in which the bourgeoisie to an ever-increasing degree lives on the proceeds of capital exports and by 'clipping coupons'. It would be a mistake to believe that this tendency to decay precludes the rapid growth of capitalism. It does not. In the epoch of imperialism, certain branches of industry, certain strata of the bourgeoisie and certain countries betray, to a greater or lesser degree, now one and now another of these tendencies. On the whole, capitalism is growing far more rapidly than before; but this growth is not only becoming more and more uneven in general, its unevenness also manifests itself, in particular, in the decay of the countries which are richest in capital (England) . . .

When a big enterprise assumes gigantic proportions, and, on the basis of an exact computation of mass data, organises according to plan the supply of primary raw materials to the extent of two-thirds, or three-fourths of all that is necessary for tens of millions of people; when the raw materials are transported in a systematic and organised manner to the most suitable place of production, sometimes hundreds of thousands of miles; when a single centre directs all the consecutive stages of work right up to the manufacture of numerous varieties of finished articles; when these products are distributed according to a single plan among tens and hundreds of millions of consumers (the marketing of oil in America and Germany by the American 'oil trust') – then it becomes evident that we have socialisation of production, and not mere 'interlocking'; that private economic and private property relations constitute a shell which no longer fits its contents, a shell which must inevitably decay if its removal is artificially delayed, a shell which may remain in a state of decay for a fairly long period (if, at the worst, the cure of the opportunist abscess is protracted), but which will inevitably be removed . . .

Source: Lenin, 'Imperialism, the Highest Stage of Capitalism', January–June 1916, Selected Works, pp. 171, 172, 260, 262.

The theory was not entirely coherent, since many countries that lacked surplus capital also participated in colonial adventures; and a large proportion of British capital went to areas outside its direct control (in particular South America and the United States). More political, indeed psychological, factors help explain the upsurge of colonial rivalry in the age of the 'new imperialism' from the 1880s. In an essay on Lenin's imperialism ('The Sociology of Imperialism', 1918–19) Joseph Schumpeter described imperialism as an atavism, a holdover from the age of absolutism and not a necessary form for capitalism to take. Lenin's central argument, however, was clear: the concentration of capital in ever fewer hands in the domestic economy and the increased socialisation of labour prepared the way for the socialist organisation of the economy. The introduction of the notion of a 'labour aristocracy' bought off with the 'superprofits' of imperialism in the 1920 preface was a way of explaining the absence of revolution in the West, of why the Western proletariat had not followed the Russian example and overthrown their bourgeoisies.

Document 1.22   Bukharin on the Imperialist State

During the First World War Nikolai Bukharin (1888–1938) became increasingly alarmed about the monstrous powers of the modern militarised state. His arguments were first outlined in his *Imperialism and World Economy* in 1915, and summarised in 1916 in the article extracted below. From this perspective he led a 'left-Bolshevik' group that argued for the total revolutionary destruction of the modern state to avoid the development of the Leviathan of 'state capitalism'. While for Lenin the concentration of capital in the form of 'state monopoly capitalism' prepared the way for socialism, for Bukharin this was a nightmare vision. The war (imperialist) organisation of capitalism for Lenin represented a model of the socialist economy, but for Bukharin it was a ghastly subversion of the socialist principle of self-managed socialism.

Even the most superficial glance at social-economic life reveals the colossal growth of the economic significance of the state. This is reflected above all in the growth of the *state budget*. The complicated apparatus of contemporary state organisation requires enormous expenses which increase with astonishing swiftness . . .

The greatest role in this increase of the budget is undoubtedly played by militarism, one of the aspects of *imperialist* politics, which in turn stems necessarily from the structure of *finance capitalism*. But not only militarism in the narrow sense of the word. The cause of this is the growing intervention of state power in all branches of social life, beginning with the sphere of production and ending with the higher forms of ideological creativity. If the pre-imperialist period – the period of liberalism, which was the political expression of industrial capitalism – was characterised by the non-interference of state power, and the formula *laissez-faire* was a symbol of the belief of the ruling circles of the bourgeoisie, who allowed the 'free play of economic forces', our time is characterised by the directly opposite tendency, which has as its logical conclusion state capitalism, sucking everything into the arena of state regulation . . .

State power thus sucks in almost all branches of production; it not only preserves the general conditions of the process of exploitation; the state becomes more and more a direct exploiter, which organises and directs production as a collective, composite capitalist . . . The anarchic commodity market is to a significant degree replaced by the organised distribution of output, in which state power is again the supreme authority . . .

In war socialism [*Kriegssozialismus*, the highly militarised German war economy] class contradictions are not only not eliminated, but are brought to their maximum intensity. In the ideal type of the imperialist state the process of exploitation is not obscured by any secondary forms; the state casts off the mask of a supraclass institution which treats everyone equally. This fact is a basic fact, and it completely refutes the arguments of the renegades [i.e., the pro-war Social Democrats]. For socialism is the regulation of production directed by society, not by the state (state socialism is like soft-boiled boots); it is the annihilation of class contradictions, not their intensification. The regulation of production by itself does not mean socialism at all; it exists in any sort of economy, in any slave-owning group with a natural economy. What awaits us in the immediate future is in fact *state capitalism* . . .

The general pattern of the state's development is as follows. At first the state is the only organisation of the dominant class. Then other organisations arise, whose numbers are especially increased in the epoch of finance capitalism, and the state is transformed from the only organisation of the dominant class into one of its organisations which exist simultaneously – an organisation which is distinguished by its most general character. Finally the third stage arrives, *when the state absorbs these organisations and again becomes the only overall organisation of the dominant class, with a technical division* of labour within it; the formerly independent organisational groupings are transformed into divisions of a gigantic state mechanism, which descends with crushing force upon the obvious and internal enemy. Thus arises the final type of the contemporary imperialist bandit state, the iron organisation which with its grasping, prehensile claws seizes the living body of society. It is a new Leviathan, in the face of which the fantasy of Thomas Hobbes seems like child's play . . .

Source: Nikolai Bukharin, 'K teorii imperialisticheskogo gosudarstva' ('On the Theory of the Imperialist State'), 1916, Revolyutsiya prava: sbornik pervi (Moscow, 1925), pp. 5–32.

2 | 1917: From revolution to revolution

The overthrow of tsarism in February 1917* was long anticipated but unexpected when it came. A Provisional Government was established under Prince Lvov that appeared to open the way for Russia's 'bourgeois' democratic development. The Bolshevik party in Russia was confused over the stance to take, with most of the leadership (including Stalin) favouring cooperation with the government as long as it sought an end to the war. On his return Lenin took a sharply critical stance, insisting that the 'bourgeois' revolution could be transformed into a socialist one, but only if certain conditions were met. The Provisional Government staggered from crisis to crisis until finally overthrown in October.

Revolution and War

The Provisional Government, dominated at first by liberals and in particular the Constitutional Democratic Party headed by Pavel Milyukov, had to share power with the newly recreated soviets of workers' and soldiers' deputies, organised by all the self-styled 'democratic' parties (the Mensheviks, Bolsheviks and Socialist Revolutionaries – the last known as the SRs, being the party established in 1902 as the successor to the Populists). Lenin dubbed the relationship between the two sources of authority 'dual power'. The soviets came to symbolise for Lenin the kernel of an alternative form of state organisation – if only the Bolsheviks could win dominance in them, something achieved on the eve of the October revolution.

Document 2.1 Order No. 1

The central issue was control over the armed forces, and this resolution undermined the new government's authority over the armed forces. If control over the coercive apparatus is one of Max Weber's basic defining features of a state, then according to this criterion the Provisional Government was an incomplete state in 1917.

---

* March in the new style (Gregorian) calendar that came into effect on 1 (14) February 1918. In 1917 Russia's Julian calendar was 13 days behind the rest of Europe. In this chapter old-style dates are used, and when necessary new style dates are given in brackets after the old-style dates.

The Soviet of Workers' and Soldiers' Deputies resolves:

1 In all companies, battalions, regiments, depots, artillery positions, cavalry regiments, other military service units and on the ships of the navy immediately to elect committees of selected representatives of the lower ranks of the above-mentioned military units.

2 In all military units that have not yet elected their representatives to the Soviet of Workers' Deputies, elect one representative from companies, who are to appear with written credentials in the State Duma building by 10 a.m. on 2 March.

3 In all of their political actions military units are subordinate to the Soviet of Workers' and Soldiers' Deputies and their committees.

4 Orders of the Military Commission of the State Duma must be obeyed, except when they contradict orders and decisions of the Soviet of Workers' and Soldiers' Deputies.

5 All types of arms like rifles, machine-guns, armoured vehicles and others must be at the disposal and under the supervision of company and battalion committees and in no case to be given to officers even when they ask for them.

6 In line units and in fulfilling military duties soldiers must observe strict discipline, but outside service and line duties in their political, civic and private lives soldiers cannot in the slightest manner be deprived of those rights which are enjoyed by any citizen. In particular, standing at the front and the compulsory saluting on leave is abolished.

7 Equally, the use of titles for officers is abolished: your excellency, highness, etc. are replaced by Mr General, Mr Colonel, and so on.

Rude behaviour to soldiers of whatever military rank is forbidden, in particular the use of the familiar 'you', and any infringement of this [is forbidden], and in the event of any misunderstandings between officers and soldiers, the latter are obliged to inform the company committees.

Source: Izvestiya Petrogradskogo Soveta rabochikh i soldatskikh deputatov, *2 March 1917.*

Document 2.2   Lenin's 'April Theses'

Lenin returned to Russia in a 'sealed carriage' across Germany – 'the bacillus of revolution' as the German High Command considered him. Arriving in Petrograd on the evening of 3 April, he immediately condemned the conciliatory attitude adopted by Stalin and Lev Kamenev towards the other socialist parties. Lenin, who had been working on these ideas in Switzerland, denounced any compromises with the new democratic government and insisted on the continuation of the revolution. Note in particular the theoretical statement in the second thesis.

1 In our attitude towards the war not the slightest concession must be made to 'revolutionary defencism', for under the new government of Lvov and co., owing to the capitalist nature of this government, the war on Russia's part remains a predatory imperialist war.

The class-conscious proletariat may give its consent to a revolutionary war actually justifying revolutionary defencism, only on condition (a) that all power be transferred to the proletariat and its ally, the poorest section of the peasantry; (b) that all annexations be renounced in deeds, not merely in words; (c) that there be a complete break, in practice, with all interests of capital.

In view of the undoubted honesty of the mass of rank and file representatives of revolutionary defencism who accept the war only as a necessity and not as a means of conquest, in view of their being deceived by the bourgeoisie, it is necessary most thoroughly, persistently, patiently to explain to them their error, to explain the inseparable connection between capital and the imperialist war, to prove that without the overthrow of capital it is *impossible* to conclude the war with a really democratic, non-oppressive peace.

This view is to be widely propagated among the army units in the field. Fraternisation.

2 The peculiarity of the present situation in Russia is that it represents a *transition* from the first stage of the revolution, which, because of the inadequate organisation and insufficient class-consciousness of the proletariat, led to the assumption of power by the bourgeoisie, to its second stage which is to place power in the hands of the proletariat and the poorest strata of the peasantry.

This transition is characterised, on the one hand, by a maximum of legality (Russia is now the freest of all the belligerent countries of the world); on the other, by the absence of oppression of the masses, and, finally, by the trustingly ignorant attitude of the masses toward the capitalist government, the worst enemy of peace and socialism.

This peculiar situation demands of us an ability to adapt ourselves to the specific conditions of party work amid vast masses of the proletariat just awakened to political life.

3 No support to the Provisional Government; exposure of the utter falsity of all its promises, particularly those relating to the renunciation of annexations. Unmasking, instead of admitting, the illusion-breeding 'demand' that *this* government, a government of capitalists, cease being imperialistic.

4 Recognition of the fact that in most of the Soviets of Workers' Deputies our party constitutes a minority, and a small one at that, in the face of the *bloc* of all the petty-bourgeois opportunist elements, from the People's Socialists, Socialist-Revolutionists, down to the Organisation Committee (Chkheidze, Tsereteli, etc., Steklov, etc.), who have yielded to the influence of the bourgeoisie and have been extending this influence to the proletariat as well.

It must be explained to the masses that the Soviet of Workers' Deputies is the only possible form of revolutionary government and that, therefore, our task is, while this government is submitting to the influence of the bourgeoisie, to present a patient, systematic, and persistent analysis of its errors and tactics, an analysis especially adapted to the practical needs of the masses.

While we are in the minority, we carry on the work of criticism and of exposing errors, advocating throughout the necessity of transferring the entire power of state to the Soviets of Workers' Deputies, so that the masses might learn from experience how to rid themselves of errors.

5 Not a parliamentary republic – a return to it from the Soviet of Workers' Deputies would be a step backward – but a republic of Soviets of Workers' and Poor Peasants' Deputies throughout the land, from top to bottom.

Abolition of the police, the army, the bureaucracy. (Substituting for the standing army the universal arming of the people.)

All officers to be elected and to be subject to recall at any time, their salaries not to exceed the average wage of a competent worker.

6 In the agrarian programme, the emphasis must be shifted to the Soviets of Poor Peasants' Deputies.

Confiscation of all private lands.

Nationalisation of all lands in the country, and management of such lands by local Soviets of Poor Peasants' Deputies. A separate organisation of the Soviets of Deputies of Poor Peasants. Creation of model agricultural establishments out of large estates (from one hundred to three hundred *desiatinas* [one *desyatina* equals 2.7 acres or just over one hectare], in accordance with local and other conditions and with the estimates of local institutions) under the control of the Soviet of Poor Peasants' Deputies, and at public expense.

7 Immediate merger of all the banks in the country into one general national bank, over which the Soviet of Workers' Deputies should have control.

Source: Lenin, 'The Tasks of the Proletariat in the Present Revolution' ('April Theses'), Pravda, 7 April 1917; Robert Paul Browder and Alexander F. Kerensky (eds), The Russian Provisional Government 1917: Documents, *vol. III (Stanford, Stanford University Press, 1961), pp. 1206–7.*

The Bolsheviks were by no means united over policy and Lenin was forced to wage a vigorous struggle to have his view accepted. The April Theses sharply rejected as outmoded the orthodox social democratic advocacy (to which the Mensheviks remained loyal) of a two-stage revolution: the 'bourgeois' revolution had to be completed before socialism could be considered. Lenin insisted that a socialist revolution was on the agenda in Russia on the grounds that (1) alliance with the peasantry would give the working class strength to overthrow the old system and (2) the theory of imperialism saw the revolution as only the first step in the world revolution, which would then come to the assistance of backward Russia. The first all-Russian conference of Bolsheviks (7–12 May 1917) adopted, though against considerable opposition, Lenin's views on the transfer of power to the soviets, the immediate giving of land to the peasants, workers' control in industry and the end of the war by spreading the revolution. The Bolshevik slogan of 'Bread, Peace, Land' accurately reflected popular aspirations at this time.

Policy towards the war became the defining issue of the months between February and October. In a note in April 1917 to the Allies the foreign minister, Milyukov, pledged that Russia would fight until 'decisive victory'. This was misjudged, to say the least, and aroused a storm of protest and a government reshuffle. The Provisional Government considered the February revolution a protest against the inept conduct of the war by the tsarist regime and not directed against the war itself. Milyukov's note led to the fall of the government and the creation of the first coalition government, still under Lvov, which lasted from May to July. The new government included liberals and socialists, with the SR Alexander Kerensky as minister of war. The moderate socialists took a 'defencist' position in the war: insisting on the defence of Russian territory but rejecting any annexations or indemnities from the defeated powers. In June, under pressure from the French to divert German forces from the hard-pressed Western Front, Kerensky launched an ill-fated offensive in Galicia, hoping to take advantage of the expected revolutionary enthusiasm. On 15 July tensions between the moderate socialists and the bourgeois parties led to the resignation of Lvov and four Kadet (Constitutional Democratic Party) ministers and a second coalition government was formed headed by Kerensky.

The sheer scale of Russia's commitment to the war on the side of the Entente powers is sometimes forgotten. In 1917 15,798,000 people, about half of all those able to work, were servicing military needs of one sort or another, while the active army on 1 September 1917 comprised 7,060,700 men, some 45 per cent of those mobilised. Military losses were 775,400 killed, 348,000 wounded and 3,343,900 prisoners (*Svobodnaya mysl'*, no. 9, 1997, p. 102). The endless requisitions and the economic disruption of the regions along the front undermined the whole economy, provoking inflation that hit the poor particularly hard. The official Russian war aims were to destroy Germany's armed might, to incorporate the lower reaches of the River Neman, Galicia, part of Silesia and, later (as mentioned in Milyukov's note), Turkish Armenia and Constantinople and its environs. These were hardly tasks to inspire great enthusiasm among the masses, especially when offensives were launched prematurely to relieve the pressure on the Western Front – twice Paris was saved by Russia's enormously costly efforts in the East. Even this was not enough for the Entente powers (in particular France), endlessly pressurising Russia through official and informal channels to make yet more sacrifices. In this sense, it can be argued that the Russian revolution was made in Paris.

Document 2.3 Lenin and the Imperialist War

Lenin understood that war weariness was at the root of the revolution and Bolshevik anti-war agitation found a receptive audience. For Lenin, the war, irrespective of whether it was fought by the tsar or by democrats, was a manifestation of capitalist imperialism. He continued to call for international war to be converted into class war, believing that only an international proletarian revolution could put an end to the bloodletting.

The war is not a product of the evil will of rapacious capitalists although it is undoubtedly being fought *only* in their interests and they alone are being enriched by it. The war is a product of half a century of development of world capital and of its billions of threads and connections. It is *impossible* to escape from the imperialist war at a bound, it is *impossible* to achieve a democratic, non-coercive peace without overthrowing the power of capital and transferring state power to *another* class, the proletariat.

The Russian revolution of February–March 1917 was the beginning of the conversion of the imperialist war into a civil war. This revolution took the *first* step towards ending the war; but it requires a *second* step, namely, the transfer of state power to the proletariat, to make the end of the war a *certainty*. This will be the beginning of a 'breach in the front' on a world-wide scale, a breach in the front of the interests of capital; and only after having broken through *this* front *can* the proletariat save humanity from the horrors of war and endow it with the blessings of a durable peace.

It is directly to such a 'breach in the front' of capital that the Russian revolution has already brought the Russian proletariat by creating the Soviets of Workers' Deputies . . .

Source: Lenin, 'The Tasks of the Proletariat in Our Revolution: Draft of a Platform for the Proletarian Party', Pravda, 30 April (13 May) 1917.

Policy Issues and the Way Ahead

The Provisional Government found itself overwhelmed by urgent domestic problems. In three areas in particular the government's response was found wanting: the nationality question, the agrarian crisis, and industrial relations.

The immediate reason for the fall of Lvov's government in July 1917 was the violent disagreement over nationality policy. A number of countries took advantage of the weakness of central authority to break away. Finland declared itself independent, and the Ukrainians set up their own government in the form of the Rada. It was disagreement over recognising the autonomy of the Ukraine that led to the fall of the Lvov government. Muslim national movements developed rapidly in the course of 1917, while in the Caucasus the foundations were laid of an independent Georgia and Armenia. Nationalist demands within a multinational empire, in which Russians made up barely half of the population, were to remain a constant source of tensions for the Provisional Government and its successor.

From May 1917 soldiers left the fronts to participate in what was increasingly a spontaneous wave of land seizure. The peasant communes in conjunction with the newly elected district committees became the effective rulers of the countryside. Victor Chernov, head of the SR party and now also minister of agriculture, was in a unique position to implement his party's land programme. This called for the socialisation of land, its transfer to the peasant communes to be distributed equally for personal use, and the banning of the hire of paid labour. However, wary of encouraging further desertions from the army by peasants eager to take part in land redistribution and intimidated by the complexity of land reform, the government made the fatal mistake of refusing to implement this programme in its entirety until sanctioned by the Constituent Assembly. The government thereby failed to gain the support of the peasantry, who ultimately simply took the land.

In industry workers began to organise factory committees to defend themselves and to keep the factories open in the face of economic disruption and lock-outs. The movement for workers' *kontrol'* (the Russian word means 'supervision' rather than, control, in the English sense) represented a revolution within the revolution. The Bolsheviks supported the workers' revolution in 1917 as long as it was directed against the employers and the Provisional Government, but in 1918 (as we shall see) in effect disowned the movement for self-management and imposed a more centralised system. In October 1917, however, the Bolsheviks appeared to be the only party offering a viable economic and social alternative to economic catastrophe and bourgeois dominance.

Document 2.4   Tsereteli at the First Congress of Soviets

The Provisional Government was overwhelmed by the sheer number of policy crises at a time of war. It had, moreover, to share authority with the soviets. The way ahead was debated at the First Congress of Soviets in June 1917. Irakli Tsereteli was one of the leaders of the Menshevik party. At the time of the congress in June 1917 he was minister for posts and telegraph in the Provisional Government, and later became minister for internal affairs and attended the Constituent Assembly. The speech was interesting for two reasons. First, the belief shared by defencist Mensheviks like Tsereteli that the revolution's primary task was to complete the agenda set by the autocracy, to concentrate all resources on winning the war, in the belief that 'organised democracy' could do this better than the tsarist authorities. The second interesting element was Lenin's famous cry from the body of the hall interrupting his speech: there was a party ready to take power.

For the first time before the All-Russian Congress we, representatives of organised democracy, are reporting on the general policies which we have pursued as members of the Provisional Government . . .

We, socialist ministers . . . are preparing laws which would facilitate securing the interests of the state through the creation of a central body that would be able to intervene and regulate production in all those branches where required with the greatest powers. All other leading countries, those allied with us or fighting us, in the light of the unprecedented hardships imposed by the war on countries, have been able in one way or another to adapt the state and economic organism to these demands. These profound financial transformations have taken place and the economy is regulated as much as is required. Only in Russia at the present time after three years of disruption, which was made even worse by the irresponsible policies of the autocracy, we finally have to deal with this problem and we will have to force the resolution of the question because on the speed of its solution depends the fate of the revolution . . .

At the present moment, there is not a political party in Russia which would say: Hand the power over to us, resign, and we will take your place. Such a party does not exist in Russia. (Lenin from his seat: 'It does exist.') . . . they [the Bolsheviks] say: When we have a majority, or when the majority comes over to our point of view, then the power should be seized, Comrade Lenin, you said that. At least the Bolsheviks and you with them say it in their official statements.

Gentlemen, until now, there has not been a single party in Russia which has come out openly for getting for itself all power at once, although there have been such cries by irresponsible groups on the Right and the Left . . . The Right says, let the Left run the Government, and we and the country will draw our conclusions; and the Left says, let the Right take hold, and we and the country will draw our conclusions . . . Each side hopes that the other will make such a failure, that the country will turn to it for leadership.

But, gentlemen, this is not the time for that kind of play . . . In order to solve the problems of the country, we must unite our strength and must have a strong Government . . . strong enough to put an end to experiments dangerous for the fate of the revolution, . . . experiments that may lead to civil war . . . This, gentlemen, is our policy . . .

Source: Pervyi vserossiiskii s"ezd Sovetov rabochikh i soldatskikh deputatov: stenograficheskii otchet *(Moscow and Leningrad, 1930), pp. 54–67; Browder and Kerensky (eds)*, The Russian Provisional Government 1917, *vol. III, pp. 1301–2.*

Document 2.5 Lenin Addresses the First Congress of Soviets, 4 June 1917

Lenin's was the next speech, in which he amplified his views on Russia's preparedness for socialism and the Bolsheviks' readiness to take power.

The first and main question facing us is this: where are we? What are these soviets which have gathered together here for the All-Russian Congress, what is that revolutionary democracy, about which so much has been spoken here that would insult any understanding and provoke a complete revulsion from it . . . Soviets are an institution that does not and cannot exist within, or alongside of, the ordinary bourgeois-parliamentary state . . . It comes down to one of two things: either a bourgeois government with those 'plans' of reform, which have been described to us and which have dozens of times in all countries been proposed and remained on paper, or that institution which is now suggested, a new type of 'government', created by the revolution . . . This is that new, more democratic type of state which we called in our party resolutions a peasant-proletarian democratic republic, in which the entirety of power would belong to the Soviets of Workers' and Soldiers' Deputies. Such an institution would mark the transition to a republic that would create a strong authority without police, without a standing army not in words but in deed, which in Western Europe cannot exist, a power without which the Russian revolution cannot triumph in the sense of a victory over the landlords, in the sense of victory over imperialism . . .

They say to us, can socialism be introduced in Russia, can any profound transformations take place at once. All these are empty excuses, comrades. The doctrine of Marx and Engels, as they always explained, reduces to the following: 'our teaching is not a dogma, but a guide to action'. Pure capitalism, moving into pure socialism, is nowhere to be found in the world and cannot be found at a time of war, but there is something in the middle, something new, unheard of . . . He [Tsereteli] said that there is no political party in Russia ready to take power entirely into its hands. I answer: 'Such a party exists! No party has a right to refuse power, and our party does not refuse it. Our party is ready at any moment to take all power into its hands.' (*Applause, laughter.*)

Source: Pravda, *28, 29 June 1917;* Khrestomatiya po istorii Rossii *1917–1940 (Moscow, Aspekt Press, 1995), pp. 25–7.*

Document 2.6 Kerensky's Response

Kerensky's speech of 4 June 1917 reveals the degree to which the influence of the French revolution hung over events in Russia. Here Kerensky presciently warns of the consequences of the Bolsheviks' revolutionary extremism and their attempt to resolve economic problems by political means.

Comrades:

You have been told of 1792 and of 1905. How did 1792 end in France? It ended in the fall of the republic and the rise of a dictator. How did 1905 end? With the triumph of reaction. And now, in 1917, we are doing that which we could have done earlier. The problem of the Russian socialist parties and of the Russian democracy is to prevent such an end as was in France – to hold on to the revolutionary conquests already made; to see to it that our comrades who have been released from prison do not return there; that Comrade Lenin, who has been abroad, may have the opportunity to speak here again, and not be obliged to flee back to Switzerland. (*Applause.*)

We must see to it that the historic mistakes do not repeat themselves; that we do not bring on a situation that would make possible the return of the reaction, the victory of force over democracy. Certain methods of fighting have been indicated to us. We have been told that we should not fight with words, not talk of annexation, but should show by deeds that we are fighting against capitalism. What means are recommended for this fight? To arrest Russian capitalists. (*Laughter.*) Comrades, I am not a Social Democrat. I am not a Marxist, but I have the highest respect for Marx, his teaching, and his disciples. But Marxism has never taught such childlike and primitive means. I suspect that Citizen Lenin has forgotten what Marxism is. He cannot call himself a socialist, because socialism nowhere recommends the settling of questions of economic war, of the war of classes in their economic relations, the question of the economic reorganisation of the state, by arresting people, as is done by Asiatic despots . . . Every Marxist who knows his socialism would say that capitalism is international, that the arrest of a few capitalists in a certain state would not affect the iron law of the economic development of a given period . . . You Bolsheviks recommend childish prescriptions – 'arrest, kill, destroy.' What are you – socialists or the police of the old regime? (*Uproar.* Lenin: 'You should call him to order.')

This gathering of the flower of the Russian democracy understands its problems. Such prescriptions do not excite it, but among the masses such words will be taken seriously. We do not cater to the mob; we are not demagogues. What we say now, we said ten years ago . . .

You [Bolsheviks] recommend that we follow the road of the French revolution of 1792. You recommend the way of further disorganisation of the country . . . When you, in alliance with reaction, shall destroy our power, then you will have a real dictator. It is our duty, the duty of the Russian democracy, to say: Don't repeat the historic mistakes. You are asked to follow the road that was once followed by France, and that will lead Russia to a new reaction, to a new shedding of democratic blood.

Source: Browder and Kerensky (eds), The Russian Provisional Government 1917, vol. III, pp. 1305–6.

In his speech to the First Congress of Soviets Lenin insisted that socialism was on the agenda in Russia. Some of his followers interpreted this to mean the immediate seizure of power. The events of the 'July Days' are still not entirely clear, but the pressure from below for an end to 'dual power' undoubtedly precipitated the violent uprising of exasperated workers and soldiers in Petrograd on 3–5 July 1917.

Bolshevik activists at the grass roots were heavily involved in transforming the accumulating tensions into a challenge to the government itself, a step which the Bolshevik leadership only reluctantly endorsed and which Lenin considered premature. The moderate socialist leadership of the soviets categorically refused to take power and the insurrection was crushed by forces loyal to the Provisional Government at a cost of some 400 killed or wounded. Lenin and his colleague G. E. Zinoviev were forced to go into hiding, Kamenev was arrested and *Pravda* banned. Alexander Kerensky came to head the government and sought to outlaw the Bolsheviks. Lenin and some other Bolshevik leaders went into exile in Finland.

Document 2.7 Lenin's *State and Revolution*

While hiding in Finland Lenin drafted his famous work *The State and Revolution*, in effect a commentary on the views of Marx and Engels on the state, but distilling from them a radical critique of the 'bourgeois' state. Although he had disagreed with Bukharin's view of the capitalist Leviathan state (see Document 1.22) earlier, Lenin now echoed Bukharin's ideas. Lenin argued that the 'bourgeois' state could not simply be taken over by the victorious proletariat but had to be completely 'smashed', and an entirely new type of revolutionary authority created modelled on the Paris Commune of 1871 (or at least the representation of it in Marx's *The Civil War in France*), whose kernel was the already-established soviets. In the short term this new authority would have to be strong enough to overcome the resistance of the old exploiting class, and only then would the socialist state begin to 'wither away' (to use the phrase made famous by Engels).

The state is a product and a manifestation of the *irreconcilability* of class antagonisms. The state arises where, when and insofar as class antagonisms objectively *cannot* be reconciled . . . According to Marx, the state is an organ of class *rule*, an organ for the *oppression* of one class by another . . . If the state is a product of the irreconcilability of class antagonisms, if it is a power standing *above* society and '*alienating* itself *more and more* from it', it is obvious that the liberation of the oppressed class is impossible not only without a violent revolution, *but also without the destruction* of the apparatus of state power which was created by the ruling class and which is the embodiment of this 'alienation' . . .

Revolution alone can 'abolish' the bourgeois state. The state in general, i.e., the most complete democracy, can only 'wither away' . . . The necessity of systematically imbuing the masses with *this* and precisely *this* view of violent revolution lies at the root of the *entire* theory of Marx and Engels . . . The supersession of the bourgeois state by the proletarian state is impossible without a violent revolution. The abolition of the proletarian state, i.e., of the state in general, is impossible except through the process of 'withering away' . . . Only the proletariat – by virtue of the economic role it plays in large-scale production – is capable of being the leader of *all* the working and exploited people . . . The overthrow of the bourgeoisie can be achieved only by the proletariat becoming the *ruling class*, capable of crushing the inevitable and desperate resistance of the bourgeoisie, and of organising *all* the working and exploited people for the new economic system . . .

But since the proletariat needs the state as a *special* form of organisation of violence *against* the bourgeoisie, the following conclusion suggests itself: is it conceivable that such an organisation can be created by the bourgeoisie *for themselves?* . . . The conclusion is extremely precise, definite, practical and palpable: all previous revolutions perfected the state machine, whereas it must be broken, smashed . . .

In the usual arguments about the state, the mistake is constantly made against which Engels warned . . . it is constantly forgotten that the abolition of the state means also the abolition of democracy; that the withering away of the state means the withering away of democracy . . . No, democracy is *not* identical with the subordination of the minority to the majority. Democracy is a *state* which recognises the subordination of the minority to the majority, i.e., an organisation for the systematic use of *force* by one class against another, by one section of the population against another . . .

Freedom in capitalist society always remains about the same as it was in the ancient Greek republics: freedom for the slave-owners . . . During the *transition* from capitalism to communism suppression is *still* necessary, but it is now the suppression of the exploiting minority by the exploited majority . . . Only communism makes the state absolutely unnecessary, for there is *nobody* to be suppressed . . . So long as the state exists there is no freedom. When there is freedom, there will be no state . . . Under socialism *all* will govern in turn and will soon become accustomed to no one governing.

Source: Lenin, The State and Revolution, *August–September 1917 (Moscow, Progress Publishers, 1949), pp. 9, 10, 19, 22, 25, 26, 27, 75, 79, 82, 83, 87, 106.*

While Lenin insisted that socialism was on the agenda in Russia, the actual organisation of the new system was at best vague. His vision of a state based on soviets proved popular, but the role of the Bolshevik Party in the new system of government remained unclear. These ambiguities were not cleared up in *The State and Revolution*. While the work is often considered to be 'anti-authoritarian', indeed it has even been taken to suggest an 'anarchist' streak in Lenin, a close reading of the text reveals that the only state to be smashed was the bourgeois one; but that the revolutionary state would retain the capacity of 'crushing' the resistance of the bourgeoisie. Lenin transformed what for Marx was a *social* category, the dictatorship (i.e., social dominance) of the proletariat, into an outright *political* form, the physical and coercive dictatorship of the revolutionary proletariat. The left wing of the party remained loyal to the vision of a self-managing republic, but the bulk followed Lenin and supported the recreation of a traditional state apparatus, albeit in a 'proletarian' guise.

The Road to Power

The Bolsheviks took the credit for defeating the Kornilov putsch and were rescued from the doldrums in which they had languished since the July Days. In September they gained majorities in the Petrograd and Moscow city soviets. Kerensky's attempts to broaden the base of the regime by forming a third coalition government in late September failed to overcome the alienation of left and right.

Document 2.8   The Kornilov 'Revolt'

On 26 August the military high command under General L. G. Kornilov called for the surrender of the Provisional Government and planned to form a government under his personal direction, a military dictatorship. Kerensky refused the demand and on 27 August called for popular resistance to come to the defence of the Provisional Government. Kornilov's forces were repulsed by the Petrograd soviet and the city's workers organised in Red Guard units. Kornilov brusquely rejected charges that he sought to overthrow the government, and in language remarkably reminiscent of that of the putschists of August 1991 (see pp. 474–82), he outlined his position.

People of Russia! Our great motherland is dying. The hour of her death is near. Forced to speak openly, I, General Kornilov, declare that under the pressure of the Bolshevik majority of the Soviets, the Provisional Government acts in complete harmony with the plans of the German general staff, and simultaneously with the forthcoming landing of the enemy forces on the Riga shores, it is killing the army and undermines the very foundation of the country.

The heavy sense of the inevitable ruin of the country commands me in these ominous moments to call upon all Russian people to come to the aid of the dying motherland. All in whose breasts a Russian heart is beating, who believe in God, in Church, pray to the Lord for the greatest miracle, the saving of our native land!

I, General Kornilov, son of a Cossack peasant, declare to all and sundry that I want nothing for myself, except the preservation of a Great Russia, and I vow to bring the people by means of victory over the enemy to the Constituent Assembly, where they will themselves decide their fate and choose their new form of government. But it is quite impossible for me to betray Russia into the hands of her ancient enemy, the German race, and to turn the Russian people into German slaves. I prefer to die on the battle-field of honor rather than see the disgrace and infamy of the Russian land.

Russian people, the life of your motherland is in your hands! August 27 1917. General Kornilov.

Source: Browder and Kerensky (eds), The Russian Provisional Government 1917, vol. III, p. 1573.

Document 2.9   Lenin – *The Bolsheviks Must Seize Power*

When the soviets were dominated by opponents of the Bolsheviks, the slogan 'all power to the soviets' had been quietly dropped (although not without much resistance from rank-and-file communists), but with the tide turning in their favour, the slogan was restored.

Having obtained a majority in the Soviets of Workers' and Soldiers' Deputies of both capitals, the Bolsheviks can and *must* take power into their hands.

They can do so because the active majority of the revolutionary elements of the people of both capitals is sufficient to attract the masses, to overcome the resistance of the adversary, to vanquish him, to conquer power and to retain it. For, in offering immediately a democratic peace, in giving the land immediately to the peasants, in re-establishing the democratic institutions and liberties which have been mangled and crushed by Kerensky, the Bolsheviks will form a government which *nobody* will overthrow.

The majority of the people is *with* us. This has been proved by the long and difficult road from 19 May to 12 August and 25 September: the majority in the Soviets of the capitals is the *result* of the people's progress *to our side*. The vacillation of the Socialist-Revolutionaries and Mensheviks, and the strengthening of internationalists among them, is proof of the same thing . . .

To 'wait' for the Constituent Assembly would be wrong. By surrendering Petrograd, Kerensky and Co. can always *destroy* the Constituent Assembly. Only our party, having assumed power, can secure the convocation of the Constituent Assembly; and, after assuming power, it could blame the other parties for delaying it and could substantiate its accusations . . .

We must recall and ponder the words of Marx on uprising: '*Uprising is an art*', etc.

It would be naive to wait for a 'formal' majority on the side of the Bolsheviks; no revolution ever waits for *this* . . . History will not forgive us if we do not assume power now.

No apparatus? There is an apparatus: the Soviets and democratic organisations. The international situation *just now*, on the *eve* of a separate peace between the English and the Germans, is *in our favour*. It is precisely now that to offer peace to the peoples means to *win*.

Assume power *at once* in Moscow and in Petrograd (it does not matter which begins; perhaps even Moscow may begin); we will win *absolutely and unquestionably*.

Source: Lenin, Bol'sheviki dolzhny vzyat' vlast' *(The Bolsheviks Must Seize Power), 12–14 (25–7) September 1917, PSS, vol. 34, pp. 239, 240, 241–2.*

Document 2.10   Lenin's 'Marxism and Insurrection'

Lenin's calls for an immediate insurrection to overthrow the Provisional Government became ever more insistent. On the question of ending the war, Lenin believed that the Germans would grant the Bolsheviks, at the very least, an armistice. In this, as we shall see, Lenin was wrong.

One of the more vicious and probably most widespread distortions of Marxism resorted to by the dominant 'socialist' parties is the opportunist lie that preparation for insurrection, and generally the treatment of insurrection as an art, is 'Blanquism' . . .

To be successful, insurrection must rely not upon conspiracy and not upon a party, but upon the advanced class. That is the first point. Insurrection must rely upon a *revolutionary upsurge of the people*. That is the second point. Insurrection must rely upon that *turning point* in the history of the growing revolution when the activity of the advanced ranks of the people is at its height, and when the *vacillations* in the ranks of the enemy and *in the ranks of the weak, half-hearted and irresolute friends of the revolution* are strongest. That is the third point. And these three conditions for raising the question of insurrection distinguish *Marxism from Blanquism.*

Once these conditions exist, however, to refuse to treat insurrection as an *art* is a betrayal of the revolution . . .

On 3–4 July it could have been argued, without violating the truth, that the correct thing to do was to take power, for our enemies would in any case have accused us of insurrection and ruthlessly treated us as rebels. However, to have decided on this account in favour of taking power at that time would have been wrong, because the objective conditions for the victory of the insurrection did not exist . . .

We could not have retained power politically on 3–4 July because, *before the Kornilov revolt*, the army and the provinces could and would have marched against Petrograd.

Now the picture is entirely different . . .

All the objective conditions exist for a successful insurrection . . .

And another thing. By immediately proposing a peace without annexations, by immediately breaking with the Allied imperialists and with all imperialists, either we shall at once obtain an armistice, or the entire revolutionary proletariat will rally to the defence of the country, and a really just, really revolutionary war will then be waged by revolutionary democrats under the leadership of the proletariat . . .

Source: Lenin, 'Marxism and Insurrection: A Letter to the Central Committee of the RSDWP', 13–14 (26–7) September 1917, Selected Works, pp. 357, 358, 360–1.

Document 2.11   Lenin – 'Can the Bolsheviks Retain State Power?'

In the last days of September 1917 Lenin continued to urge the revolutionary seizure of power, but he also sought to answer those who argued that the Bolsheviks had no constructive policies and would not last long in power. All that the Bolsheviks had to do, according to Lenin, was smash the 'bourgeois' democratic political system of the old regime, and convert its economic apparatus to socialist purposes. In his view, the German war economy had already shown how this could be done: this was his model of a socialist economy. This was an extraordinarily naive view of how a modern economic system works.

On what are all trends agreed . . . They all agree that the Bolsheviks will either never dare take over full state power alone, or, if they dare, and do take power, they will not be able to retain it even for the shortest while . . .

No. We must not allow ourselves to be frightened by the screams of the frightened bourgeoisie. We must bear firmly in mind that we have never set ourselves 'insoluble' social problems, and as for the *perfectly* soluble problem of taking immediate steps towards socialism, which is the only way out of the exceedingly difficult situation, that will be *solved only* by the dictatorship of the proletariat and poor peasants. Victory, and lasting victory, is now more than ever, more than anywhere else, assured for the proletariat in Russia if it takes power . . .

The proletariat *cannot* 'lay hold of' the 'state apparatus' and 'set it in motion'. But it can *smash* everything that is oppressive, routine, incorrigibly bourgeois in the state apparatus and substitute its *own*, new apparatus. The Soviets of Workers', Soldiers' and Peasants' Deputies are exactly this apparatus . . .

This brings us to another aspect of the question of the state apparatus. In addition to the chiefly 'oppressive' apparatus – the standing army, the police and the bureaucracy – the modern state possesses an apparatus which has extremely close connections with the banks and syndicates, an apparatus which performs an enormous amount of accounting and registration work, if it may be expressed in this way. This apparatus must not, and should not be *cut off, lopped off, chopped away from* this apparatus; it must be *subordinated* to the proletarian Soviets; it must be expanded, made more comprehensive, and nation-wide, and this *can* be done by utilising the achievements already made by large-scale capitalism (in the same way as the proletarian revolution can, in general, reach its goal only by utilising these achievements).

Capitalism has created an accounting *apparatus* in the shape of the banks, syndicates, postal service, consumers' societies and office employees' unions. *Without big banks socialism would be impossible.*

The big banks *are* the 'state apparatus' which we *need* to bring about socialism, and which we *take ready-made* from capitalism; our task here is merely to *lop off* what *capitalistically mutilates* this excellent apparatus, to make it *even bigger*, even more democratic, even more comprehensive. Quantity will be transformed into quality. A single State Bank, the biggest of the big, with branches in every rural district, in every factory, will constitute as much as nine-tenths of the *socialist* apparatus. This will be country-wide *book-keeping*, country-wide *accounting* of the production and distribution of goods, this will be, so to speak, something in the nature of the *skeleton* of socialist society . . .

    Compulsory syndication, i.e., compulsory amalgamation in associations under state control – this is what capitalism has prepared the way for, this is what has been carried out in Germany by the Junkers' state, this is what can be easily carried out in Russia by the Soviets, by the proletarian dictatorship, and this is what will *provide us with a state apparatus* that will be universal, up-to-date, and non-bureaucratic . . .

Source: Lenin, 'Can the Bolsheviks Retain State Power?', late September 1917, Selected Works, pp. 363, 366, 372–3, 375–6, 377.

Document 2.12 Lenin Again Calls for the Seizure of Power

In a letter to the Bolshevik party's Central Committee (CC) and other party organisations on 1 (14) October 1917 Lenin urged the seizure of power. The Second Congress of Soviets was due to convene at the end of October, but Lenin insisted that the Bolsheviks could not wait that long.

Dear comrades! Events so clearly indicate the task for us that any delay would be tantamount to a crime. The agrarian movement is growing. The government is intensifying wild repression, in the army sympathy towards us is growing . . . In Germany it is clear that the revolution has begun, especially after the shooting of the sailors. The elections in Moscow, with 47 per cent voting for the Bolsheviks, is a gigantic victory. With the Left SRs we are clearly a majority in the country. The railway workers and post office employees are in conflict with the government . . .

    The Bolsheviks do not have the right to wait for the congress of soviets, they must take *power immediately*. In this way they will save the world revolution . . . and the Russian revolution.

Source: Lenin, 'Pis'mo v TsK, MK, PK i chlenam sovetov pitera i moskvy bol'shevikam', 1 (14) October 1917, PSS, vol. 34, p. 340.

Document 2.13 Kamenev and Zinoviev Denounce Lenin's Plans for Insurrection

Coming in disguise to the Central Committee's session of 10 (23) October 1917 Lenin urged preparations to be made for the seizure of power. It was at that meeting that a Political Bureau (Politburo) of seven leading Bolsheviks (Lenin, Zinoviev, Kamenev, Trotsky, Stalin, Sokolnikov and Bubnov) was established, though the existence of such a body was only formalised in 1919. The momentous decision to launch an armed insurrection was taken by a vote of 10 for and 2 against, largely at Lenin's instigation. The resolution, however, was opposed by Kamenev and Zinoviev at sessions of the Central Committee on the grounds that the Bolsheviks had neither the mass support nor the international backing to ensure success. They continued to agitate against the motion in the following days. In an article in Maksim Gorkii's journal *Novaya zhizn'* (*New Life*) on 18 (31) October Kamenev denied that the party had taken any decision to launch an uprising, insisting that it would be 'inadmissible to launch an armed uprising in the present circumstances, independently and a few days before the Congress of Soviets'. In an impassioned statement on 11 (24) October Kamenev and Zinoviev argued the case against insurrection, making points that remain valid despite the success of the Bolshevik seizure of power on 25 October.

There is a tendency becoming established and gaining ground in workers' circles to see the immediate declaration of an armed insurrection as the only way out. All the timetables have now come together that if one talks of such an insurrection, it has to be fixed directly and then for the very near future. The subject is already being discussed in one form or another in all the periodicals and at workers' meetings and it occupies the minds of a large circle of Party workers. We, in our turn, regard it as our duty and our right to express ourselves on this matter with complete frankness.

We are deeply convinced that to proclaim an armed insurrection now is to put at stake not only the fate of our Party but also the fate of the Russian and the international revolution.

There is no doubt that historical circumstances do exist when an oppressed class has to recognise that it is better to go on to a defeat than surrender without a fight. Is the Russian working class in just such a position today? *No, a thousand times no!!!*

As a result of the enormous growth in our Party's influence in the towns and particularly in the army, a position has been reached at the present moment where it is becoming more and more impossible for the bourgeoisie to block the Constituent Assembly . . . Our Party's chances in the Constituent Assembly elections are excellent. We regard the talk put about that the influence of Bolshevism is beginning to decline and suchlike as totally without foundation . . . The influence of Bolshevism is growing. Whole sections of the working population are still only beginning to be swept up in it . . .

The Constituent Assembly cannot by itself, of course, change the real relationship between social forces. But it will prevent this relationship being disguised as at present. There is no getting rid of the Soviets, which have taken root in the life we live. Already the Soviets in practice exercise power in a number of places.

The Constituent Assembly, too, can only rely on the Soviets in its revolutionary work. The Constituent Assembly plus the Soviets – here is that mixed type of state institution we are going towards. Based on this, our Party's policy gets a tremendous chance of a real victory.

We have never said that the Russian working class *on its own*, relying only on its own resources, can successfully accomplish the present revolution. We did not forget, and still must not forget, that between us and the bourgeoisie stands a huge third camp: the petty bourgeoisie. This camp aligned itself with us in the days of the Kornilov revolt and brought us victory. It will join us again, more than once. One must not allow oneself to be mesmerised by what exists at a given moment. There is no doubt that now this camp is far nearer to the bourgeoisie than it is to us. But the present position is not eternal and immutable. And it only takes one careless step, some ill-considered move which makes the whole fate of the revolution depend on an immediate insurrection, for the proletarian party to push the petty bourgeoisie into Miliukov's arms *for a long time*.

They say: 1. The majority of the people in Russia are already on our side and 2. the majority of the international proletariat is on our side. Alas! Neither one nor the other is true, and that is the whole point.

In Russia we have the majority of the workers and a considerable section of the soldiers on our side. But all the rest are doubtful. We are all convinced, for example, that if things now get as far as the Constituent Assembly elections, the peasants will vote in the main for the SRs . . .

And now we come to the second assertion – that the majority of the international proletariat now supports us. Unfortunately, it is not so. The revolt in the German navy has enormous significance as a symptom. The first signs of a serious movement exists in Italy. But from this to any active support of proletarian revolution in Russia, declaring war on the whole bourgeois world, is still a very long way. It can do great harm to overestimate one's strength . . .

It is against this fatal policy that we raise our voice in warning.

Source: The Bolsheviks and the October Revolution: Minutes of the Central Committee of the Russian Social-Democratic Labour Party (bolsheviks), August 1917–February 1918, *translated from the Russian by Ann Bone (London, Pluto Press, 1974), pp. 89–95.*

The Seizure of Power

In October the Bolsheviks cut short the evolutionary option and launched the country on the path of radical transformation. The October revolution was a classical Leninist revolution, with bodies of armed men waving red flags seizing power in violent insurrection. The weakness of the Provisional Government might not have mattered so much if it had not had the misfortune of having its own resolute executioner to hand, the Bolsheviks headed by a leader of genius, Lenin. Only they offered a clear political and social alternative, however demagogic in detail it might have been. The demand to transfer power to the soviets offered the prospect of a break with old patterns of authority. It appeared to present an opportunity of improving their economic conditions and status.

Driven by Lenin's urgings and against the warnings of Kamenev and Zinoviev, on the night of 24–5 October (6–7 November) the Bolsheviks organised by Trotsky moved to take power. Against weak resistance and with the majority of the population passive, the Bolsheviks took control of Petrograd and besieged the remaining ministers in the Winter Palace which, after a few salvoes from the war-ship *Aurora* in the Neva, was occupied by insurgent forces on the evening of 25 October. Already by late in the evening of 24–5 October they presented the Second Congress of Soviets, meeting in Petrograd with a Bolshevik majority, with a *fait accompli*: power belonged to the Bolsheviks in the name of the soviets. In the event, the Bolsheviks struck not only against 'the bourgeoisie', but also against the soviets and the Constituent Assembly. The Petrograd soviet in effect pre-empted the decisions of the Second Congress of Soviets in voting for a proletarian government.

Document 2.14 John Reed on the Second Congress of Soviets, 25 October (7 November) 1917

John Reed (1887–1920) was an American journalist whose eyewitness account of the revolutionary events in Petrograd, *Ten Days That Shook the World*, has become a classic of the genre. On his return to America he helped establish the Communist Party of the USA in 1919. In the following year he was once again drawn to Soviet Russia, but covering a congress of the communist organisations of the peoples of the East in Baku in November 1920 he contracted typhus and died. He was buried in the Kremlin Wall in Red Square alongside other revolutionary heroes. Lenin wrote an enthusiastic introduction to Reed's account of the revolution, but later Stalin suppressed the book since the work contained powerful descriptions of Lenin, Trotsky, Kamenev and others, but nothing on Stalin.

The massive façade of Smolny blazed with lights as we drove up, and from every street converged upon it streams of hurrying shapes dim in the gloom . . . There was an atmosphere of recklessness. A crowd came pouring down the staircase, workers in black blouses and round black fur hats, many of them with guns slung over their shoulders, soldiers in rough dirt-coloured coats and grey fur *shapki* pinched flat, a leader or so – Lunacharsky, Kameniev – hurrying along in the centre of a group all talking at once, with harassed anxious faces, and bulging portfolios under their arms. The extraordinary meeting of the Petrograd Soviet was over. I stopped Kameniev – a quick-moving little man, with a wide, vivacious face set close to his shoulder . . .

It was 10.40 p.m.

Dan, a mild-faced, baldish figure in a shapeless military surgeon's uniform, was ringing the bell. Silence fell sharply, intense, broken by the scuffling and disputing of the people at the door . . .

'We have the power in our hands,' he began sadly, stopped for a moment, and then went on in a low voice. 'Comrades! The Congress of Soviets is meeting in such unusual circumstances and in such an extraordinary moment that you will understand why the Tsay-ee-kah [Central Executive Committee of the Soviet] considers it unnecessary to address you with a political speech. This will become much clearer to you if you will recollect that I am a member of the Tsay-ee-kah, and that at this moment our Party comrades are in the Winter Palace under bombardment, sacrificing themselves to execute the duty put on them by the Tsay-ee-kah.' (*Confused uproar.*)

'I declare the first session of the Second Congress of Soviets of Workers' and Soldiers' Deputies open!'

The election of the presidium took place amid stir and moving about. Avanessov announced that by agreement of the Bolsheviki, Left Socialist Revolutionaries [the SR was in the throes of a split], and Mensheviki Internationalists, it was decided to base the presidium upon proportionality. Several Mensheviki leaped in their feet protesting. A bearded soldier shouted at them, 'Remember what you did to us Bolsheviki when we were in the minority!' Result – 14 Bolsheviki, 7 Socialist Revolutionaries, 3 Mensheviki, and 1 Internationalist (Gorky's group). Hendelmann, for the right and centre Socialist Revolutionaries, said that they refused to take part in the presidium, the same from Khinchuk, for the Mensheviki; and from the Mensheviki Internationalists, that until the verification of certain circumstances, they too could not enter the presidium. Scattering applause and hoots. One voice, 'Renegades, you call yourself Socialists!' A representative of the Ukrainian delegates demanded, and received, a place. Then the old Tsay-ee-kah stepped down, and in their places appeared Trotsky, Kameniev, Lunacharsky, Madame Kollontai, Nogin. . . . The hall rose, thundering. How far they had soared, these Bolsheviki, from a despised and hunted sect less than four months ago, to this supreme place, the helm of great Russia in full tide of insurrection!

The order of the day, said Kameniev, was first, Organization of Power; second, War and Peace; and third, the Constitutional Assembly. Lozovsky, rising, announced that upon agreement of the bureaux of all factions, it was proposed to hear and discuss the report of the Petrograd Soviet, then to give the floor to members of the Tsay-ee-kah and the different parties, and finally to pass to the order of the day.

But suddenly a new sound made itself heard, deeper than the tumult of the crowd, persistent, disquieting – the dull shock of guns. People looked anxiously towards the clouded windows, and a sort of fever came over them. Martov, demanding the floor, croaked hoarsely, 'The civil war is beginning, comrades! The first question must be a peaceful settlement of the crisis. On principle and from a political standpoint we must urgently discuss a means of averting civil war. Our brothers are being shot down in the streets! At this moment, when before the opening of the Congress of Soviets the question of Power is being settled by means of a military plot organized by one of the revolutionary parties – ' for a moment he could not make himself heard above the noise, 'All of the revolutionary parties must face the fact!' . . .

On behalf of the Mensheviki, Khinchuk then announced that the only possibility of a peaceful solution was to begin negotiations with the Provisional Government for the formation of a new Cabinet, which would find support in all strata of society. He could not proceed for several minutes. Raising his voice to a shout he read the Menshevik declaration:

'Because the Bolsheviki have made a military conspiracy with the aid of the Petrograd Soviet, without consulting the other factions and parties, we find it impossible to remain in the Congress, and therefore withdraw, inviting the other groups to follow us and to meet for discussion of the situation!'

'Deserter!' At intervals in the almost continuous disturbance Hendel-mann, for the Socialist Revolutionaries, could be heard protesting against the bombardment of the Winter Palace . . . 'We are opposed to this kind of anarchy . . .'

Scarcely had he stepped down when a young, lean-faced soldier, with flashing eyes, leaped to the platform, and dramatically lifted his hand:

'Comrades!' he cried, and there was a hush. 'My *familia* (name) is Peterson – I speak for the Second Lettish Rifles. You have heard the statements of two representatives of the Army Committees; these statements would have some value *if their authors had been representatives of the Army* – ' Wild applause. '*But they do not represent the soldiers!*' Shaking his fist. 'The Twelfth Army has been insisting for a long time upon the re-election of the Great Soviet and the Army Committee, but just as your own Tsay-ee-kah, our Committee refused to call a meeting of the representatives of the masses until the end of September, so that the reactionaries could elect their own false delegates to this Congress. I tell you now, the Lettish soldiers have many times said, "No more resolutions! No more talk! We want deeds – the Power must be in our hands!" Let these imposter delegates leave the Congress! The Army is not with them!'

The hall rocked with cheering. In the first moments of the session, stunned by the rapidity of events, startled by the sound of cannon, the delegates had hesitated. For an hour hammer-blow after hammer-blow had fallen from that tribune, welding them together but beating them down. Did they stand then alone? Was Russia rising against them? Was it true that the Army was marching on Petrograd? Then this clear-eyed young soldier had spoken, and in a flash they knew it for the truth. . . . *This* was the voice of the soldiers – the stirring millions of uniformed workers and peasants were men like them, and their thoughts and feelings were the same. . . .

Kameniev jangled the bell, shouting, 'Keep your seats and we'll go on with our business!' And Trotsky, standing up with a pale, cruel face, letting out his rich voice in cool contempt, 'All these so-called Socialist Revolutionaries, *Bund* – let them go! They are just so much refuse which will be swept away into the garbage-heap of history!'

Source: John Reed, Ten Days That Shook the World *(Harmondsworth, Penguin Books, 1966), pp. 96, 99–100, 102–3, 104.*

Document 2.15 'To the Citizens of Russia'

The announcement of the victory of 'the revolution' came not from the Congress of Soviets itself, but from the Military Revolutionary Committee of the Petrograd Soviet.

The Provisional Government has been deposed. State power has passed into the hands of the organ of the Petrograd Soviet of Workers' and Soldiers' Deputies, the Military Revolutionary Committee, which leads the Petrograd proletariat and garrison.

The cause for which the people have fought, namely, the immediate offer of a democratic peace, the abolition of land ownership, workers' control over production, and the establishment of Soviet power – this cause has been secured.

Long live the revolution of workers, soldiers and peasants!

Source: 'To the Citizens of Russia', Proclamation of the Military Revolutionary Committee, 25 October (7 November) 1917, in Lenin, PSS, vol. 35, p. 1.

Document 2.16 Lenin on the Significance of the Revolution

The Second Congress of Soviets endorsed the Bolshevik seizure of power, despite the protests of the minority, and the power of soviets was proclaimed in the centre and the localities. Executive authority was entrusted to an exclusively Bolshevik government, the Council of People's Commissars (Sovnarkom), headed by Lenin. Lenin addressed the congress on the night of 25–6 October. In keeping with his theory of imperialism and 'April Theses', Lenin staked everything on an alliance with the peasantry and aid from revolution abroad.

Comrades, the workers' and peasants' revolution, about the necessity of which the Bolsheviks have been speaking all the time, has come to pass.

What is the significance of this workers' and peasants' revolution? First of all, the significance of this revolution is that we shall have a Soviet Government, our own organ of power, without the participation of any bourgeois. The oppressed masses will form a government themselves. The old State machinery will be uprooted and a new machinery of government will be created, embodied in the Soviet organizations.

This is the beginning of a new period in the history of Russia, and the present, third Russian revolution must ultimately lead to the victory of socialism.

One of our immediate tasks is the necessity of ending the war at once. But in order to end this war, which is closely bound up with the present capitalistic system, it is clear to all that it is necessary to overcome capitalism itself.

We will be aided in this work by the world workers' movement, which is already beginning to develop in Italy, England, and Germany.

A just and immediate offer of peace by us to the international democracy will find everywhere a fervent response among the masses of the international proletariat. In order to strengthen this confidence of the proletariat, it is necessary to publish at once all secret treaties.

An enormous part of the peasantry within Russia has said: enough of playing games with the capitalists – we will go with the workers. We shall win the confidence of the peasantry by one decree, which will abolish *pomeshchik* [landlord] landownership. The peasants will understand that their only salvation lies in an alliance with the workers.

We will institute real workers' control over production.

You have now learned how to work together in harmony, as evidenced by the revolution that has just occurred. We now possess the strength of a mass organization, which will triumph over everything and which will lead the proletariat to world revolution.

In Russia we must now devote ourselves to the construction of a proletarian socialist state.

Long live the socialist world revolution. (*Storm of applause.*)

Source: Browder and Kerensky (eds), The Russian Provisional Government 1917, *vol. III, p. 1793.*

Document 2.17   More Warnings

The last issue of *Izvestiya* before the Bolsheviks took it over condemned the seizure of power.

Yesterday we called the Bolshevik uprising an insane venture. Today, when the attempt was crowned with success in Petrograd, we have not changed our mind. We repeat that this is not a transfer of power to the Soviets, but a seizure of power by one party – the Bolsheviks. Yesterday we were saying that this means the thwarting of the greatest gain of the revolution – the Constituent Assembly. Today we must add that it means the thwarting of the Congress of Soviets and, very probably, of the whole Soviet organization. These are the facts: the Socialist Revolutionary Party and the Mensheviks of the Social Democratic Party (the defensists as well as the Internationalists) have found it impossible, under the present circumstances, to participate in the Congress. The representatives from the front adhere to the same opinion. When these factions depart from the Congress, it will be left only with what it should have been left as a result of a complete Bolshevik overthrow, i.e., with only the Bolsheviks. They can call themselves whatever they please, but this will not alter the fact that the Bolsheviks alone participated in the uprising. All the other socialist and democratic parties are protesting against it . . .

To date, the Bolsheviks have seized Petrograd but not all of Russia. The danger of a bloody civil war is threatening. Bloodshed and pogroms – this is what we must prepare ourselves for. This can only be averted, if it is not already too late, by one event: if a democratic government, recognized by all democratic elements and parties, is formed anew, and if the Bolsheviks agree to submit to such a government.

The entire responsibility for the future of the country now falls on them alone.

Source: Izvestiya, 26 October (8 November) 1917, p. 1; Browder and Kerensky (eds), The Russian Provisional Government 1917, *vol. III, p. 1801.*

Bolsheviks in Power – First Steps

Neither the February nor the October revolution was caused by rising social classes bursting into prominence (the Marxist view); rather, a specific set of conjunctural factors was abetted by long-term social and political strains. The Bolsheviks in October 1917 were the beneficiaries of a broad coalition united only in despair at the ineffectiveness of the Provisional Government. In October 1917 the aims of the social movements and those of the Bolsheviks coincided; together they swept away the old government and took the destiny of Russia into their hands. Power was in the hands of the Bolsheviks, but what would they do with it? On coming to power the Bolshevik government issued a flurry of decrees dealing with the most urgent issues facing the country. The attempt to end the war by simply declaring Russia's refusal to fight did not prove an effective strategy, while inside the country the Civil War gathered pace.

Document 2.17   Decree on Peace

The day after seizing power the Bolsheviks called for all the belligerent governments to end the war, threatening them with overthrow by their own proletariats if they failed to respond.

The workers' and peasants' government created by the revolution of 24–5 October and relying on the Soviets of Workers', Soldiers' and Peasants' Deputies calls upon all the belligerent peoples and their governments to start immediate negotiations for a just, democratic peace.

By a just or democratic peace, for which the overwhelming majority of the working and toiling classes of all the belligerent countries, exhausted, tormented and racked by the war, are craving – a peace that has been most definitely and insistently demanded by the Russian workers and peasants ever since the overthrow of the tsarist monarchy – by such a peace the government means an immediate peace without annexations (i.e., without the seizure of foreign lands, without the forcible incorporation of foreign nations) and without indemnities.

This is the kind of peace the government of Russia proposes to all the belligerent nations to conclude immediately, and expresses its readiness to take all the resolute measures immediately, without the least delay, pending the final ratification of all the terms of such a peace by authoritative assemblies of the people's representatives of all countries and all nations . . .

The government abolishes secret diplomacy, and, for its part, announces its firm intention to conduct all negotiations quite openly under the eyes of the whole people. It will immediately proceed to the full publication of the secret treaties endorsed or concluded by the government of landlords and capitalists from February to 25 October 1917. The government proclaims the absolute and immediate annulment of everything contained in these secret treaties in so far as it is aimed, as is mostly the case, at securing advantages and privileges for the Russian landlords and capitalists and at the retention, or extension, of the annexations made by the Great Russians . . .

In proposing an immediate armistice, we appeal to the class-conscious workers of the countries that have done so much for the development of the proletarian movement. We appeal to the workers of France, who have in repeated uprisings displayed the strength of their class-consciousness, and to the workers of Germany, who waged the fight against the Anti-Socialist Law and have created powerful organisations.

Source: 'Decree on Peace', 26 October (8 November) 1917, Lenin, PSS, vol. 35, pp. 13–14, 15, 17.

Document 2.18   Decree on Land

The Decree on Land helped stabilise Bolshevik rule in the countryside. The Socialist Revolutionary land programme was adopted in its entirety, legalising peasant seizures of land but prohibiting the private ownership of land.

1 Landlord ownership of land is immediately abolished without compensation.
2 The landed estates, as well as crown, monastery and church lands, with their livestock, implements, buildings and everthing associated with them, is to be placed at the disposal of the *volost'* [parish] Land Committees and the *uezd* [district] Soviets of Peasants' Deputies pending the convocation of the Constituent Assembly . . .
5 The land of ordinary peasants and ordinary Cossacks shall not be confiscated. . . .

Peasant Mandate on Land

1 Private ownership of land shall be abolished forever; land shall not be sold, purchased, mortgaged or otherwise alienated.

Source: 'Decree on Land', 26 October (8 November) 1917, written by Lenin, PSS, vol. 35, p. 24.

Document 2.19   The Sovnarkom 'Decree on the Press'

Two days after seizing power the Bolsheviks issued a decree limiting press freedom, and although proclaimed as a 'temporary and emergency measure', it remained in force until the 1990 press law once again restored freedom of speech.

In the serious decisive hour of revolution and the days that immediately followed, the Military Revolutionary Committee had to undertake a whole number of measures against the counter-revolutionary press of all hues. Immediately from all sides cries were raised that the new socialist authorities had in this way violated the basic principle of their programme by encroaching on the freedom of the press.

The Workers' and Peasants' Government points out that in our society, behind this liberal screen, in fact there is only freedom for the property-owning classes, seizing the lion's share of the press, freely poisoning minds and introducing confusion in the consciousness of the masses. Everyone knows that the bourgeois press is one of the most powerful weapons of the bourgeoisie. Especially in critical moments when the new power, the power of the workers and peasants, is only just gaining a foothold, it is impossible to leave this weapon entirely in the hands of the enemy at this time, when it is no less dangerous than bombs and machine-guns. That is why temporary and extraordinary measures have been adopted to cut off the stream of filth and lies in which the yellow and green press would gladly drown the youthful victory of the people.

As soon as the new order is consolidated, all administrative restrictions on the press will be lifted; it will be allowed full freedom within the limits of responsibility before the courts according to the widest and most progressive laws in this respect. Considering, however, that only the absolutely necessary limits on the press, even in critical moments, are permissible, the Council of People's Commissars decrees as follows:

General Regulations on the Press

1 Press organs to be closed are only those: (a) calling for open resistance or insubordination to the Workers' and Peasants' Government; (b) sowing confusion by the obvious distortion of facts; (c) calling for openly criminal actions, i.e., of a criminally punishable character.
2 The temporary or permanent banning of press organs is carried out only by a resolution of the Council of People's Commissars.
3 The present regulation is temporary and will be revoked by a special decree with the onset of normal conditions of social life.

Chairman of the Council of People's Commissars
Vladimir Ul'yanov (Lenin)

Source: 'Decree on the Press', 27 October (9 November) 1917, Pravda, 28 October 1917; in Istoriya sovetskoi politicheskoi tsenzury: dokumenty i kommentarii (Moscow, Rosspen, 1997), pp. 27–8.

Document 2.20 Declaration of the Rights of the Peoples of Russia

One of the most important issues facing the new government was the national question. The following extract outlined the principles of Bolshevik policy.

The unworthy policy of distrust and falsehood must be ended. Henceforth it must be replaced by an open and honest policy to create mutual trust among the peoples of Russia. Only as a result of such trust can there be formed an open and honest union of the peoples of Russia. Only as the result of such a union can the toilers and peasants of the peoples of Russia be forged into one revolutionary force able to resist all the attempts by the imperialist and annexationist bourgeoisie.

Emerging from these principles, the First Congress of Soviets in June of this year proclaimed the right of the peoples of Russia to free self-determination. The Second Congress of Soviets in October of this year reaffirmed this inalienable right of the peoples of Russia more decisively and firmly. The united will of these congresses, and the Council of People's Commissars, resolve to base their work on the question of the nationalities of Russia on the following principles:

1 The equality and sovereignty of the peoples of Russia.
2 The right of the peoples of Russia to free self-determination, even up to the point of separation and the creation of an independent state.
3 The abolition of any and all national and national-religious privileges and restrictions.
4 The free development of national minorities and ethnographic groups living on the territory of Russia.

The specific decrees that arise from these principles will be immediately formulated after the establishment of a Commission of Nationality Affairs . . .

Chairman of the Council of People's Commissars, V. Ul'yanov (Lenin)
People's Commissar on Nationality Affairs, Josef Djugashvili (Stalin)

Source: 'Declaration of the Rights of the Peoples of Russia', 2 (15) November 1917, mimeo, n.d.

Reactions to the Bolshevik Coup

The Bolshevik revolution not only struck against the 'bourgeoisie' but also offended a great swathe of the socialist movement.

Document 2.21   Plekhanov on the Bolshevik Revolution

The veteran leader of Russian Social Democracy, Georgii Plekhanov, felt deeply that the Bolshevik revolution represented a betrayal of the working class itself. He vented his feelings in a letter to the Bolshevik leadership on 27 October in which he referred to Engels's famous warning about the fate of a revolutionary party that seizes power prematurely.

Dear Comrades,

There is no doubt that some of you are pleased with the events that led to the fall of the Provisional Government of A. F. Kerenskii and that political power has been transferred into the hands of the Petrograd Soviet of Workers' and Soldiers' Deputies. I will tell you directly: these events distress me. They distress me not because I do not want the triumph of the working class, but on the contrary, because I support this with all the strength of my spirit . . .

In the last few months we, Social Democrats, have frequently had to remind ourselves of Engels's observation that for the working class there cannot be a greater historical misfortune than to seize political power at a time when it is not yet ready for it . . . Our working class is still far from ready to benefit either itself or the country by taking into its hands the entirety of political power. To foist such power on it means to put it on the path of the greatest historical misfortune, which would be at the same time the greatest misfortune for Russia.

In the population of our country the proletariat does not represent *the majority, but a minority*. It would be able to practise dictatorship effectively only if it represented the majority. No serious socialist would dispute this. True, the working class can count on the support of the peasantry, who make up the larger part of the Russian population, but the peasantry requires land, not the replacement of capitalism by socialism . . . It could well turn out that the peasantry is a completely unreliable ally of the worker in building the socialist form of production . . . If, having seized power, our proletariat tried to make the 'social revolution', then the very economy of our country would consign it to the severest defeat.

They say that what the Russian worker begins, will be completed by the German. But this is a great mistake. There is no doubt that in the economic sense Germany is much more developed than Russia. The 'social revolution' is closer in Germany than in Russia. But even in Germany it is not on the agenda today. All sensible German Social Democrats, whether of the left or right wing, perfectly well understood this even before the war. And the war itself has even further reduced the chances of the social revolution in Germany because of the sad fact that the majority of the German proletariat headed by Scheiderman supported the German imperialists. At present in Germany there is hope neither for the 'social' nor even for the political revolution. This is recognised by Bernstein, by Haase, by Kautsky, and probably Karl Liebknecht agrees with this . . . Seizing political power prematurely, the Russian proletariat will not accomplish the social revolution but will only provoke civil war, which will ultimately force it to retreat further back from positions won in February and March this year.

The government should be based on a coalition of all living forces in the country, that is, on all classes and strata which do not want to see the restoration of the old order.

Yours, G. Plekhanov

Source: Edinstvo, *28 October (8 November) 1917.*

Document 2.22   Maksim Gorky and the Bolshevik Revolution

Gorky was the most popular 'proletarian' writer in early twentieth-century Russia. In the first months following the Bolshevik seizure of power he used his enormous authority to criticise the Bolsheviks, and the anti-war journal he edited, *Novaya zhizn'* (*New Life*), was one of the main thorns in the side of the new authorities. Established in April 1918, up to September 1917 the journal reflected the views of the Menshevik-Internationalists led by Martov and had provided a platform for 'right Bolsheviks' like Kamenev and Zinoviev. At the end of the Civil War Gorky went into exile. Wooed back by Stalin, he returned for extended periods from the late 1920s, until his exit was blocked in 1934. In 1936 it appears he was murdered by agents of Stalin.

Pravda stated that 'Gorky has begun to talk the language of the enemies of the working class'. This is not true. Appealing to the most conscious representatives of the working class I say: fanatics and superficial fantasists, arousing in the working class hopes that cannot be fulfilled in the given historical circumstances, will lead the Russian proletariat to defeat and destruction, and the defeat of the proletariat will provoke a long and sad period of reaction in Russia . . .

In whomsoever's hands power is, I retain my human right to criticise it. And I am especially suspicious, especially distrustful of a Russian in power – not long ago a slave, he becomes an unbridled despot as soon as he gains the possibility of lording over his own.

Source: Novaya zhizn´, *19 November 1917.*

Document 2.23   Bogdanov on the Bolshevik Revolution

Gorky's reservations were given a much firmer scholarly foundation by Bogdanov, who outlined a broad theory of Bolshevism as a response to and consequence of total war – what he called 'war communism' by which he meant a 'communism of war', the mobilisation and regulation by the state of all social resources to prosecute the war. In a letter to Anatoly V. Lunacharskii on 19 November 1917 he outlined his views about the emergence of a 'socialism of the barracks'.

I see nothing extraordinary in the sometimes strange but almost always necessary things you have to do. I think that you have not fully grasped the tragedy of our situation. I will try in my own way to explain it.

The root of everthing is the war. It gave rise to two basic facts:

(1) Economic and cultural decline; (2) the gigantic development of war communism.

War communism, developing from the front to the rear, has temporarily restructured society: the multi-million commune of the army, rations for the family of soldiers, the regulation of demand, the norming of distribution, production. The whole system of state capitalism is nothing other than a mongrel of capitalism and consumers' war communism, something which contemporary economists do not understand, not understanding organisational analysis. The atmosphere of war communism has engendered maximalism . . .

Maximalism has developed further in Russia than in Europe because capitalism here is weaker and the influence of war communism as an organisational form, correspondingly, stronger. The socialist workers' party earlier was Bolshevik. But the revolution, under pressure from the soldiery, made demands on it that profoundly distorted its nature. It was forced to organise the pseudo-socialist mass of soldiers (peasants, torn from production and living at the expense of the state in barrack communes). Why they? Simply because it was the party of peace, the ideal of the soldiery at the present time. The party became worker-soldier. But what does this mean? There is a tectological law that states that if a system is composed of higher and lower organised parts, its relationship to the surrounding world is determined by the lesser organised part . . . The position of the party, comprised of heterogeneous class fractions, is defined by its backward wing. A worker-soldier party is objectively simply a soldiers' party. And the degree to which the Bolshevik party has been transformed is striking . . . It has absorbed the whole logic of the barracks, all of its methods, all of its specific culture and ideals.

The logic of the barracks, by contrast with the logic of the factory, is characterised by the fact that it understands any task as a question of shock force, and not as a question of organisational experience and labour. Smashing the bourgeoisie – that's socialism. Seize power, then we can do anything. Agreement? Why? Share the spoils? How can it be otherwise? Alright, then let's share. But wait! We're once again stronger! Then we won't, and so on.

There will not be a socialist revolution in Europe now: its working class is not at the right level of culture and organisation, its level is clearly demonstrated by the history of the war. There will be a number of revolutions there of a liquidationist character, to overcome the legacy of the war, authoritarianism (oligarchy, the dictatorship of the authorities), indebtedness (consequently, the extreme development of rent-seeking), the suppression of newly created nations spawned by the war and the isolation of nations reinforced by state capitalism, and so on – there is much to do. In Russia the soldier-communist revolution is rather more opposed to socialism than something leading to it . . .

Source: A. A. Bogdanov, Voprosy sotsializma (Problems of Socialism) *(Moscow, Politicheskaya literatura, 1990), pp. 352–5.*

The Struggle for a Coalition Government

Plekhanov was right to recall Engels's warning that the premature seizure of power by the working class would be disastrous and lead to civil war. His calls for a coalition government were reflected in desultory attempts to forge some sort of broader government. Most socialists, including many Bolsheviks, hoped that a coalition government would be formed based on the socialist parties represented in the soviets. Lenin, however, was ill-disposed to attempts to dilute his power, while most Mensheviks and Right Socialist Revolutionaries would have found it hard to swallow Lenin as leader anyway. The moderate wing of the Bolshevik party, including Kamenev, Zinoviev and the future prime minister, Alexei Rykov, also sought to broaden the one-party government, and threatened to resign. Lenin's response was typically vituperative, and the moderates therefore fulfilled their threat and resigned from the Bolshevik Central Committee and from Sovnarkom.

Document 2.24 Attempts to Create a Coalition Government

A resolution adopted by the Central Committee on 1 (14) November 1917 allowed the negotiations to proceed but held out little chance of success.

Considering, on the basis of its experience of previous talks, that the conciliation parties are pursuing these negotiations not to create a united Soviet power but to cause a split among the workers and the soldiers, to undermine Soviet power and finally to attach the Left SRs to a policy of conciliation with the bourgeoisie,

The CC resolves: to allow the members of our Party, in view of the decision already taken by the *TsIK*, to take part today in a last attempt by the Left SRs to form a so-called homogeneous power in order to expose the unviability of this attempt for the last time and to put a conclusive end to further negotiations on a coalition power.

Source: The Bolsheviks and the October Revolution, *p. 136.*

Document 2.25 Session of the Petersburg Committee of the RSDLP(b)

Lenin made his position clear at a meeting of the Petersburg Committee of the RSDLP(b) on 1 (14) November 1917. This is from a recently opened archival report.

[When] comrades Zinoviev and Kamenev began to agitate against the uprising, they were considered strike-breakers. I even wrote a letter to the Central Committee proposing their expulsion from the party . . . I did not want to be too harsh with them.

I look upon Kamenev's negotiations with the Central Executive Committee on coalition benevolently, since we are not opposed in principle.

When, however, the Social Revolutionaries refused to join the government, I understood that they did this after Kerensky had rallied the opposition. The situation has become difficult in Moscow. Our supporters . . . have plunged into pessimism . . . and then the idea of coalition emerged.

Bolsheviks . . . have often been too benevolent. If the bourgeoisie was victorious, it would act as it did in 1848 and 1871. Who thought that we would not encounter the sabotage of the bourgeoisie? . . . We must use force: arrest the directors of banks and so on. Even short-term arrests have already given positive results . . .

Thus Lenin set out on the path of the violent maintenance of power. At the same meeting Nogin warned of the consequences.

How can it be so: spill blood together, but govern separately? Can we refuse the soldiers power? Civil war will last for years. You will not go far with bayonets with the peasantry . . . What will happen if we rebuff all the other parties?

Source: Khrestomatiya po istorii Rossii, *1917–1940, pp. 82–3.*

Document 2.26 The Central Committee on Opposition Within the Party

On the next day, 2 (15) November 1917, the Central Committee met to discuss the issue of coalition.

The Central Committee recognises that the present meeting is of historic importance and therefore finds it necessary to set out clearly the two positions which have been revealed here.

1 The Central Committee takes the view that the opposition which has arisen within the CC totally disregards all the fundamental tenets of Bolshevism and the proletarian class struggle in general, repeating deeply unMarxist phrases about a socialist revolution being impossible in Russia and the need to yield to ultimatums and threats of resignation made by an obvious minority in the Soviet organisation, and in so doing frustrates the will and the decision of the Second All-Russian Congress of Soviets and sabotages the dictatorship of the proletariat and the poor peasants which has been inaugurated.

2 The Central Committee considers that this opposition must take full responsibility for the way revolutionary work has been hampered and for vacillations criminal at a moment like this and invites it to remove itself from practical work it does not believe in and to transfer its discussion and its scepticism to the press. For apart from a fear of the bourgeoisie and a state of mind which reflects that of the exhausted (and not the revolutionary) section of the population, there is nothing in this opposition.

3 The Central Committee confirms that there can be no repudiation of the purely Bolshevik government without betraying the slogan of Soviet power, since a majority of the Second All-Russian Congress of Soviets, barring no one from the Congress, entrusted power to this government.

4 The Central Committee affirms that if the slogan of rule by the Soviets of Workers', Soldiers' and Peasants' Deputies is not to be betrayed, there can be no resort to petty haggling over the affiliation to the Soviets of organisations which are not of the Soviet type, that is, of organisations which are not voluntary associations of the revolutionary vanguard of the masses fighting to overthrow the landowners and the capitalists.

5 The Central Committee affirms that to give in to ultimatums and threats from the minority in the Soviets amounts to a complete renunciation not

only of Soviet Power but of democracy, too, for such concessions add up to a fear of the majority to use its majority, inviting anarchy and new ultimatums from any minority.

6 The Central Committee affirms that, not having excluded anyone from the Second All-Russian Congress of Soviets, it is fully prepared even now to reinstate those who walked out and to agree to a coalition within the Soviets with those who left; therefore the claim that the Bolsheviks do not want to share power with anyone is absolutely false.

7 The Central Committee affirms that on the day the government was formed, some hours before that formation, the CC invited the representative of the Left Socialist Revolutionaries to its meeting and formally proposed that they join the government. The Left SRs' refusal, although temporary and conditional, means that all responsibility for the failure to reach an agreement with them must be put fairly and squarely on these Left SRs.

8 The Central Committee recalls that the Second All-Russian Congress of Soviets adopted a resolution moved by the Bolshevik group which said that it was prepared to supplement the Soviet with soldiers from the trenches and peasants from the localities, from the villages – and therefore the assertion that the Bolshevik government is against a coalition with the peasants is completely false. On the contrary, the CC declares that our government's land law, embodying the SR mandate, has proved in practice that the Bolsheviks are completely and very sincerely ready to establish a coalition with the vast majority of Russia's population.

9 The Central Committee affirms, finally, that no matter what the difficulties, the policy of the present government must be continued unswervingly if the victory of socialism both in Russia and in Europe is to be assured. The Central Committee expresses its complete faith in the victory of this socialist revolution and invites all sceptics and waverers to abandon their hesitations and give wholehearted and energetic support to the activity of this government.

Source: 'Resolution of the CC RSDWP(b) on Opposition in the Party', 2 (15) November 1917, in Lenin, PSS, vol. 35, pp. 44–6.

Document 2.27 The Resignation of a Group of People's Commissars

On 4 (17) November 1917 a group resigned, warning darkly of civil war.

It is our view that a socialist government must be formed from all the parties in the soviet. We consider that only if such a government is formed will there be an opportunity for the fruits of the heroic struggle waged by the working class and the revolutionary army in the October and November days to be made secure.

We believe that, apart from this, there is only one other path: the retention of a purely Bolshevik government by means of political terror. The Council of People's Commissars has embarked on that path. We cannot and will not take it. It will lead to the mass proletarian organisations becoming cut off from the leadership of political life, to the establishment of an unaccountable regime and to the destruction of the revolution and the country. We cannot be responsible for this policy and so, before the *TsIK*, we relinquish our titles of People's Commissars.

> People's Commissar of Trade and Industry – V. Nogin.
> People's Commissar of Internal Affairs – A. Rykov.
> People's Commissar of Agriculture – V. Milyutin.
> People's Commissar for the Food Supply – Teodorovich.

Associating themselves with this statement:

> D. Ryazanov . . .
> Director of the department of legisl. Chm. Commissar – L. Iu. Larin.

While I endorse the general assessment of the political situation with regard to the need for an agreement, I consider it inadmissible to relinquish my responsibility and obligations.

> People's Commissar for Labour – A. Shlyapnikov.

Source: Izvestiya TsIK i Petrogradskogo Soveta Rabochikh i Sovetskikh Deputatov, *no. 217, 5 November 1917.*

Document 2.28 Lenin on the Rebels

On 5 or 6 (18 or 19) November 1917 Lenin made his views clear.

From the Central Committee of the Russian Social-Democratic Labour Party (bolsheviks)
To Comrades Kamenev, Zinoviev, Ryazanov and Larin.

The CC has already presented one ultimatum to the most prominent representatives of your policy (Kamenev and Zinoviev) demanding that they submit fully to decisions of the CC and to its policy line, renouncing the sabotage of its work, and stop their disruptive activity.

In leaving the CC but remaining in the party, the exponents of your policy put themselves under an obligation to obey CC resolutions. Yet you have not confined yourselves to criticism within the party but are disrupting the ranks of the people fighting an insurrection which is still not over and you continue, in defiance of party discipline, to thwart CC decisions outside our party, in the soviets, in municipal institutions, in trade unions, etc., and to obstruct the CC's work.

In view of this, the CC is forced to repeat its ultimatum and to suggest that you either undertake immediately in writing to submit to CC decision and to promote its policy in all your speeches, or withdraw from all public party activity and resign all responsible posts in the workers' movement until the party congress.

If you refuse to make either of these pledges, the CC will be obliged to raise the question of your immediate expulsion from the party.

Source: Lenin, PSS, vol. 35, pp. 70–1.

Document 2.29   Lenin Defends the Bolsheviks Going it Alone

Lenin was willing to accept the principle of coalition, in particular with the Left Socialist Revolutionaries, but on his own terms. In a circular letter addressed to all party members and workers issued in the name of the CC he insisted (somewhat misleadingly) that Bolshevik one-party government had been forced upon them.

Comrades!

Everyone knows that the majority of the delegates at the Second All-Russian Congress of Workers' and Soldiers' Deputies were from the Bolshevik party.

This fact is fundamental to an understanding of the revolution which has just taken place and triumphed in Petrograd and Moscow and in Russia as a whole. Yet this fact is constantly forgotten and ignored by supporters of the capitalists and their unwitting helpers. They are undermining the basic principle of the new revolution – *all power to the soviets.* There must be no other government in Russia but a *soviet government.* Soviet power has been won in Russia and the government can be transferred out of the hands of one soviet party into the hands of another party without any revolution, simply by a decision of the soviets, simply by new elections of deputies to the soviets. The Bolshevik party was in the majority at the Second All-Russian Congress of Soviets. Only a government formed by that party is, therefore, a soviet government. And everyone knows that a few hours before the new government was formed and before the list of its members was proposed to the Second All-Russian Congress of Soviets, the Central Committee of the Bolshevik party called three of the most prominent members of the Left SR group, comrades Kamkov, Spiro and Karelin, to its meeting *and invited them* to join the new government. We are extremely sorry that the Left SR comrades refused, for we consider such a refusal unthinkable for revolutionaries and workers' advocates. We are always ready to include Left SRs in the government, but we declare that, as the majority party in the Second All-Russian Congress of Soviets, we have the right and the obligation to the people to form a government.

Everyone knows that the Central Committee of our Party submitted a purely Bolshevik list of People's Commissars to the Second All-Russian Congress of Soviets and that the *Congress approved this list of a purely Bolshevik government.*

The fraudulent statements to the effect that a Bolshevik government is not a soviet government are therefore complete lies and can only come from enemies of the people, from enemies of Soviet power. On the contrary, *only* a Bolshevik government now, after the Second All-Russian Congress of Soviets and until the convocation of the third or new elections to the soviets or until the Central Executive Committee forms a new government – only a Bolshevik government can now be regarded as a *Soviet* government . . .

Source: Lenin, 'From the CC RSDRP(b) to all Party Members and Working Class in Russia', 5–6 (18–19) November 1917, PSS, vol. 35, pp. 72–3.

The coalition debate was the first serious split in the Bolshevik party after coming to power. It represented the fear that without allies the Bolsheviks would be overthrown, but also reflected more profound misgivings over the nature of the power that would emerge if the Bolsheviks tried to monopolise politics. These fears were more than justified: *soviet* power (the power of the soviets) became *Soviet* power (communists ruling in the name of the soviets).

1917 in Perspective

Despite the many failings of the Provisional Government it made possible Russia's development as a modern representative democracy. The government, however, moved too slowly to establish the institutions of constitutional democracy and undermined its own legitimacy by temporising over key policy issues. The new administrative machinery remained rudimentary and the government was forced to rely on the voluntary cooperation of the soviets and other bodies. Its popular support gradually eroded to leave it vulnerable to a coup from right or left. The moderate socialist parties, the Mensheviks and the Socialist Revolutionaries, failed to provide effective leadership. The Mensheviks remained locked in their two-stage view that leadership in the revolution should go to the 'bourgeois democratic' parties, and only after a considerable period could socialism be placed on the agenda in Russia. Liberal parties, primarily the Kadets, adopted increasingly intransigent positions and failed to define an adequate response to the fact that the Russian revolution was as much a social as a political revolution. In different circumstances – an end to the war, some economic stability, better leadership from the moderate socialists – then the February 'bourgeois' revolution might have survived. In the event the problems that had overwhelmed the tsarist government engulfed the Provisional Government as well.

Document 2.30 Trotsky Writes about the Revolution

Trotsky expresses some of the hopes of 1917 while becoming himself one of its most prominent victims. In his captivating yet misleading analysis of the revolution of 1917 Trotsky sought to place the events in historical perspective. Writing fifteen years later, Trotsky sought to establish a version of events free from later Stalinist distortions. He contrasted the spontaneity of the February revolution with the planned nature of the October seizure of power, in which he took a prominent part. Trotsky's history stresses his closeness to Lenin and the orthodoxy of his views, in particular his denigration of what later became the Stalinist concept of 'socialism in one country' contrasted with his own defence of the 'permanent revolution', the internationalist approach to establishing socialism. His question 'Do the consequences of a revolution justify in general the sacrifices it involves?' is one we return to at the end of the next chapter.

A remarkable consecutiveness of stages is to be observed in the development of the Russian revolution – and this for the very reason that it was an authentic popular revolution, setting in motion tens of millions. Events succeeded each other as though obeying laws of gravitation. The correlation of forces was twice verified at every stage: first the masses would demonstrate the might of their assault, then the possessing classes, attempting revenge, would reveal their isolation the more clearly.

In February the workers and soldiers of Petrograd rose in insurrection – not only against the patriotic will of all the educated classes, but also contrary to the reckonings of the revolutionary organisations. The masses demonstrated that they were unconquerable. Had they themselves been aware of this, they would have become the government. But there was not yet a strong and authoritative revolutionary party at their head . . . The Mensheviks and Social Revolutionaries could make no other use of the confidence of the masses but to summon to the helm the liberal bourgeoisie, who in their turn could only place the power slipped to them by the Compromisers at the service of the interests of the Entente . . .

The chief task of a political régime, according to an English aphorism, is to put the right people in the right positions . . . From the 25th of October the man at the head of Russia was Lenin, the greatest figure in Russian political history. He was surrounded by a staff of assistants who, as their most spiteful enemies acknowledge, knew what they wanted and how to fight for their aims . . .

The historic ascent of humanity, taken as a whole, may be summarised as a succession of victories of consciousness over blind forces – in nature, in society, in man himself. Critical and creative thought can boast of its greatest victories of consciousness over blind forces – in nature, in society, in man himself . . . The physico-chemical sciences have already reached a point where man is clearly about to become master of matter. But social relations are still forming in the manner of the coral islands. Parliamentarism illumined only the surface of society, and even that with a rather artificial light. In comparison with monarchy and other heirlooms from the cannibals and cave-dwellers, democracy is of course a great conquest, but it leaves the blind play of forces in the social relations of men untouched. It was against this deeper sphere of the unconscious that the October revolution was the first to raise its hand. The Soviet system wishes to bring aim and plan into the very basis of society, where up to now only accumulated consequences have reigned.

Enemies are gleeful that fifteen years after the revolution the Soviet country is still but little like a kingdom of universal well-being. Such an argument, if not really to be explained as due to a blinding hostility, could only be dictated by an excessive worship of the magic power of socialist methods. Capitalism required a hundred years to elevate science and technique to the heights and plunge humanity into the hell of war and crisis. To socialism its enemies allow only fifteen years to create and furnish a terrestrial paradise. We took no such obligation upon ourselves. We never set these dates. The process of vast transformations must be measured by an adequate scale.

But the misfortunes which have overwhelmed living people? The fire and bloodshed of the civil war? Do the consequences of a revolution justify in general the sacrifices it involves? The question is teleological and therefore fruitless. It would be as well to ask in face of the difficulties and griefs of personal existence: Is it worth while to be born? Melancholy reflections have not so far, however, prevented people from bearing or being born. Even in the present epoch of intolerable misfortune only a small percentage of the population of our planet resorts to suicide. But the people are seeking the way out of their unbearable difficulties in revolution.

It is not remarkable that those who talk most indignantly about the victims of social revolutions are usually the very ones who, if not directly responsible for the victims of the world war, prepared and glorified them, or at least accepted them? It is our turn to ask: Did the war justify itself? What has it given us? What has it taught? . . .

The language of the civilised nations has clearly marked off two epochs in the development of Russia. Where the aristocratic culture introduced into world parlance such barbarisms as *czar*, *pogrom*, *knout*, October has internationalised such words as *Bolshevik*, *soviet*, and *piatiletka* [five-year plan]. This alone justifies the proletarian revolution, if you imagine that it needs justification.

Source: Leon Trotsky, The History of the Russian Revolution, *translated by Max Eastman (London, Victor Gollancz, 1934), pp. 1188, 1191–2, 1193.*

Document 2.31   Semyon Frank on the Meaning of the Russian Revolution

S. L. Frank (1877–1950) was one of the most profound and broad-ranging of Russia's religious philosophers. He was expelled from Russia in 1922 by Lenin, together with a number of other leading figures, and settled in Berlin, and from 1937 in Paris. His view evolved from Populism, through 'Legal Marxism' to idealism and the universalist ideas of Vladimir Soloviev, and ended with views close to Martin Heidegger's. His contribution to the *Vekhi* collection (see Document 1.16), 'The Ethics of Nihilism', stressed the Russian intelligentsia's radicalism that ignored spiritual and moral absolutes, while his contribution to *From the Depths* (a collection that in 1918 continued the debate begun in *Vekhi*, see pp. 21–2) argued that the reason for the failure of liberalism in Russia was spiritual, 'the lack of a viable, positive *social worldview*', and it was thus crushed by a 'completely blind and thus secular nihilism' that was insensitive to human complexity. The absolutisation of social factors provoked a 'principled revolutionism' that considered the total destruction of the existing order the main condition for human emancipation. His fears were borne out by the Bolshevik revolution, and much of the rest of his work examined the reasons for the failure of liberalism and conservatism to take root in Russia, and he developed an original conception of 'liberal conservatism'. In the extract below, first published in 1924, he reflects on the revolution.

The national distinctiveness of the Russian revolution is determined by the peculiarities of Russian history, taking an entirely different path than that of the Western world, and the exceptional features of the Russian national character, mind and beliefs, which make the Russian person somehow enigmatic, closed and secret not to the Western European, but also for the Russian brought up on Western ways of thinking . . .

We can briefly formulate the Russian revolutionary faith as *nihilistic rationalism*, the combination of disbelief and rejection of all objective foundations linking human will with belief in human arbitrariness . . . Socialism is only the expression of this nihilistic rationalism in the socio-economic sphere. That which is only timidly dreamed about by the Western European masses and their leaders and which in their own consciousness encounters unsurpassable spiritual barriers in the form of deeply rooted systems of law and culture – the attempt to subordinate all of life, including its most profound, so to speak physiological, basis in the form of the economic circulation of social mechanisms – this was without doubt tried out in Russia. Here there was sufficient lack of faith in the suprarational basis of culture, including the individual as an economic subject, and enough belief in straightforward human intelligence that, with the help of the fist and the lash for the depraved and lacking in understanding, there was a belief that human life could easily and simply be remade.

The Russian revolution is the last effective and national manifestation of nihilism – this primordial Russian frame of mind, closely associated with universal developments of modernity . . . Russia missed out on the Renaissance and the Reformation, and even the rationalism and enlightenment in that profound and spontaneous sense that these movements entailed in the West. Russia lacked the dominance of liberal-bourgeois democracy, whose completion and at the same time repudiation is socialism.

Source: S. L. Frank, 'Religiozno-istoricheskii smysl russkoi revolyutsii', in M. A. Maslin (ed.), Russkaya ideya *(Moscow, Respublika, 1992), pp. 327, 333, 335.*

3 | The birth of the Soviet state, 1917–1921

In October 1917 several streams of revolutionary activism – peasant, worker, soldier, nationalist – converged, and it was Lenin's genius to seize the unique opportunity to knot them together in a single revolutionary moment. It must be stressed, however, that the Bolshevik revolution was directed as much against the moderate 'evolutionary' socialists as it was against the decaying authority of the 'bourgeois' Provisional Government. The revolution, moreover, appeared to run counter to Marx's own views on the necessary developmental foundations for socialism – a mature economy and an advanced society. For Lenin – as for so many other revolutionaries in the twentieth century – the revolution appeared to be the key to development, and not vice versa. Once in power the revolutionary knot began to unravel, with open dissension within the party over various issues throughout the Civil War. It was only in March 1921 that the Leninist discipline, which had been so much discussed earlier, was finally imposed in practice. The aims of the other revolutionary threads also diverged, while 'democracy' as an aspiration, not only for the defenders of the Constituent Assembly but also for revolutionary workers and sailors in Kronstadt, did not disappear. Lenin's second stroke of genius, then, was not only to have made a revolution but to have forged a 'Leninist' party-state out of a fissiparous revolutionary socialist movement.

The Consolidation of Power

The Kadet Party was banned on 28 November 1917. On 9 December 1917 the Left SRs agreed to join Sovnarkom and took three ministerial appointments, including Steinberg as People's Commissar of Justice, and two without portfolio. Despite the broadening of the government, repression continued. One of the first acts of all twentieth-century revolutionary socialist governments was to establish a secret police, and the Bolsheviks led the way in this.

Document 3.1 Establishment of the Secret Police

Having already banned the opposition press and right-wing parties, Sovnarkom on 7 (20) December 1917 moved against not only actual but also possible sources of opposition, establishing the Extraordinary Commission to Fight Counter-Revolution, better known by the acronym of the first two words, the Cheka.

The Commission is to be named the All-Russian Extraordinary Commission and is to be attached to the Council of People's Commissars. [This commission] is to make war on counter-revolution and sabotage . . .

The duties of the Commission will be:

1 To persecute and break up all acts of counter-revolution and sabotage all over Russia, no matter what their origin.
2 To bring before the Revolutionary Tribunal all counter-revolutionists and saboteurs and to work out a plan for fighting them.
3 To make preliminary investigation only – enough to break up [the counter-revolutionary act]. The Commission is to be divided into sections: (a) the information section, (b) the organisation section (in charge of organising the fight against counter-revolution all over Russia) with branches, and (c) the fighting section.

The Commission will be formed tomorrow (December 21) . . . The Commission is to watch the press, saboteurs, strikers, and the Socialist-Revolutionists of the Right. Measures [to be taken against these counter-revolutionists are] confiscation, confinement, deprivation of [food] cards, publication of the names of the enemies of the people, etc.

Source: James Bunyan and H. H. Fisher, The Bolshevik Revolution, 1917–1918: Documents and Materials *(Stanford, Stanford University Press, 1934), pp. 297–8.*

Headed by Felix Dzerzhinskii, the Cheka soon emerged as a largely independent body, despite the attempts by Bolshevik leaders like Kamenev to regulate and bring its activities under political control. Applying the death penalty at will, the Cheka came into its own during the 'Red Terror' in autumn 1918, following the attempted assassination of Lenin by the Left Socialist Revolutionary Fanny Kaplan, on 30 August 1918. At various points thereafter the Cheka and its successors enjoyed the right to arrest and summarily to execute. In 1922 the Cheka became the GPU (State Political Administration); in 1924 OGPU (Unified State Political Administration); in 1934 the interior and secret police ministries merged to create Stalin's killing machine, the NKVD (People's Commissariat of Internal Affairs); after the war the ministry was split to create the MVD (Ministry of Internal Affairs, which lasts to this day), and the MGB (Ministry of State Security); following Stalin's death the latter changed to the KGB (the Committee for State Security), which led the struggle against dissent and saw out the Soviet Union.

Document 3.2   Dissolution of the Constituent Assembly

The Constituent Assembly was intended to establish forms of governance and to devise a new constitution. It was elected on the basis of universal proportional election in the autumn of 1917, the first completely free national elections in Russia's history. Fifty per cent of the electorate took part. In the country as a whole some 9 million people voted for the Bolsheviks (25 per cent of the vote), in the 67 *guberniya* provincial centres 36.5 per cent and in the Petrograd garrison 79.2 per cent. Some 715 people were elected to the Assembly, of whom 370 were SRs, 40 Left SRs, 175 Bolsheviks, 17 Kadets, 15 Mensheviks, 2 Popular Socialists, 1 non-party and 86 from national groups. The Assembly opened on the afternoon of 5 (18) January 1918, and then in the early hours of 6 January the sentry Zheleznyakov anounced that 'The guard is tired'. The Assembly retired for the night to meet late next afternoon. In the event, it never met again and on the night of 6–7 (19–20) January VTsIK (All-Russian Central Executive Committee (of the Soviets)) decided to dissolve the Constituent Assembly on the grounds that the October revolution had rendered it redundant and that it now represented a counter-revolutionary threat to the soviets.

Although Russia had been waiting for a democratic asembly for over a century, Lenin insisted that it had outlived its usefulness. His language was redolent of class war and the need to use violence against whole classes of vaguely specified people. The dissolution of the Constituent Assembly met with some resistance, including demonstrations of workers and students in Petrograd and Saratov that were dispersed with violence.

The Constituent Assembly, elected on the basis of lists drawn up prior to the October revolution, was an expression of the old relation of political forces which existed when power was held by the compromisers and the Kadets. When the people at that time voted for the candidates of the Socialist-Revolutionary Party, they were not in a position to choose between the Right Socialist-Revolutionaries, the supporters of the bourgeoisie, and the Left Socialist-Revolutionaries, the supporters of socialism. Thus the Constituent Assembly, which was to have been the crown of the bourgeois parliamentary republic, could not but become an obstacle in the path of the October revolution and the Soviet power.

The October revolution, by giving power to the Soviets, and through the Soviets to the toiling and exploited classes, aroused the desperate resistance of the exploiters, and in the crushing of this resistance it fully revealed itself as the beginning of the socialist revolution. The toiling classes learnt by experience that the old bourgeois parliamentarism had outlived its purpose and was absolutely incompatible with the aim of achieving socialism, and that not national institutions, but only class institutions (such as the Soviets), were capable of overcoming the resistance of the propertied classes and of laying the foundations of a socialist society. To relinquish the sovereign power of the Soviets, to relinquish the Soviet republic won by the people, for the sake of bourgeois parliamentarism and the Constituent Assembly, would now be a retrograde step and cause the collapse of the October workers' and peasants' revolution . . .

The Right Socialist-Revolutionary and Menshevik parties are in fact waging outside the walls of the Constituent Assembly a most desperate struggle against the Soviet power, calling openly in their press for its over-throw and characterising as arbitrary and unlawful the crushing by force of the resistance of the exploiters by the toiling classes, which is essential in the interests of emancipation from exploitation. They are defending the saboteurs, the servitors of capital, and are going to the length of undisguised calls to terrorism, which certain 'unidentified groups' have already begun to practise. It is obvious that under such circumstances the remaining part of the Constituent Assembly could only serve as a screen for the struggle of the counter-revolutionaries to overthrow the Soviet power.

Accordingly, the Central Executive Committee resolves: The Constituent Assembly is hereby dissolved.

*Source: Lenin, 'Draft Decree on the Dissolution of the Constituent Assembly',
6 (19) January 1918, PSS, vol. 35, pp. 235–6, 236–7.*

Document 3.3   From the 'Declaration of the Rights of the Toiling and Exploited People'

With the Constituent Assembly out of the way, the Third Congress of Soviets on 12 January declared Russia 'a republic of soviets'. Classic notions of the separation of powers and the like were abolished in favour of a single national system of soviets, to whom *all* power belonged. The role of the Communist Party in this system remained undefined. The first steps were taken towards the construction of Russia as a federal system. The same declaration abolished the private ownership of land and socialised it, declaring land a national asset. At the same time universal labour duty was introduced 'to eliminate the parasitical layers of society'.

1 Russia is declared to be a Republic of Soviets of Workers', Soldiers' and Peasants' Deputies. All power in the centre and localities belongs to these soviets.
2 The Soviet Russian Republic is established on the basis of the free union of free nations, as a federation of Soviet national republics.

Source: Izvestiya, 19 January 1918.

Document 3.4   Church and State

Relations between Church and state throughout the Soviet years veered from the murderous to the uncomfortable. Marx's views on religion as the 'opiate of the people' under the Bolsheviks took the form of a militant atheism that sought to destroy the social sources of the power of the Church, and to extirpate religious belief as a social phenomenon. Under the slogan of separating Church and state, the Bolsheviks in effect expropriated church property and dramatically limited the Church's ability to conduct a normal religious life. On 19 January 1918 Patriarch Tikhon (1865–1925), the first Patriarch of the Russian Orthodox Church after the restoration of the Patriarchate in 1917, pronounced an anathema on the Bolsheviks.

> The Holy Orthodox Church of Christ in the Russian lands is undergoing hard times now . . . Every day we receive news about awful and bestial beatings of innocents and even people on their sick beds, guilty only of honestly fulfilling their duty to the motherland, doing all they can to serve the good of the people, and all this takes place not only under the cover of darkness but even in broad daylight, with hitherto unheard-of audacity and with merciless cruelty, without any trial and flouting all laws and legality. This is taking place today in nearly all towns and corners of our native land, in the capitals and in distant regions . . . Come to your senses, madmen, stop your massacres. What you are doing is not only cruel: it is truly Satan's work . . .
> Patriarch of Moscow and All Russia Tikhon

Source: Khrestomatiya po istorii Rossii, 1917–1940, *pp. 99–101.*

Document 3.5   Sovnarkom Decree 'On Freedom of Conscience, Church and Religious Associations'

On 20 January Sovnarkom issued a decree separating the Church from the state, formally guaranteeing people the right to practise the religion of their choice, or none at all. The decree, however, insisted that religious belief could not be used as an excuse not to fulfil one's 'civic duty', and the teaching of religion in state schools was banned, as it was in private general educational schools.

1 The Church is separated from the state . . .
12 No church or religious association has the right to own property. They do not have the right to act as a legal entity.
13 All property in Russia belonging to churches or religious societies is declared a public resource. Buildings and religious objects used for worship are allowed, by special permission of local or state authorities, to be used by the relevant religious association.

Source: Pravda, *21 January 1918.*

Peace and War

Away from internal and inter-party wrangling, the Great War continued. Taking advantage of the chaos in Russia, the Germans had launched an offensive in the West. On coming to power the Bolsheviks agreed an armistice with Germany, but the problem still remained of how to extricate the country from the war. The Decree on Peace (see Document 2.17) tried to achieve a unilateral peace, calling for the cessation of hostilities against Russia and renouncing cooperation with the Allies. The failure of this initiative led to negotiations at the Polish border town of

Brest-Litovsk where the Soviet delegation, headed by Trotsky, adopted the unconventional negotiating tactic of calling for the overthrow of the state with which it was negotiating. Trotsky's tactic of 'neither war nor peace' did not impress the Germans, who threatened a new offensive. Lenin in January 1918 advocated acceptance of the German terms, insisting that Russia needed a 'breathing spell' (*peredyshka*) to protect the gains of the revolution. This was not accepted by the party, and the Germans thereupon seized great swathes of territory. In desperation, the government then accepted even more humiliating peace terms, provoking a controversy that nearly destroyed the Communist Party (as the Bolsheviks were renamed in March 1918). A Left Communist group emerged, joined by Bukharin, that condemned the idea of peace with the imperialists and urged Soviet Russia to launch a 'revolutionary war' against the occupying forces. Instead, Lenin's view on the need for peace triumphed, despite the humiliating terms. At the same time the country began forming a traditional army.

Document 3.6   Lenin on the Brest-Litovsk Peace Treaty

On 23 February 1918 the Central Committee finally voted by the narrowest of margins (five to four) to accept the German peace terms, sacrificing land – Poland, the Ukraine and the Baltic – for time. The treaty was signed on 3 March but at the Seventh Party Congress held a few days later the party nearly split. Lenin insisted that the Brest-Litovsk Treaty was preferable to a war which Soviet Russia could not win. The treaty would allow the regime to survive until the world revolution began.

The revolution will not come as quickly as we expected. History has proved this, and we must be able to take this as a fact, to reckon with the fact that the world socialist revolution began in Russia – in the land of Nicholas and Rasputin, the land in which an enormous part of the population was absolutely indifferent as to what peoples were living in the outlying regions, or what was happening there. In such a country it was quity easy to start a revolution, as easy as lifting a feather.

But to start without preparation a revolution in a country in which capitalism is developed, in which it has produced a democratic culture and organisation, provided it to everybody, down to the last man – to do so would be wrong, absurd. There we are only just approaching the painful period of the beginning of socialist revolutions. This is a fact. We do not know, no one knows; perhaps – it is quite possible – it will triumph within a few weeks, even within a few days, but we cannot stake everything on that. We must be prepared for extraordinary difficulties, for severe defeats, which are inevitable, because the revolution in Europe has not yet begun, although it may begin tomorrow, and when it does begin then, of course, we shall not be tortured by doubts, there will be no question about a revolutionary war, but just one continuous triumphal march. That will be, it will inevitably be so, but it is not so yet. This is the simple fact that history has taught us, with which she has hit us quite painfully – and a man who has been thrashed is worth two that haven't. That is why I think that after history has given us a very painful thrashing, because of our hope that the Germans cannot attack and that we can get everything by shouting 'hurrah!', this lesson, with the help of our Soviet organisations, will be very quickly brought home to the masses all over Soviet Russia . . .

Source: Lenin, 'Political Report of the CC', Seventh Emergency Congress of the RCP(b), 7 March 1918, PSS, vol. 36, pp. 15–16.

Document 3.7   The Left Communists Condemn the Brest-Litovsk Peace

The Left Communists led by Bukharin advocated a revolutionary war, Trotsky took a middle line, while the majority led by Lenin argued that the treaty was essential for the survival of the regime. In a declaration the Left Communists insisted that there was an alternative.

In response to the offensive by the German imperialists, openly declaring their aim of crushing the proletarian revolution in Russia, the party's CC responded by agreeing to making peace on those conditions that a few days earlier had been rejected by the Soviet delegation at Brest. This agreement, accepted on the first onslaught of the enemies of the proletariat, represents the capitulation by the leading section of the international proletariat before the international bourgeoisie . . .

We consider that after seizing power, after the complete crushing of the last bastions of the bourgeoisie, there inevitably arises before the proletariat the task of fomenting civil war on an international scale, a task for whose fulfilment it cannot stop in the face of any danger. Refusal to fulfil this will lead to its destruction by internal degeneration, the equivalent of suicide . . .

Source: Protokoly TsK RSDRP(b): avgust 1917–fevral' 1918 (Moscow, Politizdat, 1958), p. 178.

For the Bolshevik regime to have been able to put up any military resistance to the Germans, the war would have had to have been fought not so much as a revolutionary war but as a *national* war, as Stalin did indeed fight the Great Patriotic War of 1941–5. But to have done so would have forced the Bolsheviks to ally precisely with those forces that they were intent upon destroying, threatening the Bolshevik hold on power in the process. The Brest-Litovsk Peace Treaty was ratified by the Fourth (Emergency) Congress of Soviets on 15 March 1918. The Left SRs refused to recognise the peace and withdrew their representatives from Sovnarkom. The Bolsheviks also committed themselves to the cessation of revolutionary propaganda. A further agreement signed in Berlin on 27 August 1918 committed Russia to paying Germany a total of 6 million marks. The Brest peace was annulled by the Soviet government on 13 November 1918.

Document 3.8　Trotsky and the Red Army

Soon after establishing the Cheka, the Soviet authorities moved to create their own army – the tsarist army having in effect dissolved. On 23 February 1918 the Red Army was formally established, and Trotsky, who had resigned as Foreign Affairs Commissar at the time of the Brest-Litovsk negotiations, was appointed Commissar of Military Affairs. While the Left Communists harked back to Marx's strictures against a standing army, favouring a revolutionary volunteer militia army using guerrilla tactics, the election of officers and democratic decision-making, Trotsky insisted on the reimposition of traditional discipline and the employment of so-called 'military specialists', former tsarist officers, under the *kontrol'* (supervision) of communist commissars.

The misfortune of the working class is that it has always been in the position of an oppressed class. This is reflected in everything: both in its level of education, and in the fact that it does not have those habits of rule which the dominant class has and which it bequeaths to its heirs through its schools, universities, etc. The working class has none of this, but must acquire it. Having come to power, it has had to view the old state apparatus as an apparatus of class oppression. But at the same time it must draw from this apparatus all the worthwhile skilled elements which are technically necessary, put them where they belong, and heighten its proletarian class power by using these elements. This, Comrades, is the task which now stands before us for our overall growth . . .

Here I turn to a ticklish point which to a familiar degree has now assumed major importance in our party life. This is one of the questions of the organisation of the army, specifically the question of recruiting military specialists – i.e., to speak plainly, former officers and generals – to create the army and to run it. All basic, guiding institutions of the army are now set up so that they consist of one military specialist and two political commissars. Such is the present basic tone of the leading organs of the army . . .

There is still another question in the area of the organisation of the army: the so-called elective principle. In general, all it means is to struggle against the old officers' corps, to control the commanding staff. As long as power was in the hands of a class that was hostile to us, when the commanding staff was an instrument in the hands of this power, we were obliged to strive to smash the class resistance of the commanding personnel by way of the elective principle. But now political power is in the hands of that same working class from whose ranks the army is recruited. Under the present regime in the army – I tell you this in all frankness – the elective principle is politically pointless and technically inexpedient, and has in fact already been set aside by decree . . .

Source: Trotsky, 'Labour, Discipline, Order', speech to the 27 March 1918 Moscow City Conference of the Russian Communist Party, in Daniels, Communism in Russia, *p. 93.*

Industrial Democracy and State Capitalism

Industrial democracy was at the heart of the aspirations of the workers' movement in 1917, yet following the Bolshevik assumption of power the two trends of the revolution – from above and from below – increasingly came into conflict. Having exploited the aspirations of the workers in 1917, Lenin during the 'breathing space' following the Brest-Litovsk peace soon reverted to type and insisted on strict hierarchy, discipline, and even the reimposition of piece rates, something detested by workers at this time.

Document 3.9   Workers' Control

The following decree was issued on 14 (27) November 1917 and appeared to grant workers' demands, yet the rights of workers were limited. As mentioned above (p. 38), the Russian word *kontrol'* means 'supervision', not 'control' in the English sense.

1 In the interests of a systematic regulation of national economy, Workers' Control is introduced in all industrial, commercial, agricultural (and similar) enterprises which are hiring people to work for them in their shops or which are giving them work to take home. This control is to extend over the production, storing, buying and selling of raw materials and finished products as well as over the finances of the enterprise.
2 The workers will exercise this control through their elected organizations, such as factory and shop committees, soviets of elders, etc. The office employees and the technical personnel are also to have representation in these committees.
3 Every large city, province and industrial area is to have its own Soviet of Workers' Control, which, being an organ of the S(oviet) of W(orkers'), S(oldiers'), and P(easants') D(eputies), must be composed of representatives of trade-unions, Factory, shop and other workers' committees and workers' co-operatives . . .
6 The organs of Workers' Control have the right to supervise production, fix the minimum of output, and determine the cost of production.
7 The organs of Workers' Control have the right to control all the business correspondence of an enterprise. Owners of enterprises are legally responsible for all correspondence kept secret. Commercial secrets are abolished. The owners have to show to the organs of Workers' Control all their books and statements for the current year and for the past years.
8 The rulings of the organs of Workers' Control are binding on the owners of enterprises and can be annulled only by decisions of the higher organs of Workers' Control.

Source: Bunyan and Fisher, The Bolshevik Revolution, 1917–1918, *pp. 308–10.*

Instead of the direct control of enterprises, this decree allowed 'supervision' over the workplace. In practice, faced with lockouts and the like, workers were forced to seize their enterprises. In the 'red guard attack on capital' following the seizure of power Lenin tolerated this, but later imposed a more centralised state-directed model of industrial management. The ideal of workers' self-management of the economy was later espoused by the Workers' Opposition, and was in part implemented in the Yugoslav model of self-managing socialism.

Document 3.10   Lenin and 'State Capitalism'

Early hopes that the October revolution would usher in workers' self-management were soon dismissed as Utopian. Following the Brest-Litovsk peace Lenin turned to the problem of shaping the transitional Soviet economic order, and (once again to the disappointment of the Left Communists) advocated the retention of the rudiments of capitalist management – with any surviving capitalists under the supervision of the Soviet state. Measures included the reintroduction of one-man management, labour discipline and piecework incentive payments, together with the employment of 'bourgeois' technical and managerial 'specialists' (known as '*spetsy*' in Soviet jargon). 'Accounting and control' became the slogan of the new period.

Thanks to the peace which has been achieved – despite its extremely onerous character and extreme instability – the Russian Soviet Republic has gained an opportunity to concentrate its efforts for a while on the most important and most difficult aspect of the socialist revolution, namely, the task of organisation . . .

It also goes without saying that we shall be able to render effective assistance to the socialist revolution in the West, which has been delayed for a number of reasons, only to the extent that we are able to fulfil the task of organisation confronting us . . .

For the first time in human history a socialist party has managed to complete in the main the conquest of power and the suppression of the exploiters, and has managed to *approach directly* the task of *administration*. We must prove worthy executors of this most difficult (and most gratifying) task of the socialist revolution . . .

The decisive thing is the organisation of the strictest and country-wide accounting and control of production and distribution of goods. And yet, we have *not yet* introduced accounting and control in those enterprises and in those branches which we have taken away from the bourgeoisie; and without this there can be no thought of achieving the second and equally essential material condition for introducing socialism, namely, raising the productivity of labour on a national scale . . .

Now we have to resort to the old bourgeois method and to agree to pay a very high price for the 'services' of the top bourgeois specialists. All those who are familiar with the subject appreciate this, but not all ponder over the significance of this measure being adopted by the proletarian state. Clearly, such a measure is a compromise, a departure from the principles of the Paris Commune and of every proletarian power, which call for the reduction of all salaries to the level of the wages of the average worker, which call for fighting careerism, not with words, but with deeds.

Moreover, it is clear that such a measure not only implies the cessation – in a certain field and to a certain degree – of the offensive against capital (for capital is not a sum of money, but a definite social relation); it is also *a step backward* on the part of our socialist Soviet state power, which from the very outset proclaimed and pursued the policy of reducing high salaries to the level of the wages of the average worker . . .

It becomes immediately clear that while it is possible to capture the central government in a few days, while it is possible to suppress the military resistance (and sabotage) of the exploiters even in different parts of a great country in a few weeks, the capital solution of the problem of raising the productivity of labour requires, at all events (particularly after a most terrible and devastating war), several years. The protracted nature of the work is certainly dictated by objective circumstances . . .

The Russian worker is a bad worker compared with people in advanced countries. It could not be otherwise under the tsarist regime and in view of the persistence of the hangover from serfdom. The task that the Soviet government must set the people in all its scope is – learn to work. The Taylor system, the last word of capitalism in this respect, like all capitalist progress, is a combination of the refined brutality of bourgeois exploitation and a number of the greatest scientific achievements in the field of analysing mechanical motions during work, the introduction of the best system of accounting and control, etc. The Soviet republic must at all costs adopt all that is valuable in the achievements of science and technology in this field. The possibility of building socialism depends exactly upon our success in combining the Soviet power and the Soviet organisation with the up-to-date achievements of capitalism . . .

It would be extremely stupid and absurdly Utopian to assume that the transition from capitalism to socialism is possible without coercion and without dictatorship. Marx's theory very definitely opposed this petty bourgeois-democratic and anarchist absurdity long ago. And Russia of 1917–18 confirms the correctness of Marx's theory in this respect so strikingly, palpably and imposingly that only those who are hopelessly dull or who have obstinately decided to turn their backs on the truth can be under any misapprehension concerning this. Either the dictatorship of Kornilov (if we take him as the Russian type of bourgeois Cavaignac [the general who had suppressed the uprising of Paris workers in June 1848]) or the dictatorship of the proletariat – any other choice is *out of the question* for a country which has gone through an extremely rapid development with extremely sharp turns and amidst desperate ruin created by one of the most horrible wars in history . . .

There is absolutely *no* contradiction in principle between Soviet (*that is*, socialist) democracy and the exercise of dictatorial powers by individuals. The difference between proletarian dictatorship and bourgeois dictatorship is that the former strikes at the exploiting minority in the interests of the exploited majority, and that it is exercised – *also through individuals* – not only by the toiling and exploited masses, but also by organisations which are built in such a way as to rouse these masses to the work of history-making. (The Soviet organisations are organisations of this kind.)

Sources: Lenin, 'The Immediate Tasks of the Soviet Government', April 1918, Selected Works, pp. 401, 402, 404, 406, 409, 415, 417, 420, 424; 'Ocherednye zadachi sovetskoi vlast', PSS, vol. 36, pp. 167, 168, 173, 175, 179, 187–8, 189–90, 194, 199.

Document 3.11   The Left Communists and Economic Management

The Left Communists were not willing to accept what appeared to them to be the fundamental repudiation of the aspirations of October. The issues raised earlier by Bogdanov about the role of the party and the proletariat in the revolutionary process were once again aired. The Left Communists advocated revolutionary construction from below and argued that workers should retain a high degree of independent initiative through workers' control. They condemned the trend towards centralism and dictatorial leadership in the new system, and thus once again, as Bogdanov had done earlier, challenged the fundamental postulates of Lenin's view of the vanguard role of leadership. In a series of 'Theses on the Present Moment' presented to a conference of party leaders on 4 April 1918, the Left Communists outlined what they saw as the stark choices facing the country.

10 The party of the proletariat is faced by a choice between two paths. One is the path of preserving and strengthening the part of the Soviet state that remains intact, which is at present from the economic perspective – considering that the revolution remains partial – only an organisation for the transition to socialism (in views of incomplete nationalisation of the banks, capitalist forms of finance enterprises, the partial nationalisation of enterprises, the predominance of small-scale farming and small property-holding in the village, and the efforts of the peasants to solve the land question by dividing up the land). But from the political viewpoint this path may, under cover of the dictatorship of the proletariat supported by the poorest peasantry, transform itself into an instrument for the political rule of the semi-proletarian petty bourgeois masses, and become merely a transitional stage to the complete rule of finance capital.

This path can be justified – in words – as an attempt to preserve at all costs the revolutionary forces and Soviet power for the international revolution, even if in 'Great Russia' alone. In this case every effort will be directed towards strengthening the development of productive forces towards 'organic construction', while rejecting the further smashing of capitalist production relations and even their partial restoration.

11 . . . The economic policy which corresponds to such a course will have to develop in the direction of agreements with capitalistic businessmen, both 'native' and the international ones who stand behind them . . .

The policy of administering enterprises on the principle of broad participation of capitalists and semi-bureaucratic centralisation is naturally accompanied by a labour policy directed at the establishment among workers of discipline disguised as 'self-discipline', the introduction of obligatory labour for workers (such a project was proposed by the rightist Bolsheviks), piecework payment, lengthening of the working day, etc.

The form of state control of enterprises must develop in the direction of bureaucratic centralisation, of rule by various commissars, of the deprivation of local soviets of their independence, and in practice the rejection of the type of 'commune state' administered from below. Many facts demonstrate that a definite tendency in this direction is already taking shape (decree on the control of the railways . . .)

12 The introduction of labour discipline in connection with the restoration of capital leadership in production cannot essentially increase the productivity of labour, but it will lower the class autonomy, activity and degree of organisation of the proletariat. It threatens the enslavement of the working class, and provokes the dissatisfaction both of the backward parts and of the vanguard of the proletariat. To impose this system with the intense class hatred prevalent in the working class against 'capitalists and saboteurs', the Communist Party would have to gain the support of the petty bourgeoisie against the workers and thereby put an end to itself as the party of the proletariat . . .

13 Proletarian communists consider a different political course essential. Not the policy of preserving a Soviet oasis in the north of Russia with the help of concessions that transform it into a petty-bourgeois state. Not a transition to 'organic internal work', under the consideration that the 'acute period' of the civil war is over.

The acute period of civil war is over only in the sense of the absence of an acute necessity to apply predominantly the sharpest physical measures of revolutionary violence. Once the bourgeoisie is beaten and is no longer capable of open fighting, 'military' methods are for the most part inappropriate. But the sharpness of the class contradiction between the proletariat and the bourgeoisie cannot diminish; as before, the proletariat's attitude towards the bourgeoisie is total negation, its annihilation as a class. The end of the acute period of the civil war cannot mean that deals are possible with the remaining forces of the bourgeoisie, and the 'organic construction' of socialism, which is undoubtedly the pressing task of the moment, can be accomplished only by the efforts of the proletariat itself, with the participation of qualified technical experts and administrators, but not by any kind of collaboration with the 'privileged elements' as such.

The Russian workers' revolution cannot 'save itself' by leaving the path of international revolution, constantly avoiding battle and retreating in the face of the onslaught of international capital, and making concessions to 'native capital'.

From this point of view three things are necessary: a decisive class internationalist policy, combining international revolutionary propaganda by word and deed, and strengthening the organic links with international socialism (and not with the international bourgeoisie); decisive resistance to all interference by imperialists in the internal affairs of the Soviet republic; refusal of political and military agreements which make the Soviet republic a tool of the imperialist camp . . .

The administration of enterprises must be placed in the hands of mixed bodies of workers and technical personnel, under the control and leadership of local economic councils. All economic life must be subjected to the organised influence of these councils, elected by workers without the participation of the 'privileged elements', but with the participation of the unions of technical and service personnel in the enterprise.

No capitulation to the bourgeoisie and its petty-bourgeois intellectual henchmen, but defeat of the bourgeoisie and the final smashing of sabotage. The final liquidation of the counterrevolutionary press and counterrevolutionary bourgeois organisations. The introduction of labour duty for qualified specialists and intellectuals; the organisation of consumer communes; the limitation of consumption by the prosperous classes and the confiscation of their surplus property. In the countryside the organisation of an attack by the poorest peasants on the rich ones, the development of large-scale socialised agriculture, and support for forms of working the land by the poor peasants which are transitional to socialised farming . . .

The granting of broad independence to local soviets and not the restricting of their activities by commissars sent by the central authorities. Soviet power and the party of the proletariat must find their support in the class initiative of the broad masses, to the development of which all efforts must be directed . . .

15 The proletarian communists define their attitude toward the majority of the party as the position of the left wing of the party and vanguard of the Russian proletariat, maintaining full unity with the party insofar as the policy of the majority does not provoke an unbridgeable split in the ranks of the proletariat itself. They define their attitude toward the Soviet power as a position of unqualified support of that power at a time of necessity, by means of participating in it insofar as the confirmation of the peace has removed

from the agenda the question of responsibility for this decision and has created a new objective situation. This participation is possible only on the basis of a definite political programme, which would prevent the deviation of the Soviet power and the majority of the party on the ruinous path of petty-bourgeois policies. In the event of such a deviation the left wing of the party will have to adopt the position of an effective and responsible proletarian opposition.

Source: Kommunist, *no. 1, 20 April 1918, in Ronnie Kowalski (ed.),* Kommunist: A Weekly Journal of Economic, Political and Social Opinion, *Publications of the Study Group on the Russian Revolution 9 (Millwood, NY, Kraus International Publications, 1990), pp. 18, 19, 20, 21–2, 22–3, 23, 24.*

Document 3.12   Workers Protest Against Bolshevik Dictatorship over Workers

Worker and student protests against the dissolution of the Constituent Assembly had already been dispersed by force in Petrograd and elsewhere in January 1918. In the spring of that year worker protests against Bolshevik dictatorship continued, in particular on the railways (whose union had most firmly favoured coalition in November 1917). In Petrograd this took the form of the establishment of assemblies of worker 'plenipotentiaries' [upolonomochennykh] elected from the workplace – they deliberately avoided using the word 'soviet'. A delegation of Petrograd workers to Moscow sent the following report back to their comrades.

Comrade workers,

Fulfilling your instructions, we set out for Moscow to inform Moscow workers about the difficult condition of the Petrograd proletariat and to consult with their representatives about ways and means of improving the condition of the working class of all Russia, restoring its independent organisations, saving our sinking revolution, and freeing Russia from the foreign yoke and fragmentation.

In Moscow we found much in common with Petrograd. The workers are similarly impoverished and similarly lack class organisations that would defend their interests. Constant lack of food is becoming genuine famine, the Soviets have become isolated from the workers and have become the mouthpieces of the anti-worker and anti-revolutionary policies of the Council of People's Commissars and only take into account the will and orders of the government bosses and least of all the wishes and aspirations of the workers down below. Martial law has been declared. Newspapers are being closed by the dozen. Freedom of speech has been suffocated. Meetings have been banned. Arrests are being made among workers. The Okhrana-type organisation called 'the commission for the struggle against counter-revolution' [the Cheka] has been granted the right to shoot without trial or the least investigation and is widely using this right . . .

Protest against repression. Free yourselves from the captivity of the Bolshevik autocracy . . .

Source: M. S. Bernshtam (ed.), Nezavisimoe rabochee dvizhenie v 1918 godu: dokumenty i materialy *(Paris, YMCA-Press, 1981), pp. 204–5, 207.*

Attempts by the Petrograd delegation to meet with Moscow workers were impeded by the Cheka, and ultimately the delegation itself was arrested. At this point the Bolsheviks, recognising a direct threat to their power, decided to eliminate the threat posed by an independent workers' organisation and arrested groups of workers involved in the plenipotentiary movement, often in the workshop itself. There could be no more clear evidence of the divergence between the workers' and the Bolshevik revolution – the temporary (and grudging) alliance of October 1917 was over. All that remained was the Bolshevik rhetoric of worker power. It was at this time (14 June 1918) that the Right and Centre SRs and the Mensheviks were expelled from the central and local soviets.

Critics of the Bolshevik Revolution

Plekhanov, in October 1917, had argued that there was no chance for a political revolution in Germany, but it took another year of pointless mass slaughter on the Western Front for the German revolution to break out, leading to the overthrow of the Hohenzollern monarchy and the establishment of a republic. Attempts to transform this 'political' revolution into a 'social' one met the resolute hostility not only of the property-owning classes, but of the moderate social democrats. The German revolutionaries, notably Luxemburg and Kautsky, still had time to comment on the Russian revolution.

Document 3.13 Luxemburg on the Russian Revolution

While welcoming Lenin's achievement in having 'put socialism on the agenda', she warned that Lenin's methods of seizing and retaining power would undermine the very purposes of socialism. For her, socialism was inseparable from democracy, and she remained to the end of her life an ardent believer in the creative capacity of humanity. Socialism, as she saw it, was to extend democracy beyond the limits imposed by bourgeois capitalist rule, not to eliminate even that limited democracy. While recognising that revolutions were not made in salons, she nevertheless regarded the dictatorial elements as temporary and to be balanced by the extension of democracy. No party, for her, had a monopoly on wisdom: a revolution was to reflect the free spontaneous creativity of the masses. All this was a far cry from Lenin's dictatorship.

Lenin says: the bourgeois state is an instrument of oppression of the working class; the socialist state, of the bourgeoisie. To a certain extent, he says, it is only the capitalist state stood on its head. This simplified view misses the most essential thing: bourgeois class rule has no need of the political training and education of the entire mass of the people, at least not beyond certain narrow limits. But for the proletarian dictatorship that is the life element, the very air without which it is not able to exist . . .

Freedom only for the supporters of the government, only for the members of one party – however numerous they may be – is no freedom at all. Freedom is always and exclusively freedom for the one who thinks differently. Not because of any fanatical concept of 'justice' but because all that is instructive, wholesome and purifying in political freedom depends on this essential characteristic, and its effectiveness vanishes when 'freedom' becomes a special privilege . . .

The tacit assumption underlying the Lenin–Trotsky theory of the dictatorship is this: that the socialist transformation is something for which a ready-made formula lies completed in the pocket of the revolutionary party, which needs only to be carried out energetically in practice. This is, unfortunately – or perhaps fortunately – not the case. Far from being a sum of ready-made prescriptions which have only to be applied, the practical realization of socialism as an economic, social and juridical system is something which lies completely hidden in the mists of the future. What we possess in our program is nothing but a few main signposts which indicate the general direction in which to look for the necessary measures, and the indications are mainly negative in character at that. Thus we know more or less what we must eliminate at the outset in order to free the road for a socialist economy. But when it comes to the nature of the thousand concrete, practical measures, large and small, necessary to introduce socialist principles into economy, law and all social relationships, there is no key in any socialist party program or textbook. That is not a shortcoming but rather the very thing that makes scientific socialism superior to the utopian varieties . . .

The negative, the tearing down, can de decreed; the building up, the positive, cannot . . . Only experience is capable of correcting and opening new ways. Only unobstructed, effervescing life falls into a thousand new forms and improvisations, brings to light creative force, itself corrects all mistaken attempts. The public life of countries with limited freedom is so poverty-stricken, so miserable, so rigid, so unfruitful, precisely because, through the exclusion of democracy, it cuts off the living sources of all spiritual riches and progress . . .

Decree, dictatorial force of the factory overseer, draconic penalties, rule by terror – all these things are but palliatives. The only way to a rebirth is the school of public life itself, the most unlimited, the broadest democracy and public opinion. It is rule by terror which demoralizes . . .

But with the repression of political life in the land as a whole, life in the soviets must also become more and more crippled. Without general elections, without unrestricted freedom of press and assembly, without a free struggle of opinion, life dies out in every public institution, becomes a mere semblance of life, in which only the bureaucracy remains as the active element. Public life gradually falls asleep, a few dozen party leaders of inexhaustible energy and boundless experience direct and rule. Among them, in reality only a dozen outstanding heads do the leading and an elite of the working class is invited from time to time to meetings where they are to applaud the speeches of the leaders, and to approve proposed resolutions unanimously – at bottom, then, a clique affair – a dictatorship, to be sure, not the dictatorship of the proletariat, however, but only the dictatorship of a handful of politicians, that is a dictatorship in the bourgeois sense, in the sense of the rule of the Jacobins . . . such conditions must inevitably cause a brutalization of public life.

Source: Rosa Luxemburg, The Russian Revolution *(Ann Arbor, University of Michigan Press, 1961), pp. 68, 69, 70, 71, 72.*

Having gained German citizenship through marriage, from 1900 Luxemburg focused her activities on the German Social-Democratic Party (SPD), and later helped establish the radical Spartacus League, which became the core of the German Communist Party in 1919. The Spartacist uprising in the first days of 1919 was crushed, and its leaders, Karl Liebknecht and Luxemburg, were murdered by reactionary officers 'while taking them to prison' on 16 January 1919.

Document 3.14   Kautsky on the Russian Revolution

Karl Kautsky was one of the leading figures of German social democracy, a luminary of the Second International and long the butt of Lenin's cruel invective. His pamphlet, *The Dictatorship of the Proletariat*, published in Vienna in 1918, criticised the Bolshevik revolution from the perspective of social democratic Marxism, insisting that parliamentary democracy had an important part to play in the transition from capitalism to socialism. For socialists, he insisted, democracy was more than an instrument in the struggle for power, but an essential part of socialism itself. The work marked an important stage in the division between social democracy and communism. As far as he was concerned the Russian revolution was not part of a broader anti-capitalist movement but a result of exceptional circumstances born of war and Russian conditions. This in part explains Lenin's vitriolic response to Kautsky's arguments.

The present Russian Revolution has, for the first time in the history of the world, made a Socialist Party the rulers of a great Empire. A far more powerful event than the seizing of control of the town of Paris by the proletariat in 1871. Yet, in one important aspect, the Paris Commune was superior to the Soviet Republic. The former was the work of the entire proletariat. All shades of the Socialist movement took part in it, none drew back from it, none was excluded.

On the other hand, the Socialist Party which governs Russia today gained power in fighting against other Socialist Parties, and exercises its authority while excluding other Socialist Parties from the executive.

The antagonism of the two Socialist movements is not based on small personal jealousies: it is the clashing of two fundamentally distinct methods, that of democracy and that of dictatorship. Both movements have the same end in view: to free the proletariat, and with it humanity, through socialism. But the view taken by the one is held by the other to be erroneous and likely to lead to destruction.

It is impossible to regard so gigantic an event as the proletarian struggle in Russia without taking sides. Each of us feels impelled to violent partisanship. And the more so because the problem which to-day occupies our Russian comrades will to-morrow assume practical significance for Western Europe, and does already decisively influence the character of our propaganda and tactics.

It is, however, our party duty not to decide for one or the other side in the Russian internal quarrel before we have thoroughly tested the arguments of both. In this many comrades would hinder us. They declare it to be our duty blindly to pronounce in favour of the section now at the helm. Any other attitude would endanger the Revolution, and socialism itself. This is nothing less than to ask us to accept as already proved that which is still to be examined, viz., that one of the sections has struck out in the right path, and we must encourage it by following.

We place ourselves, of course, by asking for the fullest discussion, already on the ground of democracy. Dictatorship does not ask for the refutation of contrary views, but the forcible suppression of their utterance. Thus, the two methods of democracy and dictatorship are already irreconcilably opposed before the discussion has started. The one demands, the other forbids it.

In the meantime, dictatorship does not yet reign in our Party; discussion amongst us is still free. And we consider it not only as our right, but as our duty to express our opinions freely, because an appropriate and fruitful decision is only possible after hearing all the arguments. One man's speech is notoriously no man's speech. Both sides must be listened to.

We will, therefore, examine the significance which democracy has for the proletariat – what we understand by the dictatorship of the proletariat – and what conditions dictatorship, as a form of government, creates in the struggle for freedom of the proletariat . . .

For us, therefore, socialism without democracy is unthinkable. We understand by modern socialism not merely social organization of production, but democratic organization of society as well. Accordingly, socialism is for us inseparably connected with democracy. No socialism without democracy.

But this proposition is not equally true if reversed. Democracy is quite possible without socialism. A pure democracy is even conceivable apart from socialism, for example, in small peasant communities, where complete equality of economic conditions for everybody exists on the basis of participating in privately owned means of production . . .

In the struggle for the political rights referred to modern democracy arises, and the proletariat matures. At the same time a new factor appears, viz., the protection of minorities, the opposition in the State. Democracy signifies rule of the majority, but not less the protection of minorities . . .

What significance the protection of minorities has for the early stages of the Socialist Party, which everywhere started as a small minority, and how much it has helped the proletariat to mature, is clear. In the ranks of the Socialist Party the protection of minorities is very important. Every new doctrine, be it of a theoretical or a tactical nature, is represented in the first place by minorities. If these are forcibly suppressed, instead of being discussed, the majority is spared much trouble and inconvenience. Much unnecessary labour might be saved – a doctrine does not mean progress because it is new and championed by a minority. Most of what arises as new thought has already been discussed long before, and recognized as untenable, either by practice or by refutation.

Ignorance is always bringing out old wares as if they were something new. Other new ideas may be original, but put in a perverted shape. Although only a few of the new ideas and doctrines may spell real progress, yet progress is only possible through new ideas, which at the outset are put forward by minorities. The suppression of the new ideas of minorities in the Party would only cause harm to the proletarian class struggle, and an obstacle to the development of the proletariat. The world is always bringing us against new problems, which are not to be solved by the existing methods.

Tedious as it may be to sift the wheat from the chaff, this is an unavoidable task if our movement is not to stagnate, and is to rise to the height of the tasks before it. And what is needful for a party is also needful for the State. Protection of minorities is an indispensable condition for democratic development, and no less important than the rule of the majority . . .

It is quite false to say that the proletariat in the democracy ceases to be revolutionary, that it is contented with giving public expression to its indignation and its sufferings, and renounces the idea of social and political revolution. Democracy cannot remove the class antagonisms of capitalist society, nor prevent the overthrow of that society, which is their inevitable outcome. But if it cannot prevent the Revolution, it can avoid many reckless and premature attempts at revolution, and render many revolutionary movements unnecessary . . .

In his letter criticizing the Gotha party programme, written in May, 1875, it is stated: 'Between capitalist and communist society lies the period of the revolutionary transformation of the one into the other. This requires a political transition stage, which can be nothing else than the revolutionary dictatorship of the proletariat.'

Marx had unfortunately omitted to specify more exactly what he conceived this dictatorship to be. Taken literally, the word signifies the suspension of democracy. But taken literally it also means the sovereignty of a single person, who is bound by no laws. A sovereignty which is distinguished from a despotism by being regarded as a passing phase, required by the circumstances of the moment, and not a permanent institution of the State.

The expression 'Dictatorship of the Proletariat,' that is the dictatorship not of a single person, but of a class, excludes the inference that Marx thought of dictatorship in the literal sense.

He speaks in the passage above quoted not of a form of government, but of a condition which must everywhere arise when the proletariat has conquered political power. That he was not thinking of a form of government is shown by his opinion that in England and America the transition might be carried out peacefully. Of course, Democracy does not guarantee a peaceful transition. But this is certainly not possible without Democracy . . .

What are the grounds for thinking that the sovereignty of the proletariat must necessarily take a form which is incompatible with democracy? . . .

A government so strongly supported by the masses has not the least occasion to interfere with democracy. It cannot dispense with the use of force when this is employed to suppress democracy. Force can only be met by force. But a government which knows that the masses are behind it would only use force to protect democracy, and not to subvert it. It would be committing suicide to cast aside such a strong support as universal suffrage, which is a powerful source of moral authority.

A subversion of democracy by dictatorship can therefore only be a matter for consideration in exceptional cases, when an extraordinary combination of favourable circumstances enables a proletarian party to take to itself political power, while the majority of the people are either not on its side, or are even against it . . .

A dictatorship of a minority which grants to the people the fullest freedom of organization undermines its own power by so doing. Should it seek, on the other hand, to maintain its authority by restricting this freedom, it impedes development towards socialism, instead of furthering it.

Source: Karl Kautsky, The Dictatorship of the Proletariat *(Michigan, Ann Arbor Paperback, 1964), pp. 1–3, 6–7, 30, 33–4, 36, 42–3, 46, 47–8, 51.*

Document 3.15 Lenin's Response to Kautsky

Lenin was at his best in polemics, and in his response to Kautsky he surpassed himself, writing a classic of what Stalin later was to dub Marxism-Leninism. Lenin insisted that proletarian dictatorship was at the heart of Marxist teaching, even though Kautsky had quite rightly pointed out that Marx and Engels had never really elaborated on their concept of the dictatorship of the proletariat. For Lenin, democracy was always restricted to the ruling class, while for the ruled it always appeared as dictatorship. Lenin's concept of politics had always been crude, but here he advanced a formula that was fraught with danger. His particularly abusive and dismissive tone suggested that Lenin realised the importance of Kautsky's points, but, lacking substantive arguments to rebut them, focused on attacking the man.

Kautsky's pamphlet, *The Dictatorship of the Proletariat*, recently published in Vienna . . . is the clearest lucid example of that utter and ignominious bankruptcy of the Second International about which all honest socialists in all countries have been talking for a long time. The proletarian revolution is now becoming a practical issue in a number of countries, and an examination of Kautsky's renegade sophistries and his complete renunciation of Marxism is therefore essential . . .

In substance, the chief theoretical mistake Kautsky makes in his pamphlet on the dictatorship of the proletariat lies in those opportunist distortions of Marx's ideas on the state, which I exposed in detail in my pamphlet, *The State and Revolution* . . .

How Kautsky Turned Marx into a Common Liberal

The fundamental question discussed by Kautsky in his pamphlet is that of the very essence of proletarian revolution, namely, the dictatorship of the proletariat. This is a question that is of the greatest importance for all countries, especially for the advanced ones, especially for those at war, and especially at the present time. One may say without fear of exaggeration that this is the key problem of the entire proletarian class struggle. It is, therefore, necessary to pay particular attention to it.

Kautsky formulates the question as follows: 'The contrast between the two socialist trends' (i.e., the Bolsheviks and non-Bolsheviks) 'is the contrast between two radically different methods: the *dictatorial* and the *democratic*' (p. 3) . . .

The question of the dictatorship of the proletariat is a question of the relation of the proletarian state to the bourgeois state, of proletarian democracy to bourgeois democracy. One would think that this is as plain as day. But Kautsky, like a schoolmaster who has become as dry as dust from quoting the same old textbooks on history, persistently turns his back on the twentieth century and his face to the eighteenth century, and for the hundredth time, in a number of paragraphs, in an incredibly tedious fashion chews the old cud over the relation of bourgeois democracy to absolutism and medievalism!

It sound just as though he were chewing rags in his sleep!

But this means he utterly fails to understand what is what! One cannot help smiling at Kautsky's effort to make it appear that there are people who preach 'contempt for democracy' (p. 11) and so forth. That is the sort of rubbish Kautsky uses to befog and confuse the issue, for he talks like the liberals, speaking of democracy in general, and not of *bourgeois* democracy; he even avoids using this precise, class term, and, instead, tries to speak about 'presocialist' democracy. This windbag devotes almost one-third of his pamphlet, twenty pages out of sixty-three, to this twaddle, which is so agreeable to the bourgeoisie, for it is tantamount to embellishing bourgeois democracy, and obscures the question of the proletarian revolution.

But, after all, the title of Kautsky's pamphlet is '*The Dictatorship of the Proletariat*'. Everybody knows that this is the very *essence* of Marx's doctrine; and after a lot of irrelevant twaddle Kautsky *was obliged* to quote Marx's words on the dictatorship of the proletariat.

But the way in which he the 'Marxist' did it was simply farcical! Listen to this:

'This view' (which Kautsky dubs 'contempt for democracy') 'rests upon a single word of Karl Marx's.' This is what Kautsky literally says on page 20. And on page 60 the same thing is repeated even in the form that they (the Bolsheviks) 'opportunely recalled the little word' (that is literally what he says – *des Wörtchens*!!) 'about the dictatorship of the proletariat which Marx once used in 1875 in a letter.'

Here is Marx's 'little word': 'Between capitalist and communist society lies the period of the revolutionary transformation of the one into the other. Corresponding to this is also a political transition period in which the state can be nothing but the revolutionary dictatorship of the proletariat.' [Marx, *Critique of the Gotha Programme*.]

First of all, to call this classical reasoning of Marx's, which sums up the whole of his revolutionary teaching, 'a single word' and even 'a little word', is an insult to and complete renunciation of Marxism. It must not be forgotten that Kautsky knows Marx almost by heart, and, judging by all he has written, he has in his desk, or in his head, a number of pigeon-holes in which all that was ever written by Marx is most carefully filed so as to be ready at hand for quotation. Kautsky must know that both Marx and Engels, in their letters as well as in their published works, *repeatedly* spoke about the dictatorship of the proletariat, before and especially after the Paris Commune. Kautsky must know that the formula 'dictatorship of the proletariat' is merely a more historically concrete and scientifically exact formulation of the proletariat's task of 'smashing' the bourgeois state machine, about which both Marx and Engels, in summing up the experience of the Revolution of 1848, and still more so, of 1871, spoke *for forty years*, between 1852 and 1891 . . .

To transform Kautsky's liberal and false assertion into a Marxist and true one, one must say: dictatorship does not necessarily mean the abolition of democracy for the class that exercises the dictatorship over other classes; but it does mean the abolition (or very material restriction, which is also a form of abolition) of democracy for the class over which, or against which, the dictatorship is exercised.

Source: Lenin, 'Proletarskaya revolyutsiya i renegat Kautskii'
('The Proletarian Revolution and the Renegade Kautsky'), PSS, vol. 37,
pp. 237, 239, 240, 240–2, 243–4.

War Communism and its Critics

As predicted by the coalitionists, the Bolshevik monopoly on power provoked civil war. Talk of 'state capitalism' was abandoned and a policy that was later dubbed 'War Communism' emerged. Industry was nationalised by a series of increasingly radical decrees and placed under the control of centralised agencies (*glavki*) under the Supreme Economic Council. Class war in the countryside was encouraged while food supplies were forcibly requisitioned to feed the starving cities and the army. War Communism was characterised by extreme centralisation of production and distribution, the banning of free trade, and food requisitioning from the peasants. Although some of this was repudiated in early 1921, in the late 1920s Stalin returned to War Communist themes. It is remarkable just how quickly the main outlines of the Soviet system emerged and how durable they proved to be. The political system essentially established in the first period of Bolshevik rule was the one that fell in August 1991.

Document 3.16   The Party Programme of 1919

The Eighth Party Congress in March 1919 summarised the aims and purposes of the Russian Communist Party (bolsheviks) (RCP(b)), as the party had been renamed in March 1918. The programme stressed the superior democratic character of the communist state, outlined measures that sought to avert the bureaucratisation of the party, condemned religion, and stressed that the unions had to play a key economic role in the socialist economy together with the employment of 'bourgeois' specialists.

2 In contrast to bourgeois democracy, which concealed the class character of the state, the Soviet authority openly acknowledges that every state must inevitably bear a class character until the division of society into classes has been abolished and all government authority disappears. By its very nature, the Soviet state directs itself to the suppression of the resistance of the exploiters, and the Soviet constitution does not stop short of depriving the exploiters of their political rights, bearing in mind that any kind of freedom is a deception if it is opposed to the emancipation of labour from the yoke of capital. The aim of the party of the proletariat consists in carrying on a determined suppression of the resistance of the exploiters, in struggling

against the deeply rooted prejudices concerning the absolute character of bourgeois rights and freedom, and at the same time explaining that deprivation of political rights and any kind of limitation of freedom are necessary as temporary measures in order to defeat the attempts of the exploiters to retain or to re-establish their privileges. With the disappearance of the possibility of the exploitation of one human being by another, the necessity for these measures will also gradually disappear and the Party will aim to reduce and completely abolish them . . .

8 The proletarian revolution, owing to the Soviet organisation of the state, was able at one stroke finally to destroy the old bourgeois, official and judicial state apparatus. The comparatively low standard of culture of the masses, the absence of necessary experience in state administration on the part of responsible workers who are elected by the masses, the pressing necessity owing to the critical situation of engaging specialists of the old school and the calling up to military service of the more advanced section of city workmen, all this led to the partial revival of bureaucratic practices within the Soviet system.

The All-Russian Communist Party, carrying on a resolute struggle with bureaucratism, suggests the following measures for overcoming this evil:

1 Every member of the Soviet is obliged to perform a certain duty in state administration.
2 These duties must change in rotation, so as gradually to embrace all the branches of administrative work.
3 All the working masses without exception must be gradually induced to take part in the work of state administration.

Religion

. . . 13 With reference to religion, the All-Russian Communist Party does not content itself with the already decreed separation of Church from state, i.e. measures which are one of the items of the programmes of bourgeois democracy, which was, however, never fulfilled owing to many and various ties binding capital with religious propaganda.

The All-Russian Communist Party is guided by the conviction that only the realisation of conscious and systematic social and economic activity of the masses will lead to the disappearance of religious prejudices. The aim of the Party is finally to destroy the ties between the exploiting classes and the organisation of religious propaganda, at the same time helping the toiling masses actually to liberate their minds from religious superstitions, and organising on a wide scale scientific-educational and anti-religious propaganda. It is, however, necessary carefully to avoid offending the religious susceptibilities of believers, which leads only to the strengthening of religious fanaticism.

Economics

1 Undeviatingly to continue and finally to realise the expropriation of the bourgeoisie that was begun and which has already been largely completed, the transforming of all means of production and exchange into the property of the Soviet republic, i.e. the common property of all toilers . . .

5 The organising apparatus of socialised industry must first of all rest upon the trade unions. The latter must free themselves from their narrow guild outlook and transform themselves into large productive combinations which will unite the majority and ultimately all the workers in a given branch of production.

8 Moreover, for the development of the productive forces the immediate, wide and full utilisation of all specialists in science and technology bequeathed to us by capitalism is necessary, in spite of the fact that the majority of the latter are inevitably imbued with bourgeois ideas and habits. The party considers that the period of sharp struggle with this group, owing to organised sabotage on their part, is ended as the sabotage is in the main subdued.

Source: 'Programma RKP(b) (The Programme of the Russian Communist Party (Bolsheviks), adopted by the Eighth Congress of the RKP(b)', 18–23 March 1919, in Lenin, PSS, vol. 38, p. 424, 427, 433, 435, 436.

It was at the Eighth Congress that the party took on its definitive organisational form, with the formal creation of the Politburo, the Orgburo and the Secretariat with authority over the whole party membership. Prompted by the exigencies of the Civil War, the aim was to improve decision-making and implementation, focusing above all on the creation of a centralised cadre of party secretaries. The RCP(b) was a unitary body directing the work of its 'regional' committees in Latvia, Lithuania and Ukraine.

Document 3.17 The ABC of Communism

In mid-1919 Bukharin and Yevgeny Preobrazhensky collaborated to produce a popular manual of communism for the masses. The result was *The ABC of Communism*, a remarkable window into the thinking of the Bolsheviks of this time into what communism would look like. The first, theoretical, part was mainly written by Bukharin and described the decline and fall of capitalism and the emergence of the communist revolution, while in the second, more 'practical' part, Preobrazhenskii examined the dictatorship of the proletariat and the development of the communist order. Later Bukharin and Preobrazhenskii were to become bitterly divided over developmental strategies for the country. The extract below reveals some of the 'Utopianism' of the thinking of this period and advances a view that Stalin was forcefully to repudiate.

In communist society there will be no classes. But if there will be no classes, this implies that *in communist society there will likewise be no State*. We have previously seen that the State is a class organization of the rulers. The State is always directed by one class against the other. A bourgeois State is directed against the proletariat, whereas a proletarian State is directed against the proletariat. In the Communist social order there are neither landlords, nor capitalists, nor wage workers; there are simply people – comrades. If there are no classes, then there is no class war, and there are no class organizations. Consequently the State has ceased to exist. Since there is no class war, the State has become superfluous. There is no one to be held in restraint, and there is no one to impose restraint.

But how, they will ask us, can this vast organization be set in motion without any administration? Who is going to work out the plans for social administration? Who will distribute labour power? Who is going to keep account of social income and expenditure? In a word, who is going to supervise the whole affair?

It is not difficult to answer these questions. The main direction will be entrusted to various kinds of book-keeping offices or statistical bureaux. There, from day to day, account will be kept of production and all its needs; there also it will be decided whither workers must be sent, whence they must be taken, and how much work is to be done . . . There will be no need for special ministers of state, for police and prisons, for laws and decrees – nothing of the sort . . . The bureaucracy, the permanent officialdom, will disappear. The State will die out . . .

The communist method of production will signify an enormous development of productive forces. As a result, no worker in communist society will have to do as much work as of old. The working day will grow continually shorter, and people will be to an increasing extent freed from the chains imposed on them by nature.

Source: N. Bukharin and E. Preobrazhensky, The ABC of Communism, *introduction by E. H. Carr (Harmondsworth, Penguin Books, 1969), pp. 117–18, 121.*

Document 3.18   Trotsky on Terror and Militarisation

Trotsky became one of the most eloquent exponents of dictatorial centralisation and brutal discipline (cf. Document 3.8). Carried away by War Communism, he advocated unlimited coercion not only to defend the workers' state but also to manage it. In early 1920, in connection with the anticipated end of the Civil War, he had suggested a rethinking of policy, but once this had been rejected by the party leadership he veered to the opposite extreme. He now rejected the whole concept of 'free labour' and called for universal compulsory labour duty and the militarisation of the economy.

Who aims at the end cannot reject the means. The struggle must be carried on with such intensity as actually to guarantee the supremacy of the proletariat . . . It follows that the dictatorship must be guaranteed at all costs . . . The man who repudiates terrorism in principle – i.e., repudiates measures of suppression and intimidation towards determined and armed counter-revolution, must reject all idea of the political supremacy of the working class and its revolutionary dictatorship. The man who repudiates the dictatorship of the proletariat repudiates the socialist revolution, and digs the grave of socialism.

The theoretical apostasy of Kautsky lies just in this point: having recognised the principle of democracy as absolute and eternal, he has stepped back from Marxist dialectics to natural law. That which was exposed by Marxism as the passing mechanism of the bourgeoisie, and was subjected only to temporary utilisation with the object of preparing the proletarian revolution, has been newly sanctified by Kautsky as the supreme principle standing above classes, and unconditionally subordinating to itself the methods of the proletarian struggle. The counter-revolutionary degeneration of parliamentarianism finds its most perfect expression in the deification of democracy by the decaying theoreticians of the Second International . . .

The question of the form of repression, or of its degree, of course, is not one of 'principle'. It is a question of expediency . . . But terror can be very efficient against a reactionary class which does not want to leave the scene of operations. *Intimidation* is a powerful weapon of policy, both internationally and internally. War, like revolution, is founded upon intimidation. A victorious war, generally speaking, destroys only an insignificant part of the conquered army, intimidating the remainder and breaking their will. The revolution works in the same way: it kills individuals, and intimidates thousands. In this sense, the Red Terror is not distinguishable from the armed insurrection, the direct continuation of which it represents. The state terror of a revolutionary class can be condemned 'morally' only by a man who, as a principle, rejects (in words) every form of violence whatsoever – consequently, every war and every rising. For this one has to be merely and simply a hypocritical Quaker.

'But, in that case, in what do your tactics differ from the tactics of Tsarism?' we are asked, by the high priest of Liberalism and Kautskianism.

You do not understand this, holy men? We shall explain to you. The terror of Tsarism was directed against the proletariat. The gendarmerie of Tsarism throttled the workers who were fighting for the Socialist order. Our Extraordinary Commissions shoot landlords, capitalists, and generals who are striving to restore the capitalist order. Do you grasp this – distinction? Yes? For us Communists it is quite sufficient . . .

The further we go, however, the more do the unions recognise that they are organs of production of the Soviet state, and assume responsibility for its fortunes – not opposing themselves to it, but identifying themselves with it. The unions become the organisers of labour discipline . . . The very principle of compulsory labour service is for the Communist quite unquestionable.

Source: Leon Trotsky, Terrorism and Communism: A Reply to Karl Kautsky, *first published 1920 (London, New Park Publications, 1975), pp. 45–6, 46–7, 63, 78–9, 124, 146.*

Document 3.19   The Democratic Centralists

Trotsky's views did not go unchallenged. The Democratic Centralists, the successors to the Left Communists, as a group had first emerged in December 1918, and thereafter advocated a type of 'Bolshevik constitutionalism', the regulation and thus the ordering of what had become capricious and arbitrary personalised rule and bureaucratised decision-making by committees far removed from the lives and concerns of the workers themselves. They condemned the tendency for party 'centres' to substitute for the activity of the whole party, and in particular condemned the way that the party had usurped the role of the soviets. One of their most eloquent spokesmen was V. V. Osinskii, who had been a leading Left Communist in 1918.

I propose to make a series of amendments and additions to Comrade Trotsky's theses . . . First of all I want to give the basis for the amendment which we are introducing on the question of militarisation.

What is happening now at the congress is the clash of several cultures. Our system has given birth to different cultures: we have created a military-Soviet culture, a civil-Soviet culture, and the trade unions have created theirs. Each of these forms of our movement has its own approach to things and has created its own practices. Comrade Trotsky has posed the question from the point of view of a man coming from the sphere of military culture; we approach it from the point of view of the civil sphere, and, finally, the trade union comrades pose it in their own way. They have presented it the most poorly, insofar as they have for a long time been considering only the need to protect the workers from militarisation and to keep labour free, etc.

I want first of all to establish that we approached the question of militarisation earlier than those from the other cultures, and from the other side . . . I radically reject the proposition that we oppose militarisation *per se* . . . We are against the excessive extension of the concept of militarisation, we are against the blind imitation of military models . . .

Comrade Lenin has revealed here today a very original understanding of democratic centralism . . . Comrade Lenin says that all democratic centralism consists of is that the congress elects the Central Committee, and the Central Committee governs . . . With such an original definition we cannot agree. We consider that democratic centralism – a very old concept, a concept clear to every Bolshevik and fixed in our rules – consists of carrying out the directives of the Central Committee through local organisation; the autonomy of the latter; and their responsibility for individual spheres of work. If party work is broken down into several branches with special departments, and if these departments are under the general direction of the local organisation, just as the departments of the soviets are under the authority and direction of the provincial executive committee – this is democratic centralism, i.e., the execution of the decisions of the centre through local organs which are responsible for all the particular spheres of work in the provinces. This is the definition of democratic centralism, a system of administration preserved from bureaucratism and closely associated with the principle of collegia . . .

If you reduce the collegial principle to nothing in our institutions, this entails the downfall of the entire system of democratic centralism. I advise careful thought about this, although the speakers following me may try to 'besmirch' this argument. Bearing this in mind, we will conduct an unyielding struggle against the principle of one-person management . . .

Source: V. V. Osinskii, 'Minority Report on Building the Economy', Ninth Party Congress, March 1920, Devyatyi s''ezd RKP(b) (mart–aprel' 1920g): protokoly *(Moscow, Politizdat, 1960), pp. 115, 116, 121–2, 123.*

Document 3.20   Lenin Condemns Leftist 'Infantilism'

Once again, Lenin's response to criticisms within Russia and in the Third Communist International (Comintern), established in March 1919, of over-centralisation and expediency was robust. He accused of 'petty bourgeois infantilism' those who criticised compromises, going so far as to suggest that those who objected to the draconian discipline that was being imposed on the party were effectively agents of imperialism.

At the present moment in history, however, it is the Russian model that reveals to *all* countries something – and something highly significant – of their near and inevitable future. Advanced workers in all lands have long realised this; more often than not, they have grasped it with their revolutionary class instinct rather than realised it. Herein lies the international 'significance' (in the narrow sense of the word) of Soviet power, and of the fundamentals of Bolshevik theory and tactics . . .

It is, I think, almost universally realised at present that the Bolsheviks could not have retained power for two and a half months, let alone two and a half years, without the strictest, truly iron discipline in our party, or without the fullest and unreserved support from the entire mass of the working class, that is, from all thinking, honest, devoted and influential elements in it, capable of leading or carrying with them the backward strata.

The dictatorship of the proletariat means a most determined and most ruthless war waged by the new class against a *more powerful* enemy, the bourgeoisie, whose resistance is increased *tenfold* by their overthrow (even if only in a single country), and whose power lies, not only in the strength of international capital, the strength and durability of their international connections, but also in the *force of habit*, in the strength of *small-scale production* . . .

As a current of political thought and as a political party, Bolshevism has existed since 1903. Only the history of Bolshevism during the *entire* period of its existence can satisfactorily explain why it has been able to build up and maintain, under most difficult conditions, the iron discipline needed for the victory of the proletariat . . .

The conclusion is clear: to reject compromises 'on principle', to reject the permissibility of compromises in general, no matter of what kind, is childishness, which it is difficult even to consider seriously. A political leader who desires to be useful to the revolutionary proletariat must be able to distinguish *concrete* cases of compromises that are inexcusable and are an expression of opportunism and treachery; he must direct all the force of criticism, the full intensity of merciless exposure and relentless war, against *these concrete* compromises, and not allow the past masters of 'practical' socialism and the parliamentary Jesuits to dodge and wriggle out of responsibility by means of disquisitions on 'compromises in general' . . .

There are different kinds of compromises. One must be able to analyse the situation and the concrete conditions of each compromise, or of each variety of compromise. One must learn to distinguish between a man who has given up his money and firearms to bandits so as to lessen the evil they can do and to facilitate their capture and execution, and a man who gives his money and firearms to bandits so as to share in the loot. In politics this is by no means always as elementary as it is in this childishly simple example. However, anyone who is out to think up for the workers some kind of recipe that will provide them with cut-and-dried solutions for all contingencies, or promises that the policy of the revolutionary proletariat will never come up against difficult or complex situations, is simply a charlatan . . .

Repudiation of the party principle and of party discipline – this is what the opposition has *arrived at*. And this is tantamount to disarming the proletariat completely *in the interest of the bourgeoisie*. It all adds up to that petty-bourgeois diffuseness and instability, that incapacity for sustained effort, unity and organised action, which, if encouraged, must inevitably destroy any proletarian revolutionary movement.

Source: Lenin, '"Left-Wing" Communism – An Infantile Disorder', April 1920, Selected Works, pp. 516–17, 518, 519, 529, 534.

Bolshevism Abroad

The third Communist International (Comintern) was established in Moscow in March 1919. Already by that time it was becoming clear that the German revolution of November 1918 was not going to take the Bolshevik route, although hopes remained in Moscow until the final defeat of the communist insurrection in the early 1920s. Only in Hungary was a Soviet-type republic established under the leadership of Béla Kun, lasting from 21 March, when Hungary was declared a Soviet republic, to 1 August 1919 when it was overthrown by Admiral Horthy, who remained in power until the Second World War. In mid-1920 Lenin's hopes were raised once again by the Red Army's advance on Warsaw. He hoped that this would open the path to Berlin and the West, but defeat by Marshal Piłsudski and the retreat of Soviet forces meant that the Soviet revolution remained isolated.

Document 3.21 Discipline in the Comintern

The discipline that was imposed on the Communist Party at home was extended at this time to the international arena. The Second Comintern Congress (19 July–7 August 1920) laid down '21 conditions' of membership in the Comintern. Drafted by Zinoviev ('but, to the last detail, inspired by Lenin'), they sought to impose the Russian pattern of a violent revolution led by a disciplined elite party on the rest of the communist movement. The interests of the Soviet republic were considered paramount for all member communist parties, who were subordinated to the decisions of the centralised, disciplined and ideologically pure Soviet-dominated International. The aim was to split Western socialist parties and ensure that the emerging communist parties would be under Soviet influence.

The Second Congress of the Communist International establishes the following conditions of membership in the Communist International:
1 All *propaganda* and *agitation* must have a truly communist character, and correspond to the programme and resolutions of the Communist International . . .
 Periodical and nonperiodical publications as well as all party publishing houses must be completely subordinate to the party executive committee . . . It is impermissible for the publishing houses to misuse their autonomy to pursue policies that do not correspond entirely to those of the party . . .
2 Every organization wishing to join the Communist International must consistently and systematically remove reformists and centrists from all positions of any responsibility in the workers' movement . . . and replace them with reliable Communists . . .
3 In almost every country of Europe and America the class struggle is entering the phase of civil war. Under such conditions the Communists can place no faith in bourgeois legality . . . In all countries where a state of siege or emergency laws make it impossible for Communists to carry out all their work legally, it is absolutely necessary that legal and illegal activity be combined.
4 The duty to disseminate communist ideas carries with it a special obligation to conduct vigorous and systematic propaganda in the army . . .
5 Systematic and consistent agitation is necessary in the countryside. The

working class cannot be victorious unless it has the support of the rural proletariat and at least a part of the poorest peasants . . .

6 Every party that wishes to belong to the Communist International is duty-bound to expose not only overt social patriotism but also the duplicity and hypocrisy of social pacifism . . .

7 Parties wishing to belong to the Communist International are duty-bound to recognize the need for a complete break with reformism and the policies of the Centre and must conduct propaganda for this among the broadest layers of the party membership. Without this, no consistent communist policy is possible.

8 The Communist International demands unconditionally and as an ultimatum that this break be carried out at the earliest possible date. The Communist International cannot accept that notorious opportunists as, for example, Turati, Modigliani, Kautsky . . . and MacDonald should have the right to consider themselves members of the Communist International . . .

9 Every party wishing to belong to the Communist International must carry out systematic and persistent activity in the trade unions . . . and other mass workers' organizations. In these organizations it is necessary to organize communist cells that win the unions . . . to the cause of communism through persistent and unremitting work . . .

10 Every party that belongs to the Communist International has the obligation to wage a tenacious struggle against the Amsterdam 'International' of Yellow trade unions [the successor to the Second International]. It must conduct forceful propaganda among workers organized in unions on the need to break with the Yellow Amsterdam International . . .

12 Parties belonging to the Communist International must be organized on the basis of the principle of democratic centralism. In the present epoch of intensified civil war, the Communist Party will be able to fulfil its duty only if it is organized in the most centralized way possible and governed by iron discipline, and if its central leadership, sustained by the confidence of the party membership, is strong, authoritative, and endowed with the fullest powers.

13 Communist parties of those countries in which the Communists pursue their work legally must from time to time carry out purges (re-registrations) of the party membership in order to systematically cleanse the party of the petty-bourgeois elements that worm their way into it.

14 Every party that wishes to belong to the Communist International is obligated to render unconditional assistance to every soviet republic struggling against the forces of counterrevolution . . .

16 All decisions by congresses of the Communist International as well as decisions by its Executive Committee are binding on all parties . . . The Communist International, working under conditions of most acute civil war, must be organized in a far more centralized way than was the Second International. At the same time, of course, in all their activity the Communist

International and its Executive Committee must take into account the diverse conditions under which each party has to struggle and work, adopting universally binding decisions only on questions in which such decisions are possible.

17 Taking all this into consideration, all parties that wish to belong to the Communist International must change their name. . . . [to] Communist Party of such and such country (Section of the Communist International) . . .

21 Party members who reject on principle the conditions and theses laid down by the Communist International must be expelled from the party . . .

Source: 'Theses on the Conditions for Admission to the Communist International', adopted by the Second Congress, 6 August 1920, in Kevin McDermott and Jeremy Agnew, The Comintern: A History of International Communism from Lenin to Stalin *(Basingstoke and London, Macmillan, 1996), pp. 226–8.*

From Reform to Kronstadt

War Communism represented the attempt to concentrate the whole economic life of the country in the hands of the state economic apparatus. At a time of war, grain was expropriated from the peasants without their being granted anything in return, and guards were placed at the entrances to cities to prevent 'bagmen' (*meshochniki*) bringing in food to be sold in the markets. The markets themselves were frequently raided and by the end of 1920 mostly closed down. Unrest among what remained of the industrial labour force in the cities was accompanied by the full-scale peasant uprisings in the countryside, in particular the revolt led by Antonov in the Tambov region.

In the last months of 1920 and into early 1921, the final period of War Communism, Bolshevik rule faced its sternest test. Within the party, reformers hoped to modify the extremes of hierarchical centralisation that had taken hold during the Civil War. In the cities the Bolsheviks' own base, the working class, was increasingly alienated, while in the countryside the policy of grain requisitions (confiscation) provoked an increasingly desperate (and hungry) peasantry to revolt. This period culminated in the revolt of the sailors and workers in Kronstadt, the naval base at the mouth of the Gulf of Finland that had once been a symbol of Bolshevik revolutionism. In response to Kronstadt's calls for 'soviets without Bolsheviks', the party launched ferocious repression, a policy that had decisive effects on the Communist Party itself.

Document 3.22   Attempts at Party Reform

Victory in the Civil War was accompanied by demands in the party for an end to the hyper-centralisation and stifling of criticism that had become prevalent in the organisation. This movement for party reform peaked at the Ninth

Party Conference in September 1920, when the depth of the problem was acknowledged by the leadership. The resolution adopted by the conference represented the most serious attempt to 'democratise' the party, above all by reducing the powers of appointment from above and allowing more autonomy for lower party bodies. The reforms, however, lacked focus, with the 'Makhaevist' attack on *spetsy* continuing, and were distorted by the belief that workerisation on its own would in some unspecified way solve the ills of bureaucratisation. Quite apart from the inadequacies of the reforms themselves, the implementation of party democracy was derailed by the onset of the trade union debate.

It is essential to realise in the internal life of the party broader criticism of the central as well as local institutions of the party; to commission the Central Committee to point out by circulars the means for broadening intra-party criticism at general meetings; to create publications which are capable of realising broader and more systematic criticism of the mistakes of the party and general criticism within the party (discussion sheets, etc.) . . .

Recognising in principle the necessity of appointment to responsible offices in exceptional cases, it is necessary to propose to the Central Committee that in the assignment of functionaries in general it replace appointment with recommendation.

[It is necessary] to point out that in the mobilisation of comrades it is not permissible for party organs and individual comrades to be guided by any considerations except business ones. Any repression whatsoever against comrades because they dissent about some question or another decided by the party is not permissible. . . .

[It is necessary] to work out fully effective practical measures to eliminate inequality (in conditions of life, the wage scale, etc.) between the *spetsy* and the responsible functionaries on the one hand and the toiling masses on the other . . . This inequality violates democratism and is the source of disruption in the party and of reduction in the authority of communists . . .

Sources: 'On the Coming Tasks of Building the Party', IX konferentsiya RKP(b), sentyabr' 1920g: protokoly *(Moscow, 1972), pp. 278–82;* KPSS v rezolyutsiyakh i resheniyakh, *vol. I, pp. 507, 509, 511–12.*

Instead of focusing on party reform, the political elite was engulfed by a debate over the role of trade unions in economic management and their relationship to the political authorities. Provoked by Trotsky's plans to militarise industrial life and to 'governmentalise' the unions, the Workers' Opposition (yet another successor organisation to the Left Communists) demanded the opposite, the transfer of the entire management of the economy into the hands of the trade unions. The most eloquent exponent of these ideas was Alexandra Kollontai.

Document 3.23 Kollontai's *The Workers' Opposition*

Distributed to delegates at the Tenth Party Congress in March 1921, the work analysed the bureaucratic degeneration of the Soviet state. The analysis was mistaken, blaming the influence of bourgeois specialists (the so-called *spetsy*) for stifling the initiative of workers and reducing them to apathy when in fact the party apparatus was to blame. Kollontai called for a return to the principle of election and hoped to eliminate bureaucracy by making officials responsible to the public. She advocated greater openness within the party, freedom of speech and greater democracy. She also called on the party to purge itself of non-proletarian elements and to make itself a genuine workers' party, recalling Marx's dictum that 'the liberation of the working class was the task of the working class itself', a principle which contradicted Lenin's views on the vanguard role of the party. The attempt to find a *social* explanation for what was essentially a *political* problem only muddled the issue and inhibited the development of an adequate response. A gulf opened up between the aspiration and the prescription.

1 The Workers' Opposition sprang from the depths of the industrial proletariat of Russia. It is an outgrowth not only of the unbearable conditions of life and labour in which seven million industrial workers find themselves, but it is also a product of vacillation, inconsistencies, and outright deviations of our Soviet policy from the early expressed class consistent principles of the communist programme. 2 The Opposition did not originate in some particular centre, was not a fruit of personal strife and controversy, but, on the contrary, covers the whole extent of Soviet Russia and meets with a resonant response . . .

[W]ho shall develop the creative powers in the sphere of economic reconstruction? Shall it be purely class organs, directly connected by vital ties with the industries – that is, shall industrial trade unions undertake the work of reconstruction – or shall it be left to the Soviet machine which is separated from direct vital industrial activity and is mixed in its composition? This is the root of the break . . .

And the more our industrial establishments and unions are drained of their best elements by the party (which sends them either to the front or to Soviet institutions), the weaker becomes the direct connection between the rank-and-file workers and the directing party centres. A chasm is growing. At present, this division manifests itself even in the ranks of the party itself. The workers, through their Workers' Opposition, ask: Who are we? Are we really the prop of the class dictatorship? Or are we just an obedient flock that serves as a support for those who, having severed all ties with the masses, carry out their own policy and build up industry without any regard to our opinions and creative abilities under the reliable cover of the party label? . . .

The whole controversy boils down to one basic question: who shall build the communist economy, and how shall it be built? . . . *The Workers'*

Opposition sees in the unions the managers and creators of the communist economy, whereas Bukharin, together with Lenin and Trotsky, leave them only the role of 'schools of communism' and no more . . . Only workers can generate in their minds new methods of organising labour as well as running industry . . . The Workers' Opposition asserts that administration of the people's economy is the trade unions' job and, therefore, that the Opposition is more Marxist in thought than the theoretically trained leaders . . . This consideration, which should be very simple and clear to every practical man, is lost sight of by our party leaders: *it is impossible to decree communism.* It can be treated only in the process of practical research, through mistakes, perhaps, but only by the creative powers of the working class itself . . .

The task is clear: it is to arouse initiative and self-activity in the masses. But what is being done to encourage and develop that initiative? Nothing at all. Quite the contrary . . . Every comrade can easily recall scores of instances when workers themselves attempted to organise dining-rooms, day nurseries for children, transportation of wood, etc. Each time a lively, immediate interest in the undertaking died from the red tape, interminable negotiations with the various institutions that brought no results, or resulted in refusals, new requisitions, etc. Whenever there was an opportunity under the impetus of the masses themselves – for the masses using their own efforts – to equip a dining-room, to store a supply of wood, or to organise a nursery, refusal always followed refusal from the central institutions . . . How much bitterness is generated among working men and women when they see and know that if they had been given the right, and an opportunity to act, they could themselves have seen the project through . . . As a result there is generated a most harmful division: *we* are the toiling people, *they* are the Soviet officials, on whom everything depends. This is the whole trouble . . .

Restrictions on initiative are imposed, not only in regard to the activity of the non-party masses (this would only be a logical and reasonable condition, in the atmosphere of the civil war). The initiative of party members themselves is restricted. Every independent attempt, every new thought that passes through the censorship of our centre, is considered as 'heresy', as a violation of party discipline, as an attempt to infringe on the prerogatives of the centre, which must 'foresee' everything and 'decree' everything and anything. If anything is not decreed one must wait, for the time will come when the centre at its leisure will decree. Only then, and within sharply restricted limits, will one be allowed to express one's 'initiative'. What would happen if some of the members of the Russian Communist Party – those, for instance, who are fond of birds – decided to form a society for the preservation of birds? The idea itself seems useful. It does not in any way undermine any 'state project'. But it only seems this way. All of a sudden there would appear some bureaucratic institution which would claim the right to manage this particular undertaking . . .

Fear of criticism and of freedom of thought, by combining together with bureaucracy, often produce ridiculous results. There can he no self-activity without freedom of thought and opinion, for self-activity manifests itself not only in initiative, action, and work, but in independent thought as well. We give no freedom to class activity, we are afraid of criticism, we have ceased to rely on the masses: hence we have bureaucracy with us. That is why the Workers' Opposition considers that bureaucracy is our enemy, our scourge, and the greatest danger to the future existence of the communist party itself.

In order to do away with the bureaucracy that is finding its shelter in the Soviet institutions, we must first of all get rid of all bureaucracy in the party itself . . .

In the name of party regeneration and the elimination of bureaucracy from the Soviet institutions, the Workers' Opposition, together with a group of responsible workers in Moscow, demand complete realisation of all democratic principles, not only for the present period of respite, but also for times of internal and external tension. This is the first and basic condition for the party's regeneration, for its return to the principles of its programme, from which it is more and more deviating in practice under the pressure of elements that are foreign to it.

The second condition, the vigorous fulfilment of which is insisted upon by the Workers' Opposition, is the expulsion from the party of all non-proletarian elements . . .

The third decisive step towards democratisation of the party is the elimination of all non-working-class elements from administrative positions. In other words, the central, provincial, and county committees of the party must be so composed that workers closely acquainted with the conditions of the working masses should have the preponderant majority therein . . .

The fourth basic demand of the Workers' Opposition is that the party must reverse its policy in relation to the elective principle.

Appointments are permissible only as exceptions. Lately they have begun to prevail as a rule. Appointments are very characteristic of bureaucracy, and yet at present they are a general, legalised and well-recognised daily occurrence. The procedure of appointments produces a very unhealthy atmosphere in the party. It disrupts the relationship of equality amongst the members by rewarding friends and punishing enemies, and by other no less harmful practices in party and Soviet life . . .

Wide publicity, freedom of opinion and discussion, the right to criticise within the party and among the members of the trade unions – such are the decisive steps that can put an end to the prevailing system of bureaucracy. Freedom of criticism, right of different factions freely to present their views at party meetings, freedom of discussion – are no longer the demands of the Workers' Opposition alone. Under the growing pressure from the masses a whole series of measures that were demanded by the rank and file long before the [ninth] party conference are now recognised and officially promulgated . . . the building of communism can and must be the work of the toiling masses themselves. The building of communism belongs to the workers.

Source: Alexandra Kollontai, The Workers' Opposition in Russia *(London, Dreadnought Publishers, 1923).*

In the event the 'centrist' position advanced by Lenin, Zinoviev, Stalin and others sought to remove the unions from economic administration altogether, insisting that they focus on educational and social support functions. This was the position adopted at the Tenth Party Congress in March 1921, which met against the background of urban and rural insurgency. Members of the Workers' Opposition actively participated in the bloody suppression of the Kronstadt revolt against the party bureaucracy.

Document 3.24 Programme of the Kronstadt Insurgents: 'What We Are Fighting For'

Although Bolshevik propaganda claimed that the insurgents in the naval fortress of Kronstadt, in the Gulf of Finland, were counter-revolutionaries in the pay of the White emigration, in fact the Kronstadt sailors, formerly the shock troops of Bolshevism itself in 1917, remained loyal to a vision of a genuine participatory and non-bureaucratised form of popular power represented by the soviets. Their programme can be summed up as 'soviets without Bolsheviks'.

After carrying out the October revolution, the working class had hoped to achieve its emancipation. But the result was an even greater enslavement of the human personality. The power of the police and gendarme monarchy passed into the hands of the Communist usurpers, who, instead of giving the people freedom, instilled in them the constant fear of falling into the torture chambers of the Cheka, which in their horrors far exceed the gendarme administration of the tsarist regime. The bayonets, bullets, and gruff commands of the Cheka *oprichniki* [a reference to Ivan the Terrible's sixteenth-century personal police] – these are what the working man of Soviet Russia has gained after so much struggle and suffering. The glorious emblem of the workers' state – the sickle and hammer – has in fact been replaced by the Communist authorities with the bayonet and barred window, for the sake of maintaining the calm and carefree life of the new bureaucracy of Communist commissars and functionaries.

But most infamous and criminal of all is the moral servitude which the Communists have created: they have laid their hands also on the inner world of the toilers, forcing them to think in the Communist way. With the help of the bureaucratised trade unions, they bound the workers to their benches, so that labour has become not a joy but a new form of slavery. To the protests of the peasants, expressed in spontaneous uprisings, and those of the workers, whose living conditions have driven them out on strike, they answer with mass executions and bloodthirstiness, in which they have not been surpassed even by the tsarist generals. Russia of the toilers, the first to raise the red banner of the liberation of labour, is drenched in the blood of those martyred for the glory of Communist domination. In this sea of blood the Communists are drowning all the great and glowing pledges and slogans of the workers' revolution. The picture has been drawn more and more sharply, and now it is clear that the Russian Communist Party is not the defender of the toilers that it pretends to be. The interests of the working people are alien to it. Having gained power, it is afraid only of losing it, and therefore deems every means permissible: slander, violence, deceit, murder, vengeance upon the families of rebels.

The long-suffering patience of the toilers is at an end. Here and there the land is lit up by the fires of insurrection in a struggle against oppression and violence. Strikes by the workers have flared up, but the Bolshevik *okhrana* agents have not been asleep and have taken every measure to forestall and suppress the unavoidable third revolution. But it has come nevertheless, and it is being made by the hands of the toilers themselves. The generals of Communism see clearly that it is the people who have risen, convinced that the ideas of socialism have been betrayed. Yet, trembling for their skins and aware that there is no escape from the wrath of the workers, they still try, with the help of their *oprichniki*, to terrorise the rebels with prison, firing squads, and other atrocities. But life under the yoke of the Communist dictatorship has become more terrible than death . . .

There can be no middle ground. Victory or death! The example is being set by Red Kronstadt, threatening the counter-revolutionaries of the right and of the left. The new revolutionary upheaval has been launched here. Here is raised the banner of rebellion against the three-year-old violence and oppression of Communist rule, which has overshadowed the three hundred-year yoke of monarchism. Here at Kronstadt the first stone of the third revolution has been laid, striking the last fetters from the toiling masses and opening a broad new road for socialist creativity.

This new revolution will rouse the toiling masses of the East and of the West, by serving as an example of the new socialist construction as opposed to the Communists' barrack-room 'creativity'. The toiling masses abroad will see with their own eyes that everything created here up to now by the will of the workers and peasants was not socialism. Without a single shot, without a drop of blood, the first step has been taken. The toilers do not need blood. They will shed it only in self-defence. In spite of all the outrageous acts of the Communists, we have enough restraint to confine ourselves only to isolating them from public life so that their malicious and false agitation will not hinder our revolutionary work.

The workers and peasants steadfastly march forward, leaving behind them the bourgeois Constituent Assembly, with its bourgeois regime, and the dictatorship of the Communist Party, with its Cheka and its state capitalism, whose hangman's noose encircles the necks of the labouring masses and threatens to strangle them to death. The present overturn at last provides the toilers with the opportunity to have their freely elected soviets, operating without the slightest force of party pressure, and to remake the bureaucratised trade unions into free associations of workers, peasants and the labouring intelligentsia. At last the policeman's club of the Communist autocracy has been broken.

Source: Paul Avrich, Kronstadt 1921 *(Princeton, Princeton University Press, 1970), pp. 241–3, translation modified by the present author.*

The Bolshevik authorities launched a wave of calumny against the insurgents, who had asked for no more than a return to the ideals of the October revolution. These demands, striking at the heart of the Bolshevik legitimacy, threatened their power in a more subversive way than any number of White manifestos. The assault was led by Trotsky across the ice of the gulf, and many delegates (including oppositionists) to the Tenth Party Congress, meeting at the time in Petrograd, joined in the suppression of the insurgents. Their defeat was followed by mass executions and a wall of lies over what the real aims of the movement had been.

Document 3.25   Bolshevik Bureaucratism Condemned

Alexander Berkman was an American anarchist-communist deported along with hundreds of other radicals of Russian origin (including Emma Goldman) in late 1919. His faith in Russian communism was soon tempered by the realities of Soviet Russia. The libertarian critique of Bolshevik rule was forceful and accurate. His diary chronicles the ups and downs of his time in Russia (he returned with Goldman to America in 1922), but ends with thorough disillusionment.

2 April 1920 – The Bolsheviki claim they need good workers, but if you are not a Communist they don't want you. We've been called counter-revolutionists, and the Chief of the Tcheka has even threatened to send us to prison . . . 'The Communists won't stand for independent initiative', one of the women remarked; 'it's dangerous for their regime'.

'No, my friends, it's no use deluding yourselves,' a tall, bearded man retorted. 'Russia is not ripe for Communism. Social revolution is possible only in a country with the highest industrial development. It was the greatest crime of the Bolsheviki that they forcibly suspended the Constituent Assembly. They usurped governmental power, but the whole country is against them. What can you expect under such circumstances? They have to resort to terror to force the people to do their bidding, and of course everything goes to ruin' . . .

Easter week – Notwithstanding all the faults and shortcomings of the Bolsheviki, I feel that Russia is still the hearth of the Revolution. It is the torch whose light is visible throughout the world, and proletarian hearts in every land are warmed by its glow . . .

6 March 1921 – Today Kronstadt sent out by radio a statement of its position. It reads: 'Our cause is just, we stand for the power of Soviets, not parties. We stand for freely elected representatives of the laboring masses. The substitute Soviets manipulated by the Communist Party have always been deaf to our needs and demands; the only reply we have ever received was shooting . . . Comrades! They deliberately pervert the truth and resort to most despicable fabrications . . . In Kronstadt the whole power is exclusively in the hands of the revolutionary sailors, soldiers and workers – not with counter-revolutionaries led by some Kozlovsky, as the lying Moscow radio tries to make you believe . . . Do not delay, Comrades! Join us, get in touch with us: demand admission to Kronstadt for your delegates. Only they will tell you the whole truth and will expose the fiendish calumny about Finnish bread and Entente offers.

Long live the revolutionary proletariat and the peasantry!

Long live the power of freely elected Soviets.'

7 March – Distant rumbling reaches my ears as I cross the Nevsky. It sounds again, stronger and nearer, as if rolling toward me. All at once I realize that artillery is being fired. It is 6pm. Kronstadt has been attacked!

Days of anguish and cannonading. My heart is numb with despair; something has died within me. The people on the streets look bowed with grief, bewildered. No one trusts himself to speak. The thunder of heavy guns rends the air.

17 March – Kronstadt has fallen today.

Thousands of sailors and workers lie dead in its streets. Summary executions of prisoners and hostages continues . . .

30 September – Gray are the passing days. One by one the embers of hope have died out. Terror and despotism have crushed the life born in October. The slogans of the Revolution are forsworn, its ideals stifled in the blood of the people. The breath of yesterday is dooming millions to death; the shadow of today hangs like a black pall over the country. Dictatorship is trampling the masses under foot. The Revolution is dead; its spirit cries in the wilderness.

High time the truth about the Bolsheviki were told. The whited sepulcher must be unmasked, the clay feet of the fetish beguiling the international proletariat to fatal will o' the wisps exposed. The Bolshevik myth must be destroyed.

I have decided to leave Russia.

Source: Alexander Berkman, The Bolshevik Myth *(London, Pluto Press, 1989), pp. 115–16, 302–3, 318–19.*

Document 3.26   'The Party' and the People

Attached to the British Embassy in Petrograd, Paul Dukes was a witness to the February revolution and later conducted relief work with the American YMCA in 1918. In that year he was recalled to London and directed to work with the Secret Intelligence Service attached to the Foreign Office. His duty was to report on the attitudes of the Russian people towards Soviet power, the development of Bolshevik policy, the possibility of a change of regime and the role of foreign powers. He travelled the country clandestinely, and at various points was accused by the Soviet authorities of instigating all sorts of conspiracies. In an argument prefiguring Solzhenitsyn's *Letter to the Soviet Leaders* (see Document 9.23), he called on the Bolsheviks to give up their ideology and place themselves at the head of a *national* movement. His evidence about the lifelessness of the soviets demonstrated the accuracy of earlier warnings by Luxemburg, Kautsky and others, while his comments on the futility of foreign intervention are noteworthy. The poem by Tiutchev with which the work ends is one of the most powerful observations on Russia, and widely quoted to this day.

One might ask why the Bolsheviks, while suppressing all free soviets, still maintain the farce of elections, since they cause a lot of bother. 'Soviets', however, in some form or other, are indispensable in order that the government may continue to call itself for propagandist purposes the 'Soviet' Government. If the soviet or freely elected council system did work unshackled in Russia today, Bolshevism would long ago have been abolished. In fact one of the demands frequently put forward during strikes is for a restoration, side by side with the free co-operative societies, of the soviet system which is now virtually suppressed. Paradoxical though it be, Bolshevism is in reality the complete negation of the soviet system. It is by no means impossible that the downfall of the Communists may result in a healthy effort being made to set the soviets to work in some form for the first time. If this book serves no other purpose than to impress this vitally important fact upon the reader, I shall feel I have not written in vain.

Whenever it is possible, that is, whenever no serious opposition to a Communist candidate is expected, the Bolsheviks allow an election to take its normal course, except that the secret ballot has been almost universally abolished. Before they rose to power the secret ballot was a cardinal principle of the Bolshevist programme. The argument, so typical of Bolshevist reasoning, now put forward in justification of its abolition is that secret voting would be inconsistent in a proletarian republic that has become 'free'.

The number of Communists who are elected without opposition is very considerable, and strangely enough, it is upon the bourgeoisie, engaged in the multifarious clerical tasks of the bureaucratic administration, that the authorities are able to rely for the least opposition. Employees of the government offices mostly miss the elections if they can, and if they cannot, acquiesce passively in the appointment of Communists, knowing that the proposal of opponents will lead, at the last, to extreme unpleasantness. A partial explanation of this docility and the general inability of the Russian people to assert themselves is to be found in sheer political inexperience. The halcyon days of March, 1917, before the Bolsheviks returned, was the only period in which they have known liberty, and at the elections of that time there was little or no controversy. In any case, political experience is not to be acquired in the short space of a few weeks . . .

Alas! there is but one way to bridge the gulf dividing the party from the people. It is for Russian Communists to cease to be first Communists and then Russians, and to become Russians and nothing else. To expect this of the Third International, however, is hopeless . . . The creation of the Third International was perhaps inevitable, embodying as it does the essentials of the Bolshevist creed. It was a fatal step. If the present administration lays any claim to be a *Russian* government, then the Third International is its enemy . . .

There are many reasons why, in the event of a modification of régime, the retention of some organized machine, even that established by the Communists, is desirable. In the first place there is no alternative ready to supplant it. Secondly, the soviet system has existed hitherto only in name, the Bolsheviks have never permitted it to function, and there is no evidence to prove that such a system of popular councils properly elected would be a bad basis for at least a temporary system of administration. Thirdly, Bolshevist invitations to non-Bolshevist experts to function on administrative bodies, especially in the capitals, began at an early date as I have already pointed out. For one reason or other, sometimes under compulsion, sometimes voluntarily, many of these invitations have been accepted. Jealously supervised by the Communist Party, experts who are anything but Communists hold important posts in government departments. They will obviously be better versed in the exigencies of the internal situation than outsiders. To sweep away the entire apparatus means to sweep away such men and women with it, which would be disastrous. It is only the purely political organizations – the entire paraphernalia of the Third International and its department of propaganda, for instance, and, of course, the Extraordinary Commission – that must be consigned bag and baggage to the rubbish heap . . .

The fact that warring against the Red régime has greatly fortified its power is now a universally recognized fact; and this has resulted not because the Red armies, as such, were invincible, but because the politics of the Reds' opponents were selfish and confused, their minds seemed askew, and their failure to propose a workable alternative to Bolshevism served to intensify the nausea which overcomes the Russian intellectual in Petrograd and Moscow whenever he is drawn into the hated region of party politics. So great indeed is the aversion of the bourgeois intellectual for politics that he may have to be pushed back into it, but he must first be strengthened physically and the country aided economically.

Whether the intervention should be of an economic or philanthropic character was a year ago a secondary question. The Bolshevist régime being based almost entirely on abnormalities, it needed but the establishment of any organization on normal lines for the latter ultimately to supersede the former . . .

I make no excuse for concluding this book with the oft-quoted lines of 'the people's poet', Tiutchev, who said more about his country in four simple lines than all other poets, writers, and philosophers together. In their simplicity and beauty the lines are quite untranslatable, and my free adaptation to the English, which must needs be inadequate, I append with apologies to all Russians:

> Umom Rossii nie poniatj;
> Arshinom obshchym nie izmieritj
> U niei osobiennaya statj –
> V Rossiu mozhno tolko vieritj.

> Seek not by Reason to discern
> The soul of Russia: or to learn
> Her thoughts by measurements designed
> For other lands. Her heart, her mind,
> Her ways in suffering, woe, and need,
> Her aspirations and her creed,
>   Are all her own –
>   Depths undefined,
> To be discovered, fathomed, known
>   By Faith alone.

Source: Paul Dukes, Red Dusk and the Morrow: Adventures and Investigations in Red Russia *(London, Williams and Norgate, 1923), pp. 274–5, 295, 296, 299, 308.*

Putting the Lid on the Opposition

Lenin, fearing that power was slipping from his grasp, next turned his attention to the party itself. The discipline that had long been claimed was now at last imposed on the party. Note that this was not at a time of civil war – the last of the White forces had in late 1920 been defeated in the Crimea and General Wrangel and the remnants of his forces had gone into exile. Peace threatened Bolshevik rule perhaps more than war, and thus Lenin took the necessary action in two resolutions adopted by the Tenth Party Congress that defined the way that the party would work until Gorbachev began to make changes in the late 1980s. The Congress did make some economic concessions which turned into the New Economic Policy (NEP) (see chapter 4).

Document 3.27 The 'Ban on Factions'

At the Tenth Congress, in the wake of the Kronstadt rebellion, two resolutions were passed at Lenin's insistence that were to have epochal significance, closing down the scope for debate in the party. The language used to denounce the Kronstadt insurgents was imported into intra-party discourse. The first was the resolution 'On Party Unity' (better known as the 'ban on factions').

1 The Congress calls the attention of all members of the party to the fact that the unity and solidarity of the ranks of the party, ensuring complete mutual confidence among party members and genuine team work, genuinely embodying the unanimity of will of the vanguard of the proletariat, are particularly essential at the present juncture when a number of circumstances are increasing the vacillation among the petty-bourgeois population of the country.

2 Notwithstanding this, even before the general party discussion on the trade unions certain signs of factionalism had been apparent in the party, viz. the formation of groups with separate platforms, striving to a certain degree to segregate and create their own group discipline. Such symptoms of factionalism were manifested, for example, at a party conference in Moscow (November 1920) and in Kharkov, both by the so-called 'Workers' Opposition' group, and partly by the so-called 'Democratic Centralism' group.

All class-conscious workers must clearly realise the perniciousness and impermissibility of factionalism of any kind, for no matter how the representatives of individual groups may desire to safeguard party unity, in practice factionalism inevitably leads to the weakening of team work and to intensified and repeated attempts by the enemies of the party, who have fastened themselves on to it because it is the governing party, to widen the cleavage and to use it for counter-revolutionary purposes.

The way the enemies of the proletariat take advantage of every deviation from the thoroughly consistent Communist line was perhaps most strikingly shown in the case of the Kronstadt mutiny, when the bourgeois counter-revolutionaries and White Guards in all countries of the world immediately expressed their readiness to accept even the slogans of the Soviet system, if only they might thereby secure the overthrow of the dictatorship of the proletariat in Russia, and when the Socialist Revolutionaries and the bourgeois counter-revolutionaries in general resorted in Kronstadt to slogans calling for an insurrection against the Soviet government of Russia ostensibly in the interest of Soviet power. These facts fully prove that the White Guards strive, and are able, to disguise themselves as Communists, and even as the most Left Communists, solely for the purpose of weakening and overthrowing the bulwark of the proletarian revolution in Russia . . .

4 In the practical struggle against factionalism, every organisation of the party must take strict measures to prevent any factional actions whatsoever.

Criticism of the party's shortcomings, which is absolutely necessary, must be conducted in such a way that every practical proposal shall be submitted immediately, without any delay, in the most precise form possible, for consideration and decision to the leading local and central bodies of the party. Moreover, everyone who criticises must see to it that the form of his criticism takes into account the position of the party, surrounded as it is by a ring of enemies, and that the content of his criticism is such that, by directly participating in Soviet and party work, he can test the rectification of the errors of the party or of individual party members in practice . . .

5 . . . While ruthlessly rejecting unpractical and factional pseudo-criticisms, the party will unceasingly continue – trying out new methods – to fight with all the means at its disposal against bureaucracy, for the extension of democracy and initiative, for detecting, exposing and expelling from the party elements that have wormed their way into its ranks, etc.

6 The Congress therefore hereby declares dissolved and orders the immediate dissolution of all groups without exception that have been formed on the basis of one platform or another (such as the 'Workers' Opposition' group, the 'Democratic-Centralism' group, etc.). Non-observance of this decision of the Congress shall involve absolute and immediate expulsion from the party.

7 In order to ensure strict discipline within the party and in all Soviet work and to secure the maximum unanimity in removing all factionalism the Congress authorises the Central Committee, in cases of breach of discipline or of a revival or toleration of factionalism, to apply all party penalties, including expulsion, and in regard to members of the Central Committee to reduce them to the status of alternate members and even, as an extreme measure, to expel them from the party. A necessary condition for the application of such an extreme measure to members of the Central Committee, alternate members of the Central Committee and members of the Control Commission is the convocation of a plenum of the Central Committee, to which all alternate members of the Central Committee and all members of the Control Commission shall be invited. If such a general assembly of the most responsible leaders of the party, by a two-thirds majority, deems it necessary to reduce a member of the Central Committee to the status of alternate member, or to expel him from the party, this measure shall be put into effect immediately.

Source: Lenin, 'O edinstve partii' ('On Party Unity'), Resolution of the Tenth Congress of the RCP(b), March 1921, PSS, vol. 43, pp. 89–93.

Document 3.28   The End of the Trade Union Debate

The second resolution, 'On the Syndicalist and Anarchist Deviation in our Party', abruptly terminated the debate over the role of the scope of Soviet trade unions.

1 In the past few months a syndicalist and anarchist deviation has been definitely revealed in our party, and calls for the most resolute measures of ideological struggle and also for purging and restoring the health of the party.

2 The said deviation is due partly to the influx into the party of former Mensheviks and also of workers and peasants who have not yet fully assimilated the communist world outlook; mainly, however, this deviation is due to the influence exercised upon the proletariat and on the Russian Communist Party by the petty-bourgeois element, which is exceptionally strong in our country, and which inevitably engenders vacillation towards anarchism, particularly at a time when the conditions of the masses have sharply deteriorated as a consequence of the crop failure and the devastating effects of war, and when the demobilisation of the army numbering millions releases hundreds and hundreds of thousands of peasants and workers unable immediately to find regular means of livelihood.

3 The most theoretically complete and formulated expression of this deviation [see source note, p. 109] are the theses and other literary productions of the so-called 'Workers' Opposition' group. Sufficiently illustrative of this is, for example, the following thesis propounded by this group: 'The organisation of the administration of the national economy is the function of an All-Russian Producers' Congress organised in industrial trade unions, which elect a central organ for the administration of the entire national economy of the Republic.'

The ideas at the bottom of this and numerous analogous statements are radically wrong in theory, and represent complete rupture with Marxism and communism as well as with the practical experience of all semi-proletarian revolutions and of the present proletarian revolution . . .

Marxism teaches – and this tenet has not only been formally endorsed by the whole of the Communist International in the decisions of the Second (1920) Congress of the Comintern on the role of the political party of the proletariat, but has also been confirmed in practice by our revolution – that only the political party of the working class, i.e. the Communist Party, is capable of uniting, training and organising a vanguard of the proletariat and of the whole mass of the working people that alone will be capable of withstanding the inevitable petty-bourgeois vacillations of this mass and the inevitable traditions and relapses of narrow craft unionism or craft prejudices among the proletariat, and of guiding all the united activities of the whole of the proletariat, i.e. of leading it politically and, through it, the whole mass of the working people. Without this the dictatorship of the proletariat is impossible. . . .

5 In addition to theoretical fallacies and a radically wrong attitude towards the practical experience of economic construction already begun by the Soviet government, the Congress of the Russian Communist Party discerns in the views of these and analogous groups and persons a gross political

mistake and a direct political danger to the very existence of the dictatorship of the proletariat.

In a country like Russia, the overwhelming preponderance of the petty-bourgeois element and the devastation, impoverishment, epidemics, crop failures, extreme want and hardship inevitably resulting from the war engender particularly sharp vacillations in the moods of the petty-bourgeois and semi-proletarian masses. At one moment the wavering is in the direction of strengthening the alliance between these masses and the proletariat, and at another moment in the direction of bourgeois restoration. The whole experience of all revolutions in the eighteenth, nineteenth and twentieth centuries shows with utmost and absolute clarity and conviction that the only possible result of these vacillations – if the unity, strength and influence of the revolutionary vanguard of the proletariat is weakened in the slightest degree – can be the restoration of the power and property of the capitalists and landlords.

Hence, the views of the 'Workers' Opposition' and of like-minded elements are not only wrong in theory, but in practice are an expression of petty-bourgeois anarchist wavering, in practice weaken the consistency of the leading line of the Communist Party, and in practice help the class enemies of the proletarian revolution.

6 In view of all this, the Congress of the Russian Communist Party, emphatically rejecting the said ideas which express a syndicalist and anarchist deviation, deems it necessary:

First, to wage an unswerving and systematic ideological struggle against these ideas;

Second, the Congress regards the propaganda of these ideas as being incompatible with membership of the Russian Communist Party.

Instructing the Central Committee of the party strictly to enforce these decisions the Congress at the same time points out that space can and should be devoted in special publications, symposiums, etc., for a most comprehensive interchange of opinion among party members on all the questions herein indicated.

Source: Lenin, 'O sindikalistskom i anarkhistskom uklone v nashei partii'
('On the Syndicalist and Anarchist Deviation in our Party'), Resolution of the
Tenth Congress of the RCP(b), March 1921, PSS, vol. 43, pp. 93–7.

Bolshevism in Perspective

In a letter to Lunacharsky on 22 September 1920, the writer V. Korolenko had noted that 'Russia stands at the crossroads between two Utopias: the Utopia of the past and the Utopia of the future, and is deciding into which Utopia to throw itself.' The only option that appeared excluded was 'normal' practical development.

Document 3.29 Sukhanov, *Notes on the Revolution*

Nikolai Sukhanov had been a witness to the revolution of 1917 and in 1922 produced one of the most perceptive analyses of the revolutionary events and of Lenin personally.

There can be no doubt, above all, that Lenin is an extraordinary phenomenon. He is a man with extraordinary mental powers . . . If I had to find a term or epithet, I would not hesitate to call Lenin a genius, bearing in mind what is meant by the term genius. A genius is, as is well known, an 'abnormal' person, who is 'not quite right in the head'. More concretely, he is a person with an extremely narrow sphere of mental activity, but who in that sphere works with extraordinary force and productivity. A genius is an extremely narrow person, a chauvinist to the core, who is not receptive to and is unable to understand the most simple and straightforward things . . . Lenin is undoubtedly like this, whose mind cannot understand many elementary truths, even in the field of social movements. From this arose an endless number of elementary mistakes by Lenin both in the period of his agitation and demagogy and in the period of his dictatorship. But in the sphere of the intellect Lenin had a few 'core ideas' that he pursued with amazing force, with superhuman endeavour, to ensure his enormous influence among socialists and revolutionaries . . .

The Bolshevik party was Lenin's work and his alone. Dozens and hundreds of people passed through in responsible posts, changing one after the other the revolutionary generations, but Lenin unshakeably stood at his post, defining alone the physiognomy of the party and sharing power with no one . . . Developing 'leftism', his shameless radicalism, primitive demagogy, held back by neither learning nor common sense, later guaranteed him success among the proletarian-peasant masses, having no experience other than the tsarist whip . . .

A Utopianist and fantasist, focused on abstractions, Lenin was also a brilliant realist politician, both in the large and the small. 'To set Europe alight', to provoke the 'worldwide socialist revolution', to secure the flag of socialism by Lenin's methods was not possible and will not be. But to conquer one's own party, putting aside all one's own knowledge, this Lenin was able to do brilliantly, taking advantage of all favourable circumstances, invoking to assist him the shades of Bonaparte and Machiavelli.

Source: N. Sukhanov, Zapiski o revolyutsii, *cited in* Literaturnaya gazeta: dos'e, *no. 5, 1992, p. 8.*

Document 3.30 Communism and the Salvation of Society

In mid-1920 Bertrand Russell visited Russia, and in November of that year his thoughts on the visit were published, supplemented, as he puts it in the preface to the book, 'by much reading and discussion' (p. 10). His analysis provides a commentary on all that had gone before. He stressed that 'To understand Bolshevism it is not sufficient to know facts; it is necessary also to enter with sympathy and imagination into a new spirit' (p. 15). He wrote one of the most perceptive accounts of the Soviet experience up to that time, providing an analysis that has enduring value.

Three questions arise in regard to this method of reaching Utopia. First, would the ultimate state foreshadowed by the Bolsheviks be desirable by itself: Secondly, would the conflict involved in achieving it by the Bolshevik method be so bitter and prolonged that its evils would outweigh the ultimate good? Thirdly, is this method likely to lead, in the end, to the state which the Bolsheviks desire, or will it fail at some point and arrive at a quite different result? If we are to be Bolsheviks, we must answer all these questions in a sense favourable to their programme.

As regards the first question, I have no hesitation in answering it in a manner favourable to Communism. It is clear that the present inequalities of wealth are unjust. In part, they may be defended as affording an incentive of useful industry, but I do not think this defence will carry us very far. However, I have argued this question before in my book on *Roads to Freedom*, and I will not spend time upon it now. On this matter, I concede the Bolshevik case. It is the other two questions that I wish to discuss.

Our second question was: Is the ultimate good aimed at by the Bolsheviks sufficiently great to be worth the price that, according to their own theory, will have to be paid for achieving it? If anything human were absolutely certain, we might answer this question affirmatively with some confidence. The benefits of Communism, if it were once achieved, might be expected to be lasting; we might legitimately hope that further change would be towards something still better, not towards a revival of ancient evils. But if we admit, as we must do, that the outcome of the Communist revolution is in some degree uncertain, it becomes necessary to count the cost; for a great part of the cost is all but certain.

Since the revolution of October, 1917, the Soviet Government has been at war with almost all the world, and has had at the same time to face civil war at home. This is not to be regarded as accidental, or as a misfortune which could not be foreseen. According to Marxian theory, what has happened was bound to happen. Indeed, Russia has been wonderfully fortunate in not having to face an even more desperate situation. First and foremost, the world was exhausted by the war, and in no mood for military adventures.

Next, the tsarist régime was the worst in Europe, and therefore rallied less support than would be secured by another capital Government. Again, Russia is vast and agricultural, making it capable of resisting both invasion and blockade better than Great Britain or France or Germany . . .

Now the price that Russia is having to pay is very great. The almost universal poverty might be thought to be a small evil in comparison with the ultimate gain, but it brings with it other evils of which the magnitude would be acknowledged even by those who have never known poverty and therefore make light of it. Hunger brings an absorption in the question of food, which, to most people, makes life almost purely animal. The general shortage makes people fierce, and reacts upon the political atmosphere. The necessity of inculcating Communism produces a hot-house condition, where every breath of fresh air must be excluded: people are to be taught to think in a certain way, and all free intelligence becomes taboo. The country comes to resemble an immensely magnified Jesuit College. Every kind of liberty is banned as being '*bourgeois*' but it remains a fact that intelligence languishes where thought is not free . . .

This brings us to our third question: Is the system which Communists regard as their goal likely to result from the adoption of their methods? This is really the most vital question of the three.

Advocacy of Communism by those who believe in Bolshevik methods rests upon the assumption that there is no slavery except economic slavery, and that when all goods are held in common there must be perfect liberty. I fear this is a delusion.

There must be administration, there must be officials who control distribution. These men, in a Communist State, are the repositories of power. So long as they control the army, they are able, as in Russia at this moment, to wield despotic power even if they are a small minority. The fact that there is Communism – to a certain extent – does not mean that there is liberty. If the Communism were more complete, it would not necessarily mean more freedom; there would still be certain officials in control of the food supply, and these officials could govern as they pleased so long as they retained the support of the soldiers. This is not mere theory: it is the patent lesson of the present condition of Russia. The Bolshevik theory is that a small minority are to seize power, and are to hold it until Communism is accepted practically universally, which, they admit, may take a long time. But power is sweet, and few men surrender it voluntarily. It is especially sweet to those who have the habit of it, and the habit becomes most ingrained in those who have governed by bayonets, without popular support. Is it not almost inevitable that men placed as the Bolsheviks are placed in Russia, and as they maintain that the Communists must place themselves wherever the social revolution succeeds, will be loath to relinquish their monopoly of power, and will find reasons for remaining until some new revolution ousts them? Would it not be fatally easy for them, without altering economic structure, to decree large salaries for high Government officials, and so reintroduce the old inequalities of wealth? What motive would they have for not doing so? What motive is possible except idealism, love of mankind, non-economic motives of the sort that Bolsheviks decry? The system created by violence and the forcible rule of a minority must necessarily allow of tyranny and exploitation; and if human nature is what Marxians assert it to be, why should the rulers neglect such opportunities of selfish advantage?

It is sheer nonsense to pretend that the rulers of a great empire such as Soviet Russia, when they have become accustomed to power, retain the proletarian psychology, and feel that their class-interest is the same as that of the ordinary working man. This not the case in fact in Russia now, however the truth may be concealed by fine phrases. The Government has a class-consciousness and a class-interest quite distinct from those of the genuine proletarian, who is not to be confounded with the paper proletarian of the Marxian scheme. In a capitalist state, the Government and the capitalists on the whole hang together, and form one class; in Soviet Russia, the Government has absorbed the capitalist mentality together with the governmental, and the fusion has given increased strength to the upper class. But I see no reason whatever to expect equality or freedom to result from such a system, except reasons derived from a false psychology and a mistaken analysis of the sources of political power.

I am compelled to reject Bolshevism for two reasons: First, because the price mankind must pay to achieve Communism by Bolshevik methods is too terrible; and secondly because, even after paying the price, I do not believe the result would be what the Bolsheviks profess to desire.

Source: Bertrand Russell, The Practice and Theory of Bolshevism *(London, George Allen & Unwin, 1920), pp. 148–51, 153–6.*

The paths diverge, 1921–1929 | 4

Two issues dominated political debates in the 1920s. The first focused on political developments within the party, with an undercurrent of protest against the dominance of the bureaucracy. This debate after Lenin's death in January 1924 became bound up with the issue of the succession. The second issue was the status of the New Economic Policy (NEP): was it a betrayal of communist aspirations or did it offer a viable long-term path of socialist development? By the end of the decade Stalin resolved both issues by consolidating his own power and launching the programme of crash industrialisation and forced collectivisation.

Launching the New Economic Policy

While NEP represented a concession to the market, in particular to the peasantry, no commensurate concessions were made in the political sphere. In fact, both within the party and in society the early NEP was accompanied by the final extirpation of political resistance. The few remaining islands of support for non-Bolsheviks in the soviets were eliminated, non-Bolshevik trade unions were crushed, and the remnants of the Mensheviks and Socialist Revolutionaries were imprisoned or exiled. A trial of the Right SRs in mid-1922 signalled a new stage in the use of 'show trials' for political opponents. The leadings lights of the non-Bolshevik intelligentsia (including Nikolai Berdyaev) were shipped into exile in autumn 1922. The political tone of the period is reflected in Lenin's letter urging repressive measures against the Church.

Document 4.1   'On the Replacement of Requisitioning by a Tax in Kind'

Accompanying the two resolutions on party discipline and the trade unions at the Tenth Congress, Lenin made concessions to the broader movement united in hostility to War Communism. Above all, the policy of requisitioning was to be replaced by a 'tax in kind', a set tax payable in grain with the surpluses able to be marketed. A monetary economy was restored and some private capitalism in industry allowed, while the state remained in control of the 'commanding heights' of the economy. By the end of 1921 War Communism had given way to the New Economic Policy based on the *smychka* (union) between peasants and workers.

1 To ensure the correct and peaceful management of the economy on the basis of the freer disposal by landholders of their economic resources, to strengthen the peasant economy and to raise their productivity and also for the accurate fulfilment of state obligations, requisitioning as a way of collecting supplies, raw materials and forage is replaced by a tax in kind . . .
3 The tax will be collected in the form of a percentage and proportionate collection of agricultural products, taking into account the harvest, the number of mouths to feed and the real number of livestock on the holding . . .
8 All surpluses of food, raw materials and forage remaining with the landholder after fulfilment of the tax is at their entire disposal and can be used by then to improve and strengthen their holding, to raise their personal consumption and to exchange for manufactured and craft products and agricultural machinery.

Source: 'O zamene razverstki natural'nym nalogom', KPSS v rezolyutsiyakh s''ezdov, konferentsii i plenumov TsK *(Moscow, Politizdat, 1983), pp. 370–1.*

Document 4.2   Lenin on the 'Tax in Kind'

Defending the concession to the market, Lenin insisted that War Communism had not represented the fulfilment of Marxian socialism but had been no more than a 'temporary' measure and not 'a policy that corresponded to the economic tasks of the proletariat'. He argued that NEP represented a return to the policies of mid-1918, interrupted by the exigencies of the Civil War.

The most urgent thing at the present time is to take measures that will immediately increase the productive forces of peasant farming. Only in *this way* will it be possible to improve the conditions of the workers and strengthen the alliance between the workers and peasants, to strengthen the dictatorship of the proletariat. The proletarian or representative of the proletariat who *refused* to improve the conditions of the workers in *this way* would *in fact* prove himself to be an accomplice of the White Guards and the capitalists; because to refuse to do it in this way would mean putting the craft interests of the workers above their class interests, would mean sacrificing the interests of the whole of the working class, of its dictatorship, its alliance with the peasantry against the landlords and capitalists, its leading role in the struggle for the emancipation of labour from the yoke of capital, for the sake of the immediate, momentary and partial gain of the workers.

Thus the first thing required is immediate and serious measures to raise the productive forces of the peasantry.

This cannot be done without a serious modification of our food policy. Such a modification was the substitution of the surplus-appropriation system by the tax in kind, which implies free trade, at least in local economic exchange, after the tax has been paid.

The essence of this distinctive 'War Communism' was that we practically took from the peasant all the surplus grain – and sometimes even not only surplus grain, but part of the grain the peasant required for food – to meet the requirements of the army and sustain the workers. We took most of it on credit, for paper money. Otherwise we would not have been able to defeat the landlords and capitalists in a devastated petty bourgeois country . . .

We were forced to resort to 'War Communism' by war and ruin. It was not, nor could it be, a policy that corresponded to the economic tasks of the proletariat. It was a temporary measure. The correct policy of the proletariat, which is exercising its dictatorship in a small-peasant country, is to obtain grain in exchange for the manufactured goods the peasant requires. Only such a food policy corresponds to the tasks of the proletariat; only such a policy can strengthen the foundations of socialism and lead to its complete victory.

Source: Lenin, 'O prodovol'stvennom naloge' ('The Tax in Kind'), 21 April 1921, PSS, vol. 43, pp. 218–19, 219–20.

Document 4.3   Lenin Puts NEP in Perspective

Not all were convinced by Lenin's arguments and the left of the party, above all those associated with the Workers' Opposition, condemned NEP as a betrayal of socialist principles. Here Lenin suggested that NEP was indeed a retreat, but it was not clear what form the 'leap forward' would take. Stalin at the end of the 1920s could with some justification use these statements to claim that NEP in Lenin's view had only been envisaged as a temporary policy. This speech, incidentally, was Lenin's last public oration; he never again addressed a large audience.

But as regards home policy, the change we made in the spring of 1921, which was necessitated by such extremely powerful and convincing circumstances that no debates or disagreements arose among us about it – that change continues to cause us some difficulties, great difficulties, I would say. Not because we have any doubts about the need for the turn – no doubts exist in that respect – not because we have any doubts as to whether the test of our New Economic Policy has yielded the successes we expected. No doubts exist on that score – I can say this quite definitely – either in the ranks of our Party or in the ranks of the huge mass of non-Party workers and peasants.

In this sense the problem presents no difficulties. The difficulties we have stem from our being faced with a task whose solution very often requires the services of new people, extraordinary measures and extraordinary methods. Doubts still exist among us as to whether this or that is correct. There are changes in one direction or another. And it should be said that both will continue for quite a long time. 'The New Economic Policy!' A strange title. It was called a New Economic Policy because it turned things back. We are now retreating, going back, as it were; but we are doing so in order, after first retreating, to take a running start and make a bigger leap forward. It was on this condition alone that we retreated in pursuing our New Economic Policy. Where and how we must now regroup, adapt and reorganise in order to start a most stubborn offensive after our retreat, we do not yet know. To carry out all these operations properly we need, as the proverb says, to look not ten but a hundred times before we leap. We must do so in order to cope with the incredible difficulties we encounter in dealing with all our tasks and problems . . .

We can see why we, who eighteen months ago took the path of the so-called New Economic Policy, are finding it so incredibly difficult to advance along that path. We live in a country devastated so severely by war, knocked out of anything like the normal course of life, in a country that has suffered and endured so much, that willy-nilly we are beginning all our calculations with a very, very small percentage – the pre-war percentage. We apply this yardstick to the conditions of our life, we sometimes do so very impatiently, heatedly, and always end up with the conviction that the difficulties are vast. The task we have set ourselves in this field seems all the more vast because we are comparing it with the state of affairs in any ordinary bourgeois country. We have set ourselves this task because we understood that it was no use expecting the wealthy powers to give us the assistance usually forthcoming under such circumstances. After the Civil War we have been subjected to very nearly a boycott, that is, we have been told that the economic ties that are customary and normal in the capitalist world will not be maintained in our case . . .

We still have the old machinery, and our task now is to remould it along new lines. We cannot do so at once, but we must see to it that the Communists we have are properly placed. What we need is that they, the Communists, should control the machinery they are assigned to, and not, as so often happens with us, that the machinery should control them. We should make no secret of it, and speak of it frankly. Such are the tasks and the difficulties of that practical path, when we must not approach socialism as if it were an icon painted in festive colours. We need to take the right direction, we need to see that everything is checked, that the masses, the entire population, check the path we follow and say: 'Yes, this is better than the old system.' That is the task we have set ourselves. Our Party, a little group of people in comparison with the country's total population, has tackled this job. This tiny nucleus has set itself the task of remaking everything, and it will do so. We have proved that this is no Utopia but a cause which people live by . . .

We have brought socialism into everyday life and must here see how matters stand. That is the task of our day, the task of our epoch. Permit me to conclude by expressing confidence that difficult as this task may be, new as it may be compared with our previous task, and numerous as the difficulties may be that it entails, we shall all – not in a day, but in a few years – all of us together fulfil it whatever the cost, so that NEP Russia will become socialist Russia. (*Stormy, prolonged applause.*)

Source: Lenin, 'Speech at a Plenary Session of the Moscow Soviet', 20 November 1922, Selected Works, pp. 675, 676, 679, 680.

Document 4.4   Lenin Attacks the Church

While concessions were made in the economic sphere, there was no 'New Political Policy' and instead War Communist repression was intensified. The following letter from Lenin to Molotov of 19 March 1922 was kept secret until Gorbachev's *glasnost* finally allowed it to be published. Marked '*Strictly secret*', the letter was provoked by disturbances among Orthodox believers in the town of Shui in response to the looting of church valuables by the authorities, allegedly to be used to assist famine victims. The Orthodox hierarchy at this time in fact had made it quite clear that they would donate valuables to be sold to buy food, but that sacramental items were not to be touched. Lenin saw that the incident could be exploited, using the famine on the Volga as an instrument to discredit and ruin the Orthodox Church. Lenin's policy had already been prefigured by his callous attitude to the famine of 1891, when he had argued that aid ought to be denied the peasants to provoke a revolutionary crisis. The letter was distributed to members of the Politburo and Mikhail Kalinin, who from March 1919 was chairman of VTsIK (the All-Russian (later All-Soviet) Central Executive Committee of the Soviets) and remained the figurehead president of the Soviet Union throughout Stalin's reign until his death in 1946. As an exercise in cynicism and bloodthirstyness, the letter is hard to beat. The whole practice of Bolshevik power is contained therein.

Strictly secret
Do not in any circumstances make a copy, and every Politburo member (and Comrade Kalinin) make notes on the document itself.

To Comrade Molotov for the Members of the Politburo

In connection with the events in Shui, which have already been discussed by the Politburo, it seems to me that we have to take a firm decision about the general plan of struggle on the given matter. I doubt whether I will personally be able to attend the Politburo meeting of 20 March and therefore I am sending my thoughts in a written form.

The events in Shui should be seen in connection with the information recently sent out by ROSTA [Russian Telegraph Agency] to newspapers not for publication giving news of the resistance being prepared by the Black Hundreds in Peter against the decree on the confiscation of church valuables. If we compare this fact with what the nespapers are writing about the attitude of the priesthood to the decree on the confiscation of church valuables, and also with what we know of the illegal proclamation by Patriarch Tikhon, then it becomes absolutely clear that the Black Hundred clergy headed by its leader are fully consciously pursuing a plan to resist us now on this issue.

It is obvious that at secret meetings of influential Black Hundred clergy this plan was thought out and firmly adopted. The events in Shui are only one manifestation of the implementation of this general plan.

I think that here our enemy is making a huge strategic mistake, trying to draw us into a decisive struggle which for them is particularly hopeless and especially difficult. On the contrary, the time for us is particularly suitable, and indeed a unique moment when we can with a probability of 99 out of a 100 completely successfully smash our opponents and secure for us our position for many decades. Precisely now and only now, when in the famine areas they are eating people and where hundreds if not thousands of corpses are lying in the streets, we can (and therefore should) undertake the confiscation of church valuables with the utmost violence and merciless energy, without hesitation crushing all resistance whatsoever. Precisely now and only now the vast majority of the peasant masses will be either for us, or in any case will be in no condition to give any strong support to that handful of Black Hundred clergy and reactionary urban petty bourgeoisie, which can and want to try out a policy of violent resistance to the Soviet decree.

Whatever happens, we must confiscate church valuables in the most decisive and speediest way, securing for ourselves a fund of several hundred million gold roubles (we mustn't forget how enormously wealthy some monasteries are). Without this fund no state work in general, and no economic reconstruction in particular, and especially no backing to our position in Genoa [see below], are at all possible. We must get this fund of several hundred million gold roubles (and perhaps, several billion) into our hands whatever happens. And we can do this successfully only now. Everything suggests that later we will not be able to do this since no other moment apart from desperate hunger will provide us with such a mood among the wide peasant masses, which will either provide us with the sympathy of these masses, or at the very least, will neutralise these masses in the sense that victory in the struggle to confiscate valuables will undoubtedly and completely be with us.

A wise writer on problems of state [Machiavelli] said that if a series of cruel actions must be carried out to achieve a certain political objective, then they must be carried out in the most energetic fashion and in as short a time as possible, because the popular masses will not tolerate a long period in which cruel actions are taken. These considerations are reinforced by the fact that the international situation for Russia will probably, after Genoa, make harsh measures against the reactionary clergy politically irrational, and possibly even excessively dangerous. Now complete victory over the reactionary clergy is certainly within our grasp. Moreover, the struggle against us by most of our foreign opponents among Russian émigrés abroad, i.e., the

SRs and Milyukovites, will be made more difficult if we act precisely at this time, in connection with the famine, and pursue with maximum speed and mercilessness the crushing of the reactionary clergy.

Therefore, I have reached the firm conclusion that we must now at this moment undertake a decisive and merciless struggle against the Black Hundred clergy and suppress their opposition with so much cruelty that they will not forget it for several decades. I envisage the implementation of the plan taking the following form:

Only Comrade Kalinin should officially come up with some measure or other – never and in no way should Comrade Trotsky speak in the press or should he in any other way address the public.

The telegram already sent by the Politburo about the temporary suspension of the confiscations should not be rescinded. It is useful for us, in that it will sow amongst our opponents the idea that we are wavering, as if he [the enemy] was able to scare us (the enemy certainly will soon learn about this secret telegram, precisely because it is secret).

Send one of the most energetic, sensible and effective members of VTsIK or other representatives of the central authorities (better one, than several), giving him verbal instructions through a Politburo member. These instructions should essentially state that in Shui he should arrest as many as possible, no fewer than several dozen representatives of the local clergy, the local petty bourgeoisie and the local bourgeoisie on suspicion of direct or indirect participation in violent resistance to the VTsIK decree on the confiscation of church valuables. As soon as he has finished this work he must return to Moscow and personally report to a full meeting of the Politburo or to two plenipotentiaries appointed by the Politburo for this. On the basis of this report the Politburo should issue a detailed directive to the judicial authorities, also verbally, so that the trial against the Shui rebels, resisting help for the hungry, is conducted with the maximum speed and ends in no other way than the shooting of a very large number of the most influential and dangerous Black Hundredists in the town of Shui, and if possible not only in that town but also in Moscow and several other religious centres.

It would be expedient not to touch Patriarch Tikhon himself, I think, although undoubtedly he stands at the head of this whole rebellion of slaveowners. Concerning him, we should immediately issue a secret order to the GPU [Main Political Directorate, secret police] to monitor closely and report his communications. Order Dzerzhinskii and Unshlikht personally to report on this weekly to the Politburo.

Organise a secret meeting at the [Eleventh] Party Congress [27 March–2 April 1922] of all or nearly all delegates on this question, together with the main officials of the GPU, NKYu [Ministry of Justice] and the Revtribunal [Revolutionary Tribunal]. At this meeting adopt a secret congress resolution stating that the confiscation of valuables, in particular from the wealthiest monasteries and churches, should be conducted with merciless decisiveness, unconditionally not stopping for anything and in the shortest possible period. The greater the number of representatives of the reactionary clergy and the reactionary bourgeoisie that we succeed in shooting for this reason, the better. It is precisely now that we must teach these people a lesson, so that for several decades they will not even dare to think of any resistance.

To oversee the swift and successful implementation of these measures appoint at the congress, i.e., at the secret meeting, a special commission with the obligatory participation of Comrade Trotsky and Comrade Kalinin without any announcement about this commision to ensure that the whole operation subordinated to it is achieved and conducted not in the name of the commission, but in a general-Soviet and all-party format. Appoint the best and particularly responsible workers to implement this measure in the richest monasteries and churches.

19.III.22   Lenin

Source: Izvestiya TsK KPSS, *no. 4, 1990, pp. 190–3.*

The Genoa economic and political conference was held from 10 April to 19 May 1922 with twenty-nine countries attending to discuss economic cooperation between Soviet Russia and the capitalist world, with disarmament also an item on the agenda. The major stumbling block was the insistence by the Western powers that Russia pay all the tsarist debts, including pre-war debts, the return of nationalised enterprises to their former owners and much more that was obviously unacceptable to the Soviet government. The conference broke up early without agreement. Even while the conference at Genoa was dragging on, Soviet Russia and Germany (the two outcast nations of the interwar years) signed a treaty at Rapallo (near Genoa) on 16 April 1922. The two countries reciprocally renounced all claims arising from the First World War and Germany gave up attempts to have its nationalised property restored as long as Soviet Russia did not satisfy similar claims by other countries. Diplomatic relations and a favourable trade regime were established between the two countries. In this way the two outcast nations of the early interwar years, Soviet Russia and Weimar Germany, broke out from their diplomatic isolation.

Document 4.5   Establishing the 'Ministry of Censorship'

We saw above (Document 2.19) how two days after seizing power the Bolsheviks closed down some newspapers and placed restrictions on the rest as a 'temporary' measure. In mid-1922 a 'Main Administration for Matters of Literature and Publishing' (Glavlit) was established to oversee censorship. Glavlit remained active until the late 1980s when Gorbachev allowed a degree of freedom of the press. The decree was held in secret archives until recently released.

1 With the aim of uniting all forms of censorship over printed materials, a Main Administration for Matters of Literature and Publishing under the

People's Commissariat of Education and its local organs, the *guberniya* Departments of Education, is to be formed.

2 The responsibilities of the Main Adminstration for Matters of Literature and Publishing and its local organs are:

(a) The preliminary review of all materials designated for publication or for distribution, including manuscripts as well as periodical and non-periodical publications, photographs, drawings, maps and so on;

(b) The licensing of the publication of individual materials, as well as periodical and non-periodical press organs;

(c) Compiling lists of publications that are forbidden to be sold or distributed;

(d) Issuing instructions and regulations about publishing matters, obligatory for all press bodies, publishers, printworks, libraries and book shops.

3 The Main Adminstration for Matters of Literature and Publishing and its organs forbid the publication and distribution of materials:

(a) Containing agitation against Soviet power;

(b) Revealing the republic's military secrets;

(c) Arousing public opinion by the dissemination of false information;

(d) Having a pornographic character.

Source: 'Regulations on the Main Adminstration for Matters of Literature and Publishing (Glavlit)', 6 June 1922, Istoriya sovetskoi politicheskoi tsenzury: dokumenty i kommentarii *(Moscow, Rosspen, 1997), pp. 35–6.*

Who would decide what constituted 'agitation against Soviet power' was not specified, nor what the definition of 'false information' would be. The decree represented an important step in the consolidation of the Bolshevik dictatorship. What had previously been justified as emergency measures at a time of war now became standard practice in peacetime.

Political Controversy

The ban on factions in 1921 did not put an end to discussion within the Communist Party, but it did render them more oblique ('Aesopian') and inhibited open discussion of important issues. One of the legacies of Lenin's polemical style was that theoretical debates became bound up with issues of political power: the stronger could impose ideological uniformity rather than winning arguments in open debate.

Document 4.6   Lukács on Party Organisation

Georg Lukács, the Hungarian philosopher, literary critic and Commissar of Education in the short-lived Hungarian proletarian dictatorship in 1919, was one of the first to understand the deepest meaning of the Leninist style of politics and its implications. Lukács revised Marxist theory to argue that ideas and power were as important as economics in determining revolutionary development. Obviously stimulated by the experience of the Bolshevik revolution, where 'voluntarist' factors like leadership had exerted a determining effect on outcomes, Lukács laid bare the profound essence of the theoretical shift signified by Bolshevism, although Lenin himself was reluctant to embrace the theoretical consequences of his own thinking. Lukács understood the immanence of Stalinism in Bolshevik rule, and thus became the theorist of Stalinist voluntarism. His comment, cited below, that 'The party is divided into an active and a passive group in which the latter is only occasionally brought into play and then only at the behest of the former' in effect became the slogan of numerous oppositions. Lukács was too explicit in drawing out the nature of party leadership and was censured by the Soviet authorities when his essays were published in the early 1920s.

If the Menshevik parties are the organised form of the ideological crisis of the proletariat, the Communist Party is the organised form of the conscious approach to this leap and hence the first *conscious* step towards the realm of freedom . . . Above all one thing must be made clear: freedom here does not mean the freedom of the individual . . . The *conscious* desire for the realm of freedom can only mean consciously taking the steps that will really lead to it. And in the awareness that in contemporary bourgeois society individual freedom can only be corrupt and corrupting because it is a case of unilateral privilege based on the unfreedom of others, this desire must entail the renunciation of individual freedom. It implies the conscious subordination of the self to that collective will that is destined to bring real freedom into being and that today is earnestly taking the first arduous, uncertain and groping steps towards it. This conscious collective will is the Communist Party. And like every aspect of a dialectical process it too contains the seeds, admittedly in a primitive, abstract and undeveloped form, of the determinants appropriate to the goal it is destined to achieve: namely freedom in solidarity.

The unifying factor here is *discipline*. Only through discipline can the party be capable of putting the collective will into practice, whereas the introduction of the bourgeois concept of freedom prevents this collective will from forming itself and so transforms the party into a loose aggregate of individuals incapable of action. More importantly, even for the individual it is only discipline that creates the opportunity of taking that first step to the freedom that is already possible even though it is freedom of a very primitive sort, corresponding as it does to the stage of societal development. This is the freedom that works at overcoming the present.

What was novel in the formation of the Communist Parties was the new relation between spontaneous action and conscious, theoretical foresight . . . This conflict between individual and class consciousness in every single worker is by no means a matter of chance. For the Communist Party shows itself here to be superior to every other party organisation in two ways: firstly, for the first time in history the active and practical side of class consciousness directly influences the specific actions of every individual, and secondly, at the same time it consciously helps to determine the historical process . . .

Corresponding to this is the necessary appearance simultaneously of two complementary but equally false views of the course of history: the voluntaristic overestimation of the active importance of the individual (the leader) and the fatalistic underestimation of the importance of the class (the masses). The party is divided into an active and a passive group in which the latter is only occasionally brought into play and then only at the behest of the former. The 'freedom' possessed by the members of such parties is therefore nothing more than the freedom of more or less peripheral and never fully engaged observers to pass judgement on the fatalistically accepted course of events or the errors of individuals. Such organisations never succeed in encompassing the total personality of their members, they cannot even attempt to do so. Like all the social forms of civilisation these organisations are based on the exact mechanised division of labour, on bureaucratisation, on the precise delineation and separation of rights and duties. The members are only connected with the organisation by virtue of abstractly grasped aspects of their existence and these abstract bonds are objectivised as rights and duties.

Really active participation in every event, really practical involvement of all the members of an organisation can only be achieved by engaging the whole personality. Only when action within a community becomes the central personal concern of everyone involved will it be possible to abolish the split between rights and duties, the organisational form of man's separation from his own socialisation and his fragmentation at the hands of the social forces that control him . . .

Flexibility, the ability to change and adapt one's tactics and a tightly knit organisation are just two sides of one and the same thing. The whole trajectory of this, the deepest meaning of the communist form of organisation is rarely grasped in its entirety even in communist circles. And this despite the fact that both the possibility of right action and the Communist Party's inner capacity for development depend on it.

Source: Georg Lukács, 'Towards a Methodology of the Problem of Organisation', September 1922, in History and Class Consciousness *(London, Merlin Press, 1971), pp. 314, 315–16, 317–18, 318–19, 320, 335.*

Document 4.7   The Declaration of the Twenty-Two

The Workers' Opposition continued the struggle against the NEP, which they insisted represented a betrayal of the working class, by appealing above the heads of the party leadership in Soviet Russia to the Comintern.

Dear Comrades:

We have learned from our newspapers that the International Conference of the Communist International is considering the question of the 'united Workers' front', and we consider it our Communist duty to make it known to you that in our country things stand unfavorably with the united front, not only in the broad sense of the term, but even in applying it to the ranks of our party.

At a time when the forces of the bourgeois element press on us from all sides, when they even penetrate into our party, whose social content (40% workers and 60% nonproletarians) favors this, our leading rentiers are conducting an unrelenting, disruptive struggle against all, especially proletarians, who allow themselves to have their own judgment, and against the expression of this within the party they take all kinds of repressive measures.

The effort to draw the proletarian masses closer to the state is declared to be 'anarcho-syndicalism,' and its adherents are subjected to persecution and discredit.

In the area of the trade-union movement there is the very same picture of suppression of the workers' independence and initiative, and a struggle using every means against heterodoxy. The combined forces of the party and trade-union bureaucracies, taking advantage of their position and power, are ignoring the decisions of our congresses about carrying out the principles of workers' democracy. Our [Communist] fractions in the unions, even the fractions of entire [trade-union] congresses, are deprived of the right to express their will in the matter of electing their centers. Tutelage and pressure by the bureaucracy lead to the members of the party being constrained by the threat of expulsion and other repressive measures to elect not those whom these Communists themselves want, but those whom the higher-ups, ignoring them, want. Such methods of work lead to careerism, intrigue, and toadying, and the workers answer this by quitting the party.

Sharing the idea of a united workers' front . . . we turn to you in the sincere hope of ending all the abnormalities which stand in the way of the unity of this front, above all within our Russian Communist Party . . .

Source: 'Declaration of the Twenty-Two Members of the Russian Communist Party to the International Conference of the Communist International', February 1922, in Daniels, Communism in Russia, *pp. 146–7.*

Document 4.8   Appeal of the 'Workers' Truth' Group

The 'Workers' Truth' group of Gavriil Myasnikov drew on the thinking of both Machajski and Bogdanov, condemning the exploitation of the workers by the new 'state capitalist' regime made up of the intelligentsia and 'organisers'. This group, like others of the type emerging at this time condemning the 'new exploitation of the proletariat', was ruthlessly crushed by the GPU.

Message to the Revolutionary Proletariat and to All Revolutionary Elements Who Remain Faithful to the Struggling Working Class:

... The working class of Russia, small in numbers, unprepared, in a peasant country, accomplished in October 1917 the historically necessary October revolution. Led by the Russian Communist Party, it has overthrown and destroyed the power of the ruling classes; during long years of revolution and civil war it has firmly resisted the pressure of international and Russian reaction.

In spite of the unprecedentedly heavy losses sustained by the working class, the October revolution remains a decisive and heroic event in the history of the struggle of the Russian proletariat. The Russian October revolution has given the struggling international proletariat an experience of tremendous value for its struggle against capital.

As a result of the October revolution all the obstacles in the path of economic development were eliminated; there is no longer any oppression by the landlords, the parasitic tsarist bureaucracy, and the bourgeoisie, which relied on reactionary groups of European capitalists. After the successful revolution and civil war, broad perspectives opened before Russia, of rapid transformation into a country of progressive capitalism. In this lies the undoubted and enormous achievement of the revolution in October.

But what has changed in the position of the working class? The working class of Russia is disorganised; confusion reigns in the minds of the workers: are they in a country of the 'dictatorship of the proletariat', as the Communist Party ceaselessly reiterates by word of mouth and in the press? Or are they in a country of arbitrary rule and exploitation, as life tells them at every step? The working class is leading a miserable existence at a time when the new bourgeoisie (i.e. the responsible functionaries, plant directors, heads of trusts, chairmen of executive committees, etc.) and the Nepmen [capitalist entrepreneurs] live in luxury and recall in our memory the picture of the life of the bourgeoisie of all times. And again long and difficult years of the struggle for existence lie ahead. But the more complicated the circumstances, the more clarity and organisation are necessary for the struggling proletariat. To introduce class clarity into the ranks of the working class of Russia, to aid in every way the organisation of the revolutionary powers of the struggling proletariat – this is our task ...

The Communist Party, which during the years of the revolution was a party of the working class, has become the ruling party, the party of the organisers and directors of the governmental apparatus and economic life on capitalistic lines, with the general backwardness and lack of organisation of the working class. The party has more and more lost its tie and community with the proletariat. The soviet, party, and trade-union bureaucracies and organisers find themselves with material conditions which are sharply distinguished from the conditions of existence of the working class. Their very well-being and the stability of their general position depend on the degree to which the toiling masses are exploited and subordinated to them. All this makes a contradiction between their interests and a break between the Communist Party and the working class inevitable.

The social existence of the Communist Party itself inevitably determines the corresponding social consciousness, interests and ideals, which contradict the interests of the struggling proletariat.

The Russian Communist Party has become the party of the organiser intelligentsia. The abyss between the Russian Communist Party and the working class is getting deeper and deeper, and this fact cannot be glossed over by any resolutions or decisions of the communist congresses and conferences.

Source: 'Appeal of the "Workers' Truth" Group', 1922, Sotsialisticheskii vestnik, 31 January 1923, pp. 12–14.

The Formation of the USSR

The structure of the multinational state became the most contentious constitutional issue facing the country. During the Civil War a number of countries had enjoyed various periods of independence (e.g. Ukraine, Georgia and Armenia), and it was clear that some concessions had to be made to their aspirations for sovereignty. While Lenin had earlier condemned federalism, he now accepted that this was the only realistic way forward. Stalin, however, who as Commissar of Nationalities headed the commission responsible for drawing up a plan for the new state structure, favoured 'autonomisation', the enlargement of Soviet Russia as a unitary state while allowing significant 'autonomy' for national groups. Lenin came to favour a federal solution, a view confirmed in his mind by the behaviour of Stalin and other Moscow leaders with regard to the leadership of the Georgian Communist Party. In the event, Stalin's plan, by limiting the sovereignty of national units and thus rejecting the principle of ethno-federalism, might have avoided the break-up of the Soviet state in 1991.

Document 4.9   Autonomisation versus Federalism

The kernel of Stalin's autonomisation plan of August–September 1922 sought the 'adhesion' of Belorussia, Ukraine, Armenia, Azerbaijan and Georgia to the Russian Soviet Federated Socialist Republic (RSFSR). In other words, what were hitherto in form independent states would join Russia as autonomous republics and become subordinated to the Russian federation government and its institutions. Its Central Executive Committee and Sovnarkom would take over responsibility for the enlarged country. Although the Politburo commission responsible adopted the plan on 24–5 September 1922, only Armenia and Azerbaijan were in favour. On 26 September 1922 Lenin wrote to Kamenev to pass on to the Politburo his views on the shape of the future union.

Comrade Kamenev! You will no doubt have received from Stalin the resolution of his commission concerning the incorporation of the independent republics in the RSFSR. If you have not yet received it, please collect it from the secretary and read it immediately. I have already discussed it with Sokolnikov, spoken about it today with Stalin and will be seeing Mdivani (the Georgian communist suspected of *nezavisimstvo* [seeking independence]) tomorrow.

In my opinion, the question is of enormous importance. Stalin is in rather too much of a hurry. You must – since you did at one time intend to take up the question and have even studied it to some extent – think about it seriously and Zinoviev likewise. Stalin has already agreed to make a concession, that of replacing the term 'adhesion' to the RSFSR in paragraph 1 by 'formal union with the RSFSR within the framework of a Union of the Soviet Republics of Europe and Asia'. I hope the significance of this concession is clear: we recognise that we are equals in law with the SSR [Soviet Socialist Republic] of the Ukraine etc., and join it on an equal footing in a new Union, a new Federation, the 'Union of the Soviet Republics of Europe and Asia'.

In this case, paragraph 2 must also be altered to create, parallel with the sessions of the VTsIK [Central Executive Committee] of the RSFSR, something in the nature of a 'federal VTsIK of the Union of Soviet Republics of Europe and Asia'. If the first organisation is to meet once a week and the second similarly (or even if they meet every two weeks), it will not be very difficult to combine their activities. It is important not to give grist to the mill of the *nezavisimtsy*, not to destroy their independence, but to establish a new echelon, a Federation of Republics with equal rights.

Source: Lenin, 'Ob obrazovanii SSSR' ('On Forming the USSR'), PSS, vol. 45, pp. 211–13.

Document 4.10   Amended Plans for the Union

Stalin was forced to make concessions, and on 6 October 1922 he submitted a revised project to the Central Committee incorporating Lenin's amendments. This became the cornerstone of the final agreement of the new union. Ukraine, Belorussia, the Transcaucasian Federation (Armenia, Azerbaijan and Georgia), and the RSFSR were to create a new Union of Soviet Socialist Republics, each with the right to secede from the 'alliance'. A new Central Executive Committee and other state and governmental bodies were to be created. This was not the end of the matter, however, and although debilitated by sickness, Lenin was forced to return to the question. The debate over the shape of the union became bound up with a violent incident in Georgia when Sergei Ordzhonikidze struck the Georgian party leader, Mdivani. Lenin drew the conclusion that the greatest danger came from Russian chauvinism in relations with the many peoples of the country whereas in practice it was communist arrogance that was at the root of the problem.

I suppose I have been very guilty *vis-à-vis* the workers of Russia for not having intervened energetically and decisively enough in the notorious question of autonomisation, which, it appears, is officially called the question of the Union of Soviet Socialist Republics.

When this question arose last summer, I was ill; and then in autumn I relied too much on my recovery and on the October and December plenary meetings giving me an opportunity of intervening in this question. However, I did not manage to attend the October plenary meeting (when this question came up) or the one in December, and so the question passed me by almost completely.

I have only had time for a talk with Comrade Dzerzhinsky, who came from the Caucasus and told me how this matter stood in Georgia. I have also managed to exchange a few words with Comrade Zinoviev and express my apprehension on this matter. From what I was told by Comrade Dzerzhinsky, who was at the Georgian incident, I could only draw the gravest conclusions. If matters had come to such a pass that Ordzhonikidze could go to the extreme of applying physical violence, as Comrade Dzerzhinsky informed me, we can imagine what a mess we have got ourselves into. Obviously the whole business of 'autonomisation' was radically wrong and ill-timed.

It is said that a united apparatus was needed. Where did that assurance come from? Did it not come from that same Russian apparatus which, as I pointed out in one of the preceding sections of my diary, we took over from tsarism and slightly anointed with Soviet oil?

There is no doubt that that measure should have been delayed somewhat until we could say that we vouched for our apparatus as our own. But now, we must, in all conscience, admit the contrary; the apparatus we call ours is, in fact, still quite alien to us; it is a bourgeois and tsarist hotch-potch and there has been no possibility of getting rid of it in the course of the past five years without the help of other countries and because we have been 'busy' most of the time with military engagements and the fight against famine.

It is quite natural that in such circumstances the 'freedom to secede from the union' by which we justify ourselves will be a mere scrap of paper, unable to defend the non-Russians from the onslaught of that really Russian man, the Great-Russian chauvinist [Lenin uses the word Derzhimorda, the aggressive policeman in Gogol's play *The Inspector General*], in substance a rascal and a tyrant, such as the typical Russian bureaucrat is. There is no doubt that the minute percentage of Soviet and sovietised workers will drown in that tide of chauvinistic Great-Russian riffraff like a fly in milk.

It is said in defence of this measure that the People's Commissariats directly concerned with national psychology and national education were set up as separate bodies. But the question arises: can these People's Commissariats be made quite independent? And second: were we careful enough to take measures to provide the non-Russians with a real safeguard against the truly Russian bully? I do not think we took such measures although we could and should have done so.

I think that Stalin's haste and his infatuation with pure administration, together with his spite against the notorious 'socialist-nationalism', played a fatal role here. In politics spite generally plays the basest of roles.

I also fear that Comrade Dzerzhinsky, who went to the Caucasus to investigate the 'crime' of those 'socialist-nationalists', distinguished himself there by his truly Russian frame of mind (it is common knowledge that people of other nationalities who have become Russified overdo this Russian frame of mind) and that the impartiality of his whole commission was typified well enough by Ordzhonikidze's 'physical violence'. I think that no provocation or even insult can justify such Russian physical violence and that Comrade Dzerzhinsky was inexcusably guilty in adopting a light-hearted attitude towards it.

For all the citizens in the Caucasus Ordzhonikidze was the authority. Ordzhonikidze had no right to display that irritability to which he and Dzerzhinsky referred. On the contrary, Ordzhonikidze should have behaved with a restraint which cannot be demanded of any ordinary citizen, still less of a man accused of a 'political' crime. And, to tell the truth, those socialist-nationalists were citizens who were accused of a political crime, and the terms of the accusation were such that it could not be described otherwise.

Here we have an important question of principle: how is internationalism to be understood?

Lenin

Source: Lenin, 'K voprosu o natsional'nostyakh ili ob "avtonomizatsii"' ('On the Question of the Nationalities or of "Autonomisation"', 30–1 December 1922, PSS, vol. 45, pp. 356–8.

Document 4.11   The 1924 USSR Constitution

A treaty on union between four founding republics (RSFSR, Ukraine, Belorussia and the Transcaucasian Federation) was signed on 30 December 1922. After much discussion a constitution for the new Union of Soviet Socialist Republics was adopted in January 1924. The USSR was a federal alliance that preserved the formal sovereignty of the republics, including their right to secede, but the Communist Party remained unitary and thus many of the rights enjoyed by the republics remained purely formal until the party's power itself began to wane in the late 1980s.

Part I: Declaration

Since the foundation of the Soviet Republics, the States of the world have been divided into two camps; the camp of Capitalism and the camp of Socialism.

There, in the camp of Capitalism: national hate and inequality, colonial slavery and chauvinism, national oppression and massacres, brutalities and imperialistic wars.

Here, in the camp of Socialism: reciprocal confidence and peace, national liberty and equality, the pacific co-existence and fraternal collaboration of peoples.

The attempts made by the capitalistic world during the past ten years to decide the question of nationalities by bringing together the principle of the free development of peoples with a system of exploitation of man by man have been fruitless. In addition, the number of national conflicts becomes more and more confusing, even menacing the capitalistic regime. The bourgeoisie has proven itself incapable of realising a harmonious collaboration of the peoples.

It is only in the camp of the Soviets; it is only under the conditions of the dictatorship of the proletariat that has grouped around itself the majority of the people, that it has been possible to eliminate the oppression of nationalities, to create an atmosphere of mutual confidence and to establish the habit of a fraternal collaboration of peoples . . .

Part II: Treaty

The Russian Socialist Federated Soviet Republic, the Socialist Soviet Republic of the Ukraine, the Socialist Soviet Republic of Belorussia, and the Socialist Soviet Republic of Transcaucasia (comprising the Socialist Soviet Republic of Azerbaijan, the Socialist Soviet Republic of Georgia, and the Socialist Soviet Republic of Armenia) unite themselves in one federal State – 'The Union of Soviet Socialist Republics' . . .

Chapter II: Sovereign Rights of the Member Republics

Article 3   The Sovereignty of the member Republics is limited only in the matters indicated in the present Constitution, as coming within the competence of the Union. Outside of those limits, each member Republic exerts its public powers independently; the Union of S.S.R. protects the rights of member Republics.

Article 4   Each one of the member Republics retains the right freely to withdraw from the Union.

Source: 'Constitution of the USSR', ratified by the Second Congress of Soviets of the USSR, 13 January 1924, in Daniels, Communism in Russia, pp. 166–7.

In the 1920s the policy of *korenizatsiya* (indigenisation) allowed the republics wide latitude in cultural affairs. This was reflected above all in cultural policy, allowing native languages to flourish in this period. By the early 1930s, however, Stalin imposed 'Russianisation' on the country, identifying the 'Soviet' Union as a whole with Russia, a policy that reversed indigenisation but did little to benefit Russians themselves. The stifling of the national aspirations of the main peoples making up the USSR engendered tensions that ultimately destroyed the Union.

Lenin's Bequest

Struck down by a stroke in May 1922, followed by two more in late 1922 and March 1923, Lenin retreated ever more from the day-to-day leadership of the country. A 'triumvirate' comprising Kamenev, Zinoviev and Stalin came together to thwart what they feared were Trotsky's leadership ambitions. Stalin had been appointed General Secretary of the party in April 1922, and he used what had hitherto been little more than an extended membership filing system to build up a body of supporters beholden to him for promotion (the 'circular flow of power'), while punishing those whom he distrusted. Lenin died on 21 January 1924, and his bequest was far more than a specific set of policies but above all a style of politics. It must not be forgotten that the Soviet system of labour camps was set up by Lenin, including the notorious camp in the former Solovetskii monastery on an island in the White Sea. In his last period Lenin wrote on a number of crucial issues, but together they add up to less than clear directives for development than a confused legacy open to conflicting interpretations.

Document 4.12   Lenin's Style of Politics

With the onset of *glasnost* under Gorbachev from 1985 the image of the Lenin of the early NEP, allegedly favouring the gradual move towards socialism, was used as a corrective against later 'deviations'. As the pace of truth-telling intensified, however, Lenin's own image came under scrutiny. This was facilitated by the publication of his writings that had hitherto been suppressed. One of the most notorious cases of this type of manipulation of Lenin's image, as we have seen above, was the suppression of Lenin's letter to Molotov of 19 March 1922 about the events in Shui. In another example, Lenin's works before *perestroika* had published what appeared to be a straightforward recommendation to Trotsky:

Should we not mobilise another 20,000 Petrograd workers and obtain a mass attack on Yudenich [the White Army commander]?

In the original letter in the archives this takes on a far more bloodthirsty tone:

Should we not mobilise another 20,000 Petrograd workers, *plus about 10,000 bourgeois, put machine guns behind them, shoot a few hundred*, and obtain a mass attack on Yudenich?

The phrase in italics had simply been deleted by the editors (*Komsomolskaya pravda*, 12 February 1992). The writer Vladimir Soloukhin compiled a collection of Lenin's gruesome statements, mainly concerning relations with the peasantry and in particular the supply dictatorship that allowed grain to be expropriated at will, often leaving the peasants with nothing to eat themselves (one of the factors that had exacerbated the famine on the Volga in 1921–2). The booklet represents a devastating critique of the Leninist style of politics. The following example begins with a quotation from Lenin followed by Soloukhin's commentary.

Lenin writes:

The Bolsheviks resolved the problem of seizing power in the capital as well as in the main industrial centres of Russia relatively easily. But in the provinces, in places far from the centre, Soviet power had to overcome resistance that took military forms and only now, some four months after the October revolution, this is coming to an end. At the present time the task of overcoming and suppressing resistance in Russia is broadly speaking over. *The Bolsheviks have conquered Russia.*

Soloukhin comments as follows:

When one country conquers another, as when the Russian empire conquered Central Asia, whatever the merits of the case, the purpose was clear and was not hidden by the conquerors themselves . . . Thus when one country conquers another and imposes there a harsh occupational regime, allowing it to crush popular resistance and maintain that conquered country under its control, a clear if not benign aim is pursued: to unite the conquered country with the metropolis.

But here Russia was conquered by a group, a handful of people. This group then pursued in the country the harshest occupational regime which no other age in the history of humanity has seen. This regime was pursued to maintain themselves in power. Suppress all and everyone to stay in power. They saw that practically the whole population was against them, apart from a very thin layer of 'advanced' workers, that is, a tiny percentage of the population of Russia, but kept suppressing, cutting, shooting, imposing famine, raped at will, to keep that country in their hands. Why? What for? With what aim? To achieve in their conquered country their political principles. Universal accounting and control of manufactured goods, a state monopoly of all types of goods and their controlled distribution. But this would have been only a half-victory. From a deep reading of Lenin we learn that this accounting and distribution was only a means and not an end. The aim was to achieve universal labour duty in the country, that is, to force people to work, to force them to subordinate themselves to a single leader, dictator, that is, a means to turn the whole population of the country into a single subservient mechanism.

Source: Vladimir Soloukhin, Chitaya Lenina (Reading Lenin) *(Moscow, samizdat mimeo), pp. 37–8.*

Document 4.13   Lenin's Last Testament

Lenin had always shielded Stalin from criticism but he was forced to change his mind when he heard about the incident of 22 December 1922; Stalin had subjected Lenin's wife, Nadezhda Krupskaya, to a 'storm of the coarsest abuse' (as she put it in a note to Kamenev the next day). It was at this time that Lenin, in preparation for the Twelfth Party Congress, made a number of recommendations of an organisational and of a personal nature. The themes of his organisational proposal were developed in his article 'Better Fewer, But Better', while his reflections on the personalities of his colleagues became known as his 'Last Testament'. Alarmed by the bitterness of personal conflict around him, Lenin commented on the qualities of his colleagues. Published abroad in 1926 as his 'Testament', they only became widely known in the USSR after Khrushchev's denunciation of Stalin in 1956. In identifying the weak points of the main leadership contenders, the comments could not but exacerbate the conflicts. The postscript was penned after Stalin's abuse of Krupskaya became known to Lenin.

23 December 1922

I would urge strongly that at this Congress a number of changes be made in our political structure. I want to tell you of the considerations to which I attach most importance. At the head of the list I set an increase in the number of Central Committee members to a few dozen or even a hundred. It is my opinion that without this reform our Central Committee would be in great danger if the course of events were not quite favourable for us (and that is something we cannot count on).

Then, I intend to propose that the Congress should on certain conditions invest the decisions of the State Planning Commission [Gosplan, established in 1921] with legislative force, meeting, in this respect, the wishes of Comrade Trotsky – to a certain extent and on certain conditions.

As for the first point, i.e., increasing the number of CC members, I think it must be done in order to raise the prestige of the Central Committee, to do a thorough job of improving our administrative machinery and to prevent conflicts between small sections of the CC from acquiring excessive importance for the future of the Party. It seems to me that our Party has every right to demand from the working class fifty to one hundred CC members, and that it could get them from it without unduly taxing the resources of that class.

Such a reform would considerably increase the stability of our Party and ease its struggle in the encirclement of hostile states, which, in my opinion, is likely to, and must, become much more acute in the next few years. I think that the stability of our Party would gain a thousandfold by such a measure.

Continuation of the Notes: 'Lenin's Last Testament', 24–5 December 1922

By stability of the Central Committee, of which I spoke above, I mean measures against a split, as far as such measures can at all be taken. For, of course, the White Guard in *Russkaya Mysl* (it seems to have been S. E. Oldenburg) was right when, in the first place, in his play against Soviet Russia he banked on the hope of a split in our party, and when, in the second place, he banked for that split on serious disagreements in our party.

Our party rests upon two classes, and for that reason its instability is possible, and if there cannot exist agreement between those classes its fall is inevitable. In such an event it would be useless to take any measures or in general to discuss the stability of our Central Committee. In such an event no measures would prove capable of preventing a split. But I trust that is too remote a future, and too improbable an event, to talk about.

I have in mind stability as a guarantee against a split in the near future, and I intend to examine here a series of considerations of a purely personal character.

I think that the fundamental factor in the matter of stability – from this point of view – is such members of the Central Committee as Stalin and Trotsky. The relation between them constitutes, in my opinion, a big half of the danger of that split, which might be avoided, and the avoidance of which might be promoted, in my opinion, by raising the number of members of the Central Committee to fifty or one hundred.

Comrade Stalin, having become General Secretary, has concentrated an enormous power in his hand; and I am not sure that he always knows how to use that power with sufficient caution. On the other hand Comrade Trotsky, as was proved by his struggle against the Central Committee in connection with the question of the People's Commissariat of Ways of Communication, is distinguished not only by his exceptional abilities – personally he is, to be sure, the most able man in the present Central Committee – but also by his too far-reaching self-confidence and disposition to be too much attracted by the purely administrative side of affairs.

These two qualities of the two most able leaders of the present Central Committee might, quite innocently, lead to a split; if our party does not take measures to prevent it, a split might arise unexpectedly.

I will not further characterise the other members of the Central Committee as to their personal qualities. I will only remind you that the October episode of Zinoviev and Kamenev was not, of course, accidental, but that it ought as little to be used against them personally as the non-Bolshevism of Trotsky.

Of the younger members of the Central Committee I want to say a few words about Bukharin and Pyatakov. They are, in my opinion, the most able forces (among the youngest), and in regard to them it is necessary to bear in mind the following: Bukharin is not only the most valuable and leading theoretician of the party, but also may legitimately be considered the favourite of the whole party, but his theoretical views can only with the very greatest doubt he regarded as fully Marxist, for there is something scholastic in him (he never has learned, and I think never has fully understood, the dialectic).

And then Pyatakov – a man undoubtedly distinguished in will and ability, but too much given over to administration and the administrative side of things to be relied on in a serious political question.

Both of these remarks, of course, are made only for the present, on the assumption that both of these outstanding and devoted party workers fail to find an occasion to enhance their knowledge and amend their one-sidedness.

Postscript, 4 January 1923

Stalin is too rude, and this defect, although quite tolerable in our midst and in dealings among us Communists, becomes intolerable in a General Secretary. That is why I suggest that the comrades think about a way of removing Stalin from that position and appointing another man in his stead who in all other respects differs from Comrade Stalin in having only one advantage, namely, that of being more tolerant, more loyal, more polite and more considerate to the comrades, less capricious, etc. This circumstance may appear to be a negligible detail. But I think that from the standpoint of safeguards against a split and from the standpoint of what I wrote above about the relationship between Stalin and Trotsky it is not a detail, or it is a detail which can assume decisive importance.

Sources: Lenin, PSS, vol. 45, pp. 343–6; Selected Works, pp. 681–3.

This letter was circulated among delegates at the Thirteenth Party Congress, held after Lenin's death in January 1924, but the proposals contained therein, above all Stalin's transfer from the post of General Secretary, were not discussed. The Fifteenth Party Congress in 1927 returned to the matter, and while the letter was published in the verbatim report of the congress, Lenin's recommendations on internal party changes were not. Only after 1956 were these latter materials made available and published in Lenin's collected works.

Document 4.14   Lenin's Advocacy of Co-operatives

Faced with a wartorn and relatively backward economy, in a society dominated by peasants, and in the retreat conditions of NEP, Lenin began to see the way forward in the development of 'socialist' co-operatives. This work has been taken as an indication of Lenin's conversion to the merits of gradualism in the transition to socialism, and thus by implication to a long-term future for NEP. Lenin's notion of a 'cultural revolution' was used in a distinctive sense, to signal the gradual acceptance of the organised and efficient collective management of the economy.

It seems to me that not enough attention is being paid to the co-operative movement in our country. Not everyone understands that now, since the time of the October revolution and quite apart from NEP (on the contrary, in this connection we must say – because of NEP), our co-operative movement has become one of great significance. There is a lot of fantasy in the dreams of the old co-operators. Often they are ridiculously fantastic. But why are they fantastic? Because people do not understand the fundamental, the rock-bottom significance of the working-class political struggle for the overthrow of the rule of the exploiters. We have overthrown the rule of the exploiters, and much that was fantastic, even romantic, even banal in the dreams of the old co-operators is now becoming unvarnished reality.

Indeed, since political power is in the hands of the working class, since this political power owns all the means of production, the only task, indeed, that remains for us is to organise the population in co-operative societies. With most of the population organised in co-operatives, the socialism which in the past was legitimately treated with ridicule, scorn and contempt by those who were rightly convinced that it was necessary to wage the class struggle for political power, etc., will achieve its aim automatically. But not all comrades realise how vastly, how infinitely important it is now to organise the population of Russia in co-operative societies on a sufficiently large scale, for we have now found that degree of combination of private interest, of private commercial interest, with state supervision and control of this interest, that degree of its subordination to the common interests which was formerly the stumbling-block for very many socialists. Indeed, the power of the state over all large-scale means of production, political power in the hands of the proletariat, the alliance of this proletariat with the many millions of small and very small peasants, the assured proletarian leadership of the peasantry, etc. – is this not all that is necessary to build a complete socialist society out of co-operatives, out of co-operatives alone, which we formerly ridiculed as huckstering and which from a certain aspect we have the right to treat as such now, under NEP? Is this not all that is necessary to build a complete socialist society? It is still not the building of socialist society, but it is all that is necessary and sufficient for it . . .

There is another aspect to this question. From the point of view of the 'enlightened' (primarily, literate) European there is not much left for us to do to induce absolutely everyone to take not a passive, but an active part in co-operative operations. Strictly speaking, there is 'only' one thing we have left to do and that is to make our people so 'enlightened' that they understand all the advantages of everybody participating in the work of the co-operatives, and organise this participation. *Only* that. There are now no other devices needed to advance to socialism. But to achieve this 'only', there must be a veritable revolution – the entire people must go through a period of cultural development. Therefore, our rule must be: as little philosophising and as few acrobatics as possible. In this respect NEP is an advance, because it is adjustable to the level of the most ordinary peasant and does not demand anything higher of him. But it will take a whole historical epoch to get the entire population into the work of the co-operatives through NEP. At the best we can achieve this in one or two decades. Nevertheless, it will be a distinct historical epoch, and without this historical epoch, without universal literacy, without a proper degree of efficiency, without training the population sufficiently to acquire the habit of book-reading, and without the material basis for this, without a certain sufficiency to safeguard against, say, bad harvests, famine, etc. – without this we shall not achieve our object. The thing now is to learn to combine the wide revolutionary range of action, the revolutionary enthusiasm which we have displayed, and displayed abundantly, and crowned with complete success – to learn to combine this with (I am almost inclined to say) the ability to be an efficient and capable trader, which is quite enough to be a good co-operator. By ability to be a trader I mean the ability to be a cultured trader. Let those Russians, or peasants, who imagine since they are good traders, get that well into their heads. This does not follow at all. They do trade, but that is far from being cultured traders. They now trade in an Asiatic manner, but to be a good trader one must trade in the European manner. They are a whole epoch behind in that . . .

Now the emphasis is changing and shifting to peaceful, organisation, 'cultural' work. I should say that emphasis is shifting to educational work, were it not for our international relations, were it not for the fact that we have to fight for our position on a world scale. If we leave that aside, however, and confine ourselves to internal economic relations, the emphasis in our work is certainly shifting to education.

Two main tasks confront us, which constitute the epoch – to reorganise our machinery of state, which is utterly useless, and which we took over in its entirety from the preceding epoch; during the past five years of struggle we did not, and could not, drastically reorganise it. Our second task is educational work among the peasants. And the economic object of this educational work among the peasants is to organise the latter in co-operative societies. If the whole of the peasantry had been organised in co-operatives, we would by now have been standing with both feet on the soil of socialism. But the organisation of the entire peasantry in co-operative societies presupposes a standard of culture among the peasants (precisely among the peasants as the overwhelming mass) that cannot, in fact, be achieved without a cultural revolution.

Our opponents told us repeatedly that we were rash in undertaking to implant socialism in an insufficiently cultured country. But they were misled by our having started from the opposite end to that prescribed by theory (the theory of pedants of all kinds), because in our country the political and social revolution preceded the cultural revolution, that very cultural revolution which nevertheless now confronts us.

This cultural revolution would now suffice to make our country a complete socialist country; but it presents immense difficulties (for to be cultured we must achieve a certain development of the material means of production, must have a certain material base).

Source: Lenin, 'On Co-operation', 4, 6 January 1923, Pravda, 26, 27 May 1923, in Selected Works, pp. 690–1, 692–3, 695.

Bukharin was to interpret this and other final writings of Lenin as the assertion of a gradualist path to socialism. As Bukharin put it in conversation with Boris Nicolaevsky in 1936: 'The main point of his testament was that it is possible to arrive at Socialism without applying more force to the peasantry' (Nicolaevsky, 1965, p. 13). The central issue was indeed the relationship of Soviet power with the peasants, who comprised 80 per cent of the population.

Document 4.15   Lenin on the Possibility of Socialism in Russia

In commenting on the memoirs of the Menshevik Sukhanov, Lenin conceded that Russia lacked the material conditions for socialism, but insisted that the Communist government could by its own endeavours create them. Once again Lenin's voluntarism triumphed over classical Marxist materialism.

I have lately been glancing through Sukhanov's notes on the revolution. What strikes one most is the pedantry of all our petty-bourgeois democrats and of all the heroes of the Second International. Apart from the fact that they are all extremely faint-hearted, and that when it comes to the minutest deviation from the German model, even the best of them fortify themselves with reservations – apart from this characteristic, which is common to all petty-bourgeois democrats and has been abundantly manifested by them throughout the revolution, what strikes one is their slavish imitation of the past . . .

Infinitely stereotyped, for instance, is the argument they learned by rote during the development of West European Social Democracy, namely, that we are not yet ripe for socialism, that, as certain 'learned' gentlemen among them put it, the objective economic premises for socialism do not exist in our country. It does not occur to any of them to ask: but what about a people that found itself in a revolutionary situation such as that created during the first imperialist war? Might it not, influenced by the hopelessness of the situation, fling itself into a struggle that would offer it at least some chance of securing conditions for the further development of civilisation that were somewhat unusual? . . .

If a definite level of culture is required for the building of socialism (although nobody can say just what that definite 'level of culture' is, for it differs in every West European country), why cannot we begin by first achieving the prerequisites for that definite level of culture in a revolutionary way, and *then*, with the aid of the workers' and peasants' government and the Soviet system, proceed to overtake the other nations?

You say that civilisation is necessary for the building of socialism. Very good. But why could we not first create such prerequisites of civilisation in our country as the expulsion of the landlords and the Russian capitalists, and then start moving towards socialism? Where, in what books, have you read that such variations of the customary historical order of events are impermissible or impossible?

Napoleon, I think, wrote: *On s'engage et puis . . . on voit.* Rendered freely this means: 'First engage in a serious battle and then see what happens.' Well, we did first engage in a serious battle in October 1917, and then saw such details of development (from the standpoint of world history they were certainly details) as the Brest peace, the New Economic Policy, and so forth. And now there can be no doubt that in the main we have been victorious.

Source: Lenin, 'Our Revolution (Apropos of N. Sukhanov's Notes)',
16–17 January 1923, Pravda, 30 May 1923, in Selected Works,
pp. 696–8.

Document 4.16 Lenin's 'Better Fewer, But Better'

In this classic analysis Lenin condemned the bureaucratic morass in which the Soviet state found itself mired. The flaws in his analysis of the problem (however trenchant the condemnation might have been) were reflected in the inadequacy of his proposals for reform; thus, as with Kollontai earlier (Document 3.23), his suggested remedies only undermined his aspirations. He fundamentally failed to understand the root causes of the inefficiency and extreme bureaucratisation of Soviet life, seeing the cultural legacy of the past as the main problem whereas the Soviet system itself spawned the ills which so vexed him in the last year of his life. Disappointed by the delay in the revolution in the West, Lenin began to look to the East for support.

Our state apparatus is so deplorable, not to say wretched, that we must think very carefully how to combat its defects, bearing in mind that these defects are rooted in the past, which, although it has been overthrown, has not yet been overcome, has not reached the stage of a culture that has receded into the distant past. I say culture deliberately, because in these matters we can only regard as achieved what has become part and parcel of our culture, of our social life, our habits. We might say that the good in our social system has not been properly studied, understood and taken to heart; it has been hastily grasped at; it has not been verified or tested, corroborated by experience, and not made durable, etc. Of course, it could not be otherwise in a revolutionary epoch, when development proceeded at such breakneck speed that in a matter of five years we passed from tsarism to the Soviet system . . .

It is time we did something about it. We must show sound scepticism for too rapid progress, for boastfulness, etc. We must give thought to testing the steps forward we proclaim every hour, take every minute and then prove every second that they are flimsy, superficial and misunderstood. The most harmful thing here would be haste. The most harmful thing would be to rely on the assumption that we know at least something, or that we have any considerable number of elements necessary for the building of a really new state apparatus, one really worthy to be called socialist, Soviet, etc.

No, we are ridiculously deficient of such an apparatus, and even of the elements of it, and we must remember that we should not stint time on building it, and that it will take many, many years . . .

In order to renovate our state apparatus we must at all costs set out, first, to learn, secondly, to learn, and thirdly, to learn, and then see to it that learning shall not remain a dead letter, or a fashionable catch-phrase (and we should admit in all frankness that this happens very often with us), that learning shall really become part of our very being, that it shall actually and fully become a constituent element of our social life. In short, we must not make the demands that are made by bourgeois Western Europe, but demands that are fit and proper for a country which has set out to develop into a socialist country . . .

We have been bustling for five years trying to improve our state apparatus, but it has been mere bustle, which has proved useless in these five years, or even futile, or even harmful. This bustle created the impression that we were doing something, but in effect it was only clogging up our institutions and our brains.

It is high time things were changed.

We must follow the rule: Better fewer, but better. We must follow the rule: Better get good human material in two or even three years than work in haste without hope of getting any at all . . .

I think that the time has at last come when we must work in real earnest to improve our state apparatus and in this there can scarcely be anything more harmful than haste. That is why I would sound a strong warning against inflating the figures. In my opinion, we should, on the contrary, be especially sparing with figures in this matter. Let us say frankly that the People's Commissariat of the Workers' and Peasants' Inspection [Rabkrin] does not at present enjoy the slightest authority. Everybody knows that no other institutions are worse organised than those of our Workers' and Peasants' Inspection, and that under peasant conditions nothing can be expected from this People's Commissariat. We must have this firmly fixed in our minds if we really want to create within a few years an institution that will, first, be an exemplary institution, secondly, win everybody's absolute confidence, and, thirdly, prove to all and sundry that we have really justified the work of such a highly placed institution as the Central Control Commission. In my opinion, we must immediately and irrevocably reject all general figures for the size of office staffs. We must select employees for the Workers' and Peasants' Inspection with particular care and only on the basis of the strictest test. Indeed, what is the use of establishing a People's Commissariat which carries on anyhow, which does not enjoy the slightest confidence, and whose word carries scarcely any weight? I think that our main object in launching the work of reconstruction that we now have in mind is to avoid all this . . .

In all spheres of social, economic and political relationships we are 'frightfully' revolutionary. But as regards precedence, the observance of the forms and rites of office management, our 'revolutionariness' often gives way to the mustiest routine. On more than one occasion, we have witnessed the very interesting phenomenon of a great leap forward in social life being accompanied by amazing timidity whenever the slightest changes are proposed . . .

The system of international relationships which has now taken shape is one in which a European state, Germany, is enslaved by the victor countries. Furthermore, owing to their victory, a number of states, the oldest states in the West, are in a position to make some insignificant concessions to their oppressed classes – concessions which, insignificant though they are, nevertheless retard the revolutionary movement in those countries and create some semblance of 'class truce'.

At the same time, as a result of the last imperialist war, a number of countries of the East, India, China, etc., have been completely jolted out of the rut. Their development has definitely shifted to general European capitalist lines. The general European ferment has begun to affect them, and it is now clear to the whole world that they have been drawn into a process of development that must lead to a crisis in the whole of world capitalism.

Thus, at the present time we are confronted with the question – shall we be able to hold on with our small and very small peasant production, and in our present state of ruin, until the West European capitalist countries consummate their development towards socialism? But they are consummating it not as we formerly expected. They are not consummating it through the gradual 'maturing' of socialism, but through the exploitation of some countries by others, through the exploitation of the first of the countries vanquished in the imperialist war combined with the exploitation of the whole of the East. On the other hand, precisely as a result of the first imperialist war, the East has been definitely drawn into the revolutionary movement, has been definitely drawn into the general maelstrom of the world revolutionary movement . . .

In the last analysis, the outcome of the struggle will be determined by the fact that Russia, India, China, etc., account for the overwhelming majority of the population of the globe. And during the past few years it is this majority that has been drawn into the struggle for emancipation with extraordinary rapidity, so that in this respect there cannot be the slightest doubt what the final outcome of the world struggle will be. In this sense, the complete victory of socialism is fully and absolutely assured . . .

We must strive to build up a state in which the workers retain the leadership of the peasants, in which they retain the confidence of the peasants, and by exercising the greatest economy remove every trace of extravagance from our social relations.

We must reduce our state apparatus to the utmost degree of economy. We must banish from it all traces of extravagance, of which so much has been left over from tsarist Russia, from its bureaucratic capitalist state machine.

Source: Lenin, 'Better Fewer, But Better', 2 March 1923, Pravda, 4 March 1923, in Selected Works, pp. 701, 702–3, 708, 711.

The 'New Course' Debate

In the summer of 1923 strikes broke out in a number of important industrial areas, provoked by delays in the payment of wages of up to three months. The State Bank in August sought to reduce industrial prices by cutting credits to industrial enterprises, while at the same time reducing prices for food products, thus undermining the peasant economy. In response to the mounting crisis at the end of September 1923 the Central Committee established three special commissions: one to examine the 'scissors' that had opened up between industrial and agricultural prices; one to investigate the wages issue; and one headed by Dzerzhinsky to find ways of overcoming factional activity within the party itself. It was in response to the latter's attempts to impose unity in the party that Trotsky launched the 'New Course' controversy.

Document 4.17   Trotsky's Letter to the CC

Losing the initiative in his struggle against the triumvirate (Stalin, Kamenev and Zinoviev, the dominant group in Lenin's declining year), Trotsky sought to outflank them by launching a debate over the lack of democracy within the party. His opening salvo was a letter delivered to the Central Committee on 8 October 1923, many of whose themes were reiterated by the 'Letter of the 46'. A further letter by Trotsky called 'The New Course' gave the whole debate its title.

One of the proposals of Comrade Dzerzhinsky's commission declares that we must make it obligatory for Party members knowing about groupings in the Party to communicate the fact to the GPU, the Central Committee and the Central Control Commission. It would seem that to inform the Party organizations of the fact that its branches are being used by elements hostile to the Party is an obligation of Party members so elementary that it ought not to be necessary to introduce a special resolution to that effect six years after the October Revolution. The very demand for such a resolution is an extremely startling symptom alongside of others no less clear . . . The demand for such a resolution means: (a) that illegal oppositional groups have been formed in the Party, which may become dangerous to the revolution; (b) that there exist such states of mind in the Party as to permit comrades knowing about such groups not to inform the Party organizations. Both these facts testify to an extraordinary deterioration of the situation within the Party from the time of the Twelfth Congress.

In the fiercest moment of War Communism, the system of appointment within the Party did not have one-tenth of the extent that it has now. Appointment of the secretaries of provincial committees is now the rule. That creates for the secretary a position essentially independent of the local organization . . .

The Twelfth Congress of the Party was conducted under the sign of democracy. Many of the speeches at that time spoken in defence of workers' democracy seemed to me exaggerated, and to a considerable extent demagogish, in view of the incompatibility of a fully developed workers' democracy with the regime of dictatorship. But it was perfectly clear that the pressure of the period of War Communism ought to give place to a more lively and broader Party responsibility. However, this present regime – which began to form itself before the Twelfth Congress, and which subsequently received its final reinforcement and formulation – is much farther from workers' democracy than the regime of the fiercest period of War Communism. The bureaucratization of the Party apparatus has developed to unheard-of proportions by means of the method of secretarial selection. There has been created a very broad stratum of Party workers, entering into the apparatus of the government of the Party, who completely renounce their own Party opinion, at least the open expression of it, as though assuming that the secretarial hierarchy is the apparatus which creates Party opinion and Party decisions. Beneath this stratum, abstaining from their own opinions, there lies the broad mass of the Party, before whom every decision stands in the form of a summons or a command. In this foundation-mass of the Party there is an unusual amount of dissatisfaction . . . This dissatisfaction does not dissipate itself by way of influence of the mass upon the Party organization (election of Party committees, secretaries, etc.), but accumulates in secret and thus leads to interior strains . . .

It is known to the members of the Central Committee and the Central Control Commission that while fighting with all decisiveness and definiteness within the Central Committee against a false policy, I decisively declined to bring the struggle within the Central Committee to the judgment even of a very narrow circle of comrades, in particular those who in the event of a reasonably proper Party course ought to occupy prominent places in the Central Committee. I must state that my efforts of a year and a half have given no results. This threatens us with the danger that the Party may be taken unawares by a crisis of exceptional severity . . . In view of the situation created, I consider it not only my right, but my duty to make known the true state of affairs to every member of the Party whom I consider sufficiently prepared, matured and self-restrained, and consequently able to help the Party out of this blind alley without factional convulsions.

Sources: Trotsky, Letter of 8 October 1923, Documents of the 1923 Opposition *(London, New Park Publications, 1975), pp. 2–3;* Izvestiya TsK, *no. 5, 1990, pp. 165–73.*

Document 4.18   Declaration of the Forty-Six

A few days after Trotsky had sent his letter, forty-six leading Bolsheviks set out their own platform criticising the policies of the triumvirate. The platform was presented to the Politburo on 15 October 1923. The immediate demand was for the convocation of a special conference of the Central Committee and the opposition to deal with the issues disturbing the party. While many of the criticisms of the forty-six coincided with Trotsky's, there was no prior consultation.

To the Politburo of the Central Committee of the Russian Communist Party

The extreme seriousness of the situation compels us (in the interests of our party, in the interests of the working class) to state openly that a continuation of the policy of the majority of the Politburo threatens grievous disasters for the whole party. The economic and financial crisis beginning at the end of July of the present year, with all the political, including internal party, consequences resulting from it, has inexorably revealed the inadequacy of the leadership of the party, both in the economic domain, and especially in the domain of internal party relations . . .

Similarly in the domain of internal party relations we see the same incorrect leadership paralysing and breaking up the party; this appears particularly clearly in the period of crisis through which we are passing.

We explain this not by the political incapacity of the present leaders of the party; on the contrary, however much we differ from them in the estimate of the position and in the choice of means to alter it, we assume that the present leaders could not in any conditions fail to be appointed by the party to the outstanding posts in the workers' dictatorship. We explain it by the fact that beneath the external form of official unity we have in practice a one-sided recruitment of individuals, and a direction of affairs which is one-sided and adapted to the views and sympathies of a narrow circle. As a result of a party leadership distorted by such narrow considerations, the party is to a considerable extent ceasing to be that living independent collectivity which sensitively seizes living reality because it is bound to this reality with a thousand threads. Instead of this we observe the ever increasing, and now scarcely concealed, division of the party between a secretarial hierarchy and the 'quiet folk', between professional party officials recruited from above and the general mass of the party which does not participate in the common life.

This is a fact which is known to every member of the party. Members of the party who are dissatisfied with this or that decision of the Central Committee or even of a provincial committee, who have this or that doubt on their minds, who privately note this or that error, irregularity or disorder, are afraid to speak about it at party meetings, and are even afraid to talk about it in conversation, unless the partner in conversation is thoroughly reliable from the point of view of 'discretion'; free discussion within the party has practically vanished, the public opinion of the party is stifled. Nowadays it is not the party, not its broad masses, who promote and choose members of the provincial committees and of the Central Committee of the RCP. On the contrary, the secretarial hierarchy of the party to an ever greater extent recruits the membership of conferences and congresses, which are becoming to an ever greater extent the executive assemblies of this hierarchy.

The regime established within the party is completely intolerable; it destroys the independence of the party, replacing the party by a recruited bureaucratic apparatus which acts without objection in normal times, but which inevitably fails in moments of crisis, and which threatens to become completely ineffective in the face of the serious events now impending.

Source: 'The Platform of the 46', 15 October 1923, in E. H. Carr, The Interregnum *(London, Macmillan, 1954), pp. 374, 375–6.*

Document 4.19 Trotsky, *The New Course*

The triumvirate appeared to acknowledge the validity of some of the criticisms, and on 7 November Zinoviev announced that the pages of *Pravda* would be thrown open for the discussion. Following vigorous exchanges, Kamenev, Stalin and Trotsky appeared to reach agreement on a 'new course' for intra-party 'workers' democracy' and economic planning, outlined in a Politburo resolution of 5 December. Three days later, however, Trotsky elaborated on this resolution in a letter to party meetings that he could not address personally through illness. His assault now went much further than simply attacks against the bureaucratic 'old guard' in the party, and compared the current degeneration with that of the pre-war German Social Democratic Party, one of the most offensive analogies he could have devised.

The centre of gravity which was mistakenly placed in the apparatus by the old course, has now been transferred by the new course, proclaimed in the resolution of the Central Committee, to the activity, the initiative and the critical spirit of all the party members, as the organised vanguard of the proletariat. The new course does not at all signify that the party apparatus is charged with decreeing, creating or establishing a democratic regime at such and such a date. No. This regime will be realised by the party itself.

To put it briefly: *the party must subordinate to itself its own apparatus* without for a moment ceasing to be a centralized organisation.

In the debates and articles of recent times, it has been underlined that 'pure', 'complete', 'ideal' democracy is not realisable and that in general for us it is not an end in itself. That is incontestable. But it can be stated with just as much reason that pure, absolute centralism is unrealisable and incompatible with the nature of a mass party, and that it can no more be an end in itself than can the party apparatus. Democracy and centralism are two faces of party organisation. The question is to harmonise them in the most correct manner, that is, the manner best corresponding to the situation. During the last period there was no such equilibrium. The centre of gravity wrongly centred in the apparatus. The initiative of the party was reduced to the minimum. Thence, the habits and the procedures of leadership, fundamentally contradicting the spirit of revolutionary proletarian organisation. The excessive centralisation of the apparatus at the expense of initiative engendered a feeling of uneasiness, an uneasiness which, at the extremities of the party, assumed an exceedingly morbid form and was translated, among other things, in the appearance of illegal groupings directed by elements indubitably hostile to communism. At the same time, the whole of the party disapproved more and more of apparatus-methods of solving questions. The idea, or at the very least the feeling, that bureaucratism threatened to get the party into a blind alley, had become pretty general. Voices were raised to point out the danger. The resolution on the new course is the first official expression of the change that has taken place in the party. It will be realised to the degree that the party, that is, its four hundred thousand members, will want to realise it and will succeed in doing so . . .

The application of workers' democracy cannot be made dependent upon the degree of 'preparation' of the party members for this democracy . . . It is not necessary to speak of the immense authority of the group of party veterans, not only in Russia but internationally; that is universally recognised. But it would be a crude mistake to regard it as absolute. It is only by a constant active collaboration with the new generation, within the framework of democracy, that the old guard will preserve the old guard as a revolutionary factor. Of course, it may ossify and become unwittingly the most consummate expression of bureaucratism.

History offers us more than one case of degeneration of 'the old guard'. Let us take the most recent and striking example: that of the leaders of the parties of the Second International . . . We saw that on the eve of the war, the formidable apparatus of the Social Democracy, covered with the authority of the old generation, had become the most powerful brake upon revolutionary progress.

Before the publication of the decision of the Central Committee on the 'new course', the mere pointing out of the need of modifying the internal party regime was regarded by bureaucratic apparatus functionaries as heresy, as factionalism, as an infraction of discipline. And now the bureaucrats are ready formally to 'take note' of the 'new course', that is, to nullify it bureaucratically. The renovation of the party apparatus – naturally within the clear-cut framework of the statutes – must aim at replacing the mummified bureaucrats with fresh elements closely linked with the life of the collectivity, or capable of assuring such a link. And before anything else, the leading posts must be cleared out of those who, at the first word of criticism, of objection, or of protest, brandish the thunderbolts of penalties before the critic. The 'new course' must begin by making everyone feel that from now on nobody will dare terrorise the party.

*Source: Trotsky, 'The New Course (A Letter to Party Meetings)',
8 December 1923, in* The New Course, *annotated and translated by Max Shachtman (London, New Park Publications, 1956),
pp. 76–7, 78, 79–80.*

Document 4.20   The End of the 'New Course'

Meeting in the week before Lenin's death in January 1924, the Thirteenth Party Conference voted overwhelmingly to denounce the opposition – Stalin's behind-the-scenes manipulation of delegate selection triumphed. Note how the ban on factions imposed by Lenin at the Tenth Party Congress in March 1921 was now being used by Stalin to silence criticism within the party. It should be stressed, however, that the critique by Trotsky and the left by no means included an extension of democracy to society; indeed, they tended to oppose the concessions granted by NEP, with its associated emergence of a rich class of 'Nepmen' and growing inequalities.

The opposition, headed by Trotsky, advanced the slogan of smashing the party apparatus, and sought to shift the focus of the struggle against bureaucratism in the governmental apparatus to 'bureaucratism' in the party apparatus. Such wholesale criticism and direct attempts to discredit the party apparatus cannot objectively lead to anything other than the emancipation of the governmental apparatus from party influence upon it, to the separation of governmental institutions from the party . . .

All shades of the opposition have revealed a completely un-Bolshevik approach to the question of party discipline. The actions of a number of representatives of the opposition represent a clear violation of party discipline, reminiscent of the period when Lenin had to struggle against the 'anarchism of the intellectuals' in organisational questions and defend the foundations of proletarian discipline in the party.

The opposition clearly violated the decision of the Tenth Congress of the Russian Communist Party [March 1921] which prohibited the formation of factions within the party. The opposition has replaced the Bolshevik view of the party as a monolithic whole with the view of the party as the sum of all possible tendencies and factions. These tendencies, factions and groupings, according to the 'new' view of the opposition, must have equal rights in the party, and the Central Committee of the party must not so much lead the party as act as a simple secretary and intermediary between the tendencies and groupings. This view of the party has nothing in common with Leninism. The factional work of the opposition cannot but become a threat to the unity of the state apparatus. The factional moves of the opposition strengthened the hopes of all enemies of the party, including the West European bourgeoisie, for a split in the ranks of the Russian Communist Party. These factional moves again sharply pose before the party the question of whether the Russian Communist Party, since it is in power, can allow the formation of factional groupings within the party.

Source: 'On the Results of the Discussion and on Petty Bourgeois Deviation in the Party', Resolution of the Thirteenth Conference of the RCP, 18 January 1924, KPSS v rezolyutsiyakh i resheniyakh, vol. I, pp. 780–2.

Creating 'Stalinism'

Lenin's theory of the smashing of the bourgeois state was accompanied by the denigration of the autonomous status of law: from this perspective law was no more than a manifestation of the class struggle and would wither away together with the state. Stalin himself consciously sought to assume the mantle of intellectual leadership, recognising that in the Bolshevik context claims to power were couched in the idiom of knowledge about the real needs of the movement and interpretations of the nature of the historical epoch. To this end Stalin launched a number of theoretical innovations. Despite attempts by Trotskyists to portray Stalin as an intellectual dullard, in fact he had a remarkable intuition in understanding the authoritative components of political rule.

Document 4.21   Soviet Law – Pashukanis

Evgeny Pashukanis, one of the leading authorities in Soviet legal science in the 1920s, took up the themes of Marx's 'On the Jewish Question' and Lenin's 'The State and Revolution' to devise a critique of the role of law in capitalist societies from the historical materialist perspective. Pashukanis was one of the leading exponents of the early Soviet 'legal nihilist' tendency; he recognised the need for law in the new system but no longer defined as a set of absolute norms but as a flexible set of standards. In his major work, published in 1924, he outlined the dominant view of law at that time.

In bourgeois society, jurisprudence has always held a special, privileged place. Not only is it first among the other social sciences, but it also leaves its mark on them. Not for nothing did Engels call the juridical way of looking at things the classical world view of the bourgeoisie, a kind of 'secularisation of the theological', in which 'human justice takes the place of dogma and divine right, and the state takes the place of the church'.

By destroying the bourgeois state and overturning property relations, the proletarian revolution created the possibility of liberation from the fetters of legal ideology. 'The workers' lack of property' – wrote Engels in the piece quoted from above – 'was matched only by their lack of illusions'.

But the experiences of the October Revolution have shown that even after the foundations of the old legal order have collapsed, after the old laws, statutes and regulations have been transformed into a heap of waste paper, old mental habits still exhibit an extraordinary tenacity. Even now, the struggle against the bourgeois legal view of the world represents a task of pressing importance for the jurists of the Soviet Republic today . . .

The constitutional state [*Rechtsstaat*] is a mirage, but one which suits the bourgeoisie very well, for it replaces withered religious ideology and conceals the fact of the bourgeoisie's hegemony from the eyes of the masses. The ideology of the constitutional state is even more convenient than religious ideology, because, while it does not entirely reflect objective reality, it is still based on this reality. Power as the 'collective will', as the 'rule of law', is realised in bourgeois society to the extent that this society represents a market . . .

A certain discrepancy between legal truth and the truth to which historical and sociological research aspires is unavoidable. This is due not only to the fact that the dynamic of social life overturns rigidified legal forms and that, as a result, the jurist is condemned always to complete his analysis far too late; even if he does remain up to date with the facts in his assertions, he renders these facts differently than the sociologist. For, so long as he remains a jurist, he starts from the concept of the state as an autonomous force, set apart from all other individual and social forces. From the historical and political point of view, the resolutions of an influential class or party organisation have a significance as great, and sometimes greater, than the decisions of parliament or of any other state organisation. From the legal point of view, facts of the first kind are, as it were, non-existent. In contrast to this, one can, by ignoring the legal standpoint, see in every parliamentary resolution not an act of state, but a decision reached by a particular group or clique . . .

Coercion as a protective measure is an act of pure expediency, and as such, can be governed by technical regulations . . . The concepts of crime and punishment are, as is clear from what has been said already, necessary determinants of the legal form, from which people will be able to liberate themselves only after the legal superstructure itself has begun to wither away. And when we begin to overcome and to do without these concepts in reality, rather than merely in declarations, that will be the surest sign that the narrow horizon of bourgeois law is finally opening up before us.

Source: Evgeny B. Pashukanis, Law and Marxism: A General Theory: Towards a Critique of the Fundamental Juridical Concepts *(London, Pluto Press, 1989), pp. 33, 146, 147, 187, 188.*

For Pashukanis, law was no more than a reflection of the commodity relations of bourgeois society. He thus gave no autonomy either to law or the state, reflecting the materialist reductionism already marked in the works of Marx and Engels. There was no room here for morality or the autonomy of politics in any form other than Bolshevik voluntarism. Pashukanis sought to root his legal nihilism in Marxist theory; for Stalin, this was not enough, requiring subordination not to abstract theory but to Bolshevik practice – as interpreted by Stalin. Consequently, Pashukanis in 1937 fell victim to the system he had helped create.

Document 4.22   Stalin – on Leninism, the Party and Dictatorship

Following Lenin's death on 21 January 1924 the struggle was on not only for the organisational dominance of the party, but also for its ideological leadership. In formal terms, Alexei Rykov replaced Lenin as chairman of Sovnarkom, while Stalin (still controlling the party Secretariat) and Zinoviev dominated the party. To establish himself as the heir to Lenin's mantle as chief theoretician, Stalin delivered a series of lectures in April 1924 on 'Leninism'. The very notion of 'Leninism' paved the way for 'Stalinism'.

Leninism was born and developed in conditions of imperialism, when the contradictions in capitalism reached their extreme point, when the proletarian revolution became a directly practical question, when the old period of the preparation of the working class for revolution was consolidated and grew into the new period of the direct assault against capitalism . . .

The party is not only the *vanguard* detachment of the working class. If it really seeks to direct the struggle of the class it must at the same time be the organised detachment of its class. The party's tasks under capitalism are immense and diverse. The party must direct the struggle of the proletariat under the exceptionally difficult conditions of internal and external development; it must lead the proletariat in the offensive when the situation calls for an offensive; it must lead the proletariat in retreat when the situation calls for retreat to ward off the blows of the powerful enemy; it must imbue the millions of unorganised non-party workers with the spirit of discipline and order in the struggle, with the spirit of organisation and endurance. But the party can fulfil these tasks only if it is itself the embodiment of discipline and organisation, if it is itself the *organised* detachment of the proletariat. Without these conditions there can be no question of the party genuinely leading the multi-million mass of the proletariat. The party is the organised detachment of the working class . . .

But the proletariat needs the party not only to achieve the dictatorship, it is even more necessary for the maintenance of the dictatorship, to strengthen and develop it for the complete victory of socialism . . . The achievement and maintenance of the dictatorship of the proletariat is impossible without a party strong by virtue of its cohesion and iron discipline. But iron discipline in the party is inconceivable without unity of will, without complete and unconditional unity of action of all members of the party. This does not mean, of course, that the possibility of differing views within the party is thereby precluded. On the contrary, iron discipline does not preclude but assumes criticism and differing views within the party. Least of all does it mean that discipline must be 'blind'. On the contrary, iron discipline does not preclude but presupposes conscious and voluntary submission, for only conscious discipline can be truly iron discipline. But after a contest of views has been closed, after criticism has been exhausted and a decision has been arrived at, unity of will and unity of action of all party members are the necessary conditions without which neither party unity nor iron discipline in the party are conceivable . . .

It follows from this that the existence of factions is incompatible either with the unity of the party or with its iron discipline. It hardly needs proving that the existence of factions leads to the existence of a number of centres, and the existence of a number of centres signifies the absence of a single centre in the party, the destruction of the unity of will, the weakening and disintegration of discipline, the weakening and disintegration of the dictatorship . . .

The source of factionalism in the party is its opportunist elements. The proletariat is not an introverted class. It is constantly replenished by the influx of peasants, petty bourgeois and intellectuals proletarianised by the development of capitalism . . . All these petty bourgeois groups enter one way or another into the party, spreading there the spirit of wavering and opportunism, the spirit of disintegration and unsureness . . . Therefore, the merciless struggle with these elements, their expulsion from the party, is the preliminary condition for the successful struggle against imperialism . . . The path of development and strengthening of proletarian parties lies in purging themselves of opportunists and reformists, social-imperialists and social-pacifists . . .

Leninism is a school of theory and practice producing a distinctive type of party and state worker, creating a distinctive Leninist style of work. What are the characteristic features of this style? What are its distinctive features?

It has two distinctive features: (a) Russian revolutionary sweep, and (b) American efficiency. The style of Leninism is a combination of these two distinctive features in party and state work.

Russian revolutionary sweep is an antidote to inertia, routine, conservatism, mental stagnation and slavish submission to ancestral traditions. Russian revolutionary sweep is the life-giving force which stimulates thought, impels things forward, smashes the past and opens up perspectives. Without it no progress is possible. But Russian revolutionary sweep has every chance of degenerating in practice into empty 'revolutionary' Manilovism if it is not combined with American efficiency in work . . . American efficiency is that indomitable force which neither knows nor recognises obstacles; which with its businesslike perseverance pushes aside all obstacles; which continues with a task once started until it is finished, even if it is a minor task; and without which serious constructive work is impossible. But American efficiency has every chance of degenerating into narrow and unprincipled commercialism if it is not combined with the Russian revolutionary sweep . . .

The combination of Russian revolutionary sweep with American efficiency is the essence of Leninism in party and state work. Only this combination produces the finished type of Leninist worker, the style of Leninism in work.

Source: Stalin, 'The Foundations of Leninism', lectures delivered at the Sverdlovsk University, April 1924, Voprosy Leninizma (Problems of Leninism), *3rd edn (Moscow, Gosizdat, 1931), pp. 7, 82–3, 90, 91, 92, 93.*

Document 4.23   Stalin – Against 'Permanent Revolution'

Against the background of the failure of the German socialist revolution – sporadic uprisings against the inflation-ridden Weimar republic were repressed in 1923 – Stalin by the end of 1924 had devised the notion of 'socialism in one country'. The concept was also clearly directed against Trotsky who, recovering somewhat from his depression of early 1924 provoked by the counter-productive outcome of the 'new course' debate, argued that the isolated Soviet regime, not reinforced by the international revolution, was in danger of losing its socialist character. Stalin responded by condemning Trotsky's theory of 'permanent revolution', contrasting Lenin's alleged views on the possibilities of autonomous Soviet development with Trotsky's apparent pessimism that the Russian revolution was fatally dependent on the world revolution. For good measure, Stalin insisted that the Russian revolutionary experience was a model for the rest of the world.

The Leninist theory of the dictatorship of the proletariat is not a purely 'Russian' theory, but a theory obligatory for all countries. Bolshevism is not just a Russian phenomenon . . .

According to Lenin, the revolution draws its strength above all from the workers and peasants of Russia itself. According to Trotsky, the required strength can *only* be found 'in the area of the world proletarian revolution'. But what if the world revolution is fated to arrive with some delay? Is there any ray of hope for our revolution? Trotsky offers no ray of hope, for 'the contradictions in the situation of the workers' government . . . can *only* be resolved . . . in the arena of the world proletarian revolution'. According to this plan, there is only one prospect left for our revolution: to vegetate in its own contradictions and rot away while waiting for the world revolution . . .

'Permanent revolution' is not merely an underestimation of the revolutionary potential of the peasant movement. 'Permanent revolution' is an underestimation of the peasant movement which leads to the *repudiation* of Lenin's theory of the dictatorship of the proletariat. Trotsky's 'permanent revolution' is a variety of Menshevism . . .

Studying imperialism, particularly during the period of war, Lenin devised the law of uneven and combined economic and political development of capitalist countries . . . In the light of this the victory of socialism in one country, even if this country is less developed than the capitalist ones and with the retention of capitalism in other countries, even if these countries are more capitalistically developed, is quite possible and feasible . . .

The second distinctive feature of the October revolution is that this revolution represents a model for the practical application of the Leninist theory of proletarian revolution. Those who have not understood this distinctive feature of the October revolution will never understand either the international nature of this revolution, or its colossal international strength, or its distinctive foreign policy . . .

Trotsky's 'permanent revolution' is the denial of Lenin's theory of proletarian revolution; and conversely, the Leninist theory of proletarian revolution is the denial of the theory of 'permanent revolution'. Lack of faith in the strength and possibilities of our revolution, lack of faith in the strength and possibilities of the Russian proletariat, that is what lies at the root of the theory of 'permanent revolution' . . .

In what way does Trotsky's theory differ from the customary Menshevik theory that the victory of socialism in one country, and in a backward one at that, is impossible without the prior victory of the proletarian revolution 'in the principal countries of Western Europe'? Essentially, there is no difference. There can be no doubt. Trotsky's theory of 'permanent revolution' is a variety of Menshevism.

Source: Stalin, 'Oktyarbr'skaya revolyutsiya i taktika russkikh kommunistov' ('The October Revolution and the Tactics of Russian Communists'), Voprosy Leninizma, *pp. 99, 101, 102, 103–4, 109–10.*

Document 4.24 Stalin – 'Socialism in One Country'

The long-standing Bolshevik belief that the Russian revolution could not survive unless it spread to the more developed countries encountered the reality that the revolution could survive on its own. What, then, was to be done? At the heart of 'Stalinism' was the belief that the building of socialism could not only *begin* in Russia, but that it could be *completed* using internal resources alone. Here Stalin says it was 'possible' to build socialism in one country; later he would insist that it was 'necessary'. The slogan of 'socialism in one country' suggested stability, especially when contrasted with Trotsky's notion of 'permanent revolution' (although at this time Trotsky modified his position), and identified the cause of socialism with Russia's developmental tasks.

What do we mean by the *possibility* of the victory of socialism in one country?

We mean the possibility of solving the contradictions between the proletariat and the peasantry with the aid of the internal forces of our country, the possibility of the proletariat assuming power and using that power to build a complete socialist society in our country, with the sympathy and the support of the proletarians of other countries, but without the preliminary victory of the proletarian revolution in other countries.

Without such a possibility, the building of socialism is building without prospects, building without being sure that socialism will be built. It is no use building socialism without being sure that we can build it, without being sure that the technical backwardness of our country is not an *insuperable* obstacle to the building of a complete socialist society. To deny such a possibility is to display lack of faith in the cause of building socialism, to abandon Leninism.

Source: Stalin, 'On the Problems of Leninism', 25 January 1926,
Problems of Leninism *(Moscow, Foreign Languages Publishing House, 1947),*
pp. 159–60.

At the root of the conflict between Trotsky and Stalin lay important theoretical issues. The same cannot be said of the swirling currents of the intra-party struggle for power, usually dressed up in fancy theoretical language. Having defeated Trotsky, in 1925 the triumvirate split, and Kamenev and Zinoviev (and with him the Leningrad Party Organisation, which he headed) went into opposition against the majority led by Stalin, Bukharin and Rykov. At the Fourteenth Party Congress in December 1925 Zinoviev warned of the dangers of 'state capitalism', while Kamenev denounced the trend towards the emergence of a *vozhd* (*Führer*, or leader) in the party, condemning the fusion of political and organisational functions in the hands of the Secretariat. The two defeated oppositional groups (Trotskyist and Zinovievite) came together in 1926 to form the United Opposition. Accused of factionalism, they argued that the growth of bureaucratism was the problem and called for accelerated industrialisation to develop state industry and to undermine what they saw as the growing predominance of the 'rich peasants' (*kulaks*) in the countryside. It was impossible to disentangle the political and developmental debates.

The End of NEP

Two main developmental strategies were advanced in the party at this time. From the left came Yevgeny Preobrazhensky's argument that, given the lack of investment funds, only the systematic exploitation of the small-scale producer (i.e. primarily peasant) sector could provide the resources for industrialisation. It was this strategy of 'primary socialist accumulation', shorn of its nuances, that was later implemented by Stalin. On the right, Bukharin became the main defender of a gradualist 'growing into socialism', allowing a healthy peasant sector to develop and then taxing its reserves for investment. At first, needing his support in his struggle against the various oppositions, Stalin sided with Bukharin in the great developmental debate. At the Fifteenth Party Congress in December 1927 the opposition leaders were defeated, most of them removed from their posts and the leaders expelled from the party. Zinoviev and Kamenev soon after recanted and were temporarily re-admitted to the party while the Trotskyists were exiled to Siberia, with Trotsky himself being sent out of the country altogether in February 1929. With his hands freed, Stalin began to question the viability of the NEP. A trial of 'specialists' (the Shakhty case) signalled the beginning of a wave of arrests of the old intelligentsia. For Stalin 'The Shakhty case represents a new serious offensive by international capital and its agents in our country against Soviet power. This is economic intervention in our internal affairs' (PSS, vol. 11, p. 63).

Document 4.25 Preobrazhenskii, 'Primary Socialist Accumulation'

Preobrazhenskii's view was elaborated in a paper delivered to the Communist Academy in August 1924 entitled 'The Fundamental Law of Socialist Accumulation'.

As we have seen, primary capitalist accumulation took place on the basis of feudalism, but primary socialist accumulation cannot take place on the basis of capitalism. It follows that if socialism has its prehistory, it only begins with the assumption of power by the proletariat. The nationalisation of large-scale industry is the first act of socialist accumulation . . . Socialist accumulation, in the real sense of the word, i.e., accumulation on the technical-economic base of a socialist economy, already developing all of its inherent characteristics and advantages, can only begin after the Soviet economy has passed through the phase of primary accumulation . . . In these conditions to rely only on accumulation within the socialist part of the economy means risking the very existence of the socialist economy or risk extending to infinity the period of preliminary accumulation . . . In any case, the idea that the socialist economy can develop on its own, not touching the resources of the petty-bourgeois economy, including that of the peasantry, is undoubtedly a reactionary petty-bourgeois Utopia.

Source: E. A. Preobrazhenskii, 'Osnovnoi zakon sotsialisticheskogo nakopleniya', in Puti razvitiya: diskussi 20-x godov (Leningrad, Lenizdat, 1990), pp. 57, 58, 66.

Document 4.26   Stalin and the Grain Crisis

The NEP had periodically suffered from food shortages in the cities. Grain collection depended on the sensitive management of market forces, above all a pricing policy for grain that would encourage peasants to market their surpluses. For Bolshevik enthusiasts, it appeared that the peasants were able to hold the revolution to ransom. The rupture of the *smychka* (alliance) between workers and peasants would both free the Bolsheviks of this incubus and provide resources for industrialisation. An additional advantage for Stalin in this policy was that it would embarrass his erstwhile allies, Bukharin and Rykov. The year 1928 saw ever more use of administrative measures to confiscate grain from the peasantry, representing an abandonment of NEP's use of the market.

The basic cause of our grain difficulties is that the increase in the production of grain for the market is not keeping pace with the increase in the demand for grain. Industry is growing. The number of workers is growing. Towns are growing. And, finally, regions producing industrial crops (cotton, flax, sugar beet, etc.) are growing, creating a demand for grain. All this leads to a rapid increase in our requirements for grain, for marketable grain. But the production of grain for the market is increasing at a disastrously slow rate . . .

The reason is primarily and mainly the change in the structure of our agriculture brought about by the October revolution, the change from large-scale landlord and large-scale kulak farming, which provided the largest amount of marketed grain, to small and middle peasant farming, which provides the smallest proportion of marketed grain. The mere fact that before the war there were 15–16 million individual peasant farms, whereas at present there are 24–5 million peasant farms, reveals that now the basis of our agriculture is essentially small peasant farming, which provides a minimum amount of grain for the market . . .

What is the way out of this situation?

There are some who see the way out of this situation in a return to kulak farming, in the development and extension of kulak farming. These people dare not advocate a return to landlord farming, for they realise, evidently, that to talk of these things in our times is dangerous. All the more eagerly, therefore, they urge the utmost development of kulak farming in the interest of Soviet power. These people think that Soviet power can simultaneously rely on two opposed classes – the class of the kulaks, whose economic principle is the exploitation of the working class, and the class of the workers, whose economic principle is the abolition of all exploitation. A trick worthy of reactionaries. There is no need to prove that these reactionary 'plans' have nothing in common with the interests of the working class, with the principles of Marxism, with the tasks of Leninism . . .

What, then, is the way out of the situation?

1 The way out lies, above all, in the transition from small, backward and scattered peasant farms to amalgamated, large-scale socialised farms, equipped with machinery, armed with scientific knowledge and capable of producing the greatest quantity of grain for the market. The solution lies in the transition from individual peasant farming to collective, socialised farming . . .
2 The way out lies, second, in expanding and strengthening the old state farms, and in organising and developing new, large state farms . . .
3 Finally, the way out lies in systematically increasing the yield of the small and middle individual-peasant farms. We cannot and should not lend any support to the individual large kulak farms. But we can and should assist the individual small- and middle-peasant farms, helping them to increase their crop yields and drawing them into co-operative organisations . . .

Thus, if all these tasks are fulfilled, the state can in three or four years have at its disposal 250–300 million additional poods [4.1–4.9 million tonnes] of marketable grain, more or less enough to enable us to give us freedom of action within the country as well as abroad.

Source: Stalin, 'On the Grain Front', Talk to Students of the Institute of Red Professors, the Communist Academy and the Sverdlov University, 28 May 1928, Voprosy Leninizma, *pp. 386–7, 388, 390–1, 393, 394.*

Document 4.27   Bukharin Warns against Stalin

The Fifteenth Party Congress adopted plans for increasing the tempo of indus-trialisation, and taken together with Stalin's shift towards a more punitive approach towards the peasants, Bukharin, Rykov and others were increasingly alarmed. They formed what their opponents later called the 'Right Deviation'. Bukharin sought a rapprochement with his erstwhile opponents in the left opposition. Visiting Kamenev on 11 July 1928, Bukharin poured out his fears about Stalin.

Kamenev: Is the struggle really serious?

Bukharin: That's precisely what I wanted to talk about. We feel that Stalin's line is disastrous for the whole revolution. We could be overthrown on account of it. *The disagreements between us and Stalin are many times more serious than the disagreements which we used to have with you.* Rykov, Tomsky and I are unanimous in formulating the situation thus: 'It would be much better if Zinoviev and Kamenev were in the Politburo instead of Stalin.' I spoke with Rykov and Tomsky about this quite frankly. I have not spoken with Stalin for several weeks. He is an unprincipled intriguer, who sub-ordinates everything to the preservation of his own power. He changes his theory according to whom he needs to get rid of. In the 'seven' [the leadership group], our arguments with him reached the point of saying, 'false,' 'you lie', etc. Now he has made concessions, so that he can cut our throats. We understand this, but he manoeuvres so as to make us appear to be the sectarians . . . This is the line which he pronounced at the plenum: (1) Capitalism developed through colonies, or loans, or the exploitation of the workers. We have no colonies, we can get no loans, therefore our basis is tribute from the peasantry. You understand that this is just what Preobrazhensky's theory is; (2) The more socialism grows, the greater will be the resistance [to it] . . . This is idiotic illiteracy; (3) Since tribute is necessary and resistance will grow, we need firm leadership. Self-criticism should not apply to the leadership, but only to those who carry out orders. Self-criticism is in fact aimed at Tomsky and Uglanov [the rightist secretary of the Moscow Party Organisation]. As a result we are getting a police regime. This is not a 'cuckoo' matter, but will really decide the fate of the revolution. With this theory everything can be lost . . .

The Petersburg [Leningrad] people are in general with us, but they got scared when the discussion moved on to the possibility of removing Stalin . . . Our potential forces are vast, but: (1) the middle-ranking Central Committee member still does not understand the depth of the disagreements; and (2) there is a terrible fear of a split. Therefore, when Stalin conceded on the extraordinary measures, he made it difficult for us to attack him. We don't want to appear as sectarians, for then they would slaughter us. But Tomsky in his latest speech showed clearly that Stalin is the sectarian.

Source: Notes by Kamenev, in Yu. G. Fel'tshtinskii, Razgovory s Bukharinym *(Moscow, Izd-vo gumanitarnoi literatury, 1993), pp. 32, 33.*

Document 4.28   Bukharin – *Notes of an Economist*

In addition to condemning Stalin personally, Bukharin denounced plans for accelerated industrialisation, calling for caution and equilibrium, in particular for a greater balance between consumer and investment spending. In his *Notes of an Economist* Bukharin insisted that sustained industrial growth could best be achieved within the framework of the NEP and with the balanced development of agriculture.

The growth of our economy and the undoubted growth of *socialism* is accompanied by distinctive 'crises' . . . To attain the most favourable possible march of social reproduction (the most crisis-free), and to attain the systematic growth of socialism, and, in consequence, to attain the most favourable possible situation for the proletariat in the relations of class forces in the country, it is necessary to achieve a coordination of the basic elements of the national economy, to 'balance' them, arrange them in such fashion that they best fulfil their respective functions, and actively influence the develoment of economic life and the class struggle so as to attain the best possible balance or equilibrium . . .

In their simplicity, the ideologists of Trotskyism assume that the maximum annual pumping out of resources from the peasant economy into industry will assure the maximum tempo of the development of industry. But that is clearly not so. The greatest not temporary but continuous tempo can be attained by such a coordination in which industry develops on the foundations of a rapidly growing agricultural economy. It is then that industry attains its own record-breaking figures in its development . . .

What the Trotskyists fail to comprehend is that the development of industry is dependent on the development of agriculture.

Source: N. I. Bukharin, 'Zametki ekonomista', Pravda, 30 September 1928, in Put' k sotsializmu (Novosibirsk, Nauka, 1990), pp. 336–66.

Document 4.29   Nadezhda Mandelstam – 'Hope Abandoned'

Nadezhda Mandelsham was the companion and wife of the poet Osip Mandelstam, who was exiled and imprisoned following his denuncation of Stalin in the early 1930s. Following his death in 1938 Nadezhda survived, like so many others, by teaching in faraway provincial towns. In 1956 she was allowed to return to Moscow where she wrote two volumes of memoirs, *Hope against Hope* (a play on her first name, which means 'hope' in Russian), and *Hope Abandoned* about her and Osip's life together. It is both a powerful literary memoir and an important historical source, providing a movingly intelligent impression of the times. The incident described below helps put Lenin's letter on the events in Shui (Document 4.4) in perspective, while the extract ends with a powerful corrective to those who considered (and consider) NEP as some sort of golden age coming between the Civil War and Stalinist terror.

There were rumours about the famine on the Volga, and a letter about it from Patriarch Tikhon, who wanted to organize aid for the victims, was passed from hand to hand. The Muscovites flippantly dismissed it as a joke, saying that the new State did not need any help from priests. In Bogoslovski Street, not far from where we were living, there was a little church. I remember how once, stopping at the sight of a small crowd gathered outside, we were told that all church property was being confiscated. I do not know whether it was the same everywhere else, but here it was being done quite openly. No one tried to bar our way as we went inside. An elderly, dishevelled priest was trembling all over, large tears rolling down his cheeks, as the icons were stripped of their coverings and flung to the ground. The people doing all this were simultaneously carrying on loud anti-religious propaganda while old women wept, and the crowd jeered, hugely enjoying the spectacle. The church, as we all know, belongs to the 'superstructure', and it was now being destroyed together with the old 'basis'.

We are always hearing it said that old Russian painting, previously hidden under the icon coverings, was exposed to view for the first time after the Revolution, but nobody mentions the way in which it was done. We also prefer to gloss over the fact that untold numbers of icons were destroyed and chopped to pieces, and that many churches in Moscow and all over the country were razed to the ground. The best was if a church was converted into a warehouse – it then had some chance of survival . . .

The church, he went on, really would have helped the starving, but Tikhon's proposal had been turned down, and now they were shrieking that the church people had no pity for the starving and were hoarding their treasures. In this way, they were killing two birds with one stone: while vilifying the church, they were also grabbing its gold. He also doubted that the funds thus obtained would be spent on the needs of the starving rather than on 'World Revolution'. Recently, one of our journals, the most 'progressive', published the memoirs of a woman who had seen the effects of the 'confiscation' of church property from another angle: she was one of those who were sent to distribute aid in the famine areas. They were not able to give the peasants food, only seed grain, and somehow keeping alive by eating weeds, nearly dropping from hunger, the people did manage to sow their crops. The woman in question is a real follower of Lenin, and her humane heart bled from pity. It did not occur to her to ask why all the wealth of the church, stored up during the ages, had not sufficed to feed the hungry even in that relatively small and under-populated region – if she had given it any thought she would no doubt have blamed the 'grasping church people'. Who now remembers the hungry crowds in the cities and the peasants silently dying on their cold, crumbling stoves? In Russia people die in silence.

We had gone into that church quite by chance and heard the jeering of the mob and the wailing of the old women. Similar disconnected scenes from daily life appeared kaleidoscopically like this before our eyes, never forming into a complete picture. Everything we learned was a chance detail, the result of a momentary glimpse. Conflicting rumours provided a commentary on events from different points of view. The twenties are still looked back upon as a period of the rule of law and general prosperity . . . I am often accused of subjectivism, because I keep harping not only on 1937 but also on earlier phases of the suppression of 'alien elements': the church, the Freemasons, idealist philosophers, peasants, engineers, ordinary people held in prison cells until they yielded up their gold, collectors of anecdotes, and suspect intellectuals . . .

Many people failed to notice the transition from the popular upheaval of the Revolution, with all its spontaneous barbarity, to the carefully planned, machine-like callousness that followed. People who had tended to find excuses for the first of these phases also reconciled themselves to the second.

Source: Nadezhda Mandelstam, Hope Abandoned, *translated by Max Hayward (Harmondsworth, Penguin Books, 1974), pp. 156–7, 158, 405.*

5 | Building socialism, 1929–1939

The 'revolution from above' launched at the end of the 1920s is often considered as completing the October 1917 revolution. In foreign policy, agriculture, industry and culture policies were radicalised, sometimes with disastrous consequences. A new type of Stalinist conservatism emerged that was traditional in its tastes, repressive in its social attitudes and nationalistic in its tone. Stalin's personal predominance was firmly established at the time of his fiftieth birthday in 1929, and thereafter his rule was marked by an extreme form of the 'cult of the personality'. Issues of military security came to the fore after Hitler came to power in Germany in 1933. Stalin's personal pre-eminence took increasingly morbid forms as mass terror was launched on the country, peaking with the 'Yezhovshchina' (named after the head of the NKVD at the time, Nikolai Yezhov) in 1937. The inner logic, if any, of the great purges is still disputed. With the West suffering the effects of the Great Depression and the rise of fascism, for the Soviet Union the 1930s were the grandest and the most terrible of years.

Foreign Policy

Soviet foreign policy always followed the twists and turns of domestic policy, but never with more devastating consequences than in the early 1930s. Diplomatic relations with Great Britain were broken off in May 1927, and with the defeat of Chinese communism in that month the USSR's isolation appeared complete.

Document 5.1   The 'Third Period'

As Stalin intensified the struggle against Bukharin and the 'Right Deviationists' at home, so, too, abroad he launched through the Comintern at its Sixth Congress in August 1928 a 'left turn', justified as a response to the 'third period' of post-war capitalism. Stalin believed that this period would be marked by the sharpening of the class struggle and a new round of imperialist wars and interventions.

After the first world imperialist war the international labour movement passed though a series of historical phases of development, expressing various phases of the general crisis of the capitalist system.

The *first* period was the period of extremely acute crisis of the capitalist system, and of direct revolutionary action on the part of the proletariat. This period reached its apex of development in 1921, and culminated, on the one hand, with the victory of the USSR over the forces of foreign intervention and internal counter-revolution and with the consolidation of the Communist International. On the other hand, it ended with a series of severe defeats for the Western European proletariat and the beginning of the general capitalist offensive. The final link in the chain of events in this period was the defeat of the German proletariat in 1923. This defeat marked the starting point of the *second* period, a period of gradual and partial stabilization of the capitalist system, of the restoration of capitalist economy, of the development and expansion of the capitalist offensive and of the continuation of the defensive battles fought by the proletarian army weakened by severe defeats. On the other hand, this was a period of rapid restoration in the USSR, of extremely important successes in the work of building up socialism, and also of the growth of the political influence of the Communist Parties over the broad masses of the proletariat. Finally came the *third* period, which, in the main, is the period in which capitalist economy is exceeding the pre-war level, and in which the economy of the USSR is also almost simultaneously exceeding the pre-war level . . . For the capitalist system this is the period of rapid development of technique and accelerated growth of cartels and trusts, and in which tendencies of development towards State capitalism are observed. At the same time, it is a period of intense development of the contradictions of world capitalism . . . This third period, in which the contraction of markets become particularly accentuated, is inevitably giving rise to a fresh series of imperialist wars; among the imperialist States themselves, wars of the imperialist States against the USSR, wars of national liberation against imperialism and imperialist intervention, and to gigantic class battles. The intensification of all international antagonisms (antagonisms between the capitalist States and the USSR, the military occupation of Northern China – which is the beginning of the partition of China – the mutual struggles between the imperialists, etc.), the intensification of the *internal* antagonisms in capitalist countries (the swing to the left of the masses of the working class, growing acuteness of the class struggle), and the wide development of *colonial movements* (China, India and Syria), which are taking place in this period, will inevitably lead – through the further development of the contradictions of capitalist stabilization – to capitalist stabilization becoming still more precarious and to the severe intensification of the general crisis of capitalism.

Source: 'Communism and the International Situation', Theses of the Sixth Congress of the Comintern, 19 August 1928, in McDermott and Agnew, The Comintern, *pp. 234–5.*

Having purged 'Trotskyists' from the leadership of foreign communist parties, Stalin now targeted Bukharin's sympathisers, eliminating the vestiges of the original communist leaderships and suppressing the final sparks of independence. 'Third period' extremism condemned the German Social Democrats as 'social fascists', so driving a wedge between the opponents of Nazism and facilitating Hitler's rise to power. Leading the largest party in the Reichstag, President Hindenburg appointed Hitler Chancellor in January 1933 as a counterweight to the socialists and communists (who themselves were bitterly divided as a result of Stalin's policies).

Document 5.2   The Popular Front Policy

In the face of the rise of Nazi power in Germany, the Seventh (and last) Comintern Congress in August 1935 resolved to promote cooperation with liberal and socialist groups to establish 'Popular Fronts' against fascism. The transitional strategy was also rethought, including (in the short term at least) the use of parliamentary democracy. Revolution was to be deferred as the USSR advanced the policy of 'collective security' against the common threat. Popular Front governments came to power in Spain and France, the former overthrown by Franco's rebels supported by Italy and Germany.

In the face of the towering menace of fascism to the working class and all the gains it has made, to all toilers and their elementary rights, to the peace and liberty of the peoples, the Seventh Congress of the Communist International declares that at the present historical stage it is the main and immediate task of the international labour movement to establish the united fighting front of the working class. For a successful struggle against the offensive of capital, against the reactionary measures of the bourgeoisie, against fascism, the bitterest enemy of all the toilers, who, without distinction of political views, have been deprived of all rights and liberties, it is imperative that unity of action be established between all sections of the working class, irrespective of what organization they belong to, even before the majority of the working class unites on a common fighting platform for the overthrow of capitalism and the victory of the proletarian revolution. But it is precisely for this very reason that this task makes it the duty of the Communist Parties to take into consideration the changed circumstances and to apply the united front tactics in a new manner, by seeking to reach agreements with the organizations of the toilers of various political trends for joint action on a factory, local, district, national and international scale.

Source: Resolution on 'Fascism, Working Class Unity, and the Tasks of the Comintern', of the Seventh World Congress of the Communist International, 20 August 1935, in McDermott and Agnew, The Comintern, p. 223.

Collectivisation

Bukharin's warnings were ignored and Stalin launched a coercive campaign for the collectivisation of the peasantry. Tsarism's emancipation of the peasants had never been complete, and it was only during the NEP that their liberation had been achieved. This brief period of freedom now came to an end and a second enserfment, as the peasants called collectivisation, was imposed.

Document 5.3 Stalin on 'The Liquidation of the Kulaks as a Class'

Lenin had envisaged collectivisation as a gradual and relatively non-coercive process; from mid-1929 Stalin transformed it into a brutally violent campaign. Resistance within the party was condemned as part of the 'Right Deviation', and in the countryside as counter-revolution. From December 1929 under the guise of 'the liquidation of the kulaks as a class' a war of the regime against the mass of the peasantry was launched in which over half the peasantry was 'collectivised', a euphemism for mass dispossession and deportation.

The so-called theory of 'equilibrium' between the sectors of our national economy is still current among Communists. This theory has, of course, nothing in common with Marxism. Nevertheless, this theory is advocated by a number of people in the camp of the right. This theory is based on the assumption that to begin with we have a socialist sector – which is, as it were, one compartment – and that in addition we have a non-socialist or, if you like, capitalist sector – which is another compartment. These two 'compartments' move on different rails and glide peacefully forward, without touching one another. Geometry teaches that parallel lines do not meet. But the authors of this remarkable theory believe that these parallel lines will meet eventually, and that when they meet we will have socialism. This theory overlooks the fact that behind these so-called 'compartments' there are classes, and that these compartments move as a result of a fierce class struggle, a life-and-death struggle, a struggle on the principle of 'who will win?' [*kto kogo*].

It is not difficult to see that this theory has nothing in common with Leninism. It is not difficult to see that, objectively, the purpose of this theory is to defend the position of individual peasant farming, to arm kulak elements with a 'new' theoretical weapon in their struggle against collective farms and to discredit them . . .

And so, the question stands as follows: either one way or the other, either *back* – to capitalism, or *forward* – to socialism. There is no third way, nor can there be. The 'equilibrium' theory is an attempt to indicate a third way. And precisely because it is based on a third (non-existent) way, it is Utopian and anti-Marxist . . .

The characteristic feature in our work during the past year is that we, as a party, as Soviet power: (a) have launched an offensive along the whole front against the capitalist elements in the countryside; (b) that this offensive, as you know, has brought about and is bringing about very palpable, *positive* results. What does this mean? It means that we have passed from the policy of *restricting* the exploitative tendencies of the kulaks to the policy of *liquidating* the kulaks as a class. This means that we have made, and are still making, one of the decisive turns in our whole policy . . .

Now that we have the material base with which to beat the kulaks, to break their resistance, to eliminate them as a class and to *replace* their output with the output of the collective and state farms . . . Now, the kulaks are being expropriated by the masses of poor and middle peasants themselves, by the masses who are putting solid collectivisation into practice. Now, the expropriation of the kulaks in the regions of mass collectivisation is no longer just an administrative measure. Now, the expropriation of the kulaks is an integral part of the formation and development of the collective farms. Consequently it is now ridiculous and foolish to go on about the expropriation of the kulaks. You do not lament the loss of the hair of one who has been beheaded.

There is another question which seems no less ridiculous: whether the kulaks should be permitted to join the collective farms. Of course not, for they are sworn enemies of the collective-farm movement.

Source: Stalin, 'Problems of Agrarian Policy in the USSR', Speech at a Conference of Marxist Students of the Agrarian Question, 27 December 1929, Voprosy Leninizma, *3rd edn, pp. 547, 549, 563–4, 565, 566–7.*

The whole notion of 'kulak', it must be stressed, was largely a political one (anyone resisting Bolshevik policies, be they rich or poor peasants) rather than a social one. Most so-called kulaks were indistinguishable from the great mass of peasants except in their harder work and more successful farms. In 1928 Stalin unexpectedly announced that 5 per cent of all peasants were kulaks (1.2 million peasant households, 6.2 million of the rural population), while studies in 1927 had suggested that kulaks represented at most 3.5 per cent. Of the USSR's 125 million peasants on 25 million farms, no more than some 750,000 farms were owned by kulaks averaging 10 hectares of arable land with usually no more than 3 cows and 3 working animals.

Document 5.4 Horror in the Village

Victor Kravchenko, who at the time was an engineering student but who later became one of Stalin's industrial managers, was sent from his institute to assist with collectivisation in the villages of the Ukraine. He was one of the 'twenty-thousanders', industrial workers who helped in the collectivisation of agriculture. His account vividly illustrates the tragic implementation of 'Bolshevik firmness', and not least the traumatic effect it had on all the participants.

Comrade Hatayevich, a member of the Central Committee of the Party, made a speech. It only increased our nervousness. We had half expected to hear a technical discourse on agriculture and village economy. Instead we listened to a fiery summons to go forth and do battle in a do-or-die spirit.

'Comrades,' he said, 'you are going into the country for a month or six weeks. The Dniepropetrovsk Region has fallen behind. The Party and Comrade Stalin ordered us to complete collectivisation by spring, and here we are at the end of summer with the task unfinished. The local village authorities need an injection of Bolshevik iron. That's why we are sending you.

'You must assume your duties with a feeling of the strictest Party responsibility, without whimpering, without any rotten liberalism. Throw your bourgeois humanitarianism out of the window and act like Bolsheviks worthy of Comrade Stalin. Beat down the kulak agent wherever he raises his head. It's war – it's them or us! The last decayed remnant of capitalist farming must be wiped out at any cost!

'Secondly, comrades, it is absolutely necessary to fulfil the government's plan for grain delivery. The kulaks, and even some middle and "poor", peasants, are not giving up their grain. They are sabotaging the Party policy. And the local authorities sometimes waver and show weakness. Your job is to get the grain at any price. Pump it out of them, wherever it's hidden, in ovens, under beds, in cellars or buried away in back yards.

'Through you, the Party brigades, the villages must learn the meaning of Bolshevik firmness. You must find the grain and you will find it. It's a challenge to the last shred of your initiative. Don't be afraid of taking extreme measures. The Party stands four-square behind you. Comrade Stalin expects it of you. It's a life-and-death struggle; better to do too much than not enough.

'Your third important task is to complete the threshing of the grain, to repair the tools, ploughs, tractors, reapers and other equipment.

'The class struggle in the village has taken the sharpest forms. This is no time for squeamishness or sentimentality. Kulak agents are masking themselves and getting into the collective farms where they sabotage the work and kill the livestock. What's required from you is Bolshevik alertness, intransigence and courage. I am sure you will carry out the instructions of the Party and the directives of our beloved Leader.' The final words, conveying a threat, were drowned in obedient applause.

'Are there any questions? Is everything clear?'

There were no questions.

'Then wait right here. You will soon be called separately to see Comrade Brodsky.'

I asked myself: Can this be all the 'instructions' we will receive? Is it possible that a lot of students and industrial officials are expected to solve the tremendous economic and political problems of the agrarian village just by applying more and more 'Bolshevik firmness'? How can a group like this, youngsters and most of us ignorant of farm problems, be entrusted to decide the fate of hundreds of thousands of peasants? . . .

Evening was falling when I drove into the village, with several companions. Immediately we realised that something was happening. Agitated groups stood around. Women were weeping. I hurried to the Soviet building.

'What's happening?' I asked the constable.

'Another round-up of kulaks,' he replied. 'Seems the dirty business will never end. The GPU and District Committee people came this morning.'

A large crowd was gathered outside the building. Policemen tried to scatter them, but they came back. Some were cursing. A number of women and children were weeping hysterically and calling the names of their husbands and fathers. It was all like a scene out of a nightmare.

Inside the Soviet building, Arshinov was talking to a GPU official. Both of them were smiling, apparently exchanging pleasantries of some sort. In the back yard, guarded by GPU soldiers with drawn revolvers, stood about twenty peasants, young and old, with bundles on their backs. A few of them were weeping. The others stood there sullen, resigned, hopeless.

So this was 'liquidation of the kulaks as a class'! A lot of simple peasants being torn from their native soil, stripped of all their worldly goods, and shipped to some distant lumber camps or irrigation works. For some reason, on this occasion, most of the families were being left behind. Their outcries filled the air. As I came out of the Soviet house again, I saw two militiamen leading a middle-aged peasant. It was obvious that he had been manhandled – his face was black and blue and his gait was painful; his clothes were ripped in a way indicating a struggle.

As I stood there, distressed, ashamed, helpless, I heard a woman shouting in an unearthly voice. Everyone looked in the direction of her cry and a couple of GPU men started running towards her. The woman, her hair streaming, held a flaming sheaf of grain in her hands. Before anyone could reach her, she had tossed the burning sheaf onto the thatched roof of the house, which burst into flame instantaneously.

'Infidels, murderers!' the distraught woman was shrieking. 'We worked all our lives for our house. You won't have it. The flames will have it!' Her cries turned suddenly into crazy laughter.

Peasants rushed into the burning house and began to drag out furniture. There was something macabre, unreal, about the whole scene – the fire, the wailing, the demented woman, the peasants being dragged through the mud and herded together for deportation. The most unreal touch of all, for me, was the sight of Arshinov and the GPU officer looking on calmly, as if this were all routine, as if the burning hut were a bonfire for their amusement.

I stood in the midst of it, trembling, bewildered, scarcely in control of my senses. I had an impulse to shoot – someone, anyone, to relieve the un-bearable tension of my emotions. Never before or since have I been so close to losing my mind. I reached under my coat for my revolver. Just then a strong hand gripped my arm. It was my host, Stupenko. Perhaps he had guessed my thoughts.

'You must not torment yourself, Victor Andreyevich,' he said. 'If you do anything foolish, you'll only hurt yourself without helping us. Believe me, I'm an old man and I know. Take a hold of yourself. You'll do more good if you avoid trouble, since this is beyond your control. Come, let's go home. You're as white as a sheet. As for me, I'm used to it. This is nothing. The big round-ups last year were worse.' . . .

In war, there is a palpable difference between those who have been in the front lines and the people at home. It is a difference that cannot be bridged by fuller information and a lively sympathy. It is a difference that resides in the nerves, not in the mind.

Those of the Communists who had been directly immersed in the horrors of collectivisation were thereafter marked men. We carried the scars. We had seen ghosts. We could almost be identified by our taciturnity, by the way we shrank from discussion of the 'peasant front'. We might consider the subject among ourselves, as Seryozha and I did after our return, but to talk of it to the uninitiated seemed futile. With them we had no common vocabulary of experience.

Source: Victor Kravchenko, I Chose Freedom: The Personal and Political Life of a Soviet Official *(London, Robert Hale, 1947), pp. 91–2, 104–5, 107.*

Document 5.5 Stalin – 'Dizzy with Success'

Stalin's 'liquidation' speech encouraged ever greater violence in the countryside as officials feared lagging behind in the campaign. Volunteers from the cities who knew nothing of the countryside added to the mayhem. Hostility to the regime took ever more violent forms, leading Stalin himself in March 1930 to call a temporary retreat, blaming the over-enthusiasm of local officials for the excesses.

Everybody is now talking about the successes of Soviet power in the field of the collective farm movement. Even enemies have been forced to recognise major successes. And these successes are great indeed.

It is a fact that by 20 February of this year 50 per cent of peasant households in the USSR have been collectivised. This means that we *over-fulfilled* the five-year plan by 20 February 1930 by double . . . What does this mean? It means that *the fundamental turn of the countryside towards socialism can be considered achieved* . . .

But successes have their dark side, especially when they are achieved relatively 'easily', as it were, 'unexpectedly'. These successes sometimes lead to a spirit of self-importance and conceit: 'We can do anything!', 'Nothing can stop us!'. These successes sometimes make people drunk, people's heads become dizzy with success, the sense of measure is lost, the ability to understand reality is lost, the tendency to overestimate one's abilities appears and with it the underestimation of the strength of the opponent, adventuristic attempts to resolve all questions of socialist construction 'in one step' appears. Here there is no room for concern about how to *consolidate* the successes achieved and to *use* them in a planned way for further movement ahead . . .

Thus the task of the party is to conduct a decisive struggle with these dangerous and harmful opinions and to expel them from the party . . .

A few facts: The success of our collective farm policy is explained among other things in that it is based on the *voluntary* nature of the collective farm movement and *taking into account the diversity of conditions* in various parts of the USSR. Collective farms should not be imposed by force . . .

The art of leadership is a serious matter. One must not lag behind the movement, for to lag means to separate from the masses. But one should not race ahead, for to race ahead means to lose contact with the masses. Whoever wants to lead the movement and to retain links with the masses of millions has to fight on two fronts – against those lagging behind and against those racing ahead.

Source: Stalin, 'Dizzy with Success', Pravda, 3 March 1930, in Voprosy Leninizma, *pp. 574, 575, 580.*

Collectivisation proceeded thereafter at a more measured pace, with peasants being allowed to keep a small private plot. These private plots in effect became the mainstay of Soviet agriculture; although occupying only a very small proportion of the land, they came to produce a large proportion of market produce and allowed the peasants to survive and, later, earn something on the side when they took their vegetables, fruit, honey and milk to market.

Document 5.6   Declaration of the Bolshevik-Leninist Opposition

Defeated at home, the remnants of the Trotskyist left in exile subjected the Soviet power system to merciless critique, notably in the pages of the *Bulletin of the Opposition*. Christian Rakovsky, the Romanian-born former prime minister of Ukraine and Soviet ambassador to Britain, took up some of the themes of the opposition of the early 1920s, above all detailing the social degeneration of the workers' state, which in his view had come under the domination of a ruling bureaucracy that pursued its own class interests. This theme was later developed by Trotsky in his *The Revolution Betrayed* (Document 5.26), and by Milovan Djilas in *The New Class* (Document 8.14). Stalin's policies were criticised by the left as well as the right, and the following extracts from their theses in 1929 and declaration of April 1930 summarise their arguments.

The Party Leadership and the Party Regime

In 1923 the opposition foresaw that enormous damage to the dictatorship would derive from the distortion of the party regime. Events have fully justified this prognosis: the enemy has climbed in through the bureaucratic window.

Now more than ever it is necessary to say out loud that the correct democratic party regime *is the touchstone of a genuine left course* . . .

Centrism [as the left opposition called the Stalinist group] did not create bureaucracy. It inherited it, together with the other general social, cultural (etc.) conditions of our country. However, instead of fighting bureaucratism, centrism turned it into a system of government, transferred it from the Soviet apparatus into the party apparatus and gave the latter completely unprecedented forms and dimensions, completely unjustified by the role of *political* leadership that the party must play. Above all the centrist leadership has elevated into communist dogma ('the organised principles of leninism') methods of command and coercion, refining and polishing them to produce a bureaucratic virtuosity rarely attained in history. With the help of precisely these demoralizing methods, turning thinking communists into machines, killing off will, character and human dignity, the centrist leadership has succeeded in transforming itself into an inviolable oligarchy which cannot be removed from office, and has substituted itself for class and party.

'Declaration of April 1930', C. Rakovsky, V. Kossior, N. Muralov, V. Kasparova

In its declaration to the CC and the Central Control Commission of 4 October last year, the Bolshevik-leninist opposition warned against the extraordinary administrative measures being taken in the countryside, and of their inevitable political consequences. We also warned against the harmful theory that it is possible to build a socialist society in one country. This theory could only arise in the imagination of a bureaucracy and has been put forward since Lenin's death by Stalin and Bukharin . . .

The CC issued a directive which in itself was *the most flagrant deviation from socialism*. The slogan of *complete* collectivization – irrespective of whether this was to be accomplished in fifteen years, as at first, or in one year, as was later decided – is itself the greatest economic nonsense. We are marxists, and we know that new forms of property can be founded only on the basis of new productive relations. But these new productive relations *still do not exist*. There are 50,000 tractors in the whole of the Union and the bulk of them belong to state farms. Taken together they cannot plough even 5 per cent of the existing sown area. Yet without a high technical basis, even collective farms obtaining state credit and possessing a poor peasant class character are liable to collapse.

The decree abolishing NEP and the kulaks as a class is another economic absurdity . . . Intensive collectivization was not necessary, just as the expansion of NEP is not necessary . . . On this question the difference between the centrists and the rightists is one of tempo: the rightists are proposing a consistently rightist policy, the centrists a policy with ultra-left intervals . . .

The whole political wisdom of the centrist and right-centrist leadership has consisted in suppressing the masses' feelings of political independence, human dignity and pride, and in encouraging and organizing the autocracy of the apparatus. The exceptional ingenuity of the centrist leadership and especially of the general secretary has been entirely devoted – and still is – to establishing this autocracy. The strength of the party leadership is in the party apparatus, but it is also the source of its weakness.

Source: Christian Rakovsky, Selected Writings on Opposition in the USSR *(London, Allison & Busby, 1980), pp. 162–3, 166, 168, 170, 173.*

While in certain respects accurate, above all in its characterisation of the new ruling elite, this analysis was also spectacularly misconceived: the so-called 'centrists' were pursuing far more than 'a policy with ultra-left intervals'. The damage inflicted on the rural economy contributed to the devastating famine of 1932–3 in Ukraine and the Kuban. Stalin continued to export grain, placed soldiers around the affected region, and refused to release strategic grain reserves until too late for the millions who died or who were reduced to cannibalism.

Industrialisation and the Creation of a New Intelligentsia

Collectivisation was justified on the grounds that grain could be exported to provide vital investment resources and to provide cheap food for the growing industrial working class, quite apart from its primary aim of eliminating the 'peasant contradiction', a workers' state dependent for supplies on a commodity-producing private peasantry. Grain collection in 1929 surpassed that of 1928 by 1.5 times, and in 1930 was double the 1928 level, most of which was exported to buy machines. The first five-year plan (FYP) was launched in 1928, yet its targets were soon doubled, tripled and accelerated to a fevered pace of industrial construction. This was not 'planning' in any serious sense but a command economy in the hands of leaders drugged by the power of steel. There was an enormous amount of waste and disruption that actually led to falls in output in some areas. Yet the first FYP was completed (officially) in four years and three months (January 1933), and the USSR joined the ranks of the industrial superpowers.

Document 5.7   Stalin on Industrialisation

Industrialisation was proceeding at a breakneck and equally wasteful pace. This was a period marked by huge achievements in terms of industrial objects built, but also by chaos and the wasteful use of resources. In the speech below Stalin outlined the need for traditional discipline and managerial authority, while at the same time stressing the security rationale for accelerated industrialisation.

A Bolshevik's word is his bond. Bolsheviks are in the habit of fulfilling their pledges. But what does the pledge to fulfil the control figures for 1931 mean? It means ensuring a general increase of industrial output by 45 per cent. And this is a very big task. More than that. Such a pledge means that you not only promise to fulfil our Five-Year Plan in four years – that is decided, and no more resolutions are needed on that score – *it means that you promise to fulfil it in three years in all the basic, decisive branches of industry* . . .

How is it that we Bolsheviks, who have made three revolutions, who emerged victorious from the bitter Civil War, who have swung the peasantry to the path of socialism – how is it that in the matter of directing production we bow to a slip of paper? The reason is that it is easier to sign papers than to direct production . . .

Life itself has more than once signalled that not all was well in this field. The Shakhty case showed that the Party organizations and the trade unions lacked revolutionary vigilance. It showed that our business executives were disgracefully backward in regard to the knowledge of technology; that some of the old engineers and technicians, working without supervision, were more prone to engage in wrecking activities, especially as they were constantly being besieged by 'offers' from our enemies abroad . . .

Hence, the task is for us to master technique ourselves, to become the masters of the job ourselves. This is the sole guarantee that our plans will be carried out in full, and that one-man management will be established.

This, of course, is no easy matter; but it can certainly be accomplished. Science, technical experience, knowledge, are all things that can be acquired. We may not have them today, but tomorrow we will. The main thing is to have the passionate Bolshevik desire to master technique, to master the science of production. Everything can be achieved, everything can be overcome, if there is a passionate desire to do so.

It is sometimes asked whether it is not possible to slow down the tempo somewhat, to put a check on the movement. No, comrades, it is not possible! The tempo must not be reduced! On the contrary, we must increase it as much as is within our powers and possibilities. This is dictated to us by our obligations to the workers and peasants of the USSR. This is dictated to us by our obligations to the working class of the whole world.

To slacken the tempo would mean falling behind. And those who fall behind get beaten. But we do not want to be beaten. No, we refuse to be beaten! One feature of the history of old Russia was the continual beatings she suffered because of her backwardness. She was beaten by the Mongol khans. She was beaten by the Turkish beys. She was beaten by the Swedish feudal lords. She was beaten by the Polish and Lithuanian gentry. She was beaten by the British and French capitalists. She was beaten by the Japanese barons. All beat her – for her backwardness: for military backwardness, for cultural backwardness, for political backwardness, for industrial backwardness, for agricultural backwardness. She was beaten because to do so was profitable and could be done with impunity . . . Such is the law of the exploiters – to beat the backward and the weak. It is the jungle law of capitalism. You are backward, you are weak – therefore you are wrong; hence, you can be beaten and enslaved. You are mighty – therefore you are right; hence, we must be wary of you.

That is why we must no longer lag behind.

In the past we had no fatherland, nor could we have one. But now that we have overthrown capitalism and power is in our hands, in the hands of the people, we have a fatherland, and we will defend its independence. Do you want our socialist fatherland to be beaten and to lose its independence? If you do not want this you must put an end to its backwardness in the shortest possible time and develop genuine Bolshevik tempo in building up its socialist system of economy. There is no other way. That is why Lenin said no on the eve of the October Revolution: 'Either perish, or overtake and outstrip the advanced capitalist countries.'

We are fifty or a hundred years behind the advanced countries. We must make good this distance in ten years. Either we do it, or we shall be crushed . . .

In ten years at most we must make good the distance which separates us from the advanced capitalist countries. We have all the 'objective' possibilities for this. The only thing lacking is the ability to take proper advantage of these possibilities. And that depends on us. *Only* on us! It is time we learned to take advantage of these possibilities. It is time to put an end to the rotten policy of non-interference in production. It is time to adopt a new policy, a policy adapted to the present times – the policy of interfering in everything. If you are a factory manager, then interfere in all the affairs of the factory, look into everything, let nothing escape you, learn and learn again. Bolsheviks must master technique. It is time Bolsheviks themselves became experts. In the period of reconstruction technique decides everything. And a business executive who does not want to study technique, who does not want to master technique, is a joke and not an executive.

It is said that it is hard to master technique. That is not true! There are no fortresses which Bolsheviks cannot capture. We have assumed power. We have built up a huge socialist industry. We have swung the middle peasants to the path of socialism. We have already accomplished what is most important from the point of view of construction. What remains to be done is not so much: to study technique, to master science. And when we have done that we will develop a tempo of which we dare not even dream at present. And we can do this if we really want to.

Source: Stalin, 'The Tasks of Business Executives', speech at the First All-Union Conference of Managers of Socialist Industry, 4 February 1931, in Problems of Leninism, *pp. 350, 354–5, 355–5, 357–8.*

Document 5.8   Against Wage Equality and the Creation of a New Intelligentsia

Traditional socialist notions of wage equality and collectivism were now jettisoned in favour of individual responsibility and incentives, a theme Stalin returned to later (Document 5.18). In June 1931 Stalin condemned *uravnilovka* ('wage-levelling' or 'equality-mongering'), allowing the development of wide wage differentials. What this had in common with Marxism remains disputed, and certainly reversed the Utopianism of *The ABC of Communism* (Document 3.17). In Soviet parlance *uravnilovka* joined the pantheon of sins against the Soviet state. The remnants of the tsarist intelligentsia were to be replaced by new Soviet-trained specialists. A 'proletarian advancement' (*vydvyzhenie*) movement was launched whereby workers were promoted to become engineers and administrators through a process of accelerated training. Universities and colleges were opened up to adults even if they lacked the necessary prerequisites. A massive new cohort of 'red specialists' (of whom Kravchenko was one) replaced the old generation of specialists and retained leadership positions for the next two generations. A new 'Soviet' intelligentsia came into being.

What is the cause of the heavy turnover of labour power?

The cause is the wrong structure of wages, the wrong wage scales, the 'leftist' practice of wage equalization. In a number of our factories wage scales are drawn up in such a way as practically to wipe out the difference between skilled and unskilled labour, between heavy and light work. The consequence of wage equalization is that the unskilled worker lacks the incentive to become a skilled worker and is thus deprived of the prospect of advancement; as a result he feels himself a 'sojourner' in the factory, working only temporarily so as to 'earn a little' and then go off to 'seek his fortune' elsewhere. The consequence of wage equalization is that the skilled worker is obliged to wander from factory to factory until he finds one where his skill is properly appreciated.

Hence, the 'general' drift from factory to factory; hence, the heavy turnover of labour power.

In order to put an end to this evil we must abolish wage equalization and discard the old wage scales. In order to put an end to this evil we must draw up wage scales that will take into account the difference between skilled and unskilled labour, between heavy and light work . . .

No ruling class has managed without its own intelligentsia. There are no grounds for believing that the working class of the USSR can manage without its own industrial and technical intelligentsia.

The Soviet government has taken this fact into account and has opened wide the doors of all the higher educational institutions in every branch of national economy to members of the working class and labouring peasantry. You know that tens of thousands of working class and peasant youths are now attending higher educational institutions. Formerly, under capitalism, the higher educational institutions were the monopoly of the scions of the rich – today, under the Soviet system, the working class and peasant youth predominate in these institutions. There is no doubt that our educational institutions will soon be turning out thousands of new technicians and engineers, new leaders for our industries.

Source: Stalin, 'New Conditions – New Tasks in Economic Construction', speech at a conference of business executives, 23 June 1931, in Problems of Leninism, *pp. 362–3, 369.*

Document 5.9   The Stakhanovite Movement

The Stakhanovite movement from 1935 served important functions in disciplining and inspiring workers. The subject of innumerable frenzied speeches and articles, the whole movement was a fraud from beginning to end. As an industrial manager, Kravchenko saw at first hand its artificial and disruptive character.

In September, 1935, a 'miracle' occurred in the Donetz Basin coal region. A worker named Stakhanov mined 102 tons of coal in one shift – fourteen times the normal output per miner! Few events in all modern history have been greeted with such sustained, hysterical and histrionic acclaim. It was, to be sure, a quite mundane miracle and a bit shabby at the edges. To a practical engineer the elements of deceit in it were fairly transparent. It was obvious that special conditions and special tools and assistance had been provided to enable Stakhanov to achieve the record. It was a miracle made to order for the Kremlin in launching a new religion – the religion of speed-up.

What Stakhanov had done, all miners could do! What miners could do all other industries could do! There you have a summary of the new religion. Doubters were damned and would not have to wait for the next life for their share of inferno. Technicians who raised practical objections were defeatists, enemies of Stakhanovism! Workers who could not toe the mark set by the Donetz miner were slackers!

Moscow screamed the new Stakhanovite slogans. Telegraphic orders began to pour into Nikopol from Kharkov and Moscow headquarters. Every order was a blunt threat. We must instantly create Stakhanovite brigades, as pace-setters for the slowpokes. Engineers or superintendents who raised objections would be treated as saboteurs . . .

In the end, in my own sub-plant, I was obliged to resort to artificial speed-up which, in my heart, I considered a crime against the machines and the workers alike. On direct orders from the Party Committee, I regrouped my labour, putting the best workers, foremen and engineers into one shift. Then we selected the best tools and materials, setting them aside for the special shift. Having thus stacked the cards, we gave the signal for the specious game to start.

At eleven o'clock one evening, with reporters and photographers present, the 'Stakhanovite' shift got under way. As expected, it 'overfulfilled' the normal quota by 8 per cent. There were flaming headlines. Congratulations arrived from officials in the capitals. Everyone breathed more freely – we had diverted the lightning. As the responsible technical leader I was given a lot of the credit.

But this 'victory' on the industrial front merely left me heartsick. It was, at bottom, fraudulent and must boomerang. The other two shifts, deprived of their best personnel and their best tools, lost more than the fevered group had won. By contrast they seemed ineffective if not actually 'lazy'. They naturally resented being made the scapegoats. They cursed the lucky ones and the officials.

Throughout the Soviet land the speed-up drive turned into a furious campaign unfolded in the familiar atmosphere of fright and repressions. Thousands of administrators were dismissed, many of them were arrested, for sabotage of the new 'socialist production' and for 'failure to provide the proper Stakhanovite conditions'. Every lag in output was blamed upon the engineers and technicians. The picture created in the public mind was that of workers eager to step up production but intentionally 'held back' by scheming managers.

A wedge was thus driven between workers and technical staffs.

Even to the simplest-minded factory hand or miner it was apparent that the new records set by forced speed-up would soon be set up as 'norms' for everybody.

Source: Kravchenko, I Chose Freedom, *p. 188.*

Cultural Transformation

Cultural transformation was an essential part of the revolution from above. The 1920s were marked by the relative diversity of intellectual life and a degree of tolerance of different views. This period came to an end at this time and strict controls were imposed over all aspects of creative work. The only approach allowed was that of class war. Communists and non-communists alike who evinced any independence from the party line were purged or imprisoned. Philosophers were among the first in the firing line, but the main emphasis was on controlling history.

Document 5.10   Bringing History to Order

In the infamous letter reproduced below Stalin brought the historical profession to heel. Condemning an article that had questioned Lenin's infallibility, Stalin made it clear that the pursuit of truth was no more than 'rotten liberalism', and that in future it would be the party that decided what was true or not.

Dear Comrades!

I emphatically protest against the publication in *Proletarskaya Revolyutsiya* (no. 6, 1930) of Slutsky's anti-party and semi-Trotskyite article, 'The Bolsheviks on German Social Democracy in the Period of its Prewar Crisis', as a discussion article.

Slutsky asserts that Lenin (the Bolsheviks) underestimated the danger of *centrism* in German Social Democracy and in prewar Social Democracy in general; that is, he underestimated the danger of camouflaged opportunism, the danger of conciliation with opportunism. In other words, according to Slutsky, Lenin (the Bolsheviks) did not wage a relentless struggle against opportunism, for, in essence, underestimation of centrism is tantamount to the renunciation of a forceful struggle against opportunism. Thus, it is suggested that in the period before the war Lenin was not yet a real Bolshevik; that it was only in the period of the imperialist war, or even at the close of that war, that Lenin became a real Bolshevik.

This is the tale Slutsky tells in his article. And you, instead of branding this new-found 'historian' as a slanderer and falsifier, enter into discussion with him, provide him with a forum. I cannot refrain from protesting against the publication of Slutsky's article in your journal as a discussion article, for the question of Lenin's *Bolshevism*, the question as to whether Lenin *did* or *did not* wage a relentless principled struggle against centrism as a certain form of opportunism, the question as to whether Lenin *was* or *was not* a real Bolshevik, cannot be made the subject of discussion . . . .

Everyone knows that Leninism was born, grew up and became strong in its ruthless struggle against opportunism of every brand, including centrism in the West (Kautsky) and centrism in our country (Trotsky, etc.). This cannot be denied even by the outspoken enemies of Bolshevism. It is an axiom. But you are trying to drag us back by turning an axiom into a problem requiring 'further analysis'. Why? On what grounds? Perhaps through ignorance of the history of Bolshevism? Perhaps for the sake of a rotten liberalism, so that the Slutskys and other disciples of Trotsky may not be able to say that they are being gagged? A rather strange sort of liberalism, this, exercised at the expense of the vital interests of Bolshevism . . . The more reliable method of testing the Bolsheviks by their deeds would have upset Slutsky's whole position in a flash.

Because a test of the Bolsheviks by their deeds would have shown that the Bolsheviks are the *only* revolutionary organisation in the world which has completely smashed the opportunists and centrists and driven them out of the Party . . . Because a test of the Bolsheviks by their deeds would have exposed Slutsky once and for all as a falsifier of the history of our party, who is trying to cover up the centrism of prewar Trotskyism by slanderously accusing Lenin and the Bolsheviks of underestimating the danger of centrism.

That, comrade editors, is how matters stand with Slutsky and his article. As you see, the editorial board made a mistake in permitting a discussion with a falsifier of the history of our party. What induced the editorial board to take this wrong road? I think that they were induced to take that road by the rotten liberalism which has spread to some extent among a section of the Bolsheviks. Some Bolsheviks think that Trotskyism is a faction of communism – one which makes mistakes, it is true, which does many foolish things, is sometimes even anti-Soviet, but which, nevertheless, is a faction of communism. Hence, there is a somewhat liberal attitude towards the Trotskyites and Trotskyite-minded people. It need hardly be proved that such a view of Trotskyism is profoundly wrong and pernicious. As a matter of fact, Trotskyism has long ceased to be a faction of communism. As a matter of fact, Trotskyism is the vanguard of the counter-revolutionary bourgeoisie which is fighting communism, fighting the Soviet regime, fighting the building of socialism in the USSR.

Source: Stalin, 'Some Questions Concerning the History of Bolshevism', Letter to the Editorial Board of Proletarian Revolution, no. 6, 1931, in Problems of Leninism, pp. 378, 379, 368–9.

Document 5.11   Teaching History

In reaction against M. N. Pokrovskii's Marxist materialist and anti-nationalist version of Russian history, Stalin insisted on a far more conventional narrative form, no longer emphasising so much the role of class forces as the achievements of individual rulers. This was accompanied by the rehabilitation of Russian history as such, of its national achievements, with less emphasis on its exploitative role in social and national relations.

The Council of People's Commissars of the USSR and the Central Committee of the All-Union Communist Party (Bolsheviks) find that the teaching of history in schools of the USSR is not conducted satisfactorily. The textbooks and the instruction have an abstract, schematic character. Instead of the teaching of civil history in a lively, engaging form with an exposition of the most important events and facts in their chronological sequence, with characterisations of historical personages, the pupils are presented with abstract definitions of socio-economic formations, which thus replace the connected exposition of civic history with abstract sociological schemes.

The decisive condition of a firm mastery of the history course by the pupils is the observance of historical and chronological sequence in the exposition of historical events, with mandatory consolidation in the pupils' memory of important historical events, historical personages, and chronological dates. Only such a history course can ensure to the pupils the necessary understanding, clarity, and concreteness of historical material, on which basis alone is it possible to have the correct analysis and correct generalisations about historical events that will lead pupils to a Marxist understanding of history.

*Source: Decree 'On the Teaching of Civic History in the Schools of the USSR',
16 May 1934*, Pravda, *17 May 1934, in Daniels,* Communism in Russia, *p. 242.*

Pokrovskii died in 1932 and thus escaped the purges, although this did not prevent his posthumous denunciation in 1936. The Soviet attempt to shape history was part of the strategy of maintaining power over society. The loss of control over the past, as we shall see in our discussion of *glasnost*, contributed to the loss of power in the present.

Document 5.12   Socialist Realism

Literature was clearly a central concern of the attempt to create a new Soviet culture. In 1934 a Union of Soviet Writers was established that superseded the rich network of literary organisations with a single bureaucratically organised body. Writers, as Gorky put it at the founding congress, were to become 'engineers of the human soul'. The only acceptable literary style became 'socialist realism'.

The party leadership of literature must be thoroughly purged of all philistine influences. Party members active in literature must not only be the teachers of ideas which will muster the energy of the proletariat in all countries for the last battle for its freedom; the party leadership must, in all its conduct, show a morally authoritative force. This force must imbue literary workers first and foremost with a consciousness of their collective responsibility for all that happens in their midst. Soviet literature, with all its diversity of talents, and the steadily growing number of new and gifted writers, should be organised as an integral collective body, as a potent instrument of socialist culture.

The Writers' Union is not being created merely for the purpose of bodily uniting all artists of the pen, but so that professional unification may enable them to comprehend their corporate strength, to define with all possible clarity their varied tendencies, creative activity, guiding principles, and harmoniously to merge all aims in that unity which is guiding all the creative working energies of the country . . .

The proletarian state must educate thousands of first-class 'craftsmen of culture', 'engineers of the soul'. This is necessary in order to restore to the whole mass of the working people the right to develop their intelligence, talents and faculties – a right of which they have been deprived everywhere else in the world. This aim, which is a fully practicable one, imposes on us writers the need of strict responsibility for our work and our social behaviour. This places us not only in the position, traditional to realist literature, of 'judges of the world and men', 'critics of life', but gives us the right to participate directly in the construction of a new life, in the process of 'changing the world'. The possession of this right should impress every writer with a sense of his duty and responsibility for all literature, for all the aspects in it which should not be there.

Source: Gorky, 'Soviet Literature', speech at the First All-Union Congress of Soviet Writers, August 1934, in Daniels, Communism in Russia, *pp. 245–6, 247.*

Social Conservatism

Timasheff called this period 'the great retreat', as the Stalinist system became more socially conservative, repudiating the revolutionary maximalism of the left radicals and coopting the force of nationalism. But this can only be termed a 'retreat' in a very abstract sense of the term; in practice, the Stalinist system consolidated itself as a new social order. In response to the horrors of collectivisation and the brutalisation of political life, Bukharin returned to 'proletarian humanist' themes.

Document 5.13   Social Policy

In social policy the earlier libertarian approach gave way to socially conservative policies. Abortion was banned and a new stress was placed on the sanctity of the family.

The published draft of the law prohibiting abortion and providing material assistance to mothers has provoked a lively reaction throughout the country. It is being heatedly discussed by tens of millions of people and there is no doubt that it will serve as a further strengthening of the Soviet family. Parents' responsibility for the education of their children will be increased and a blow will be dealt at the lighthearted, negligent attitude toward marriage.

When we speak of strengthening the Soviet family, we are speaking precisely of the struggle against the survivals of a bourgeois attitude toward marriage, women and children. So-called 'free love' and all disorderly sex life are bourgeois through and through, and have nothing to do with either socialist principles or the ethics and standards of conduct of the Soviet citizen. Socialist doctrine shows this, and it is proved by life itself.

The *elite* of our country, the best of the Soviet youth, are as a rule also excellent family men who dearly love their children. And *vice versa*: the man who does not take marriage seriously, and abandons his children to the whims of fate, is usually also a bad worker and a poor member of society . . .

More than once the enemies of the people suggested to us the foul and poisonous ideal of liquidating the family and disrupting marriage. The bourgeoisie has tried to use it as a weapon in the struggle against socialist progress. It is enough to recall with what persistence they spread the slander about the 'nationalisation of women'. And during the great move to collectivise the villages, the kulaks again broadcast this favourite bourgeois allegation. The kulaks used it to scare the peasants: 'In the collective farms you will all sleep under the same 30-yard-wide blanket.'

Source: Discussion of the Law on the Abolition of Legal Abortion, editorials in Pravda, *28 May and June 1936, in Daniels,* Communism in Russia, *pp. 247–8.*

Document 5.14   Consolidating Soviet Nationalism

An essential part of the 'great retreat' was the assertion of a distinctive type of Soviet nationalism that used Russian symbols to consolidate the Soviet system. Militant Soviet nationalism was the basis of the purges in which 'betrayal of the motherland' was as heinous a crime as 'counter-revolutionary activity'. The attempt to escape *out* of the country was considered as undesirable as attempts to infiltrate in. Note how family members were held responsible for the acts of one of its members, and the draconian nature of the penalties.

The defence of the fatherland is the supreme law of life. And he who raises his hand against his country, he who betrays his country should be destroyed. Today we publish the decree of the Central Executive Committee of the USSR regarding the supplementing of the statutes of the state criminal code with articles on treason. The Soviet country is very dear to the workers and kolkhozniks [collective farmers]. They have paid for it dearly in blood and suffering in their struggle with exploiters and interventionists and they will not allow anyone to betray their country and will not allow anyone to bargain with her interests.

For high treason, for acts detrimental to the country's military might, or state independence, or inviolability of her territories, for espionage, for divulging military or state secrets, for deserting to the enemy, or escaping across the border, the Soviet court will punish the guilty by shooting or by confiscating all his property. In the case of a civilian, some leniency will be shown according to circumstances, and for the death penalty will be substituted the confiscation of his property or imprisonment for ten years. For a person in military service, however, for treason there will be only one measure of punishment – execution by shooting with confiscation of all his property. Individual members of his family are also responsible for the acts of traitors. In the case of the escape or flight across the border of a person in military service, all mature members of his family, if they are implicated in aiding the criminal, or knew of his intentions and did not report them to the authorities, are punished by imprisonment for five to ten years with confiscation of all their property. The other members of the family of the traitor and all his dependants at the time he committed treason are subject to disfranchisement and exile to some remote region in Siberia for five years.

Source: 'For the Fatherland!', Pravda, 9 June 1934, in Daniels, Communism in Russia, *pp. 243–4.*

Document 5.15   The Assault on Religion Continues

John Brown was a labour activist who went to Germany and Soviet Russia to see for himself how the Nazi and communist systems worked in practice. His Soviet trip was funded by Lord Nuffield, formerly Sir William Morris, the founder and pro-prietor of the huge Morris Motors works in Oxford. One of his companions on the ship to Russia was Lord Passfield (Sidney Webb), whose lecture to the passengers was 'The Experiment in the USSR' in which he argued that the rebuilding of the state after the anarchy of 1917 was the 'extremity of gradualness' (p. 180). By experiment he meant that the system 'was still working out' (p. 181). Brown considered himself a man of the people and his account of life in the Soviet Union has an unusual immediacy and directness.

Religion is being definitely stamped out everywhere in the USSR – of that there can be no question, in spite of official denials and ambiguities. Communist apologists repeatedly declare that in Russia the churches are still open. No one is prevented from worshipping, they say, the only changes being the withdrawal of State grants to the Church and the ban on religious instruction in the schools.

There was a certain amount of justification for these apologetics up to 1933, but in the last two years anti-religious pressure has been greatly extended, and the absolute extinction of all forms of religion is promised for 1937.

Even before 1933 all kinds of indirect anti-religious influence had been exerted. Thus no believers could be members of the Communist Party, and this rule debarred them from positions of even local importance.

Priests and others who practised religious ceremonies were denied citizenship and refused ration cards – being compelled to live on charity or as salesmen in the 'open market' – which brought them into fresh difficulties.

The continual militantly atheistical Press, cinema, and radio propaganda, the closing of many of the churches, the ridiculing of Christianity in the schools, and the opening of anti-God museums in every town had a cumulative effect on the mass mind which displayed itself in excesses in various republics . . .

In Kazan, capital of the Tartar Republic, where Mohammedanism was very strong well after 1917, the mosques were shut up, although I was told that one of them was still used. In this city in 1917 there had been sixty

Russian churches. Today there are six – and these are to be transformed into 'public offices' in the next two years.

In the southern towns many of the older people are still believers, but the younger generation, which has been trained in the atheist schools, is bitterly hostile to all forms of worship, and any kind of spiritual faith is ridiculed as '*bourgeois* ideology'.

Source: John Brown, I Saw for Myself *(London, Selwyn and Blount, n.d.), pp. 218–19, 219–20.*

Document 5.16   The Defeat of Time

Stalinism represented the triumph of human endeavour over the physical environment. One of the classics of early Stalinist literature celebrating the building of socialism was Kataev's novel *Forward, Oh Time!*, reflecting the belief that through the hard work of this generation in building a modern industrial infrastructure, generations to come would enjoy a better life. Happiness was measured in tons of steel produced, a theme reflected in another representative novel of the time, Nikolai Ostrovsky's *How the Steel Was Tempered*. Note the staccato, breathless style considered proper for a direct, proletarian approach in the school of socialist realism.

There would be a flagstone under the fifth battery. On the flagstone sixty-nine coke ovens would be erected. Blast furnaces need coke. The blast furnaces were being put together. The mountain would be blown up. The ore would be extracted. The ore would go into the blast furnaces. The coke would be lighted. Molten iron would flow. The molten iron would be boiled into steel. They would make rails, wagons, saws, axes, ploughs, machines.

And all this would be for the needs, for the happiness of 'him'.

To make life happy, it was not enough to say good words. It was not enough. One needed steel, steel, steel! With steel, there will be a new, happy life, a life that has never been before, a life that has never been seen before!

And all this was for 'him'. And 'he' – that is I. And 'he' and I – are we. And we – that is life!

Until now, life had gone by like a river, from backwater to backwater, from lake to lake. Time was life. Life flowed as it wished. When it wished, it flowed slowly. When it wished, it flowed swiftly.

Now Ishchenko opened his eyes, and, for the first time in his life, looked down the entire length of time. It flowed too slowly. But it flowed for him. The past flowed for the future.

And it lay securely in his hands.

Oh, how good life was, after all!

Source: Valentine Kataev, Forward, Oh Time!, *translated by Charles Malamuth (London, Victor Gollancz, 1934), pp. 175–6.*

Anticipating the Terror

The debate over the origins and logic of the purges continues. Were they provoked by Stalin's paranoia and morbid suspiciousness, or was there a deeper purpose behind them? Alarmed by the rise of Nazism in Germany, was Stalin securing the rear by destroying all potential opponents, or were the purges no more than the logical outcome of the establishment of an all-powerful bureaucratic system?

Document 5.17   The 'Ryutin Group'

Amid the imagined plots against Stalin there were genuine expressions of dissatisfaction with his personalised regime of terror. Already in late 1929 Beso Lominadze and Sergei Syrtsov, formerly Stalin's supporters, gave voice to their concerns; they were denounced and expelled from the Central Committee. In 1932 a group around Mikhail Ryutin, calling itself 'The Union of Marxists-Leninists', called for a shift of priorities from industry and agriculture to consumer goods. There appeared to be growing pressure for a relaxation of the pressure against society following the successful completion of collectivisation and the first stages of industrialisation. Alarmed by the analysis reproduced below, for the first time Stalin demanded the death penalty against a ranking party oppositionist; the Politburo refused his wish and Ryutin was sentenced to ten years in the Gulag. This was to be one of the last times that Stalin's bloodthirsty vengefulness was thwarted.

Stalin and the Crisis of the Proletarian Dictatorship

A regime of unheard of terror and colossal spying, achieved through an extraordinarily centralised and ramified gigantic apparatus, concentrating in its hands all the material resources of the country and placing in direct dependence on itself the physical survival of tens of millions of people, this is the main basis of Stalin's dictatorship. The whole state apparatus, including the party, terrorises others and at the same time itself lives under the constant Damocles sword of terror, is like a machine, despite the consciousness of each individual cell, forced to move and fulfil the will of the 'mechanic'.

But having entered a dead end and established throughout the country, in the most diverse forms, the dominance of terror, Stalin has deprived himself of any path of retreat or the possibility of an evolutionary outcome of the crisis. He has placed himself on a pedestal like an infallible pope and cannot admit either the criminality of his policies or even the smallest mistake. The dictator cannot make a mistake – only his subordinates can be at fault . . .

In practice the sum of measures required to remove the party and the country from the crisis and the dead end can be summarised as follows:

I In the party sphere.
1 The elimination of Stalin's dictatorship and that of his clique.
2 The immediate replacement of the entire leadership of the party apparatus and new elections to party organs on the basis of genuine intra-party

democracy and the establishment of firm organisational guarantees against the usurpation of the rights of the party by the party apparatus.

3 An immediate emergency party congress.

4 The decisive and immediate return of the party to Leninist principles on all questions.

II In the state sphere.

1 Immediate new elections to the soviets with the decisive and genuine removal of appointees.

2 The replacement of the judicial apparatus and the introduction of strict revolutionary legality.

3 The replacement and severe purge of the GPU apparatus.

III In the sphere of industrialisation.

1 The immediate end of anti-Leninist methods of industrialisation and playing with tempos at the expense of the impoverishment of the working class, employees and the countryside, provided for by direct and indirect, open and masked but equally intolerable taxes and inflation. The achievement of industrialisation on the basis of the genuine and steady growth in the well-being of the masses.

2 Bringing investment and capital construction into correspondence with the general condition of all available resources of the country.

Sources: Reabilitatsiya: politicheskie protsessy 30–50gg *(Moscow, Politizdat, 1989), pp. 434, 440;* Istoriya otechestva v dokumentakh 1917–1993gg, *vol. 2 (Moscow, Ilbi, 1994), pp. 119–21.*

Document 5.18   'The Congress of Victors'

The Seventeenth Party Congress met in January 1934. The storm of collectivisation appeared over, at enormous cost the first stages of the country's industrialisation had been completed, but Stalin insisted that vigilance against 'the remnants of capitalism' should not only be maintained but intensified. As far as Stalin was concerned, 'cadres decide everything'. Stalin remained associated with a policy of pressure and the intensification of the class struggle. Sergei Kirov, the leader of the Leningrad party organisation since 1926 when he had replaced Zinoviev, emerged as the putative leader of a policy of reconciliation and the end of Stalin's personal tyranny.

Comrades, more than three years have passed since the Sixteenth Congress. That is not a very long period. But it has been fuller in content than any other period . . .

While in the capitalist countries the economic crisis is still raging, the USSR is advancing steadily both in the sphere of industry and in the sphere of agriculture. While in the capitalist countries feverish preparations are in progress for a new war, for a new redivision of the world and of spheres of influence, the USSR is continuing its systematic and persistent struggle against the menace of war and for peace; and it cannot be said that the efforts of the USSR in this sphere have been entirely unsuccessful . . .

During this period, the USSR has become radically transformed and has cast off the integument of backwardness and medievalism. From an agrarian country it has become an industrial country. From a country of small individual agriculture it has become a country of collective, large-scale mechanized agriculture. From an ignorant, illiterate and uncultured country it has become – or rather it is becoming – a literate and cultured country covered by a vast network of higher, intermediate and elementary schools teaching in the languages of the nationalities of the USSR . . .

More than 200,000 collective farms and 5,000 state farms have been organized, with new district centres and industrial centres serving them . . . Unemployment, that scourge of the working class, has disappeared . . . With the disappearance of kulak bondage, poverty in the countryside has disappeared . . .

I now come to the question of the Party . . . The anti-Leninist Trotskyite group has been defeated . . . The anti-Leninist group of Right deviationists have been defeated and scattered . . . The national deviationist groups have been defeated and scattered . . . Everyone now sees that the line of the Party has triumphed. (*Loud applause.*) . . .

A number of problems of Leninism could be taken to demonstrate the tenacity of the survivals of the ideology of the defeated anti-Leninist groups in the minds of certain Party members. Take, for example, the problem of building a *classless Socialist society* . . . It goes without saying that a classless society cannot come of itself, spontaneously, as it were. It has to be achieved and built by the efforts of all the working people, by strengthening the organs of the dictatorship of the proletariat, by intensifying the class struggle, by abolishing classes, by eliminating the remnants of the capitalist classes, and in battles with enemies both internal and external . . .

These people evidently think that Socialism calls for levelling the requirements and the individual lives of the members of society. Needless to say, such an assumption has nothing in common with Marxism, with Leninism. By equality Marxism means, not equalization of individual requirements and individual life, but the abolition of class . . .

Or take, for example, the *national problem* . . . It should be observed that the survivals of capitalism in people's minds are much more tenacious in the sphere of the national problem than in any other sphere. They are more tenacious because they are able to disguise themselves well in national costume . . . The deviation towards nationalism reflects the attempts of 'one's own' 'national' bourgeoisie to undermine the Soviet system and to restore capitalism . . .

As you see, here too, in the sphere of deviations from the line of the Party – regardless of whether they are deviations on general policy or deviations on the national problem – the survivals of capitalism in people's minds, including the minds of certain members of our Party, are quite tenacious . . .

Now that the correctness of the Party's political line has been confirmed by the experience of a number of years, and that there is no longer any doubt as to the readiness of the workers and peasants to support this line, the part played by so-called objective conditions has been reduced to a minimum; whereas the part played by our organizations and their leaders has become decisive, exceptional. What does this mean? It means that from now on nine-tenths of the responsibility for the failures and defects in our work rests, not on 'objective' conditions, but on ourselves, and on ourselves alone . . . the main thing in organizational work is – *choosing the right people and keeping a check on the fulfilment of decisions.*

Source: Stalin, 'Report on the Work of the CC to the Seventeenth Congress of the CPSU(b)', 26 January 1934, in Problems of Leninism, *pp. 454, 455, 470, 471, 489, 497, 499, 506, 508, 510, 512.*

Document 5.19   The Murder of Kirov

The murder of Kirov in December 1934 signalled the beginning of the great purges. He was shot by a disaffected former Zinovievite called Leonid Nikolaev, apparently with Stalin's connivance and probably with his support. Kirov appeared to support a relaxation of coercive policies of the type suggested by Ryutin. At the Seventeenth Party Congress (the 'congress of victors') in February 1934 he emerged as a popular alternative to Stalin. The depth of disenchantment is revealed by Kravchenko's comment about this period.

But whatever the immediate cause or the deeper motivations of Nicolayev's shot, to thinking Communists it seemed a symbol of the desperations under the policed surface of their country's life. Each of us knew the bitterness and despair in his own heart. Sometimes we dared to share our doubts in twos and threes. It took the murder of one of Stalin's closest associates to make us conscious that our private griefs were part of the great subterranean river of discontent flowing through the heart of a vast nation.

Outwardly everything was tranquil. Critics from the Left and the Right had been crushed and Stalin, Our Sun, shone benignly over a united Party. The peasant had been whipped into surly submission by firing squads and famine. No murmur of protest was any longer heard about the killing tempo of industrialisation, the food shortage, the hardships, the mass arrests. But inwardly many in the Party and the nation seethed with resentment. Under the stupor of indifference, under the crust of silent despair, there was the hot lava of primitive angers.

This should be made clear to the world in ordinary justice to the Russian people. They were impotent in their suffering; weakened by twenty years of war, revolution, undernourishment and systematic persecutions, dizzied by slogans and bewildered by lies; cut off completely from the outside world. Yet they never approved the brutality of their rulers. The bitterness was deepest in the Party itself, because it was mixed with a feeling of guilt and churned by galling helplessness against the rulers and their might.

It was no accident that Nicolayev and those accused of direct complicity in his crime were all young people, products of the Soviet epoch, mostly students. Traditionally the higher schools of Russia have been the breeding ground of revolutionary idealism. Now such idealism was called counter revolutionary but it was still in the same tradition.

Source: Kravchenko, I Chose Freedom, *p. 168.*

Document 5.20   Bukharin's Assessment of Kirov and Stalin

Boris Nicolaevsky was a former Menshevik who had emigrated to Paris. On a visit there in 1936 at the head of a Soviet delegation Bukharin apparently shared his feelings with Nicolaevsky. The conversation was published in the form of a 'Letter of an Old Bolshevik', which gives a vivid picture of the politics of the period, although it might appear that some of the statements were more the product of wishful thinking than fact. Nicolaevsky in this and other works revealed the depth of the intra-party struggle against Stalin between 1932 and 1934, the background to Kirov's murder and its significance.

Kirov played an important part in the Politburo. He was a 100 percent supporter of the general line and distinguished himself during its operation by great energy and inflexibility. This caused Stalin to value him highly. But there was always a certain independence in Kirov's attitude which annoyed Stalin. The story is that Stalin had prevented Kirov from attending the meetings of the Politburo in Moscow for several months under the pretext that his presence in Leningrad was indispensable. However, Stalin could never make up his mind to take strong measures against Kirov. It would have been folly to add to the already large number of the dissatisfied an important party leader such as Kirov, especially since Kirov had succeeded in surrounding himself in Leningrad with reliable and devoted aides. A new conflict with the Leningrad party might have been more fatal now than in Zinoviev's day. In the winter of 1933–34, Kirov had so strengthened his position that he could afford to follow his own line. He aimed not only at a 'Western orientation' in foreign policy, but also at the conclusions which would follow logically from this new orientation as far as home policy was concerned . . .

Kirov stood for the idea of *abolition of the terror*, both in general and inside the Party. We do not desire to exaggerate the importance of his proposals. It must not be forgotten that when the first Five-Year Plan was being put into effect, Kirov was one of the heads of the Party, that he was among those who inspired and carried through the notoriously ruthless measures against the peasants and the wiping out of the kulaks. The Kem and Murmansk coasts, with their prison camps, and so forth, were under his jurisdiction. Furthermore, he was in charge of the construction of the Baltic–White Sea Canal. This is enough to make it clear that Kirov could not be reproached with any undue tenderness in the manner in which he disposed of human lives. But this very fact added to his strength in the official circles in which he had to defend his point of view. That he had so large a share of responsibility in the horrors of the First Five-Year Plan made it possible for him to come forward as a leader and protagonist of the policy of moderating the terror during the Second Five-Year Plan. Kirov's line of thought ran as follows: The period of destruction, which was necessary to extirpate the small proprietor elements in the villages, was now at an end; the economic position of the collectives was consolidated and made secure for the future. This constituted a firm basis for future development, and as the economic situation continued to improve, the broad masses of the population would become more and more reconciled to the government; the number of 'internal foes' would diminish. It was now the task of the party to rally those forces which would support it in the new phase of economic development, and thus to broaden the foundation upon which Soviet power was based. Kirov, therefore, strongly advocated reconciliation with those Party elements who, during the period of the First Five-Year Plan, had gone over to the Opposition, but who might be induced to cooperate on the new basis, now that the 'destructive' phase was over . . .

Hence, early in the summer of 1933, when it became certain that the harvest would be good, Kamenev, Zinoviev and a number of other former members of the Opposition were once again readmitted as members of the Party. They were even permitted to choose their spheres of work, and some of them actually received invitations to the [seventeenth] party congress (February, 1934).

At that congress Kirov appeared in triumph . . . Kirov received an extraordinarily enthusiastic reception. He was cheered, the entire assembly rising to its feet on hearing his report. During the recess there was discussion as to who had the more tumultuous reception, Kirov or Stalin. This very comparison shows how strong Kirov's influence had already become . . .

More could be said about Kirov's murder that would undoubtedly make very interesting reading, for this unfortunate shot ushered in a new period in the history of the Soviet Union . . .

In these circumstances, it looked at first as though the continued terror inside the Party was only an unpleasant accident, a belated and exaggerated aftermath of Nikolaev's shot, and not a symptom of the impending radical change in the entire policy of the Party. All were convinced that the logic of the policy of reconciliation with the intelligentsia would ultimately be bound to induce the Party leadership to take the path of internal Party reconciliation as well. All that was necessary (it was believed) was for Stalin's acute crisis of morbid mistrust to pass. To this end, it was maintained, the loyalty of the Party to its present leadership must be stressed as often and as emphatically as possible; that the thing to do was to burn incense before Stalin and extol his person on all occasions. The argument ran as follows: He has a weakness for such adulation and his vengefulness can be appeased only by huge doses of flattery, laid on with a trowel; there is nothing else to be done about it. Moreover, it was added, we must learn to forgive these trifles because of the big things Stalin has done for the Party in guiding it through the critical years of the First Five-Year Plan, and at the same time we must speak ever louder and with increasing emphasis of the tremendous changes now taking place, of the new 'happy days' into which we were now entering, of the new Party policy, the basis of which was to cultivate in the masses feelings of human dignity, respect for human personality, and the development of 'proletarian humanism.' Alas, how naive were all these hopes of ours! Looking back now, we find it hard to understand how we could have failed to note the symptoms which indicated that the trend was in quite the opposite direction: not toward reconciliation inside the Party, but toward intensification of the terror inside the Party to its logical conclusion, to the stage of *physical extermination of all those whose Party past might make them opponents of Stalin or aspirants to his power.* Today, I have not the slightest doubt that it was at that very period, between the murder of Kirov and the second Kamenev trial, that Stalin made his decision and mapped out his plan of 'reforms,' an essential component part of which was the trial of the sixteen and other trials yet to come. If, before the murder of Kirov, Stalin still had some hesitation as to which road to choose, he had now made up his mind.

The determining reason for Stalin's decision was his realization, arrived at on the basis of reports and information reaching him, that the mood of the majority of the old Party workers was really one of bitterness and hostility toward him.

The trials and investigations which followed the Kirov affair had demonstrated unmistakably that the Party had not reconciled itself to Stalin's personal dictatorship; that, in spite of all their solemn declarations, the old Bolsheviks rejected Stalin in the depths of their hearts, that this attitude of hostility, instead of diminishing, was growing, and that the majority of those who cringed before him, protesting devotion, would betray him at the first change of the political atmosphere.

Source: Boris Nicolaevsky, 'Letter of an Old Bolshevik', in Power and the Soviet Elite *(New York, Praeger, 1965), pp. 31–5, 37, 59–60.*

Document 5.21   Bukharin on Humanism

Nicolaevsky's account of his discussions with Bukharin presents the latter as a man who had finally understood that the logic of Bolshevik terror would hasten him and many more other supporters of the revolution to an early grave. His turn to 'humanism', together with his earlier advocacy of a gradualist path to socialism through NEP, made him a symbol of an unfulfilled alternative path of Soviet development, an alternative that finally appeared to be realised by Alexander Dubček in the 'Prague spring' of 1968 and under Gorbachev in the 1980s. By then, however, it was at least fifty years too late.

On another occasion in Paris, he [Bukharin] was to deliver a speech on the goals of Communism. In this speech, which was never published in Russian, he emphasized the humanist idea even more forcefully. I happened to go to see him while he was finishing his preparation of this speech. 'If you like,' he said, 'I'll read you what I've been writing just now. It has a direct relation to our conversations.' I said that of course I wanted to hear it, and he read some passages to me. When he finished, I said to him, 'Nikolai Ivanovich, that's what we've been talking about – humanism, the return to humanism.' He replied that in the early days they had rebelled against humanism. And indeed, if we take the literature of 1917–20, this was a revolt against humanism, and not only by Bukharin, not only by Gorky, but also by the poet Alexander Blok and many others. Bukharin went on to say that everything passes through difficult stages. Earlier, destructiveness was necessary and the struggle against humanism inevitable. But now we have entered a different period, he said, when we are faced by tasks of construction. They demand the reorganization of our entire outlook. Not only our Communism but also your Socialism must, he continued, become rooted in this humanist base, like the Communism of Marx.

I made no objection to these ideas. I myself had arrived at them before, during Hitler's attack on German democracy. In February, 1933, on the eve of Hitler's accession to power, a friend and I put out a book about the young Marx, the main idea of which was that he was a humanist. Bukharin read my little book and I think that to a certain extent he shared my feelings.

Source: Nicolaevsky, 'An Interview With Boris Nicolaevsky', in Power and the Soviet Elite, *pp. 17–19.*

Document 5.22   The 1936 Constitution

Bukharin was secretary of the commission that drafted the 1936 constitution and he was its guiding spirit. The new constitution was adopted on 5 December 1936, and the first elections to the new Supreme Soviet were held in December of the following year. Universal and equal suffrage was introduced and the principle of the equality of all citizens before the law conceded, thus ending formal discrimination against non-proletarians. Special privileges for the Communist Party were not incorporated in the constitution, and there had even been talk of allowing multi-candidate elections. As part of his 'return to humanism', Bukharin now appeared to advocate the need for a second party composed of the intelligentsia, not opposed to the regime but acting as a force for innovation and remedies. In conversation with Nicolaevsky Bukharin said:

> Some second party is necessary. If there is only one election slate and there is no contest, it is the same as Nazism. In order to differentiate ourselves in the minds of the peoples of both Russia and the West, we must institute a system of two electoral slates as opposed to the one-party system.
>
> (Nicolaevsky, p. 15)

This did not take place, and, as Nicolaevsky puts it, 'Bukharin underestimated his opponent and did not foresee how cunningly Stalin would apply these principles, perverting equality of all before the law into the equality of Communists and non-Communists before the absolute dictatorship of Stalin' (Nicolaevsky, p. 22).

Chapter I: The Structure of Society

Article 1. The Union of Soviet Socialist Republics is a socialist state of workers and peasants.

Article 2. The political foundation of the USSR consists of soviets of working people's deputies, which grew up and became strong as a result of the overthrow of the power of landlords and capitalists and the winning of the dictatorship of the proletariat.

Article 3. All power in the USSR belongs to the working people of town and country as represented by soviets of working people's deputies.

Article 4. The economic foundation of the USSR consists of the socialist economic system and the socialist ownership of the tools and means of production, firmly established as a result of the liquidation of the capitalist economic system, the abolition of private ownership of the tools and means of production, and the abolition of the exploitation of man by man.

Article 5. Socialist property in the USSR has either the form of state property (the wealth of the whole people) or the form of cooperative-collective property (property of separate collective farms, property and cooperative associations) . . .

Article 11. The economic life of the USSR is determined and directed by a state plan of national economy in the interests of increasing the public wealth, of steadily raising the material and cultural standard of the working people, and of strengthening the independence of the USSR and its capacity for defence.

Article 12. Work in the USSR is a duty and a matter of honour for every able-bodied citizen, on the principle: He who does not work shall not eat.

Chapter II: The Structure of the State

Article 13. The Union of Soviet Socialist Republics is a federal state, formed on the basis of the voluntary union of the following Soviet Socialist Republics equal in rights: . . .

Article 15. The sovereignty of the constituent republics shall be restricted only within the limits set forth in Article 14 of the constitution of the USSR. Outside of these limits, each constituent republic shall exercise state power independently. The USSR shall protect the sovereign rights of the constituent republics.

Article 16. Each constituent republic shall have its own constitution, which shall take into account the peculiarities of the republic and be drawn up in full conformity with the constitution of the USSR.

Article 17. The right freely to secede from the USSR is reserved to each constituent republic.

Article 18. The territory of the constituent republics may not be altered without their consent.

Article 19. The laws of the USSR shall have like force in the territories of all constituent republics.

Article 20. In case of conflict between a law of a constituent republic and a law of the Union, the All-Union law shall prevail.

Article 21. A single Union citizenship is established for all citizens of the USSR. Every citizen of a constituent republic is a citizen of the USSR . . .

Chapter X: Basic Rights and Duties of Citizens

Article 118. Citizens of the USSR have the right to work, that is, the right to guaranteed employment and payment for their work in accordance with its quantity and quality.

The right to work is ensured by the socialist organisation of the national economy, the steady growth of the productive forces of soviet society, the elimination of the possibility of economic crises, and the abolition of unemployment.

Article 119. Citizens of the USSR have the right to rest.

The right to rest is ensured by the reduction of the working day to seven hours for the overwhelming majority of the workers, the institution of annual vacations with pay for workers and other employees, and the provision of a wide network of sanatoria, rest homes and clubs serving the needs of the working people.

Article 120. Citizens of the USSR have the right to material security in old age, and also in case of sickness or loss of capacity to work.

This right is ensured by the wide development of social insurance of workers and other employees at state expense, free medical service for the working people, and the provision of a wide network of health resorts at the disposal of the working people.

Article 121. Citizens of the USSR have the right to education.

This right is ensured by universal compulsory elementary education, by education free of charge including higher education, by a system of state stipends for the overwhelming majority of students in higher schools, by instruction in schools in the native language, and by the organisation in factories, state farms, machine-tractor stations and collective farms of free industrial, technical and agricultural education for the working people.

Article 122. Women in the USSR are accorded equal rights with men in all spheres of economic, state, cultural, social and political life.

The realisation of these rights of women is ensured by affording women equally with men the right to work, payment for work, rest, social insurance and education, and by state protection of the interests of mother and child, pregnancy leave with pay, and the provision of a wide network of maternity homes, nurseries and kindergartens.

Article 123. Equal rights for citizens of the USSR, irrespective of their nationality or race, in all spheres of economic, state, cultural, social and political life, shall be an irrevocable law.

Any direct or indirect limitation of these rights, or, conversely, any establishment of direct or indirect privileges for citizens on account of their race or nationality, as well as any propagation of racial or national exclusiveness or hatred and contempt, shall be punished by law.

Article 124. In order to ensure to citizens freedom of conscience, the church in the USSR shall be separated from the state, and the school from the church. Freedom of religious worship and freedom of anti-religious propaganda shall be recognised for all citizens.

Article 125. In accordance with the interests of the working people, and in order to strengthen the socialist system, the citizens of the USSR are guaranteed by law:

(a) Freedom of speech;
(b) Freedom of the press;
(c) Freedom of assembly and meetings;
(d) Freedom of street processions and demonstrations.

These rights of citizens are ensured by placing at the disposal of the working people and their organisations printing shops, supplies of paper, public buildings, the streets, means of communication and other material requisites for the exercise of these rights.

Article 126. In accordance with the interests of the working people, and for the purpose of developing the organised self-expression and political activity of the masses of the people, citizens of the USSR are ensured the right to unite in public organisations – trade unions, cooperative associations, youth organisations, sport and defence organisations, cultural, technical, and scientific societies; and the most active and politically conscious citizens from the ranks of the working class and other strata of the working people unite in the All-Union Communist Party (of Bolsheviks), which is the vanguard of the working people in their struggle to strengthen and develop the socialist system, and which represents the leading nucleus of all organisations of the working people, both social and state.

Article 127. Citizens of the USSR are guaranteed inviolability of the person. No one may be subject to arrest except by an order of the court or with the sanction of a state attorney.

Article 128. The inviolability of the homes of citizens and secrecy of correspondence are protected by law . . .

Chapter XI: The Electoral System

Article 135. The elections of deputies shall be universal: all citizens of the USSR who have reached the age of 18, irrespective of race and nationality, religion, education qualifications, residence, social origin, property status or past activity, shall have the right to take part in the elections of deputies and to be elected, with the exception of insane persons and persons sentenced by court with deprivation of electoral rights.

Article 136. The elections of deputies shall be equal: every citizen shall have one vote; all citizens shall take part in the elections on an equal basis.

Article 137. Women shall have the right to elect and to be elected on equal terms with men.

Source: 'The New Constitution of 1936', in Sidney and Beatrice Webb, The Truth about Soviet Russia *(London, Longmans, 1942), pp. 55–6, 56–7, 58, 71–3, 73–4.*

The Great Terror

The great purges emerged out of the general reregistrations of party membership. The one in early 1935 saw the expulsion of nearly 300,000 communists from the party, with the usual consequence of an investigation by the secret police. Following Kirov's assassination simplified judicial procedures were introduced allowing NKVD troikas to decide cases on their own and to impose the death penalty without the right of appeal. The delegates to the Seventeenth Party Congress, as Khrushchev later reported (Document 8.4), were decimated. Three 'show trials' provide the enduring image of the purges: the first in August 1936 saw Kamenev and Zinoviev joined together in death as in life; the second in January–February 1937 featured Radek and Pyatakov; and the third in March 1938 (see Documents 5.24 and 5.25) included Bukharin and the former head of the NKVD, Genrikh Yagoda.

Document 5.23 The Purge Plenum

The Central Committee plenum of 23 February–5 March 1937 is considered to be the one that formally approved the policy of mass terror. Little, however, is known about its deliberations, perhaps indicating some resistance to Stalin's policy of mass liquidation. The report encouraged denunciations from below, particularly in the workplace.

The plenum of the Central Committee of the VKP(b) [All-Union Communist Party] cannot countenance the objectionable phenomenon that a number of the organs of industry and transport remain passive in the face of the very exposure and unmasking of trotskyite diversionists, after the diversionist work of the trotskyites becomes evident. Usually the trotskyites are unmasked by the organs of the NKVD and individual party members – volunteers. In this situation the organs of industry themselves, and also, to some extent, of transport, display neither action nor, more important, initiative. Moreover, certain organs of industry even retard in this matter . . . [Ellipsis in original.]

The bureaucratic distortion of the principle of one-man authority (as contrasted with collective management, which was formerly practised) consists of the fact that many leaders in the economy think that one-man authority makes them entirely free of the control by the public opinion of the masses and the rank and file of workers in the economy. They do not think it necessary to be guided by these activists. They cut themselves off from the activists and thereby deprive themselves of the support of the activists in the matter of exposing and liquidating inadequacies and lapses that are exploited by the enemies for their diversionist work.

Source: Pravda, *21 April 1937, in McNeal (ed.),* Resolutions and Decisions of the CPSU, *vol. 3,* The Stalin Years: 1929–1953, *pp. 182–3.*

Document 5.24 Vyshinsky and the Show Trials

In 1938 in the third of the great 'show trials' Bukharin and Rykov were in the dock together with the Trotskyites Rakovsky and Krestinsky and the former NKVD leader Yagoda. As before, elaborate chains of conspiracy were alleged along with fantastic accusations. In his final speech Bukharin confessed to enormous crimes but denied any specific offence, thus apparently exposing the absurdity of the charges. Most of the defendants were shot, and the rest perished in the Gulag. Andrei Vyshinsky, a Menshevik up to the early 1920s, was the chief prosecutor in this as in earlier trials. His call to 'shoot the mad dogs' became the slogan of the purges.

The Trotskyites and Bukharinites, that is to say, the 'bloc of Rights and Trotskyites', the leading lights of which are now in the prisoners' dock, is not a political party, a political tendency, but a band of felonious criminals, and not simply felonious criminals, but of criminals who have sold themselves to enemy intelligence services, criminals whom even ordinary felons treat as the basest, the lowest, the most contemptible, the most depraved of the depraved . . .

Our people and all honest people throughout the world are waiting for your just verdict. May this verdict of yours resound through the whole of our great country like a bell calling to new feats of heroism and to new victories! May your verdict resound as the refreshing and purifying thunderstorm of just Soviet punishment!

Our whole country, from young to old, is awaiting and demanding one thing: the traitors and spies who were selling our country to the enemy must be shot like dirty dogs!

Our people are demanding one thing: crush the accursed reptile!

Source: Daniels, Communism in Russia, *pp. 269, 270.*

At this time Pashukanis was purged and his radical Marxist theory on the withering away of law was replaced by Vyshinsky's formulations that the proletariat required the state and a strengthened socialist legal order to regulate the new Soviet system – the 'legalising' of illegality. Law, like the state, would only wither away in the highest stage of communism, when capitalist encirclement had been overcome and the community could regulate its own affairs without the aid of constraint.

Document 5.25 The Show Trials – an American View

Joseph E. Davies was the US ambassador to the Soviet Union from 1936 to 1938, the period of the most intense terror. Supported by a sophisticated intelligence-gathering network and many personal contacts in the hierarchy, Davies nevertheless gave credence to the charges laid against former Bolshevik leaders in the three great show trials. In the third the 'rightists' Bukharin and Rykov were charged with heinous crimes. In a letter to his daughter of 8 March 1938 Davies gives his view of the event; in the second extract he comments on the verdict in a confidential cable of

17 March to the US Secretary of State; and in a note written in 1941 he looks back at the trials and repressions of his time in Moscow and marvels at the foresight of the Soviet government in clearing the country of all potential 'fifth columnists'.

For the last week I have been attending daily sessions of the Bukharin treason trial. No doubt you have been following it in the press. It is terrific. I have found it of much intellectual interest, because it brings back into play all the old critical faculties involved in assessing the credibility of witnesses and sifting the wheat from the chaff – the true from the false – which I was called upon to use for so many years in the trial of cases, myself.

All the fundamental weaknesses and vice of human nature – personal ambitions at their worst – are shown up in the proceedings. They disclose the outlines of a plot which came very near to being successful in bringing about the overthrow of this government.

This testimony now makes clear what we could not understand and what happened last spring and summer. You will recall that the folks at the chancery were telling us of extraordinary activity around the Kremlin, when the gates were closed to the public; that there were indications of much agitation and a changing of the character of the soldiers on guard. The new guards, you will remember we were told, consisted almost entirely of soldiers recruited from Georgia, Stalin's native land.

The extraordinary testimony of Krestinsky, Bukharin, and the rest would appear to indicate that the Kremlin's fears were well justified. For it now seems that a plot existed in the beginning of November, 1936, to project a coup d'état, with Tukhatchevsky at its head, for May of the following year. Apparently it was touch and go at the time whether it actually would be staged.

But the government acted with great vigour and speed. The Red Army generals were shot and the whole party organization was purged and thoroughly cleansed. Then it came out that quite a few of those at the top were seriously infected with the virus of the conspiracy to overthrow the government, and were actually working with the Secret Service organizations of Germany and Japan.

This situation explains the present official attitude of hostility towards foreigners, the closing of various foreign consulates in this country and the like. Quite frankly, we can't blame the powers-that-be much for reacting in this way if they believed what is now being divulged at the trial.

On March 13, 1938, at approximately five o'clock in the morning, all the defendants in the trial were adjudged guilty and the sentences were imposed. Three of the defendants were condemned to imprisonment and the remainder to death through shooting. Eight of the most prominent former members of the Soviet government, including a former premier, six former cabinet officers, one of the most prominent party leaders and members of the Politburo, and also a former president of one of the constituent republics were condemned to be shot. Condemned to imprisonment were a former Ambassador to England and France, a former Counsellor of the Soviet Embassy in Berlin, and one famous heart specialist.

Notwithstanding a prejudice arising from the confession evidence and a prejudice against a judicial system which affords practically no protection for the accused, after daily observation of the witnesses, their manner of testifying, the unconscious corroborations which developed, and other facts in the course of the trial, together with others of which a judicial notice could be taken, it is my opinion, so far as the political defendants are concerned, that sufficient crimes under Soviet law, among those charged in the indictment, were established by the proof and beyond a reasonable doubt to justify the verdict of guilty of treason and the adjudication of the punishment provided by Soviet criminal statutes. The opinion of those diplomats who attended the trial most regularly was general that the case had established the fact that there was a formidable political opposition and an exceedingly serious plot, which explained to the diplomats many of the hitherto unexplained developments of the last six months in the Soviet Union. The only difference of opinion that seemed to exist was the degree to which the plot had been implemented by different defendants and the degree to which the conspiracy had become centralized . . .

All of these trials, purges and liquidations, which seemed so violent at the time and shocked the world, are now quite clearly a part of a vigorous and determined effort of the Stalin government to protect itself from not only revolution from within but from attack from without. They went to work thoroughly to clean up and clean out all treasonable elements within the country. All doubts were resolved in favour of the government.

There were no Fifth Columnists in Russia in 1941 – they had shot them. The purge had cleansed the country and rid it of treason.

Source: Joseph E. Davies, Mission to Moscow *(London, Victor Gollancz, 1942), pp. 177, 178–9, 184.*

The purge of the military included the shooting of General M. Tukhachevskii on 11 June 1937 (on the basis of a false lead provided by German counter-intelligence), one of the USSR's most brilliant military leaders, an event that was followed by the mass slaughter of Red Army officers and NCOs including the top generals V. Blyukher, A. Egorov, I. Yakir (whose son was later to become a dissident) and I. Unschlicht. According to recent evidence, out of 733 higher commanders and political commissars, 579 were 'repressed' (79 per cent), leaving only 154. As a result, when war began only 7 per cent of commanders had higher military education, and 37 per cent had not even completed basic military training courses (V. M. Kulish, *Ob urokakh i pravde istorii* (Moscow, 1989), pp. 283–4). The purge of the military undermined the credibility of Soviet calls for intervention to defend Czechoslovakia at the time of Munich in September 1938. They also reduced Germany's fear of the USSR and debilitated the Soviet army when war began.

The New 'Civilisation'

The nature of the system that had come to power in 1917 and what it had become under Stalin was (and indeed remains) the subject of a voluminous and fascinating literature. Here we will give no more than an indication of some of the contrasting contemporary views.

Document 5.26   Trotsky – *The Revolution Betrayed*

In this work (published in 1936) Trotsky rejected the view that the Soviet Union had become a form of 'state capitalism' since the means of production remained socialised: there had been no reversion to private ownership. The Soviet state remained a workers' state, albeit a 'degenerated' one, where the 'dictatorship of the proletariat' had not been repudiated. Although in his view the bureaucracy had usurped political control from the workers, largely as a result of Russia's backwardness, it did not constitute a class but merely a ruling stratum or caste which used Stalin as its tool. However misguided, Trotsky's analysis must be the starting point of any study of Stalinism. Note the role that the 'Leninist Levy', a mass influx of workers following Lenin's death in 1924, played, according to Trotsky, in precipitating the degeneration of the party, together with the demobilisation of the Red Army after the Civil War.

Russia was not the strongest, but the weakest link in the chain of capitalism. The present Soviet Union does not stand above the world level of economy, but is only trying to catch up to the capitalist countries. If Marx called that society which was to be formed upon the basis of a socialization of the productive forces of the most advanced capitalism of its epoch, the lowest stage of communism, then this designation obviously does not apply to the Soviet Union, which is still today considerably poorer in technique, culture and the good things of life than the capitalist countries. It would be truer, therefore, to name the present Soviet regime in all its contradictoriness, not a socialist regime, but a *preparatory* regime *transitional* from capitalism to socialism.

There is not an ounce of pedantry in this concern for terminological accuracy. The strength and stability of regimes are determined in the long run by the relative productivity of their labor. A socialist economy possessing a technique superior to that of capitalism would really be guaranteed in its socialist development for sure – so to speak, automatically – a thing which unfortunately it is still quite impossible to say about the Soviet economy . . .

The regime of proletarian dictatorship from its very beginning thus ceases to be a 'state' in the old sense of the word – a special apparatus, that is, for holding in subjection the majority of the people. The material power, together with the weapons, goes over directly and immediately into the hands of workers' organizations such as the soviets. The state as a bureaucratic apparatus begins to die away from the first day of the proletarian dictatorship. Such is the voice of the party program – not voided to this day. Strange: it sounds like a spectral voice from the mausoleum.

However you may interpret the nature of the present Soviet state, one thing is indubitable: at the end of its second decade of existence, it has not only not died away, but not begun to 'die away.' Worse than that, it has grown into a hitherto unheard of apparatus of compulsion. The bureaucracy not only has not disappeared, yielding its place to the masses, but has turned into an uncontrolled force dominating the masses. The army not only has not been replaced by an armed people, but has given birth to a privileged officers' caste, crowned with marshals, while the people, 'the armed bearers of the dictatorship,' are now forbidden in the Soviet Union to carry even nonexplosive weapons. With the utmost stretch of fancy it would be difficult to imagine a contrast more striking than that which exists between the schema of the workers' state according to Marx, Engels and Lenin, and the actual state now headed by Stalin. While continuing to publish the works of Lenin (to be sure, with excerpts and distortions by the censor), the present leaders of the Soviet Union and their ideological representatives do not even raise the question of the causes of such a crying divergence between program and reality. We will try to do this for them . . .

We have thus taken the first step toward understanding the fundamental contradiction between Bolshevik program and Soviet reality. If the state does not die away, but grows more and more despotic, if the plenipotentiaries of the working class become bureaucratized, and the bureaucracy rises above the new society, this is not for some secondary reasons like the psychological relics of the past, etc., but is a result of the iron necessity to give birth to and support a privileged minority so long as it is impossible to guarantee genuine equality . . .

It is sufficiently well known that every revolution up to this time has been followed by a reaction, or even a counter-revolution. This, to be sure, has never thrown the nation all the way back to its starting point, but it has always taken from the people the lion's share of their conquests. The victims of the first reactionary wave have been, as a general rule, those pioneers, initiators, and instigators who stood at the head of the masses in the period of the revolutionary offensive. In their stead people of the second line, in league with the former enemies of the revolution, have been advanced to the front . . .

The axiomlike assertions of the Soviet literature, to the effect that the laws of bourgeois revolutions are 'inapplicable' to a proletarian revolution, have no scientific content whatever. The proletarian character of the October revolution was determined by the world situation and by a special correlation of internal forces. But the classes themselves were formed in the barbarous circumstances of tzarism and backward capitalism, and were anything but made to order for the demands of a socialist revolution. The exact opposite is true. It is for the very reason that a proletariat still backward in many respects achieved in the space of a few months the unprecedented leap from a semifeudal monarchy to a socialist dictatorship, that the reaction in its ranks was inevitable. The revolution got no direct help from the west. Instead of the expected prosperity of the country an ominous destitution reigned for long. Moreover, the outstanding representatives of the working class either died in the civil war, or rose a few steps higher and broke away from the masses. And thus after an unexampled tension of forces, hopes and illusions, there came a long period of weariness, decline and sheer disappointment in the results of the revolution. The ebb of the 'plebeian tide' made room for a flood of pusillanimity and careerism. The new commanding caste rose to its place upon this wave.

The demobilization of the Red Army of five million played no small role in the formation of the bureaucracy. The victorious commanders assumed leading posts in the local soviets, in economy, in education, and they persistently introduced everywhere that regime which had ensured success in the civil war. Thus on all sides the masses were pushed away gradually from actual participation in the leadership of the country . . .

It would be naïve to imagine that Stalin, previously unknown to the masses, suddenly issued from the wings fully armed with a complete strategical plan. No indeed. Before he felt out his own course, the bureaucracy felt out Stalin himself. He brought it all the necessary guarantees: the prestige of an old Bolshevik, a strong character, narrow vision, and close bonds with the political machine as the sole source of his influence. The success which fell upon him was a surprise at first to Stalin himself. It was the friendly welcome of the new ruling group, trying to free itself from the old principles and from the control of the masses, and having need of a reliable arbiter in its inner affairs. A secondary figure before the masses and in the events of the revolution, Stalin revealed himself as the indubitable leader of the Thermidorian bureaucracy, as first in its midst . . .

Together with the theory of socialism in one country, there was put into circulation by the bureaucracy a theory that in Bolshevism the Central Committee is everything and the party nothing. This second theory was in any case realized with more success than the first. Availing itself of the death of Lenin, the ruling group announced a 'Leninist Levy.' The gates of the party, always carefully guarded, were now thrown wide open. Workers, clerks, petty officials, flocked through in crowds. The political aim of this maneuver was to dissolve the revolutionary vanguard in raw human material, without experience, without independence, and yet with the old habit of submitting to the authorities. The scheme was successful. By freeing the bureaucracy from the control of the proletarian vanguard, the 'Leninist Levy' dealt a death blow to the party of Lenin. The machine had won the necessary independence. Democratic centralism gave way to bureaucratic centralism . . .

Of party democracy there remained only recollections in the memory of the older generation. And together with it had disappeared the democracy of the soviets, the trade unions, the co-operatives, the cultural and athletic organizations. Above each and every one of them there reigns an unlimited hierarchy of party secretaries. The regime had become 'totalitarian' in character several years before this word arrived from Germany . . .

We have defined the Soviet Thermidor as a triumph of the bureaucracy over the masses. We have tried to disclose the historic conditions of this triumph. The revolutionary vanguard of the proletariat was in part devoured by the administrative apparatus and gradually demoralized, in part annihilated in the civil war, and in part thrown out and crushed. The tired and disappointed masses were indifferent to what was happening on the summits. These conditions, however, important as they may have been in themselves, are inadequate to explain why the bureaucracy succeeded in raising itself above society and getting its fate firmly into its own hands. Its own will to do this would in any case be inadequate; the arising of a new ruling stratum must have deep social causes . . .

The present Soviet society cannot get along without a state, nor even – within limits – without a bureaucracy. But the cause of this is by no means the pitiful remnants of the past, but the mighty forces and tendencies of the present. The justification for the existence of a Soviet state as an apparatus of compulsion lies in the fact that the present transitional structure is still full of social contradictions, which in the sphere of *consumption* – most close and sensitively felt by all – are extremely tense, and forever threaten to break over into the sphere of production. The triumph of socialism cannot be called either final or irrevocable.

The basis of bureaucratic rule is the poverty of society in objects of consumption, with the resulting struggle of each against all . . .

The attempt to represent the Soviet bureaucracy as a class of 'state capitalists' will obviously not withstand criticism. The bureaucracy has neither stocks nor bonds. It is recruited, supplemented and renewed in the manner of an administrative hierarchy, independently of any special property relations of its own. The individual bureaucrat cannot transmit to his heirs his rights in the exploitation of the state apparatus. The bureaucracy enjoys its privileges under the form of an abuse of power. It conceals its income; it pretends that as a special social group it does not even exist. Its appropriation of a vast share of the national income has the character of social parasitism. All this makes the position of the commanding Soviet stratum in the highest degree contradictory, equivocal and undignified, notwithstanding the completeness of its power and the smoke screen of flattery that conceals it . . .

To define the Soviet regime as transitional, or intermediate, means to abandon such finished social categories as *capitalism* (and therewith 'state capitalism') and also *socialism*. But besides being completely inadequate in itself, such a definition is capable of producing the mistaken idea that from the present Soviet regime *only* a transition to socialism is possible. In reality a backslide to capitalism is wholly possible. A more complete definition will of necessity be complicated and ponderous . . .

Caesarism, or its bourgeois form, Bonapartism, enters the scene in those moments of history when the sharp struggle of two camps raises the state power, so to speak, above the nation, and guarantees it, in appearance, a complete independence of classes – in reality, only the freedom necessary for a defense of the privileged. The Stalin regime, rising above a politically atomized society, resting upon a police and officers' corps, and allowing of no control whatever, is obviously a variation of Bonapartism – a Bonapartism of a new type not before seen in history.

Caesarism arose upon the basis of a slave society shaken by inward strife. Bonapartism is one of the political weapons of the capitalist regime in its critical period. Stalinism is a variety of the same system, but upon the basis of a workers' state torn by the antagonism between an organized and armed Soviet aristocracy and the unarmed toiling masses.

As history testifies, Bonapartism gets along admirably with a universal, and even a secret, ballot. The democratic ritual of Bonapartism is the *plebiscite*. From time to time, the question is presented to the citizens: *for* or *against* the leader? And the voter feels the barrel of a revolver between his shoulders. Since the time of Napoleon III, who now seems a provincial dilettante, this technique has received an extraordinary development. The new Soviet constitution which establishes *Bonapartism on a plebiscite basis* is the veritable crown of the system.

In the last analysis, Soviet Bonapartism owes its birth to the belatedness of the world revolution. But in the capitalist countries the same cause gave rise to fascism. We thus arrive at the conclusion, unexpected at first glance, but in reality inevitable, that the crushing of Soviet democracy by an all-powerful bureaucracy and the extermination of bourgeois democracy by fascism were produced by one and the same cause: the dilatoriness of the world proletariat in solving the problems set for it by history. Stalinism and fascism, in spite of a deep difference in social foundations, are symmetrical phenomena. In many of their features they show a deadly similarity. A victorious revolutionary movement in Europe would immediately shake not only fascism, but Soviet Bonapartism. In turning its back to the international revolution, the Stalinist bureaucracy was, from its own point of view, right. It was merely obeying the voice of self-preservation.

Source: Leon Trotsky, The Revolution Betrayed *(London, New Park Publications, 1973), pp. 47–48, 51–2, 55, 87–8, 89–90, 92–3, 97–8, 99–100, 105, 108, 111–12, 249–50, 254, 277–9.*

The bureaucracy, in Trotsky's view, was therefore no more than a temporary aberration destined to be swept away by a new proletarian revolution. The social sources of this bureaucracy remained vague in Trotsky's thinking, other than some veiled references to its bourgeois and petty-bourgeois roots. The political roots of the bureaucracy are even less satisfactorily explained. Like Khrushchev later in his denunciation of Stalinism, Trotsky failed to make a Marxist analysis of the phenomenon. A new class of rulers had usurped the proletariat's governing status, yet the system remained a 'dictatorship of the proletariat'. As we shall see later (Document 8.14), Milovan Djilas in his *The New Class* (1957) began with Trotsky's criticism of the Stalinist bureaucracy but took the argument to its logical conclusion – the party bureaucracy and its acolytes had constituted themselves as a new ruling class based not on ownership but the administrative exploitation of common property.

Document 5.27 Berdyaev on the Russian Revolution

Nicholas Berdyaev had been one of the contributors to the *Landmarks* (*Vekhi*) volume in 1909 and was expelled from Soviet Russia in 1922 to take up residence in Paris where he edited the liberal Orthodox review *The Way* (*Put'*). He was haunted by the meaning of the Russian revolution, considering Russia's intellectual traditions and society as responsible as Marxism. In the interwar years he fell under the influence of the prevalent anti-parliamentarianism and the distaste for effete and pointless bourgeois civilisation. From his Christian perspective, however, he could never reconcile himself with the communist repudiation of religion. For him, communism was both a Russian and a universal phenomenon which could only be understood through a process of *katharsis*, interior purification. Berdyaev was one of Russia's most original thinkers of the twentieth century, to the end insisting that 'The Russian question is at present above all a spiritual question.' In his view both Russia and the world were going through a profound spiritual crisis. Few would disagree with that judgement.

The most remarkable of Russian philosophers in the nineteenth century, a Christian philosopher, Vladimir Solovyev, once said that to defeat what is false in Socialism one must recognise what is true in it. The same must be said of Communism, which is one of the extreme forms of Socialism. In Communism there is a great untruth, an anti-Christian untruth, but it also contains much truth, and even many truths. In Communism there are many truths which one might formulate in a whole series of paragraphs, and only one untruth; but that untruth is so enormous that it outweighs all the truths and spoils them . . .

What is true in Communism? One can lay down a whole series of assertions in which truth is on its side. First of all there is its negative truth, its criticism of the falsehood of *bourgeois* capitalist civilisation, of its contradictions and diseases. Then there is the truth of its denouncement of a degenerate, decadent pseudo-Christianity, adapted to the interests of the *bourgeois* epoch of history. But there is also positive truth in its scheme for organising and regulating the economic life of society, on which men's lives depend, and which can no longer be abandoned to the free play of individual interests and arbitrariness. The idea of methodically planning out the norms of economic life is, on principle, a right idea. The liberal principle of formal freedom in such matters produces enormous injustices and deprives a considerable portion of humanity of all real liberty. The truth contained in Communism is that society ought to be a working society of labourers, and that the working-classes ought to be called to play their part in history and share its culture (though it is true that Communism has not a right understanding of the qualitative hierarchy of labour) . . .

Communism states before the whole world the great problem of its radical social reconstruction. The whole world is burning, thirsting for transformation, seeking a new and better life. The strength of Communism lies in its having a complete design for reconstructing the world's life, in which theory and practice, thought and will are at one. And in that respect it resembles the theocratic design of the Middle Ages. For Communism subjects the life of individual man to a great, worldwide, super-individual man to a great, worldwide, super-individual end. It goes back again to the concept of life as a service – an idea completely lost in the de-Christianised *bourgeois* liberal epoch. Every young man feels he is building up a new world. It may very well be the building of the Tower of Babel, but it fills the life of the very least among men with something super-individual which sweeps him on and sustains him. Economics are no longer a private affair, they are a world affair. Man is being forcibly freed from private life, he is reconstructing the world. Communism denies individual man but it accepts collective man as omnipotent. Every human being is called to reconstruct the world collectively. The weight of the past, of history and tradition, which are so strong in the West, is thrown aside. It is as though the creation of the earth were beginning afresh . . .

The Russian Revolution has given proof of enormous vital strength. But its force cannot be entirely attributed to Communism, which is merely its conventional formula; it is above all the vital strength of the Russian people, a force formerly held in leash and now unchained.

But the untruth in Communism is greater than its truth. It has even disfigured that truth. It is above all a spiritual, not a social falseness. What is false and terrible is the very spirit of Communism. Its spirit is the negation of spirit, the negation of the spiritual principle in man. Its untruth is its rejection of God. Everything flows from that source. Godlessness cannot go unpunished. Communism is inhuman, for denial of God leads to denial of man.

Source: Nicholas Berdyaev, The Russian Revolution *(London, Sheed & Ward, 1931), pp. 53–4, 77–8, 79–80, 80–1.*

Document 5.28 Berdyaev on the Origins of Russian Communism

Berdyaev's book *The Origin of Russian Communism*, published in 1937, returned to some of his earlier themes but now focused more specifically on the role of the intelligentsia, the nature of revolutions in general, and the roots of the Russian revolution in the Russian messianic idea.

Russian communism is difficult to understand on account of its twofold nature. On the one hand it is international and a world phenomenon; on the other hand it is national and Russian. It is particularly important for Western minds to understand the national roots of Russian communism and the fact that it was Russian history which determined its limits and shaped its character. A knowledge of Marxism will not help in this. The Russian people in their spiritual make-up are an Eastern people. Russia is the Christian East, which was for two centuries subject to the powerful influences of the West, and whose cultured classes assimilated every Western idea. The fate of the Russian people in history has been an unhappy one and full of suffering. It has developed at a catastrophic tempo through interruption and change in its type of civilization . . .

The whole history of the Russian intelligentsia was a preparation for communism. Into communism there entered the well-known traits – thirst for social righteousness and equality, a recognition of the working classes as the highest type of humanity, aversion to capitalism and the bourgeoisie, the striving after an integrated outlook and an integrated relation to life, sectarian intolerance, a suspicious and hostile attitude to the cultural *élite*, an exclusive this-worldliness, a denial of spirit and of spiritual values, a well-nigh religious devotion to materialism. All these had always belonged to the Russian radical intelligentsia. If the remnants of the old intelligentsia which remain and have not joined up with bolshevism have not recognized their proper character-istics in those against whom they have rebelled, this is a historical aberration, a loss of memory due to emotional reaction. The old revolutionary intelli-gentsia simply did not think about what it would be like when it acquired power. It was accustomed to accept itself as powerless and oppressed, and power and ability to oppress seemed to it to be a child of another wholly alien type, while all the while it was its own child. Here lies the paradox of the final stage in the development of the Russian inteliigentsia, its transformation in a victorious revolution. Part of it was converted to communism and adapted its psychology to the new conditions. Another part of it did not accept the socialist revolution and forgot its own past . . .

Any judgment on the Russian revolution presupposes a judgment on revolution in general, as an entirely special and, in the last resort, spiritual phenomenon in the destinies of peoples. Rationalist and moralist judgments on revolution are entirely fruitless and so are such judgments on war, which is very like revolution. Revolution is irrational; it is a sign of the dominance of irrational forces in history. The makers of revolution may consciously profess the most rational theories and make the revolution on those grounds, but revolutions are always a symptom of the growth of irrational forces, and this must be understood in a twofold sense. It means the old régime has become entirely irrational and no longer justifiable in any sense; and that the revolution itself comes into being through the unshackling of the irrational elements in the masses. The organizers of a revolution always desire to rationalize the irrational element in revolution, but all the same they are its instruments. Lenin was an extreme rationalist; he believed in the possibility of finally rationalizing social life, but still he was a man of destiny, a man of fate, i.e., of the irrational in history. Revolution is destiny and fate . . .

The whole fashion assumed by Russian and world communism was due to the War. Had there been no war, then all the same there would have been a Russian revolution in the end, but probably it would have come later and it would have been different. The unsuccessful war created the most favourable conditions for the victory of the bolsheviks. The Russians are by nature prone to maximalism, and the maximalist character of the Russian revolution was very true to type. Contradictions and cleavages had reached their maximum intensity in Russia, but it needed the atmosphere of war to produce the type of victorious bolshevik among us, the new type of the bolshevik conqueror. It was the War with its experiences and methods which regenerated the type of Russian intelligentsia. War methods were transferred to the internal life of the country. A new type appeared, that of the militarized youth; in contrast with the old members of the intelligentsia he is clean shaven, alert, with a firm vigorous gait; he looks like a conqueror; he makes no bones about the methods he uses; he is always ready for violence; he is possessed by the will-to-power; he forces his way to the front; he wants to be not only destructive but also constructive and an organizer. It was only with the help of such young men drawn from the peasants, the workmen and the semi-intelligentsia, that the communist revolution could be brought about; it could not be done with the dreamy compassionate person who belonged to the old intelligentsia, and who was always ready to suffer.

But it is very important to remember that the Russian communist revolution came to birth in misery and from misery, the misery of a dis-integrating war; it was not born of a creative abundance of strength . . .

In this book I have tried to show that Russian communism is more traditional than is commonly thought and thus it is a transformation and deformation of the old Russian messianic idea. Communism in Western Europe would be an entirely different phenomenon in spite of the similarity of Marxist theories. To the traditional Russian character of communism are due both its positive and its negative sides: On the one hand the search for the Kingdom of God and integrated truth and justice, capacity for sacrifice and the absence of the bourgeois spirit; on the other hand, the absoluteness of the State, the despotism, feeble grasp of the rights of man and the danger of a featureless collectivism. In other countries communism, in the event of an attempt to bring it into existence, may be less integrated, make less claim to take the place of religion, may be more secular and more bourgeois in its spirit. The problems of communism stimulate the awakening of the Christian conscience and should lead to the development of a creative social Christianity, not in the sense of understanding Christianity as a social religion, but in the sense of revealing Christian truth and justice in relation to social life. This will mean emancipation from social slavery, that social slavery in which Christian consciousness finds itself. The world is living through the danger of a dehumanization of social life, the dehumanization of man himself. The very existence of man is in danger from all the processes which are going on in the world. Only the spiritual strengthening of man can combat this danger. When Christianity appeared in the world it defended man from the danger arising from demonolatry. Man was in the power of cosmic forces, of demons and spirits of Nature which tormented him. Christianity focused man spiritually and subjected his fate to God; thus was prepared the possibility of man's power over Nature. At the present time Christianity is again called upon to protect man, to protect his whole image from a demonolatry which torments him anew, from servitude to the old cosmic and the new technical forces. But this can only be done by a re-juvenated Christianity which is true to its prophetic spirit and which is turned towards the Kingdom of God.

Source: Nicholas Berdyaev, The Origin of Russian Communism *(Michigan, Ann Arbor Paperback, 1960), pp. 7, 122, 129, 138–9, 187–9.*

Document 5.29   Sidney and Beatrice Webb

Sidney Webb (Lord Passfield) had been one of the driving forces in modernising the Fabian Society to accept constitutional socialism, while Beatrice Potter, 'a society lady of the political plutocracy' (as Bernard Shaw put it), was a gifted social researcher. Together they wrote a monumental history of British trade unionism, an analysis of industrial democracy, a multi-volume study of local government, and helped establish the London School of Economics. The Webbs had long had an interest in Russia. In 1935 they brought out a massive two-volume work called *Soviet Communism: A New Civilisation?* Two years later they issued a revised version, taking into account the changes in the Soviet system of government made by the adoption of the 'Stalin' constitution in 1936. The title of the revised version was *Soviet Communism: A New Civilisation*; the question mark had been dropped. At a time of mass terror and arbitrary personal dictatorship, the Webbs dropped their earlier equivocations and declared that a new civilisation had been built in the USSR. This is perhaps the most famous question mark in history. The Webbs had taken the Soviet constitution at face value. Their approach to Soviet politics was strictly legal and constitutional, examining the institutional forms of power but failing to look deeper at the informal ways in which the system operated, and not recognising the need to examine the behaviour of individuals in the political process. The institutional approach to the study of politics was for a generation discredited by the Webbs in favour of behavioural and functionalist approaches. The tone of their approach is revealed in the following extract from a work published in 1942.

The New Civilisation

Since the signing of the German–Soviet Pact in 1939 I have been frequently asked by bewildered friends: Is there any distinction between the status and activities of Stalin on the one hand and Hitler and Mussolini on the other? Are these three men all alike dictators? And secondly, have these three sovereign states similar constitutions by law established: or is the Soviet Union, unlike Germany and Italy, a political democracy similar in essence, if not in detail, to the political democracies of the USA and Great Britain? And assuming that the Soviet Union is a political democracy, has democratic control of the instruments of production, distribution and exchange been added so that the government should be, not merely a government of the people by the people, but also a government for the good of the people? Finally, is it right to suggest that Soviet Communism is a new civilisation which will, in spite of the crudities and cruelties inherent in violent revolution and fear of foreign aggression, result in maximising the wealth of the nation and distributing it among all the inhabitants on the principle of from each man according to his faculty and to each man according to his need?

Is Stalin a Dictator?

To answer the first question – Is Stalin a dictator? – we must agree on what meaning is to be attached to the term *dictator*: otherwise argument is a waste of time. Assuming that we accept the primary meaning of the term *dictator*, as it is defined in the *New English Dictionary* – 'a ruler or governor whose word is law; an absolute ruler of the state – and who authoritatively prescribes a course of action or dictates what is to be done' (the example given being the Dictators of ancient Rome) – Stalin is not a dictator. So far as Stalin is related to the constitution of the USSR, as amended in 1936, he is the duly elected representative of one of the Moscow constituencies to the Supreme Soviet of the USSR. By this assembly he has been selected as one of the thirty members of the Presidium of the Supreme Soviet of the USSR, accountable to the representative assembly for all its activities. It is this Presidium which selects the Council of Commissars (Sovnarkom) and, during the intervals between the meetings of the Supreme Soviet, controls the policy of the Sovnarkom, of which Molotov has been for many years the Prime Minister, and, since 1939, also the Foreign Secretary. In May 1941, Stalin, hitherto content to be a member of the Presidium, alarmed at the menace of a victorious German army invading the Ukraine, took over, with the consent of the Presidium, the office of Prime Minister and Minister of Defence, leaving Molotov as Foreign

Secretary; in exactly the same way, and for a similar reason – the world war – that Winston Churchill, with the consent of the House of Commons, became Prime Minister and Minister of Defence with Chamberlain, the outgoing Prime Minister, as a prominent member of the British Cabinet. As Prime Minister I doubt whether Stalin would have offered, as Churchill did, to amalgamate the USSR on terms of equality with another Great Power without consulting the Presidium of which he was a member. Neither the Prime Minister of the British Cabinet nor the presiding member of the Sovnarkom has anything like the autocratic power of the President of the USA, who not only selects the members of his Cabinet subject to the formal control of the Senate, but is also Commander-in-Chief of the American armed forces and, under the Lease-Lend Act, is empowered to safeguard, in one way or another, the arrival of munitions and food at the British ports. By declaring, in May this year, a state of unlimited national emergency, President Roosevelt legally assumes a virtual dictatorship of the United States. He has power to take over transport, to commandeer the radio for the purposes of propaganda, to control imports and all exchange transactions, to requisition ships and to suspend laws governing working hours, and, most important of all, to decide on industrial priorities and, if necessary, to take over industrial plants.

In what manner, then, does Stalin exceed in authority over his country's destiny the British Prime Minister or the American President? The office by which Stalin keeps his livelihood and owes his predominant influence is that of general secretary of the Communist Party, a unique organisation the characteristics of which, whether good or evil, I shall describe later on in this pamphlet. Here I will note that the Communist Party, unlike the Roman Catholic and Anglican Church, is not an oligarchy; it is democratic in its internal structure, having a representative congress electing a central committee which in its turn selects the Politbureau and other executive organs of the Communist Party. Nor has Stalin ever claimed the position of a dictator or fuehrer. For otherwise; he has persistently asserted in his writings and speeches that as a member of the Presidium of the Supreme Soviet of the USSR he is merely a colleague of thirty other members, and that so far as the Communist Party is concerned he acts as general secretary under the orders of the executive. He has, in fact, frequently pointed out that he does no more than carry out the decisions of the Central Committee of the Communist Party. Thus, in describing his momentous article known as 'Dizzy with Success', he expressly states that this was written on 'the well-known decisions of the Central Committee regarding the fight 'against Distortions of the Party Line' in the collective farm movement . . . In this connection', he continues, 'I recently received a number of letters from comrades, collective farmers, calling upon me to reply to the questions contained in them. It was my duty to reply to the letters in private correspondence; but that proved to be impossible, since more than half the letters received did not have the addresses of the writers (they forgot to send their addresses). Nevertheless the questions raised in these letters are of tremendous political interest to our comrades . . . In view of this I found myself faced with the necessity of replying to the comrades in an open letter, i.e., in the press . . . I did this all the more willingly since I had a direct decision of the Central Committee for this purpose.'

Is the USSR a Political Democracy?

In answer to the second question – is the USSR a political democracy? – it is clear that, tested by the Constitution of the Soviet Union as revised and enacted in 1936, the USSR is the most inclusive and equalised democracy in the world. The Supreme Soviet of the USSR consists of two chambers – the Soviet of the Union and the Soviet of Nationalities. The Soviet of the Union is directly elected by the citizens in electoral districts of one deputy for three hundred thousand inhabitants, the number of deputies today being over twelve hundred. The Soviet of Nationalities, with over six hundred deputies, also directly elected, aims at giving additional representation to ethnical groups whether manifested in colour or figure, language or literature, religion or manners, inhabiting large areas of the USSR. These separate Constituent Republics (now sixteen, formerly eleven) are supplemented by smaller local areas also distinguished by racial characteristics, termed Autonomous Republics or Autonomous Regions, to all of whom are allotted a smaller number of deputies to the Soviet of Nationalities. The two chambers which make up the Supreme Soviet of the USSR have equal rights, and their sessions begin and terminate simultaneously. Joint sessions of both chambers are needed to ratify legislation and meet twice a year, and are convened by the Presidium of the Supreme Soviet at its direction, or on demand of one of the Constituent Republics. All these assemblies, whether the Soviet of the Union or the Soviet of Nationalities, together with a network of subordinate provincial, municipal and village soviets, are directly elected by secret ballot, by all the inhabitants over eighteen years of age, without distinction of sex, race or religion, or political or social opinion. For instance the 'deprived class' of the earlier constitutions, former landlords and capitalist profit-makers, relations of the late Tsar, or members of a religious order, are now included on the register of voters. I may add that nearly fifty thousand practising priests of the Greek Orthodox Church, together with several hundreds of Roman Catholics, Evangelicals, Mohammedans and Buddhist officiants, were enfranchised by the Constitution of 1936.

Source: Sidney and Beatrice Webb, The Truth about Soviet Russia, *pp. 14–17.*

Document 5.30 Raskolnikov's Letter to Stalin

Fedor Raskolnikov had joined the party in 1910 and participated in the October uprising at the head of the Kronstadt sailors. He had then worked in the Soviet military establishment until taking up diplomatic work in the 1930s. In 1939 he was declared an 'enemy of the people' and escaped abroad where he wrote this letter denouncing Stalin, and he died that year in Nice.

Stalin, you have declared me 'outside the law'. With this act you have made me equal in rights – more accurately, in rightlessness – with all Soviet citizens, whom under your rule live beyond the law . . . Your 'socialism', under whose triumph there is room only behind camp wires for its builders, is so far from true socialism as the arbitrariness of your personal dictatorship has nothing in common with the dictatorship of the proletariat . . .

No one in the Soviet Union feels themselves secure. No one, going to bed, can be sure that they will not be arrested at night. There is no mercy for anyone. The innocent and the guilty, hero of October and enemy of the revolution, Old Bolshevik and non-party people, kolkhoz peasant and political representative, people's commissar and worker . . . are all equally under your whip, all on the same devilish and bloody carousel . . . You are the cook of hot dishes, intolerable for the stomachs of normal people.

You have destroyed the party of Lenin, and on its bones you have built a new 'party of Lenin and Stalin', which serves as a cover for your one-man rule . . . You are a renegade who has betrayed your past, betraying Lenin's work. With the cruelty of a sadist you are beating cadres who are useful and necessary for the country. They appear to you dangerous to your personal dictatorship. On the eve of war you are destroying the Red Army, the love and pride of the country, the foundation of its strength . . . You have deprived the kolkhoz peasant of any incentive whatsoever to work . . . There is not a corner or area where one can quietly get on with anything . . .

Your social base is narrowing every day. Your mindless bacchanalia cannot continue much longer. The list of your crimes is endless. The list of your victims is endless. It is not possible to list them all.

Source: Fedor Raskolnikov's Letter to Stalin, 17 August 1939, in Vozvrashchenie k pravde: reabilitirovan posmertno *(Moscow, Yuridicheskaya literatura, 1988), p. 198.*

Document 5.31   *The God that Failed*

This was the title of a book edited by Richard Crossman that came out in 1950 in which six former communists or communist sympathisers (Arthur Koestler, Ignazio Silone, Richard Wright, André Gide, Louis Fischer and Stephen Spender) described how they came to support the movement, and their subsequent disillusionment. Since the early 1920s Gide (1869–1951) had sympathised with the struggle of the young Soviet regime to establish itself. Finally, in June 1936 he visited the object of his admiration, and was deeply shocked.

Some years ago I wrote of my love and admiration for the Soviet Union where an unprecedented experiment was being attempted, the thought of which inflamed my heart with expectation and from which I hoped a tremendous advance, and impulse capable of sweeping along the whole of humanity. It was certainly worth while to be alive at such a moment to be able to witness this rebirth and to give one's whole life to further it. In my heart, I bound himself resolutely, in the name of future culture, to the fortunes of the Soviet Union . . .

Like many other visitors I saw model factories, clubs, pleasure-grounds, at which I marvelled. I asked for nothing better than to be carried away with admiration and to convert others as well. And so, as it is very pleasant to be enraptured and to persuade others, if I protest against all this enchantment, I must have serious grounds for doing so. I only began to see clearly when, abandoning the government transport, I travelled alone through the country in order to be able to get into direct contact with the people. I had read too much Marxist literature to feel a fish out of water in Russia, but I had also read too many accounts of idyllic trips and too many enthusiastic apologies. My mistake, at first, was to believe all the praise that I heard and everything which might have enlightened me was always said in a spiteful tone of voice. It happens too often that the friends of the Soviet Union refuse to see anything bad there – or at least to recognize it – so it happens that truth is spoken with hatred and falsehood with love. My mind is constituted in such a way that my greatest severity is directed especially towards those of whom I would like always to approve and I do not think that it is the best way to express one's love to be content with praise alone. I think that I do more service to the cause which the Soviet Union represents by speaking without pretence and without too much circumspection and consideration. I certainly had personally nothing to complain of in the course of my trip, in spite of all the spiteful explanations which were invented subsequently to invalidate my criticism, which was too often interpreted as the result and expression of personal pique and disappointment – that is most absurd of all . . .

Certainly it seemed to me quite natural that they should want to receive a guest as well as possible and to show him the best of everything, but nevertheless it surprised me to find so great a difference between the best and the common lot, such excessive privileges beside such depths of poverty. It is on account of my admiration for the Soviet Union and the marvels she has already accomplished by herself, that my criticism is going to be severe; because of what we expect from her and what she gave us reason to hope from her. I trusted her and so, in Russia, what distressed me most was not what was not yet perfect, but rather to find there everything from which all my longing was directed; it was a land where I imagined Utopia was in process of becoming reality. The Soviet Union, is, however, at an early stage of construction – that needs to be remembered constantly – and we are present at the parturition of the future. There are both good and bad points – I should say both the best and the worst; one moves from the brightest to the darkest with alarming and disconcerting suddenness. Much has already been accomplished which has filled our hearts with joy, and this, doubtless, made me exacting. It seemed at first to me as if the most difficult [tasks] had already been achieved and I was ready to throw myself with all my heart into the contract, as it were, into which I had entered with the Soviet Union in the name of all suffering mankind. I felt myself so much committed that failure was not to be contemplated.

I admired particularly in Russia the extraordinary impulse towards education and culture. But the sad thing is that the education the people receive only informs them on what leads them to flatter themselves on the present state of affairs and to believe in the Soviet Union 'Ave spes unica.' Culture is directed towards one aim only, the glorification of the Soviet Union; it is not disinterested and critical discrimination is entirely lacking. I know well that they make a parade of self-criticism, and at first I believed and hoped in that, thinking that it might lead to great results if it was applied with integrity. But I soon discovered that criticism consists solely in inquiring whether such or such a work is in agreement with the Party line. It is not the Party line which is discussed or criticized, but only the question whether a certain theory tallies or not with this sacred line. No state of mind is more dangerous than this, nor more likely to imperil real culture. Soviet citizens remain in the most complete ignorance of everything outside their own country and – what is worse – have been persuaded that everything abroad is vastly inferior to everything at home. On the other hand, although they are not interested in what prevails outside their country, they are very much interested in what foreigners think of them. What they are very anxious to know is whether they are sufficiently admired abroad; what they fear above all else is that foreigners may not be sufficiently well informed concerning their merits; what they want from them is praise and not information . . .

In the Soviet Union it is accepted once and for all that on every subject – whatever may be the issue – there can only be one opinion, the right one. And each morning *Pravda* tells the people what they need to know, and must believe and think . . .

The disappearance of capitalism has not brought freedom to the Soviet workers – it is essential that the proletariat abroad should realize this fully. It is of course true that they are no longer exploited by share-holding capitalists, but nevertheless, they are exploited, and in so devious, subtle and twisted a manner that they do not know any more whom to blame. The largest number of them live below the poverty line and it is their starvation wages which permit the swollen pay-packets of the privileged workers – the pliant yes-men. One cannot fail to be shocked by the indifference shown by those in power towards their inferiors, and the servility and obsequiousness on the part of the latter – I almost said the poor. Granted that there are no longer any classes nor class distinctions in the Soviet Union, but the poor are still with them – and there are far too many of them . . .

Although the long-heralded dictatorship of the proletariat has not materialized there is nevertheless dictatorship of one kind – dictatorship of the Soviet bureaucracy. It is essential to recognize this and not to allow oneself to be bamboozled. This is not what was hoped for – one might almost say that it is precisely the last thing in the world that was hoped. The workers have no longer even the liberty of electing their own representatives to defend their threatened interests. Free ballot – open or secret – is a derision and a sham; the voters have merely the right of electing those who have been chosen for them beforehand. The workers are cheated, muzzled and bound hand and foot, so that resistance has become wellnigh impossible. The game has been well played by Stalin, and Communists the whole world over applaud him, believing that in the Soviet Union at least they have gained a glorious victory, and they call all those who do not agree with them public enemies and traitors. But in Russia this has led to treachery of a new sort. An excellent way of earning promotion is to become an informer; that puts you on good terms with the dangerous police which protects you while using you. Once you have started on that easy, slippery slope no question of friendship or loyalty can intervene to hold you back; on every occasion you are forced to advance, sliding further into the abyss of shame. The result is that everyone is suspicious of everyone else and the most innocent remarks – even of children – can bring destruction, so that everyone is on his guard and no one lets himself go . . .

The Soviet Union has deceived our fondest hopes and shown us tragically in what treacherous quicksand an honest revolution can founder. The same old capitalist society has been re-established, a new and terrible despotism crushing and exploiting man, with all the abject and servile mentality of serfdom.

Source: Richard Crossman (ed.), The God That Failed: Six Studies in Communism *(London, Hamish Hamilton, 1950), pp. 179, 181–2, 182–4, 184–5, 185–6, 187–8, 198.*

Document 5.32 Anna Akhmatova

There can be no more eloquent conclusion to a discussion of the Soviet 1930s than to draw on one of the greatest of Russia's poets. In a cycle of poems under the general rubric 'Requiem', some of which were written some years later, Anna Akhmatova gave profound poetic voice to the victims of Stalin's terror. Yezhov was head of the Soviet secret police, the NKVD, from September 1936 to December 1938. Known as 'the bloody dwarf', he oversaw the great purges of those years, which are forever inscribed in folk memory as the 'Yezhovshchina'.

Requiem

No, it wasn't under a foreign heaven,
It wasn't under the wing of a foreign power, –
I was there among my countrymen,
I was where my people, unfortunately, were.

1961

INSTEAD OF A PREFACE

In the awful years of Yezhovian horror, I spent
seventeen months standing in line in front of various
prisons in Leningrad. One day someone 'recognized' me.
Then a woman with blue lips, who was standing behind me, and
who, of course, had never heard my name, came out of the stupor
which typified all of us, and whispered into my ear (everyone there
spoke only in whispers):
       – Can you describe this?
    And I said:
       – I can.
       Then something like a fleeting smile passed over what once
had been her face.

1 April 1957
Leningrad

DEDICATION

Faced with this grief, mountains sink down,
The great river has to languish,
But the hasps of the prison are made of iron,
And behind them the 'concentration den'
And deadly anguish.
Cool winds are stroking someone's hair,
And the sun is shining on someone's head –
We don't know, we're the same everywhere,
The gnashing of keys is all we hear
And the soldiers' booted tread.
We get up as if there were priests to assist,
We cross the rebrutalized city squares,
More breathless than the dead, we come to the tryst,
The sun is lower and the Neva's all mist,
And far off, the song of hoping flares.
Sentence . . . And at once the tears will start,
How different from the others one's already grown,
It's as if they took the life out of the heart,
Like being thrown backwards on a jolting cart,

. . . She's coming . . . Staggering . . . Alone . . .
Where now are all the chance-met people,
Friends during those two years in hell?
Of which Siberian storms are they full?
What phantoms do they see in the lunar circle?
It's to them I am sending this farewell.

1940

INTRODUCTION

This happened when only the dead wore smiles –
They rejoiced at being safe from harm.
And Leningrad dangled from its jails
Like some unnecessary arm.
And when the hosts of those convicted,
Marched by – mad, tormented throngs,
And train whistles were restricted
To singing separation songs.
The stars of death stood overhead,
And guiltless Russia, that pariah,
Writhed under boots, all blood-bespattered,
And the wheels of many a black maria.

1935

Source: Anna Akhmatova, Poems, *selected and translated by Lyn Coffin, Introduction by Joseph Brodsky (New York, W. W. Norton & Co., 1983), pp. 82–4.*

6 | The road to Berlin, 1939–1945

Following the Munich agreement of September 1938, in which Britain and France sought to appease Hitler by allowing him to occupy the German-settled Sudetenland in Czechoslovakia, the USSR began negotiations with Germany which led to the non-aggression treaty (the Nazi–Soviet pact) of 23 August 1939. Vyacheslav Molotov was at the time both prime minister (he was chairman of Sovnarkom from 1930 to 1941) and foreign minister (1939–49, and 1953–6). The pact threw the communist world into confusion and strained the loyalties of all but the most slavishly pro-Moscow communist parties. In the immediate aftermath of the pact Stalin incorporated eastern Poland into the USSR, provoked a war with Finland, and occupied the Baltic republics and Bessarabia. Stalin ignored all warnings and punctiliously adhered to the terms of the pact, allowing Hitler to absorb much of Eastern Europe and then to defeat the Low Countries and France. All the while, Hitler was preparing for war with his nominal ally, and when he struck on 22 June 1941 the USSR was caught thoroughly unprepared. There are suggestions that Stalin had been preparing for an offensive war against Hitler, possibly to be launched in July 1941, and thus left his defences woefully unprepared and his best forces and equipment lined up on the border, most of which was destroyed in the first days of the German offensive. The war in the East was fought with unprecedented brutality, forging a reconciliation between the Stalinist regime and its own people – but only for the duration of hostilities and even then at the minimum level possible to ensure victory. The war appeared to have been won not because of the system and Stalin but despite them. Too often political concerns were placed over strategic and tactical requirements resulting in the wasteful loss of life. Victory gave the regime a legitimacy that it had hitherto lacked, but hopes for a permanent reconciliation between regime and society were disappointed.

The Diet of Dictators

After Munich Stalin pursued a dual foreign policy: while still trying to establish an anti-Hitler collective security pact with Britain and France, he prepared the ground for an agreement with Hitler. Following the signing of the Nazi–Soviet pact on 23 August 1939, a war was launched against Finland, ensuring its lasting hatred, the Baltic republics were swallowed up, and up to 2 million Polish men, women and children were deported from eastern Poland ('western Belorussia' and 'western

Ukraine' in Soviet parlance). The trains were full of these hapless victims in the first days of war, jamming the network and preventing the rapid deployment of reserves. Warnings of the imminent German attack were ignored, suggesting that Stalin saw the pact as something more than a temporary expedient. Grain and oil deliveries continued to be made to Germany right up to the invasion itself. The main concentrations of Soviet forces were deployed right on the new border with Germany, leaving them exposed to the devastating German hammer blow in the first days of the war.

Document 6.1   Stalin Provokes the War

Materials that have become available since 1991 force us to revise some aspects of the old historiography. In particular, Stalin's hitherto unpublished speech to the Politburo of 19 August 1939 revealed a cynical understanding of the possibilities open to him.

If we sign a mutual assistance treaty with France and Great Britain, Germany will forsake Poland and will try to find a 'modus vivendi' with the Western powers. War will be averted, but later events could take a dangerous turn for the USSR. If we accept Germany's proposal and sign a non-aggression pact with her, Germany will attack Poland, and the intervention of France and England in that war will become inevitable. Western Europe will suffer serious uprisings and disturbances. In these conditions we will have a great possibility of remaining on the sidelines in the conflict, and we can reckon on our successful entry into the war.

The experience of the last twenty years demonstrates that in peacetime it is impossible in Europe to have a communist movement strong enough for a Bolshevik party to seize power. The dictatorship of such a party is possible only as a result of a great war. We are making our choice, and it is clear. We must accept the German proposal and politely send back the Anglo-French mission. The first advantage which we will gain will be the destruction of Poland right up to the gates of Warsaw, including Ukrainian Galicia.

Germany is giving us complete freedom of action in the Baltic states and does not object to the return of Bessarabia to the USSR. She is willing to grant us a sphere of influence in Romania, Bulgaria and Hungary. The question of Yugoslavia remains open . . . At the same time, we must consider the consequences arising from either the defeat or the victory of Germany. In the event of its defeat the Sovietisation of Germany will inevitably follow and a communist government will be formed. We must not forget that a Sovietised Germany will be in great danger if this Sovietisation is a result of Germany's defeat in a short war. England and France will be strong enough to seize Berlin and destroy Soviet Germany. And we will not be strong enough to come to the assistance of our Bolshevik comrades in Germany.

Our task, therefore, is to ensure that Germany can fight the war for as long as possible so that an exhausted and debilitated England and France are in no condition to destroy a Sovietised Germany. Maintaining a position of neutrality and waiting for its moment, the USSR will support today's Germany, supplying it with raw materials and foodstuffs . . .

At the same time we must conduct active communist propaganda, especially in the Anglo-French bloc and primarily in France. We must be prepared for the eventuality that during the war the party will have to renounce legal work and go underground. We know that this work will require many victims, but our French comrades will have no doubts. Their primary task will be to disorganise and demoralise the army and the police . . . For the realisation of our plans the war must last as long as possible . . .

Let us now consider the second possibility, i.e., Germany's victory. Some hold the view that this outcome is a great threat to us. There is some truth in this, but it would be a mistake to think that this danger is as close and so great, as some imagine it to be. If Germany is victorious, she will emerge from the war too exhausted to be able to start a military conflict with the USSR, at least for a decade . . .

Comrades! It is in the interests of the USSR, the homeland of workers, that war breaks out between the Reich and the capitalist Anglo-French bloc. We must do everything possible to ensure that this war lasts as long as possible to ensure the exhaustion of both parties.

Source: Drugaya voina 1939–1945 *(Moscow, RGGU, 1996), pp. 73–5.*

Stalin thus accepted that at some point the USSR would enter the war, and he sought the best possible opportunity to do so. Indeed, he understood that war could advance Soviet interests, and thus feared that Germany might make peace (find a 'modus vivendi') with the Western powers. Thus the Nazi–Soviet pact was designed not only to buy the USSR breathing space, but to ensure that the war was not averted.

Document 6.2 Treaty on Non-Aggression between Germany and the Soviet Union

The day before military negotiations between the USSR, France and Britain due on 12 August, the Politburo decided on a fundamental change in foreign policy priorities, agreeing to establish close links with Nazi Germany. It was for this purpose that the German foreign minister Joachim von Ribbentrop flew to Moscow on 23 August, and the Nazi–Soviet pact was signed by him and Molotov late that evening. Of two documents signed that day, the Non-Aggression Treaty had an open character. The meeting was attended by Stalin and the German ambassador, Count Friedrich Werner von der Schulenburg. It was clear that Stalin wanted his share of the spoils of Nazi aggression.

The government of the USSR and the German government, guided by the desire to strengthen peace between the USSR and Germany and in keeping with the treaty on neutrality between the USSR and Germany of April 1926, have agreed the following:

Article 1

Both Signatory Parties agree to refrain from any violence, from any agressive action and any attack on the other, either individually or together with other powers.

Article 2

In the event of one of the Signatory Parties becoming the object of military activities by a third power, the other Signatory Party will not in any way support this power.

Article 3

The governments of both Signatory Parties will remain in contact with each other.

Article 4

Neither of the Signatory Parties will participate in any grouping of powers either directly or indirectly directed against the other side.

Article 5

In case of conflict between the Signatory Parties over any particular issue both sides will resolve these quarrels or conflicts by exclusively peaceful means in the form of friendly exchanges or when necessary by the creation of commissions to regulate the conflict.

Article 6

This treaty is signed for ten years with the provision that if neither of the Signatory Parties annuls it within a year of its expiry, the treaty will be considered automatically renewed for another five years.

Article 7

This treaty is to be ratified as soon as possible. The exchange of ratified documents will take place in Berlin. The treaty comes into force immediately after it is signed. Composed in two original copies in German and Russian in Moscow.

On behalf of the USSR government, V. Molotov
For the German government, I. Ribbentrop

Source: Pravda, *24 August 1939.*

Document 6.3   Secret Supplementary Protocol to the Nazi–Soviet Pact

The key points, however, were in the secret supplementary protocol, which was kept secret for over half a century. The two sides agreed on a division of spheres of influence in neighbouring countries. Almost every single article contradicted principles of international law and damaged Soviet state interests.

23 August 1939

In signing the Non-Aggression Treaty between Germany and the Union of Soviet Socialist Republics the signatory plenipotentiaries of both sides held strictly confidential discussions over the demarcation of spheres of interest in Eastern Europe. These discussions led to the following results:

1   In case of the territorial–political restructuring of regions in the Baltic states (Finland, Estonia, Latvia, Lithuania), the northern border of Lithuania is simultaneously the border between the sphere of interests of Germany and the USSR. At the same time, both sides recognise the Lithuanian claim on the Vilnius region.

2   In case of the territorial-political restructuring of regions in the Polish state, the border between the spheres of interests of Germany and the USSR will approximately follow the line of the Nareva, Vistula and Sana rivers.

The question of whether it is in the interests of both sides to preserve an independent Polish state and what the borders of such a state would be can be definitively clarified only in the course of further political developments.

In any case both governments will decide this question in friendly mutual agreement.

3   Concerning South-east Europe the Soviet side affirms the interest of the USSR in Bessarabia. The German side declares its complete political lack of interest in this region.

4   This protocol is to be preserved by both sides in the strictest secrecy.

On behalf of the USSR government, V. Molotov
For the German government, I. Ribbentrop

Source: Voprosy istorii, *no. 1, 1993, p. 6.*

Molotov and von der Schulenburg on 28 August signed a clarification to the secret supplementary protocol, modifying the line demarcating Soviet and German 'spheres of interest' outlined in the first paragraph of point 2, above. This line later changed several times. In a speech to the Supreme Soviet on 31 August 1939 Molotov insisted that the pact eliminated 'the danger of war between Germany and the Soviet Union'. Two main factors had allowed the conclusion of the pact, he argued: the impasse reached in negotiations with France and Great Britain; and the change in German foreign policy seeking 'good neighbourly relations with the Soviet Union'. He noted that 'Stalin hit the nail on the head when he exposed the machinations of the Western European politicians who were trying to set Germany and the Soviet Union at loggerheads'. He admitted, however, 'that there were some short-sighted people even in our own country who, carried away by over-simplified fascist propaganda, forgot about this provocative work of our enemies' (Daniels, *Communism and the World*, pp. 118–19).

Document 6.4   The Soviet Occupation of Eastern Poland

With their hands freed by the Nazi–Soviet pact, Hitler gave the order for the German invasion of Poland to commence at 4.45 a.m. on 1 September 1939. For the first time a country fell victim to the new military tactic of *Blitzkrieg*. The Soviet leadership was taken by surprise by the swift and dramatic collapse of resistance; not that the Polish forces did not fight with enormous valour, but the sides were too unevenly matched. The USSR swiftly sought to take advantage of the new situation and on 17 September Molotov made the following broadcast.

The USSR government this morning handed a note to the Polish ambassador in Moscow which announced that the Soviet government directed the Supreme Command of the Red Army to order their forces to cross the border and to undertake the defence of the life and property of the population of western Ukraine and western Belorussia.

The Soviet government also declared in the note that it is simultaneously resolved to undertake all measures to free the Polish people from the ill-fated war into which it was dragged by its unwise leadership, and to give it the possibility to begin to live a peaceful life.

Source: Vneshnyaya politika SSSR: sbornik dokumentov, *vol. IV (Moscow, Gospolitizdat, 1946), p. 447.*

Document 6.5   German–Soviet Treaty on Friendship and Borders between the USSR and Germany

Soviet forces entered Poland on 17 September under the guise of 'liberating' the eastern parts that were now joined with the Soviet republics of Ukraine and Belorussia. With the defeat and division of Poland complete, a further agreement with Germany was reached at a meeting in Moscow on 28 September, transforming what might have been justified as a security pact into a barely comprehensible 'friendship' pact. The open part of the pact divided Poland between the two powers, while one confidential and two secret protocols discussed matters that were long kept hidden.

The government of the USSR and the German government after the dissolution of the former Polish state consider their task to be the restoration of peace and order on this territory and to secure for the peoples living there a peaceful existence, corresponding to their national traits. To this end they have agreed the following:

Article 1

The government of the USSR and the German government establish as the border between their respective state interests on the territory of the former Polish state a line drawn on the enclosed map and which will be described in more detail in a supplementary protocol.

Article 2

Both sides recognise the border established in article 1 of their respective state interests as final and remove any interference by a third power in this decision.

Article 3

The necessary state restructuring on territory to the west of the line established in article 1 will be carried out by the German government, on territories to the east of this line by the USSR government.

Article 4

The government of the USSR and the German government consider the above-mentioned restructuring a reliable basis for the further development of friendly relations between their peoples.

Source: Pravda, *29 September 1939.*

Over the corpse of Poland Soviet–German friendship was thus built. One of the two secret protocols attached to this document redivided Polish territory: in exchange for including Lithuania in the 'sphere of interest of the USSR', Stalin offered Hitler Lublin and part of the Warsaw region. A map was appended with the changes. The protocol stated that as soon as the USSR 'undertakes on Lithuanian territory special measures to defend its interests', then the current German–Lithuanian border would be 'corrected', with part of south-west Lithuania being ceded to Germany (*Voprosy istorii*, no. 1, 1993, p. 9). The other secret protocol stated: 'Neither side will allow on their territory any Polish agitation originating from the territory of another country. They will liquidate the roots of such agitation on their territory and will inform each other of the necessary measures to be taken for this' (*Voprosy istorii*, no. 1, 1993, p. 10).

Document 6.6   The Deportation of the Poles: *The Dark Side of the Moon*

In 1946 Zoë Zajdlerowa, who had been associated with General Sikorski, head of the Polish government-in-exile in London, brought out this collection of testimonies of the deportation of Poles from their homes in the eastern part of the country.

Later Alexander Solzhenitsyn would use the same technique of collecting eye-witness accounts and as much documentary evidence as possible to compile his monumental account of the Soviet labour camps in his *The Gulag Archipelago*. The deportations continued right up to the Nazi invasion on 22 June 1941; indeed, the whole western Soviet rail network was jammed with cattle-trucks bearing their dangerous cargo of women and children to Siberia, the Soviet Arctic and Central Asia, regions 'as remote from the Western observer as the dark side of the moon from the stargazer's telescope', as Arthur Koestler put it. The new edition of the work ends with a comparison of Nazi and Soviet 'death camps'. The destruction of the Polish state and the attempted elimination of the active part of the nation in the 'fourth partition' of Poland ranks as one of the greatest tragedies of the twentieth century.

In the present chapter . . . I shall set down . . . as much as I can of the emotions and sensations through which we lived while the events were taking shape.

For this I must begin at midnight on September the 16–17th [1939], when, with my companions, in a small house on the edge of the Pripet Marshes, I listened to the broadcast from Moscow which announced that Soviet divisions, with armour and air cover, had crossed our eastern frontier.

From this night onwards the Moscow radio broadcast almost uninter-ruptedly that 'the internal bankruptcy of the Polish State had been revealed', that 'the Polish State and its Government have ceased to exist', that 'Warsaw no longer exists as the capital of Poland', and that 'therefore the Agreement concluded between the Soviet Union and Poland had ceased to operate'. It is noteworthy that the first German siege of Warsaw was at this time still going on, and that on September the 19th the capital was still bearing itself in such a way as to receive the broadcast message from 'the people of Britain to the city of Warsaw' which declared: 'All the world is admiring your courage', and that Poland had become 'the standard-bearer of liberty in Europe'.

The stupefaction in Poland was so great that many units were surrounded and taken prisoner before they could fight back. Others fought desperately on, but there was not now the slightest hope for our shattered forces, caught between the two heaviest and most powerful armies in the world. Of the civilian population, very many – the majority – as we know, believed in the first hours that the Russians had come as friends, that they were to fight the Germans and join up with the Polish divisions re-forming in the marshes.

From this time onward, we found ourselves in a night of doubt and confusion. Great mists of grief and horror oppressed our minds. The stream of refugees which had flowed east now began to flow back again towards the west. The millstones moved relentlessly together, and hundreds of thousands of people were caught between them, enduring every kind of progressive wretchedness and horror. As well as the tens of thousands of refugees on the roads, tens of thousands of soldiers and marines now began retreating westward again, standing here and there to fight and retreat again: more often to lie where they had fought or to be taken as prisoners to the Soviet Union. These men were desperately weary, famished, and short of everything; shortest of all of sleep. Many of them had been marching fifty or sixty kilometres a day. Rumour of course came with them. They knew even less than ourselves. Many of them kept right on believing that when the Russian and German armies met they would fight each other. Half of the men were too exhausted to talk at all. The worst thing was the condition of their feet. Too exhausted to be roused, they were incapable even of surveying their own bivouac fires; the chill of the autumn nights, following on the fantastically hot and cloudless days, barely reached them in this deathlike sleep. Only the very sick rested anywhere for more than a few hours. Polish and Soviet patrols were stumbling over each other here and there; some of them had talked together. More than once, a Red soldier had produced tobacco from his own pockets and given it to the tobacco-starved Poles. Many of them had said that they did not know what to make of this war. They had been told they were to march straight through against the Germans. They had had no idea that their leaders were sending them in to secure their share of a new partition of Poland. Later, I was to hear this story over and over again. I do not know if what they said was true. The perfect autumn weather added to the horror of all that was taking place . . .

This abyss of difference between the standards of Soviet citizens and the standards of the poorest or most primitive Polish home became fully apparent with the arrival in Poland of wives and families from the Union. The state to which these families could reduce a normal lodging within a few hours of taking possession, the accumulating filth in which they were satisfied to live, their total lack of discipline in respect of physiological functions, the crowded promiscuity of all the arrangements they made, the complete absence we observed in them of any instinct towards any other order of things – all this, we felt and felt with truth, had brought Asia into our homes . . .

All this, however, was still too little. A secret registration was simultaneously being prepared of persons to be deported to Soviet territory by a series of mass deportations, and to be there confined within Soviet penal institutions. From February the 10th [1940] onwards more than a million men, women, and children were so carried off; and many more would have followed them but for the German invasion of Russia in 1941.

The lists included all of university standing, teachers, doctors, engineers, the forestry services, well-to-do peasants and very many very poor peasants, certain categories of workmen, the families of soldiers of all ranks who were thought to be with the Polish Army or interned abroad, refugees from the German-occupied parts of Poland, and 'speculators' – a term applied to small merchants and traders.

Both the registration and the deportations which followed it automatically included the families also of all persons enumerated above, again a perfectly normal proceeding under the Soviet code . . .

In none of the cars, however, were there now enough of these bunks left to accommodate more than about ten or fifteen persons. In the majority there were none left at all. The extreme filth, recognizably human (for human filth always has something in it which is quite different from the filth of other animals), of the walls and floors, showed that the cars had been long and lately in use, probably for carrying troops. Dust, too, lay along all the folds of clothing and worked its way into lungs whose resistance became weaker every day. This was not so awful a problem in winter as it became in the April and June of the same year, when the roofs and walls of the cars were red-hot from the burning rays of the sun. Space was by common consent allotted first of all to the very old and to the most feeble and to mothers with very young children or women who were pregnant. The hole in the middle of the floor was screened by a blanket or two. This hole was of necessity extremely filthy and repulsive and, from the very beginning, this question of physiological processes loomed larger, probably, than any other. It is a recurring question which it will not be possible to omit from this record. Not only in the trains or on marches, but later in the penal institutions of every kind, the whole endless torturing business of the body's needs, and the absolute lack of any kind of decency or privacy in which these needs could be satisfied, pressed with accumulating cruelty not only on the poor body, but also on the mind . . .

On their way to these settlements, after twenty, thirty and sometimes forty days spent on the NKVD trains, hundreds of thousands of these exiles from the green fields, friendly towns and ancient parishes of Poland waited whole days on the naked steppe for the convoys to take them on the last stages of their route. Ragged, emaciated, filthy, prisoners of the Soviet East, they gasped under a pitiless sun all day or shivered with cold, without food or covering, all night: never again, at sunrise or sunset, to watch with joy the scented wood smoke rise above the Polish villages, the windows of Polish homes beckon with hospitable lights or the great white, fraternal Polish storks sink down upon or rise from their rooftop nests with serene and fondly familiar deployments of their immaculate wings . . .

[Afterword by the editors]

The people of Poland suffered intensely during the Second World War, irrespective of social class and ethnicity. The Nazis and the Soviet authorities were equally blameworthy, although Nazi atrocities received more publicity in the immediate post-war years . . .

Nevertheless, there have been attempts, if not to exculpate the Soviets, at least to show them in a relatively favourable light in comparison with the Nazis. Needless to say, such apologiae have not generally originated with the

Poles. Interviews with survivors of deportation place the perpetrators of death and terror in some sort of hierarchy with the Nazis at the top and the Soviets further down. These survivors are not prepared to accept that there is any distinction, from the viewpoint of the sufferers, between the destroyers of a national group and the eliminators of a social and political category. They cannot accept that there was any qualitative difference between camps in Germany and in the Soviet Union. All were death camps, and though life was prolonged in the Soviet Union, death's progress was inexorable, as Solzhenitsyn, who should know, has argued:

> The main thing is: avoid *general-assignment work*. Avoid it from the day you arrive. If you land in *general-assignment work* that first day, then you are lost, and this time for keeps . . . that is the main and basic work performed in any given camp. Eighty per cent of the prisoners work at it, and they all die off. All . . . The only ones who *survive* in camps are those who try at any price not to be put on general-assignment work. From the first day.

Similarly there was no hope of release in either system. The Poles believed fervently that they would get out, but they were in an exceptional position. The Russian prisoners had no expectations at all of release or survival, and were amazed when Poles were let out after the amnesty. If, by some chance, you survived your eight years, the NKVD would slap a repeat sentence on you. Death came fast or lingeringly, but it assuredly came. To assert, as [Primo] Levi does [in his *If This is a Man*, 1957] that death was not expressly sought in the Soviet camp system is a partial truth. Re-education and labour were other aims, but it was self-deception or misunderstanding on the prisoners' part not to accept that an eight-year sentence was tantamount to a sentence of execution. It is widely accepted that the camps were an ugly stain on Soviet socialism. But while socialism and camps were not generally regarded as indivisible, the same cannot be said about Nazism and camps. Neither can it be said about Stalinism and camps. [Jan] Gross has used the term 'spoiler state' [in her *Revolution from Abroad* (Princeton, 1988)] to describe the Soviet Union, and quotes Stalin's maxim that 'the State under communism wages war on society', commenting that the Stalinist system 'predicated a massive extermination of its subjects', comparable to 'wars between sovereign states'.

Hence, while the Nazis eliminated or enslaved enemies of the Aryan race and those who obstructed the achievement of Nazi strategic objectives, the Soviets liquidated or enslaved enemies of the people or party and those who stood in the way of *their* strategic goals.

Source: Zoë Zajdlerowa, The Dark Side of the Moon, *first published 1946, this edition edited by John Coutouvidis and Thomas Lane (London, Harvester Wheatsheaf, 1989), pp. 47–8, 54, 55, 67, 137, 171–2.*

Document 6.7 Churchill's Radio Broadcast of 1 October 1939

The spectacle of the two former enemies coming together left the Western powers bewildered. Churchill tried to make sense of events by arguing that 'the key is Russian national interest'. Churchill was never known to have used the terms 'Soviet Union' or 'USSR'; as far as he was concerned, Russia was synonymous with the larger USSR, a confusion that caused (and continued to cause) considerable distress among the non-Russian peoples making up the Soviet Union. Churchill implicitly supported the later Stalin line that the pact had bought time to prepare for war, although inadequate preparations were in fact made.

Poland has again been overrun by two of the Powers which held her in bondage for a hundred and fifty years but were unable to quench the spirit of the Polish nation. The heroic defence of Warsaw shows the soul of Poland is indestructible, and that she will rise again like a rock, which may for a time be submerged by a tidal wave, but which remains a rock.

Russia has pursued a policy of cold self-interest. We could have wished that the Russian armies should be standing on their present line as the friends and allies of Poland instead of as invaders. But that the Russian armies should be standing on this line was clearly necessary for the safety of Russia against the Nazi menace. At any rate, the line is there, and an Eastern front has been created which Nazi Germany does not dare assail . . .

I cannot forecast to you the action of Russia. It is a riddle wrapped in a mystery inside an enigma. But perhaps there is a key. That key is Russian national interest. It cannot be in accordance with the interest or safety of Russia that Germany should plant herself upon the shores of the Black Sea, or that she should overrun the Balkan States and subjugate the Slavonic peoples of South-eastern Europe. That would be contrary to the historic life-interests of Russia.

Source: Winston Churchill, The Second World War: The Gathering Storm *(London, Cassell/The Reprint Society, 1948), p. 363.*

Document 6.8 The Winter War

Its appetite whetted, the Soviet government on 26 November staged a provocation on the Finnish border. That evening Molotov handed a protest note to the Finnish ambassador in Moscow demanding that Finland remove its troops 20–5 kilometres from the Karelian isthmus. The Finnish government on 27 November responded by stating that the shellfire mentioned in the Soviet note had in fact come from the Soviet side of the border, but that it was willing to enter negotiations for the mutual withdrawal of forces from the border. Khrushchev later commented on these events in the following way.

The general opinion was that Finland would be delivered an ultimatum of a territorial nature that she had already rejected in the negotiations, and if she did not agree then military action would begin. Stalin held this view and I, obviously, did not object. I also thought that this was right. It was enough to state loudly our demands, and if they did not listen, then we would shoot and the Finns would put up their hands and agree to our demands . . . Then Stalin said: 'Today the business will begin'.

We stayed up rather late because the hour had already been set. Stalin was sure, and we believed it too, that there would be no war, that the Finns would accept our proposals and that we would attain our goals without war. The goal was our security in the North.

A telephone call suddenly came through stating that we had started shooting. The Finns responded with an artillery salvo. War in effect had begun. I am saying this because there is another version: that the Finns shot first, and therefore we had to respond. Did we have the juridical and moral right for such an action? We had no juridical right, of course. From the moral point of view the desire to ensure one's security, to come to terms with our neighbour justified our actions to ourselves.

Source: Ogonek, *no. 30, 1989, p. 11.*

Soviet forces invaded Finland on 30 November and established what they hoped would become the new government of Finland, the People's Government of the Finnish Democratic Republic headed by Otto Kuusinen and made up of representatives of various leftist groups, above all the Finnish Communist Party. A 'treaty of mutual assistance and friendship' signed between the 'Finnish Democratic Republic' and the USSR envisaged the transfer of 70,000 square kilometres in northern Karelia, populated mainly by Karelians, in return for the cession of 3,970 square kilometres to the north-west of Leningrad, thus pushing back the border along the Karelian isthmus away from the city. After early Soviet advances the Finns fought back and inflicted incommensurate losses on Soviet forces. The USSR suffered 87,506 men killed compared to Finland's 48,243, with another 39,369 Soviet soldiers disappearing without trace compared to Finland's 3,273, while 5,000 Soviet soldiers were taken prisoner, compared to 1,100 Finns. What became known as the 'Winter War' revealed the loss of the Red Army's fighting potential inflicted by Stalin's purge of the officer corps in 1937–8 and its poor equipment. The sheer weight of numbers, however, led to Finland agreeing to peace on 12 March 1940 whereby the whole of the Karelian isthmus, including the town of Vyborg, was transferred to the USSR. In the wake of the war the Soviet Ministry of Defence revealed the parlous state of its forces (*Izvestiya TsK KPSS*, no. 1, 1990, pp. 193–208). It was the Winter War rather than the German threat that provoked the reorganisation of Soviet armed forces. At the same time, the working day was lengthened, labour discipline tightened, the unauthorised change of jobs forbidden and modern arms production stepped up.

Document 6.9 Stalin's Attitude to Alliance with Hitler

Why did Stalin sign the Nazi–Soviet pact and stick to its terms so pedantically right up to the end? The usual reason was that Stalin sought to gain time to prepare his own defences, yet there is little evidence of these preparations actually taking place. Indeed, with the advance of the Soviet borders into Poland the old defences were dismantled but new ones were not constructed so as not to alarm Hitler. In Leningrad, where Andrei Zhdanov had taken over as party boss after Kirov's assassination, any sign of preparing for war was regarded as treasonable activity. The curators of the palace at Pushkin (formerly Tsarskoe Selo) could only clandestinely, and at great personal risk, begin packing and preparing the most valuable items for safekeeping. Stalin's constant interference in the choice of equipment and design had lamentable consequences in the early days of the war. It was only in the first half of 1941 that the modern T-34 and KV tanks and Yak-1 and MiG-3 fighters entered mass production. The real basis for the pact was probably psychological: Hitler was possibly the only man Stalin ever trusted. Kravchenko details some of the consequences of the pact.

In the light of future events, one thing should be made clear. Stalin entered into his compact with Hitler in earnest. Had the Kremlin played with the idea that we must ultimately fight Germany anyhow, some part of the existing hatred of the Nazis would have been preserved; our antifascist propaganda would not have been so completely abandoned in favor of 'anti-imperialist' (meaning anti-British and anti-American) propaganda. At least the more trusted Party officials in the Kremlin itself, many of whom I knew intimately, would have been apprised of the continuing Nazi danger.

Nothing of the sort happened. On the contrary, any whisper against Germany, any word of sympathy for Hitler's victims, was treated as a new species of counter-revolution. The French, British, Norwegian 'warmongers' were getting their deserts.

The theory that Stalin was merely 'playing for time' while feverishly arming against the Nazis was invented much later, to cover up the Kremlin's tragic blunder in trusting Germany. It was such a transparent invention that little was said about it inside Russia during the Russo-German war; only after I emerged into the free world did I hear it seriously advanced and believed. It was a theory that ignored the most significant aspect of the Stalin–Hitler arrangement: the large-scale economic undertakings which drained the USSR of the very products and materials and productive capacity necessary for its own defense preparations.

The simple fact is that the Soviet regime did not use the interval to arm itself effectively. I was close enough to the defense industries to know that there was a slackening of military effort after the pact. The general feeling, reflecting the mood in the highest official circles, was that we could afford to feel safe thanks to the statesmanship of Stalin. Not until the fall of France did doubts arise on this score; only then was the tempo of military effort stepped up again.

Source: Kravchenko, I Chose Freedom, *p. 355.*

Document 6.10   The Incorporation of the Baltic Republics

By June 1940 Stalin was ready to cash in his stake in the Baltic republics granted him by the treaties with Germany. On 14 June 1940 he issued an ultimatum to Lithuania for its government to disband, and the next day Soviet forces attacked and soon occupied all of Lithuania. Rigged elections on 14 July gave a figleaf of constitutionality to Lithuania's incorporation into the USSR. For Estonia, 14 June is a day of mourning. On that day in 1941 more than 10,000 Estonian citizens – men, women and children – were deported to slave labour and subsequent death in the Soviet Union. The day also commemorates the further 20,000 who suffered a similar fate in 1949. At Christmas 1941 the Estonian poet Marie Under, who witnessed the first deportation, wrote a poem in memory of the event – the poem is sometimes printed in Estonian newspapers on 14 June. The late Russian poet Joseph Brodsky, who supported the aspirations of the Baltic peoples for freedom, used to say that 'in art there are no sides', a truth reflected in Under's poem.

> I walk the silent, Christmas-snowy path,
> that goes across the homeland in its suffering.
> At each doorstep I would like to bend my knee:
> there is no house without mourning.
> The spark of anger flickers in sorrow's ashes,
> the mind is hard with anger, with pain tender:
> there is no way of being pure as Christmas
> on this white, pure-as-Christmas path.
> Alas, to have to live such stony instants,
> to carry on one's heart a coffin lid!
> Not even tears will come any more –
> that gift of mercy has run out as well.
> I'm like someone rowing backwards:
> eyes permanently set on past –
> backwards, yes – yet reaching home at last . . .
> my kinsmen, though, are left without a home . . .
> I always think of those who were torn from here . . .
> The heavens echo with the cries of their distress.
> I think that we are all to blame
> for what they lack – for we have food and bed!
> Shyly, almost as in figurative language,

I ask without believing it can come to pass:
Can we, I wonder, ever use our minds again
for the sake of joy and happiness?

1941

Source: Mimeo, translation by Leopoldo J. Niilus and David McDuff.

Document 6.11   Katyn

After occupying half of Poland following its intervention on 17 September 1939, several thousand Polish officers were interned, the great majority of whom came from intelligentsia families – teachers, doctors and officials. They were mobilised at the beginning of the war largely from the eastern region, and had barely fought before Poland capitulated. By March 1940, as Lavrentii Beria (head of the NKVD) states in his note to Stalin, 14,736 were held in Soviet camps. In addition, another 10,685 Poles were held in camps in western Belorussia and Ukraine. The largest camps holding the Polish officers were at Kozielsk, Starobielsk and Ostaszkov. In the spring of 1940 rumours circulated that these camps had closed, with their inmates transferred to an unknown destination. Three years later mass graves were found on territory occupied by the Germans in the Katyn forest near Smolensk. An inquiry set up by them found that several thousand Polish officers, mainly from the Kozielsk camp, had been shot by the NKVD. The Soviet government vigorously denied its involvement in the killings, accusing the occupying forces of perpetrating the atrocity. To add insult to injury, they accused the Polish government-in-exile in London of having staged a provocation, and broke off diplomatic relations with it.

Beria's Memorandum to Stalin

Top Secret
5.III.1940

Comrade Stalin,
In the prisoner-of-war camps of the USSR NKVD and in the prisons of the western regions of Ukraine and Belorussia at the present time there are a great number of former Polish Army officers, former workers of the Polish police and secret service bodies, members of Polish nationalistic c[ounter]-r[evolutionary] parties, members of secret c-r rebel organisations, deserters and others. They are all accursed enemies of Soviet power, filled with hate for the Soviet order.

The officer prisoners of war and policemen in the camps try to continue their c-r work, conducting anti-Soviet agitation. Every one of them is only waiting for his release to be able to enter actively in the struggle against Soviet power.

The NKVD organs in the western regions of the Ukraine and Belorussia have exposed a number of c-r rebel organisations. In all these c-r activities an active leading role was played by the former officers of the former Polish army, former policemen and gendarmes.

Among the detained deserters and those who have crossed the border illegally there have also been caught a significant number of people who are members of c-r espionage and rebel organisations.

In the prisoner-of-war camps there are a total (excluding soldiers and non-commissioned officers) of 14,736 former officers, civil servants, landlords, policemen, gendarmes, prison officers, intelligence officers – by nationality over 97 per cent Polish . . .

Since they are all inveterate, incorrigible enemies of Soviet power, the USSR NKVD considers necessary:

I To direct the USSR NKVD:
1 The cases of the 14,700 former Polish officers, civil servants, landlords, policemen, intelligence officers, gendarmes and prison officers held in prisoner-of-war camps,
2 And also the cases of those arrested and held in camps in the western regions of the Ukraine and Belorussia numbering 11,000 people, members of various espionage and diversionary organisations, former landlords, factory owners, former Polish officers, civil servants and deserters –
– to examine them as a matter of urgency, with the application of the highest measure of punishment – shooting.

II To examine the cases without summoning those arrested and without presenting charges, stating the ending of the investigation and summing up – in the following way:
1 for those in prisoner-of-war camps – according to documents presented by the Board for Prisoner-of-war Affairs of the USSR NKVD,
2 for the arrested – from documents from the files presented by the UkSSR and BSSR NKVD.

III The examined cases and decisions to be presented to a troika consisting of Comrades Merkulov, Kobulov and Bashtakov (the head of the First Special Department of the USSR NKVD).

The People's Commissar of Internal Affairs of the USSR (L. Beria)

Source: Voprosy istorii, *no. 1, 1993, pp. 17–18.*

The Politburo on 5 March 1940 agreed to all of Beria's proposals: the cases were to be resolved in the absence of the accused, without any charges to be laid and with the sentences agreed beforehand – shooting. Without further ceremony the Politburo ordered NKVD troikas to examine the cases of 25,700 imprisoned Poles, Belorussians and west Ukrainians and to shoot them. From notes on the first page of the report we know that Stalin, Molotov, Voroshilov and Mikoyan were directly involved in the decision, and from marginal notes that Kalinin and Kaganovich agreed to the action. Why the Soviet authorities needed to murder these people, already imprisoned in camps or prisons, remains unclear, although the language used by Beria suggested that the undying hatred felt by the Poles for the Soviet atrocities was part of the reason.

On 3 March 1959 the head of the KGB, A. Shelepin, sent Khrushchev a hand-written note (he did not even trust the typist) giving more details of the victims' fate at the hands of the special NKVD troika in 1940. A total of 21,857 were executed: 4,421 in the Katyn forest in Smolensk region; 3,820 in Starobielsk camp near Kharkov; 6,311 in Ostaszkov camp in Kalinin region; and 7,305 were shot in other camps and prisons of western Ukraine and western Belorussia (*Voennye Arkhivy Rossii*, no. 1, 1993, pp. 124–8). All the files had been kept in a sealed form. Shelepin argued that the documents were of no historical or material interest for the Soviet authorities and, on the contrary, 'some unforeseen eventuality could lead to the operation becoming known with all of the unpleasant consequences for our state. Moreover, there is an official version in regard to those shot in the Katyn forest, confirmed by the commission set up by the Soviet organs of power in 1944' that had found the 'German-fascist occupiers' guilty. This version, Shelepin argued, had been well publicised in the Soviet and foreign press and had become part of international public opinion and nothing should allow this view to be challenged. He therefore recommended that all the materials associated with the 1940 operation, except those of the troika and the death sentences, be destroyed (*Voprosy istorii*, no. 1, 1993, pp. 20–1).

In the post-war years the whole Katyn incident was a taboo subject for the communist authorities, although for Poles both at home and in emigration it remained a live issue. One of the more tragic aspects of the case is the willingness of Western authorities to go along with Soviet lies for so long, refusing even to allow Polish émigrés to put up a monument to the victims with the date '1940'. Only under Gorbachev did the truth emerge and during the visit by the Polish president, Wojciech Jaruzelski, to Moscow in April 1990 the Soviet Union formally acknowledged responsibility for the murders and apologised to Poland. Soviet policy in this period was later defended by Gorbachev (Document 10.8).

The Titans Go To War

While Stalin was murdering Poles, attacking Finland and occupying the Baltic republics and Bessarabia, Hitler was preparing for war against the USSR. It appears that in July 1940 he effectively abandoned plans to invade Britain (Operation Sealion) and turned his attention to the East. On 18 December 1940 he insisted that 'German armed forces must be ready to smash Soviet Russia in a short campaign even before the war against England is over (the "Barbarossa variant")' (*Rossiya, kotoruyu my ne znali*, p. 37).

6.12   Hitler's War Aims

At a meeting on 30 March 1941 Hitler defined Germany's tasks in relation to Russia as:

[T]he utter defeat of its armed forces and the destruction of the state . . . This is a struggle between two ideologies: the death sentence on Bolshevism is not a social crime . . . This war will be very different from war in the West. In the East brutality itself is of benefit for the future. Commanders must sacrifice much to overcome their doubts.

Source: Rossiya, kotoruyu my ne znali, *pp. 38–9.*

6.13 'None so Deaf as Will Not Hear'

From the summer of 1940 to 22 June 1941 the NKVD received a mass of information about Germany's preparations for the invasion of the USSR. German reconnaissance planes flew deep over Soviet territory over 200 times, always over military and defence objects, and one of these planes when forced to land was found to be carrying aerial photographic equipment (*Izvestiya TsK KPSS*, no. 4, 1990, pp. 216–18). Despite warnings from General G. Zhukov, the Soviet spy Richard Sorge in the German embassy in Tokyo, Winston Churchill and others about the concentration of German forces on the Soviet border, the Soviet information agency TASS issued the following disclaimer.

1 Germany has made no demands on the USSR and is not proposing any new, closer, agreement and thus negotiations on this subject could not have taken place.
2 According to Soviet information, Germany is undeviatingly fulfilling the conditions of the Soviet–German non-aggression pact, as is the Soviet Union; in view of this, in Soviet opinion, rumours that Germany plans to tear up the pact and attack the USSR lack any substance, and the recent transfer of German forces, freed from operations in the Balkans, to eastern and north-eastern regions of Germany is linked, one must suppose, with motives having nothing to do with Soviet–German relations.
3 Arising out of its peaceful policy, the USSR has observed and will observe the conditions of the Soviet–German non-aggression pact, thus rumours that the USSR is preparing for war with Germany are lies and provocations.

Source: Pravda, *14 June 1941.*

The very strength of the disclaimer is in itself suspicious. Was Stalin preparing to launch an offensive war against Germany? We noted above (Document 6.1) that even in signing the Nazi–Soviet pact in August 1939 Stalin had in mind only a temporary truce to buy time before war with Germany, and thus (contrary to the old version) Stalin had no absolute faith in the pact. While Germany might have been preparing for war against the USSR from July 1940, Stalin had been preparing for war against Germany from October 1939; and from November 1940 their relations entered into a new phase when both sides prepared for war while formally maintaining the terms of their non-aggression pact. Stalin's speech of 5 May 1941 to military graduates gave a signal to the Soviet agitprop apparatus to prepare the army psychologically for war. However, the bulk of evidence suggests that there could have been no thought of a Soviet offensive in 1941. Although between 1 January 1939 and 22 June 1941 Soviet forces increased from 1.9 to 5.7 million, rising from 136 to 303 divisions, from 18,400 to 23,300 tanks, and from 17,500 to 22,400 warplanes (*Drugaya voina 1939–1945*, p. 98), most of its equipment was outdated and its officer corp unprepared after the purges. Even after the attack, according to Dmitrii Volkogonov on the basis of super-secret documents, Stalin used Bulgarian intermediaries to offer Hitler huge territories in return for a cessation of the attack (Lev Gintsberg, *Nezavisimaya gazeta*, 21 June 1996, p. 5).

Document 6.14 'Secret Number One'

Shortly before the invasion the Soviet ambassador to Berlin, V. G. Dekanozov, returned to Moscow for a visit and was invited to dine with von Schulenburg. Schulenburg made the following statement.

Mr ambassador, perhaps this has never yet taken place in the history of diplomacy, but I intend to reveal to you state secret number one: pass this on to Mr Molotov, and I hope he will inform Mr Stalin; Hitler has decided on 22 June to start a war against the USSR. You ask, why am I doing this? I was brought up in the spirit of Bismarck, and he was always against war with Russia.

Source: Pravda, *22 June 1989.*

Dekanozov hurried to tell Molotov, and that very day Stalin called the Politburo together to discuss Schulenburg's information. Stalin declared: 'We consider that disinformation has now reached up to the level of ambassadors.'

6.15 More Disclaimers

In a note to Stalin on 21 June 1941 Lavrentii Beria, still the head of the Soviet secret police (the NKVD), fawned:

I once again insist on the recall and punishment of our ambassador in Berlin, Dekanozov, who as before is bombarding me with 'disinformation' that Hitler is allegedly preparing to attack the USSR. He stated that this 'attack' will begin tomorrow . . . But I and my people, Joseph Vissarionovich, firmly remember your wise prognosis: Hitler will not attack us in 1941!

Source: Argumenty i fakty, *no. 4, 1989.*

Document 6.16   Molotov's Radio Broadcast of 22 June 1941

The German blow, when it came on 22 June, was total and devastating. The best Soviet forces were captured, the air force largely destroyed on the ground, masses of military equipment captured, and a large proportion of Soviet industrial plant lost. Stalin disappeared from view (although he was far from inactive – in the days following the invasion he held to a gruelling regime of meetings and decision-taking), leaving it to Molotov to rally the people.

Citizens of the Soviet Union!

The Soviet government and its head, Comrade Stalin, have commissioned me to make the following announcement:

Today at four in the morning, without any ultimatum against the Soviet Union, without a declaration of war, German forces invaded our country, attacked our borders in many places and their planes bombed our towns – Zhitomir, Kiev, Sevastopol, Kaunas and some others, with some 200 people being killed. Enemy flights and artillery bombardments also took place from Romanian and Finnish territory . . .

Now that the attack on the Soviet Union has taken place, the Soviet government has ordered our forces to repulse the wretched attack and expel the German forces from the territory of our Motherland . . .

This is not the first time that our people has had to deal with an attacking enemy. Our people responded to Napoleon's campaign in Russia with the Patriotic War, and Napoleon was defeated and ultimately destroyed. And the same will happen to the arrogant Hitler, declaring a new campaign against our country. The Red Army and our whole people will once again conduct a victorious Patriotic War for the Motherland, for honour, for freedom . . .

The government calls on you, citizens of the Soviet Union, to unite even closer around our glorious Bolshevik party, around our Soviet government, around our great leader Comrade Stalin.

Our cause is just! The enemy will be defeated! Victory will be ours!

Sources: Pravda, *23 June 1941;* Izvestiya, *24 June 1941.*

Document 6.17   Stalin's Radio Broadcast of 3 July 1941

From the first the struggle was conducted under patriotic rather than communist slogans. The very term of address to the people as 'citizens' rather than comrades symbolised the way that the war would be fought. Stalin himself disappeared for some ten days, apparently suffering some sort of nervous attack (but, as noted, he remained active), leaving the call to the Soviet people in Molotov's hands. Only on 3 July did Stalin address the Soviet people.

Comrades, citizens, brothers and sisters, men of our Army and Navy!

My words are addressed to you, dear friends!
The perfidious military attack by Hitlerite Germany on our Fatherland, begun on 22 June, is continuing. In spite of the heroic resistance of the Red Army, and although the enemy's finest divisions and finest air force units have already been smashed and have met their doom on the field of battle, the enemy continues to push forward, hurling fresh forces to the front . . .

How could it have happened that our glorious Red Army surrendered a number of our cities and districts to the fascist armies? Is it really true that the German-fascist forces are invincible, as the braggart fascist propagandists are ceaselessly blaring forth?

Of course not! History shows that there are no invincible armies and never have been . . . The same must be said of Hitler's German-fascist army of today. This army has not yet met with serious resistance on the continent of Europe. Only on our territory did it meet with serious resistance . . .

As to part of our territory having nevertheless been seized by the German-fascist troops, this is chiefly due to the fact that the war of fascist Germany against the USSR began in conditions that were favourable for the German forces and unfavourable for the Soviet forces. The fact of the matter is that the troops of Germany, a country at war, were already fully mobilized . . . Of no little importance in this respect was the fact that fascist Germany suddenly and treacherously violated the non-aggression pact which she had concluded in 1939 with the USSR . . . It may be be asked, how could the Soviet government have consented to conclude a non-aggression pact with such perfidious people, such fiends as Hitler and Ribbentrop? Was this not an error on the part of the Soviet government? Of course not! Non-aggression pacts are pacts of peace between two states. It was such a pact that Germany proposed to us in 1939. Could the Soviet government have refused such a proposal? I think that not a single peace-loving state could decline a peace treaty with a neighbouring state even though the latter were headed by such monsters and cannibals as Hitler and Ribbentrop . . .

What did we gain by concluding the non-aggression pact with Germany? We secured our country peace for a year and a half and the opportunity of preparing our forces to repulse fascist Germany should she risk an attack our country despite the pact.

Sources: Pravda, *3 July 1941; Generalissimo Stalin,* War Speeches *(London, Hutchinson, n.d.), pp. 7, 8.*

Document 6.18   Stalin's Conduct of the War

Stalin was clearly being disingenuous and covering his tracks in his broadcast, since as we have seen little was done to prepare Soviet forces in the nearly two years of peace. Yet as a war leader Stalin showed himself, as did the Soviet system as a whole, at his and its best. The war, as Stalin argued in the same broadcast, would be fought as a national endeavour allied with Western powers. He even hinted that democracy would be restored in the case of victory.

In areas occupied by the enemy, guerilla units, mounted and on foot, must be formed; sabotage groups must be organized to combat enemy units, to foment guerilla warfare everywhere, blow up bridges and roads, damage telephone and telegraph lines, set fire to forests, stores and transports. In occupied regions conditions must be made unbearable for the enemy and all his accomplices. They must be hounded and annihilated at every step, and all their measures frustrated.

The war with fascist Germany cannot be considered an ordinary war. It is not only a war between two armies, it is also a great war of the entire Soviet people against the German-fascist armies. The aim of this national patriotic war in defence of our country against the fascist oppressors is not only to eliminate the danger hanging over our country, but also to aid all the European peoples groaning under the yoke of German fascism. In this war of liberation we shall not be alone. In this great war we shall have true allies in the peoples of Europe and America, including the German people which is enslaved by the Hitlerite misrulers. Our war for the freedom of our country will merge with the struggle of the peoples of Europe and America for their independence, for democratic liberties. It will be a united front of the peoples standing for freedom against enslavement and threats of enslavement by Hitler's fascist armies. In this connection the historic utterance of the British Prime Minister, Mr Churchill, regarding aid to the Soviet Union and the declaration of the United States government signifying readiness to render aid to our country, which can only evoke a feeling of gratitude in the hearts of the peoples of the Soviet Union, are fully comprehensible and symptomatic . . .

In order to ensure the rapid mobilization of all the forces of the peoples of the USSR, and to repulse the enemy who has treacherously attacked our country, a State Committee of Defence [GKO] has been formed and the entire state authority has been vested in it . . .

All the forces of the people for the destruction of the enemy!
Forward to victory!

Source: Stalin, War Speeches, *pp. 11, 12.*

The resolution of 18 July 1941, 'On the Organisation of Fighting in the Rear of German Troops', called on the occupied population to form partisan units to harry the enemy in the rear: to destroy communications, transport and even armed units. The partisan war did indeed take on a mass character, but by the same token provoked mass reprisals against the civilian population.

Document 6.19   The Unexpected War

Stalin's speech at last admitted what those at the front already knew: that the Germans had seized vast Soviet territories in the first week of the war. The 'suddenness' of the attack was obviously made up by Stalin, having been warned according to a recent account by no fewer than seventy-six different sources (Lev Gintsberg, *Nezavisimaya gazeta*, 21 June 1996, p. 5), although the idea remains current in the literature. The speech nevertheless proved inspirational. Stalin was able to take advantage of the offers of assistance from the Western powers, while internally the GKO effectively began to mobilise resources for the war effort. This included the mass evacuation of industry and personnel to the East. In keeping with the national rather than communist tone of the war effort the slogan 'Proletarians of the world, unite' was removed from the mastheads of newspapers and other literature and replaced by 'Death to the German occupier' on the grounds that the old slogan 'could disorient some of the soldiery' (*Rodina*, nos. 6–7, 1991, p. 73). Kravchenko, however, took a sober view of Soviet efforts in the early days of the war.

A lot of to-do would subsequently be made in the Soviet propaganda about the factories evacuated to Siberia from White Russia and the Ukraine. In truth only a minor part was removed. Nothing would be said of the hundreds of plants left as a present to Hitler. Virtually every factory I had worked in or been connected with – in Dniepropetrovsk, Krivoi Rog, Zaparozhe, Taganrog – fell to the enemy almost intact. The same was more or less true of Kiev, Odessa, Kharkov, Mariupol, Stalino, Lugansk. Stalin's mistake in trusting Hitler was responsible for the fact that we abandoned to the enemy industry with a capacity of about ten million tons of steel a year, plus about two million tons in finished steel. It was all returned to us in time in the form of death-dealing tanks, guns, shells and bombs. The story was no less tragic for other industries.

During the period of the pact, Stalin helped Hitler conquer Europe by providing him with metal, ores, oil, grain, meat, butter, and every conceivable type of material, in accordance with their economic pact. After the invasion, Stalin helped him by leaving him immense riches in military goods and productive capacity and – most shameful of all – tens of millions of people.

Failure to prepare will be held against the Stalin regime by history despite the ultimate victory. It was to blame for millions of unnecessary casualties, for human wretchedness beyond calculation. Why was not the population of Leningrad evacuated? This 'oversight' is ignored by the hallelujah-shouters, though up to May 1, 1943, more than 1,300,000 died of hunger and cold, and the rest will carry the marks of their suffering to the grave, in three successive winters of terrifying siege. It was an exposed city. The preparations for saving its inhabitants should have been made long in advance, but they were not undertaken even after the war started. Responsibility for the gruesome sufferings of Leningrad rests directly on two members of the Politburo – Voroshilov, as the then commander of the Leningrad front, and Zhdanov, the supreme master of the Leningrad region.

Source: Kravchenko, I Chose Freedom, *pp. 364–5.*

Document 6.20   Hitler's Conduct of the War

Hitler's assault on the USSR was indeed a war of a new type. At a secret meeting on 16 July 1941 Hitler stressed that to the world at large German war aims in Soviet Russia should be presented as no different from those in occupied Norway, Denmark, Holland and Belgium, namely:

[T]o restore order and and impose security . . . The main thing is that we ourselves know what we want . . . it should not be made known that the heart of the matter is the final solution . . . but nevertheless we must apply all necessary measures, shootings, deportations, and so on . . .

In Hitler's view the order to start a partisan war in the rear:

[H]as its advantages: it gives us the opportunity to exterminate all those who rise up against us.

The Crimea was to be cleansed of all 'aliens' and settled with Germans, while Galicia was to become a region of the German empire.

Source: From notes taken by Martin Borman, in Rossiya, kotoruyu my ne znali, *pp. 62–2.*

Others talked not just of the destruction of the Russian state but of the total extermination of the Russian people, with the possible exception of 'those with clear signs of the Nordic race' (from a memorandum on the 'Ost' plan to the SS Reichsführer from Doctor Wetzel 'On Future Relations with the Russian Population', Berlin, 27 April 1942, in V. I. Dashichev, *Bankrotstvo strategii germanskogo fashizma,* vol. 2 (Moscow, 1973), pp. 36–8). In a secret letter to the Nazi ideologue Alfred Rosenberg, Martin Borman, head of Hitler's chancellery, insisted that it would be 'enough to teach the local population . . . only to read and write', and he was particularly concerned to keep the population to manageable levels by encouraging abortions and not offering German medical services to non-Germans (letter of 23 July 1942, in *Voenno-istoricheskii zhurnal,* no. 1, 1965, pp. 82–3). While older people, in the German view, 'expressed hatred of the old Bolshevik system', those between 17 and 21 were considered 'the most dangerous age group. They are 99 per cent infected and are to be struck from the list of the living.' Occupied areas were to be Germanised and settled with Germans, in particular Belorussia, Estonia, Latvia, Lithuania, Crimea and Ingermanland (north-west Russia). Thus 83 million Germans sought to dominate 200 million Russians and other Soviet peoples.

Document 6.21   The 'Final Solution' in the USSR

The inhumanity of the Germans to the Soviet Slav population was reminiscent of the attitudes of Europeans to the native peoples of America, but the scale and thoroughness of the attempt to impose the 'final solution' on the Jewish population was something new in history. From the first, Jews were forced to wear a yellow Star of David, forbidden to walk on pavements, enter parks or public spaces, and so on. In occupied areas of the USSR 'special action' troops systematically murdered the Jewish population. In a ravine on the outskirts of Kiev known as Babii Yar over a quarter of a million people were killed, a large proportion of them Jews. In the mid-1960s Anatoly Kuznetsov, an adolescent eyewitness of the 778 days that Kiev was occupied, published his account of the German occupation (*Babi Yar: A Documentary Novel*, London Sphere Books, 1969), but the most famous and powerful commemoration of the events was Yevgeny Yevtushenko's poem 'Babii Yar'.

No monument stands over Babii Yar.
A drop sheer as a crude gravestone.
I am afraid.
      Today I am as old in years
as all the Jewish people.
Now I seem to be
      a Jew.
Here I plod through ancient Egypt.
Here I perish crucified, on the cross,
and to this day I bear the scars of nails.
I seem to be
      Dreyfus.
The Philistine
      is both informer and judge.
I am behind bars.
      Beset on every side.
Hounded,
      spat on,
      slandered.
Squealing, dainty ladies in flounced Brussels lace
stick their parasols into my face.
I seem to be then
      a young boy in Byelostok.
Blood runs, spilling over the floors.
The bar-room rabble-rousers
give off a stench of vodka and onion.
A boot kicks me aside, helpless.
In vain I plead with these pogrom bullies.

While they jeer and shout,
                    'Beat the Yids. Save Russia!'
some grain-marketeer beats up my mother.
O my Russian people!
                    I know
                         you
are international to the core.
But those with unclean hands
have often made a jingle of your purest name.
I know the goodness of my land.
How vile these anti-Semites –
                         without a qualm
they pompously called themselves
'The Union of the Russian People!'
I seem to be
                    Anne Frank
transparent
             as a branch in April.
And I love
             And have no need of phrases.
My need
         is that we gaze into each other.
How little we can see
                    or smell!
We are denied the leaves,
                    we are denied the sky.
Yet we can do so much –
                    tenderly
embrace each other in a dark room.
They're coming here?
                    Be not afraid. Those are the booming
sounds of spring:
                    spring is coming here.
Come then to me.
                    Quick, give me your lips.
Are they smashing down the door?
                              No, it's the ice breaking . . .
The wild grasses rustle over Babii Yar.
The trees look ominous,
                    like judges.
Here all things scream silently,
                    and, baring my head,
slowly I feel myself
             turning gray.

And I myself
              am one massive, soundless scream
above the thousand thousand buried here.
I am
        each old man
                      here shot dead.
I am
        every child
                      here shot dead.
Nothing in me
              shall ever forget!
The 'Internationale', let it
                              thunder
when the last anti-Semite on earth
is buried forever.
In my blood there is no Jewish blood.
In their callous rage, all anti-Semites
must hate me now as a Jew.
For that reason
              I am a true Russian!

Source: 'Babii Yar', 19 September 1961, in Yevgeny Yevtushenko: Early
Poems, *translated by George Reavey (London, Marion Boyars, 1989).*

The Soviet War

There were in effect two wars being fought simultaneously: the war against the Nazi aggressor; and the continuing war of the Stalinist regime to stay in power. The second war was tempered at moments of threat, but never ceased. Fearing that the German settlements on the Volga would act as a diversionary fifth column, the order was issued in August 1941 for the deportation of the entire population to Kazakhstan and to the eastern regions of the USSR. With victory in sight it intensified, taking the form of mass deportation of minority ethnic groups, the punishment of former prisoners of war, and yet more persecution of those who had had the misfortune to find themselves in occupied territory. The Soviet losses were quite staggering, totalling some 27 million in all. The USSR did not sign the Geneva Convention on prisoners of war, so captured troops were given no protection from Nazi brutality and received no food parcels.

Document 6.22   From the Supreme Command of the Red Army, 16 August 1941

In the first days of the war whole units surrendered *en masse*. The Germans at first shot all those who surrendered, even those who were wounded, but in early July

Hitler changed the policy to encourage further desertions. In all a total of some 5,263,566 Soviet soldiers were taken prisoner between 22 June 1941 and 1 May 1944, of whom some 816,230 were freed and another 1,155,055 remained alive: some 3,292,281 were shot or died in some other way, nearly two-thirds of all those captured (*Rodina*, nos. 6–7, 1991, p. 100). Stalin's refusal to sign the Geneva Convention on the treatment of prisoners of war was paid for in the lives of millions. In the early days of the war draconian discipline was imposed on the army where the concept of surrender was identified with betrayal.

Recently some disgraceful cases of surrender to the enemy have taken place. Some generals have given a bad example to soldiers . . .
 It is ordered:

1 Commanders and political workers who during a battle hide their identity tags, desert to the rear or surrender to the enemy are to be considered malicious deserters. Their families are to be arrested as the relatives of deserters who have broken their oaths of service and betrayed their motherland. All commanders and commissars are to shoot deserters in leadership positions on the spot.
2 Units and sub-units that are surrounded by the enemy are to fight self-lessly to the last man, look after *matériel* as their most precious possession, and try to get back through to the rear of enemy forces to inflict blows upon the fascist dogs.

Source: Sovetskii soyuz v gody Velikoi otechestvennoi voiny, 1941–1945: tyl, okkupatsiya, soprotivlenie *(Moscow, Politizdat, 1993), p. 63.*

By October 1941 the Germans were approaching Moscow and foreign missions, government offices and the military command were evacuated to Kuibyshev (Samara). On 15 October the GKO gave the order for the government to be evacuated, noting 'Comrade Stalin will be evacuated tomorrow or later, depending on circumstances' (*Izvestiya TsK KPSS*, no. 12, 1990, p. 217). In the event the German army was halted and the Battle of Moscow began.

Document 6.23   Stalin's Speech, 6 November 1941

Facing an unprecedented crisis, the regime was forced to reach out for support in ways that had hitherto been unacceptable. On the occasion of the twenty-fourth anniversary of the Russian revolution, with the Nazis some 40 miles from Moscow, Stalin appealed to Russian national pride rather than Marxism-Leninism as the inspiration for resistance. He characterised the war as a just war of liberation, vowed that the Germans would be defeated just as the Teutonic Knights, Tatars, Poles and Napoleon had been, and praised the positive features of his British and other allies. The utter savagery of the German army in Russia remains difficult to comprehend.

In our country the German invaders, i.e., the Hitlerites, are usually called fascists. The Hitlerites, it appears, consider this wrong and obstinately continue to call themselves 'National-Socialists' . . . Can the Hitlerites be regarded as *socialist*? No, they cannot. Actually, the Hitlerites are the sworn enemies of socialism, arrant reactionaries and Black Hundreds, who have robbed the working class and the peoples of Europe of the most elementary democratic liberties. In order to cover up their reactionary, Black Hundred essence, the Hitlerites denounce the internal regime of Britain and America as plutocratic regimes. But in Britain and the United States there are elementary liberties, there exist trade unions of workers and employees, there exist workers' parties, there exist parliaments; whereas in Germany, under the Hitler regime, all these institutions have been destroyed. One only needs to compare these two sets of facts to perceive the reactionary nature of the Hitler regime and the utter hypocrisy of the German-fascist pratings about a plutocratic regime in Britain and in America. In point of fact the Hitler regime is a copy of that reactionary regime which existed in Russia under tsardom . . .

'I emancipate man', says Hitler, 'from the humiliating chimera which is called conscience. Conscience, like education, mutilates man. I have the advantage of not being restrained by any considerations of a theoretical or moral nature' . . . In one of the declarations of the German command to the soldiers, found on the dead body of Lieutenant Gustav Ziegel, a native of Frankfurt-on-Main, it is stated: 'You have no heart or nerves; they are not needed in war. Eradicate every trace of pity and sympathy from your heart – kill every Russian, every Soviet person. Do not stop even if before you stands an old man or woman, girl or boy, kill! By this you will save yourselves from destruction, ensure the future of your family and win eternal glory.' There you have the programme and instructions of the leaders of the Hitlerite party and of the Hitlerite command, the programme and instructions of men who have lost all semblance of human beings and have sunk to the level of wild beasts . . . The German invaders want a war of extermination with the peoples of the USSR. Well, if the Germans want to have a war of extermination, they will get it. (*Loud and prolonged applause.*) . . .

Lenin distinguished between two kinds of war – predatory, and therefore unjust wars, and wars of liberation – just wars. The Germans are now waging a predatory war, an unjust war, aimed at seizing foreign territory and subjugating foreign peoples. That is why all honest people must rise against the German invaders as their enemies. Unlike Hitlerite Germany, the Soviet Union and its allies are waging a war of liberation, a just war, for the purpose of liberating the enslaved peoples of Europe and the USSR from Hitler's tyranny. That is why all honest people must support the armies of the USSR, Great Britain and the other allies, as armies of liberation.

We have not, and cannot have, such war aims as the seizure of foreign territories and the subjugation of foreign peoples – whether it be the peoples and territories of Europe or the peoples and territories of Asia, including Iran. Our first aim is to liberate our territories and our peoples from the German-fascist yoke. We have not, and cannot have, any such war aims as that of imposing our will and our regime upon the Slavonic or other enslaved nations of Europe, who are expecting our help. Our aim is to help these nations in the struggle for liberation they are waging against Hitler's tyranny and then to leave it to them quite freely to organize their life on their lands as they think fit. No interference in the internal affairs of other nations!

Sources: Pravda, *7 November 1941; Stalin,* War Speeches, *18–19, 19–20, 22–3.*

One of the coldest winters of the twentieth century took a heavy toll on German forces unprepared for the rigours of a Russian winter. Soviet forces destroyed all habitable buildings to deprive the enemy of shelter. In December the German advance on Moscow was turned and in early 1942 pushed back from the city. German forces had raced towards Leningrad in August 1941 but there, too, Soviet forces refused to surrender. The siege of Leningrad began on 8 September 1941 and lasted until January 1944 – known as 'the 1,000-day siege'. Vital supplies came in along the 'Road of Life', the only link with the outside world cut across the frozen Lake Ladoga. The choice facing the authorities was whether to provide food for the starving population or materials for the arms factories.

Document 6.24 The People's War

Kravchenko provides a vivid picture of how the war was fought by the Soviet people. He presents the important argument that the Germans might have been welcomed as liberators if they had not proved themselves even more vile than the Soviet regime. For example, instead of returning the land to the peasants, they proceeded to use the collective farm system and fulfilled its potential as one of the most efficient instruments of peasant exploitation known to humanity. At the same time, Kravchenko acknowledged that there was little desire for the restoration of the pre-revolutionary order of 'landlords and capitalists'.

It took months of direct experience with German brutality to overcome the moral disarmament of the Russian people. They had to learn again to detest the Nazis, after two years in which Hitler had been played up as a friend of Russia and a friend of peace. Let it not be forgotten that in the early weeks entire Red Army divisions fell prisoners to the enemy almost without a struggle.

Had the invaders proved to be human beings and displayed good political sense they would have avoided a lot of the fierce guerilla resistance that plagued them day and night. Instead the Germans, in their fantastic racial obsessions, proceeded to kill, torture, burn, rape and enslave. Upon the collectivization which most peasants abhorred the conquerors now imposed an insufferable German efficiency. In place of the dreaded NKVD, the Germans brought their dreadful Gestapo. Thus the Germans did a magnificent job for Stalin. They turned the overwhelming majority of the people, whether in captured territory or in the rear, and all of the armed forces against themselves. They gave the Kremlin the materials for arousing a burning national hatred against the invaders.

Refugees and escaped prisoners disseminated the bloody tidings of German atrocities and high-handed stupidity. The Nazi barbarians, we learned, treated all Slavs as a sub-human species. I know from my own emotions that indignation against the Germans drove out resentments against our own regime. Hitler's hordes succeeded in inflaming Russian patriotism more effectively than all the new war cries of race and nation launched from the Kremlin.

Had we been at war with a democratic country, humane and enlightened, bringing us a gift of freedom and sovereign independence within a family of free nations, the whole story would have been different. But the Russians were merely given a choice between their familiar tyranny and an imported brand. The fact that they preferred the native chains is scarcely an item in which the Soviet dictators should take excessive pride.

In its propaganda to the armed forces and the population at large the Kremlin insisted that the invaders were intent on restoring landlords and capitalists. This was an effective morale builder and, indeed, offered the most solid common ground on which the regime and the people could meet. Except for a negligible minority, it should be understood, the Russians categorically did not desire such a restoration, under any disguise, no matter how sincerely they might detest the political and economic despotism of the Soviet system. Anti-capitalist education and indoctrination during a quarter of a century had sunk deep roots in the Russian mind.

But millions who fought courageously against the Nazis, on battlefronts and in guerilla actions, did dream that a new Russia, freed from a dictatorship of one party or one person, blessed with democratic freedoms, would rise from the ashes of the holocaust. The government nurtured this illusion, especially in the territories overrun by the enemy, as long as the war was going against us. The texts of the Atlantic Charter and Mr Roosevelt's Four Freedoms were published in our press, quietly and without comment; even that thrilled us with new hope. In the propaganda beamed to the conquered areas, these documents were exploited to the limit, to give the partisans an implied assurance that they were fighting for a new Russia, not for the one that had betrayed them by its terror and one-party tyranny. In their suffering and despair people were eager to accept the smoke of agitation for the incense of freedom.

The regime and the people both strove to save the country – but their hopes and purposes were as far apart as the poles. The dominant purpose of the regime was to save itself and its system for the further development of its Communist adventures at home and abroad; the people were moved by unadulterated love of their fatherland and the hope of achieving elementary political and economic freedoms.

The guerilla movement and the 'scorched earth' tactics have been depicted by some romantic writers as spontaneous phenomena. Actually they were carefully planned and at all times controlled from Moscow. In his radio speech of July 3 [see Document 6.18] Stalin . . . also proclaimed that in the retreat all valuable property which could not be taken along must be 'unconditionally destroyed.' By this time it is no secret that many peasants and city dwellers resisted this policy, fiercely and sometimes bloodily. The scorching was done, in the main, not by civilians but by the military forces.

Source: Kravchenko, I Chose Freedom, *pp. 365–7.*

Document 6.25   From the Head of the Gulag of the USSR NKVD

The labour camp system was turned to the war effort. A report in August 1944 described the changes.

At the beginning of the war the total number of prisoners in corrective-labour camps and colonies was 2,300,000. On 1 July 1944 the number of prisoners had fallen to 1,200,000.

In three years of war 2,900,000 prisoners left the camps and 1,800,000 entered.

At the same time the composition of the prisoners changed by the type of crime. If in 1941 the proportion sentenced for counter-revolutionary and other especially dangerous crimes was only 27 per cent of the total number of those imprisoned in camps and colonies, then by July 1944 the number imprisoned in this category had risen to 43 per cent . . . The proportion of men has decreased while that of women has increased. In 1941 men represented 93 per cent, whereas now there are 74 per cent men, 26 per cent women . . .

In the three years of war the general output of all types of ammunition by the NKVD's Gulag was 70,700,000 units, or 104 per cent of the plan.

Source: Rossiya, kotoruyu my ne znali, p. 127.

Document 6.26   'Plans for Imprisonment'

Kravchenko once again provides a vivid commentary on the way that the Gulag provided an essential source of labour for the Soviet economy.

In pressing commissariats for speedy output, I was continually balked by man-power shortages at critical points. People's Commissars knew the situation better than I did; they frequently asked Pamfilov for additional manpower from the NKVD reserves and he in turn made demands on the NKVD for working hands to supply this or that key factory; sometimes he put the problems up directly to Vosnessensky, Molotov, Beria. The Central Administration of forced labor camps – known as GULAG – was headed by the NKVD General Nedosekin, one of Beria's assistants. Nedosekin received orders for slave contingents from the State Defense Committee over the signatures of Molotov, Stalin, Beria and other members and acted accordingly.

I recall vividly an interview which I arranged on Utkin's orders with one of the top administrators of GULAG. He was to supply a certain commissariat some hundreds of prisoners for a rush assignment. We were under terrific pressure from Pamfilov, who was, in turn, of course, being pushed from higher up, and I had summoned the GULAG official for a showdown on this manpower.

'But Comrade Kravchenko, be reasonable,' he interrupted my speech. 'After all, your Sovnarkom is not the only one howling for workers. The State Defense Committee needs them, Comrade Mikoyan makes life miserable for us. Malenkov and Vosnessensky need workers, Voroshilov is calling for road builders. Naturally everyone thinks his own job is the most important. What are we to do? The fact is *we haven't as yet fulfilled our plans for imprisonments.* Demand is greater than supply.'

Plans for imprisonments! The fantastic, cold-blooded cynicism of the phrase still makes me shudder. What made it more uncanny was the fact that this official was entirely unconscious of the frightfulness of his remark. The seizure and enslavement of human beings had become a routine affair in his life. Of course, he did not mean that arrests were actually planned to meet labor demands. He was merely complaining, in Soviet lingo, about the fact that the multi-million armies of forced labor were not enough to meet all requests.

Source: Kravchenko, I Chose Freedom, *pp. 405–6.*

Document 6.27   Dissolution of the Comintern

The war was not to be revolutionary but patriotic. To confirm this, in May 1943 the Comintern was dissolved on the grounds that conditions in each country were so different that a single revolutionary centre was no longer required. The resolution below avoided stating the real reason for the dissolution of the Comintern, and its dissolution in practice did not weaken Stalin's control over national communist parties.

The historic role of the Communist International, which was founded in 1919 as a result of the political union of the great majority of the old, pre-war working-class parties, consisted in upholding the principles of Marxism from vulgarization and distortion by the opportunist elements in the working-class movement, in helping to promote the consolidation in a number of countries of the vanguard of the foremost workers in real working-class parties, and in helping them to mobilize the workers for the defence of their economic and political interests and for the struggle against fascism and the war the latter was preparing and for support of the Soviet Union as the chief bulwark against fascism . . .

But long before the war it became more and more clear that, with the increasing complications in the internal and international relations of the various countries, any sort of international centre would encounter insuperable obstacles in solving the problems facing the movement in each separate country. The deep differences of the historic paths of development of various countries, the differences in their character and even contradictions in their social orders, the differences in the level and tempo of their economic and political development, the differences, finally, in the degree of consciousness and organization of the workers, conditioned the different problems facing the working class of the various countries.

The whole development of events in the last quarter of a century, and the experience accumulated by the Communist International, convincingly showed that the organizational form of uniting the workers chosen by the first congress of the Communist International answered the conditions of the first stages of the working-class movement but has been outgrown by the growth of this movement and by the complication of its problems in separate countries, and has even become a drag on the further strengthening of the national working-class parties.

The World War that the Hitlerites have let loose has still further sharpened the differences in the situation of the separate countries, and has placed a sharp dividing line between those countries which fell under the Hitlerite tyranny and those freedom-loving peoples who have united in the powerful anti-Hitlerite coalition . . .

Guided by the judgement of the founders of Marxism-Leninism, communists have ever been supporters of the conservation of organizational forms that have outlived themselves . . .

In consideration of the above, taking into account the growth and political maturity of the communist parties and their leading cadres in the separate countries, and also having in view the fact that during the present war some sections have raised the question of the dissolution of the Communist International as the directing centre of the international working-class movement . . .

The Presidium of the Executive Committee of the Communist International . . . puts forward the following proposal for ratification by the sections of the Communist International.

The Communist International . . . is to be dissolved, thus freeing the sections . . . from their obligations arising from the statutes and resolutions of the congresses of the Communist International.

Source: 'Resolution of the ECCI Presidium Recommending the Dissolution of the Communist International', 15 May 1943, in McDermott and Agnew, The Comintern, *pp. 248–9.*

Document 6.28   The War and the Orthodox Church

As for the patriotic side, in September 1943 an unofficial concordat was reached between the Soviet state and the Russian Orthodox Church in an attempt to broaden traditionalist support for the regime in the war. The office of Patriarch was revived and the organisational life of the Church was allowed as long as there were no aspirations to independence.

On 8 September in Moscow there was held the Council of Bishops of the Orthodox Church, convened to elect a Partiarch of Moscow and All Russia and to form a Holy Synod under the Patriarch.

The Council of Bishops unanimously elected Metropolitan Sergei as Patriarch of Moscow and All Russia.

The Council furthermore adopted unanimously the statement addressed by Metropolitan Sergei to the Government of the USSR expressing thanks for its attention to the needs of the Russian Orthodox Church. Archbishop Grigory of Saratov read a statement to the Christians of the whole world. This document, containing an appeal for the unification of all forces in the struggle against Hitlerism, was also adopted unanimously by the Council . . .

Statement of the Council of the Most Reverend Hierarchy of the Russian Orthodox Church to the Soviet Government (September 8, 1943)

Deeply moved by the sympathetic attitude of our national Leader and Head of the Soviet Government, J. V. STALIN, toward the needs of the Russian Orthodox Church and toward our modest works, we, his humble servants, express to the Government our council's sincere gratitude and joyful conviction that, encouraged by this sympathy, we will redouble our share of work in the nationwide struggle for the salvation of the motherland.

Let the Heavenly Head of the Church bless the works of the Government with the Creator's blessing and let him crown our struggle in a just cause with the victory we long for and the liberation of suffering humanity from the dark bondage of fascism.

(Signed by Sergei, Metropolitan of Moscow and Kolomna, and eighteen other metropolitans, archbishops and bishops.)

Source: Daniels, Communism in Russia, *pp. 289–90.*

Document 6.29   Stalingrad, *Life and Fate*

Having been rebuffed before Moscow and stalemated around Leningrad, Hitler in 1942 turned his forces to the south-east, splitting them with one occupying the north Caucasus in the quest for Caspian oil and the other driving on towards Stalingrad (formerly Tsaritsyn, now Volgograd). By August 1942 the Sixth Tank Army commanded by von Paulus had reached the outskirts of the city, but to the astonishment of the Germans the entire population of Stalingrad took up arms. Workers in overalls repulsed the German tanks and soldiers fought grimly to defend every inch of territory. The Germans never reached the Volga. At this critical point Stalin took numerous measures to build up the authority of the Red Army: the system of military commissars was abolished, thus establishing the undivided authority (*edinonachalie*) of commanders, and traditional medals, ranks and other tsarist symbols were restored. The Soviet counter-offensive began on 19 November, and on 23 November von Paulus urged Hitler to order an immediate retreat from Stalingrad. Mesmerised by victory and incapable of believing that the hitherto invincible German forces could be defeated, on the 24th Hitler refused.

Vasilii Grossman's novel *Life and Fate* has a legitimate claim to be considered the greatest novel of the twentieth century. Focused on the Battle of Stalingrad, it is an extended meditation not only on the whole Soviet system but on the status of science in the twentieth century, the limits and nature of human loyalty and love, the malleability of time and history, the self-sacrifice and duty of soldiers, patriotism, Jewishness and Russianness, the beliefs of communists in Nazi and Soviet prison camps, the place of the prison camp in modernity, the role of the security police, and much more besides. Just as Leo Tolstoy's novel *War and Peace* is more than a discussion of the Battle of Borodino and the suffering Napoleon inflicted on Russia, so Grossman's novel transcends its ostensible subject-matter to present us with a mirror of the twentieth century written in the blood of the Soviet experience. Like Tolstoy, Grossman discusses the relationship between the individual leader and broader historical processes.

'Look where all your Chernyshevskys and Herzens have got us! Don't you remember what Chaadayev wrote in his *Third Philosophical Letter*?'

'I detest you and your mystical obscurantism as much as I detest the organizers of this camp,' replied Stepanov in a schoolmasterly tone. 'Both they and you forget the third and most natural path for Russia: the path of democracy and freedom' . . .

Sokolov's brother-in-law, the historian Madyarov, spoke calmly and unhurriedly. He never openly defended Trotsky or the senior Red Army officers who had been shot as traitors to the Motherland; but it was clear from the admiration with which he spoke of Krivoruchko and Dubov, from the casual respect with which he mentioned the names of commissars and generals who had been liquidated in 1937, that he did not for one moment believe that Marshals Tukhachevsky, Blücher and Yegorov, or Muralov, the commander of the Moscow military district, or Generals Levandovsky, Gamarnik, Dybenko and Bubnov, or Unschlicht, or Trotsky's first deputy, Sklyansky, had ever really been enemies of the people and traitors to the Motherland.

No one had talked like this before the war. The might of the State had constructed a new past. It had made the Red cavalry charge a second time. It had dismissed the genuine heroes of long-past events and appointed new ones. The State had the power to replay events, to transform figures of granite and bronze, to alter speeches long since delivered, to change the faces in a news photograph.

A new history had been written. Even people who had lived through those years had now had to relive them, transformed from brave men to cowards, from revolutionaries to foreign agents.

Listening to Madyarov, however, it seemed clear that all this would give way to a more powerful logic – the logic of truth . . .

Three major events formed the basis for this new vision of human relationships and of life itself: collectivization, industrialization and the year 1937. These events, like the October Revolution itself, involved the displacement of vast sections of the population, displacements accompanied by the physical extermination of numbers of people far greater than had accompanied the liquidation of the Russian aristocracy and the industrial and commercial bourgeoisie.

These events, presided over by Stalin himself, marked the economic triumph of the builders of the new Soviet State, the builders of 'Socialism in One Country'. At the same time, these events were the logical result of the October Revolution itself.

This new social order – this order which had triumphed during that period of collectivization, industrialization and the year 1937 with its almost complete change of leading cadres – had preferred not to renounce the old ideological concepts and formulae. The fundamental characteristic of the new order was State nationalism, but it still made use of a phraseology that went back to the beginning of the twentieth century and the formation of the Bolshevik wing of the Social Democratic Party.

The war accelerated a previously unconscious process, allowing the birth of an overtly national consciousness. The word 'Russian' once again had meaning.

To begin with, during the retreat, the connotations of this word were mainly negative: the hopelessness of Russian roads, Russian backwardness, Russian confusion, Russian fatalism . . . But a national self-consciousness had been born; it was waiting only for a military victory.

National consciousness is a powerful and splendid force at a time of disaster. It is splendid not because it is nationalist, but because it is human. It is a manifestation of human dignity, human love of freedom, human faith in what is good. But this consciousness can develop in a variety of ways.

No one can deny that the head of a personnel department protecting his Institute from 'cosmopolitans' and 'bourgeois nationalists' is expressing his national consciousness in a different manner to a Red Army soldier defending Stalingrad.

This awakening of national consciousness can be related to the tasks facing the State during the war and the years after the war: the struggle for national sovereignty and the affirmation of what is truly Russian, truly Soviet, in every area of life. These tasks, however, were not suddenly imposed on the State; they appeared when the events in the countryside, the creation of a national heavy industry and the complete change in the ruling cadres marked the triumph of a social order defined by Stalin as 'Socialism in One Country'.

The birthmarks of Russian social democracy were finally erased.

And this process finally became manifest at a time when Stalingrad was the only beacon of freedom in the kingdom of darkness.

A people's war reached its greatest pathos at the time of the defence of Stalingrad; the logic of events was such that Stalin chose this moment to proclaim openly his ideology of State nationalism . . .

Stalin! The great Stalin! Perhaps this man with the iron will had less will than any of them. He was a slave of his time and circumstances, a dutiful, submissive servant of the present day, flinging open the doors before the new age.

Yes, yes, yes . . . And those who didn't bow down before the new age were thrown on the scrapheap.

He knew now how a man could be split apart. After you've been searched, after you've had your buttons ripped off and your spectacles confiscated, you look on yourself as a physical nonentity. And then in the investigator's office you realize that the role you played in the Revolution and the Civil War means nothing, that all your work and all your knowledge is just so much rubbish. You are indeed a nonentity – and not just physically.

The unity of man's physical and spiritual being was the key to the investigators' almost uninterrupted run of success. Soul and body are two complementary vessels; after crushing and destroying a man's physical defences, the invading party nearly always succeeded in sending its mobile detachments into the breach in time to triumph over a man's soul, to force him into unconditional capitulation.

He didn't have the strength to think about all this; neither did he have the strength not to think about it.

Who had betrayed him? Who had informed on him? Who had slandered him? Somehow these questions no longer interested him . . .

Katsenelenbogen was a poet, the laureate of the State security organs.

He recounted with admiration how, during a break at the last [Eighteenth] Party Congress, Stalin had asked Yezhov why he had carried punitive measures to such extremes; Yezhov, confused, had replied that he had been obeying Stalin's own orders. Stalin had turned to the delegates around him and said, 'And he's a Party member.'

He talked about the horror Yagoda had felt . . .

He reminisced about the great Chekists, connoisseurs of Voltaire, experts on Rabelais, admirers of Verlaine, who had once directed the work of his vast, sleepless building [the Lubyanka, headquarters of the Soviet secret police].

He talked about a quiet, kind, old Lett who had worked for years as an executioner; how he always used to ask permission to give the clothes of a man he had just executed to an orphanage. The next moment he would start talking about another executioner who drank day and night and was miserable if he didn't have any work to do; after his dismissal he began visiting State farms around Moscow and slaughtering pigs; he used to carry bottles of pig's blood around with him, saying it had been prescribed by a doctor as a cure for anaemia.

He told of how, in 1937, they had executed people sentenced without right of correspondence every night. The chimneys of the Moscow crematoria had sent up clouds of smoke into the night, and the members of the Communist youth organization enlisted to help with the executions and subsequent disposal of the bodies had gone mad.

He told Krymov about the interrogation of Bukharin, about how obstinate Kamenev had been. Once, when he was developing a theory of his, trying to generalize, the two of them talked all through the night . . .

Life inside the camps could be seen as an exaggerated, magnified reflection of life outside. Far from being contradictory, these two realities were symmetrical.

Now Katsenelenbogen spoke not like a poet, not like a philosopher, but like a prophet.

If one were to develop the system of camps boldly and systematically, eliminating all hindrances and shortcomings, the boundaries would finally be erased. The camp would merge with the world outside. And this fusion would signal the maturity and triumph of great principles. For all its inadequacies, the system of camps had one decisive point in its favour: only there was the principle of personal freedom subordinated, clearly and absolutely, to the higher principle of reason. This principle would raise the camp to such a degree of perfection that finally it would be able to do away with itself and merge with the life of the surrounding towns and villages.

Katsenelenbogen had himself supervised the work of a camp design office; he was convinced that, in the camps, scientists and engineers were capable of solving the most complicated problems of contemporary science or technology. All that was necessary was to provide intelligent supervision and decent living conditions. The old saying about there being no science without freedom was simply nonsense.

'When the levels become equal,' he said, 'when we can place an equals sign between life on either side of the wire, repression will become unnecessary and we shall cease to issue arrest warrants. Prisons and solitary-confinement blocks will be razed to the ground. Any anomalies will be handled by the

Culture and Education Section. Mahomed and the mountain will go to meet each other.

'The abolition of the camps will be a triumph of humanitarianism, but this will in no way mean the resurgence of the chaotic, primeval, cave-man principle of personal freedom. On the contrary, that will have become completely redundant.'

After a long silence he added that after hundreds of years this system might do away with itself too, and, in doing so, give birth to democracy and personal freedom.

'There is nothing eternal under the moon,' he said, 'but I'd rather not be alive then myself.'

'You're mad,' said Krymov. 'That's not the heart of the Revolution. That's not its soul. People say that if you work for a long time in a psychiatric clinic you finally go mad yourself. Forgive me for saying this, but it's not for nothing you've been put inside. You, comrade Katsenelenbogen, ascribe to the security organs all the attributes of the deity. It really was time you were replaced.'

Katsenelenbogen nodded good-humouredly.

'Yes, I believe in God. I'm an ignorant, credulous old man. Every age creates the deity in its own image. The security organs are wise and powerful; they are what holds sway over twentieth-century man. Once this power was held by earthquakes, forest-fires, thunder and lightning – and they too were worshipped. And if I've been put inside – well, so have you. It was time to replace you too. Only the future will show which of us is right.'

Source: Vasily Grossman, Life and Fate *(London, The Harvill Press, 1995), pp. 187, 274–5, 664–5, 842, 843, 845–6.*

Document 6.30 The Fruits of Industrialisation and Assistance from the West

Victory at Stalingrad was followed by the great Soviet offensive, including the world's largest tank battle around Kursk in July 1943 in which 1.3 million Soviet soldiers with 3,444 tanks, 2,900 aircraft and 19,000 guns faced 900,000 Germans with 2,700 tanks, 2,000 aircraft and 10,000 guns. Victory at Kursk led to the liberation of Orel, Belgorod, and opened the path to the Ukraine and the West. Yegor Ligachev, and with him the generation that had sacrificed themselves to achieve liberation, later defended these achievements. A leading 'conservative' under Gorbachev, Ligachev upheld the wartime Soviet achievement against the detractors who were given free rein during *glasnost*. His arguments reflected the views of many in the last years of the Soviet Union as they saw their sacrifices and lives dissolve before them.

So much untruth and slander has been splashed on our great victory. Some say we did not fight properly and that the country's leadership panicked.

Politicians remind me of a critical fly on the wall of a beautiful building that sees only the unevenness of the wall's brick and so naturally is unable to appreciate the beauty of the building as a whole. Our ill-wishers do not want to recognize the greatness of our victory or the superiority of the Soviet order over Hitler's tyranny; they see rotten twigs and fail to notice the healthy tree. They disown their own people, the victor, their own Fatherland, with all its joys and misfortunes . . .

It is for good reason that our Communist Party was called a fighting party. Three million Communists perished on the fronts of World War II in the fighting between the Soviet people and the German aggressors. The Communists took the lead in both battle and labor . . .

In 1941, in a matter of a mere six months, the country was moved east – to the Urals, to Siberia. More than a thousand enterprises were moved 4,000 kilometers; in early 1942 they started turning out airplanes, tanks, artillery, and ammunition for the front. This was a great achievement for the people and the Party!

Source: Yegor Ligachev, Inside Gorbachev's Kremlin *(Boulder, Westview Press, 1996), pp. 354–5.*

Although the Soviet industrialisation drive had provided the basis for defence industries, and in the event the Soviet T-34 was superior to the American Sherman tank, the American Lend-Lease programme was essential for the Soviet war effort, amounting to $11.3 billion by the end of the war (a staggering $90 billion in 1998 dollars). The material was transported in British convoys to the northern ports of Arkhangel and Murmansk; attacked by German U-boats and from the air, they suffered enormous losses. Allied deliveries supplied 58 per cent of the aviation fuel, 53 per cent of all explosives, and almost half of the entire wartime supply of copper, aluminium and tyres. More crucially, Lend-Lease provided some 20,000 military aircraft, 10,000 tanks, 57 per cent of the rails, 1,900 locomotives, 11,075 rail wagons and 425,000 trucks, representing well over half of the Soviet fleet of light trucks and jeeps, as well as radios and radio tubes. Enough food was supplied to provide every single Soviet soldier with half a pound of solid nourishment for every day of the war (see Overy, 1998). According to Khrushchev, the debt was acknowledged by Stalin: 'If we had to deal with Germany one-to-one we would not have been able to cope because we lost so much of our industry' (*The Khrushchev Tapes*).

Document 6.31   The Deportations

No sooner was the end of the war in sight than Stalin turned his wrath once again against his own people. In 1944 the Crimean Tatars, Kalmyks and various north Caucasian peoples – the Cherkess, Karachai, Balkars and Kabardins, Ingush and Chechens – in formerly occupied territory were targeted for expulsion from their homelands to Central Asia. They were accused by Beria of collaboration with the

German occupiers and deported. On 8 March 1944, for example, the entire Balkar population was rounded up and loaded into trains and sent to Central Asia. Of the 40,000 deported, 14,000 died during the journey or in the harsh early days of exile, transported into empty steppe and told to build their own shelter. As thousands more Balkars returned from fighting in the Soviet army to their former homes they were picked up and transported. The sheer scale and clinical bureaucratised horror of the operation is revealed by the following strictly secret telegram from Beria to Stalin on 29 February 1944.

This is to report the results of the resettlement operation of the Chechens and Ingush. The resettlement began on 23 February in the majority of districts, with the exception of high mountain areas.

By 29 February 478,479 people, including 91,250 Ingush, had been evicted and loaded on to special trains. One hundred and seventy-seven special trains had been loaded, of which 159 have already been sent to the new place of settlement.

Today special trains departed carrying former leaders and religious authorities of Chechen-Ingushetia, who were used in carrying out the operation . . .

Party leaders and Soviet organs of north Ossetia, Dagestan and Georgia have already started work on the assimilation of the new districts that have gone to them.

Source: Rossiya, kotoruyu my ne znali, *pp. 156–7.*

Document 6.32   Beria on the Crimean Tatars

On the pretext of alleged collaboration with the Nazis during the German occupation of the peninsula between 1941 and 1944, the mass relocation of the Crimean Tatars was conducted with extreme brutality resulting in a high death toll. It is estimated that nearly half of the 240,000 Crimean Tatars selected for expulsion died in the process or soon after. On 10 May 1944 Stalin received the following telegram from Beria.

Taking into account the treacherous activity of the Crimean Tatars against the Soviet people and the undesirability of the further habitation of the Crimean Tatars in border zones of the USSR, the USSR NKVD presents for your consideration a draft resolution of the State Committee of Defence on the resettlement of all Tatars from the Crimea.

We consider it expedient to resettle the Crimean Tatars as special settlers in regions of the Uzbek S[oviet] S[ocialist] R[epublic] to be used for agricultural work, kolkhozes and sovkhozes, and also in industry and transport . . .

According to preliminary data the population of the Crimea at present is

140,00–160,000. The resettlement operation will begin on 20–1 May and be completed by 1 July . . .

USSR People's Commissar of Internal Affairs, L. Beria

Source: Rossiya, kotoruyu my ne znali, *p. 152.*

Towards the Post-war Order

Even before the war was over the Allies began to prepare for the post-war order. A series of conferences sought to avoid conflict between the Allies, culminating in the Yalta conference of February 1945. Stalin expertly exploited differences between Roosevelt and Churchill; whereas the Americans wished to see a world opened up to trade after the war, Churchill tried to salvage as much as possible for the British Empire.

Document 6.33 Declaration of the Three Powers of 1 December 1943

Meeting in Teheran in November 1943 Churchill, Roosevelt and Stalin agreed that the second front would be opened in the West as soon as possible. The conference declared that the wartime spirit of collaboration would be maintained in peacetime.

We, the president of the United States, the prime minister of Great Britain and the premier of the Soviet Union, have met over the last four days in the capital of our ally, Iran, and formulated and confirmed our common policy. We express our determination that our countries will work together both in war and in the following period of peace.

Source: Izvestiya, *7 December 1943.*

Document 6.34 The Percentages Agreement, 9 October 1944

In April 1944 the last of Soviet territory was liberated and Soviet forces entered Romania, signalling the start of a new offensive phase in the USSR's war as it pursued the enemy across neighbouring countries. Although Stalin continued to express hopes that the wartime alliance would continue, it soon became clear that in the wake of the Red Army Stalin sought to install local communists in power to ensure 'friendly' and 'democratic' regimes, ably assisted by the NKVD. Following the D-Day landings in Normandy on 6 June 1994 the Allies from East and West advanced towards each other. The race was on not only to reach Berlin first but to ensure a modicum of agreement for the post-war settlement. Churchill flew to Moscow in early October 1944 to discuss various problems with Stalin, in particular the division of spheres of influence in South-eastern Europe. Churchill describes the meeting as follows.

We alighted at Moscow on the afternoon of October 9, and were received very heartily and with full ceremonial by Molotov and many high Russian personages. This time we were lodged in Moscow itself, with every care and comfort. I had one small, perfectly appointed house, and Anthony [Eden] another near by. We were glad to dine alone together and rest. At ten o'clock that night we held our first important meeting in the Kremlin. There were only Stalin, Molotov, Eden, Harriman and I, with Major Birse and Pavlov as interpreters . . .

The moment was apt for business, so I said, 'Let us settle about our affairs in the Balkans. Your armies are in Rumania and Bulgaria. We have interests, missions, and agents there. Don't let us get at cross-purposes in small ways. So far as Britain and Russia are concerned, how would it do for you to have ninety per cent predominance in Rumania, for us to have ninety per cent of the say in Greece, and go fifty–fifty about Yugoslavia?' While this was being translated I wrote out on a half-sheet of paper:

Rumania	
Russia	90%
The others	10%
Greece	
Great Britain	90%
(in accord with USA)	
Russia	10%
Yugoslavia	50–50%
Hungary	50–50%
Bulgaria	
Russia	75%
The others	25%

I pushed this across to Stalin, who had by then heard the translation. There was a slight pause. Then he took his blue pencil and made a large tick upon it, and passed it back to us. It was all settled in no more time than it takes to set down.

Of course we had long and anxiously considered our point, and were only dealing with immediate war-time arrangements. All larger questions were reserved on both sides for what we then hoped would be a peace table when the war was won.

After this there was a long silence. The pencilled paper lay in the centre of the table. At length I said, 'Might it not be thought rather cynical if it seemed we had disposed of these issues, so fateful to millions of people, in such an offhand manner? Let us burn the paper.' 'No, you keep it,' said Stalin.

Source: Winston Churchill, The Second World War: Triumph and Tragedy *(Boston, Houghton Mifflin, 1953), pp. 226–8.*

Later, Major Birse, Churchill's interpreter, advised that the existence of the 'naughty document' be omitted from official records, as giving the impression that 'these very important discussions were conducted in a most unfitting manner'. However high-handed it might appear, the agreement represented an attempt by Churchill to retain at least some influence for the Western powers in Eastern Europe and to avoid civil wars and bloodshed. The next day Molotov amended the figures for Bulgaria and Hungary in favour of the USSR. As the occupying power, the USSR's bargaining position was strong and the West's options limited. Note that the status of Poland was not mentioned in this paper, but figured largely in the discussions during this visit, with the Lublin Poles (the communist-dominated Polish National Committee) acting as pawns of the USSR, particularly over the question of the Polish border. The Curzon Line was basically accepted by the London Poles represented by M. Mikolajczyk, the Polish prime minister.

Document 6.35   Yalta: Peace and Betrayal

The Yalta conference of Churchill, Roosevelt and Stalin met on 6–11 February 1945. By the time of the conference the Soviet Army already occupied Bulgaria, Romania, Poland, Hungary, part of Czechoslovakia and some of Germany. Poland was discussed at seven out of the eight plenary sessions. On the face of it the Yalta agreement of 11 February appeared reasonable, with the Western Allies making concessions to Stalin over the line of the Polish border, German reparations and the Soviet role in the post-war order, while Stalin promised to support the principles of the Atlantic Charter, the establishment of the United Nations and to join in the war effort against Japan. The problem, however, was that the high principles (in particular the sections dealing with Poland) proved in practice unenforceable. The Second World War was not followed by a Versailles-type conference but instead the Yalta conference of the three great powers decided the fate of the post-war world. The word 'Yalta' became a synonym for the disposal by large nations of the fate of small ones without their participation.

The Crimea Conference of the Heads of the Government of the United States of America, the United Kingdom, and the Union of Soviet Socialist Republics which took place from February 4th to 11th came to the following conclusions.

I World Organisation

It was decided:
   that a United Nations Conference on the proposed world organisation should be summoned for Wednesday, 25th April, 1945, and should be held in the United States of America . . .

II Declaration on Liberated Europe

The following declaration has been approved:

'The Premier of the Union of Soviet Socialist Republics, the Prime Minister of the United Kingdom and the President of the United States of America have consulted with each other in the common interests of the peoples of their countries and those of liberated Europe. They jointly declare their mutual agreement to concert during the temporary period of instability in liberated Europe the policies of their three governments in assisting the peoples liberated from the domination of Nazi Germany and the peoples of the former Axis satellite states of Europe to solve by democratic means their pressing political and economic problems.

'The establishment of order in Europe and the re-building of national economic life must be achieved by processes which will enable the liberated peoples to destroy the last vestiges of Nazism and Fascism and to create democratic institutions of their own choice. This is a principle of the Atlantic Charter – the right of all peoples to choose the form of government under which they will live – the restoration of sovereign rights and self-government to those peoples who have been forcibly deprived of them by the aggressor nations.

'To foster the conditions in which the liberated peoples may exercise these rights, the three governments will jointly assist the people in any European liberated state or former Axis satellite state in Europe where in their judgment conditions require (a) to establish conditions of internal peace; (b) to carry out emergency measures for the relief of distressed peoples; (c) to form interim governmental authorities broadly representative of all democratic elements in the population and pledged to the earliest possible establishment through free elections of governments responsive to the will of the people; and (d) to facilitate where necessary the holding of such elections . . .'

III Dismemberment of Germany

It was agreed that Article 12(a) of the Surrender Term for Germany should be amended to read as follows:

'The United Kingdom, the United States of America and the Union of Soviet Socialist Republics shall possess supreme authority with respect to Germany. In the exercise of such authority they will take such steps, including the complete disarmament, demilitarisation and the dismemberment of Germany as they deem requisite for future peace and security.'

The study of the procedure for the dismemberment of Germany was referred to a Committee, consisting of Mr Eden (Chairman), Mr Winant and Mr Gousev. This body would consider the desirability of associating with it a French representative.

IV Zone of Occupation for the French and Control Council for Germany

It was agreed that a zone in Germany, to be occupied by the French Forces, should be allocated to France. This zone would be formed out of the British and American zones and its extent would be settled by the British and Americans in consultation with the French Provisional Government.

It was also agreed that the French Provisional Government should be invited to become a member of the Allied Control Council for Germany.

V *Reparation*

The following protocol has been approved:

1 Germany must pay in kind for the losses caused by her to the Allied nations in the course of the war. Reparations are to be received in the first instance by those countries which have borne the main burden of the war, have suffered the heaviest losses and have organised victory over the enemy.

2 Reparation in kind is to be exacted from Germany in three following forms:

(a) Removals within 2 years from the surrender of Germany or the cessation of organised resistance from the national wealth of Germany located on the territory of Germany herself as well as outside her territory (equipment, machine-tools, ships, rolling stock, German investments abroad, shares of industrial, transport and other enterprises in Germany etc.), these removals to be carried out chiefly for purpose of destroying the war potential of Germany.

(b) Annual deliveries of goods from current production for a period to be fixed.

(c) Use of German labour.

3 For the working out on the above principles of a detailed plan for exaction of reparation from Germany an Allied Reparation Commission will be set up in Moscow. It will consist of three representatives – one from the Union of Soviet Socialist Republics, one from the United Kingdom and one from the United States of America.

4 With regard to the fixing of the total sum of the reparation as well as the distribution of it among the countries which suffered from the German aggression the Soviet and American delegations agreed as follows:

'The Moscow Reparation Commission should take in its initial studies as a basis for discussion the suggestion of the Soviet Government that the total sum of the reparation in accordance with the points (a) and (b) of the paragraph 2 should be 20 billion dollars and that 50% of it should go to the Union of Soviet Socialist Republics.'

The British delegation was of the opinion that pending consideration of the reparation question by the Moscow Reparation Commission no figures of reparation should be mentioned.

The above Soviet–American proposal has been passed to the Moscow Reparation Commission as one of the proposals to be considered by the Commission.

VI Major War Criminals

The Conference agreed that the question of the major war criminals should be the subject of enquiry by the three Foreign Secretaries for report in due course after the close of the Conference.

VII Poland

The following Declaration on Poland was agreed by the Conference:
'A new situation has been created in Poland as a result of her complete liberation by the Red Army. This calls for the establishment of a Polish Provisional Government which can be more broadly based than was possible before the recent liberation of the Western part of Poland. The Provisional Government which is now functioning in Poland should therefore be reorganised on a broader democratic basis with the inclusion of democratic leaders from Poland itself and from Poles abroad. This new Government should then be called the Polish Provisional Government of National Unity.

Mr Molotov, Mr Harriman and Sir A. Clark Kerr are authorised as a commission to consult in the first instance in Moscow with members of the present Provisional Government and with other Polish democratic leaders from within Poland and from abroad, with a view to the reorganisation of the present Government along the above lines. This Polish Provisional Government of National Unity shall be pledged to the holding of free and unfettered elections as soon as possible on the basis of universal suffrage and secret ballot. In these elections all democratic and anti-Nazi parties have the right to take part and to put forward candidates.

When a Polish Provisional Government of National Unity has been properly formed in conformity with the above, the Government of the USSR, which now maintains diplomatic relations with the present Provisional Government of Poland, and the Government of the United Kingdom and the Government of the USA will establish diplomatic relations with the new Polish Provisional Government of National Unity, and will exchange Ambassadors by whose reports the respective Governments will be kept informed about the situation in Poland.

The three Heads of Government consider that the Eastern frontier of Poland should follow the Curzon Line with digressions from it in some regions of five to eight kilometres in favour of Poland. They recognise that Poland must receive substantial accessions of territory in the North and West. They feel that the opinion of the new Polish Provisional Government of National Unity should be sought in due course on the extent of these accessions and that the final delimitation of the Western frontier of Poland should thereafter await the Peace Conference . . .'

Agreement Regarding Entry of the Soviet Union into the War against Japan

TOP SECRET AGREEMENT

The leaders of the three Great Powers – the Soviet Union, the United States of America and Great Britain – have agreed that in two or three months after Germany has surrendered and the war in Europe has terminated the Soviet Union shall enter into the war against Japan on the side of the Allies on condition that:

1 The status quo in Outer-Mongolia (The Mongolian People's Republic) shall be preserved;
2 The former rights of Russia violated by the treacherous attack of Japan in 1904 shall be restored, viz:

(a) the southern part of Sakhalin as well as all the islands adjacent to it shall be returned to the Soviet Union,

(b) the commercial port of Dairen shall be internationalised, the pre-eminent interests of the Soviet Union in this port being safeguarded and the lease of Port Arthur as a naval base of the USSR restored,

(c) the Chinese-Eastern Railroad and the South-Manchurian Railroad which provides an outlet to Dairen shall be jointly operated by the establishment of a joint Soviet–Chinese Company, it being understood that the pre-eminent interests of the Soviet Union shall be safeguarded and that China shall retain full sovereignty in Manchuria;
3 The Kuril islands shall be handed over to the Soviet Union.

It is understood that the agreement concerning Outer-Mongolia and the ports and railroads referred to above will require the concurrence of Generalissimo Chiang Kai-Shek. The President will take measures in order to obtain this concurrence on advice from Marshal Stalin.

The Heads of the three Great Powers have agreed that these claims of the Soviet Union shall be unquestionably fulfilled after Japan has been defeated.

For its part the Soviet Union expresses its readiness to conclude with the National Government of China a pact of friendship and alliance between the USSR and China in order to render assistance to China with its armed forces for the purpose of liberating China from the Japanese yoke.

Source: British and Foreign State Papers, *1947, Part II, vol. 148 (London, Her Majesty's Stationery Office, 1955), pp. 80, 82 3, 83 6, 88 9.*

Document 6.36   Stalin on Poland at Yalta

The composition of the Polish government was at the centre of attention at Yalta. Churchill sought to limit Soviet influence, and in particular to return the Polish government-in-exile in London to Poland to counter the communist 'Committee of National Liberation', which formed itself into a government in Lublin backed by the Soviet Army. Roosevelt was more inclined to make a deal with Stalin, abhorring what he understood as the cynicism of British imperialism's 'sphere of influence' policy. The Americans sought an open door for their trade. Even if Churchill and Roosevelt had been united, it is not clear whether they would have been able to rally their populations for a new confrontation, this time against their former Soviet ally. The Declaration on Poland on paper conceded some of what the West had wanted, but in the months that followed the agreement unravelled and the West appeared to lack the will to ensure that Stalin fulfilled its spirit and letter.

Marshal Stalin then gave the following summary of his views on the Polish question: Mr Churchill had said that for Great Britain the Polish question was one of honor and that he understood, but for the Russians it was a question both of honor and security. It was one of honor because Russia had many past grievances against Poland and desire to see them eliminated. It was a question of strategic security not only because Poland was a bordering country but because throughout history Poland had been the corridor for attack on Russia. We have to mention that during the last thirty years Germany twice has passed through this corridor. The reason for this was that Poland was weak. Russia wants a strong, independent and democratic Poland . . . It is not only a question of honor for Russia, but one of life and death.

Source: Martin McCauley, The Origins of the Cold War *(Harlow, Longman, 1983), pp. 101–2.*

Flag over Berlin

In the early afternoon of 30 April 1945 Soviet soldiers raised the Red Flag over the Reichstag. A few hundred yards away at that very moment Hitler and Eva Braun committed suicide, and their bodies were burned in the courtyard of their bunker. Although victory had been achieved it remained unclear which country had won: the Poles had not regained their full independence; Eastern Europe remained occupied by new forces; and the Soviet Union entered a new period of repression. The laurels of victory undoubtedly fell to Stalin and his regime.

Document 6.37   'The Prague Manifesto' of the Vlasov Movement

In the first months of the war millions of Soviet troops fell into German hands, some of them surrendering with barely a fight. Some limited organisation among them was allowed under the leadership of Andrei Vlasov, a Red Army lieutenant-general who had been captured in 1942 while attempting to break the siege of Leningrad. In 1944 this was organised as the 'Committee for the Liberation of the Peoples of Russia', with the movement adopting the so-called 'Prague Manifesto' in November of that year calling for a democratic Russia while recognising the socialised economy. The only serious military action in which the Vlasovites participated was the liberation of Prague in May 1945 – from the Germans! Captured by the Red Army or returned by the British and American forces, Vlasov and the other leaders were executed for treason and the rank and file sent to the Gulag.

Fellow-countrymen! Brothers and Sisters!

In this hour of great trial we must decide the fate of our Motherland, our peoples and our own fate.

Mankind is going through an era of the greatest upheavals. The present world war is a fight to the finish between opposing political systems.

It is fought by the powers of imperialism, led by the plutocrats of England and the USA, whose greatness is based on the oppression and exploitation of other countries and peoples. It is fought by the powers of internationalism, led by Stalin's clique, who dream of world revolution and the destruction of the national independence of other countries and peoples. It is being fought by freedom-loving nations, who yearn to live their own way of life, determined by their own historical and national development . . .

What then are the peoples of Russia fighting for? Why are they condemned to countless sacrifices and suffering? . . .

The peoples of Russia have experienced the burden of Bolshevik tyranny for more than a quarter of a century.

In the revolution of 1917 the peoples who inhabited the Russian Empire sought to realise their aspirations for justice, for the general welfare and national liberty . . . The Bolshevik Party promised to create a social system in which the people would live happily. To attain this the people made incalculable sacrifices. It is not the fault of the people that the Bolshevik Party not only did not realise the demands of the people, but by gradually strengthening the coercive nature of the administrative apparatus, robbed the people of the rights which they had won, and forced them into permanent misery, into lawlessness and exploited them most unscrupulously . . .

The Bolsheviks condemned the peoples of our homeland to permanent poverty, hunger and extinction and to spiritual and physical slavery, and finally they forced them into a criminal war for causes alien to them.

All this is being camouflaged with lies about the democratic nature of Stalin's constitution and the building of a socialist society. No other country in the world has ever had such a low standard of living, while its material wealth is so vast. No other country has known such interference with the personal freedom of the individual and such humiliation as has occurred and continues to occur under the Bolshevik system.

The peoples of Russia have lost their faith in Bolshevism forever. It is a system where the state is the all-devouring machine and the people have become indigent slaves deprived of their belongings and their legal rights . . .

The Committee for the Liberation of the Peoples of Russia has as its aim:

(a) The overthrow of the tyranny created by Stalin, the liberation of the peoples of Russia from the Bolshevik system, and the restitution to the peoples of Russia of those rights which they won in the national revolution of 1917;
(b) An end to the war and the conclusion of an honourable peace with Germany;
(c) The creation of a new free popular state system without Bolsheviks and exploiters.

Source: 'Manifesto of the Committee for the Liberation of the Peoples of Russia', 14 November 1944, in Catherine Andreyev, Vlasov and the Russian Liberation Movement: Soviet Reality and Emigré Theories *(Cambridge, Cambridge University Press, 1987), pp. 216, 217, 218, 219.*

Document 6.38   Denikin on the Anniversary of the Volunteer Army

The alliance between patriotism and the Soviet system that was forged during the war now took on specifically Russian nationalist features. This was reflected in a speech by Denikin, one of the leaders of the White armies during the Russian Civil War of 1918–20. For some in the emigration, Stalin's victory proved the viability of the Soviet regime and appeared to justify the arguments of the National Bolsheviks earlier that the communist regime was in a perverse way fulfilling Russian national tasks. Denikin, however, reminds these people that the Soviet Union remained outside the international system and that its people remained in thrall to an inhuman power system.

15 November 1917–1944

We are remembering the twenty-seventh anniversary of the foundation of the Volunteer Army in very different conditions from those that have prevailed over the last four years. But these conditions are no less complicated, evoking a whole range of contradictory feelings and forcing the Russian emigration once again into new divisions. And its dregs, yesterday's obscurantists, defeatists, Hitlerite apologists, are already changing their faces and praise without measure, without a twinge of conscience, the new masters of the situation . . .

The international situation has fundamentally changed. The enemy has been thrown beyond the borders of the motherland. We – and herein lies the unavoidable pathos of our situation – are only witnesses and not participants of events that have shaken our motherland in the last years. We could only follow with the deepest sadness the sufferings of our people and with pride its great feats. We suffered in the days of the army's defeat, even though it is called 'Red' and not Russian, and happiness in the days of its victory. And now, when the world war is still not over, with all our hearts we wish it a victorious conclusion to free our country from encroachments from beyond.

But the situation within Russia has not changed. At a time when the whole world is restructuring its life on to new principles of international cooperation, social fairness, freeing people's labour and activity from the exploitation of capital and the state, the peoples of Russia cannot remain in a serf-like condition. They cannot live and work without the most basic requirements for human existence:

1 basic freedoms;
2 the emancipation of labour;
3 the abolition of the bloodthirsty arbitrariness of the NKVD;
4 independent courts, equal for all, based on justice and the law, freed from the Party's partiality and administrative influence.

As long as there is none of this we will pursue our previous path, promised to the founders of the Volunteer Army, whatever clouds might darken our path. The fate of Russia is more important than the fate of the emigration.

Source: Rodina, *nos. 6–7, 1991, p. 105.*

Hopes that victory in war would lead to an end of oppression at home were disappointed. The Allies did all they could to appease Stalin in this period, including the forced repatriation not only of Vlasovites, Cossacks and released Soviet prisoners of war, but also many who had gone into emigration a generation earlier (for a discussion of these 'victims of Yalta', see Bethell, 1974; Tolstoy, 1979; Elliot, 1982). The Cold War in international relations was accompanied by a cold peace in domestic affairs.

Document 6.39 Stalin's Victory Toast

On 24 May 1945 at a reception in the Kremlin for Red Army commanders Stalin acknowledged the primacy of the 'Great Russians' in the Soviet order and their part in the victory. The sufferings of all the other peoples and their contribution to victory was not recognised. In this, as in so many other ways, Stalin set the clock ticking for the disintegration of the Soviet Union forty-six years later.

Comrades, permit me to propose one more, last toast.

I should like to propose a toast to the health of our Soviet people, and in the first place, the Russian people. (*Stormy and prolonged applause and shouts of 'hurrah!'.*)

I drink in the first place to the health of the Russian people because it is the most outstanding nation of all the nations forming the Soviet Union.

I propose a toast to the health of the Russian people because it has won in this war universal recognition as the leading force of the Soviet Union among all the peoples of our country.

I drink to the health of the Russian people not only because it is the leading people, but also because it possesses a clear mind, a staunch character, and patience.

Our government made not a few errors, we experienced at moments a desperate situation in 1941–1942, when our Army was retreating, abandoning our own villages and towns in the Ukraine, Belorussia, Moldavia, the Leningrad region, the Baltic area and the Karelian-Finnish republic, abandoning them because there was no other way out. A different people might have said to the government: 'you have not lived up to our expectations, get out, we shall establish another government which will make peace with Germany and secure us a quiet life'. But the Russian people did not take this path because it trusted the correctness of the policy of its government and was prepared to make sacrifices to ensure Germany's defeat. And this confidence by the Russian people in the Soviet government proved to be that decisive force which ensured the historic victory over the enemy of humanity, over fascism.

Thanks to you, the Russian people, for this trust!

To the health of the Russian people! (*Stormy and extended applause.*)

Sources: Speech at the Reception in the Kremlin in Honour of the Commanders of the Red Army Troops, 24 May 1945, Pravda, *25 May 1945; Stalin,* War Speeches, *pp. 138–9.*

The cold peace, 1945–1953

Like the victory of Alexander I against Napoleon in 1812, the Soviet triumph in 1945 legitimated and reinforced the system that had delivered victory in war but fostered illusions about its viability and durability in peace. Victory gave rise to expectations that the peacetime Soviet system of government would change. These hopes, however real or imaginary, were crushed by the Stalinist counter-attack against the nascent pluralism led by Andrei Zhdanov.

The Onset of the Cold War

The Stalinist system was able to win the war but was increasingly unable to manage the peace. In practice, the need for an enemy was so essential to the Soviet system that the defeat of one enemy, Germany, appeared to give rise to an array of new ones.

Document 7.1   Djilas on Stalin

Milovan Djilas was a leading Yugoslav communist, joining the Politburo of the Yugoslav Communist Party in 1940 and fighting with the partisans led by Tito following the German invasion in 1941. He led a military mission to Moscow in 1944 and later reported on his conversation with Stalin.

Stalin presented his views on the distinctive nature of the war that was being waged: 'This war is not as in the past; whoever occupies a territory also imposes on it his own social system. Everyone imposes his own system as far as his army has power to do so. It cannot be otherwise.'

He also pointed out, without going into long explanations, the meaning of his Pan-Slavic policy. 'If the Slavs keep united and maintain solidarity, no one in the future will be able to move a finger. Not even a finger!' he repeated, emphasising his thought by cleaving the air with his forefinger.

Someone expressed doubt that the Germans would be able to recuperate within fifty years. But Stalin was of a different opinion. 'No, they will recover, and very quickly. It is a highly developed industrial country with an extremely skilled and numerous working class and technical intelligentsia. Give them twelve to fifteen years and they'll be on their feet again. And this is why the unity of Slavs is important. But even apart from this, if the unity of the Slavs exists, no one will dare move a finger.'

At one point he got up, hitched up his trousers as though he was about to wrestle or to box, and cried out emotionally, 'The war will soon be over. We shall recover in fifteen or twenty years, and then we'll have another go at it.'

There was something terrible in his words: a horrible war was still going on. Yet there was something impressive, too, about his realisation of the paths he had to take, the inevitability that faced the world in which he lived and the movement that he headed.

Source: Milovan Djilas, Conversations with Stalin *(Harmondsworth, Pelican, 1969), pp. 90–1, 103.*

Document 7.2 Stalin's 'Two Camps' Speech, 9 February 1946

In his speech during the Supreme Soviet elections in February 1946 Stalin advanced the argument that later became the orthodoxy: the sacrifices of the 1930s – collectivisation, frenetic industrialisation and purges – had provided the essential foundations for victory. Stalin addressed two key issues: the first insisted that the world remained divided into 'two camps', despite the shared victory over fascism; and the second was that the new five-year plan was to restore pre-war levels of output and then to achieve new levels. The two themes were intimately linked: the danger from abroad required yet more efforts and sacrifices to build up heavy industry in case of a new war, this time with the Western democracies. The speech in tone and substance signalled continuity with pre-war policies and bitterly disappointed those who had anticipated that victory would allow the Soviet regime to relax and adapt to new circumstances.

Comrades!
Eight years have passed since the last elections to the Supreme Soviet. This was a period full of events of a decisive character. The first four years passed in intensive effort on the part of Soviet men and women to fulfil the Third Five-Year Plan. The second four years cover the events of the war against the German and Japanese aggressors, the events of the Second World War. Undoubtedly, the war was the principal event of the past period.

It would be wrong to think that the Second World War was a chance occurrence or the result of mistakes of any particular statesmen, although mistakes undoubtedly were made. The war was the inevitable result of the development of world economic and political forces on the basis of modern monopoly capitalism. Marxists have always argued that the capitalist system of world economy harbours elements of general crisis and armed conflicts and that, therefore, the development of world capitalism in our time proceeds not in the form of smooth and even progress but through crises and military catastrophes.

The unevenness of development of the capitalist countries in time provokes violent disturbances of equilibrium in the world system of capitalism; a group of capitalist countries which considers itself worse provided than others with raw materials and markets attempts to alter the situation and repartition the 'spheres of influence' in its favour by armed force. The result is a splitting of the capitalist world into two hostile camps and war between them . . .

Thus the First World War was the result of the first crisis of the capitalist system of world economy, and the Second World War was the result of a second crisis.

That does not mean of course that the Second World War is a copy of the first. On the contrary, the Second World War differs materially from the first in nature. It must be borne in mind that before attacking the Allied countries the principal fascist states – Germany, Japan and Italy – destroyed the last vestiges of bourgeois democratic liberties at home, established a brutal terrorist regime in their own countries, rode roughshod over the principles of sovereignty and free development of small countries, proclaimed a policy of seizure of alien territories as their own policy and declared for all to hear that they were out for world domination and the establishment of a fascist regime throughout the world. Moreover, by the seizure of Czechoslovakia and of the central areas of China, the Axis states showed that they were prepared to carry out their threat of enslaving all freedom-loving nations. In view of this, unlike the First World War, the Second World War against the Axis states from the very outset assumed the character of an anti-fascist war, a war of liberation, one the aim of which was also the restoration of democratic liberties. The entry of the Soviet Union into the war against the Axis states could only enhance, and indeed did enhance, the anti-fascist and liberatory character of the Second World War.

It was on this basis that the anti-fascist coalition of the Soviet Union, the United States of America, Great Britain and other freedom-loving states came into being – a coalition which subsequently played a decisive part in defeating the armed forces of the Axis states.

That is how matters stand as regards the origin and character of the Second World War.

By now I should think everyone admits that the war really was not and could not have been an accident in the life of nations, that actually this war became the war of nations for their existence, and that for this reason it could not be a quick lightning affair.

As for our country, this war was the most bitter and arduous of all wars in the history of our Motherland.

But the war was not only a curse. It was at the same time a great school in which all the forces of the people were tried and tested. The war laid bare all facts and events in the rear and at the front, it tore off relentlessly all veils and coverings which had concealed the true faces of the states, governments and parties and exposed them to view without a mask or embellishment, with all their shortcomings and merits.

The war was something like an examination for our Soviet system, for our state, for our government, for our Communist Party, and it summed up the results of their work, saying to us as it were: 'Here they are, your people and organisations, their deeds and their lives. Look at them well and reward them according to their deeds.'

This was one of the positive aspects of war . . .

Our victory means, first of all, that our Soviet social order has triumphed, that the Soviet *social order* successfully passed the ordeal in the fire of war and proved its unquestionable vitality . . . The point now is that the Soviet social order has shown itself more stable and capable of enduring than a non-Soviet social order, that the Soviet social order is a form of organisation, a society superior to any non-Soviet social order . . . Our victory means, second, that our Soviet *governmental* system triumphed, that our multinational Soviet state withstood the trials of war and proved its viability . . .

Can it be claimed that before entering the Second World War our country already commanded the necessary minimum material potential for satisfying all these requirements in the main? I think it can. In order to prepare for this tremendous job we had to carry out three Five-Year Plans of national economic development. It was precisely these three Five-Year Plans that helped us to create this material potential. Our country's position in this respect before the Second World War, in 1940, was several times better than it was before the First World War, in 1913 . . .

The main task of the new five-year plan is to rebuild the country's regions that have suffered, to restore pre-war levels of industry and agriculture and then to exceed those levels more or less substantially. Not to mention that very soon the rationing system will be abolished (*stormy, prolonged applause*), special attention will be paid to increasing the output of mass consumer goods, to raise the standard of living of toilers by the consistent lowering of the prices of goods (*stormy, prolonged applause*), and to the extensive building of all types of research institutes (*applause*) that will allow science to develop its potential (*stormy applause*).

I have no doubt that if we give the necessary support to our scientists, they will not only be able to catch up but also to soon overtake the achievements of science abroad (*prolonged applause*).

As for the more long-term plans, then the Party intends to organise a new powerful development of the economy which will allow us to raise the level of our industry, for example, three times in comparison with the pre-war level. We must ensure that our industry can produce annually up to 50 million tonnes of pig iron (*prolonged applause*), up to 60 million tonnes of steel (*prolonged applause*), up to 500 million tonnes of coal (*prolonged applause*), and up to 60 million tonnes of oil (*prolonged applause*). Only if this is achieved can we consider that our Motherland is guaranteed against any eventuality (*stormy applause*). For this no doubt three five-year plans, if not more, will be required. But this can be achieved and we must achieve it (*stormy applause*).

Source: Stalin, 'Pre-Election Speech of 9 February 1946', in R. H. McNeal (ed.), I. V. Stalin, Works, vol. 3 (16) (Stanford, Hoover Institution, 1967), pp. 1–5, 6, 7, 11, 19–20.

Document 7.3   Kennan's 'Long Telegram' of 22 February 1946

Posted to the American Embassy in Moscow, George Kennan analysed the context of Soviet policy in a document that exerted a powerful influence on Washington's view of Soviet behaviour.

At the bottom of the Kremlin's neurotic view of world affairs is traditional and instinctive Russian sense of insecurity. Originally this was insecurity of a peaceful agricultural people trying to live on vast exposed plain in neighborhood of fierce nomadic peoples. To this was added, as Russia came into contact with economically advanced West, fear of more competent, more powerful, more highly organized societies in that area. But this latter type of insecurity was one which afflicted rather Russian rulers than Russian people; for Russian rulers have invariably sensed that their rule was relatively archaic in form, fragile and artificial in its psychological foundation, unable to stand comparison for contact with political systems of Western countries. For this reason they have always feared foreign penetration, feared what would happen if Russians learned truth about world without or if foreigners learned truth about world within. And they have learned to seek security only in patient but deadly struggle for total destruction rival power, never in compacts and compromises with it.

It was no coincidence that Marxism, which had smoldered ineffectively for half a century in Western Europe, caught hold and blazed for first time in Russia. Only in this land which had never known a friendly neighbor or indeed any tolerant equilibrium of separate powers, either internal or international, could a doctrine thrive which viewed economic conflicts of society as insoluble by peaceful means. After establishment of Bolshevist regime, Marxist dogma, rendered even more truculent and intolerant by Lenin's interpretation, became a perfect vehicle for sense of insecurity with which Bolsheviks, even more than previous Russian rulers, were afflicted. In this dogma, with its basic altruism of purpose, they found justification for their instinctive fear of outside world, for the dictatorship without which they did not know how to rule, for cruelties they did not dare not to inflict, for sacrifices they felt bound to demand. In the name of Marxism they sacrificed every single ethical value in their methods and tactics. Today they cannot dispense with it. It is fig leaf of their moral and intellectual respectability. Without it they would stand before history, at best, as only the last of that long succession of cruel and wasteful Russian rulers who have relentlessly forced their country on to ever new heights of military power in order to guarantee external security for their internally weak regimes. This is why Soviet purposes must always be solemnly clothed in trappings of Marxism, and why no one should underrate the importance of dogma in Soviet affairs. Thus Soviet leaders are driven by necessities of their own past and present position to put forward a dogma which pictures the outside world as evil, hostile, and menacing, but as bearing within itself germs of creeping disease and destined to be wracked with growing internal convulsions until it is given final coup de grace by rising power of socialism and yields to new and better world. This thesis provides justification for that increase of military and police power in Russia state, for that isolation of Russian population from the outside world, and for that fluid and constant pressure to extend limits of Russian police power which are together the natural and instinctive urges of Russian rulers. Basically this is only the steady advance of uneasy Russian nationalism, a centuries-old movement in which conceptions of offense and defense are inextricably confused. But in new guise of international Marxism, with its honeyed promises to a desperate and wartorn outside world, it is more dangerous and insidious than ever before.

Sources: George F. Kennan, Memoirs 1950–63 *(New York, Bantam, 1969), pp. 549–51; McCauley,* The Origins of the Cold War, *pp. 113–14.*

Document 7.4   Churchill's 'Iron Curtain' speech

It was only after Stalin's speech (7.2) that Churchill, now in opposition, delivered his 'Iron Curtain' speech at Westminster College in Fulton, Missouri, on 5 March 1946 in the presence of President Harry Truman. He called for a partnership between Great Britain and the United States as the guarantors of peace. With powerful communist parties in France and Italy sharing power, it appeared that the days of capitalist democracy on the continent were numbered. The tone of the speech was not overtly hostile to the Soviet Union, and even less a call to war, but pointed the way to what later would be called 'containment'.

From Stettin in the Baltic to Trieste in the Adriatic, an iron curtain has descended across the continent. Behind that line lie all the capitals of the ancient states of Central and Eastern Europe. Warsaw, Berlin, Prague, Vienna, Budapest, Belgrade, Bucharest, and Sofia, all these famous cities and the populations around them lie in the Soviet sphere and all are subject, in one form or another, not only to Soviet influence but to a very high and increasing measure of control from Moscow. Athens alone, with its immortal glories, is free to decide its future at an election under British, American, and French observation . . .

However, in a great number of countries, far from the Russian frontiers and throughout the world, Communist fifth columns are established and work in complete unity and absolute obedience to the directions they receive from the Communist centre. Except in the British Commonwealth, and in the United States, where communism is in its infancy, the Communist parties or fifth columns constitute a growing challenge and peril to Christian civilization . . .

On the other hand, I repulse the idea that a new war is inevitable, still more that it is imminent. It is because I am so sure that our fortunes are in our own hands and that we hold the power to save the future, that I feel the duty to speak out now that I have an occasion to do so. I do not believe that Soviet Russia desires war. What they desire is the fruits of war and the indefinite expansion of their power and doctrines . . .

From what I have seen of our Russian friends and allies during the war, I am convinced that there is nothing they admire so much as strength, and there is nothing for which they have less respect than for military weakness. For that reason the old doctrine of a balance of power is unsound. We cannot afford, if we can help it, to work on narrow margins, offering temptations to a trial of strength. If the western democracies stand together in strict adherence to the principles of the United Nations Charter, their influence for furthering these principles will be immense and no one is likely to molest them. If, however, they become divided or falter in their duty, and if these all-important years are allowed to slip away, then indeed catastrophe may overwhelm us all.

Sources: Pravda, *11 March 1946; McCauley,* The Origins of the Cold War, *pp. 114–15.*

Document 7.5   Stalin's Response to Churchill's Speech

Stalin wilfully misrepresented Churchill's speech, accusing the West of preparing for war against the Soviet Union. His figure of 7 million Soviet deaths was revised upwards by Khrushchev to 20 million, and then under Gorbachev 27 million became the accepted figure.

A few days ago a *Pravda* correspondent asked Stalin to clarify a number of questions concerning Mr Churchill's speech. Comrade Stalin provided these clarifications, which are presented below in the form of answers to the correspondent's questions.

Question: What is your opinion of Mr Churchill's latest speech in the United States of America?

Answer: I regard it as a dangerous act, calculated to sow the seeds of discord among the Allied states and impede their collaboration.

Q. Can it be considered that Mr Churchill's speech is prejudicial to the cause of peace and security?

A. Yes, unquestionably. Essentially, Mr Churchill now adopts the position of the warmongers, and in this Mr Churchill is not alone. He has friends not only in Britain but in the United States of America as well.

A point to be noted is that in this respect Mr Churchill and his friends bear a striking resemblance to Hitler and his friends. Hitler began his work of unleashing war by proclaiming a race theory, declaring that only German-speaking people constitute a superior nation. Mr Churchill sets out to unleash war with a race theory, asserting that only English-speaking nations are superior nations, who are called upon to decide the destinies of the entire world. The German race theory led Hitler and his friends to the conclusion that the Germans, as the only superior nation, should rule over other nations. The English race theory leads Mr Churchill and his friends to the conclusion that the English-speaking nations, as the only superior nations, should rule over the rest of the nations of the world . . .

There is no doubt that the plan of Mr Churchill is a plan for war, a call to war with the Soviet Union. It is also clear that such a plan as that of Mr Churchill is incompatible with the existing treaty of alliance between Britain and the USSR . . .

Q. How do you assess that part of Mr Churchill's speech in which he attacks the democratic regime of our neighbouring European countries and in which he criticises the good neighbourly relations established between these countries and the Soviet Union?

A. This part of Mr Churchill's speech is a mix of libel with rudeness and lack of tact. Mr Churchill asserts that 'Warsaw, Berlin, Prague, Vienna, Budapest, Belgrade, Bucharest and Sofia – all these famous cities and the populations of these areas, are within the Soviet sphere and are all subjected to Soviet influence and to the increasing control of Moscow'. Mr Churchill describes this as the 'limitless expansionist' tendency of the Soviet Union. It is not hard to demonstrate that Mr Churchill crudely and shamelessly libels not only Moscow but also the above-mentioned states neighbouring the USSR.

First, it is quite absurd to speak of the exclusive control of the USSR in Vienna and Berlin, where there are Allied Control Commissions with representatives of four states, where the USSR has only a quarter of the votes. It sometimes happens that people cannot stop themselves from making libellous statements, but they should at least know the limits.

Second, the following fact should not be forgotten. The Germans made their invasion of the USSR through Finland, Poland, Romania, Bulgaria, and Hungary. The Germans were able to make their invasion through these countries because, at the time, governments hostile to the Soviet Union ruled in these countries. As a result of the German invasion the Soviet Union irretrievably lost in fighting against the Germans, and also through the German occupation and the deportation of Soviet citizens to German servitude, a total of about seven million people. In other words, the Soviet

Union's loss of life was several times greater than that of Britain and the United States of America taken together. It may be that some quarters want to forget these colossal sacrifices of the Soviet people, which secured the liberation of Europe from the Hitlerite yoke. But the Soviet Union cannot forget about them. And so what can there be surprising about the fact that the Soviet Union, anxious for its future safety, is trying to ensure that governments loyal in their attitude to the Soviet Union should exist in these countries? How can anyone, who has not taken leave of his senses, describe these peaceful aspirations of the Soviet Union as expansionist tendencies by our state? . . .

Mr Churchill further maintains that 'the communist parties were very insignificant in all these Eastern European countries but became very strong, far exceeding their earlier numbers, and are attempting to establish totalitarian states everywhere' . . . In Poland, Romania, Yugoslavia, Bulgaria and Hungary there are governing blocs composed of several parties – from four to six parties – in which the opposition, if it is more or less loyal, has the right to participate in government. Mr Churchill calls this totalitarianism, tyranny, a police state. Why, on what basis – don't expect an answer from Mr Churchill . . .

The growth of the influence of communism cannot be considered accidental. It is a normal pattern. The influence of the communists grew because during the hard years of the dominance of fascism in Europe, communists showed themselves to be reliable, daring and self-sacrificing fighters against fascist regimes for the liberty of peoples . . . Such is the law of historical development.

Of course, Mr Churchill does not like such a turn of events. He raised the alarm, appealing to force. But neither did he like the appearance of the Soviet regime in Russia after the First World War. Then, too, he raised the alarm and organised an armed expedition of fourteen states against Russia with the aim of turning back the wheel of history. History turned out to be stronger than Churchill's intervention and the quixotic antics of Mr Churchill resulted in his complete defeat. I do not know whether Mr Churchill and his friends will succeed in organising after the Second World War a new military expedition against 'Eastern Europe'. But if they succeed in this, which is unlikely since millions of 'common people' stand to defend the peace, then one can confidently assert that they will be beaten, just as they were beaten twenty-six years ago.

Sources: Pravda, *14 March 1946; Stalin,* Works, *vol. 3, pp. 35–9, 41–2, 43.*

Reimposing Orthodoxy

Any lingering hopes that the war would be followed by a thaw were dashed by a number of campaigns launched to reverse the relative openness of the war years.

Already, Soviet soldiers of victory who had seen the West were being transferred to the labour camps of the East, and on 15 February 1947 marriages between Soviet citizens and foreigners were banned. Now it was time to smash the citadels of literary freedom.

Document 7.6 'The Most Progressive Literature in the World'

The cornerstone of this attempt to reimpose ideological conformity was the campaign (the Zhdanovshchina) launched by Andrei Zhdanov, Stalin's effective second in command from 1946 until his death in August 1948, despite his obvious lack of leadership qualities in Leningrad during the siege. On 14 August 1946 Zhdanov anathematised, in the form of a Central Committee resolution, the journals *Zvezda* and *Leningrad*, and personally the poet Anna Akhmatova and the humourist Mikhail Zoshchenko. Zhdanov characterised Akhmatova as 'a harlot and a nun who mixes harlotry and prayer', while Zoshchenko was dismissed as 'a literary swindler'. The last Stalin years were characterised by cultural sterility and dogmatic intellectual closure.

The VKP(b) Central Committee notes that the literary-artistic journals *Zvezda* and *Leningrad*, published in Leningrad, are being managed in a completely unsatisfactory manner.

The journal *Zvezda* has recently published, along with successful and important works of Soviet writers, much unprincipled, ideologically harmful material. *Zvezda* made a crude error in providing a literary platform for the writer Zoshchenko, whose works are alien to Soviet literature. The editors of *Zvezda* are aware that Zoshchenko has long specialised in writing empty, insubstantial and vulgar things, propagating a rotten lack of ideological content, banality and apolitical thinking intended to disorient our youth and poison its consciousness. The latest of Zoshchenko's stories to be published (*Zvezda*, nos. 5–6, 1946) is a vulgar lampoon of Soviet daily life and of Soviet people. Zoshchenko represents Soviet ways and Soviet people in a degenerate caricatured form, libellously portraying Soviet people as primitive, uncultured, stupid, with philistine tastes and behaviour. Zoshchenko's maliciously hooligan representation of our reality is accompanied by anti-Soviet barbs . . .

The journal *Zvezda* in every way possible also popularises the works of the writer Akhmatova, whose literary and socio-political physiognomy has long been known to Soviet society. Akhmatova is a typical representative of empty non-ideological poetry, which is alien to our people. Her verse is imbued with a spirit of pessimism and decadence, reflecting the tastes of old salon poetry, frozen in the style of bourgeois-aristocratic aesthetics and decadence of 'art for art's sake', not wishing to associate with the people, and harms the task of educating our youth and cannot be tolerated in Soviet literature. . . .

The strength of Soviet literature, the most progressive literature in the world, is that it has no other interests, and cannot have any other interests than the interests of the people, the interests of the state. The task of Soviet literature is to help the state educate youth correctly, answer its questions, train the new generation to be bold, to believe in its cause and not to fear obstacles, to be ready to overcome any obstacles.

Sources: O partiinoi i sovetskoi pechati, radioveshchanii i televidenii: sbornik dokumentov i materialov *(Moscow, 1972), pp. 258–62;* Rossiya, kotoruyu my ne znali, *pp. 309–10.*

The journal *Leningrad* was suppressed and the management of *Zvezda* purged. The assault against artistic freedom was pursued into the world of films as well. The Central Committee on 4 September passed a resolution denouncing L. Lukov's film *The Big Life (Bol'shaya zhizn')*. *Pravda* on 28 January 1949 thundered against a group of theatre critics, who were accused of 'bourgeois cosmopolitanism'. It was at this time that Stalin launched an anti-Semitic campaign, using the code word 'anti-cosmopolitanism'.

Document 7.7   Party Distortion of Science – Genetics

The enormous achievements of Russian biological sciences in the 1930s were undermined by the emergence of Trofim D. Lysenko (1898–1976), who claimed to use a Marxist approach to genetics. In 1948 Lysenko's 'Michurinist' views, which asserted that acquired characteristics could rapidly be inherited (a view at variance with the standard conception of genetic inheritance), received the party's *imprimatur*, and all other views were suppressed. The horticulturalist Ivan Michurin had himself been influenced by the French geneticist Jean Lamarck, who believed that characteristics acquired in life could be passed on to offspring. Lysenko promised fantastic gains in crop productivity, and thus tapped into a powerful current in Bolshevik thinking. Just as the party believed that its will could shape society, so, too, in science it came to believe that in the struggle against nature there were 'no fortresses that the Bolsheviks could not storm'. At a genetics conference in 1937 Lysenko denounced the brilliant geneticist Nikolai Vavilov, who was arrested in 1940 and died of starvation in a prison on the Volga two years later. At the session discussed below Lysenko denounced orthodox geneticists as 'enemies of the Soviet people', describing them as 'reactionary and decadent, grovelling before Western capitalism', views that were greeted, according to *Pravda*, with a 'stormy and prolonged ovation'. Khrushchev later supported Lysenko, retarding the development of Soviet genetics, and it was only in 1965 that he was ousted as director of the Institute of Genetics.

The Session of the V. I. Lenin All-Union Academy of Agricultural Sciences (VASKhNIL) [31 July–7 August 1948] has placed a number of important problems before Soviet biological science, whose solution must contribute to the great work of socialistic construction. The Session of VASKhNIL has revealed the reactionary, anti-national nature of the Weismann–Morgan–Mendel movement in biological science, and has exposed its actual bearers. The destruction of the anti-Michurinist movement has opened new possibilities for the creative development of all branches of advanced biological science.

The materials of the VASKhNIL session have shown, with all transparency, that there has been in progress a struggle between two diametrically opposite, according to their ideological and theoretical concepts, movements in biological science: the struggle of a progressive, materialistic, Michurinist movement against a reactionary, idealistic, Weismannist–Morganist movement . . .

Michurin was discovered for our people and for advanced science through the genius of Lenin and Stalin. In an epoch of Socialism, Michurin's teaching has proved to be a powerful lever in the matter of the transformation of nature. It has received wide opportunities for its development, and popular acclaim.

If in its old form Darwinism set before itself only the problem of explanation of the evolutionary process, then Michurin's teaching, receiving further development through the works of T. D. Lysenko, has set and solves the problem of controlled alteration of hereditary characteristics of plants and animals, has set and solves the problem of controlling the process of evolution.

Source: 'On the Question of the Status and Problems of Biological Science in the Institutes and Institutions of the USSR Academy of Sciences', Resolution of the Presidium of the USSR Academy of Sciences, 26 August 1948, in Daniels, Communism in Russia, *pp. 302–3.*

Document 7.8   The Attack Against 'Cosmopolitanism'

In 1949 yet another campaign was launched, this time against 'denationalised cosmopolitanism' that failed to exalt Russia's achievements and allowed pernicious 'imperialist' influences to contaminate the Soviet mind. The teaching of history was even more to stress Russia's national greatness. The anti-Jewish element was marked, with Yiddish cultural and other organisations at this time being destroyed. The great Jewish actor, Solomon Mikhoels, was probably murdered in 1948, being struck down by a truck in mysterious circumstances. The famous picture of the flag being raised over Berlin had been taken by Evgeny Khaldai, who raced to the roof of the burning Reichstag to photograph soldiers hoisting the red flag. The event in fact had to be restaged, but this does not detract from the power of the image: of Asia in the heart of Europe, of Soviet Russia victorious over fascist Germany, brought to ruin by its aggressive policies. The picture was reproduced on millions of postcards and stamps in the USSR and distributed world-wide. Khaldei himself now became a victim of the anti-Semitic campaign that blighted the post-war USSR, being sacked from the TASS news agency in 1948.

Soviet historical science not only explains the past, but also gives the key to the correct understanding of contemporary political events and aids in understanding the perspectives of the development of society, nations, and states.

The creators of Soviet historical science, the teachers and educators of the Soviet cadres of historians, are Lenin and Stalin. In the works of Lenin and Stalin the foundations of historical science are laid down, the classical evaluations of the most important questions of world history are given, the most important questions of modern and contemporary history and especially of the history of the peoples of the USSR are worked out. Lenin and Stalin are the foundation-layers of the study of the Soviet period of the history of our country . . .

A bunch of nationless cosmopolitans have been preaching a national nihilism hostile to our world view. Defending the anti-scientific and reactionary idea of a 'single world stream' of the development of culture, the cosmopolitans declared that such concepts as national culture, national traditions, national priority in scientific and technical discoveries, were antiquated and outlived. They denied and bemoaned the national forms of socialist culture, and refused to admit that the best traditions and cultural achievements of the peoples of the USSR – above all, the traditions and cultural achievements of the Russian people – provided the basis for Soviet socialist culture. The nationless cosmopolitans have slandered the great Russian people and have propagated a false assertion about its centuries-old backwardness, about the foreign origin of Russian culture and about the absence of national traditions among the Russian people. They have denied and discredited the best achievement of Soviet culture and have tried to deprecate it in favor of the corrupt culture of the bourgeois West.

In this manner nationless cosmopolitanism is closely bound up with subservience toward things foreign. The preaching of cosmopolitan ideas is harmful and dangerous because they are aimed against Soviet patriotism, they undermine the cause of educating the Soviet people in a spirit of patriotic pride in our socialist motherland, in the great Soviet people. Therefore, it is a matter of special importance and immediacy to uproot all manifestations of cosmopolitanism, which, moreover, represents a special danger because at the present time it is an ideological weapon of the struggle of international reaction against socialism and democracy, an ideological cover for the efforts of the American imperialists to establish world domination.

The events of the last few years show what a dangerous enemy cosmopolitanism is of the freedom and independence of nations. Screening themselves with ideas about the 'world economy', a 'world state', and 'world government', and proclaiming the idea of getting rid of national sovereignty supposedly as antiquated, the cunning businessmen and politicians of Wall Street are operating in the countries of Europe and Asia to suppress the national independence of the nations and prepare war against the Soviet Union and the countries of People's Democracy.

Sources: 'On the Tasks of Soviet Historians in the Struggle with Manifestations of Bourgeois Ideology', editorial in Voprosy Istorii, *no. 2, 1949, pp. 3–6, 13; Daniels,* Communism in Russia, *pp. 304–5.*

One of the greatest acts of mass repression at the highest levels in the post-war period was the so-called 'Leningrad Affair'. Hundreds of leading party and state officials were sentenced to be shot on 1 October 1950, including the Politburo member and deputy chairman of the USSR Council of Ministers N. A. Voznesenskii. The entire party and Soviet leadership in Leningrad city and *oblast* were persecuted, including their families. They were accused of having formed an anti-party group and of setting the Leningrad party organisation against the centre. Stalin was jealous of the prestige the city had gained as a result of withstanding the 1,000-day German siege. The political purpose was to ensure an atmosphere of mutual suspicion within the party and thus to ensure his undisputed dominance.

National Relations

Stalin's nationality policy set a time bomb ticking under the USSR. While on the official level he proclaimed full equality and the Soviet media trumpeted the happiness of the Soviet multinational state, in practice Stalin waged a number of murderous 'pacification' programmes on the territories he had acquired as a result of the war, and indeed in the heartlands of the state itself. In 1946 alone 228,000 repatriated people passed through 'filtration' camps, of whom 199,000 were sent to camps or labour battalions.

Document 7.9   Stalin on the Nationality Question

In the 'two camps' speech cited above (Document 7.2) Stalin also discussed nationality issues. His argument that there was no problem was one that continued until the final days of the Soviet Union.

Our state system has been triumphant; our multinational Soviet state has withstood the trial of war. As is known, some influential foreign press commentators have frequently expressed the view that the Soviet multi-national state is an artificial and impractical construction, and that in the event of any difficulties the disintegration of the Soviet Union would be irreversible, that the Soviet Union awaits the same fate as Soviet Hungary.

The war refuted these declarations as lacking any basis. The Soviet multinational state system became even stronger during the war, because our multinational state grew up not on a bourgeois basis, stimulating feelings of national distrust and national enmity, but on a Soviet basis, which cultivates feelings of friendship and fraternal cooperation between the peoples of our state. Our system is a model of a multinational state, where problems of national cooperation have been resolved better than in any other multinational state.

Sources: Pravda, *10 February 1946;* Rossiya, kotoruyu my ne znali, *pp. 280–1.*

Document 7.10 On Deportations and 'Pacification'

This extract was written at a time when parts of the country were engulfed in numerous 'small' civil wars of national independence. The largest of these was waged in western Ukraine by Stepan Bandera at the head of the Organisation of Ukrainian Nationalists (OUN), a war that lasted until at least 1953 and with isolated acts of resistance thereafter. In 1953 there were 2,753,356 deportees (*spetspose-lentsy*) in 'special settlement' camps, of whom 1,224,931 were Germans, 316,717 Chechens (1943–4), 165,259 Crimean Tatars (1944), 139,957 deportees from the Baltic republics (1945–6), 35,838 from Moldavia (1949) and 56,746 Vlasovites. In addition, 18,104 'kulaks' were exiled from Lithuania in 1951 and 11,685 from Georgia in 1951–2 (*Argumenty i fakty*, nos. 1, 10, 1988; 38, 39, 40, 45, 1989). The struggle to pacify Lithuania alone cost 25,108 lives between 1944 and 1956 (*Izvestiya TsK KPSS*, no. 10, 1990, pp. 138–9). The following summary of the deportations and struggle to pacify areas brought under Soviet control cruelly reflects the real state of national relations in this period.

On 26 November 1948 the Presidium of the USSR Supreme Soviet adopted the following decree: Germans, Kalmyks, Ingush, Chechens, Balkars, Crimean Tatars and others have been deported to distant regions forever, and their unauthorised departure from place of settlement is punishable by hard labour for up to twenty years.

In 1948 in connection with the 'Leningrad case' practically the entire leadership of the Estonian party organisation was repressed.

In 1949 on the eve of collectivisation in Estonia over 20,000 people were deported.

On 22–3 May 1948 (by order of a resolution of the USSR Council of Ministers of 21 February 1948) 11,345 families of active participants in the armed nationalist underground and kulaks were deported from Lithuania, totalling 39,766 people (men 12,370, women 16,499 and children under fifteen, 10,897) . . .

Between 1944 and 1952 702 nationalist formations and groups in which 11,042 people participated were liquidated in Latvia. Of these 2,408 were killed, 4,341 arrested, and 4,293 gave themselves up to the authorities.

In this same period in Latvia 1,562 Soviet-Party and Komsomol activists were killed, 50 Soviet Army servicemen, 64 MVD and MGB workers, 386 soldiers in security battalions, and many members of their families . . .

On 25 March 1949 14,000 special resettlers, including old people and children, were deported from Latvia.

Source: Rossiya, kotoruyu my ne znali, *pp. 281–2.*

Stalinism Abroad

Through a gradual policy of exclusions and executions, including the export of the tried and tested Stalinist means of repression, by 1948 the majority of the Soviet-occupied countries had communist governments. The states became known as 'people's democracies', a category differing from proletarian dictatorships in claiming to represent broader strata of society than the working class alone, including the 'progressive' intelligentsia. The last to fall was Czechoslovakia, where a communist coup in February 1948 ended the bipartisan policy that had prevailed since 1945. At this moment of triumph, Stalin's overbearing attitude led to a split between Yugoslavia and the Soviet Union. In June 1948 Yugoslavia was expelled from the Cominform (Communist Information Bureau), the successor organisation to the Comintern established the previous year to link the ruling parties of Eastern Europe and those aspiring to power in Western Europe.

Document 7.11   Stalinism in Germany

For the areas occupied by Soviet forces, defeat of the Nazis by no means signified the onset of peace. From the late 1980s some of the truth about the Soviet occupation of the Eastern zone at last began to emerge. Camps like Buchenwald and Sachsenhausen, which had epitomised the cruelty of the Nazi system, were not only not closed down but continued to function until 1950, but now under new management. The subject was a forbidden one in the former GDR and in the USSR until its last days. With the end of the GDR the sites of mass burials were found, eyewitnesses were at last willing to speak out, and the Soviet authorities provided some statistical details as archival materials began to shed light on Stalinist practices in occupied Germany. The following journalistic account was published in *Moscow News*, one of the standard bearers of *glasnost* under Gorbachev.

Antifascists were also jailed

Hitlers come and go, but the German people is there to say; slogans with these words of Stalin's were hung on surviving buildings of the Soviet occupation zone. The German people that stayed were given to understand that Stalin's order was right after Hitler's, for the devil was exorcized in East Germany not without Beelzebub's help. An important feature of this process were so-called special MVD camps which were organized by NKVD/MVD in 1945, right after the Red Army entered Germany, mostly in former Nazi camps and concentration camps (which totalled nine, plus two jails). They were subordinated to the department of special camps on German territory which was established by NKVD order no. 00315 of April 15, 1945. Until

1948, when the department was included in GULAG, it was commanded by a deputy MVD minister, the omnipresent Colonel-General Ivan Serov, a legendary figure of the Soviet punitive agencies. He seemed to have taken part in all major actions of his ministry. The necessary personnel was recruited from among SMERSH (military counterintelligence) – of the First Byelorussian Group of Armies.

The inmates of special camps were known as special contingents who were mostly civilians that had actively supported the Nazi regime or engaged in espionage, sabotage and terrorism, Gestapo and SD functionaries, etc.

Statistics show that the share of people who were guilty in one way or another was great. But there were few prominent Nazis among them, to say nothing of really outstanding figures who either fled to the West or were sentenced to be deported to the USSR by military tribunals. Most of the prisoners were middling to small fry, including POWs released from allied camps and accused of espionage. The number of people arrested for espionage and convicted under Article 58 of the Soviet Criminal Code grew steadily with the onset of the cold war, and as the flywheel of what was supposed to be a law-enforcement system gathered speed, the camps began to absorb 'class enemies' from among journalists, businessmen, factory owners, etc. Participants in the antifascist resistance were also arrested. There were cases, for instance, when people were imprisoned in one Buchenwald until 1945 and in the other after 1945.

The wave of arrests swept social democrats dissatisfied by the merger of their party with the communists and members of other parties, including communists who opposed the new regime. Among the inmates of the Funfeichen camp, for example, was an old communist who had worked at the Berlin magistrate. His name was Ewald Pieck and he was the brother of Wilhelm Pieck, the future President of the GDR.

Young people were a special group among the arrested. They were imprisoned, as a rule, on suspicion of belonging to the so-called Wehrwolf [sic], an organization which was formed by the Nazis during the last months of the war for sabotage guerilla activity but which was not as widespread or influential as NKVD ascribed it to be. The myth of Wehrwolf was so persuasive that whole school classes were arrested at the slightest denunciation. The punitive agencies acted so ruthlessly that there must have been an oral instruction which was probably issued by Stalin himself. Thousands of teenagers aged from 12 to 18 were thrown into camps, not special colonies but special camps where they stayed with real criminals and where many of them died of hunger and disease. Their destiny is probably the most tragic part of this story, for yesterday's children fell victim to two totalitarian regimes.

Thousands of foreigners, displaced persons and our countrymen – former Eastern workers and Russian emigrants – also went through special camps. To them these were trans-shipment posts on the way to exile in the USSR.

For the sake of plan target figures

Arrests were made first by SMERSH groups, then by operational groups of NKVD which functioned all over Germany. People were arrested in the street, at work or at a magistrate where they were summoned for registration. One could be arrested on the strength of unsupported suspicion or denunciation which flourished in the atmosphere of fear and humiliation, of the moral catastrophe in which Germany found itself. There was no investigation as a rule since persons who were sent to special camps under order 00315 were treated according to a special procedure. Since they were not formally accused, there was no need either for sanctions of military prosecutors or for investigatory materials.

Former police stations, garages, cellars and sheds were converted into preliminary detention wards. The usual means of coercion were beating, interrogations round the clock and threats of execution. The people interrogated often could not understand what was required of them.

A. V-ya, a former interpreter of an NKVD operational group in Magdeburg, recalled during a talk with me: 'Plan target figures were the main thing on which depended stars on the shoulder straps and ranks. By the end of a month it was necessary to check who could be arrested because the task was to fill up camps. The investigator asks: "Are you a Nazi?" The German shakes his head in negation. "Have you read newspapers, listened to the radio?" The German nods. "Aha, let us write that you engaged in Nazi propaganda". So much for investigation . . .'

Many people denounced innocent persons under pressure, or names were mixed up. This happened often in the Soviet Union during a terror wave, and it was much more difficult to put German names right. There was a man, for example, in special camp Bautzen, who was a namesake of a top-ranking SS officer. Of course, they did not let him go when the mistake was found out. Another one spent three years in camp because he was S-Bahnführer, i.e. a tram driver.

From cold and hunger

Special camps were kept in the strictest secrecy. Even our own aviation was prohibited to fly over them for fear that photographs would be made from the air.

Correspondence with relatives was strictly forbidden. Prisoners' families knew practically nothing about them until 1948 when the first groups of prisoners began to be released.

Interned people were not allowed to listen to the radio, to read newspapers until 1947 and also, depending on the camp, to sing, write, read, draw, leave barracks, discuss political subjects, and so on.

The outside security was maintained by MVD units, while the order inside camps was kept by camp policemen, who were often common criminals or former Nazis. Witnesses said that this was done even by SS officers at Muhlberg camp.

There were neither tortures nor mass killings at Germany's special camps, but mortality from hunger and cold was very high. Only a few lucky ones had warm clothes, and no one was allowed to receive anything from outside, so people had to do time in what they were arrested. The prisoners of Buchenwald and Sachsenhausen wore striped clothes left by the inmates of Nazi camps.

1946 and 1947 were especially hard. From November 1946 rations were sharply reduced to 300 grams of bread and a bowl of skilly. Epidemics of typhoid and tuberculosis broke out because of hunger and lack of sanitation facilities and crowded conditions to which the Germans were not used. Tuberculosis was the most severe disease. The situation was so hard that even the camp medics had to admit: '. . . the situation in the camp as regards pulmonary tuberculosis and alimentary dystrophy is catastrophic. 30 percent of the entire special contingent suffer from tuberculosis, 11.3 percent from alimentary dystrophy . . . the total number of the diseased is 46.3 percent of the special contingent.'

You'll suffer more from your own people . . .

The turning point came at the end of 1948. Special camps began gradually to be dismantled. The last ones – Buchenwald and Sachsenhausen – closed in 1950, and 15,000 prisoners were handed over to the GDR authorities.

Seventeen-year-old Eva Fischer, sentenced by a military tribunal to ten years for anti-Soviet propaganda, who did some time in a GDR prison, recalls: 'The Russian soldiers who guarded us at the special camp were not, as a rule, vicious. They could not help us in any way, but they disliked what they saw going on in the camp. When special camp Sachsenhausen was liquidated in 1950 and we were transferred to the GDR authorities a Russian sentry told me: "You will suffer more from your own Germans". His prophecy was correct.'

The prisoners were indeed transferred 'to reliable hands'. The conditions in the GDR's prisons were so hard that a real riot broke out in Bautzen jail in 1950, when the inmates shouted through the bars, demanding improvements. As a result they were cruelly beaten up by the warders.

People released from Soviet special camps had to keep silent about what had happened to them, unless they had gone West. Nobody has been rehabilitated; this chapter has been simply deleted from the history of East Germany.

According to our archives, there were about 155,000 prisoners in special camps in Germany. About 42,000 died and 756 were sentenced to death by military tribunals. 33,000 were Soviet citizens. Documents shedding light on this chapter of our common history are kept in German, and mostly in our archives. They concern the destiny of thousands of people, many of whom are still alive. These documents should be thoroughly studied by both our and German historians. Thank God that we have lived to cooperation other than that between MGB–KGB and Stasi.

Source: Irina Shcherbakova, 'How Buchenwald Became NKVD's Torture Chamber', Moscow News, no. 23, 4 June 1993, p. 14.

Document 7.12   Djilas on the Soviet–Yugoslav Split

The Yugoslav communists under the leadership of Josef Broz Tito had come to power by their own efforts in 1945, and had thereafter pursued an independent policy although remaining loyal to a Stalinist definition of socialism. Despite their orthodoxy, the independence of the Yugoslav communists irked Stalin to such an extent that in 1948 he sought to bring them to heel, leading to a break. Only after the split did ideological differences emerge as the Yugoslavs developed an original form of 'self-managing socialism'. In Djilas's account of his conversations with Stalin (Document 7.1) special attention was paid to Stalin's views on revolution and the new socialist camp. Here Djilas comments on the break.

Except for Albania, Yugoslavia had been the only East European country to free itself from the Nazi invasion and at the same time carry out a domestic revolution without the decisive help of the Red Army . . . [T]he decision that Belgrade should be the seat of the Cominform was, on the surface, a form of recognition of the Yugoslav revolution. Behind it lay the secret Soviet intention to lull the Yugoslav leaders into a state of self-satisfaction at their own revolution and to subordinate Yugoslavia to some supposed international Communist solidarity – in fact, to the hegemony of the Soviet state, or, rather, to the insatiable demands of the Soviet political bureaucracy.

It is time something was said about Stalin's attitude to revolutions, and thus to the Yugoslav revolution. Because Moscow had always refrained at the crucial moment from supporting the Chinese, Spanish, and in many ways even the Yugoslav revolutions, the view prevailed, not without reason, that Stalin was generally against revolutions. This is, however, not entirely correct. His opposition was only conditional, and arose only when the revolution went beyond the interests of the Soviet state. He felt instinctively that the creation of revolutionary centres outside Moscow could endanger its supremacy in world Communism, and of course that is what actually happened. That is why he helped revolutions only up to a certain point – as long as he could control them – but he was always ready to leave them in the lurch whenever they slipped out of his grasp. I maintain that not even today is there any essential change in this respect in the policy of the Soviet Government.

In his own country Stalin had subjected all activities to his views and to his personality, so he could not behave differently outside. Having identified domestic progress and freedom with the interests and privileges of a political party, he could not act in foreign affairs other than as a dictator. And like everyone else he must be judged by his actual deeds. He became himself the slave of the despotism, the bureaucracy, the narrowness, and the servility that he imposed on his country.

It is indeed true that no one can destroy another's freedom without losing his own.

Source: Djilas, Conversations with Stalin, *pp. 102–3.*

Stalin moved quickly to crush any other possible outbreaks of 'national communism'. In Poland Władisław Gomułka was purged as head of the party, but survived in gaol from 1951 to 1956 when he re-emerged to defuse the crisis in Polish–Soviet relations. Elsewhere show trials were held on the Soviet model; in Hungary and Bulgaria in 1949, and in Czechoslovakia in 1952. In Yugoslavia meanwhile a new model of socialism was being developed focused on the concept of workers' self-management through workers' councils. A more decentralised economy emerged allowing private farming, foreign travel and some intellectual freedom. The Marxist critique of Soviet-type socialism generated in Yugoslavia and other communist countries in the long-run proved as devastating as any number of liberal critiques.

Containment and Beyond

The full-blown Cold War is usually reckoned to have started in 1947–8. The United States adopted the Truman Doctrine (based on a speech delivered to Congress by Truman on 12 March 1947) that sought to 'contain' Soviet expansionism in response, in part, to Kennan's arguments in his 'Mr X' article, even though he later explained that he had intended a *political* response to a *political* threat, whereas the Truman Doctrine gave it a military form. To the end Stalin was preaching the ideology of irreconcilable hostility between the capitalist world and the Soviet Union.

Document 7.13   Kennan's 'Mr X' Article

Kennan published the article anonymously, but his authorship did not remain a secret for long. In this acute analysis of the Soviet system he accurately pointed out its strengths while noting the brittle character of Soviet power.

The political personality of Soviet power as we know it today is the product of ideology and circumstances: ideology inherited by the present Soviet leaders from the movement in which they had their political origin, and circumstances of the power which they now have exercised for nearly three decades in Russia . . . tremendous emphasis has been placed on the original Communist thesis of a basic antagonism between the capitalist and Socialist worlds . . . Of the original ideology, nothing has been officially junked. Belief is maintained in the basic badness of capitalism, in the inevitability of its destruction, in the obligation of the proletariat to assist in that destruction and to take power in its own hands. But stress has come to be laid primarily on those concepts which relate most specifically to the Soviet regime itself: to its position as the sole truly Socialist regime in a dark and misguided world, and to the relationships of power within it . . .

It is always possible that another transfer of preeminent power may take place quietly and inauspiciously, with no repercussions anywhere. But again, it is possible that the questions involved may unleash, to use some of Lenin's words, one of those 'incredibly swift transitions' from 'delicate deceit' to 'wild violence' which characterize Russian history, and may shake Soviet power to its foundations . . . And if disunity were ever to seize and paralyze the Party, the chaos and weakness of Russian society would be revealed in forms beyond description. For we have seen that Soviet power is only a crust concealing an amorphous mass of human beings among whom no independent organizational structure is tolerated. In Russia there is not even such a thing as local government. The present generation of Russians have never known spontaneity of collective action. If, consequently, anything were ever to occur to disrupt the unity and efficacy of the Party as a political instrument, Soviet Russia might be changed overnight from one of the strongest to one of the weakest and most pitiable of national societies . . . the possibility remains (and in the opinion of this writer it is a strong one) that Soviet power, like the capitalist world of its conception, bears within it the seeds of its own decay, and that the sprouting of these seeds is well advanced . . .

It is clear that the main element of any United States policy towards the Soviet Union must be that of a longterm, patient but firm and vigilant containment of Russian expansive tendencies . . . It is clear that the United States cannot expect in the foreseeable future to enjoy political intimacy with the Soviet Regime. It must continue to regard the Soviet Union as a rival, not a partner, in the political arena. It must continue to expect that Soviet policies will reflect no abstract love of peace and stability, no real faith in the possibility of a permanent happy coexistence of the Socialist and capitalist worlds, but rather a cautious, persistent pressure towards the disruption and weakening of all rival influence and rival power.

Source: George Kennan (Mr X), 'The Sources of Soviet Conduct', Foreign Affairs, vol. 25, no. 4 (July 1947), pp. 566, 570, 571–2, 578–9, 580–1.

Document 7.14 Stalin's Final Bequest – War

In his last theoretical exposition Stalin noted that war was still likely between capitalist countries, but that the Soviet Union did not necessarily need to be involved.

Some comrades affirm that, as a result of new international conditions after the Second World War, war between capitalist countries is no longer inevitable. They consider that the contradictions between the socialist camp and the capitalist camp are stronger than the contradictions between capitalist states, that the United States has subordinated the other capitalist countries to itself to such an extent that it would not permit them to go to war or weaken each other, that the leading capitalist peoples have learned enough from the experience of two world wars, damaging the whole capitalist world, to allow the capitalist world once again to be drawn into war, that in view of all this war between capitalist countries is no longer inevitable.

These comrades are mistaken. They only see the superficial phenomena, but do not see those more profound forces which, even though they are at present hardly noticeable, will nevertheless determine the course of events . . .

It is said that the contradictions between capitalism and socialism are stronger than the contradictions among the capitalist countries. Theoretically, of course, that is true. It is not only true now, today; it was equally true before the Second World War. And it was more or less understood by the leaders of the capitalist countries. Yet the Second World War began not as a war with the USSR, but as a war between capitalist countries. Why? First, because war with the USSR, as a socialist land, is more dangerous to capitalism than war between capitalist countries; for whereas war between capitalist countries puts in question only the supremacy of certain capitalist countries over others, war with the USSR must certainly put in question the existence of capitalism itself. Second, because the capitalists, although they make a big fuss, for 'propaganda' purposes, about the aggressiveness of the Soviet Union, do not themselves believe that it is aggressive, because they understand the Soviet Union's peaceful policy and know that it will not itself attack capitalist countries . . .

When the United States and Britain assisted Germany's economic recovery [after the First World War], they did so with a view to setting a recovered Germany against the Soviet Union, to use her against the land of socialism. But Germany directed her forces in the first place against the Anglo-French–American bloc. And when Hitler's Germany declared war on the Soviet Union, the Anglo-French–American bloc, far from joining with Hitler's Germany, was compelled to enter into a coalition with the USSR against Hitler's Germany.

Consequently, the struggle of the capitalist countries for markets and their desire to crush their competitors proved in practice to be stronger than the contradictions between the capitalist camp and the socialist camp.

What guarantee is there, then, that Germany and Japan will not rise to their feet again, will not attempt to break out of American bondage and live their own independent lives? I think there is no such guarantee.

From this it follows that the inevitability of wars between capitalist countries remains in force.

It is said that Lenin's thesis that imperialism inevitably generates war must now be regarded as obsolete, since powerful popular forces have come forward today in defence of peace and against another world war. That is not true.

The object of the contemporary peace movement is to rouse the popular masses to fight for the preservation of peace and to prevent another world war. Consequently, the aim of this movement is not to overthrow capitalism and establish socialism – it limits itself to the democratic aim of preserving peace. In this respect, the present-day peace movement differs from the movement of the time of the First World War for the conversion of the imperialist war into civil war, since the latter movement went further and pursued socialist aims.

It is possible that in a definite conjuncture of circumstances the fight for peace will develop here or there into a fight for socialism. But then it will no longer be the contemporary peace movement; it will be a movement for the overthrow of capitalism.

Source: Stalin, Ekonomicheskie problemy sotsializma v SSSR (Economic Problems of Socialism in the USSR) *(Moscow, Gospolitizdat, 1952), pp. 32–3, 34, 35–6.*

Khrushchev and reform, 1953–1964 | **8**

The 1950s were marked by hopes that the Soviet system would find a new and more stable form of governance, less reliant on charismatic leadership. On Stalin's death on 5 March 1953, all the heirs apparent agreed that the new epoch would be marked by collective leadership. The leader of the government and party, Georgii Malenkov, at first appeared to be in the strongest position, although on 14 March he was forced to choose between his party and government posts, and chose the latter, allowing him to launch a 'New Course' somewhat modifying Stalin's economic policies. After a brief struggle the party's new First Secretary, Nikita Khrushchev, triumphed over his rival, a victory that also represented the re-establishment of the party's political dominance. Under Khrushchev's leadership the excesses of Stalinist repression were curbed and the rudiments of the rule of law were introduced. The economic system was modified to focus more on consumer needs but the results were meagre. A new system of economic management was sought while the introduction of new technology was encouraged. In agriculture some of the worst Stalinist excesses were overcome, but the legacy of forced collectivisation made the sector a permanent drain on resources. Above all, Khrushchev sought to revive the Communist Party and the ideological vitality of the regime.

The New Course and Agricultural Problems

The first task facing Stalin's successors was to eliminate the danger posed to the entire leadership from the secret police, and thus its leader, Beria, was arrested on 26 June 1953 at a meeting of the Presidium (Politburo), with the help of Marshals Zhukov and Kiril Moskalenko, and shot on 23 December of that year. Although there is no agreement, recent figures suggest that at the time of Stalin's death a total of 2.5 million were incarcerated in labour camps, of whom 582,522 were accused of 'counter-revolutionary crimes', half of whom (280,946) had been sentenced for 'betraying the Motherland' (i.e. former prisoners of war in German camps) (*Voenno-istoricheskii zhurnal*, no. 7, 1991, p. 69). Stalin's death was followed by a spate of initiatives. A more cooperative Soviet approach abroad encouraged the Chinese to accept a ceasefire ending the Korean War. It was Malenkov who first suggested that the Leninist orthodoxy of the inevitability of war between capitalist and communist countries might be obsolete in an age of nuclear weapons – a view that Khrushchev attacked as 'revisionism' but later adopted in the form of 'peaceful coexistence'.

Document 8.1 The New Course

The main debate at this time was the new balance to be struck between heavy industry and consumer goods. Malenkov called for higher standards of living and a greater priority for consumer goods. He scaled back the drive for industrialisation and focused more on the dire situation in the countryside. One of his first acts was to reduce the level of compulsory deliveries to the state from the collective farmers' private plots by reducing delivery norms; the financial burden was also reduced by writing off past debts. In a speech to the Supreme Soviet on 8 September 1953 he outlined his views.

Up to now we have not had an opportunity to develop the light and food industries at those tempos as heavy industry. At the present time we can and are therefore obliged, to ensure the more rapid improvement in the people's material and cultural standards, to force the development of light industry . . . We must significantly increase investments in the light, food and in particular the fish industries, for the development of agriculture . . . the significant increase in the output of consumer goods . . . and the further rapid growth in the production of grain. We need to change the tax system on the *kolkhoz* peasant's personal plot . . . to reduce sharply compulsory deliveries from the personal plot . . . and reduce agricultural taxes.

Source: Izvestiya, *9 September 1953.*

It was over the issue of consumer goods versus industrial investment that Malenkov was forced to resign as chairman of the Council of Ministers in February 1955. The collective leadership, about which so much was said after Stalin's death, was over. Malenkov was replaced by Nikolai Bulganin who at first shared prominence with Khrushchev, but he, too, was soon eclipsed.

Document 8.2 The Legacy of Stalinist Collectivisation: 'Crab Meat and Green Peas'

The following appeal to Khrushchev (he was not only party leader but responsible specifically for agricultural issues) reveals the scale of the problem.

Comrades think much of themselves and think little of people, of the common people. The people are living badly, and their state of mind is not to our advantage. The food situation throughout the country is dire. In practice one can only eat well in Moscow. In many regions in the shops there is only crab meat and green peas. In the countryside sugar is hardly eaten. The main thing is that the food situation from year to year does not improve.

We, Russia, buy meat from New Zealand. Just look at the yards of collective farm peasants, they are ruined. Isolated successes do not change the picture. Has it ever happened in history that people ran away from the land? And our countryside is depopulated . . .

Comrade Khrushchev! You are a bold person, gather once again your courage and admit directly that the twenty-six-year experience has demonstrated that collective farms have not justified themselves, a new organisation of agriculture is required.

Source: Izvestiya TsK KPSS, no. 6, 1989, pp. 148–9.

In September 1953 Khrushchev announced substantial increases (averaging 25–40 per cent) in the procurement prices (the fixed prices paid by the state for compulsory deliveries) and also increases in the purchase price of agricultural goods. He stressed, however: 'It should also be noted that the retail prices on livestock products, on potatoes and vegetables will not be increased, but, on the contrary, annually decrease. The policy of decreasing the retail prices of consumption items will be pursued into the future' (*Pravda*, 7 November 1953). Thus the USSR condemned itself to a reverse 'scissors crisis', with the prices paid by consumers heavily subsidised by the state, while state and collective farms were increasingly generously supported by cheap credits. Increasingly wasteful agricultural financing became a huge burden on the state budget. To the end of the Soviet period rural shops stocked little more than vodka, bread, tinned fish and Bulgarian peas.

Document 8.3   Khrushchev and the Virgin Lands Scheme

Unable to do much to improve the 'intensity' of farming, Khrushchev sought to overcome the chronic grain shortages by advocating its 'extension' to hitherto uncultivated areas, primarily the pasture-land steppe of the nomadic peoples of Kazakhstan, western Siberia, the lower Volga and (to a limited extent) in the north Caucasus. He sought within two years to expand grain planting by 13 million hectares, using intensive mechanisation. In these semi-arid terrains early successes soon gave way to serious dust-bowl problems. Later, the exploitation of these lands settled down to more sustainable levels. At this time Eduard Shevardnadze was a Komsomol (Communist Youth League) activist, and later became Georgian party leader from 1972 to July 1985, when he was made Gorbachev's foreign minister. His memoirs reveal both the enthusiasm of the period, and some of the problems with the campaign.

The campaign to develop the country's virgin lands and forests was beginning. Trains packed with young volunteers shuttled to Kazakhstan and the Altai range. I was assigned to lead the Georgian Komsomol brigade. We lived in the Kazakh steppes for several months, tilling the virgin earth, building homes and agricultural complexes. We got to know our peers from other republics. I owe much to this period of my life and retain bright memories of it. Perhaps people of my age are prone to idealise the vanished past, seeing their youth through a haze of nostalgia. But time does not distort the picture of those years or erase the remembered hardship of that life; nor do all my fellow travellers come out looking like heroes. I can clearly recall this grandiose but poorly organised 'virgin land' era, the stupid decisions, and the ill-conceived strategies that cancelled out many successes. We watched helplessly as equipment brought to the new territories from all over the country began to break down. Thousands of people worked themselves ragged but failed to gather in the gigantic harvest. The crops rotted in the fields, and there was no place to store grain. Billions of roubles and vast amounts of equipment and manpower were squandered.

Sources: Eduard Shevardnadze, Moi vybor: v zashchitu demokratii i svobody *(Moscow, Novosti, 1991), p. 57;* The Future Belongs to Freedom *(London, Sinclair-Stevenson, 1991), p. 22.*

Although the Virgin Lands scheme, the opening up of the steppe to wheat production, from 1955 provided a massive boost to output, declining fertility soon reduced the value of the new lands. The country was forced to import grain from abroad, primarily the United States, and by the late 1980s the country was facing severe food shortages. The legacy of the coercive Stalinist agricultural system and botched attempts at its reform was one of the main themes of the last years of the USSR and was one of the major contributory causes for the collapse of the Soviet system.

Destalinisation

The problem of dealing with Stalin and his legacy was never satisfactorily resolved in the Soviet period. Khrushchev bravely started the process of what became known as 'destalinisation' in his 'secret speech' to the Twentieth Party Congress in February 1956, but its limits were not greatly extended in the next thirty years. Much remained secret about Stalin's crimes, many victims (including some leading Bolsheviks like Nikolai Bukharin) were not rehabilitated, and the economic and political distortions imposed by the Stalinist system remained a permanent part of the fabric of Soviet life. The origins of the Stalinist system were allowed no sustained discussion, and the door remained open for attempts to rehabilitate Stalin himself.

Document 8.4   Khrushchev's 'Secret Speech'

The Twentieth Party Congress from 14 to 24 February 1956 was the first to be held after the death of Stalin. While many important matters were discussed in its sessions, the issue of Stalin was not placed on the agenda. With the final day's work completed on 24 February, the delegates were preparing to return home when, with the exception of foreign delegations and foreign guests, they were recalled in the evening for a closed session that lasted into the early hours of the next day. Without any preliminaries Khrushchev launched into a four-hour speech denouncing some of Stalin's excesses, above all the great purge of 1937–8 and his 'personality cult'. The speech did not remain secret for long, but although it was read to closed party meetings it was not officially published until the regime's final years.

Comrades! In the report of the Central Committee of the party at the Twentieth Congress, in a number of speeches by delegates to the Congress, as also formerly during the plenary meetings of the CC CPSU, quite a lot has been said about the cult of the individual and about its harmful consequences.

After Stalin's death the Central Committee of the party began to implement a policy of explaining concisely and consistently that it is impermissible and foreign to the spirit of Marxism-Leninism to elevate one person, to transform him into a superman possessing supernatural characteristics akin to those of a god. Such a man supposedly knows everything, sees everything, thinks for everyone, can do anything, is infallible in his behaviour.

Such a belief about a man, and specifically about Stalin, was cultivated among us for many years.

The objective of the present report is not a thorough evaluation of Stalin's life and activity. Concerning Stalin's merits, an entirely sufficient number of books, pamphlets and studies have already been written in his lifetime. The role of Stalin in the preparation and execution of the Socialist revolution, in the civil war, and in the fight for the construction of Socialism in our country is universally known. Everyone knows this well. At the present we are concerned with a question which has immense importance for the party now and in the future – (we are concerned) with how the cult of the person of Stalin has been gradually growing, the cult which became at a certain specific stage the source of a whole series of exceedingly serious and grave perversions of party principles, of party democracy, of revolutionary legality . . . [Khrushchev here cites Lenin's 'last testament', see Document 4.13]

When we analyse the practice of Stalin in regard to the direction of the party and of the country, when we pause to consider everything which Stalin perpetrated, we must be convinced that Lenin's fears were justified. The negative characteristics of Stalin, which, in Lenin's time, were only incipient, transformed themselves during the last years into a grave abuse of power by Stalin, which caused untold harm to our party.

We have to consider seriously and analyse correctly this matter in order that we may preclude any possibility of a repetition in any form whatever of what took place during the life of Stalin, who absolutely did not tolerate collegiality in leadership and in work, and who practised brutal violence, not only toward everything which opposed him, but also toward that which seemed to his capricious and despotic character contrary to his concepts.

Stalin acted not through persuasion, explanation, and patient cooperation with people, but by imposing his concepts and demanding absolute submission to his opinion. Whoever opposed this concept or tried to prove his viewpoint, and the correctness of his position, was doomed to removal from the leading collective and to subsequent moral and physical annihilation. This was especially true during the period following the Seventeenth Party Congress, when many prominent party leaders and rank-and-file party workers, honest and dedicated to the cause of Communism, fell victim to Stalin's despotism.

We must affirm that the party had fought a serious fight against the Trotskyites, Rightists and bourgeoisie Nationalists, and that it disarmed ideologically all the enemies of Leninism. This ideological fight was carried on successfully, as a result of which the party became strengthened and tempered. Here Stalin played a positive role. . . .

It was precisely during this period (1935–8) that the practice of mass repression through the Government apparatus was born, first against the enemies of Leninism – Trotskyites, Zinovievites, Bukharinites, long since politically defeated by the party – and subsequently also against many honest Communists, against those party cadres who had borne the heavy load of the Civil War and the first and most difficult years of industrialisation and collectivisation, who actively fought against the Trotskyites and the Rightists for the Leninist Party line.

Stalin originated the concept 'enemy of the people'. This term automatically rendered it unnecessary that the ideological errors of a man or men engaged in a controversy be proven; this term made possible the usage of the most cruel repression, violating all norms of revolutionary legality, against anyone who in any way disagreed with Stalin, against those who were only suspected of hostile intent, against those who had bad reputations. This concept, 'enemy of the people', actually eliminated the possibility of any kind of ideological fight or the making of one's views known on this or that issue, even those of a practical character. In the main, and in actuality, the only proof of guilt used, against all norms of current legal science, was the 'confession' of the accused himself; and, as subsequent probing proved, 'confessions' were acquired through physical pressures against the accused.

This led to glaring violations of revolutionary legality, and to the fact that many entirely innocent persons, who in the past had defended the party line, became victims. We must assert that in regard to those persons who in their time had opposed the party line, there were often no sufficiently serious reasons for their physical annihilation. The formula, 'enemy of the people', was specifically introduced for the purpose of physically annihilating such individuals.

It is a fact that many persons who were later annihilated as enemies of the party and people had worked with Lenin during his life. Some of these persons made errors during Lenin's life, but in spite of this Lenin benefited by their work, he corrected them, and he did everything possible to retain them in the ranks of the party; he induced them to follow him . . .

Stalin's wilfulness *vis-à-vis* the party and its Central Committee became fully evident after the seventeenth party congress, which took place in 1934 . . .

It became apparent that many party, Soviet and economic activists who were branded in 1937–8 as 'enemies' were actually never enemies, spies, wreckers, etc., but were always honest Communists; they were only so stigmatised, and often, no longer able to bear barbaric tortures, they charged themselves – at the order of the investigative judges, falsifiers – with all kinds of grave and unlikely crimes. The commission [established by the Central Committee to investigate the mass repressions] has presented to the Central Committee Presidium lengthy and documented materials pertaining to mass repressions against the delegates to the seventeenth party congress, and against members of the Central Committee elected at that Congress. These materials have been studied by the Presidium of the Central Committee.

It was determined that of the 139 members and candidates of the party's Central Committee who were elected at the seventeenth congress, 98 persons, i.e., 70 per cent, were arrested and shot (mostly in 1937–8). (*Indignation in the hall.*) . . . The same fate met not only the Central Committee members but also the majority of the delegates to the seventeenth party congress. Of 1,966 delegates with either voting or advisory rights, 1,108 persons were arrested on charges of anti-revolutionary crimes, i.e., decidedly more than a majority. This very fact shows how absurd, wild and contrary to common sense were the charges of counterrevolutionary crimes made out, as we now see, against a majority of participants at the seventeenth party Congress. (*Indignation in the hall.*) . . .

These and other facts show that all norms of correct party solution of problems were invalidated and everything was dependent upon the wilfulness of one man. The power accumulated in the hands of one person, Stalin, led to serious consequences during the great patriotic war . . .

Documents which have now been published show that by April 3, 1941, Churchill, through his Ambassador to the USSR., Cripps, personally warned Stalin that the Germans had begun regrouping their armed units with the intent of attacking the Soviet Union . . .

Had our industry been mobilised properly and in time to supply the Army with the necessary material, our wartime losses would have been decidedly smaller. Such mobilisation had not been, however, started in time. And already in the first days of the war it became evident that our Army was badly armed, that we did not have enough artillery, tanks, and planes to throw the enemy back . . .

When the Fascist armies had actually invaded Soviet territory and military operations began, Moscow issued the order that German fire was not to be returned. Why? It was because Stalin, despite evident facts, thought that the war had not yet started, that this was only a provocative action on the part of several undisciplined sections of the German Army, and that our reaction might serve as a reason for the Germans to begin the war . . .

As you see, everything was ignored; warnings of certain army commanders, declarations of deserters from the enemy army, and even the open hostility of the enemy. Is this an example of the alertness of the Chief of the Party and of the State at this particularly significant historical moment? . . .

It would be incorrect to forget that after the first severe disaster and defeats at the front Stalin thought that this was the end. In one of his speeches in those days he said: 'All that which Lenin created we have lost forever.' . . .

However, we speak not only about the moment when the war began, which led to serious disorganisation of our army and brought us severe losses. Even after the war began, the nervousness and hysteria which Stalin demonstrated, interfering with actual military operations, caused our army serious damage.

Stalin was very far from understanding the real situation which was developing at the front. This was natural because during the whole patriotic war he never visited any section of the front or any liberated city except for one short ride on the Mozhaisk highway during a stabilised situation at the front. To this incident were dedicated many literary works full of fantasies of all sorts and so many paintings. Simultaneously, Stalin was interfering with operations and issuing orders which did not take into consideration the real situation at a given section of the front and which could not help but result in huge personnel losses . . .

We should note that Stalin planned operations on a globe. (*Animation in the hall.*) Yes, Comrades, he used to take the globe and trace the front line on it . . .

Comrades, let us reach for some other facts. The Soviet Union is justly considered as a model of a multinational state because we have in practice assured the equality and friendship of all nations which live in the great fatherland.

All the more monstrous are the acts whose initiator was Stalin and which are crude violations of the basic Leninist principles of the nationality policy of the Soviet state. We refer to the mass deportations from their native places of whole nations, together with all Communists and Komsomols without any exception; this deportation action was not dictated by any military considerations.

Thus, already at the end of 1943, when there occurred a permanent breakthrough at the fronts of the great patriotic war in favour of the Soviet Union, a decision was taken and executed concerning the deportation of all the Karachai from the lands on which they lived. In the same period, at the end of December, 1943, the same lot befell the whole population of the Autonomous Kalmyk Republic. In March, 1944, all the Chechen and Ingush people were deported and the Chechen-Ingush Autonomous Republic was liquidated.

In April, 1944, all Balkars were deported to faraway places from the territory of the Kabardyno-Balkar Autonomous Republic and the Republic itself was renamed Autonomous Kabardyn Republic. The Ukrainians avoided meeting this fate only because there were too many of them and there was no place to which to deport them. Otherwise, he would have deported them also. (*Laughter and animation in the hall.*) . . .

The wilfulness of Stalin showed itself not only in decisions concerning the internal life of the country but also in the international relations of the Soviet Union.

The July Plenum of the Central Committee studied in detail the reasons for the development of conflict with Yugoslavia. It was a shameful role which Stalin played here. The 'Yugoslav Affair' contained no problems which could not have been solved through party discussions among comrades. There was no significant basis for the development of this 'affair', it was completely possible to have prevented the rupture of relations with that country. This does not mean, however, that the Yugoslav leaders did not make mistakes or did not have shortcomings. But these mistakes and shortcomings were magnified in a monstrous manner by Stalin, which resulted in a break of relations with a friendly country.

I recall the first days when the conflict between the Soviet Union and Yugoslavia began artificially to be blown up. Once, when I came from Kiev to Moscow, I was invited to visit Stalin who, pointing to the copy of a letter lately sent to Tito, asked me, 'Have you read this?' Not waiting for my reply he answered, 'I will shake my little finger – and there will be no more Tito. He will fall' . . .

But this did not happen to Tito. No matter how much or how little Stalin shook, not only his little finger but everything else that he could shake, Tito did not fall. Why? The reason was that, in this case of disagreement with the Yugoslav comrades, Tito had behind him a state and a people who had gone through a severe school of fighting for liberty and independence, a people which gave support to its leaders.

You see to what Stalin's mania for greatness led. He had completely lost consciousness of reality; he demonstrated his suspicion and haughtiness not only in relation to individuals in the USSR, but in relation to whole parties and nations . . .

Some comrades may ask us: where were the members of the Political Bureau of the Central Committee? Why did they not assert themselves against the cult of the individual in time? And why is this being done only now?

First of all we have to consider the fact that the members of the Political Bureau viewed these matters in a different way at different times. Initially, many of them backed Stalin actively because Stalin was one of the strongest Marxists and his logic, his strength and his will greatly influenced the cadres and party work . . .

Comrades: We must abolish the cult of the individual decisively, once and for all; we must draw the proper conclusions concerning both ideological-theoretical and practical work.

It is necessary for this purpose: . . . to return to and actually practise in all our ideological work the most important theses of Marxist-Leninist science about the people as the creator of history and as the creator of all material and spiritual good of humanity, about the decisive role of the Marxist party in the revolutionary fight for the transformation of society, about the victory of communism.

In this connection we will be forced to do much work in order to examine critically from the Marxist-Leninist viewpoint and to correct the widely spread erroneous views connected with the cult of the individual in the spheres of history, philosophy, economy and of other sciences, as well as in literature and the fine arts . . .

[It is necessary] to restore completely the Leninist principles of Soviet Socialist democracy, expressed in the Constitution of the Soviet Union, to fight the wilfulness of individuals abusing their power. The evil caused by acts violating revolutionary Socialist legality, which have accumulated during a long time as a result of the negative influence of the cult of the individual, has to be completely corrected. Comrades! The twentieth congress of the Communist party of the Soviet Union has manifested with a new strength the unshakable unity of our party, its cohesiveness around the Central Committee, its resolute will to accomplish the great task of building communism. (*Tumultuous applause.*) And the fact that we present in all their ramifications the basic problems of overcoming the cult of the individual which is alien to Marxism-Leninism, as well as the problem of liquidating its burdensome consequences, is evidence of the great moral and political strength of our party. (*Prolonged applause.*)

We are absolutely certain that our party, armed with the historical resolutions of the twentieth congress, will lead the Soviet people along the Leninist path to new successes, to new victories. (*Tumultuous, prolonged applause.*)

Long live the victorious banner of our party – Leninism! (*Tumultuous, prolonged applause ending in standing ovation.*)

Sources: The Dethronement of Stalin: Full Text of the Khrushchev Speech, *published by the Manchester* Guardian, *June 1956 from the text issued by the US Department of State on 4 June 1956 and made available through the United States Information Service and British United Press, pp. 1, 6–7, 10, 18, 19–20, 21, 23, 24–5, 31, 33. The text is also available in N. S. Khrushchev,* The Secret Speech, *introduced by Zhores Medvedev and Roy Medvedev (Nottingham, Spokesman Books, 1976); and* Khrushchev Remembers, *introduced by Edward Crankshaw, translated by Strobe Talbott (London, Book Club Associates, 1971), pp. 559–618.*

Document 8.5   Togliatti on Destalinisation

While Khrushchev's speech was courageous and devastating for what it did say, it was equally remarkable for what it omitted to discuss, above all how Stalin had managed to dominate the party so thoroughly. It might be noted, for example, that the term 'enemy of the people' was not a Stalinist innovation but was in common usage under Lenin. Note also that there was no mention of the deportation of the Crimean Tatars, or of the mass terror inflicted on ordinary citizens. The weaknesses of the speech were pointed out by Palmiro Togliatti, the leader of the Italian Communist Party (PCI).

As long as we limit ourselves, in substance, to denouncing the personal defects of Stalin as the cause of everything we remain within the realm of the 'personality cult'. At first, all that was good was attributed to the super-human, positive qualities of one man: now all that is evil is attributed to his equally exceptional and even astonishing faults. In the one case, as well as in the other, we are outside the criterion of judgment intrinsic to Marxism. The real problems, which are why and how Soviet society could reach and did reach certain forms so alien to democratic life and from the legality it had set for itself, even to the point of degeneration, are evaded . . .

It must not be forgotten that even when this power of his was established, the successes of Soviet society were not lacking . . . No one can deny that the Soviet Union in 1953 was incomparably stronger, more developed in every sense, more solid internally, and more authoritative in its foreign relations than it was, for example, at the time of the first Five-Year Plan . . . What is more important today is to respond justly, using a Marxist criterion, to the question of how the errors denounced today may have been intertwined with the development of a socialist society, and hence whether in the very development of this society there may not have been introduced, at a certain point, disturbing elements, mistakes of a general type, against which the entire socialist camp must be put on guard . . .

What the CPSU has done remains, as I said, as the first great model of building a socialist society for which a deep, decisive revolutionary break opened the way. Today, the front of socialist construction in countries where the communists are the leading party has been so broadened (amounting to a third of the human race!) that even for this part the Soviet model cannot and must not any longer be obligatory. In every country governed by the communists, the objective and subjective conditions, traditions, the organisational forms of the movement can and must assert their influence in different ways. In the rest of the world there are countries where it is desirable to move towards socialism without the communists being the leading party. In still other countries, the march toward socialism is a goal on which the efforts of various movements are concentrated, but which often have not reached either an agreement or a reciprocal understanding. The whole system becomes polycentric, and even in the communist movement itself we cannot speak of a single guide but rather of a progress that is achieved by following different roads. One general problem, common to the entire movement, has arisen from the criticisms of Stalin – the problem of the dangers of bureaucratic degeneration, of the suffocation of democratic life, of confusion between constructive revolutionary force and the destruction of revolutionary legality, of the isolation of economic and political leadership from the initiative, the criticism, and creative activity of the masses. We shall welcome competition between communist parties in power to find the best way of avoiding this danger. It will be up to us to work out our own way and method, so that we, too, may guard against the evils of stagnation and bureaucratisation, and we will learn together how to resolve the problems of freedom for the working masses and of social justice, and hence gain for ourselves ever increasing prestige and following among the masses.

Source: Palmiro Togliatti, Interview in Nuovi Argomenti, *16 June 1956, in Dan J. Jacobs,* From Marx to Mao and Marchais *(London, Longman, 1979), pp. 241, 243–4, 245, 248–9.*

Document 8.6   The Impact of the Secret Speech in Georgia

While most of the country heaved a sigh of relief, in Stalin's native Georgia matters were seen somewhat differently. Several thousand demonstrators on 5–9 March 1956 in Tbilisi in support of Stalin's memory were dispersed with tanks and armoured vehicles, leading to dozens of deaths.

Criticism of Stalin's cult of personality dealt a painful blow to my national feeling. Not just because he was a Georgian. Deliberately or not, Khrushchev permitted himself to say things that were offensive to Georgian pride. It was not enough for Nikita Sergeevich to cite facts. He gave free rein to his emotions, like a person humiliated for too long, and descended to degrading attacks on his dead master. He depicted him not only as the tyrant that he was, but as a profoundly ignorant and stupid man. But if he really were so stupid, many asked, how did he build such a powerful state and compel so many millions to follow him? How could he become a worthy adversary and partner with the leading politicians of his era? By scheming, brutality, force, and trickery alone? Impossible!

Sources: Shevardnadze, Moi vybor, p. 54; The Future Belongs to Freedom, p. 20.

Document 8.7   The 'Anti-Party' Group

In June 1957 some of the figures associated with Stalin in the Presidium (the new name for the Politburo) sought to remove Khrushchev from the leadership, fearing the concentration of power in his hands and alarmed at his policies. Khrushchev successfully counter-attacked, convening a full Central Committee plenum on 29 June (delegates were brought in on military planes provided by Zhukov), which supported him. Khrushchev then accused Kaganovich, Malenkov and Molotov, together with Dimitrii Shepilov (a member of the CC's Secretariat), of having formed an 'anti-party' group within the Presidium. They were charged with factionalism, of having undermined the course outlined by the Twentieth Party Congress, of having opposed broadening the powers of the union republics and of granting more rights to local soviets, fighting bureaucratism, resisting Khrushchev's economic reforms and opposing the denunciation of Stalin's personality cult, all matters at the heart of Khrushchevite reformism.

The Central Committee plenum of 22–29 June 1957 considered the question of the anti-party group of Malenkov, Kaganovich and Molotov, which had formed in the Presidium of the CPSU's Central Committee . . .

With the aim of changing the party's political line this group sought through anti-party factional methods to replace the party's leading bodies elected by the CC plenum.

This was no accident.

During the past three to four years, when the party has resolutely set its course at overcoming the errors and shortcomings fostered by the cult of personality, and has been waging a successful struggle against revisionists of Marxism-Leninism both in the international arena and within the country, when the party has made an enormous effort to correct past distortions of the Leninist nationality policy, the members of this anti-party group – discovered and fully exposed – kept up constant direct or indirect opposition to the course adopted by the Twentieth Congress of the CPSU. This group, effectively, sought to reverse the Leninist course towards peaceful coexistence among countries with different social systems, towards relaxing international tension and establishing friendly relations between the USSR and all peoples of the world.

They were against broadening the rights of the union republics in economic, cultural and legislative matters, and also opposed strengthening the role of local soviets in resolving these tasks. In this way the anti-party group opposed the party's resolute course towards the more rapid economic and cultural development of the Union republics, designed to consolidate further Leninist friendship among all the peoples of our country. The anti-party group not only failed to understand, but even opposed, the party's struggle against bureaucratism, designed to reduce the size of the inflated state apparatus . . .

This group stubbornly opposed and tried to undermine such important measures as the reorganisation of industrial management, the creation of economic councils [*sovnarkhozy*] and economic regions . . . On agricultural issues the members of this group failed to understand the need to increase material incentives for the collective farm peasantry to stimulate agricultural output. They opposed the˘ abolition of the old bureaucratic system of planning in collective farms and the introduction of the new system of planning to stimulate the initiative of the collective farms in running their own affairs . . . Comrade Molotov displayed conservatism and a stagnant attitude, not only failing to recognise the need to develop the virgin lands but even opposing the ploughing of 35 million hectares of virgin land, which has been of such tremendous importance in our country's economy.

Comrades Malenkov, Kaganovich and Molotov stubbornly resisted those measures, which the Central Committee and our party pursued to overcome the consequences of the cult of the personality, to eliminate the violations of revolutionary legality that had occurred and to create conditions that would preclude their recurrence.

In foreign policy this group, in particular Comrade Molotov, displayed stagnation and impeded in every way the implementation of new and pressing measures designed to alleviate international tension, to strengthen peace in the world. As foreign minister Comrade Molotov not only failed for a long time to take any measures through the ministry of foreign affairs to improve relations between the USSR and Yugoslavia, but even on occasion spoke against those measures which the Presidium of the CC pursued to improve relations with Yugoslavia . . . He impeded the conclusion of the State Treaty with Austria . . . he also opposed the normalisation of relations with Japan . . .

The CC plenum resolves:

1 To condemn as incompatible with the Leninist principles of our party the factional activities of the anti-party group of Malenkov, Kaganovich, Molotov and of Shepilov who joined them.
2 To expel Comrades Malenkov, Kaganovich and Molotov from membership of the Presidium of the Central Committee, to remove Comrade Shepilov from the post of secretary of the Central Committee and to exclude him from the list of candidates for membership in the Presidium of the Central Committee and from membership of the Central Committee. . .

Sources: Pravda, *4 July 1957;* KPSS v rezolyutsiyakh i resheniyakh, *vol. 9 (Moscow, Politizdat, 1986), pp. 184–9.*

To consolidate his power further, in October 1957 Khrushchev denounced the hero of Berlin, Georgii Zhukov, accusing him of establishing his own cult of personality in the army (*Pravda*, 10 November 1957). A year later Bulganin was dismissed and Khrushchev doubled as party leader and prime minister. The stage was set for the emergence of Khrushchev's own erratic mini-personality cult.

Document 8.8   Yevtushenko, 'The Heirs of Stalin'

The Twenty-second Party Congress in 1961 deepened the destalinisation process with yet more revelations about Stalin's rule. The Congress decreed Stalin's removal from what had become the Lenin–Stalin Mausoleum, and he was buried in the Kremlin Wall near by. In this poem of 1962 Yevtushenko (see his 'Babii Yar',

Document 6.21), who became the bard of the era, reflects the doubts of a whole generation: while Stalin might be physically dead (and in the malevolent world of the Soviets there was nothing guaranteed about this), his spirit lived on in his heirs – that is, not just the new political leadership with their arms elbow-deep in blood, but in every single Soviet citizen.

Silent the marble. Silent the glass scintillates.
Silent stand the sentries in the breeze like bronzes poured.
Thin wisps of smoke curled over the coffin.
                         And breath percolated through its chinks
as they carried him through the mausoleum doors.
Slowly floats the coffin, grazing the bayonets' edges.
He also was silent – he also! silent and terrible.
Then grimly his embalmed fist clenches,
through the chinks watches a man pretending to be dead.
He wanted to remember his pallbearers;
young recruits from Kursk and Ryazan,
so that, somehow later, collecting enough strength to sally out,
he would rise up from the grave and get those thoughtless youths.
He was scheming. Had merely dozed off.
And I turn to our government with a request;
to double, treble the guard over that gravestone slab,
so that Stalin should not rise, and with Stalin – the past.
I don't mean that past, noble and treasured,
of TurkSib, and Magnitogorsk, and the flag raised over Berlin.
I have in mind the past that is measured
by the people's good neglected,
                        the innocent slandered and arrested.
In honesty we sowed,
in honesty metal smelted,
and honestly we marched in soldierly formation.
But he feared us.
He, believing in the great goal, did not consider
                    that the means must be worthy of the ends.
He was farsighted. Skilled in the laws of struggle,
he left many heirs in this world's circumference.
It seems to me, that there is a telephone connected to that coffin:
To Enver Hoxha Stalin sends his latest instructions.
Where else does that line link up to?
No – Stalin didn't give up.
Death is to him a rectifiable mistake.
We carried him out of the mausoleum.
But how do we remove Stalin's heirs from Stalin?!
In their retirement some heirs prune roses,

but quietly believe that their retirement is only temporary.
Others from platforms even hurl abuse at Stalin,
but at night pine for the good old days.
It is not for nothing that the heirs of Stalin
                                            have heart attacks now.
The former henchmen don't like the times
                                       when prison camps are empty
and halls where people listen to poetry
                                   are overflowing.
The Party warns me against complacency.
Let some call on me to be calm
                            but I cannot be calm.
As long as Stalin's heirs on the earth exist,
It will seem to me
                that Stalin is still in the mausoleum.

Source: Samizdat mimeo, translated by the author.

National Relations

The Khrushchevite 'thaw' affected national relations as all other spheres of Soviet life. The limits of Khrushchev's modification of Stalin's policies are equally apparent.

Document 8.9   The Transfer of Crimea from Russia to Ukraine

The high-handed way that the Soviet regime dealt with its peoples also affected the arbitrary transfer of territories. One case, the transfer of Crimea to Ukraine, was to poison relations between Russia and Ukraine in the post-communist era.

The USSR Supreme Soviet resolves:

1 To confirm the decree of the Presidium of the USSR Supreme Soviet of 19 February 1954 on the transfer of Crimea *oblast* from the RSFSR to the Ukraine SSR.
2 To make the necessary changes in articles 22 and 23 of the USSR constitution.

Chairman of the USSR Supreme Soviet Presidium, K. Voroshilov
Secretary of the USSR Supreme Soviet Presidium, N. Negov
Moscow, Kremlin, 26 April 1954

Source: Rossiya, kotoruyu my ne znali, *p. 283.*

Document 8.10   Partial Lifting of Deportation Orders

In 1956 a limited amnesty lifted certain administrative restrictions from the north Caucasian peoples living in exile, but they were still not allowed to return to their original homes. Later this restriction was lifted, although there was no question of compensation. The Volga Germans and Crimean Tatars were notably excluded from the provisions of this partial amnesty.

Taking into account that the existing legal restrictions of special settler groups of Chechens, Ingush, Karachais and their family members, deported during the Great Patriotic War from the north Caucasus, are no longer necessary, the Presidium of the USSR Supreme Soviet resolves:

1 To remove from the lists of special settlers and to free from the administrative supervision of organs of the USSR Ministry of Internal Affairs Chechens, Ingush, Karachais and members of their families, resettled during the Great Patriotic War from the north Caucasus.
2 To establish that the lifting of special resettlement restrictions from people listed in article one of this resolution does not entail the return to them of property, confiscated during resettlement, and that they do not have the right to return to the place from which they were evicted.

Moscow, Kremlin, 16 July 1956
Chairman of the USSR Supreme Soviet Presidium, K. Voroshilov

Sources: Istoriya SSSR, *no. 1, 1991, p. 159;* Rossiya, kotoruyu my ne znali, *p. 282.*

Document 8.11   The New Party Programme and the National Question

In his 'secret speech' of 25 February 1956 Khrushchev had condemned Stalin's nationality policy. The CPSU's new programme of 1961 set the tone for the last Soviet years in claiming that the national question had been 'solved' in the USSR. The same programme noted that 'The borders between union republics within the USSR are increasingly losing their former significance.' While most of its other Utopian aspirations were quietly dropped from the amended programme once Brezhnev came to power in 1964, on this issue there was continuity.

The greatest achievement of socialism is the resolution of the national question. For a country like the Soviet Union, where there are over one hundred nations and peoples (*narodnosti*) this question has special significance. In a socialist society not only is the political equality of nations guaranteed, a Soviet national state has been established, but also the economic and cultural inequality inherited from the old regime has been liquidated.

Source: KPSS v rezolyutsiyakh i resheniyakh, *vol. 10, p. 91.*

The Full-scale Building of Socialism

Having overcome the worst excesses of Stalinism, the Soviet Union appeared set on a flowering of the economy, society and culture. Economic growth rates were buoyant in the 1950s and the USSR's prestige in the anti-colonial world was high. The world youth festival held in Moscow in summer 1957 revealed a new openness. On 4 October of the same year an artificial satellite (Sputnik) first circled the earth, marking the beginning of the space age, and soon afterwards the dog Laika was the first animate object in space. On 12 April 1961 Yurii Gagarin orbited the earth for 108 minutes, becoming the most famous man in the world. The chief designer of the project was the legendary Sergei Korolev. Gagarin had been chosen rather than his backup, Stepan Titov, largely for political reasons: Gagarin came from a peasant background, whereas Titov's parents were from the intelligentsia. Perhaps the most vivid expression of the optimism of the period was Khrushchev's report to the Twenty-second Party Congress on 17 October 1961, and the new Party Programme adopted at that Congress.

Document 8.12   1961 Party Programme on Achieving Communism

The new programme adopted by the CPSU to replace the 1919 version was intended to reflect the achievements of 'building socialism' in the USSR. It also reflected Khrushchev's enormous optimism that the Soviet Union was in striking distance of overtaking the USA and of achieving communism within two decades. The programme grappled with the problem of reconciling the ideal of a participatory egalitarian society with the reality of a party-dominated bureaucratised industrial society. This was perhaps the most extended and idealistic discussion of what communism would look like in practice since *The ABC of Communism* in 1919.

Communism – The Bright Future of All Mankind

The building of a communist society has become an immediate practical task for the Soviet people. The gradual development of socialism into communism is an objective law; it has been prepared by the development of Soviet socialist society throughout the preceding period.

What is communism?

Communism is a classless social system with one form of public ownership of the means of production and full social equality of all members of society; under it, the all-round development of people will be accompanied by the growth of the productive forces through continuous progress in science and technology; all the springs of co-operative wealth will flow more abundantly, and the great principle 'from each according to his ability, to each according to his needs' will be implemented. Communism is a highly organised society of free, socially conscious working people in which public self-government will be established, a society in which labour for the good of society will become the prime vital requirement of everyone, a necessity recognised by one and all, and the ability of each person will be employed to the greatest benefit of the people.

A high degree of communist consciousness, industry, discipline, and devotion to the public interest are qualities typifying the man of communist society.

Communism ensures the continuous development of social production and rising labour productivity through rapid scientific and technological progress; it equips man with the best and most powerful machines, greatly increases his power over nature and enables him to control its elemental forces to an ever greater extent. The social economy reaches the highest stage of planned organisation, and the most effective and rational use is made of the material wealth and labour reserves to meet the growing requirements of the members of society.

Under communism there will be no classes, and the socio-economic and cultural distinctions, and differences in living conditions, between town and countryside will disappear; the countryside will rise to the level of the town in the development of the productive forces and the nature of work, the forms of production relations, living conditions and the well-being of the population. With the victory of communism mental and physical labour will merge organically in the production activity of people. The intelligentsia will no longer be a distinct social stratum. Workers by hand will have risen in cultural and technological standards to the level of workers by brain.

Thus, communism will put an end to the division of society into classes and social strata, whereas the whole history of mankind, with the exception of its primitive period, was one of class society. Division into opposing classes led to the exploitation of man by man, class struggle, and antagonisms between nations and states . . .

Communism represents the highest form or organisation of public life. All production units and self-governing associations will be harmoniously united in a common planned economy and a uniform rhythm of social labour.

Under communism the nations will draw closer and closer together in all spheres on the basis of a complete identity of economic, political and spiritual interests, of fraternal friendship and co-operation.

Communism is the system under which the abilities and talents of free man, his best moral qualities, blossom forth and reveal themselves in full. Family relations will be freed once and for all from material considerations and will be based solely on mutual love and friendship.

In defining the basic tasks to be accomplished in building a communist society, the Party is guided by Lenin's great formula: '*Communism is Soviet power plus the electrification of the whole country.*'

The CPSU being a party of scientific communism, proposes and fulfils the tasks of communist construction in step with the preparation and maturing of the material and spiritual prerequisites, considering that it would be wrong to jump over necessary stages of development, and that it would be equally wrong to halt at an achieved level and thus check progress. The building of communism must be carried out by successive stages.

In the current decade (1961–70) the Soviet Union, in creating the material and technical basis of communism, will surpass the strongest and richest capitalist country, the USA, in production per head of population; the people's standard of living and their cultural and technical standards will improve substantially; everyone will live in easy circumstances; all collective and state farms will become highly productive and profitable enterprises; the demand of Soviet people for well-appointed housing will, in the main, be satisfied; hard physical work will disappear; the USSR will have the shortest working day.

The material and technical basis of communism will be built up by the *end of the second decade* (1971–80), ensuring an abundance of material and cultural values for the whole population; Soviet society will come close to a stage where it can introduce the principle of distribution according to needs, and there will be a gradual transition to one form of ownership – public ownership. Thus, *a communist society will in the main be built in the USSR*. The construction of communist society will be fully completed in the subsequent period.

The majestic edifice of communism is being erected by the persevering effort of the Soviet people – the working class, the peasantry and the intelligentsia. The more successful their work, the closer the great goal – communist society.

III The Tasks of the Party in the Spheres of State Development and the Further Promotion of Socialist Democracy

. . . *All-round extension and perfection of socialist democracy, active participation of all citizens in the administration of the state, in the management of economic and cultural development, improvement of the government apparatus, and increased control over its activity by the people constitute the main direction in which socialist statehood develops in the building of communism.* As socialist democracy develops, the organs of state power will gradually be transformed into organs of public self-government. The Leninist principle of democratic centralism, which ensures the proper combination of centralised leadership with the maximum encouragement of local initiative, the extension of the rights of the Union republics and greater creative activity of the masses, will be promoted. It is essential to strengthen discipline, constantly control the activities of all the sections of the administrative apparatus, check the execution of the decisions and laws of the Soviet state and heighten the responsibility of every official for the strict and timely implementation of these laws. . . .

VII The Party in the Period of Full-scale Communist Construction

As a result of the victory of socialism in the USSR and the strengthened unity of Soviet society, the Communist Party of the working class has become the vanguard of the Soviet people, the party of the whole people, broadening its guiding influence on all facets of social life. The party is the mind, honour and conscience of our epoch, of the Soviet people, achieving great revolutionary transformations. It looks keenly into the future and shows the people scientifically motivated roads along which to advance, arouses titanic energy in the masses and leads them to the accomplishment of great tasks.

The period of full-scale communist construction is characterised by a further *enhancement of the role and importance of the Communist Party* as the leading and guiding force of Soviet society.

Unlike all the preceding socio-economic formations, communist society does not develop spontaneously, but as a result of the conscious and purposeful efforts of the masses led by the Marxist-Leninist party. The Communist Party, which unites the most advanced representatives of the working class, of all working people, and is closely connected with the masses, which enjoys unbounded prestige among the people and understands the laws of social development, provides proper leadership in communist construction as a whole, giving it an organised, planned and scientifically based character . . .

UNDER THE TRIED AND TESTED LEADERSHIP OF THE COMMUNIST PARTY, UNDER THE BANNER OF MARXISM-LENINISM, THE SOVIET PEOPLE HAVE BUILT SOCIALISM.

UNDER THE LEADERSHIP OF THE PARTY, UNDER THE BANNER OF MARXISM-LENINISM, THE SOVIET PEOPLE WILL BUILD A COMMUNIST SOCIETY.

THE PARTY SOLEMNLY PROCLAIMS: THE PRESENT GENERATION OF SOVIET PEOPLE SHALL LIVE IN COMMUNISM!

Sources: Programme of the Communist Party of the Soviet Union, *adopted by the Twenty-second Congress of the CPSU, 31 October 1961 (Moscow, Foreign Languages Publishing House, 1961), pp. 59–60, 61–2, 92–3, 122–3, 128;* Materialy XXII s''ezda KPSS *(Moscow, Gospolitizdat, 1961), pp. 366–7, 367–8, 396–7, 423–4, 428.*

The reaffirmation of the party's 'leading role' was a central element in the programme. A number of statements became classic slogans of the late Soviet period. In particular, the assertion that 'The party is the mind, honour and conscience of our epoch' was emblazoned on a thousand posters and walls. It was at this time that the Soviet Union was declared a 'state of all the people', signalling that class conflict in the country had given way to inclusionary policies.

Intellectual Critique

A number of intellectuals, many of them former communists, began to explore the origins of Soviet-type authoritarianism. The extension of the Soviet-type communist system to Eastern Europe meant that intellectuals there were now forced to devise critiques for the systems in their countries that were equally applicable to the USSR itself.

Document 8.13   The Marxist Revisionist Critique

Leszek Kolakowski was one of Poland's foremost philosophers. In the late 1950s he was forced to leave the country and took up a teaching post in Oxford where he wrote a monumental three-volume study of Marxism. His early critique of the relationship between Marxism and morality was a searing critique of Leninist practice.

It is enough to believe in the inevitability of progress to believe simultaneously in the progressiveness of inevitability. It is enough to believe in Providence in order to bless the brick which hits one on the head. When the spirit of history assumes the difficult role of Divine Providence, it must accordingly demand humble gratitude for every blow it inflicts on its chosen. The demiurge of progress which guards the world demands the worship of his every creation and image. What could be easier than to prove that this or that national leader, this or that system of government, or of social relations, is the demiurge's anointed, even if its external appearance terrifies people with its simian hide? . . . How . . . is it possible to reconcile the conviction of the existence of historical necessity with the conviction that this necessity must be realised by brutal and terroristic means? How can this be reconciled with acceptance of any universal values, that is, with the conviction that certain actions are called for and others prohibited in all circumstances? Moral duty is the belief, perpetuated in a given social environment, that certain human actions are ends in themselves and not merely means to an end, and that other actions are counter-ends in themselves; that is, they are prohibited. If historical necessity is considered either as an unlimited process without a final end, or if an ultimate end is ascribed to it, though still unrealised and subject only to a promise of the future, and if, simultaneously, moral judgments are subject to the realisation of that necessity, then there is nothing in contemporary life which can be considered an end in itself. In other words, moral values in the strict sense of the term cease to exist altogether. Can the view of the world of reality be reconciled with the view of the world of values? . . .

The very nature of historical determinism is vague in character. I mean 'determinism' as a doctrine, describing rules of social change which can be considered valid for the future. Marx's predictions referred to a change in economic structure and were formulated in those terms. Ordinary scientific criticism did not permit going into further details so happily indulged in by Fourier and the majority of the utopians. The details of Lenin's programs, formulated before the October Revolution, went considerably further. Yet, to this very day, we cannot positively decide which part of those programs was based on peculiarly Russian conditions, and which retained, or was intended to retain, universal validity for the period of transition from capitalism to socialism. We can almost certainly take for granted Marx's fundamental assumption that the development of capitalist technology creates the tendency to endow the means of production with a collective ownership; and this assumption is confirmed, in general outline, by historical experience. However, in the course of how many revolutions won and lost, how many wars and crises, how many years and decades, according to what geographical and chronological circumstances, in the course of what progress and regress, and in what diverse forms, a Socialist way of life will be realized cannot be deduced authoritatively from a superficial knowledge of the 'laws of history.' These questions are answered by the experiences of everyday life, daily shocking us with new surprises like a virtuoso magician . . .

The philosophy of history draws its strength not from itself but from the faith invested in it, and this faith is a part of political practice and has a semi-sacred character. Even the most tattered and patched-up cloak may look like a royal ceremonial gown if it is worn by a priest the people revere. Those who foretell the future from dreams will always be believed; the faithful never falter in their belief even when it is proved to them empirically that their dreams do not come true, because believers always have one or two examples illustrating the contrary, and sufficient to support their faith. And faith never requires proof, only examples and sanctions . . .

How can we free the morality of daily life from the nightmare of the philosophy of history and from those pseudo-dialectics which, by transforming into an instrument of history, in fact make history the pretext for disgraceful behavior? . . .

Nobody is free from positive or negative responsibility because his individual actions constitute only a fragment of a specific historical process . . . If a social system exists which needs criminals for some of its tasks, one may be sure that these criminals will be found, but it does not follow that as a result of this certainty every individual criminal is freed from responsibility. In order to take upon oneself the role of such an instrument of the system, one must intrinsically be a criminal, one must voluntarily commit a specific act subject to moral judgment. We therefore support the doctrine of the total responsibility of the individual for his own deeds, and the amorality of the historical process . . .

It is not true that the philosophy of history determines our main choices in life. Our moral sensibility does this. We are not Communists because we have recognised Communism as historical necessity; we are Communists because we have joined the side of the oppressed against their masters, the side of the persecuted against their persecutors. Although we know that the correct theoretical division of society is not into rich' and 'poor,' not into 'persecuted' and 'persecutors,' when we must make a practical choice apart from the theory, that is, a fundamental option, we are then morally motivated, and not motivated by theoretical considerations. It cannot be otherwise because even the most convincing theory is not by itself capable of making us lift a finger. A practical choice is a choice of values; that is, a moral act which is something for which everyone bears his own personal responsibility.

Source: Leszek Kolakowski, 'Responsibility and History', September 1957, in Daniels, Communism and the World, pp. 246–7.

Document 8.14 The 'New Class'

Milovan Djilas, who, as we have seen, was one of the leaders of the Yugoslav revolution, by the mid-1950s had become deeply disillusioned with the actual operation of the communist system. Despite the abolition of capitalism, relations of power and dominance had not disappeared. Djilas came to realise that property ownership was far from the only social source of exploitation. The attempt to make a socialist revolution before the economic and social conditions had matured allowed a small group to act as surrogates for the historical process.

All the revolutions of the past originated after new economic or social relationships had begun to prevail, and the old political system had become the sole obstacle to further development.

None of these revolutions sought anything other than the destruction of the old political forms and an opening of the way for already mature social forces and relationships existing in the old society. Even in those cases where the revolutionists desired something else, such as the building of economic and social relationships by means of force, as did the Jacobins in the French revolution, they had to accept failure and be swiftly eliminated . . .

The case is entirely different with contemporary Communist revolutions. These revolutions did not occur because new, let us say socialist, relationships were already existing in the economy, or because capitalism was 'over-developed.' On the contrary. They did occur because capitalism was not fully developed and because it was not able to carry out the industrial transformation of the country.

In France capitalism had already prevailed in the economy, in social relationships, and even in the public conscience prior to the inception of the revolution. The case is hardly comparable with socialism in Russia, China, or Yugoslavia . . .

No revolution or party had ever set itself to the task of building social relationships or a new society. But this was the primary objective of the Communist revolution.

Communist leaders, though no better acquainted than others with the laws which govern society, discovered that in the country in which their revolution was possible, industrialization was also possible, particularly when it involved a transformation of society in keeping with their ideological hypothesis. Experience – the success of revolution under 'unfavourable' conditions – confirmed this for them; the 'building of socialism' did likewise. This strengthened their illusion that they knew the laws of social development. In fact, they were in the position of making a blueprint for a new society, and then of starting to build it, making corrections here and leaving out something there, all the while adhering closely to their plans.

Industrialization, as an inevitable, legitimate necessity of society, and the Communist way of accomplishing it, joined forces in the countries of Communist revolutions.

However, neither of these, though they progressed together and on parallel tracks, could achieve success overnight. After the completion of the revolution, someone had to shoulder the responsibility for industrialization. In the West, this role was taken over by the economic forces of capitalism liberated from the despotic political chains, while in the countries of Communist revolutions no similar forces existed and, thus, their function had to be taken over by the revolutionary organs themselves, the new authority, that is, the revolutionary party.

In earlier revolutions, revolutionary force and violence became a hindrance to the economy as soon as the old order was overthrown. In the Communist revolutions, force and violence are a condition for further development and even progress. In the words of earlier revolutionaries, force and violence were only a necessary evil and a means to an end. In the words of Communists, force and violence are elevated to the lofty position of a cult and an ultimate goal. In the past, the classes and forces which made up a new society already existed before the revolution erupted. The Communist revolutions are the first which have had to create a new society and new social forces.

Even as the revolutions in the West had inevitably to end in democracy after all the 'aberrations' and 'withdrawals,' in the East, the revolutions had to end in despotism. The methods of terror and violence in the West became needless and ridiculous, and even a hindrance in accomplishing the revolution for the revolutionaries and revolutionary parties. In the East, the case was the opposite. Not only did despotism continue in the East because the transformation of industry required so much time, but, as we shall see later, it lasted long after industrialization had taken place.

There are other basic differences between Communist revolutions and earlier ones. Earlier revolutions, though they had reached the point of readiness in an economy and a society, were unable to break out without advantageous conditions. We now know the general conditions necessary for the eruption and success of a revolution. However, every revolution has, in addition to these general conditions, its peculiarities which make its planning and execution possible . . .

The reason war was necessary for the Communist revolution, or the downfall of the state machinery, must be sought in the immaturity of the economy and society. In a serious collapse of a system, and particularly in a war which has been unsuccessful for the existing ruling circles and state system, a small but well-organized and disciplined group is inevitably able to take authority in its hands.

Thus at the time of the October Revolution the Communist Party had about 30,000 members. The Yugoslav Communist Party began the 1941 revolution with about 10,000 members. To grasp power, the support and active participation of at least a part of the people is necessary, but in every case the party which leads the revolution and assumes power is a minority group relying exclusively on exceptionally favourable conditions. Furthermore, such a party cannot be a majority group until it becomes the permanently established authority . . .

It is the bureaucracy which formally uses, administers, and controls both nationalized and socialized property as well as the entire life of society. The role of the bureaucracy in society, i.e., monopolistic administration and control of national income and national good, consigns it to a special privileged position. Social relations resemble state capitalism. The more so, because the carrying out of industrialization is effected not with the help of capitalists but with the help of the state machine. In fact, this privileged class performs that function, using the state machine as a cover and as an instrument.

Ownership is nothing other than the right of profit and control. If one defines class benefits by this right, the Communist states have seen, in the final analysis, the origin of a new form of ownership or of a new ruling and exploiting class . . .

Everything happened differently in the USSR and other Communist countries from what the leaders – even such prominent ones as Lenin, Stalin, Trotsky, and Bukharin – anticipated. They expected that the state would rapidly wither away, that democracy would be strengthened. The reverse happened. They expected a rapid improvement in the standard of living – there has been scarcely any change in this respect and, in the subjugated East European countries, the standard has even declined. In every instance, the standard of living has failed to rise in proportion to the rate of industrialization, which was much more rapid. It was believed that the differences between cities and villages, between intellectual and physical labor, would slowly disappear; instead these differences have increased. Communist anticipations in other areas – including their expectations for developments in the non-Communist world – have also failed to materialize.

The greatest illusion was that industrialization and collectivization in the USSR, and destruction of capitalist ownership, would result in a classless society. In 1936, when the new Constitution was promulgated, Stalin announced that the 'exploiting class' had ceased to exist. The capitalist and other classes of ancient origin had in fact been destroyed, but a new class, previously unknown to history, had been formed . . .

This new class, the bureaucracy, or more accurately the political bureaucracy, has all the characteristics of earlier ones as well as some new characteristics of its own. Its origin had its special characteristics also, even though in essence it was similar to the beginnings of other classes . . .

Because this new class had not been formed as a part of the economic and social life before it came to power, it could only be created in an organization of a special type, distinguished by a special discipline based on the identical philosophic and ideological views of its members. A unity of belief and iron discipline were necessary to overcome its weaknesses.

The roots of the new class were implanted in a special party, of the Bolshevik type. Lenin was right in his view that his party was an exception in the history of human society, although he did not suspect that it would be the beginning of a new class . . .

This is not to say that the new party and the new class are identical. The party, however, is the core of that class, and its base. It is very difficult, perhaps impossible, to define the limits of the new class and to identify its members. The new class may be said to be made up of those who have special privileges and economic preference because of the administrative monopoly they hold.

Since administration is unavoidable in society, necessary administrative functions may be coexistent with parasitic functions in the same person. Not every member of the party is a member of the new class, any more than every artisan or member of a middle-class party is a bourgeois.

In loose terms, as the new class becomes stronger and attains a more perceptible physiognomy, the role of the party diminishes. The core and the basis of the new class is created in the party and at its top, as well as in the state political organs. The once live, compact party, full of initiative, is disappearing to become transformed into the traditional oligarchy of the new class, irresistibly drawing into its ranks those who aspire to join the new class and repressing those who have any ideals.

The party makes the class, but the class grows as a result and uses the party as a basis. The class grows stronger, while the party grows weaker; this is the inescapable fate of every Communist party in power . . .

The monopoly which the new class establishes in the name of the working class over the whole of society is, primarily, a monopoly over the working class itself. This monopoly is first intellectual, over the so-called *avant-garde* proletariat, and then over the whole proletariat. This is the biggest deception the class must accomplish, but it shows that the power and interests of the new class lie primarily in industry. Without industry the new class cannot consolidate its position or authority.

Former sons of the working class are the most steadfast members of the new class. It has always been the fate of slaves to provide for their masters the most clever and gifted representatives. In this case a new exploiting and governing class is born from the exploited class.

When Communist systems are being critically analyzed, it is considered that their fundamental distinction lies in the fact that bureaucracy, organized in a special stratum, rules over the people. This is generally true. However, a more detailed analysis will show that only a special stratum of bureaucrats, those who are not administrative officials, make up the core of the governing bureaucracy, or, in my terminology, of the new class. This is actually a party or political bureaucracy. Other officials are only the apparatus under the control of the new class; the apparatus may be clumsy and slow but, no matter what, it must exist in every socialist society. It is sociologically possible to draw the borderline between the different types of officials, but in practice they are practically indistinguishable. This is true not only because the Communist system by its very nature is bureaucratic, but because Communists handle the various important administrative functions. In addition, the stratum of political bureaucrats cannot enjoy their privileges if they do not give crumbs from their tables to other bureaucratic categories . . . Behind Lenin, who was all passion and thought, stands the dull, gray figure of Joseph Stalin, the symbol of the difficult, cruel, and unscrupulous ascent of the new class to its final power.

After Lenin and Stalin came what had to come; namely, mediocrity in the form of collective leadership. And also there came the apparently sincere, kind-hearted, non-intellectual 'man of the people' – Nikita Khrushchev. The new class no longer needs the revolutionaries or dogmatists it once required; it is satisfied with simple personalities, such as Khrushchev, Malenkov, Bulganin, and Shepilov, whose every word reflects the average man. The new class itself is tired of dogmatic purges and training sessions. It would like to live quietly. It must protect itself even from its own authorized leader now that it has been adequately strengthened. Stalin remained the same as he was when the class was weak, when cruel measures were necessary against even those in its own ranks who threatened to deviate. Today this is all unnecessary. Without relinquishing anything it created under Stalin's leadership, the new class appears to be renouncing not his authority – only Stalin's methods which, according to Khrushchev, hurt 'good Communists.'

Lenin's revolutionary epoch was replaced by Stalin's epoch, in which authority and ownership, and industrialization, were strengthened so that the much desired peaceful and good life of the new class could begin. Lenin's *revolutionary* Communism was replaced by Stalin's *dogmatic* Communism, which in turn was replaced by *non-dogmatic* Communism, a so-called collective leadership or a group of oligarchs.

These are the three phases of development of the new class in the USSR or of Russian Communism (or of every other type of Communism in one manner or another).

Source: Milovan Djilas, The New Class *(New York, Praeger, 1957), pp. 18–19, 19–20, 21–2, 35, 37–8, 39–40, 42–3, 52–3.*

Cultural Thaw and its Limits

Stalin's death and destalinisation opened up new spaces for artists to explore the country's past and present. This generation of the liberal Soviet intelligentsia (primarily its cultural part) that came to maturity at this time came to be known as the *shestdesyatniki,* the people of the 1960s. Much vilified in later years for their apparently misplaced belief in the reformability of the Soviet system and the redemptive power of the arts, they nevertheless represented the first serious challenge to the post-Stalinist regime's claims to a monopoly on the truth. Their ideas laid a long fuse that exploded into the activism of *glasnost* under Gorbachev.

Example 8.15   Solzhenitsyn Emerges

One Day in the Life of Ivan Denisovich was first published in the November 1962 issue of *Novy mir,* edited by Andrei Tvardovskii, one of the leading figures in what was to become the trend of reform communism. The journal itself came to symbolise the liberalisation of communism. Solzhenitsyn's story appears a straightforward narrative of a day in the life of a Gulag prisoner, Shukhov, but also reveals the survival of human qualities in adverse conditions, and is a specific meditation on the quality of freedom in Soviet conditions. Its publication was due to Tvardovskii's determination and Khrushchev's own political predicament at the time, apparently labouring under the misapprehension that the story celebrated 'honest toil' by prisoners who remained loyal to the Soviet system. By the time he understood the story's full implications, hundreds of thousands of copies had already been distributed.

As usual, at five o'clock that morning reveille was sounded by the blows of a hammer on a length of rail hanging up near the staff quarters. The intermittent sounds barely penetrated the window-panes on which the frost lay two fingers thick, and they ended almost as soon as they'd begun. It was cold outside outside, and the camp-guard was reluctant to go beating out the reveille for long.

The clanging ceased, but everything outside still looked like the middle of the night when Ivan Denisovich Shukhov got up to go to the bucket. It was pitch dark except for the yellow light cast on the window by three lamps – two in the outer zone, one inside the camp itself.

And no one came to unbolt the barrack-hut door; there was no sound of the barrack-orderlies pushing a pole into place to lift the barrel of nightsoil and carry it out.

Shukhov never overslept reveille. He always got up at once, for the next ninety minutes, until they assembled for work, belonged to him, not to the authorities, and any old-timer could always earn a bit – by sewing a pair of over-mittens for someone out of old sleeve lining; or bringing some rich lag in the team his dry valenki [felt boots] – right up to his bunk, so that he wouldn't have to stumble barefoot round the heaps of boots looking for his own pair; or going the rounds of the store-huts, offering to be of service, sweeping up this or fetching that; or going to the mess-hall to collect bowls from the tables and bring them stacked to the dishwashers – you're sure to be given something to eat there, though there were plenty of others at that game, more than plenty – and, what's worse, if you found a bowl with something left in it you could hardly resist licking it out. But Shukhov had never forgotten the words of his first team-leader, Kuziomin – a hard-bitten prisoner who had already been in for twelve years by 1943 – who told the newcomers, just in from the front, as they sat beside a fire in a desolate cutting in the forest:

'Here, lads, we live by the law of taiga. But even here people manage to live. D'you know what are the ones the camps finish off? Those who lick other men's left-overs, those who set store by the doctors, and those who peach on their mates.'

As for the peachers, he was wrong there. Those people were sure to get through the camp all right. Only they were saving their own skin at the expense of other people's blood.

Shukhov always arose at reveille. But this day he didn't. He had felt queer the evening before, feverish, with pains all over his body. He hadn't been able to get warm all through the night. Even in his sleep he had felt at one moment that he was getting seriously ill, at another that he was getting better. He had longed for the morning not to come.

But the morning came as usual . . .

More than once during his life in the camps, Shukhov had recalled the way they used to eat in his village: whole saucepans of potatoes, pots of porridge and, in the early days, big chunks of meat. And milk enough to split their guts. That wasn't the way to eat, he learned in camp. You had to eat with all your mind on the food – like now, nibbling the bread bit by bit, working the crumbs up into a paste with your tongue and sucking it into your cheeks. And how good it tasted, that soggy black bread. What had he eaten for eight, no, more than eight years? Next to nothing. But how much work had he done? Ah! . . .

Shukhov ate his bread down to his very fingers, keeping only a little bit of bare crust, the half-moon-shaped top of the loaf – because no spoon is as good for scraping a bowl of porridge clean as a bread-crust. He wrapped the crust in his cloth again and slipped it into his inside pocket for dinner, buttoned himself up against the cold and prepared for work. Let them send him out now! Though of course, it would be better if they'd wait a bit longer . . .

Why, you might wonder, should prisoners wear themselves out, working hard, ten years on end, in the camps? You'd think they'd say: No thank you, and that's that. We'll shuffle through the day till evening, and then the night is ours.

But that didn't work. To outsmart you they thought up work-teams – but not teams like the ones in freedom, where every man is paid his separate wage. Everything was so arranged in the camp that the prisoners egged one another on. It was like this: either you got a bit extra or you all croaked. You're slacking, you rat – d'you think I'm willing to go hungry just because of you? Put your guts into it, scum.

And if a situation like this one turned up there was all the more reason for resisting any temptation to slack. Willy-nilly you put your back into the work. For unless you could manage to provide yourself with the means of warming up, you and everyone else would peg out on the spot . . .

But he'd had such a good day, he felt in such good spirits, that somehow he wasn't in the mood for sleep yet.

He must make his bed now – there wasn't much to it. Strip his mattress of the grubby blanket and lie on it (it must have been '41 when he last slept in sheets – that was at home; it even seemed odd for women to bother about sheets, all that extra laundering). Head on the pillow, stuffed with shavings of wood: feet in jacket sleeve; coat on top of blanket and – Glory be to Thee, O Lord. Another day over. Thank you I'm not spending tonight in the cells. Here it's still bearable.

Shukhov went to sleep fully content. He'd had many strokes of luck that day: they hadn't put him in the cells; they hadn't sent the team to the settlement; he'd pinched a bowl of kasha at dinner; the team-leader had fixed the rates well; he'd built a wall and enjoyed doing it; he'd smuggled that bit of hacksaw-blade through; he'd earned something from Tsezar in the evening; he'd bought that tobacco. And he hadn't fallen ill. He'd got over it.

A day without a dark cloud. Almost a happy day.

There were three thousand six hundred and fifty-three days like that in his stretch. From the first clang of the rail to the last clang of the rail.

The three extra days were for leap years.

Source: Alexander Solzhenitsyn, One Day in the Life of Ivan Denisovich *(Harmondsworth, Penguin, 1963), pp. 7–8, 43–4, 45, 51–2, 137.*

The cultural 'thaw' of this period was always fragile, and depended on Khrushchev's mercurial temperament. The award of the Nobel Prize to Boris Pasternak for his *Doctor Zhivago* in 1958 was accompanied by a major scandal, and Pasternak was refused permission to go to Norway to collect the prize. In 1962–3 Khrushchev condemned trends in modern art and attempts to achieve a degree of cultural autonomy for artists.

Khrushchev's Foreign Policy – to the Brink

Soviet hegemony in Eastern Europe under Stalin had been very much a personal system. His successors sought to regularise and institutionalise the relationship. The Council for Mutual Economic Assistance (CMEA, or Comecon), established in 1949, was strengthened and given broader jurisdiction over economic affairs. The inclusion of West Germany into the North Atlantic Treaty Organisation (NATO) in 1955 provoked the creation of the Warsaw Treaty Organisation (WTO, or Warsaw Pact). In May 1955 Khrushchev went to Belgrade and apologised for Yugoslavia's expulsion from the Soviet bloc, and the new willingness to allow national roads to socialism was symbolised by the dissolution of Cominform.

Document 8.16   Khrushchev and 'Peaceful Coexistence'

While the notion of peaceful coexistence had a long history in Soviet thinking, having been coined by Lenin in 1920, Khrushchev made it a central principle of his policy. At the Twentieth Congress in 1956 he proposed a reinvigorated doctrine of peaceful coexistence with capitalism, and the possibility of separate roads to socialism, including non-violent paths, depending on the conditions in each country.

When we say that the socialist system will win in the competition between the two systems – the capitalist and the socialist – this by no means signifies that its victory will be achieved through armed interference by the socialist countries in the internal affairs of capitalist countries. Our certainty of the victory of communism is based on the fact that the socialist mode of production possesses decisive superiority over the capitalist mode of production. Precisely because of this, the ideas of Marxism-Leninism are more and more capturing the minds of the broad masses of the working people in the capitalist countries, just as they have captured the minds of millions of men and women in our country and the people's democracies. (*Prolonged applause.*) We believe that all the working people on earth, once they have become convinced of the advantages communism brings, will sooner or later take the road of struggle for the construction of a socialist society. (*Prolonged applause.*) Building communism in our country, we are resolutely against war. We have always held and continue to hold that the establishment of a new social system in one or another country is the internal affair of the peoples of the countries concerned. This is our position, based on the great Marxist-Leninist teaching. The principle of peaceful coexistence is gaining ever wider international recognition. This principle has become one of the cornerstones of the foreign policy of the Chinese People's Republic and the other people's democracies. It is being actively implemented by the Republic of India, the Union of Burma, and a number of other countries. And this is natural, for there is no other way in present-day conditions. Indeed there are only two ways: either peaceful coexistence or the most destructive war in history. There is no third way . . .

As long as imperialism exists, the economic base giving rise to wars will also remain. That is why we must display the greatest vigilance. As long as capitalism survives in the world, reactionary forces, representing the interests of the capitalist monopolies, will continue their drive toward military gambles and aggression and may try to unleash war. But war is not a fatalistic inevitability. Today there are mighty social and political forces possessing formidable means to prevent the imperialists from unleashing war and, if they try to start it, to give a smashing rebuff to the aggressors and frustrate their adventurist plans. For this it is necessary for all anti-war forces to be vigilant and mobilised; they must act as a united front and not relax their efforts in the struggle for peace. The more actively the peoples defend peace, the greater the guarantee that there will be no new war. (*Stormy, prolonged applause.*)

Source: Khrushchev, 'Report of the CC to the Twentieth Party Congress, February 1956', in Daniels, Communism and the World, *pp. 225–6.*

The limits to Soviet tolerance of diversity were discovered in the aftermath of the Secret Speech. Hungarian attempts to leave the Soviet bloc were crushed by military invasion in November 1956. In Poland a military intervention was only averted by Gomułka's restoration to power and his ability to convince Khrushchev that Soviet concerns, above all strategic communications, would be safe in his hands. Yugoslavia's independent stance in 1956 once again provoked a deterioration in relations with the USSR. The attempt to achieve a modicum of unity in the international communist movement was symbolised by the staging of the conference of communist parties in November 1957, attended by all except the Yugoslavs. The distinction drawn by the conference between 'revisionism' (exemplified by Yugoslav self-managing socialism) and 'dogmatism' (unreconstructed Stalinists) appeared increasingly empty. By the time of the next conference in November 1960 relations with China had deteriorated; the struggle now was against 'dogmatism' (the Chinese) and 'sectarianism' (Albania). It was at this time that Khrushchev launched a campaign against the 'steel-eaters', the military-industrial complex, and significantly reduced Soviet conventional forces. Greater reliance was thereby placed on the nuclear deterrent.

Document 8.17   Khrushchev and the Threat from Imperialism

At the Twenty-second Party Congress in October 1961 Khrushchev took a militant line. The socialist camp had been strengthened by the establishment of a socialist community, victories in the anti-colonialist struggles, and by the struggle of the masses in capitalist countries against war.

Comrades, the chief content of the period following the Twentieth Congress of the CPSU has been the competition between the two world social systems

– the socialist and capitalist systems. This has become the pivot, the main feature of world development in the present historical period. Two lines, two historical tendencies in historical development, are becoming more and more evident. One of them is the line of social progress of peace and creative activity. The other is the line of reaction, oppression and war . . .

Comrades, important changes have come about in the alignment of world forces during the period under review. The world socialist system has become a reliable shield against imperialist military ventures not only for the peoples of the countries that are friendly to it, but for the whole of mankind. And the fact that the socialist community of nations has a preponderance of strength is most fortunate for all mankind. The peace forces, furthermore, have grown all over the world.

A few years ago there were two opposing camps in world affairs – the socialist and imperialist camps. Today an active role in international affairs is also being played by those countries of Asia, Africa and Latin America that have freed, or are freeing, themselves from foreign oppression. Those countries are often called neutralist though they may be considered neutral only in the sense that they do not belong to any of the existing military-political alliances. Most of them, however, are by no means neutral when the cardinal problem of our day, that of war and peace, is at issue. As a rule, those countries advocate peace and oppose war. The countries which have won their liberty from colonialism are becoming a serious factor in the struggle against colonialism and imperialism, and the basic issues of world politics can no longer be settled without due regard to their interests.

In the capitalist countries, too, the masses are taking more and more vigorous action against war. The working class and all working people are fighting against the arms race and the disastrous policy of the warmongers.

Thus the aggressive policy of the imperialist powers is now being opposed by growing forces. The struggle which the countries of socialism and all the forces of peace are carrying on against preparations for fresh aggression and war is the main content of world politics today . . .

Hence the peaceful coexistence of countries with different social systems can be maintained and safeguarded only through the unrelenting struggle of all peoples against the aggressive aspirations of the imperialists. The greater the strength of the socialist camp and the more vigorously the struggle for peace is waged within the capitalist countries, the more difficult it is for the imperialists to carry out their plans of aggression.

Peace and peaceful coexistence are not quite the same thing. Peaceful coexistence does not merely imply absence of war; it is not a temporary, unstable armistice between two wars but the coexistence of two opposed social systems, based on mutual renunciation of war as a means of settling disputes between states.

Historical experience shows that an aggressor cannot be placated by concessions. Concessions to the imperialists on matters of vital importance do not constitute a policy of peaceful coexistence but a policy of surrender to the forces of aggression. To that we will never agree. It is high time the imperialists understood that it is no longer they who are the arbiters of mankind's fate, and that socialism will exist, develop and gain strength whether they like it or not. But for the time being the imperialist gentry do not seem to have understood this. One may well expect of them foolhardy actions that would spell disaster for hundreds of millions of people. That is why we must curb the aggressors and not aid and abet them.

Source: Khrushchev, Report of the Central Committee to the Twenty-second Congress of the CPSU, Delivered by N. S. Khrushchev, First Secretary of the Central Committee, October 17, 1961 (London, Novosti, 1961), pp. 7, 23, 25.

Document 8.18   To the Brink – Cuba

Khrushchev's increasingly pugnacious tone, which had in 1960 led to the erection of the Berlin Wall, now led him to seek a bridgehead in the Caribbean. In December 1958 Fidel Castro had led his band of insurgents to power in Cuba, and in 1962 Khrushchev planned to install nuclear weapons on the island. American spy planes spotted the launching pads and the missiles on the decks of ships steaming westwards. President John F. Kennedy confronted Khrushchev, and in October 1962 the world stood on the verge of a nuclear exchange. After a few days of tension a deal was struck: the USSR agreed to remove its nuclear warheads from Cuba, and the United States promised not to invade the island or to place a new generation of nuclear missiles in Turkey. This face-saving deal for Khrushchev did not hide his embarrassment or the fact that his adventurism had led the world to the brink of disaster. In a letter to President Kennedy of 30 October Khrushchev sought to gain some credit for the deal.

We have received from you a promise that you will not invade Cuba and will not allow others to do so, and we on this condition will remove the weapons that you called aggressive . . . On the basis of this compromise and mutual concessions the problem is resolved . . . To our mutual satisfaction we went perhaps even further than self-interest. No doubt there will be paper-hacks who will say harsh things about our agreement, will dig out who made greater concessions to whom.

But I would say that we both gave way to reason and found a sensible resolution, which will ensure peace for all, including those who will try to find fault in it.

Source: Mezhdunarodnaya zhizn': Spetsial'nyi vypusk, *no. 4, 1992, p. 68. This issue contains most documents relevant to the crisis.*

Decline and Fall

Khrushchev's last years in power were marked by accumulating policy failures. Having restored the party to the centre of Soviet political life, Khrushchev proceeded to undermine it. Particularly unpopular was the decision in November 1962 to divide the regional party organisations into separate urban-industrial and rural-agricultural branches. Mismanagement of the economy provoked a dangerous instability in society.

There had already been bloody demonstrations in Georgia in 1956, but the single most significant outbreak of labour unrest between the end of NEP and 1989 was in Novocherkassk on 1–2 June 1962. Prices were raised on foodstuffs while at the same time a change in labour norms would have led to a wage cut. At least 7,000 workers downed tools and marched towards the centre of town and party headquarters. At first local military detachments refused to obey orders to disperse the demonstrators, and only when outside units were brought in did the shooting begin – 24 were killed outright and 30 wounded, while 105 were put on trial, of whom 7 were sentenced to be shot. Disturbances also took place at this time in three towns in the Donbass (Donetsk, Artem'evsk and Kramatorsk) leading to many casualties. In future years the Soviet regime learned to manage threats of labour unrest more effectively, at first agreeing to demands and then arresting the leaders one by one.

Document 8.19   Khrushchev's Ouster

By 1964 Khrushchev's erratic behaviour and wilfulness had alienated a large part of the Soviet leadership. While Khrushchev was on vacation in the south, the Presidium met over two days (13–14 October 1964) and adopted the following denunciatory resolution.

Recognising that as a result of mistakes and incorrect actions by Comrade Khrushchev, violating Leninist principles of collective leadership, within the CC Presidium recently there has been created a completely abnormal situation, preventing members of the CC Presidium from fulfilling responsible tasks in leading the party and the country.

Comrade Khrushchev, occupying the posts of First Secretary of the CPSU CC and Chairman of the USSR Council of Ministers and concentrating in his hands great power, in a number of ways came to escape from the control of the CC CPSU, stopped taking into account the views of members of the CC's Presidium and members of the CPSU's CC, deciding important questions without the necessary collective discussion.

Revealing intolerance and rudeness towards comrades in the Presidium and the CC, treating their views with disdain, Comrade Khrushchev made a number of major mistakes in practically fulfilling the course outlined by the resolutions of the Twentieth, Twenty-first and Twenty-second CPSU Congresses.

The Presidium of the CC considers that with these negative personal qualities in a worker of mature years and worsening health, Comrade Khrushchev is unable to remedy his mistakes and non-party methods of work.

Taking into account also Comrade Khrushchev's declaration, the Presidium of the CC CPSU resolves:

1 To satisfy the request by Comrade Khrushchev to free him of the responsibilities of First Secretary, member of the Presidium of the CC and Chairman of the USSR Council of Ministers in connection with his advanced age and worsening health.
2 To recognise the inexpediency in future of uniting in one person the duties of CC First Secretary and Chairman of the USSR Council of Ministers.
3 Considers it necessary to convene on 14 October 1964 a plenum of the CC CPSU.

Sources: Istoricheskii arkhiv, *no. 1, 1993, pp. 4–5;* Rossiya, kotoruyu my ne znali, *p. 302.*

Document 8.20   Suslov's Denunciation of Khrushchev

The Central Committee plenum met on 14 October before Khrushchev could return to Moscow. The charge that Khrushchev had been guilty of 'incorrect methods of leading the party and state' was outlined by Mikhail Suslov, who accused him of 'crudely violating Leninist norms of party leadership'.

Comrade Khrushchev, concentrating in his hands the post of First Secretary of the Central Committee of the party and Chairman of the Council of Ministers, far from always correctly used the powers and duties granted him. Crudely violating Leninist norms of party leadership, he sought on his own to decide the most important questions of party and state work. In recent times even the most important questions he in effect resolved on his own, crudely imposing his subjective and often completely incorrect judgement. He began to consider himself infallible, and claimed for himself a monopoly on the truth . . . Because of Comrade Khrushchev's behaviour, the CC's Presidium became ever less a creative collective organ of discussion and decision-making. Collective leadership in practice became impossible . . .

Could we have called him to order sooner? The members of the Presidium did this, warned him, but except for coarse rebuffs and insults they heard nothing from him, although he did not employ repression in relation to the members of the Presidium. It is harder to struggle with a living cult than with a dead one. If Stalin destroyed people physically, Khrushchev destroyed them morally. The removal of Khrushchev from power is a sign not of the weakness but of the strength of the party, and this should be a lesson.

Sources: 'Report of M. Suslov to the CC CPSU Plenum', Istoricheskii arkhiv, *no. 1, 1993, pp. 5, 7, 8;* Rossiya, kotoruyu my ne znali, *pp. 303–4.*

Document 8.21 Communiqué of the Central Committee

The message released to the country was brief and to the point.

On 14 October of this year a plenum of the CPSU Central Committee was held. The plenum approved the request of Comrade N. S. Khrushchev to be relieved of his responsibilities as First Secretary of the Central Committee of the CPSU, member of the Presidium of the CC of the CPSU, and Chairman of the USSR Council of Ministers, in connection with his advanced years and deteriorating health.

    The plenum of the CC of the CPSU elected as First Secretary of the CC of the CPSU Comrade L. I. Brezhnev.

Source: Pravda, *16 October 1964.*

Suslov went on to become the custodian of ideological dogmatism under Brezhnev. Khrushchev went into retirement and lived on to 1971, writing his memoirs, which were smuggled out and published in the West. For the first time a change of leadership had taken place according to the rules, and was not followed by repression. This alone is a measure of Khrushchev's success in stabilising the Soviet political system. His failure was not to have broadened the political establishment beyond small unaccountable groups of party bosses. Khrushchev promised a new relationship between regime and society but ultimately he failed to deliver.

Brezhnev and stagnation, 1964–1985

Leonid Brezhnev was a very different leader from Khrushchev. If the latter was ebullient and confrontational, the former was dour and (mindful of his predecessor's fate) sought to rule by consensus. Ultimately the leadership under Brezhnev appeared paralysed in the face of growing problems. The high economic growth rates of the 1950s inexorably fell until they stopped entirely in the early 1980s . In the social sphere greater resources were devoted to housing, health and education, but here, too, reforms appeared to run into the sands. Destalinisation under Khrushchev was only partial, and then under Brezhnev was effectively reversed. The full-scale rehabilitation of Stalin, sought by hardliners on the ninetieth anniversary of Stalin's birth in 1969, however, did not take place. The relative liberalisation of the thaw years came to an end. In foreign policy the principle of class warfare reigned supreme, although not unchallenged by some academic specialists. Stagnation at home was stimulated by Soviet expansionism abroad and exaggerated hopes of the economic benefits of détente. The social basis of stagnation at home was characterised by the ever-growing demand for unskilled workers, labour shortages, and declining productivity and labour discipline. Despite sporadic attempts at reform in the late 1960s and 1970s, the political system and society were marked by a growing listlessnes, alcoholism and the rise of dissent. Attempts to impose an authoritarian model of reform by Yurii Andropov (November 1982–February 1994) were cut short by his untimely death, and his successor, Konstantin Chernenko (February 1984–March 1985) had neither the desire nor energy to pursue reforms.

The Brezhnevite System

Brezhnev's eighteen years of leadership were the longest period of tranquillity that the Soviet system ever experienced. This was the system in, as it were, its normal state. It soon became clear, however, that without strong leadership to inject dynamism Soviet socialism had a tendency to relapse into stagnation. Despite Khrushchev's attempts to undermine their power by creating some one hundred regional economic councils (sovnarkhozy), the powerful economic ministries were reconstituted under Brezhnev. The system bought social peace by ensuring job security, but at the price of low productivity and relative technological stagnation. While workers had to make do with low wages and few incentives, prices also remained low due to massive state subsidies, in particular for foodstuffs. Such a system could not go on for ever and sooner or later had to confront the accumulating social and economic problems. Gagarin's fate is instructive. In the tours that followed his space flight in 1961 his charm and wit won him world-wide popularity, but with the accession to power of the Brezhnev group in 1964 his star began to fall as the new leaders became jealous of his fame. Gagarin himself appeared disgusted with the venality of the Brezhnev regime and its cranking up of the arms race once again – he represented the genuinely peaceful face of 'peaceful coexistence'. Afflicted by a growing drink problem, on 27 March 1968 Gagarin died when the MiG-15 jet he was piloting crashed. With him died the hopes of the 'children of the Twentieth Congress', those who believed in the USSR's ability to become a 'normal' open society. At the time (and for some, indeed, in retrospect), the Brezhnev years superficially appeared an oasis of calm and gradual improvement in the country's stormy twentieth century. It was, however, the calm of decay.

Document 9.1   The 1965 Reforms

The economic reforms of 1965, associated with the name of the prime minister, Alexei Kosygin, but drawing on the ideas of the economist Evsei Liberman advanced in Khrushchev's last years, soon ran into the sand of bureaucratic obstruction. They suggested a recognition of the problems, but a failure of will to resolve them. The Central Committee plenum of 27–9 September 1965 framed the reforms as follows.

The serious inadequacy in industrial management is that administrative methods predominate over economic ones. Economic cost accounting [*khozraschët*, the buzz word of all reforms] in enterprises has largely a formal character, while the rights of enterprises in economic activity are limited.

The work of enterprises is regulated by a large number of plan indicators, which limits the autonomy and initiative of the enterprise collectives and reduces responsibility for improving the organisation of production. The system of material incentives for industrial workers provides few incentives to improve the general outcome of work of the enterprise, in raising the profitability of production and improving the quality of industrial production.

The territorial management of industry, while to some degree broadening the possibility of inter-sectoral specialisation and greater cooperation of industrial production within a given region, at the same time inhibited the development of sectoral specialisation and rational production links between enterprises in different economic regions, distanced science from production, and led to the fragmentation and complexity of the management of industrial sectors, so that they lost some effectiveness in their work.

To develop further industry and raise the level of social production . . . an improvement in planning methods is required, the strengthening of economic incentives to improve industrial production, to raise the material incentives of workers to improve the work of their enterprises.

The CC plenum considers it essential that industrial management is organised on the sectoral principle, to create union republic and all-Union ministries for industrial sectors.

It is expedient to remove superfluous regulations in the work of enterprises, to reduce the number of plan indicators imposed on enterprises from above, to provide them with the necessary resources to develop and improve production, to improve the use of such economic instruments as profits, prices, bonuses and credit.

The whole system of planning, the management of enterprises and material incentives should be directed towards ensuring high rates of development of social production and to raising its efficiency. An important condition for achieving the stated aims is to create in enterprise collectives incentives to develop higher plan demands, improvements in the use of production resources, labour reserves, material and financial resources, the perfection of technology, the organisation of labour, and raising the profitability of production.

Source: Central Committee plenum resolution, 'On Improving the Management of Industry, Perfecting Planning and Strengthening Economic Incentives of Industrial Production', in KPSS v rezolyutsiyakh i resheniyakh s"ezdov, konferentsii i plenumov TsK, vol. 10 (Moscow, Politizdat, 1986), pp. 440–5.

Document 9.2 Brezhnev on the Party and the People

More often than not Brezhnev appeared to enjoy the trappings of power rather than the substance of power itself. By the early 1970s he had made himself 'first among equals', yet failed to use his authority to resolve any of the problems facing the country. He himself fell seriously ill in 1976 and became increasingly distant from all but the pomp of power. This extract from a speech he delivered to the Central Committee plenum in December 1973 is typical of his wooden style, reflecting the lifeless and dogmatic language that characterised the whole period. The slogan of 'strengthening the links between the party and the masses', as vacuous as it was universal, became the catchphrase of the Brezhnev era.

In parallel we must resolve yet another important task – the stubborn struggle for the further affirmation of a genuine party style of work, a party approach in all spheres of economic activity. We cannot approach questions of the management of the economy, to questions of the improvement of this management, from a narrowly economic position. This for us is a party matter, a political matter, whose success to an enormous extent depends on the political atmosphere in all sections of our society. A party approach is inseparable from raising personal responsibility, from changing the attitude of cadres to party decisions . . .

The Politburo of the CPSU's CC expresses its firm belief that after the confirmation of the economic plan at the session of the USSR Supreme Soviet, after the publication of the Appeal of the Central Committee, our whole party with its whole energy will take up this task, will undertake an all-people socialist emulation at such a level when not only the leaders [*peredoviki*] of production but whole collectives will undertake higher obligations and will do everything for their fulfilment.

We have 380,000 primary party organisations, about 15 million communists. This is an enormous force. We need only know how to organise it correctly, reveal its limitless possibilities, make all party organisations, all communists, conscious and active fighters for the party's policies. Then we will be able to achieve any, even the most complex, task! (*Extended applause.*)

I have already mentioned, and wish to underline yet again, that the task of party organisations consists of the constant strengthening of the links between the party and the masses, in the constant lively interaction with toilers so as to understand their needs and aspirations, so as to know how to explain to them the essence of the policies of our party, to know how to mobilise the masses to implement in practice our programme, the programme of building a communist society in our country, the programme of the struggle for peace and friendship between peoples. (*Stormy, extended applause.*)

Source: L. I. Brezhnev, Aktual'nye voprosy ideologicheskoi raboty KPSS, *vol. 1 (Moscow, Politizdat, 1978), pp. 613, 615–16.*

Document 9.3   Détente and the Helsinki Accords

Détente is the name given to the period from the late 1960s to the late 1970s marked by a reciprocal improvement and regularisation in relations between the superpowers, accompanied by intra-European détente and an improvement in intra-German relations. The high point of this period was President Richard Nixon's visit to Moscow in May 1972 to sign the ABM (Anti-Ballistic Missile) Treaty and SALT I (Strategic Arms Limitation Talks/Treaty I), followed by Brezhnev's visit to the United States the following year. The period culminated in the Conference on Security and Cooperation in Europe (CSCE), held in Helsinki in August 1975. The Helsinki conference, and above all the rights enshrined in its Final Act, was to play a crucial role in the peaceful transcendence of Soviet-type socialism. The 'three baskets' at Helsinki dealt with security, economic cooperation and human rights; the USSR was so keen on the advantages bestowed by the first two (above all, confirmation of post-war borders and acknowledgement of the principle of non-interference in the internal affairs of other states) that it signed up to the third. Critics in society could now appeal to these rights, formally undersigned by the communist authorities themselves, to hold their own governments accountable. The 'third basket' agenda undermined the systems from within and without. In short, Helsinki first of all ratified 'Yalta', and then transcended it.

I Sovereign equality, respect for the rights inherent in sovereignty

The participating States will respect each other's sovereign equality and individuality as well as all the rights inherent in and encompassed by its sovereignty, including in particular the right of every State to juridical equality, to territorial integrity and to freedom and political independence. They will also respect each other's right freely to choose and develop its political, social, economic and cultural systems as well as its right to determine its laws and regulations . . .

II Refraining from the threat or use of force

The participating States will refrain in their mutual relations, as well as in their international relations in general, from the threat or use of force against the territorial integrity or political independence of any State, or in any other manner inconsistent with the purposes of the United Nations and with the present Declaration. No consideration may be invoked to serve to warrant resort to the threat or use of force in contravention of this principle.

III Inviolability of frontiers

The participating States regard as inviolable all one another's frontiers as well as the frontiers of all States in Europe and therefore they will refrain now and in the future from assaulting these frontiers.

Accordingly, they will also refrain from any demand for, or act of, seizure and usurpation of part or all of the territory of any participating State.

IV Territorial integrity of States

The participating States will respect the territorial integrity of each of the participating States.

Accordingly, they will refrain from any action inconsistent with the purposes and principles of the Charter of the United Nations against the territorial integrity, political independence or the unity of any participating State, and in particular from any such constituting a threat or use of force.

The participating States will likewise refrain from making each other's territory the object of military occupation or other direct or indirect measures of force in contravention of international law, or the threat of them. No such occupation or acquisition will be recognised as legal.

V Peaceful settlement of disputes

The participating States will settle disputes among them by peaceful means in such a manner as not to endanger international peace and security, and justice . . .

VI Non-intervention in internal affairs

The participating States will refrain from any intervention, direct or indirect, individual or collective, in the internal or external affairs falling within the domestic jurisdiction of another participating State, regardless of their mutual relations . . .

VII Respect for human rights and fundamental freedoms, including the freedom of thought, conscience, religion or belief

The participating States will respect human rights and fundamental freedoms, including the freedom of thought, conscience, religion or belief, for all without distinction as to race, sex, language or religion. They will promote and encourage the effective exercise of civil, political, economic, social, cultural and other rights and freedoms all of which derive from the inherent dignity of the human person and are essential for his free and full development.

Within this framework the participating States will recognise and respect the freedom of the individual to profess and practise, alone or in community with others, religion or belief acting in accordance with the dictates of his own conscience.

The participating States on whose territory national minorities exist will respect the right of persons belonging to such minorities to equality before the law, will afford them the full opportunity for the actual enjoyment of human rights and fundamental freedoms and will, in this manner, protect their legitimate interests in this sphere.

The participating States recognise the universal significance of human rights and fundamental freedoms, respect for which is an essential factor for the peace, justice and well-being necessary to ensure the development of friendly relations and co-operation among themselves as among all States.

They will constantly respect these rights and freedoms in their mutual relations and will endeavour jointly and separately, including in co-operation with the United Nations, to promote universal and effective respect for them.

They confirm the right of the individual to know and act upon his rights and duties in this field.

In the field of human rights and fundamental freedoms, the participating States will act in conformity with the purposes and principles of the Charter of the United Nations and with the Universal Declaration of Human Rights. They will also fulfil their obligations as set forth in the international declarations and agreements in this field, including *inter alia* the International Covenants on Human Rights, by which they may be bound.

Source: Conference on Security and Cooperation in Europe, Final Act, Helsinki, *1 August 1975 (London, HMSO, 1975), pp. 2–5.*

Document 9.4 Developed Socialism

In Brezhnev's final years the concept of 'developed socialism' became the official orthodoxy, signifying in effect the postponement of the advent of communism in favour of a rather modest version of a participatory welfare state. Fyodor Burlatsky had been one of the key political scientists advising Khrushchev on the idea of establishing a 'state of all the people' (what he calls here the 'people's state') and he remained loyal to his vision of a modern developed socialism. Almost every postulate in his argument could be questioned, including his characterisation of national issues, the lack of any serious criticism of the electoral system, his reliance on technology (and in particular developments in computer science) to bail out the Soviet system, and above all the complacent tone of the whole 'developed socialism' approach, of which he was such an eloquent exponent. Later, during perestroika, the pusillanimity of this whole group of *shestdesyatniki* (1960s) 'reformers' at this time came to haunt them.

There are stages, periods and degrees in the development of socialist society. After the victory of the October Revolution, official documents spoke of the conquest of political power by the working class: the 1930s saw the creation of the foundation and, subsequently, the bases of socialist society; the 1950s saw the complete construction of socialism; finally, the 1970s are witnessing developed socialist society and the construction of the material and technical basis of communism . . .

Developed socialism is an independent, more or less protracted state in the transition to communism, a stage in which occur changes inherent in socialism as such, in which the advances of the scientific and technological revolution intertwine with the advantages of the socialist social system. Soviet society has just entered the period of the scientific and technological revolution, and a long period will be needed for the development of all aspects of social life on the basis of that revolution.

The idea of developed socialism is opposed to Maoist concepts of 'leaps' and 'communes' as the way to communism. These Maoist concepts ignore the fact that socialism must for a long time develop on its own base and are associated with the curtailment of socialist forms of economic and social life for the benefit of pseudo-communist (and in practice petty-bourgeois and even semi-feudal) reforms.

There is no need to dwell on the achievements of the Soviet economy. It is enough to recall the figures cited at the 24th Congress of the CPSU [March 1971]: the Soviet economy produces in one day a social product valued at two thousand million rubles, which is ten times greater than the daily output at the end of the 1930s. This provides new opportunities for the development of productive forces at the same time that society is making new demands on the economy. The economy is now developing in a more balanced and harmonious manner, and the population has a greater demand for material and cultural services.

As to qualitative indices, we should note that there are in social life key socio-political concepts that sum up the nature of a phenomenon and provide the basis for decisions important for society. Such concepts are, for example, the people's state, the scientific and technological revolution, economic reform, the intensive economy, socialist integration, scientific management. The idea of developed socialism is of especial significance: it is the most capacious and universal description of the contemporary stage of the economic, socio-political and intellectual development of Soviet society.

The fundamental sense of this concept is that it links into a single system all the key socio-political concepts mentioned above and provides a theoretical foundation for economic and social policy. Society has attained a level of maturity at which attention shifts from extensive to intensive economic development, to harmonious labor, to the optimization of decisions in order to raise national prosperity significantly. Lenin's forecast that there would be historical stages, periods and steps in the creation of the new society is well-known.

Developed socialism is simultaneously a new stage in the development of the state, of democracy and in the administration of society. It is marked by the extensive application of computer technology, the latest advances of science (especially systems analysis in decision making), integrated socio-economic planning and forecasting, the increasing involvement of social activists and all working people in administration and supervision of administration . . .

A most important prerequisite for the development of the Soviet state is strengthening the unity of the many nationalities in the country and the gradual formation of a Soviet people as a new social community. This process is expressed in state and juridical forms of strengthening the Union of Soviet Republics as the federative structure of the USSR.

From the point of view of the development of socialist democracy and administration, the emergence of socio-political activists is especially important. These include persons who have a relatively large influence on the adoption and implementation of socially significant decisions.

The most active, progressive and conscious part of the working people, as is said in the Rules of the CPSU, is joined in the Communist Party of the Soviet Union, which numbers 16 million persons. In addition, more than two million persons are elected deputies to the Soviets. Then there are the active elements of trade unions, the Komsomol and other organizations. It should be emphasized that social activists are not linked to specific social environments. They come from all classes and all strata of the working class, the collective-farm peasantry, and the intelligentsia.

Reliance on the progressive, socially and politically more active part of society, above all the most conscious part of the working class, provides the best potential for influencing the rest of the population. It is important to implement special measures that would accelerate the advancement of these strata of the population in correspondence to the demands of scientific and technological progress.

Source: Fyodor Burlatsky, The Modern State and Politics *(Moscow, Progress, 1978), pp. 100, 101–2, 104–5.*

Document 9.5   The 1977 'Brezhnev' Constitution

If the Stalin Constitution had not explicitly granted the Communist Party a privileged status, this changed in the Brezhnev Constitution adopted on 7 October 1977. Article 1 reaffirmed that the country had become a state of all the people, Article 3 the principles of democratic centralism, while Article 6 provided a general formula for the role of the Communist Party in the Soviet state.

Article 1. The Union of Soviet Socialist Republics is a socialist state of all the people, expressing the will and interests of the workers, peasants and intelligentsia, the working people of all the nations and nationalities of the country. . . .

Article 3. The Soviet state is organised and functions on the principle of democratic centralism, namely the electiveness of all bodies of state power from the lowest to the highest, their accountability to the people, and the obligation of lower bodies to observe the decisions of higher ones. Democratic centralism combines central leadership with local initiative and creative activity and with the responsibility of each state body and official for the work entrusted to them. . . .

Article 6. The leading and guiding force of Soviet society and the nucleus of its political system, of all state and public organisations, is the Communist Party of the Soviet Union. The CPSU exists for the people and serves the people.

The Communist Party, armed with Marxism-Leninism, determines the general perspectives of the development of society and the course of the home and foreign policy of the USSR, directs the great constructive work of the Soviet people, and imparts a planned, systematic and theoretically substantiated character to their struggle for the victory of communism.

All party organisations shall function within the framework of the Constitution of the USSR.

Source: Konstitutsiya (osnovnoi zakon) RSFSR *(Moscow, Politizdat, 1980), pp. 5–6.*

This only provided a general indication of the powers of the party in the system of soviets and ministries. The party–state relationship, as in other spheres of Soviet life, was governed more by convention than by statute. The CPSU was the kernel of the state, but it was potentially the state itself, although official Soviet thinking stressed that the Communist Party ruled but did not govern. The party was in effect the senior executive branch of the Soviet government where all decisions were made or confirmed; the Supreme Soviet and the Council of Ministers acted as the junior administrative branches, implementing decisions taken within the appropriate party committee. Such overlapping and lack of definition of functions was a natural consequence of the constitution's rejection of the separation of powers. As if to confirm the point, at the same time as adopting the new constitution, Brezhnev removed the chairman of the USSR Supreme Soviet, Nikolai Podgorny, and himself became head of state while remaining General Secretary of the party.

Document 9.6   Ogarkov on Technological Backwardness and Nuclear War

Despite the enormous resources the Soviet system devoted to its military-industrial complex, reaching by some accounts 40 per cent of GNP, by the late 1970s there were increasing fears that the country was lagging behind the technical achievements of its rivals. The Soviet military establishment was increasingly concerned about the widening technological gap between what Soviet military industry could produce and the advanced weaponry of the West. The military could not impose its own concerns on the defence industry, which remained locked into outmoded and unresponsive technologies. With the prospect of a rapidly modernising China emerging as a serious military rival, the head of the General Staff, Marshal Nikolai Ogarkov, brought these concerns into the open by quoting from Engels that 'Weapons, structure, organisation, tactics and strategy depend above all on the level of production and the means of communication that have been achieved at a given point in time' (*Kommunist*, no. 7, 1978, p. 112), a fairly open criticism of current policies. Long before any other senior Soviet leader he predicted that sophisticated high-technology weapons would give the United States a dangerous advantage, and advocated increased defence spending to allow the Soviet Union to develop its own 'smart' weaponry. Although the extract below reflects the traditional Soviet view, by stressing that the Soviet Union might have recourse fairly rapidly to nuclear weapons he was implicitly conceding that its conventional capacity was inadequate. He was removed from office by Chernenko for publicising these concerns, and his death in 1994 passed almost unnoticed.

Soviet military strategy views a future world war, if the imperialists manage to unleash it, as a decisive clash between two opposed world socio-economic systems – socialist and capitalist. It is supposed that in such a war simultaneously or consecutively the majority of the states in the world may become involved. It will be a global opposition of multimillion coalitional armed forces unprecedented in scale and violence and will be waged without compromise, for the most decisive political and strategic goals. In its course all the military, economic, and spiritual forces of the combatant states, coalitions and social systems will be fully used.

Soviet military strategy recognizes that world war might begin and for a certain length of time be waged with the use of just conventional weapons. However, widening military actions may lead to its escalation into general nuclear war in which nuclear weapons, primarily of strategic designation, will be the main means of waging it. At the base of Soviet military strategy lies the position that the Soviet Union, proceeding from the principles of its politics, will not use this weapon first. And it in principle is against the use of weapons of mass destruction. But any possible aggressor must clearly recognize that in the event of a nuclear rocket attack on the Soviet Union or on other countries of the social community it will receive a crushing retaliatory blow . . .

While considering the offensive as the basic kind of strategic action, Soviet military strategy at the same time recognizes the important role of defense in war, the necessity and possibility of its organization and conduct on a strategic scale for the purpose of frustrating or repulsing an enemy attack, holding (defending) certain territory, winning time to concentrate the necessary forces by economy of forces in some directions and the creation of superiority over the enemy in other directions. In doing this it is considered that defense on any scale must be active, must create conditions for going over to the offensive (counteroffensive) for the purpose of the complete destruction of the enemy.

Source: Marshal N. V. Ogarkov, 'Military Strategy', in Daniels, Communism and the World, *p. 432.*

While Ogarkov was convinced that in any nuclear conflict with the West the USSR would emerge victorious, he was equally adamant that there could not be a victor in any nuclear war. He drew the analogy between chemical weapons in the Second World War, when both sides possessed them but neither dared to use them, fearing retaliation from the other side. Ogarkov's main contribution was to alert the Soviet authorities to the importance of weapons based on new principles. He was one of the most innovative Soviet military thinkers and had opposed Moscow's intervention in Afghanistan as being against the USSR's long-term interests.

Document 9.7 Gorshkov on the Navy

Under Brezhnev the USSR developed a blue-water fleet which at last gave the country a genuinely global military reach. Much of this was unnecessary, since it was clear that at the first sign of conflict the huge Black Sea fleet would be bottled up and not allowed to enter the Mediterranean through the Dardanelles. The architect of the build-up was Sergei Gorshkov, commander-in-chief of the Soviet navy from January 1956, who had convinced Khrushchev of the need for a large naval capacity. His sudden dismissal in late 1985 and replacement by Admiral Vladimir Chernavin signalled Gorbachev's refusal to allow the huge expenditure on the fleet to continue.

The need to have a powerful Navy corresponding both to the geographical position of our country and to its political importance as a great world power has already long been understood . . . However, this question became particularly acute in the postwar years, when as a result of the alignment of forces in the world arena, the USSR and other Socialist countries found themselves surrounded on all sides by a hostile coalition of maritime states posing the serious threat of a nuclear-missile attack from the direction of the sea.

At the same time the imperialists, headed by the USA, having created a situation for the Socialist countries in which they were surrounded from the direction of the sea, did not experience a similar danger. Could the Soviet Union reconcile itself to such a situation? Could it agree to an age-long domination of the seas and oceans by the traditional western sea powers, especially under the conditions when vast areas of the oceans had become launching pads for nuclear-missile weaponry?

Of course not!

The Communist Party and the Soviet government fully appreciated both the threat to our country which is arising from the oceans, and the need to deter the aggressive aspirations of the enemy through the construction of a new, ocean-going Navy. And this need is being answered.

Source: Fleet Admiral S. G. Gorshkov, 'Some Problems in Mastering the World Ocean', in Daniels, Communism and the World, p. 442–3.

The invasion of Afghanistan in December 1979 was the logical culmination of the Soviet military build-up. Despite warnings from academics, high officials and even Ogarkov, a small group in the Brezhnev leadership committed the country to a war that proved unwinnable.

The End of the Thaw and the Rise of Dissent

The relative thaw under Khrushchev had allowed a 'cultural opposition' to emerge; in other words, the system now allowed a certain amount of criticism and intellectual debate. Even these limited openings were soon curtailed by Brezhnev. His period in office was marked by increasing disillusionment on the one hand accompanied by increasing state repression on the other. The 'period of stagnation' (*zastoi*), as it became known later, did not allow the full rehabilitation of Stalin but took on the form of a stifling 'post-totalitarianism', where full-scale repression of the old sort gave way to constant low-level repression.

Document 9.8 The Sinyavsky–Daniel trial

One of the major landmarks on the road to stagnation was the trial of Andrei Sinyavsky and Yulii Daniel in February 1966, charged with 'anti-state activity' on the grounds that they had published works abroad. The following extract is from notes taken during the course of their trial.

Morning session 10 February 1966

The decision of 4 February is announced stating that Sinyavsky and Daniel will be charged according to article 70, part one, of the RSFSR Criminal Code.

Judge: The defendant Sinyavsky, do you admit yourself guilty of the charges either fully or partially?

Sinyavsky: No, I do not admit it, either fully or partially.

Judge: The defendant Daniel, do you admit yourself guilty of the charges either fully or partially?

Daniel: No, I do not admit it, either fully or partially.

The evening questioning of Sinyavsky was interrupted and carried over to the next day. He tried to explain to the judge that in his article and three works there were presented not political views and convictions, but his writer's position, that as a writer he is close to fantastic realism with its hyperboles, irony and grotesquerie, but the procurator demanded that he stop delivering literary lectures in the courtroom. This demand was supported by the judge . . .

Procurator: Are your political view and convictions reflected in these works?

Sinyavsky: I am not a political writer. No writer uses his works to advance political views . . . You cannot ask either Pushkin or Gogol their political views. (*Disturbance in the court.*) My works reflect the way I see the world and not politics.

Procurator: I think otherwise . . .

The session continued on 12 February.

From the speech of State Prosecutor O. P. Temushkin

I accuse Sinyavsky and Daniel of anti-state activity. They wrote and published dirty libels masquerading as literary works, calling for the overthrow of order, and they circulated libels, wrapping all this up in a literary form. What they have done is not a chance mistake but an action equivalent to treachery . . . I request, taking everything into account, including the fact that they have not repented, and Sinyavsky's primary role, that Sinyavsky is sentenced to the maximum sentence possible – seven years of deprivation of freedom in a hard-labour camp, and five years of exile (*applause*), and for Daniel, five years in a hard-labour camp and three years' exile.

Source: Mif o zastoe (*Leningrad, Lenizdat, 1991*), *pp. 70–1.*

Document 9.9 Appeal against Restalinisation

The destalinisation process was reversed, and by 1967 the creeping rehabilitation of Stalin had gone so far as to provoke one of the first public acts of the emerging 'dissident' movement, a letter by the children and grandchildren of communists liquidated by Stalin during the purges. The letter remained within the spirit of within-system reform, hoping at this stage still to improve communism rather than overthrow it. The signatories including Bukharin's son and other children of people repressed in the 1930s.

At present in assemblies, in the press, on the radio and television, the 'services' of Stalin are being broadcast. This is in effect a revision of the decisions of the twentieth and twenty-second congresses of the CPSU.

This troubles us. And not only because our relatives and we ourselves, like millions of others, became victims of the criminal machine built by Stalin. It pains us to recognise that the terribly deceived masses were drawn into condoning the arbitrariness of that time. This must not be repeated. The resurrection of the past threatens the idea of communism, discredits our system, makes lawful the deaths of millions of innocent people.

Any attempt to whitewash Stalin's black deeds contains the danger of a repetition of the terrible tragedy that struck our party, our entire people and the whole communist movement . . .

Only by revealing totally the crimes of Stalin and his supporters can we generate the strength, consciousness and anger throughout society required to destroy the entire legacy of the Stalin cult and make the return of new cults and new despotisms impossible. How can one praise Stalin after all that our people have suffered because of him? This adulatory praise inhibits our movement, weakens our ranks, undermines our power, and makes the triumph of communism impossible.

We ask that what we say is taken into account and that our letter be considered part of the struggle for communism. We hope that our letter will help avert an irreparable mistake.

> Petr Yakir, son of I. E. Yakir; L. Petrovskii, son of P. G. Petrovskii; A. Antonov-Ovseenko, son of V. A. Antonov-Ovseenko; Yu. Larin-Bukharin, son of Nikolai Bukharin and grandson of Yuri Larin; Yu. Vavilov, son of Academician Nikolai Vavilov; A. Bokii, daughter of G. I. Bokii; I. A. Shlyapnikova, daughter of A. Shlyapnikov; Larisa Bogoraz, daughter of a communist, and others to total forty-three signatures.

Sources: Istochnik, *no. 2, 1994;* Rossiya, kotoruyu my ne znali, *pp. 304–5.*

Document 9.10   Appeal to Stop Political Trials

The authorities responded with more repression, reflected in the extracts from the following letter.

In recent years in our country a number of political trials have been held. The essence of the trials is that people have been tried for their convictions in violation of their basic civic rights. That is why these trials took place with crude violations of legality, chief of which is the lack of openness [glasnost].

Society no longer wants to put up with such illegality, and this has provoked indignation and protest, rising from trial to trial. A number of individual and collective letters have been sent to various judicial, government and party bodies, all the way up to the CC CPSU. These letters have remained unanswered. The response to those who protested most actively was to be sacked from work, called to the KGB and threatened with arrest, and, finally, the most scandalous form of punishment, forced incarceration in psychiatric hospitals. These illegal and inhuman actions cannot bring any positive results, but, on the contrary, increase tension and provoke new protests.

We consider it our duty to point out that there are several thousand political prisoners in camps and prisons, about whom almost no one knows. They are being kept in inhuman conditions of forced labour, on half-starvation rations, subject to administrative arbitrariness . . .

The appeal was signed by: Aleksei Kosterin, writer; Larisa Bogoraz, philologist; Pavel Litvinov, physicist; Zampira Asanova, doctor; Petr Yakir, historian; Viktor Krasin, economist; Il'ya Gabai, teacher.

Sources: Mif o zastoe, *p. 144;* Rossiya, kotoruyu my ne znali, *pp. 305–6.*

Document 9.11 *Novy mir* is Brought into Line

Pressure was now put on the journal *Novy mir*, in which Solzhenitsyn had published his novella *One Day in the Life of Ivan Denisovich*. A *Pravda* editorial of 27 January 1967 accused the journal of 'distorting the truth' by focusing on the 'dark side, on various forms of abnormality, with the painful side-effects of "tempestuous growth"'. Tvardovskii defended the *Novy mir* line at a meeting of the USSR Union of Writers on 15 March 1967, insisting that:

> *Novy mir* openly declares its ideological-aesthetic sympathies and takes as a compliment the strange accusation that it is 'following its own line'. To 'follow one's own line' means to have principles, to adhere to what you believe in hewn from that knowledge which is all-powerful because it is true.

Tvardovskii's twelve years as editor of *Novy mir* came to an end when he was forced to resign in February 1970. A platform for loyalist reformist ideas – and thus for internal renewal – was thus destroyed.

Who can read our newspapers today? Evidently only someone who has the patience to plow through the tons of empty verbiage and dross that seems to have the power to repel even the shallowest simpleton willing to swallow anything. Only someone who has learned how to detect and extract from the heaps of verbiage the subterfuges of semi-silence and the outcroppings of living, unconsoling, and unclouded truth. Only someone who has learned to divine, behind these devices, the biting, salty truth that has not been watered down. Only someone who in this way knew how to pick out the crumbs of information in our papers and had a chance to decode the ever-so-modest 'chronicle' buried in the pages of *Literaturnaya gazeta* on February 11, 1970, and to decipher nothing less than the news of the death of our best and most beloved magazine, the great friend of all progressive socialist forces in the country, the magazine that bravely and honestly told us the truth, genuine, irreplaceable, and free of quotation marks. As if by chance and just in passing, this 'chronicle' mumbles something about reassignments of personnel: some were 'relieved of their duties' and others 'confirmed in their posts'. In the process, Tvardovsky's name is mentioned as though he were one of those who carried out this act of strangulation, as though he wished to remain without those 'relieved' and with those 'confirmed'.

It was not enough that a miserly few lines stripped of any import were printed with the intention that they be noticed as little as possible. On top of that, the factual element in them was surrounded by lies. It is a barefaced lie that Tvardovsky agreed with the decision, the departure of many of his leading collaborators. In fact what they aimed at, by dismissing these people, was to force him to leave, to bring about his dismissal. The shot was carefully calculated to ricochet and hit a target they pretend they were not aiming at, at all! It is a lie that Tvardovsky agreed to this. Could anyone agree to such a thing? He did not agree to work on the magazine with people who are known to be totally alien to the spirit of *Novy mir*, people who agreed, after painting themselves up as 'members of the editorial board,' to participate in the strangulation of the magazine . . .

Deprived of *Novy mir*, many of us will now gain a better understanding of what it represented. It was the most consistent and unfailing mouthpiece we had for the tendency that revived after 1953, and especially after 1956, a tendency favoring the development of socialism free of the deformations rooted in the heritage of many centuries of Russian feudalism. It was our most outspoken voice – within the limits allowed by an increasingly thick-headed and mistrustful censorship – the voice of the people's conscience. A voice that proclaimed the irrepressible and indestructible capacity of the people to struggle for genuine socialism – and this after the decades of deadening silence and Stalinist barracks existence. It was the surest symbol of moral and human awakening, the most faithful implementer and defender of the Twentieth Congress line, which condemned the monstrous abomin-ations and crimes of barracks pseudosocialism (such as we now see raging in China) . . .

The suppression of *Novy mir* is an attempt by a handful of spiritual bankrupts to eliminate from our moral and intellectual life, from the life of the people and Party, the voice of truth that gives expression to all the socialist and progressive forces in the country, the Twentieth Congress tendency. This is an attempt to turn the country back to barracks despotism, to a state of moral and intellectual voicelessness and the silence of the grave. But there is a good chance that this attempt to bring tragedy back to us will itself turn into farce. It would be a good idea for us to think over the results and lessons of the *Novy mir* experience in order to better understand ourselves and the problematical historical work before us. That is the task of the day . . .

Source: Stephen F. Cohen (ed.), An End to Silence: Uncensored Opinion in the Soviet Union, *from Roy Medvedev's underground magazine,* Political Diary, *no. 66, March 1970 (New York, W. W. Norton, 1982), pp. 202, 203–4.*

Socialism with a Human Face

Rather than responding to appeals to end political trials and accept a degree of internal pluralism, the Soviet government intensified repression at home and abroad. The intervention in Czechoslovakia was justified by the 'Brezhnev Doctrine' of limited sovereignty, but for many foreign analysts Soviet-type socialism was an unstable compromise that could not last.

Document 9.12   The *Action Programme* of the Czechoslovak Communist Party

Czechoslovakia had been one of the most quiescent of the Soviet 'satellite' states, but burdened by economic and political stagnation, the pressure for change grew. In January 1968 the veteran hardline communist chief, Antonin Novotný, was replaced by Alexander Dubček. The new leader launched a unique attempt to renew Soviet-type socialism from within. Censorship was abolished and the country set on the path of democratisation. The key document of this period, outlining plans to establish a new relationship with society, was the party programme (*Action Programme*) adopted in April 1968.

In the past, the leading role of the party was typically defined as the monopolistic concentration of power in the hands of party bodies. This corresponded to the false thesis that the party is the instrument of the dictatorship of the proletariat. This harmful conception weakened the initiative and responsibility of the state, economic and social institutions and damaged the party's authority, and prevented it from carrying out its real functions. The party's goal is not to become the universal caretaker of society, to bind all organisations and every step taken in life by its directives. Its mission lies primarily in stimulating socialist initiative, in showing the means and real potential of communist development, and in winning over all workers for them through systematic persuasion, as well as by the personal example of communists . . .

The main thing is to reform the whole political system so that it will permit the dynamic development of socialist social relations, combine broad democracy with a scientific, highly qualified management, strengthen the social order, stabilise socialist relations and maintain social discipline. The basic structure of the political system must, at the same time, *provide firm guarantees against a return to the old methods of subjectivism and highhandedness of those in a position of power.* Party activity has, so far, not been turned systematically to that end, in fact, obstacles have frequently been put in the way of such efforts. All these changes necessarily call for . . . a new Czechoslovak constitution . . .

The implementation of constitutional *freedoms of assembly and also association* must be ensured this year so that the possibility of setting up voluntary organisations, special-interest associations, societies, etc. is guaranteed by law to meet the actual interests and needs of various strata and categories of our citizens, without bureaucratic interference and without monopoly of any individual organisation. Any restrictions in this respect can be imposed only by law and only the law can stipulate what is anti-social, forbidden, or punishable. Freedoms guaranteed by law are applicable in this sense, in compliance with the constitution, also to citizens of individual creeds and religious denominations.

The effective influence of views and opinions of the working people on all our policy, opposition to all attempts to suppress the criticism and initiative of the people, cannot be guaranteed if we do not ensure constitution-based freedom of speech and all political and personal rights of all citizens systematically and consistently, by all legal means available. *Socialism cannot mean only liberation of the working people from the domination of exploiting class relations, but must make more provisions for a fuller life of the personality than any bourgeois democracy.* The working people, who are no longer ordered about by any class of exploiters, can no longer be prescribed, by any arbitrary interpretation from a position of power, what information they may or may not be given, which of their opinions can or cannot be expressed publicly, where public opinion may play a role and where not.

Source: The Action Programme of the Czechoslovak Communist Party *(Nottingham, Spokesman Books, 1972), pp. 6, 7.*

The document is remarkable for the radicalism with which it sought to outline the principles for a humane type of pluralistic socialism, moving away from Stalinist economism where socialism was defined as the relationship between *things*: if the means of production were in state hands, it was argued, then the system was socialist, ignoring the fact that new forms of exploitation had emerged based on the relationship to the means of production, above all the supreme and arbitrary power of the bureaucracy, or what Milovan Djilas called 'the new class'. By contrast, the new humanistic socialism outlined in the *Action Programme* focused on the quality of the relationship between *people*. This threatened the very basis of communist rule in the Soviet Union, and the experiment was brutally terminated by the invasion of Warsaw Pact forces on the night of 20–1 August 1968. The Hungarian party leader János Kádár had tried to warn Dubček on the eve of the invasion: 'Do you really not know the kind of people you're dealing with?'

Document 9.13   The Brezhnev Doctrine of Limited Sovereignty

On 25 August 1968 a small group entered Red Square in protest against the invasion of Czechoslovakia. Although the numbers directly involved were not large, the invasion was a greater shock to the Soviet public than was registered at the time. Like the invasion of Afghanistan in 1979, these Soviet interventions abroad served to undermine belief in the regime's competence to manage its own affairs, let alone foreign relations. The invasion was justified by what became known as the 'Brezhnev Doctrine': the fate of socialism was the responsibility not of any one country but of the whole socialist community.

In connection with the events in Czechoslovakia, the question of the correlation and interdependence of the national interests of the socialist countries and their international duties becomes particularly topical and acute. The measures taken by the Soviet Union, jointly with other socialist countries, in defending the socialist gains of the Czechoslovak people are of great significance for strengthening the socialist community, which is the main achievement of the international working class.

We cannot ignore the assertions, advanced in some places, that the actions of the five socialist countries run counter to the Marxist-Leninist principle of sovereignty and the rights of nations to self-determination. The baselessness of such reasoning consists primarily in that it is grounded on an abstract, nonclass approach to the question of sovereignty and the rights of nations to self-determination. The peoples of the socialist countries and communist parties certainly do have and should have the freedom to determine the way forward for their respective countries.

However, none of their decisions should damage either socialism in their country or the fundamental interests of other socialist countries, and the whole working class movement, which is working for socialism. This means that each communist party is responsible not only to its own people, but also to all the socialist countries, to the entire communist movement. Whoever forgets this, in stressing only the independence of a communist party, becomes one-sided. He deviates from his international duty . . .

The sovereignty of each socialist country cannot be opposed to the interests of the world of socialism, of the world revolutionary movement. Lenin demanded that all communists struggle against small-nation narrow-mindedness, separatism and isolation, to consider the whole and the general, to subordinate the particular to the general interest . . .

Each communist party is free to apply the basic principles of Marxism-Leninism and of socialism in its country, but it cannot depart from these principles (assuming, naturally, that it remains a communist party). Concretely, this means, primarily, that in its activity each communist party cannot but take into account such a decisive fact of our time as the struggle between two opposing social systems – capitalism and socialism.

Source: S. Kovalev, 'Sovereignty and the International Duties of Socialist Countries', Pravda, 25 September 1968.

The invasion put an end to an experiment that in many ways prefigured Gorbachev's reforms two decades later. The suppression of 'socialism with a human face' in Czechoslovakia made it infinitely more difficult for Gorbachev to implement a similar programme. In a sense, the invasion of 1968 represented the destruction of the sources of renewal within the Soviet system itself. In Eastern Europe thereafter the aim of intellectual and popular resistance appeared no longer to reform socialism but to *transcend* it.

Document 9.14   The *Praxis* View of Humanistic Socialism

One of the last outbreaks of Marxist reformism was the *Praxis* school from 1964 to 1974 in Yugoslavia. The notion of *praxis* in Marxist thought denotes the unity of theory and action. Drawing on the model of self-managing socialism that had developed in Yugoslavia following the break with the USSR in 1948, a group of humanist Marxists rejected the statist model and focused on the development of a socialism that would overcome the alienation of the individual. Tito responded with heavy-handed repression and thus destroyed one of the best chances for the democratic evolution of Yugoslavia. Thereafter opposition was driven down to the level of the republics, and took on increasingly nationalistic colourings. The path to the fragmentation of Yugoslavia was being prepared.

The orthodox, *Diamat* [dialectical materialist], view that the central philosophical problem is the relation of matter and mind has been generally rejected as abstract, ahistorical, dualistic. The central problem for Marx was – how to realize human nature by producing a more humane world. The fundamental philosophical assumption implicit in this problem is that man is essentially a being of *praxis*, i.e., a being capable of free creative activity by which he transforms the world, realizes his specific potential faculties and satisfies the needs of other human individuals. *Praxis* is an essential possibility for man but under certain unfavourable historical conditions its realization may be blocked. This discrepancy between the individual's actual existence and potential essence, i.e., between what he is and what he might be – is *alienation*. The basic task of philosophy is to critically analyse the phenomenon of alienation and to indicate practical steps leading to human *self-realization*, to *praxis*.

This is believed to be the common ground of Marxist humanism . . .

A philosophy based on the notion of *praxis* will naturally pay special attention to deriving practical consequences from its principles; furthermore, these consequences essentially will be steps that have to be taken in order to make true the idea of man as essentially a *being of praxis*.

Under what social conditions, in what kind of social organization can human activity become the objectification of the individual's most creative capacities and a means of satisfying genuine individual and common needs?

This question is much more general than the one usually asked by Marxists who ignore the philosophical roots of Marx's economic and political criticism. All questions about specific social institutions, such as: private property capital, the bourgeois state and so on boil down to the fundamental issue: what happens to man, what are his relationships to other human beings, does he actualize or waste all the wealth of his potential powers?

Source: Mihailo Markovic, 'Marxist Philosophy in Yugoslavia: The Praxis Group', in Mihailo Markovic and Robert S. Cohen, The Rise and Fall of Socialist Humanism (Nottingham, Spokesman Books, 1975), pp. 31–2, 37.

Document 9.15 Meaningful Marxism

Svetozar Stojanovic was one of the most original and perceptive of the new humanistic Yugoslav socialists. His critique of Stalinism returned to the themes raised by Lukács and others, and above all focused on 'the epochal dilemma' – the relationship between socialism and democracy.

While revolutionary dictatorship is not democracy, i.e., rule of the people, it is to a great extent rule for the people. Its undemocratic form, however, soon begins to have a destructive impact upon its content. Rule in the name of the people can be rule in the interests of the people for a short time only and thereafter tends to become transformed into rule against the people . . . The abuse of revolutionary force has its limits, beyond which we can no longer speak of abuse, but rather of a change in the nature of that force: it becomes force against the revolution . . .

With Stalinism the dictatorship turned from the dispossessed classes to the revolutionary movement itself. The theory of increased external danger and class struggle in socialism was used as the pretext for this. In fact, terror was used predominantly for mutual reprisals within the revolutionary movement itself.

The growth of revolutionary dictatorship into socialist democracy is not simply one of the problems of socialism; it is *the problem of socialism*. Rosa Luxemburg perceptively warned that there can be no socialism without democracy. Just as capitalism is inconceivable without the emancipation of the forces of labor and the free movement of capital, so socialism cannot develop without social ownership and democracy.

Source: Svetozar Stojanovic, 'The Epochal Dilemma', in Between Ideals and Reality (New York, Oxford University Press, 1973), pp. 107, 108.

Document 9.16   Deutscher on the 'Unfinished Revolution'

While Trotsky had talked in terms of a 'revolution betrayed', Isaac Deutscher insisted that the revolution was 'unfinished', that is, that it retained an evolutionary potential. In his analysis of the Soviet Union on the fiftieth anniversary of the revolution, Deutscher, like many in the *Praxis* group and other dissident socialist intellectuals, used the 'gravedigger' analogy to suggest that having brought a modern industrial society and proletariat into being, the bureaucratic-statist model of socialism could give way to a more humanistic version. Based on a lecture celebrating the fiftieth anniversary of the revolution, Deutscher provided a thought-provoking analysis of the revolution itself and its evolution, and looked forward to the 'completion' of the socialist project in Russia.

What is the significance of the Russian revolution for our generation and age? Has the revolution fulfilled the hopes it aroused or has it failed to do so? It is natural that these questions should be asked anew now that half a century has passed since the fall of Tsardom and the establishment of the first Soviet government. The distance which separates us from these events seems long enough to yield a historical perspective. Even so, the distance may well be too short. This has been the most crowded and cataclysmic epoch in modern history. The Russian revolution has raised issues far deeper, has stirred conflicts more violent, and has unleashed forces far larger than those that had been involved in the greatest social upheavals of the past. And yet the revolution has by no means come to a close. It is still on the move. It may still surprise us by its sharp and sudden turns. It is still capable of re-drawing its own perspective. The ground we are entering is one which historians either fear to tread or must tread with fear . . .

But is it still the same party? Can we really speak of the revolution's continuity? Official Soviet ideologues claim that the continuity has never been broken. Others say that it has been preserved as an outward form only, as an ideological shell concealing realities that have nothing in common with the high aspirations of 1917. The truth seems to me more complex and ambiguous than these conflicting assertions suggest. But let us assume for a moment that the continuity is a mere appearance. We have still to ask what has caused the Soviet Union to cling to it so stubbornly? And how can an empty form, not sustained by any corresponding content, endure for so long? When successive Soviet leaders and rulers restate their allegiance to the original purposes and aims of the revolution, we cannot take their declarations at their face value; but neither can we dismiss them as wholly irrelevant . . .

We need not assume that the course of the Russian revolution was predetermined in all its features or in the sequence of all its major phases and incidents. But its general direction had been set not by the events of a few years or months; it had been prepared by the developments of many decades, indeed of several epochs. The historian who labours to reduce the mountain of the revolution to a few contingencies stands as helpless before it as once stood the political leaders who sought to prevent its rise . . .

No automatic economic mechanism, however, produces the final disintegration of an old established order or assures the success of a revolution. An obsolete social system may be declining in the course of decades, and the bulk of the nation may be unaware of it. Social consciousness lags behind social being. The objective contradictions of the *ancien régime* have to translate themselves into subjective terms, into the ideas, aspirations, and passions of men in action. The essence of revolution, says Trotsky, is 'the direct intervention of the masses in historic events.' It is because of that intervention – a phenomenon so real and so rare in history – that the year 1917 was so remarkable and momentous. The great mass of the people were seized by the most intense and urgent awareness of decay and rot in the established order . . .

In 1917 Russia lived through the last of the great bourgeois revolutions and the first proletarian revolution in European history. The two revolutions merged into one. Their unprecedented coalescence imparted extraordinary vitality and *élan* to the new regime; but it was also the source of severe strains and stresses and cataclysmic convulsions . . .

The Russian revolution had some streaks of irrationality in common with the bourgeois revolutions of which it was the last. This is, in a sense, the bourgeois element in its character. As the master of the purges, Stalin was Cromwell's and Robespierre's descendant. His terror was far more cruel and repulsive than theirs, for he exercised power over a much longer period, in more daunting circumstances, and in a country accustomed over the ages to barbarous brutality in its rulers. Stalin, we should remember, was also the descendant of Ivan the Terrible, Peter the Great, Nicholas I, and Alexander III. Indeed, Stalinism may be described as the amalgam of Marxism with Russia's primordial and savage backwardness. In any case, in Russia the aspirations of the revolution and its realities were far wider apart than anywhere else; and so it took far more blood and far greater hypocrisy to cover up the terrible discrepancy . . .

I have spoken about the incongruity of the attempt to establish social control over a productive process which is not social in character, and also about the impossibility of a socialism founded on want and scarcity. The whole history of the Soviet Union in these fifty years has been a struggle, partly successful and partly not, to resolve this incongruity and to overcome want and scarcity. This meant, in the first instance, intensive industrialization as a means towards an end, not an end in itself . . .

In their political life also the Russians all too often feel that they have run fast to keep in the same place. The half-freedom the Soviet Union has won since Stalin's days can indeed be even more excruciating than a complete and hermetic tyranny . . .

The failure of the official de-Stalinization is at the heart of the malaise. It is more than a decade now since, at the Twentieth Congress, Khrushchev exposed Stalin's misdeeds. That act could make sense only if it had been the prelude to a genuine clarification of the many issues raised by it and to an open nation-wide debate on the legacy of the Stalin era. This has not been the case. Khrushchev and the ruling group at large were eager not to open the debate but to prevent it. They intended the prologue to be also the epilogue of the de-Stalinization . . .

In the Soviet Union, we know, the revolution has survived all possible agents of restoration. Yet it seems to be burdened with a mass of accumulated disillusionment and even despair that in other historical circumstances might have been the driving force of a restoration. At times the Soviet Union appears to be fraught with the moral-psychological potentiality of restoration that cannot become a political actuality. Much of the record of these fifty years is utterly discredited in the eyes of the people; and no returned Romanovs are going to rehabilitate it. The revolution must rehabilitate itself, by its own efforts.

Source: Isaac Deutscher, The Unfinished Revolution: Russia 1917–1967 *(Oxford, Oxford University Press, 1967), pp. 3, 5, 8–9, 13, 21, 34, 37, 100, 101, 105.*

Within-system Reform and Beyond

There remained in the USSR hopes that the system could change from within. The samizdat *Political Diary*, edited by Roy Medvedev, for example, reflected the belief that the system retained an evolutionary socialist potential. Publishing a range of views, the journal believed that an enlightened public opinion in society, and the emergence of a reformist section in the elite, would allow the Soviet system to lose some of its coercive features while removing the restrictions that inhibited the creative potential of the economy and society.

Document 9.17 A Reformist Programme for Democratisation

An important document outlining a draft programme for the gradual democratisation of the Soviet system, echoing many of the themes of the *Action Programme* and anticipating in uncanny detail Gorbachev's reforms in the late 1980s, was a letter dated 19 March 1970. Its authors were Andrei Sakharov (1921–89), a member of the Soviet Academy of Sciences who had played a central role in developing Soviet nuclear weapons and the author of *Progress, Coexistence, and Intellectual Freedom* (1968), Valerii Turchin, also a renowned physicist, and Roy Medvedev, the historian whose work on Stalinism, *Let History Judge* (1968), broke new ground in analysing Stalin's dictatorial rule. He later summarised his ideas on the socialist democratisation of the USSR in his *On Socialist Democracy* (1971), which is cited below (Document 9.25). The letter identified the central problems in Soviet society and appealed to the leadership to achieve self-reform based on a programme of ideas that drew on many topical ideas. Its tone was loyal, internationalist and socialist. Sakharov soon abandoned hopes that the regime would reform itself, while Turchin was forced to emigrate in 1977. Quite apart from its recommendations for change, the document represented an acute and accurate portrait of the problems affecting the Soviet Union.

To L. I. Brezhnev, Central Committee of the CPSU; A. N. Kosygin, USSR Council of Ministers; N.V. Podgorny, Presidium of the Supreme Soviet of the USSR:

Respected Comrades:
We are appealing to you on a question of great importance. Our country has made great strides in the development of production, in the fields of education and culture, in the basic improvement of the living conditions of the working class, and in the development of new socialist human relationships. Our achievements have universal historical significance. They have deeply affected events throughout the world and have laid a firm foundation for the further development of the cause of communism. However, serious difficulties and shortcomings are also evident.

This letter will discuss and develop a point of view which can be formulated briefly by the following theses:

1 At the present time there is an urgent need to carry out a series of measures directed toward the further democratisation of our country's public life. This need stems, in particular, from the very close connection between the problem of technological and economic progress and scientific methods of management, on the one hand, and the problems of freedom of information, the open airing of views, and the free clash of ideas, on the other. This need also stems from other domestic and foreign political problems.
2 Democratisation must promote the maintenance and consolidation of the Soviet socialist system, the socialist economic structure, our social and cultural achievements, and socialist ideology.
3 Democratisation, carried out under the leadership of the CPSU in collaboration with all strata of society, should maintain and strengthen the leading role of the party in the economic, political, and cultural life of society.
4 Democratisation should be gradual in order to avoid possible complications and disruptions. At the same time it should be thoroughgoing, carried out consistently in accordance with a carefully worked-out programme. Without fundamental democratisation, our society will not be able to solve the problems now facing it, and will not be able to develop in a normal manner . . .

Over the past decade menacing signs of disorder and stagnation have begun to show themselves in the economy of our country, the roots of which go back to an earlier period and are very deeply ingrained. There is an uninterrupted decline in the rate of growth of the national income . . . Defects in the system of planning, accounting, and incentives often cause contradictions between the local and departmental interests and those of the state and nation. As a result, new means of developing production potential are not being discovered or properly put to use and technical progress has slowed down abruptly. For these very reasons, the natural wealth of the country is often destroyed with impunity and without any supervision or controls: forests are levelled, reservoirs polluted, valuable agricultural land inundated, soil eroded or salinised, etc. The chronically difficult situation in agriculture, particularly in regard to livestock, is well known. The population's real income in recent years has hardly grown at all; food supply and medical and consumer services are improving very slowly, and with unevenness between regions. The number of goods in short supply continue to grow. There are clear signs of inflation.

Of particular concern regarding our country's future is the lag in the development of education: our total expenditures for education in all forms are three times below what they are in the United States, and are rising at a slower rate. Alcoholism is growing in a tragic way and drug addiction is beginning to surface. In many regions of the country the crime rate is climbing systematically. Signs of corruption are becoming more and more noticeable in a number of places. In the work of scientific and scientific-technical organisations, bureaucratism, departmentalism, a formal attitude toward one's tasks, and lack of initiative are becoming more and more pronounced . . .

What is wrong? Why have we not only failed to be the pioneers of the second industrial revolution, but have in fact found ourselves incapable of keeping pace with the developed capitalist countries? Is it possible that socialism provides fewer opportunities for the development of productive forces than capitalism? Or that in the economic competition between capitalism and socialism, capitalism is winning?

Of course not! The source of our difficulties does not lie in the socialist system, but on the contrary, it lies in those peculiarities and conditions of our life which run contrary to socialism and are hostile to it. The source lies in the antidemocratic traditions and norms of public life established in the Stalin era, which have not been decisively eliminated to this day . . .

The overwhelming majority of the intelligentsia and the youth recognise the need for democratisation, and the need for it to be cautious and gradual, but they cannot understand and justify measures of a patently antidemocratic nature. And, indeed, how can one justify the confinement in prisons, camps, and insane asylums of people who hold oppositionist views but whose opposition stands on legal ground, in the area of ideas and convictions?

In many instances, there was no opposition involved, but only a striving for information, or simply a courageous and unprejudiced discussion of important social questions. The imprisonment of writers for what they have written is inadmissible. It is also impossible to understand or justify such an absurd and extremely harmful measure as the expulsion from the Soviet Writers' Union of the most significant popular writer [Solzhenitsyn], who has shown himself to be deeply patriotic and humane in all that he does. Equally incomprehensible is the purging of the editorial board of *Novy mir*, around which the most progressive forces in the Marxist-Leninist socialist tendency had rallied.

It is indispensable to speak once again about ideological problems. Democratisation, with its fullness of information and clash of ideas, must restore to our ideological life its dynamism and creativity – in the social sciences, art, and propaganda – and liquidate the bureaucratic, ritualistic, dogmatic, openly hypocritical, and mediocre style that reigns in these areas today.

A course toward democratisation would bridge the gulf between the party and state apparatus and the intelligentsia. The mutual lack of understanding will give way to close cooperation. A course toward democratisation would inspire a wave of enthusiasm comparable to that which prevailed in the 1920s. The best intellectual forces in the country would be mobilised for the solution of economic and social problems . . .

We propose the following draft programme of measures which could be realised over a four-to-five-year period:

1 A statement from the highest Party and government bodies on the necessity for further democratisation and on the rate and means of achieving it. The publication in the press of a number of articles containing a discussion of the problems of democratisation.
2 Limited distribution (through Party organs, enterprises and institutions) of information on the situation in the country and theoretical works on social problems which at the present time would not be made the object of broad discussion. Gradual increase of access to these materials until all limitations on their distribution have been lifted.
3 Extensive, planned organisation of complex industrial associations with a high degree of autonomy in matters of industrial planning, technological processes, raw material supply, sale of products, finances and personnel. The expansion of these rights for smaller productive units as well. Scientific determination after careful research of the form and degree of state regulation.
4 Cessation of interference with foreign radio broadcasts. Free sale of foreign books and periodicals. Adherence by our country to the international copyright convention. Gradual expansion and encouragement of international tourism in both directions (over a three- to four-year period),

expansion of international postal communications, and other measures for broadening international communications, with special emphasis in this regard on member nations of Comecon.

5 Establishment of an institute for public opinion research. The publication (limited at first but later complete) of materials indicating public attitudes on the most important domestic and foreign policy questions, as well as of other sociological materials.

6 Amnesty for political prisoners. An order requiring publication of the complete record of all trials of a political character. Public supervision of all prisons, camps and psychiatric institutions.

7 Introduction of measures to improve the functioning of the courts and the procuracy and to enhance their independence from executive powers, local influences, prejudices and personal ties.

8 Abolition of the indication of nationality on passports and questionnaires. Uniform passport system for the inhabitants of cities and villages. Gradual elimination of the system of passport registration, to be accomplished simultaneously with the evening up of economic and cultural inequalities between different regions of our country.

9 Reforms in education: increased appropriations for elementary and secondary schools; improving the living standard of teachers and increasing their autonomy and leeway to experiment.

10 Passage of a law on information and the press. Guaranteeing the right of social organisation and citizens' groups to establish new publications. Complete elimination of prior censorship in every form.

11 Improvement in the training of leadership cadres in the art of management. Introduction of special managerial training programmes on the job. Improvement in the information available to leading cadres at all levels, increasing their autonomy, their rights to experiment, to defend their opinions, and to test them in practice.

12 Gradual introduction of the practice of having several candidates in elections to party and Soviet bodies on every level, even for indirect elections.

13 Expansion of the rights of Soviets; expansion of the rights and the responsibilities of the Supreme Soviet of the USSR.

14 Restoration of the rights of those nationalities deported under Stalin. The re-establishment of the national autonomy of deported peoples with the opportunity for them to resettle in their homeland (in those cases where until now this has not been realised).

15 Measures directed toward increasing public discussion in the work of governing bodies, commensurate with the interests of the state. Establishment of consultative scientific committees to work with the government bodies at every level, such committees to include highly qualified specialists in the different disciplines . . .

Respected comrades! There is no way out of the difficulties now facing our country except a course toward democratisation, carried out by the Communist Party in accordance with a carefully worked-out plan. A turn to the right – that is, a victory for the forces that advocate a stronger administration, a 'tightening of the screws' – would not only fail to solve any of the problems but, on the contrary, would aggravate them to an extreme point and lead our country into a tragic impasse. The tactic of waiting passively would ultimately have the same result. Today we still have the chance to set out on the right path and to carry out the necessary reforms. In a few years it may be too late. The recognition of this is a necessity on a nationwide scale. The duty of all who see the causes of these problems and the road to their solution is to point out this road to their fellow citizens. Understanding the need for, and possibility of, gradual democratisation is the first step along the road to its achievement.

Sources: Izvestiya TsK KPSS, *no. 11, 1990, pp. 150–9; Cohen (ed.),* An End to Silence, *from* Political Diary, *no. 66, March 1970, pp. 317–19, 320–1, 322–5, 327.*

This could be taken as a blueprint for Gorbachev's reforms a generation later. By then the crisis symptoms identified here had become much sharper, and the proposed piecemeal remedies less convincing. Later that year (4 November 1970) Sakharov, Valerii Chalidze and Andrei Tverdokhlebov formed the Committee for Human Rights in an attempt to ensure that the regime obeyed its own laws in the sphere of human rights guided, as they put it, by the 'humanist principles of the Universal Declaration of Human Rights', adopted by the United Nations in 1948. Chalidze was forced to emigrate in late 1972, but Sakharov remained a thorn in the Soviet regime's side until in the early 1980s he was sent into internal exile to Gorkii (now renamed Nizhnii Novgorod).

Document 9.18   Rostropovich on Solzhenitsyn

The award to Solzhenitsyn of the Nobel Prize for literature on 8 October 1970 was treated by the party leadership as a 'provocative act', and a 'top secret' (*sovershenno sekretno*) order was given for a campaign to be launched to discredit the author and to argue that the award was not a literary but a political act. The cellist Mstislav Rostropovich sheltered Solzhenitsyn, and in an open letter on 31 October 1970 he condemned the intellectual closure of the period.

Dear Comrade Editor,
It is no longer a secret that A. Solzhenitsyn spends most of his time in my house not far from Moscow. I witnessed his expulsion from the Union of Writers at the very time when he was working hard on the novel [*August*] *1914*, and now comes the award of the Nobel Prize to him and the

newspaper campaign about this. It is the latter that forces me to take up my pen to you.

This is already the third Soviet author to receive the Nobel Prize, but in two out of the three cases [Solzhenitsyn and Boris Pasternak] we consider the award a dirty political game, but in one (Sholokhov) as the due recognition of a world-class author . . . People should not be forced to condemn what they quite simply have not read or heard. I remember with pride that I did not attend the meeting of cultural figures . . . where they abused B. Pasternak and designated a speech for me to make criticising *Doctor Zhivago* at a time when I had not even read it . . .

Every person should have the right without fear to think independently and to speak out on what they know, what they have personally thought, lived through, and not only weakly vary what has been instilled into them. We will inevitably achieve free thought without prompting and pressure . . .

Mstislav Rostropovich

Source: Reprinted in Izvestiya, *13 April 1992.*

Document 9.19   The View from Within

The KGB reported on the views of the population, and these declassified files now provide a rich source of information about the deep processes going on in Soviet society. On 21 December 1970 Andropov, the head of the KGB since 1967 and future leader of the USSR, reported on the situation, in particular the seditious attempts by parts of the intelligentsia to achieve 'democratic socialism'.

Top Secret
Among the scientific, technical and part of the creative intelligentsia documents are being passed around in which various forms of 'democratic socialism' are being propounded. According to one of these schemes of 'democratic socialism', whose author is Academician Sakharov, the evolutionary path of internal political development of the USSR will inevitably lead to the creation in the country of a 'truly democratic system'. As part of this, mathematicians and economists should in good time develop its model so that it could be a synthesis of what is positive in existing socio-political systems.

In a number of projects for the 'democratisation' of the USSR the 'restriction or liquidation of the monopoly power of the CPSU and the national development of an opposition loyal to socialism' is envisaged. Their authors and distributors consider that the current level of development of socialist democracy should allow opposition views to exist, and demand legal opportunities to express views that disagree with the official course to be made available. From this perspective they declare that criminal legislation that prosecutes anti-Soviet agitation and propaganda or the distribution of obviously false fabrications, smearing the Soviet state and its social system, is unconstitutional.

On the basis of the preparation and distribution of 'samizdat' literature there is taking place a noticeable consolidation of like-minded persons, and there are marked indications of attempts to create something like an opposition.

Approximately towards the end of 1968–early 1969 there emerged out of oppositionally minded elements a political core, called the 'democratic movement', which in their view has the three characteristics of an opposition: they 'have leaders, activists and are based on a significant number of sympathisers, not taking on the clear shape of an organisation, but set themselves clear aims and choose a suitable tactic, to gain legality'.

The main aims of the 'movement', as formulated in the thirteenth issue of *The Chronicle of Current Events* issued by the Moscow group of the 'democratic movement' headed by Yakir, is 'the democratisation of the country by developing in people democratic and scientific convictions, resistance to Stalinism, self-defence from repression, the struggle against extremism of whatever sort'.

Sources: Istochnik, *no. 2, 1994, pp. 75–6;* Rossiya, kotoruyu my ne znali, *p. 327.*

It goes without saying that Andropov stressed that the KGB was taking 'the necessary measures' to suppress the movement, but (indicative of a more sophisticated approach) called for the ideological apparatus to devise ideological and political measures to neutralise the movement and to deal with the political factors that allowed samizdat material to be distributed. On 21 June 1972 Petr Yakir was arrested and charged under article 70 of the RSFSR Criminal Code, covering 'anti-Soviet agitation and propaganda'. His father, General Iona Yakir, a hero of the Civil War, had been shot in 1937 along with most of the rest of the Red Army high command. At the time of his arrest Petr Yakir had stated: 'If I "confess", that means they have tortured me; if I "commit suicide", that means they have murdered me.' After interrogation in the notorious Lefortovo gaol he is alleged to have recanted in December 1972, and in a 'show trial' in August 1973, he and his co-defendant Viktor Krasin made public confessions and received light sentences.

Document 9.20   Bukovsky – In the Camps

Arrested as a student in the early 1960s for political activities and first sentenced in 1963, Vladimir Bukovsky spent twelve years in the Soviet nightmare world between the Gulag and psychiatric hospitals. The scene of his struggle was the Gulag, fighting for every right and benefit possible, seeking to use the system against itself. The role of the West as a conduit and echo chamber for Soviet dissident demands and concerns is highlighted here. It was pressure from the West that led to his expulsion in December 1976, in exchange for the Chilean communist leader Luis Corvalan.

Neither Zhores Medvedev nor his brother Roy thought at that time that a noisy campaign would harm our cause – would assist the 'hawks' and hinder the 'doves' in the Soviet leadership. On the contrary, having landed in trouble, they realised only too well that nothing except wide publicity would help them. Every day, Roy Medvedev issued a news bulletin on the latest developments. Exploiting his connections in the respectable world, he persuaded people who didn't usually participate in our protests to write or sign letters in support of his brother. This event had major repercussions throughout the entire world, and although the authorities surrendered fairly quickly – after nineteen days – our statements about the psychiatric method of repression were freshly confirmed. We conceived the hope that a sufficiently energetic campaign might force the authorities to abandon the use of psychiatry for repressive purposes altogether.

It was all right for Zhores Medvedev – he was well enough known in the scientific world. But what could be done for the workman Borisov, the bricklayer Gershuni, the students Novodvorskaya and Ioffe, or the stage designer Victor Kuznetsov? For them there was no prospect of academicians raising hell with the Central Committee or the world community of scientists threatening a scientific boycott. According to our information, there were hundreds of little-known individuals being held in psychiatric prisons for political reasons. Who would take up the struggle on their behalf?

I came to the conclusion that it was essential to assemble an extensive documentation, including the testimony of witnesses and the findings of the panels of doctors. The authorities' basic argument boiled down to the simple point that non-specialists could not dispute the findings of specialists. Any attempt to do so would be interpreted by them as slander. All right, I would try to find honest specialists.

Everyone contributed his bit to the documentation. The fundamental part, of course, came from our lawyers, who had defended the 'unit to plead' and had access to their case files. Only from them could we get copies of the genuine findings of the experts . . . Then came letters and testimony from prisoners still in psychiatric prisons (and from their families) about the present prison regime. To judge by their accounts, little had changed since my time, except that the 'treatment' had if anything become more intensive and more painful. We also collected evidence of the opening of new special hospitals, together with photographs of them and the names of the doctors responsible for these psychiatric abuses.

The best-known case at that time was the case of General Grigorenko. His 1969 prison diary, with its detailed description of his investigation and psychiatric examination, had already been published in the West. [(Translator's note) Major-General Pyotr Grigoryevich Grigorenko, a much-decorated Red Army commander, who in 1961 began to denounce Stalinism and call for a return to Leninist principles. In 1964 he was arrested and committed to the Leningrad Special Mental Hospital where he was held for fifteen months. He became one of the unofficial leaders of the human-rights movement, and in 1969 was arrested in Tashkent, where he had gone to give evidence in the trial of some Crimean Tartars, and again committed to a mental hospital. During his investigation he wrote his prison diary, published in *The Grigorenko Papers* (Christopher Hurst, 1976). Having been declared sane by the Tashkent doctors, he was committed to the Serbsky Institute, which at once pronounced him insane. He spent the next five years in the Chernyakhovsk Special Mental Hospital until his release in 1974. In 1978, Grigorenko was allowed to visit his son in the USA and then deprived of his Soviet citizenship.] But few people know that his first examination in Tashkent, by a panel headed by Dr Detengof, not only had concluded that he was fully fit, but had emphatically recommended that no more examinations be conducted in the future. After this the KGB hastily dispatched him to the Serbsky Institute in Moscow for a second specialist examination, where it was no trouble at all for Lunts to dress up his 'sensitivity' and 'negative attitude to residing in psychiatric clinics' as paranoia, 'accompanied by reformist ideas'.

I myself knew Grigorenko very well, knew his family intimately. Rarely in my life have I met a man who was more cautious in his judgements or more diffident and self-critical. But the trouble was that my 'honest specialists', if ever I found them, wouldn't know Grigorenko personally. I would have to rely on the findings speaking for themselves . . .

Up till the early 1970s, all the Soviet Union's political camps were situated in Mordovia. There have been political camps there since the very beginning of the Soviet regime. Practically all of Mordovia was criss-crossed with barbed wire . . .

The number of people who have died there is incalculable, and when they dig in the ground, they invariably turn up human bones. They used to say that one survivor had been in the camps from the first years to the last, a participant in the Kronstadt rising. An old, old man, taciturn and ailing, he used to walk about the compound with a pronounced roll, as if on the deck of a cruiser in a storm . . .

I was sent straight to camp 35, near the station of Vsesvyatskaya. I had spent the first year after my trial in Vladimir prison – my sentence had decreed two years in jail, five in the camps, and five years' internal exile. By the spring of 1973, when I was due to be sent to a camp, the 'Perm experiment' had been completed and I never saw Mordovia.

Our camp was a small one of about 300–350 people – and the majority of its population, as in the other political camps, consisted of 'veterans' – Ukrainians and Lithuanians who had participated in the national liberation struggles of the 1940s. Many of these prisoners had never experienced normal life in the Soviet Union, because ever since they took to arms in their youth when their lands were invaded by Soviet troops, they had been languishing in the labour camps. These were the remnants of a generation that had been completely shattered. In Lithuania alone, the 'liberators' had repressed 350,000 of the population; in the Ukraine, the total ran into millions. They had been jailed for treason to their motherland. Which motherland Stalin's military tribunal had in mind it is difficult to say . . .

The year 1973 was in a certain sense a decisive one for our movement as a whole. Having achieved a certain amount of success with the Yakir–Krasin trial, the authorities moved quickly to paralyse the entire movement. (Yakir and Krasin's public confessions in 1973 were used by the KGB to discredit the entire human-rights movement.) Dozens of people were subjected to open blackmail. They were threatened with the arrest, not of themselves but of their families and friends if they didn't put a stop to their human-rights activities. The *Chronicle of Current Events* came to a temporary halt: the KGB promised to meet each new number with fresh arrests. It was a system of taking hostages. Simultaneously, they unleashed a frenzied campaign of persecution against Solzhenitsyn and Sakharov, following their familiar recipe – from academicians to deer-breeders to milk-maids.

It is always like that, it is sufficient for one to weaken and the pressure increases on all. Ten men surrendering to blackmail can sow panic among tens of thousands. Camp life is like a barometer, and at such moments the regime is savagely tightened, achievements won by years of hunger strikes are suddenly lost again, and everyone finds himself on the edge of oblivion. A superhuman effort is required to preserve your life and your rights . . .

Outside, the turning point came later, with the deportation of Solzhenitsyn in January 1974. This event rocked everybody, and, as happens at moments of real disaster, strengthened their resolution. The *Chronicle of Current Events* started appearing again, but the authorities no longer risked using the system of hostages, and the promised arrests never took place. The blackmail ended as soon as people ceased to submit to it. But we faced a long and uphill struggle to get back everything we had lost during that term.

Source: Vladimir Bukovsky, To Build a Castle: My Life as a Dissenter, *translated by Michael Scammell (London, André Deutsch, 1978), pp. 285–7, 320–1, 333–4.*

From Under the Rubble

We have already referred (Chapter 1) to the *Landmarks* (*Vekhi*) collection of essays of 1909, in which a group of leading Russian philosophers criticised the revolutionism and narrow sectarianism of the Russian intelligentsia. A number of them contributed to a second volume in 1918 called *De Profundis* (*From the Depths*), an attempt to come to terms with the political and spiritual disaster that had overtaken Russia. In a totally different style, yet still grappling with similar issues, was the émigré movement called *Smenavekh* (Change of Landmarks), who in 1922 sought to reconcile themselves with the Bolsheviks as fulfilling certain national tasks. They were given short shrift by the Bolsheviks themselves, but the name became synonymous with capitulationism to Bolshevik power. The fourth in the series was a collection of essays edited by Solzhenitsyn in 1974 under the title *From under the Rubble* (*Iz-pod glyb*, which echoes the Russian of *De Profundis*, *Iz glubiny*). Contributors included not only Solzhenitsyn (with three articles) but Mikhail Agursky (who had written much on Russian national rebirth), and Igor Shafarevich, who later went on to write a notorious pamphlet called *Russophobia*, which presents the view that the West (and not only the West) was permeated by a profound hostility to Russia. The collection signalled a new stage in the development of Russian national consciousness.

Document 9.21 'As Breathing and Consciousness Return'

In his first contribution, 'As Breathing and Consciousness Return', Solzhenitsyn responded to some of the points developed by Sakharov in his book of 1968, *Progress, Coexistence, and Intellectual Freedom*, but at the same time developed a philosophy of freedom that stood in sharp contrast to the instrumental morality of Leninism, and indeed the consumerism of the West. He begins by commenting on the notion of 'Stalinism'.

'Stalinism' is a very convenient concept for those 'purified' Marxist circles of ours, who strive to differentiate themselves from the official line, though in reality the difference is negligible (Roy Medvedev may be mentioned as a typical example of this trend). For the same purpose the concept of 'Stalinism' is still more important and necessary to Western Communist parties – they shift onto it the whole bloody burden of the past to make their present position easier. (In this category belong such Communist theorists as G. Lukács and I. Deutscher.) It is no less necessary to those broad Left liberal circles in the West which in Stalin's lifetime applauded highly coloured pictures of Soviet life, and after the Twentieth Congress found themselves looking most painfully silly.

But close study of our modern history shows that there never was any such thing as Stalinism (either as a doctrine, or as a path of national life, or as a state system), and official circles in our country, as well as the Chinese leaders, have every right to insist on this. Stalin was a very consistent and faithful – if also very untalented – heir to the spirit of Lenin's teaching . . .

Certainly intellectual freedom in our country would immediately bring about a great transformation and help us to cleanse ourselves of many stains. Seen from the dark hole into which we are cast, that is so. But if we gaze into the far, far future – let us consider the West. The West has supped more than its fill of every kind of freedom, including intellectual freedom. And has this saved it? We see it today crawling on hands and knees, its will paralyzed, uneasy about the future, spiritually racked and dejected. Unlimited external freedom in itself is quite inadequate to save us.

Intellectual freedom is a very desirable gift, but, like any sort of freedom, a gift of conditional, not intrinsic, worth, only a means by which we can attain another and higher goal.

In accordance with his demand for freedom, Sakharov proposes to introduce the multiparty system in 'socialist' countries. Obstruction to this of course comes entirely from the regime, not from the public. But let us for our part try to rise above Western conceptions to a loftier viewpoint. Do we not discern in the multiparty parliamentary system yet another idol, but this time one to which the whole world bows down? . . . Are there no extraparty or strictly nonparty paths of national development? . . .

The multiparty parliamentary system, which some among us consider the only true embodiment of freedom, has already existed for centuries in some Western European countries. Its dangerous, perhaps mortal defects have become more and more obvious in recent decades, when superpowers are rocked by party struggles with no ethical basis; when a tiny party can hold the balance between two big ones and over an extended period determine the fate of its own and even neighbouring peoples; when unlimited freedom of discussion can wreck a country's resistance to some looming danger and lead to capitulation in wars not yet lost; when the historical democracies prove impotent, faced with a handful of snivelling terrorists. The Western democracies today are in a state of political crisis and spiritual confusion. Today, more than at any time in the past century, it ill becomes us to see our country's only way out in the Western parliamentary system. Especially since Russia's readiness for such a system, which was very doubtful in 1917, can only have declined still further in the half century since . . .

If Russia for centuries was used to living under autocratic systems and suffered total collapse under the democratic system which lasted eight months in 1917, perhaps – I am only asking not making an assertion – perhaps we should recognize that the evolution of our country from one form of authoritarianism to another would be the most natural, the smoothest, the least painful path of development for it to follow? . . .

The state system which exists in our country is terrible not because it is undemocratic, authoritarian, based on physical constraint – a man can live in such conditions without harm to his spiritual essence.

Our present system is unique in world history because over and above its physical and economic constraints, it demands of us total surrender of our souls, continuous and active participation in the general, conscious lie. To this putrefaction of the soul, this spiritual enslavement, human beings who wish to be human cannot consent. When Caesar, having exacted what is Caesar's, demands still more insistently that we render unto him what is God's – that is a sacrifice we dare not make!

The most important part of our freedom, inner freedom, is always subject to our will. If we surrender it to corruption, we do not deserve to be called human.

But let us note that if the absolutely essential task is not political liberation, but the liberation of our souls from participation in the lie forced upon us, then it requires no physical, revolutionary, social, organizational measures, no meetings, strikes, trade unions – things fearful for us even to contemplate and from which we quite naturally allow circumstances to dissuade us. No! It requires from each individual a moral step within his power – no more than that. And no one who voluntarily runs with the hounds of falsehood, or props it up, will ever be able to justify himself to the living, or to posterity, or to his friends, or to his children.

We have no one to blame but ourselves, and therefore all our anonymous philippics and programs and explanations are not worth a farthing. If mud and dung cling to any of us it is of his own free will and no man's mud is made any the less black by the mud of his neighbours.

Sources: Alexander Solzhenitsyn, 'As Breathing and Consciousness Return', in Solzhenitsyn (ed.), From under the Rubble *(London, Fontana/Collins, 1974), pp. 12, 18–19, 22–3, 24–5;* Iz-pod glyb: sbornik statei *(Moscow, Russkaya kniga, 1992), 10–11, 15–16, 18–19, 20–21.*

Document 9.22 'Repentance and Self-limitation in the Life of Nations'

Solzhenitsyn's second contribution to the collection focused on the need for repentence and 'self-limitation' in national development. His argument combined views on sustainable development with a powerful argument about the moral economy of politics.

How then can we transfer to society and the nation that which does not exist on the individual level? Perhaps this article is premature or altogether pointless? We start, however, from what seems to us beyond doubt: that true repentance and self-limitation will shortly reappear in the personal and the social sphere, that a hollow place in modern man is ready to receive them. Obviously then the time has come to consider this as a path for whole nations to follow. Our understanding of it must not lag behind the inevitable development of self-generating governmental policies.

We have so bedeviled the world, brought it so close to self-destruction, that repentance is now a matter of life and death – not for the sake of a life beyond the grave (which is thought merely comic nowadays), but for the sake of our life here and now and our very survival on this earth . . .

It is by now only too obvious how dearly mankind has paid for the fact that we have all throughout the ages preferred to censure, denounce and hate others, instead of censuring, denouncing and hating ourselves. But obvious though it may be, we are even now, with the twentieth century on its way out, reluctant to recognize that the universal dividing line between good and evil runs not between countries, not between nations, not between parties, not between classes, not even between good and bad men: the dividing line cuts across nations and parties, shifting constantly, yielding now to the pressure of light, now to the pressure of darkness. It divides the heart of every man, and there too it is not a ditch dug once and for all, but fluctuates with the passage of time and according to a man's behavior . . .

One of the peculiarities of Russian history is that our evil doing has always, even up to the present day, taken the same direction: we have done evil on a massive scale and mainly in our own country, not abroad, not to others, but at home to our own people, to ourselves. No one has borne so much of the suffering as the Russians, Ukrainians and Byelorussians. So that as we awaken to repentance we shall have to remember much that concerns only us, and for which outsiders will not reproach us . . .

What a state of disrepair twentieth-century Russian history is in, how grotesquely distorted and full of obscurities, if people so self-confidently ignorant of it can offer us their services as judges. Because of our complacency we may live to see the day when fifty or a hundred years of Russian history will have sunk into oblivion, and nobody will be able to establish any reliable record of them – it will be too late . . .

The scope of our repentance must be infinite. We cannot run away even from ancient sins; we may write off other people's sins as ancient history, but we have no right to do it for ourselves. A few pages further on I shall be talking about the future of Siberia – and whenever I do so my heart sinks at the thought of our age-old sin in oppressing and destroying the indigenous peoples. And is this really ancient history? If Siberia today were densely populated by the original national groups the only step we could ethically take would be to cede their land to them and not stand in the way of their freedom. But since there is only a faint sprinkling of them on the Siberian continent, it is permissible for us to seek our future there, so long as we show a tender fraternal concern for the natives, help them in their daily lives, educate them, and do not forcibly impose our ways on them . . .

After repentance, and once we renounce the use of force, self-limitation comes into its own as the most natural principle to live by. Repentance creates the atmosphere for self-limitation . . .

The concept of unlimited freedom is closely connected in its origin with the concept of infinite progress, which we now recognize as false. Progress in this sense is impossible on our earth with its limited surface area and resources. We shall in any case inevitably have to stop jostling each other and show self-restraint: with the population rapidly soaring, mother earth herself will shortly force us to do so. It would be spiritually so much more valuable and psychologically so much easier, to adopt the principle of self-limitation – and to achieve it through *prudent self-restriction*.

*Sources: Solzhenitsyn, 'Repentance and Self-limitation in the Life of Nations',
in Solzhenitsyn (ed.),* From under the Rubble, *pp. 107, 108, 117, 127, 129,
135, 137–8;* Iz-pod glyb, *pp. 91–2, 92, 99, 106, 107–8, 112, 114.*

Document 9.23 Solzhenitsyn's *Letter to the Soviet Leaders*

Solzhenitsyn sent this letter on 5 September 1973. He argued that the root of the
evil of Soviet Russia lay entirely in the *ideology*. The letter was an appeal to the
Soviet regime to save itself by placing itself at the head of a programme of *national*
renewal by relinquishing its obsession with Marxist-Leninist ideology. Russia could
only be liberated through the rejection of this ideology and then through universal
repentance. This is one of the most important documents of the whole late Soviet
period.

Introduction

I do not entertain much hope that you will deign to examine ideas not
formally solicited by you, although they come from a fellow-countryman of
a rare kind – one who does not stand on a ladder subordinate to your
command, who can be neither dismissed from his post, nor demoted, nor
promoted, nor rewarded by you, and who is therefore one from whom you
are almost certain to hear an opinion sincerely voiced, without any careerist
calculations, such as you are unlikely to hear from even the finest experts in
your bureaucracy. I do not entertain much hope, but I shall try to say what is
most important in a short space, namely, to set out what I hold to be for the
good and salvation of our people, to which all of you – and I myself – belong.

That was no slip of the tongue. I wish all peoples well, and the closer they
are to us and the more dependent upon us, the more fervent is my wish. But
it is the fate of the Russian and Ukrainian peoples that preoccupies me above
all, for, as the proverb says: it's where you're born that you can be most
useful. And there is a deeper reason too: the incomparable sufferings of our
people.

I am writing this letter on the *supposition* that you too are swayed by this
primary concern, that you are not alien to the origins, to your fathers,
grandfathers and great-grandfathers, to the expanse of your homeland; and
that you are conscious of your nationality. If I am mistaken, there is no point
in your reading the rest of this letter.

I am not about to plunge into the harrowing details of the last sixty years.
I try to explain the slow course of our history and what sort of one it has been
in my books, which I doubt if you have read or will ever read. But it is to you
in particular that I address this letter, in order to set out my view of the
future, which seems to me correct, and perhaps to convince you all the same.
And to suggest to you, while there is still time, a possible way out of the chief
dangers facing our country in the next ten to thirty years.

These dangers are: war with China, and our destruction, together with Western civilization, in the crush and stench of a fouled earth.

1 *The West on its Knees*

. . . The catastrophic weakening of the Western world and the whole of Western civilization is by no means solely due to the success of an irresistible, persistent Soviet foreign policy. It is, rather, the result of an historical, psychological and moral crisis affecting the entire culture and world outlook which were conceived at the time of the Renaissance and attained the acme of their expression with the eighteenth-century Enlightenment. An analysis of that crisis is beyond the scope of this letter . . .

2 *War with China*

. . . If Russia lost up to one and a half million people in the First World War and (according to Khrushchev's figures) twenty million in the Second, then war with China is bound to cost us sixty million souls at the very least, and, as always in wars, they will be the best souls – all our finest and purest people are bound to perish there. As for the Russian people, our very last root will be extirpated . . .

When war with Hitler began, Stalin, who had omitted and bungled so much in the way of military preparation, did not neglect *that* side, the ideological side. And although the ideological grounds for that war seemed more indisputable than those that face you now (the war was waged against what appeared on the surface to be a diametrically opposed ideology), from the very first days of the war, Stalin refused to rely on the putrid, decaying prop of ideology. He wisely discarded it, all but ceased to mention it, and unfurled instead the old Russian banner – sometimes, indeed, the standard of Orthodoxy – and we conquered! (Only towards the end of the war and after the victory was the Progressive Doctrine taken out of its mothballs.) . . .

Ideological dissension will melt away – and there will probably never be a Sino-Soviet war. And if there should be, then it will be in the remote future and a truly defensive, truly patriotic one. At the end of the twentieth century we cannot give up Siberian territory, that's beyond all question. But to give up an ideology can only mean relief and recovery for us!

3 *Civilization in impasse*

. . . Society must cease to look upon 'progress' as something desirable. 'Eternal progress' is a nonsensical myth. What must be implemented is not a 'steadily expanding economy' but a *zero growth economy*, a stable economy. *Economic growth is not only unnecessary but ruinous*. We must set ourselves the aim not of *increasing* national resources, but merely of *conserving* them. We must renounce, as a matter of urgency, the gigantic scale of modern technology in industry, agriculture and urban development (the cities of today are cancerous tumours). The chief aim of technology will now be to eradicate the lamentable results of previous technologies. The 'Third World', which has not yet started on the fatal path of Western civilization, can only be saved by 'small-scale technology' which requires an increase, not a reduction, in manual labour, uses the simplest of machinery, and is based purely on local materials.

4 *The Russian North-East*

. . . And herein lies Russia's hope for winning time and winning salvation: in our vast north-eastern spaces, which over four centuries our sluggishness has prevented us from mutilating by our mistakes, we can build anew: not the senseless, voracious civilization of 'progress' – no; we can set up a *stable* economy without pain or delay and settle people there for the first time according to the needs and principles of that economy. These spaces allow us to hope that we shall not destroy Russia in the general crisis of Western civilization. (And there are many lands nearer to us that have been lost through collective farm neglect.) . . .

5 *Internal, not external, development*

This switching of the focus of our attention and efforts will need to take place, of course, in more than just the geographical sense: not only from external to internal land masses, but also from external to internal problems – in all senses, from outer to inner. The actual – not the ostensible – condition of our people, our families, our schools, our nation, our spirit, our life-style and our economy demands this of you . . .

6 *Ideology*

This ideology that fell to us by inheritance is not only decrepit and hopelessly antiquated now; even during its best decades it was totally mistaken in its predictions and was never a science.

A primitive, superficial economic theory, it declared that only the worker creates value and failed to take into account the contribution of . . . organizers, engineers, transport or marketing systems. It was mistaken when it forecast that the proletariat would be endlessly oppressed and would never achieve anything in a bourgeois democracy – if only we could shower people with as much food, clothing and leisure as they have gained under capitalism! It missed the point when it asserted that the prosperity of the European countries depended on their colonies – it was only after they had shaken the colonies off that they began to accomplish their 'economic miracles'. It was mistaken through and through in its prediction that socialists could only ever come to power by an armed uprising. It miscalculated in thinking that the first uprisings would take place in the advanced industrial countries – quite the reverse. And the picture of how the whole world would rapidly be overtaken by revolutions and how states would soon wither away was sheer delusion, sheer ignorance of human nature. And as for wars being characteristic of capitalism alone and coming to an end when capitalism did – we have already witnessed the longest war of the twentieth century so far, and it was not capitalism that rejected negotiations and a truce for fifteen to twenty years; and God forbid that we should witness the bloodiest and most brutal of all mankind's wars – a war between two communist super-powers. Then there was nationalism, which this theory also buried in 1848 as a 'survival' – but find a stronger force in the world today! And it's the same with many other things too boring to list.

Marxism is not only not accurate, not only not a science, has not only failed to predict a *single event* in terms of figures, quantities, time-scales or locations (something that electronic computers today do with laughable ease in the course of social forecasting, although never with the help of Marxism) – it absolutely astounds one by the economic and mechanistic crudity of its attempts to explain that most subtle of creatures, the human being, and that even more complex synthesis of millions of people, society. Only the cupidity of some, the blindness of others and a craving for *faith* on the part of still others can serve to explain this grim humour of the twentieth century: how can such a discredited and bankrupt doctrine still have so many followers in the West! In our country there are fewest of all left! *We* who have had a taste of it are only pretending willy-nilly . . .

Cast off this cracked ideology! Relinquish it to your rivals, let it go wherever it wants, let it pass from our country like a storm-cloud, like an epidemic, let others concern themselves with it and study it, just so long as we don't! In ridding ourselves of it we shall also rid ourselves of the need to fill our life with lies. Let us all pull off and shake off from all of us this filthy sweaty shirt of ideology which is now so stained with the blood of those 66 million that it prevents the living body of the nation from breathing. This ideology bears the entire responsibility for all the blood that has been shed. Do you need me to persuade you to throw it off without more ado? Whoever wants can pick it up in our place.

7 But how can all this be managed?

. . . Yes, of course: freedom is moral. But only if it keeps within certain bounds, beyond which it degenerates into complacency and licentiousness.

And *order* is not immoral, if it means a calm and stable system. But order too has its limits, beyond which it degenerates into arbitrariness and tyranny.

Here in Russia, for sheer lack of practice, democracy survived for only eight months – from February to October 1917. The émigré groups of Constitutional Democrats and Social Democrats still pride themselves on it to this very day and say that outside forces brought about its collapse. But in reality that democracy was *their* disgrace: they invoked it and promised it so arrogantly, and then created [only] a chaotic caricature of democracy, because first of all they turned out to be ill-prepared for it themselves, and then Russia was worse prepared still. Over the last half-century Russia's preparedness for democracy, for a multi-party parliamentary system, could only have diminished. I am inclined to think that its sudden reintroduction now would merely be a melancholy repetition of 1917 . . .

Everything depends upon *what sort* of authoritarian order lies in store for us in the future. It is not authoritarianism itself that is intolerable, but the ideological lies that are daily foisted upon us. Not so much authoritarianism as arbitrariness and illegality, the sheer illegality of having a single overlord in each district, each province and each sphere, often ignorant and brutal, whose will alone decides all things. An authoritarian order does not necessarily mean that laws are unnecessary or that they exist only on paper, or that they should not reflect the notions and will of the population . . .

You may dismiss the counsels of some lone individual, some writer, with laughter or indignation. But with each passing year – for different reasons, at different times and in different guises – life itself will keep on thrusting exactly the same suggestion at you, exactly the same. Because this is the only feasible and *peaceful* way in which you can save our country and our people.

Source: Alexander Solzhenitsyn, Letter to Soviet Leaders, *translated by Hilary Sternberg (London, Collins/Harvill, 1974), pp. 7–8, 12, 13, 15, 17–18, 19, 22, 27, 33, 42–3, 47, 51–2, 53, 57.*

Document 9.24 Sakharov's Response to Solzhenitsyn

While Solzhenitsyn was urging the Soviet system to liberate itself from ideology to allow national development, Sakharov took issue with many of his arguments. In particular, he objected to Solzhenitsyn's Russian perspective, whereas Sakharov, paradoxically, could not envisage the separation of the USSR into its constituent republics. In the event, it was Solzhenitsyn's evaluation of the fragility of the Union that was closer to the truth.

However, even this critical and expository section of the letter reveals certain peculiarities in the author's approach which make me uneasy and disappointed, feelings which mount on reading further. It is, for example, very conspicuous that Solzhenitsyn singles out especially the suffering and sacrifices of the Russian people. Now, of course, anyone has a perfect right to write and be concerned about what he knows best, what touches him most nearly and personally, but we all know that the horrors of the civil war, the dekulakization, the famine, the terror, the Second World War, the historically unprecedented harsh and tyrannical repression exercised against millions of those returning from captivity, the persecution of believers, we know that all these horrors fell in absolutely equal measure upon Russian and non-Russian subjects of the Soviet empire alike. Indeed certain measures, such as forced deportation, genocide, the struggle against national liberation movements, and the repression of national cultures, were actually for the most part the privilege of the non-Russians. Today, moreover, we learn that the schoolchildren of Uzbekistan, whose progress is vaunted to foreign visitors, have to spend many months each year in the cotton plantations instead of at their lessons, and are nearly all ill from inhaling weed killers. I feel that, in discussing questions of the magnitude of those raised by Solzhenitsyn, all this cannot just be ignored. Nor must one forget that each nation in our country bears its share in our historic guilt as well as in such constructive work as has been accomplished, and that, whatever any individual may wish, their fates are bound to remain indissolubly linked for a long time to come . . .

I have outlined Solzhenitsyn's arguments here rather freely, in my own way, as I understand them. Many of his thoughts seem to me both significant and apt, and I welcome this new and talented defense of them. Nevertheless, I must state that in certain very important respects Solzhenitsyn's arguments strike me as misguided, precisely where they touch on the least trivial issues. I will begin with a question which is perhaps less significant in terms of its immediate effects, but is nevertheless very important in principle. Solzhenitsyn very aptly describes various anomalies and costly absurdities in our internal affairs and our foreign policy, and he does so with justified indignation and compassion for his countrymen. But his view of them as directly generated by ideological causes seems to me somewhat schematic. I see present-day Soviet society as being marked rather by ideological indifference and the cynical use of ideology as a convenient façade: expediency and flexibility in the manipulation of slogans go along with traditional intolerance toward free-thinking 'from below.' Stalin committed his crimes not from ideological motives but as part of the struggle for power, while he was building a new 'barrack-square' type of society (as Marx called it); in the same way, the present leaders' main criterion, when facing any difficult decisions, is the conservation of their own power and of the basic features of the system.

I also find it difficult to accept Solzhenitsyn's view of Marxism as a 'Western' and antireligious doctrine which distorted a healthy Russian line of development. The very classification of ideas as Western or Russian is incomprehensible to me. In my view, a scientific and rational approach to social and natural phenomena is only compatible with a classification of ideas and concepts as true or false. And where are we to discern this healthy Russian line of development? Has there ever been a time in the history of Russia, or any other nation, when development was possible without contradictions and upheavals?

What Solzhenitsyn says about ideological rituals and the intolerable waste of the time and energy of millions of people on drivel which only accustoms them to fatuity and hypocrisy – all this is undoubtedly true and makes a strong impression, but the point is that in our situation this hypocritical drivel is merely taking the place of an 'oath of allegiance': it binds people by mutual responsibility for the shared sin of hypocrisy. It is simply a further example of an expedient absurdity generated by the system.

I find Solzhenitsyn's treatment of the problem of progress particularly misleading. Progress is a worldwide process, which must not be equated, certainly not in the times to come, with the quantitative growth of large-scale industrial production. Given universal scientific and democratic management of the economy and of the whole of social life, including population growth, this, I am quite convinced, is not a utopia but a vital necessity. Progress must continually change its immediate forms according to need, in order to meet the requirements of human society while preserving at all costs the natural environment and the earth for our descendants. To retard scientific research, international scientific contacts, technological experiment, and the introduction of new agricultural systems can only delay the solution of these problems and create critical situations for the whole of humanity . . .

To sum up briefly some of my objections to Solzhenitsyn's letter as a whole: in my view Solzhenitsyn overestimates the role of the ideological factor in present-day Soviet society; hence his belief that the Russian people can be saved through the replacement of Marxism by a healthy ideology, which he apparently considers Orthodoxy to be. This conviction underlies his whole program. But I am convinced that in reality the nationalist and isolationist tendencies of Solzhenitsyn's thought, and his own patriarchal religious romanticism, lead him into very serious errors and render his proposals utopian and even potentially dangerous.

Solzhenitsyn addresses his letter to the country's leaders, not just rhetorically, but in the genuine expectation of meeting with at least partial understanding among them. It is difficult to quarrel with such a desire. But is there anything in his proposals which is both new and acceptable to the country's leaders? Great Russian nationalism and the enthusiastic onslaught on virgin lands – these are programs which have been tried before and are still being tried now. The appeal to patriotism could have been borrowed whole from the arsenal of semiofficial propaganda. One cannot help associating it with the 'anticosmopolitan' campaign of the recent past. During the war and up to his death, Stalin tolerated a 'tamed' Orthodoxy. All these parallels with Solzhenitsyn's proposals should not only strike us, but also put us on our guard.

It may be said that Solzhenitsyn's nationalism is not aggressive, but mild and defensive in character, only aiming to save and revive one of the most long-suffering of nations. History shows, however, that 'ideologists' are always milder than the practical politicians who follow in their footsteps. Among the Russian people and the country's leaders are a good many who sympathize with Great Russian nationalism, who are afraid of democratic reforms and of becoming dependent on the West. If they fall on such well-prepared soil, Solzhenitsyn's misconceptions could become dangerous.

Source: Sakharov, 'On Alexander Solzhenitsyn's "A Letter to the Soviet Leaders"', Kontinent (New York, Anchor Press/Doubleday, 1976), pp. 4–7, 12–13.

Document 9.25   Roy Medvedev – Democratic Socialist Dissent

It is conventional to argue that three main trends gradually emerged in alternative thinking in the USSR – patriotic, liberal and democratic socialist (with endless shadings in between). If Solzhenitsyn and Sakharov, respectively, are taken as exemplars of the first two, Roy Medvedev is considered the most eloquent exponent of the third.

We have become accustomed to speak about bourgeois democracy with disdain as something incomplete, illusory, false, designed for effect, etc. But this approach is tendentious and wrong. Bourgeois democracy is, of course, an extremely limited form of democracy and is therefore open to criticism. It is easy to demonstrate that opportunities are not equal for worker and capitalist, for the poor and the rich. The fundamental principle of bourgeois democracy is the formal equality of all citizens before the law, and there is little concern for the social rights and freedoms of working people or for material guarantees to support the rights and freedoms that have been proclaimed. This is why the programmes of communist parties in all capitalist countries, including those with the most highly developed system of bourgeois democracy, continue to put forward general democratic demands – while at the same time calling on people to struggle for socialism.

But with all these reservations, it is important to stress that the sum total of various political and social institutions which taken together form the system of bourgeois democracy is not simply a fiction, in spite of the assertions to this effect by many left-wing groups, past and present. On the contrary, all of these institutions and mechanisms are the product of decades, sometimes centuries, of stubborn struggle by the people for their rights. The democratic order of many Western countries constitutes their most important tradition, their most precious political heritage. It is democracy of this kind that makes it possible for workers in capitalist countries not only to fight for an extension of their rights or for a high standard of living under capitalism, but also to strive for the abolition of capitalism and its replacement by socialism . . .

While contrasting bourgeois with socialist democracy, one should never lose sight of the definite continuity between them, which is twofold in nature. First of all, bourgeois-democratic freedoms help the working class and its party to gather strength, to prepare their struggle for socialism. Secondly, many democratic forms and institutions, created before the socialist revolution, may and ought to be retained even after it, as long as they are given new content . . .

How democratic is contemporary Soviet society? There are two diametrically opposed views on the subject. On the one hand, it is frequently asserted that Soviet citizens have all democratic rights without exception, that our society is the most democratic in the world, etc. On the other extreme, one often hears that there is no democracy whatsoever in our country, that Soviet citizens lack all, or at least the most important, democratic rights. Both opinions are equally mistaken. If one examines the UN documents on the rights of man with an unbiased eye, it is clear that Soviet society has come a long way in terms of economic, social, and cultural rights in the fifty-three years since the October Revolution. They include the right to work and to receive vocational training, the right to organize trade unions, the right to education, social security, family and maternity benefits, medical aid, the protection of minors, the right to participate in cultural life and to benefit from the results of scientific progress. Immediately after the Revolution, the eight-hour working day was introduced, and afterwards, the seven-hour day. The right to leisure was guaranteed; child labor in industry was first restricted and then abolished. Soviet women were the first in the world to receive equal rights, and an enormous effort was made to secure their emancipation. There has been substantial progress in the drive to overcome the immense inequality between physical and mental work, and between country and town. As all socialists have traditionally demanded, every able-bodied Soviet citizen is engaged in useful labor, and it is no longer possible for the idle rich to exist by exploiting the labor of others. Both national and racial discrimination have been abolished, and much has been done to overcome the economic and cultural backwardness of the minority peoples who lived in the borderlands of tsarist Russia. During the Soviet period, the lives of working people have been enriched both materially and culturally.

It is certainly a record of remarkable social and economic achievement and could be extended. In view of the widespread misery and poverty of tsarist Russia, and the economic backwardness that made degrading dependence on the Western capitalist countries inevitable, it is easy to understand why not only the leadership but also the majority of ordinary participants in the October Revolution were concerned in the first instance with assuring social, economic, and cultural rights for workers . . .

However, although it is right to be proud of Soviet achievements with respect to social, economic, and cultural rights, it must also be recognized that Soviet society is today still very backward when it comes to the whole complex of civil and political rights. Of course there has been considerable progress, if one compares the present situation with that of tsarist Russia or with the more recent Stalinist autocracy. A great deal has been done to correct and eliminate the consequences of Stalinism. But it is not good enough to compare the present with the past. Considering the potential and the needs of a socialist society, clearly whatever advance has been made in the realm of political and civil rights is still completely inadequate . . .

For the great majority of workers, collective farmers, and intelligentsia, political participation hardly exists. This is largely because the structure of government and the way it operates reduce to a minimum any possibility for workers or intellectuals to influence the formation of economic, political, or other important policies. On almost all levels of government, the role of the individual remains a subservient one. Industrial and office workers and collective farmers to a very large extent are alienated from production and hardly participate at all in the real running of their enterprises and institutions.

We still do not possess the freedoms our socialist society deserves: freedom of speech, opinion, of the press and of thought. There is still no freedom for artistic creativity and scientific research, particularly in the social sciences. Nor is there freedom of the individual or inviolability of the person. We still do not possess freedom of movement and choice of residence. There is no freedom to travel abroad, nor is there the right to leave one's country, as laid down in the International Covenant on Civil and Political Rights. We still do not have freedom of association and organization or the right to hold peaceful meetings and demonstrations, as befits a socialist society . . .

We must, however, protest in no uncertain terms against the restrictions on human and social rights mentioned above, restrictions that reduce these rights to zero, turning them into empty declarations, paper formalities designed to deceive the people. It is absolutely not true that there is a contradiction between democratic freedom and public order, although this view is often expressed by Soviet writers and sometimes by certain foreign Marxists.

Source: Roy A. Medvedev, On Socialist Democracy, *translated and edited by Ellen de Kadt (Nottingham, Spokesman Books, 1977), pp. 32–3, 33, 35–6, 36, 38.*

Document 9.26 Amalrik, *Will the Soviet Union Survive until 1984?*

Andrei Amalrik (1938–80) was a historian, playwright and the author of perhaps the best known of all dissident writings. Expelled from Moscow State University in 1963 for his political activities, in 1965 he was sentenced to two and a half years' exile for 'parasitism'. In late 1966 he was allowed to return to Moscow but in 1970 was arrested again and, after spending three and a half years in prison and labour camps, he was once again sentenced to two years in exile in Siberia. He left the Soviet Union in 1976 and was killed in a motor car accident in Spain in November 1980. His analysis of the trajectory of post-Stalinist opposition, its social basis and the nature of the Brezhnevite regime remains a classic, while his views of the imminence of conflict with China reflect the thinking of his generation.

It can be said that over the course of the last fifteen years at least three ideological viewpoints on which opposition is founded have begun to crystallize. They are 'genuine Marxism-Leninism', 'Christian ideology' and 'liberal ideology'.

'Genuine Marxism-Leninism' contends that the regime, having perverted Marxist-Leninist ideology for its own purposes, does not practise real Marxism-Leninism, and that in order to cure the ills of our society it is essential to return to the true principles of that doctrine.

Supporters of 'Christian ideology' maintain that the life of society must return to Christian moral principles, which are interpreted in a somewhat Slavophile spirit, with a claim for a special role for Russia.

Finally, believers in 'liberal ideology' ultimately envisage a transition to a Western kind of democratic society, which would, however, retain the principle of republic or government ownership of the means of production . . .

Further, it is clear that in broader terms the basic support for the [democratic] movement comes from the intelligentsia. But since this word is too vague, defining not so much the position in society of a person, or a given social group, as the ability of members of this group to perform intellectual work, it would be better if I used the term 'middle class' . . .

Thus there exists an influential class, a stratum of society, on which the Democratic Movement could seemingly base itself. But there are at least three interrelated factors that militate strongly against such a development.

Two of these factors spring to mind immediately. First, the planned elimination from society of the most independent-minded and active of its members, which has been going on for decades, has left an imprint of greyness and mediocrity on all strata of society – and this could not fail to be reflected in the 'middle class' which is once again taking shape. This elimination, whether through emigration or exile from the country or through imprisonment or physical annihilation, has affected all strata of our people.

Second, that section of the 'middle class' which most clearly recognizes the need for democratic reforms is also the section that is most imbued with the defensive thought, 'Well, there's nothing I can do anyway' or 'You can't break down the wall by beating your head against it.' In reaction to the power of the regime, it practises a cult of its own impotence.

The third factor, although less obvious, is most interesting. As is well known, in any country the stratum of society least inclined towards change or any sort of independent action is that composed of state employees. This is natural, because every government worker considers himself too insignificant in comparison with the power apparatus of which he is only a small cog to demand of that apparatus any kind of change. At the same time, he has been relieved of all social responsibility, since his job is simply to carry out orders. Thus he always has the feeling of having performed his duty even though he had done things that he would not have done had he been given a choice . . . In our country, since all of us work for the state, we all have the psychology of government workers. Writers who are members of the Union of

Writers, scholars employed in government institutions, common labourers or collective farmers are created of this psychology just as much as are officials of the KGB or the Ministry of the Interior . . .

It goes without saying that the 'middle class' is no exception in adopting this government-employee attitude; indeed, this psychology is particularly typical of it by virtue of its position in the middle of the social scale. Many members of this class are simply functionaries of the Communist Party or governmental apparatus. They regard the regime as a lesser evil than the painful process of changing it.

Consequently we are faced with an interesting phenomenon. Although there exists in our country a social class capable of comprehending the principles of personal freedom, rule of law and democratic government, a class that needs those principles and provides the emerging Democratic Movement with its basic contingent of supporters, the vast majority of this class is so mediocre, its ways of thinking are so much those of the government employee, and its intellectually most independent members are so passive that the success of a Democratic Movement based on it seems to be gravely in doubt.

It must be said, however, that this 'paradox of the middle class' is connected in a curious way with a 'paradox of the regime'. We are aware that the regime underwent very dynamic internal changes in the five years before the war. However, the subsequent regeneration of the bureaucratic élite was carried out by the retention of those who were most obedient and unquestioning. This bureaucratic method of 'unnatural selection' of the most obedient members of the old bureaucracy, together with the elimination from the ruling caste of the boldest and most independent-minded, created over the years an increasingly weaker and more indecisive generation of élite. Accustomed to obey unconditionally and without thought in order to attain power, bureaucrats, once they have attained that power, are very good at holding on to it but have no idea how to use it. Not only are they incapable of conceiving new ideas; they regard any novel thought as an assault on their own prerogatives . . .

Self-preservation is clearly the dominant drive. The regime wants neither to 'restore Stalinism' nor to 'persecute the intelligentsia' nor to 'render fraternal assistance' to those who have not asked for it, like Czechoslovakia. The only thing it wants is for everything to go on as before: authorities to be recognized, the intelligentsia to keep quiet, no rocking of the system by dangerous and unfamiliar reforms.

The regime is not on the attack but on the defence. Its motto is: 'Don't touch us and we won't touch you.' Its aim: Let everything be as it was. This is probably the most humane objective the regime has set for itself in the last half-century, but it is also the least appealing.

Thus we have a passive bureaucratic élite opposed to a passive 'middle class'. Moreover, however passive the élite is, it really does not need to make any changes, and in theory it could remain in power for a very long time, getting away with only the slightest concessions and minor measures of repression . . .

The current process of 'widening the area of freedom' could be more aptly described as the growing decrepitude of the regime. The regime is simply growing old and can no longer suppress everyone and everything with the same strength and vigour as before; the composition of the élite is changing, as we have mentioned; the contemporary world, in which the regime is already finding it very hard to keep its bearings, is becoming more complex; and the structure of society is changing . . .

If, furthermore, one regards the evolution of the regime as analogous to the growth of entropy, then the Democratic Movement, which I analysed at the beginning of this study, could be considered an anti-entropic phenomenon. One may, of course, hope – and this will probably come true – that the emerging movement will succeed, despite persecution, in becoming influential, will work out a sufficiently concrete programme, will find the structure necessary to its goals and attract many followers. But at the same time, I think that its base in society – the 'middle class', or, more exactly, a part of the 'middle class' – is too weak and too beset by internal contradictions to allow the movement to engage in a real face-to-face struggle with the regime or, in the event of the regime's self-destruction or its collapse as a result of mass disorders, to become a force capable of reorganizing society in a new way. But will the Democratic Movement perhaps be able to find a broader base of support among the masses? . . .

Thus two ideas that the masses understand and accept – the idea of force and the idea of justice – are equally inimical to democratic ideas, which are based on individualism. To these must be added three more negative and interrelated factors: first, the continued low cultural level of the greater part of our people, especially in respect to everyday culture; second, the dominance of the many myths assiduously propagated by the mass information media; and, third, the extreme social disorientation of the bulk of people . . .

While the old social structure in both town and village has been completely destroyed, a new one is only just beginning to form. The 'ideological foundations' on which it is being built are extremely primitive: the desire for material well-being (relatively modest from a Western viewpoint) and the instinct for self-preservation. Thus the concept 'profitable' is confronted with the concept 'risky' . . .

There is, of course, a counterbalancing factor to these destructive tendencies. Contemporary Soviet society can be compared with a triple-decker sandwich – the top layer is the ruling bureaucracy; the middle layer consists of the 'middle class' or the 'class of specialists'; and the bottom layer, the most numerous, consists of the workers, peasants, petty clerks and so on. Whether Soviet society will manage to reorganize itself in a peaceful and painless way and survive the forthcoming cataclysm with a minimum of casualties will depend on how rapidly the middle layer of the sandwich expands at the expense of the other two and on how rapidly the 'middle class' and its organization grow, whether faster or slower than the disintegration of the system . . .

Summing up, it can be said that as the regime becomes progressively weaker and more self-destructive it is bound to clash – and there are already clear indications that this is happening – with two forces which are already undermining it: the constructive movement of the 'middle class' (rather weak) and the destructive movement of the 'lower classes', which will take the form of extremely damaging, violent and irresponsible action once its members realize their relative immunity from punishment. How long, though, will it be before the regime faces such an upheaval, and how long will it be able to bear the strain? . . .

Why regimes that have become internally stagnant tend to develop a militantly ambitious foreign policy I find hard to say. Perhaps they seek a way out of their domestic problems through their foreign policies. Perhaps, on the other hand, the ease with which they can suppress internal opposition creates in their minds an illusion of omnipotence. Or perhaps it is because the need to have an external enemy, deriving from internal policy aims, builds up such momentum that it becomes impossible to halt the growth of hostility. This view is supported by the fact that every totalitarian regime decays without itself noticing it . . .

The question of China needs to be considered in detail. Like our country, China has lived through a revolution and a civil war and, like ourselves, has made use of Marxist doctrine to consolidate the country. Also, as in our country, the further the revolution developed, the more Marxist doctrine became a camouflage which more or less concealed nationalist and imperialist aims . . .

Meanwhile, the relentless logic of revolution is propelling China towards a war which the Chinese leaders hope will solve the country's economic and social problems and secure for China a leading place in the modern world. (Her problems are primarily extreme overpopulation of some areas, hunger and an agriculture that needs extensive rather than intensive development and requires acquisition of new territories.)

Finally, in such a war China will be seeking national revenge for the centuries of humiliation and dependence forced on her by foreign powers. The main obstacle in the way to achieving these global goals is the existence of two superpowers, the Soviet Union and the United States, which, however, do not form a common front against China since they are themselves mutually antagonistic. Naturally, China takes this into account, and launches verbal onslaughts equally against 'American imperialism' and 'Soviet revisionism and social imperialism'. None the less, the real contradictions, and therefore the possibilities for a head-on conflict, are much greater between China and the Soviet Union than between China and the United States.

Source: Andrei Amalrik, Will the Soviet Union Survive until 1984?, *edited by Hilary Sternberg, revised and expanded edition (London, Harper Colophon Books, 1981), pp. 20, 24, 25–6, 27–8, 28–9, 34–5, 38, 42, 43, 45, 46–7.*

The larger failure of this period was that the Soviet regime systematically destroyed the sources of renewal in society, and allowed the most venal, corrupt and cowardly to thrive. Appeals for a gradual democratisation from above fell on deaf ears. Solzhenitsyn was deprived of his Soviet citizenship and exiled in February 1974. In 1978 the same fate befell Rostropovich and his wife Galina Vishnevskaya, who had given concerts in aid of émigré organisations while abroad. Whether the government had the right to remove citizenship from someone born in the USSR remained for long a moot point, and the Russian Constitution of December 1993, in direct response to such actions, formally deprives the government of this power (article 6.3).

Dissent and Nationalism

So-called dissent was not confined to Russia alone. In all the republics, to a greater or lesser extent, there remained tensions and grievances. Far from a new community of peoples emerging – 'the Soviet people' – living in harmony with each other, as the official propaganda proclaimed, as the power of the ideology waned people more, people sought their identities in traditional national forms.

Document 9.27   Leonid Plyushch – Soviet Society from the Inside

In so far as there is a classic Soviet dissident, Plyushch was one. Born into a Ukrainian working-class background in 1939 in Kirghizia, he became a brilliant mathematician. As a youngster he was a loyal Soviet citizen, but he recoiled from the huge gulf between the professed beliefs of the Soviet system and the shabby and hypocritical way in which it worked. His autobiography provides one of the most eloquent insights into Soviet realities in general, and on inter-ethnic tensions in particular. Instead of the Soviet picture of idyllic relations between the nations making up the country, Plyushch reveals a picture of systematic racism, anti-Semitism and the denigration of the status of whole peoples. He was particularly concerned over the suppression of the Ukrainian language, together with his growing anger at the lack of freedom in the USSR. Sacrificing a prestigious research fellowship, his path as a dissident led him to arrest in 1972, imprisonment and thence incarceration in a psychiatric ward for two and a half years, where the KGB used the usual range of psychotropic drugs in an attempt to modify his beliefs. The abuse of psychiatry in the Soviet Union served broader purposes than simply to punish the individuals concerned ('punishment by madness' as Tatyana Khodorovich put it), but suggested that dissidents were not only criminally mistaken but mentally deranged. Public pressure in the West forced the Soviet authorities to allow him and his family to go into exile in 1976.

In Frunze [the capital of Kirghizia] in the early 1950's boys and girls could not walk about the streets in the evening. Everyone belonged to a gang. My friends and I organized our own gang with an arsenal of one dagger. We intended to go to the militia and offer our services against the thieves and rowdies. Naturally I was the commissar of our gang.

At the Pioneer Palace I was the monitor of the zoology club. Catching field mice in winter, we saw a hand protruding from a snowdrift. I ran to get the militia. Every station refused to go out: 'It isn't our district.' Finally militiamen arrived from the city. It was a case of rape and murder. The militia captain who came out with me immediately pointed to a Gypsy encampment nearby. I believed him. Everyone knew that Gypsies were thieves and murderers.

I believed the old wives' tale about the Chechens, Ingush, Kurds, Kabardins, and other small nationalities resettled on the outskirts of Frunze: they had betrayed their motherland to the Germans. Now they were not permitted to live in the cities, and militiamen arrested them on sight. All the children – and the adults, too – believed that these 'traitors' were in the habit of murdering Russian and Ukrainian children. My friends and I went into the hills armed with a hunting rifle.

In school we were required to study the Kirghiz language. At first I proudly refused. I despised the Kirghiz teacher and had no use for the language. Then I started to study the language and made fun of the Kirghiz children. I knew only a dozen Kirghiz words, but I could effortlessly answer questions on grammar. For some reason the Kirghiz children found grammar difficult, and I always got better marks than they. No one was deliberately bringing me up to hate the natives, but prejudice was in the air. The Kirghiz and Uzbeks were not yet called 'animals,' but already half the population was Russian and Ukrainian. (The Ukrainians were dispossessed kulaks who tended to live on the outskirts.) The whites were better educated and had better jobs. They were the bearers of everything progressive and cultured.

This, too, I hold against the regime: inculcating children with chauvinism, anti-Semitism, and KGBism. It took me, a Ukrainian boy, and made me a Russian chauvinist, an oppressor of Chechens, Kurds, and Kirghizians, a white racist blinded by his mission as a *Kulturträger*. Today, when nationalism raises its head in Kirghizia, all my sympathy is on its side, even when it explodes as hatred of the Russian colonizers. The Ukrainians there are in a particularly sad and difficult position. At a time when their own land is being Russified, Ukrainians are forced to Russify Central Asia.

I had barely become acquainted with the new school when we were shaken by terrible news. Our leader Stalin had died on March 5, 1953. The teachers and pupils wept. I understood the horror of what had happened and wondered how the country would survive in a capitalist encirclement. My torments were heightened by pangs of conscience: everyone was weeping, but I couldn't force a single tear. I realized that my country was the most beautiful in the world and that Stalin had been the wisest leader of all times. But at the same time I knew that I came from the lower class. My mother earned thirty rubles a month as a cook and could not support both my sister and me. When we moved to Odessa, Ada stayed behind in Frunze with Mother's relatives, and I grew up hardly knowing her. In Odessa my mother and I huddled on a bed in a women's dormitory. Sailors and militiamen visited the girls in the evenings and stayed to sleep with them. My mother tried unsuccessfully to drown out unpleasant sounds, the way foreign radio stations are jammed in the Soviet Union. I saw a similar poverty all around me, and some of my schoolmates were even worse off. Unlike them, I could go to my mother in the kitchen and eat the patients' leftovers.

The ideology I was taught in school and the life I knew were in glaring contradiction. I could not bring myself to doubt my books and teachers and had to find another way to resolve the contradiction. The population does not know what standard of living the rulers enjoy, because it is a state secret. But we did encounter a section of the population that lived better than we did: salesclerks (they were paid little but made it up by stealing), teachers, doctors, and health-resort visitors. In Odessa at that time most of these well-to-do people were Jews. It was natural to become an anti-Semite. Blind national and social protest has often led to anti-Semitism. Engels called anti-Semitism the 'socialism of fools.' . . .

Shortly before the meeting of the Twelfth Congress of the Komsomol, several Komsomol members in the mathematics department and I wrote a letter to the Congress, describing the formalism of Komsomol activities and the way in which most members were discrediting the organization in their private lives. Our main proposal was to purge the Komsomol of petit-bourgeois good-for-nothings and raise admission standards. We also proposed various foolish projects for making Komsomol work more exciting, including the collection of funds to build a spaceship.

We anxiously awaited a reply. We were told that our letter was being discussed by the Central Committee and would be brought up at the Congress. But the Congress didn't mention the issues we had raised even in passing. Instead it abounded in drum rolls and fanfares about the great accomplishments of the Komsomol in opening up the virgin lands in the East. We knew from friends who had gone to those virgin lands that most of the press reports about the campaign were sheer demagoguery.

When our teacher of party history proposed a discussion of the resolutions of the Congress, I immediately denounced it as a 'congress of good-for-nothings.' The teacher took me aside and warned me of the trouble I could get into for such talk, to which I replied proudly that the Stalinist period was past, and now everyone had the right to speak his mind. The teacher merely shrugged his shoulders.

The Twentieth Congress of the Communist Party and the Hungarian Revolution in 1956 instigated a wave of free thinking at all the larger universities. Clandestine or semiclandestine organizations were founded in Moscow, Leningrad, and Kiev . . .

The [Twenty-first] Congress declared that the USSR was no longer a dictatorship of the proletariat but, rather, a state of all the people. In terms of classical Leninism this was nonsense, and a Marxist analysis of this new concept was needed. After all, the state is a machine that one class uses to oppress other classes. A state of all the people would be equivalent to a round square.

Political writings began to appear in *samizdat* in 1962. One of the first works that I read was Admiral Fyodor Raskolnikov's letter to Stalin, which included facts not mentioned in the official press. I was most disturbed by Raskolnikov's thesis that the famine of 1933 in Ukraine had been deliberately engineered, and set about finding people who had witnessed it. My grandfather told me that in 1933 he had seen a mountain of corpses in a village in one of the most prosperous provinces . . .

The Tatars were the first political prisoners who conducted themselves at trials in the manner of prerevolutionary political prisoners. They missed no opportunity to unmask the court and express their hatred for their torturers. They demanded that the trial be discussed in the press and – since an entire nation was on trial and not simply ten people – that observers from the Central Committee and the government be present. At first only KGB men were permitted to enter the courtroom, but when the Tatars declared that they would not participate in the trial, the public was allowed to enter. Several people began to record the proceedings, but KGB men took away their notes. The Uzbek militiamen who were guarding the courthouse quietly expressed their sympathy for the Tatars and their hatred of the Russians . . .

When one of the defendants was asked whether he had been convicted previously, he replied, 'Yes, in 1944, together with my entire people, on a charge of betraying the motherland!' Such utilization of Soviet laws was not new in the opposition movement, but the Tatars carried it to its logical conclusion and exploited every possible point of law. The judge and the KGB were furious and must have regretted that they had let the public enter the courtroom and that the defendants were being tried for slander, which allowed a maximum sentence of only three years . . . The trial lasted a month. At the end, between five and seven hundred Crimean Tatars held a sit-down demonstration at party headquarters. The militia was called in to disperse them.

Disturbed by the trial, new documents about the crimes committed in 1944, and my discussions with the Crimean Tatars, I wrote a long article about their national problem. The Tatars had been 'rehabilitated' by a decree of the Supreme Soviet in 1967, which explained that a new generation had attained maturity, thus hinting that the previous generation, an entire people, consisted of criminals who had been justly convicted. The Crimean Tatars were referred to as Tatars who had previously resided in the Crimea and thereby were denied a separate nationality. Cynically it was stated that they had taken root in Central Asia: an entire people had taken root on someone else's land by decree. Finally, the Crimeans were graciously permitted to live anywhere in the USSR in accordance with the identity-card regulations. This was done to prevent their settling in Crimean villages, where identity cards were required. Now when a Crimean Tatar settles in the Crimea without prior permission, the militia can evict him in twenty-four hours. Such are the dialectics of politics in the USSR. Any aspect of the law can be used against the citizens. Equality of the sexes is used against women; class justice against workers, peasants, and the intelligentsia; identity cards against Crimean Tatars, workers, and dissidents; and the lack of identity cards against collective farmers. Every humane and intelligent idea is turned into a new method of exploitation . . .

Or take Ilya Glazunov, the leader of the Russites in Moscow. Monarchy, Orthodoxy, truly Russian culture – Glazunov mixed together all the old slogans and rehashings of Rousseau. Back to Russia, he argued, back to peasants who wear bast shoes, light their cottages with torches, and respect the truncheon. I listened to my friends talk about Glazunov and wondered: Poor Russia, why do you need such patriots? Where are you headed, to Gogol's vision, to Dostoyevsky, to the Apocalypse? A year or two later a profile of Salvador Allende by Glazunov appeared in *Literaturnaya gazeta*. After leaving the USSR I read a report that Glazunov was traveling in the West, boasting of his assignment to paint a portrait of Brezhnev himself, the master of the Russian people and progressive humanity. The circle had closed; Glazunov had reached a new rung in his career, and Holy Mother Russia entered a new age of self-enslavement. These sad and absurd scenes did not prevent me from seeing the 'non-true Russians' – Bukovsky and Sakharov, for example – or from hoping that they would be victorious in Russia . . .

Western Ukrainians have the advantage of possessing Ukrainian books published in Poland and Germany before the war. From them I was able to learn about the nationalist movements in Western Ukraine in the 1930's. Soviet propaganda calls all nationalists fascists and Banderites [followers of the Ukrainian nationalist fighter Stepan Bandera, 1909–59], including those who had been opposed to the Banderites. It became clear to me that the populace took a hostile attitude toward the Soviet forces that occupied Western Ukraine in 1939. Some people joined with the Nazis but then turned against them when they had had a taste of fascism. The left wing of the national movement, including the Communist Party of Western Ukraine, was accused of espionage and liquidated by the NKVD.

A Western Ukrainian poet wrote a poem about the departure of Soviet troops from Lviv when the Nazis invaded. NKVD men had killed all the prisoners in the Lviv prison, and the Nazis found only blood-spattered cells when they broke in. The Nazis, not entirely stupid, informed the population about the Bolshevik crime. The poem shook me with its anger and passion and its new techniques and images. Not knowing whether the author was accused or not of writing the poem, I cannot name him . . .

The Western Ukrainian patriots have a vital advantage over their Eastern compatriots: close links with the peasants, workers, and Uniates, who are struggling to have their own Ukrainian Catholic Church. These links give the oppositionists greater credibility and make them politically more active than the people in Kiev or Kharkiv. The excessive interest in language and literature and the political indifference that so vexed me in Kiev were much less prominent in Western Ukraine. The Eastern Ukrainian abstention from politics meant that we learned about repressions in Kiev via people in Lviv or even Moscow. When a search or an arrest took place in Moscow, we learned about it that same day or at most a few days later. But when a similar event occurred in Kiev, we often heard about it only months later – or never at all.

The crackdown of January 1972 shows that the KGB is playing a positive role in one sense. It has politicized an apolitical, cultural patriotism, and it has united Eastern and Western Ukrainians and then divided them according to a new criterion: their steadfastness and resistance to betrayal. The only question is whether the KGB will succeed in embittering the Ukrainian patriots to the extent that they will become chauvinists. The *samizdat* that has come out since 1972 reveals such a tendency. On the whole, however, the Ukrainian patriots have remained democrats while increasing their political activism.

Source: Leonid Plyushch, History's Carnival: A Dissident's Autobiography *(London, Collins and Harvill Press, 1979), pp. 8–9, 16, 40, 180–1, 181–2, 185–6, 188, 189.*

Document 9.28 *Internationalism or Russification?*

This was the title of perhaps the most famous condemnation of Soviet nationality policy. Published in 1968, Ivan Dzyuba's analysis of conditions in Ukraine provided a devastating picture of the effects of Sovietisation and Russification. Both Marxism and liberalism had assumed that nationalism would progressively die out as economies were raised to ever higher levels of integration and development, but, as Dzyuba perceptively noted, this was far from being the case.

The Ukrainian people has never been aggressive and intolerant towards others; never in its history has it enslaved other peoples. To the overwhelming majority of Ukrainian intellectuals, because of their democratic spirit, narrow nationalism has always been alien and chauvinism quite unnatural. These are now all the more alien to the overwhelming majority of Ukrainians, after so many bitter lessons of history, now that socialism has become the sole philosophy of Ukrainians and is shared by dozens of peoples of the great socialist commonwealth.

It is all the more painful for a Ukrainian (if he feels the least bit as a Ukrainian) to see today that something incomprehensible and unjustifiably disgraceful is happening to his socialist nation. Not all Ukrainians are equally aware and conscious of what is taking place (for these processes themselves are of such a nature that they do not appear on the surface nor in their own guise), but almost all feel that 'something' evil is going on.

Marxism-Leninism defines a nation as an historically evolved community characterized by unity of territory, economic life, historic fate, language, and mental mould as revealed in its culture.

In all of these aspects the Ukrainian nation today is not experiencing a 'flowering', as is officially proclaimed, but a crisis, and this needs to be admitted if one takes even a moderately honest look at actual reality.

Territorial unity and sovereignty are being gradually and progressively lost through mass resettlement . . . of the Ukrainian population in Siberia, Kazakhstan, the North, etc. where it numbers millions but is quickly denationalized; through an organized mass resettlement of Russians in the Ukraine, not always with economic justification and not always motivated by economic reasons (as, for instance, in Stalin's time, particularly in the cities of Western Ukraine); through administrative divisions that remain a formality and through the doubtful sovereignty of the government of the Ukrainian SSR over the territory of the Ukraine. This latter reason, coupled with excessive centralization and a total subordination to all-Union authorities in Moscow, makes it equally difficult to speak about the *integrity and sovereignty of the economic life* of the Ukrainian nation.

A common historic fate is also being lost, as the Ukrainian nation is being progressively dispersed over the Soviet Union, and as the sense of historic national tradition and knowledge of the historic past are gradually being lost due to a total lack of national education in school and in society in general.

Ukrainian national *culture* is being kept in a rather provincial position and is practically treated as 'second-rate'; its great past achievements are poorly disseminated in society. The Ukrainian *language* has also been pushed into the background and is not really used in the cities of the Ukraine.

Finally, during the last decades the Ukrainian nation has virtually been deprived of the natural increase in population which characterizes all present-day nations. As far back as 1913 one would hear about 'the 37 million Ukrainians'. The 1926 census speaks of 29 million Ukrainians in the Ukraine; if over 7 million of the Russian SFSR are added (a figure quoted at the XII Congress of the RCP(B) in 1923), this also gives some 37 million. The same 37-million-odd appear also in the 1959 census. Even with a minimal natural increase (not to mention official tables of increase for the Ukraine), the number of Ukrainians, allowing for war losses, should have increased by 10–20 million. After all, the total population within the present boundaries of the USSR has risen from 159 million in 1913 to 209 million in 1959, and the number of Russians has doubled in spite of war losses: 55.4 million in 1897, 60–70 million in 1913, and 114.1 million in 1959.

Even if there had been no other alarming facts, this alone would have been sufficient attestation that the nation is going through a crisis. But there are countless other facts. These facts, and various aspects of the national crisis experienced by the Ukrainian people, will be the theme of the present work. We will show, in particular, how this crisis has resulted from the violation of the Leninist nationalities policy, from its replacement by Stalin's Great-Power policy and Khrushchev's pragmatism, all irreconcilable with scientific communism . . .

One way of confusing the USSR with 'Russia, one and indivisible' consists in attributing to the Russians what has been created by the common efforts of all the peoples of the USSR. Numerous Ukrainian scholars, scientists and artists of the remote and recent past are rather unceremoniously, without any reference to their nationality, labelled as Russian scholars, etc., simply because colonial conditions under tsarism in the Ukraine or their personal circumstances forced them to work beyond the boundaries of the Ukraine. So much for the past. But similar tendencies to credit the Russians with everything also exist in the present context. Formulas like 'Russians Orbit Sputnik'; 'Russians Build Aswan'; 'Russians Help Peoples of Africa and Asia' come from the bourgeois press and from foreign political phraseology – where the USSR is consistently identified with Russia and no need is felt to know other Soviet nations – into the Soviet press, and from there become imprinted on the mind of the public . . .

This socialist national consciousness, this certainty of their right and duty to give a good account of their socialist nation to humanity, this desire to see the socialist Ukraine as truly existing and genuinely equal among the socialist family of nations, this feeling of a socialist Ukraine as a national reality and not simply as an administrative geographical term and a bureaucratic stumbling-block – all this is also intensified by a number of universal factors in world history and in the world communist movement. Witness the historic reality of the socialist nations of Europe, which are experiencing an upsurge and a revitalization of their national awareness, and make the elementary comparison, which imposes itself, between their position and that of the Ukraine. Witness the fiasco of the miserable notion of nationlessness, of the nationless uniformity of communist society, under the pressure of actual historic reality, of the real historic-national multiformity of communism. Witness the Soviet reader's growing interest in, and acquaintance with, living world communist theory, the theoretical works and ideas of Marxists-Leninists from all over the world – works and ideas which turn out to be much more profound, humane and attractive than the stuff that our present newspapers keep chewing over. Finally, witness the upswing of national movements and national values all over the world, Europe included. Not so long ago *Pravda* quite justly observed that the significance of the national factor has grown in even the most industrially developed countries . . .

All over the world nations are not dying out but, on the contrary, are developing and growing stronger, in order to offer as much as possible to humanity, to contribute as much as possible to the creation of universal human values; especially the socialist nations.

And the Ukrainian nation will not become the outcast of the human race.

Source: Ivan Dzyuba, Internationalism or Russification? A Study in the Soviet Nationalities Problem *(New York, Monad Press, 1974), pp. 13–15, 92, 206.*

Document 9.29   Founding Principles of the *Ukrainsky Visnyk*

The *Ukrainsky Visnyk* (*Ukrainian Herald*) began publishing in early 1970 and, like the *Chronicle of Current Events* in Moscow, reflected the development of the democratic movement but, unlike the latter, was less focused on human rights and adopted a more explicitly pro-Soviet and pro-communist line. This did not save it and, like the *Chronicle*, it fell victim to the wave of repression against dissent launched in 1972.

The need for such an uncensored publication has been ripe for a long time in the Ukraine. There are many problems of general interest which cause concern among wide sectors of Ukrainian society and which are never dealt with in the official press. But if on rare occasions, due to the force of circumstances, the press does mention these problems, it resorts to deliberate falsification.

The *Visnyk* will present information, without generalizations, on the violations of the freedom of speech and other democratic freedoms which are guaranteed by the constitution, on judicial and extrajudicial repression in the Ukraine, on the violations of national sovereignty (instances of chauvinism and Ukrainophobia), on attempts to misinform the public, on the condition of Ukrainian political prisoners in prisons and labor camps, on various acts of protest, etc. The *Visnyk* will review, or present in full, articles, documents, literary works and other materials which have become public and have already been circulated in samvydav [samizdat].

The *Ukrainsky Visnyk* is in any case not an anti-Soviet or anticommunist publication. It is entirely legal and constitutional in its content and task. Criticism of individuals, agencies, and establishments, including the highest ones, for mistakes committed in decision-making on internal political problems, particularly the violations of the democratic rights of the individual and a nation, is not regarded by the *Visnyk* as being anti-Soviet activity, but is considered the guaranteed right and the moral duty of every citizen provided for by the [fundamental] principles of socialist democracy and the constitution. The abnormal circumstance under which the *Visnyk* is published is explained solely by the fact that there exist in our country frequent infringements of constitutional rights and illegal persecutions of individuals who are active in public affairs.

Source: George Saunders (ed.), Samizdat: Voices of the Soviet Opposition *(New York, Monad Press, 1974), pp. 421–2.*

Document 9.30   Divisions within Dissent over the National Question

The *Ukrainsky Visnyk* revealed the sharp divisions *within* the Soviet opposition, as in the following evaluation of the Russian civil rights movement. The 'Message to the Russian Nation' alluded to at the end was indeed the signal that an anti-liberal Russian nationalist backlash was emerging, although this was only one trend in the larger rebirth of Russian consciousness.

That section of Ukrainian public opinion that is familiar with Russian samizdat has taken an interest in the attitude held by the Russian oppositional forces, which have been visibly active since the second half of the 1960s, toward the national question in general and the Ukrainian question in particular . . .

In the first appeal to the CPSU Central Committee by Academician Sakharov and scientists [V.] Turchin and R. Medvedev, there is a statement to the effect that a gradual democratization of life in the USSR is necessary because that would diminish the threat of nationalism. In the same appeal there is a proposal that, instead of one's nationality, the words 'citizen of the USSR' be stamped on everyone's passport. (Similar proposals were made even under Khrushchev and were viewed in the Union Republics as attempts at further encroachment upon their sovereignty.) . . .

The Ukrainian reader has welcomed the appearance of the *Chronicle* [*of Current Events*]. It is notable for its objectivity, extensive coverage, and relative accuracy of information, providing a rounded picture of the political trials unknown to the majority of people in the USSR.

However, some have raised their voices to point out, without denying the importance of the *Chronicle*, that it has rather unilaterally and pretentiously assumed the stance of a supranational or all-union journal, when in fact it is the product of Russian (and possibly, in part, Jewish) circles. It has also been noted that the sparse informational reports from the republics are worked in as though they were supplementary to the quite extensive description of events in Russia, mostly Moscow – this in and of itself creating a false impression of the situation in the USSR . . .

Along with organizations and groups that raise the question of democratic transformations in the USSR, others have appeared that criticize the government and the 'liberals' from reactionary, openly chauvinist positions, seeking even a formal liquidation of the USSR and the creation of a military-democratic unitary state 'of all the Russians'.

Let us quote the brief description of one such document of Russian samizdat given by the *Chronicle* in its issue no. 17, 'Message to the Nation'. Signed: 'Russian patriots'. This document, a sort of declaration, is a manifesto of Russian nationalists. The authors vehemently take issue with Russian (and all) liberals, accusing them of having aims and views which are unsubstantiated, impotent, and objectively harmful. The 'Russian patriots' campaign for the purity of the white race, which is being tainted by 'random hybridization', for the rebirth of Russia ('great, united, and indivisible') and of national religion.

Source: Saunders (ed.), Samizdat, *pp. 423–4, 425.*

Document 9.31   Russification in Latvia

An open letter by a group of Latvian communists describing the impact of Soviet power in the republic first emerged in summary form in the West in January 1972. The extract provides a vivid picture of the state of affairs not only in Latvia but, to a greater or lesser extent, in other republics. The immigration of Russians, the invariable appointment of a Russian as second secretary in a republican party organisation and as head of a republic's KGB, the political use of industrial development, environmental degradation, all these (and more) were typical of Moscow's pattern of rule over the republics.

Dear comrades,

We are seventeen Latvian Communists, seeking your help. We are writing to you because we do not see any other way of affecting certain actions and events which cause great harm to the Communist movement, to Marxism-Leninism, and to our own and other small nations.

Many Communists have voiced in their party organizations the concerns we are expressing here, and some have appealed to the Central Committee of the Communist Party of the Soviet Union. Repressions have been the only results.

In order for you to understand us better, we would like to say a few words about ourselves. We are not opportunists, nor are we 'leftists' or 'rightists'. We are Communists and most of us became Communists twenty-five to thirty-five or more years ago. We wish only success for socialism, for Marxism-Leninism and for the whole of mankind. All of us were born and have lived in Latvia, and most of us have personally experienced the deficiencies of a bourgeois regime. We joined the party at a time when it was still underground. We endured repressions, were confined to prisons, and suffered under the yoke of bourgeois Latvia. The struggle to establish Soviet power and a socialistic order was our main goal in life. We all studied Marxism-Leninism. During the last world war, we were members of the Soviet armed forces or partisan groups and fought the Nazi aggressors. During the postwar years, we all actively participated in building socialism in our land. With a clear conscience, we did everything in our power to carry out the teaching of Marx, Engels, and Lenin. However, it became painfully clear to us that with each passing year their ideas became more distorted, that the teachings of Lenin are used here as a cover for Great Russian chauvinism, that deeds no longer agree with words, that we are complicating the work of Communists in other countries, that we are impeding this work instead of facilitating it.

Originally we believed that this was due simply to the errors of a few individual local officials who did not realize the harmful effects of their attitudes. With time, however, it became apparent to us that the leadership of the Soviet Communist Party had deliberately adopted a policy of Great Russian chauvinism and that the forcible assimilation of the small USSR nations had been set as one of the most immediate and important domestic policy goals . . .

Even more, in the national republics the determined program for the coercive assimilation of small nationality groups was enacted even more forcibly and consistently. What is the main course of this program and how is it enacted? The first main task is to transfer from Russia, White Russia, and the Ukraine as many Russians, White Russians, and Ukrainians as possible to Latvia (and to other Baltic states) for permanent settlement.

How is the first main task enacted? The CPSU CC did not trust the national republic CP CC. Thus:

1 For the Latvian CP CC, and likewise for all other republic CP CCs, a CPSU CC Organizational Bureau (Orgbureau) was established [staffed by Russians] for Latvian affairs. The bureau's function was to control and direct the Latvian CP CC and the republic's overall politics . . .
2 For the Latvian CP CC second secretary position Moscow appointed Ivan Lebedev and for the Latvian CP CC first secretary in cadre affairs, Fyodor Titov. These positions are still held by appointed Russians. At the present time the Latvian CP CC second secretary position is held by Belucha, a Russian sent from Leningrad.
3 The Orgbureau and these 'high commissars' from Moscow have continually directed the republic's cadre politics so that all leading positions – and primarily all party, state, and economic department head positions – are given to Russian newcomers. These people in turn grant other newcomers preference for registration in cities, provide apartments, and appoint them to better jobs.

4 To guarantee a massive influx of Russians, White Russians, and Ukrainians into the Latvian Republic, federal, interrepublican, and zonal government departments have been set up in Latvia, and the construction of new large industries, as well as expansion of existing plants, has been undertaken, disregarding any economic necessity. The construction personnel for these projects were collected and brought in from the Urals or the Don Basin . . . The imported labor force for these plants has formed a fair-sized town with almost no Latvian inhabitants . . . in every regional city new plants are being built. The construction labor, specialists, and production labor are imported, but the products are sent to the entire USSR . . .

5 Although the depletion of forests has exceeded reforestation for every year since the war, forests are being barbarically destroyed, turning large areas into swamps and leading to the importing of raw materials for the local furniture industry. For the last few years lumberjacks have been and are still being brought into Latvia from Russia, White Russia, and the Ukraine. The destruction of the forests continues and the imported lumberjacks settle permanently in the republic. This policy has led to the present situation where between 25,000 and 35,000 additional people each year become permanent residents of Riga. Total population has increased by a factor of 2.5; as a result, whereas Latvians in Latvia were 62 percent of the population in 1959 . . . only 40 percent [of the population were] Latvian in 1970. The future of such a policy can be clearly discerned from the fate of the former Karelian Soviet Socialist Republic. It exists no more, as it has been liquidated because the local nationals make up less than half of the total population of the republic. Now Karelia is a part of the Russian Soviet Federated Socialist Republic. A similar fate awaits the Kazakh SSR and Latvia.

6 Absorption of the local population into the mass of arriving Russians, White Russians, and Ukrainians is also furthered by the establishment of large bases for the armed forces and border guards on Latvian soil, as well as the building of dozens of medical clinics, rest homes, and tourist facilities for the use of the entire Soviet Union . . .

In achieving the first basic aim, the increase in the number of non-Latvians in the republic, steps are also being taken to achieve the second basic aim, which is to assimilate the Latvians and lead to the Russian way of life throughout Latvia. To achieve this the following things already have been done and are still being done:

1 The arrivals' demands for increased Russian-language radio and television programming have been met. Currently, one radio station and one television station broadcast programs only in Russian, while the others broadcast programs bilingually. Thus, approximately two-thirds of radio and television broadcasts are in Russian . . .

6 In all high schools and institutions of higher learning there are extensive study programs in Russian.

7 In newspapers, radio and television broadcasts, meetings, and books – everywhere, every day, friendship with Russians is encouraged; widely propagandized are cases where Latvian girls marry Russians or Latvian youths marry Russian girls.

Source: Saunders (ed.), Samizdat, pp. 427–8, 431–3, 434, 435.

Several important themes emerge from these accounts. First, it should be noted that although these materials are ascribed to the 'dissident' camp, at this stage the national movements were overwhelmingly loyal, seeking change within the framework of the existing system and ideology. It was the regime's failure to draw on this source of renewal that prepared the ground for the disintegration of the Union in 1991. Environmental issues were to play a large part in the emergence of a distinctive patriotic Russian literary consciousness from the 1970s. Valentin Rasputin was concerned with the pollution of Lake Baikal, the world's largest reserve of fresh water, while a number of 'village writers' described the degradation of Russian rural life. In art, as mentioned in Plyushch's memoirs, cited above, Il'ya Glazunov took up Russian national themes in his work. As we have seen, however, it was Solzhenitsyn who almost single-handedly defined a patriotic Russian identity, not so much in opposition to communism but transcending it.

The Interregnum – Andropov's Authoritarian Reform

The eighteen years of Brezhnev's stultifying regime finally came to an end in November 1982. The man who had masterminded the struggle against dissent as head of the KGB since 1967 now became General Secretary. In his former capacity Yurii Andropov was at least well informed about the problems facing the country and sought to devise a programme of authoritarian reform to deal with them. His health, however, declined rapidly and in February 1984 he died. He was strong enough to ensure a powerful role for the youngest member of the Politburo, Mikhail Gorbachev. In the event a Brezhnev protégé was selected to replace Andropov, the aged and infirm Konstantin Chernenko, who lasted barely thirteen months until March 1985, allowing Gorbachev to come to power.

Document 9.32 Andropov on Continuity and Nationality Issues

In the short time allowed him, Andropov launched a vigorous anti-corruption campaign in which many of Brezhnev's associates and relatives were implicated. On the political level he brought in new people and conceded some space for divergent views on the way forward. The campaign against dissent, however, was not halted, and indeed the struggle against absenteeism and other forms of social laxness was intensified. In his first speech as leader to the Central Committee on 22 November 1982 (*Pravda*, 23 November 1982), Andropov promised continuity, but opened the door to a renewal of détente and closer relations with China. While Andropov might have been well informed about corruption and political deviancy, he gave no indication that he understood the tension in nationality relations. The fifty-three national federal units in the USSR were ranked in a hierarchy and patterned as a matryeshka doll, with some areas contained within others. His speech on the sixtieth anniversary of the USSR on 21 December 1982 was a classic summary of the Soviet thinking of the period, but he was far too sanguine about the resolution of the national question.

The USSR: Sixty Years

Marxism revealed for the first time ever an organic link between the nationalities problem and the social, class nature of society, the prevailing type of ownership. In other words, the roots of relations between nations are embedded in the social soil. From here Marx and Engels drew their fundamental conclusion: the abolition of social oppression is an indispensable prerequisite for the abolition of ethnic oppression. '. . . Victory of the proletariat over the bourgeoisie', Marx said, 'is simultaneously a signal for the emancipation of all oppressed nations.' The immortal slogan 'Workers of the world, unite', the working people's international struggle against all forms of enslavement, both social and ethnic . . .

What looks obvious today was by no means so obvious in that stormy transitional period. The quests for concrete forms of statehood, for political institutions to embody the general ideas and prerequisites of a nationalities programme, aroused heated debates. Conflicting opinions ranged from a programme of loose, amorphous unification of the Republics in a confederation to a demand for their simple incorporation into the Russian Federation on the principle of autonomy. It took Lenin's genius and prestige to find and affirm the only correct path, that of socialist federalism . . .

All nations and national minorities living in the twenty autonomous Republics and eighteen autonomous regions and districts as one friendly family successfully bring their potentialities into play. Millions of Germans, Poles, Koreans, Kurds and members of other nationalities are fully-fledged Soviet citizens for whom the Soviet Union has long been their homeland.

The peoples of this country feel especially warm gratitude to the Russian people. Without its selfless fraternal assistance the present achievements of any of the Republics would have been impossible. A factor of exceptional significance in the economic, political and cultural life of this country, in promoting the unity of all its nations and national minorities, in giving them access to the wealth of world civilization, is the Russian language, which has naturally become part and parcel of the life of millions of people of any nationality . . .

The real qualitative changes which have taken place in relations between nations over the last sixty years is evidence that the nationalities problem in the form we inherited it from the exploiter system has been successfully resolved finally and irreversibly. For the first time in history the multinational composition of a country's population has turned from a source of its weakness into a source of its strength and prosperity.

Source: Yu. V. Andropov, Speeches and Writings, *2nd edn (Oxford, Pergamon Press, 1983), pp. 1–2, 5.*

Document 9.33 Andropov and the Need for Flexibility

In other respects, Andropov was rather more open to change and acknowledged some of the problems facing the country, although he vigorously defended Soviet achievements.

The Teaching of Karl Marx and Some Problems of Socialist Construction in the USSR

On the basis of a socialist ownership of the means of production we have built a powerful economy, which is being developed according to plan, enabling national economic and social problems of great scope and complexity to be attacked and solved effectively. Needless to say, these possibilities of ours do not mean that we can rest on our oars. Problems and grave difficulties can and do arise in this field. They vary in origin but are never associated with the essence of public, collective ownership which has been firmly established and has proved its advantages. On the contrary, some of the bottlenecks interfering at times with normal work in certain fields of our national economy are caused precisely by departures from the norms and requirements of economic life, which is based on the strong foundation of socialist ownership of the means of production . . .

We are now focusing our minds on enhancing the efficiency of production and the economy as a whole. The party and the Soviet people are profoundly aware of the importance of this problem. As far as its practical solution is concerned, however, the progress to be seen here is not as successful as it should be. What hinders this progress? Why do we fail to get sufficient returns on the enormous investments we make, and why are the achievements of science and technology applied in production at a rate that cannot satisfy us?

One could list many causes, of course. First of all, one cannot fail to see that our work in perfecting and restructuring the economic mechanism, and the forms and methods of management, is lagging behind the requirements made by the level attained by Soviet society in its material, technological, social and cultural development. This is the main thing. At the same time one can also feel the impact of such factors, for instance, as large shortfalls in supplies of farm produce over the last four years, and the need to invest growing amounts of financial and material resources in developing fuel, energy and raw materials resources in the country's northern and eastern areas.

One may again and again reiterate Marx's fundamental idea that acceleration of the progress of productive forces requires corresponding forms of organization of economic work; but matters will be at a standstill until this theoretical principle is translated into the concrete language of practice. Today, first priority is attached to the task of planning and consistently implementing measures capable of lending greater scope to the action of the colossal constructive potentials inherent in our economy . . .

One should in general handle with care the so-called fundamental truisms of Marxism, because one guilty of misunderstanding or ignoring them is severely punished by life itself. For instance, the full significance of Marx's views on distribution was only realized at the cost of great pains and even mistakes. He persistently pointed out that in the first phase of communism every worker 'receives from society after all deductions exactly as much as he himself gives society', that is, in strict accordance with the quantity and quality of his work which conforms to the basic principles of socialism: 'from each according to his abilities, to each according to his work'. A consistent democrat and humanist, Marx was a strong opponent of wage levelling and categorically rejected demagogic or naive arguments, which were fairly common in his time, depicting socialism as a society of 'universal equality' in distribution and consumption . . .

However, suffice it to take a look at the manpower shortage and the demographic situation in the country to realize clearly the economic disadvantage of further retention of a large share of manual, non-mechanized work which accounts for 40 per cent in industry alone. This is why it is so vital today to accelerate in every way the rates of scientific and technological progress, to apply its achievements more actively, primarily in those areas where labour inputs are especially great . . .

In our country exactly as, incidentally, in any country where the working class, the working people, took over political power, this meant a triumph of democracy in the most literal and precise sense of the word – a genuine triumph of government by the people. The working people finally achieved the rights and freedoms capitalism had always denied them and does deny them today, if not formally, then in fact . . .

In the course of building a new society the content of socialist democracy is enriched, restrictions imposed by historic necessity are lifted, and the forms of the exercise of people's power become more diversified. This progress is closely bound up with the development of socialist statehood which itself undergoes qualitative changes. The most important of them is the development of the state of the dictatorship of the proletariat into a state of the whole people. This is a change of enormous significance for the socialist political system. It is recorded in the Constitution of the USSR of 1977 which has provided the legislative foundation for the further intensifying of socialist democracy . . .

Soviet society has abolished the gulf between the interests of the state and the citizen existing under capitalism. Unfortunately, there are still a few individuals who attempt to impose their selfish interests on society and its other members. In this light one can clearly see the need for work in education, and sometimes in the re-education of certain individuals, for struggle against violations of socialist law and order, of the rules of our collectivist community life. This is not a violation of 'human rights', as is hypocritically alleged by bourgeois propaganda, but real humanism and democracy which means government by the majority in the interests of all working people.

Sources: Kommunist, *no. 3, 1983; Andropov, 'The Teaching of Karl Marx and Some Problems of Socialist Construction'*, Speeches and Writings, *pp. 281, 282, 285, 288, 289–90, 292.*

Document 9.34   The Role of Ideology

The death of Brezhnev permitted a profound debate over the content and role of ideology in the Soviet Union. In his speech on the hundredth anniversary of the death of Marx in January 1983, Andropov revealed a slightly more pragmatic approach in arguing for a re-evaluation of the role of ideology.

To verify one's actions by the principles of Marx, of Marxism-Leninism, is by no means to compare mechanically the process of life with certain formulas. We would be worthless followers of our teachers if we satisfied ourselves with a repetition of truths they had discovered and relied on the magic power of quotations once learned by heart. Marxism is not a dogma but a living guide to action, to independent work on complicated problems we are faced with at every new turn of history . . . We Soviet communists are proud to belong to the most influential ideological movement in the entire history of world civilization – Marxism-Leninism. Fully open to what is best and most advanced in modern science and culture, it is today the focus of the world's intellectual life and reigns over the minds of millions upon millions of people. This is the ideological creed of an ascending class liberating all mankind. This is the philosophy of social optimism, the philosophy of the present and future.

Sources: Kommunist, *no. 3, 1983; Andropov, 'The Teaching of Karl Marx and Some Problems of Socialist Construction'*, Speeches and Writings, *pp. 296, 297–8.*

While Andropov asserted that all the antagonistic contradictions had been resolved by the transition from capitalism to socialism, non-antagonistic ones remained that could not be ignored. Battle was joined at the June 1983 'ideological plenum' of the Central Committee. Andropov spoke in favour of the 'creative use of ideology'. Marxism, he argued, does not give answers in ideology once and for all. Chernenko countered, however, by asserting that 'there are eternal verities, some truths which cannot be changed'. His was the voice of an old generation unremittingly hostile to the modernisation of the ideology. Andropov, in contrast, insisted that changes in the productive forces required changes in production relations and he attacked 'formalism' and 'mechanical repetition' (Andropov, 1983, pp. 340–59).

Document 9.35   Zaslavskaya – the Novosibirsk Report

Discussions between academics at the Academy of Sciences in Novosibirsk gave rise to a report presented in April 1983 by the economic sociologist Tatyana Zaslavskaya to a closed seminar of top economic officials. Its central argument, too radical to be published at the time, suggested that the Soviet economic system had barely chaged in fifty years and had outlived its potential. Only a shift from the administrative system towards greater use of the market and decentralisation could overcome the accumulated problems. She stressed the social pathologies generated by the existing system as much as its economic deficiencies, and warned that entrenched social forces would resist reform.

Over a number of decades, Soviet society's economic development has been characterized by high rates and great stability . . . However, in the past 12–15 years a tendency towards a noticeable decline in the rate of growth of the national income began to make itself felt in the development of the economy of the USSR . . . [T]here is a more general reason at the foundation of this phenomenon. In our opinion it consists in the lagging of the system of production relations, and hence of the mechanism of state management of the economy which is its reflection, behind the level of development of the productive forces. To put it in more concrete terms, it is expressed in the inability of this system to make provision for the full and sufficiently effective use of the labour potential and intellectual resources of society.

The basic features of the present system of state management of the economy of the USSR (and thus of the system of production relations to which it gives rise) were formed roughly five decades ago. Since that time, this system has repeatedly been readjusted, renewed and improved, but not once has it undergone a qualitative restructuring which would reflect fundamental changes in the state of the productive forces . . . The structure of the national economy long ago crossed the threshold of complexity when it was still possible to regulate it effectively from one single centre . . .

Any serious reorganization of economic management must be accompanied by a certain redistribution of rights and responsibilities among various groups of workers . . . Thus, a good number of workers in the central organs of management, whose prospective role ought to be increased, is afraid that its responsibilities will become substantially more complicated, as economic [i.e. market] methods of management demand much more of highly qualified cadres than do administrative methods . . .

In the light of what has been said, we must admit that the social mechanism of economic development as it functions at present in the USSR does not ensure satisfactory results. The social type of worker formed by it fails to correspond not only to the strategic aims of a developed socialist society, but also to the technological requirements of contemporary production. The widespread characteristics of many workers, whose personal formation occurred during past five-year plans, are low labour- and production-discipline, an indifferent attitude to the work performed and its low quality, social passivity, a low value attached to labour as a means of self-realization, an intense consumer orientation, and a rather low level of moral discipline . . .

It is our conviction that both the expansion of these negative phenomena and the lowering of the rate of growth of production come about as a result of the degeneration of the social mechanism of economic development. At present, this mechanism is 'tuned' not to stimulate, but to thwart the population's useful economic activity. Similarly, it 'punishes' or simply cuts short initiatives by the chiefs of enterprises, in the sphere of production organization, aiming at the improvement of economic links. Nowadays, higher public value is placed not on the activities of the more talented, brave and energetic leaders, but on the performances of the more 'obedient' chiefs, even if they cannot boast production successes.

Source: Tatyana Zaslavskaya, 'The Novosibirsk Report', Survey, vol. 28, no. 1, Spring 1984, pp. 88, 91, 99, 106.

It was left to Gorbachev to resolve the issues raised by Zaslavskaya, beginning with the adoption of Andropov's modest opening and then dramatically extending the scope for debate and change.

Crisis and fall of the Soviet system, 1985–1991

By the early 1980s crisis symptoms were everywhere apparent. The country faced new economic challenges provoked by advanced modernisation, and political challenges stimulated by the effective extended political exclusion of the mass of the people. Life within the party itself had become formalised and dull, while the soviets were bureaucratised and lifeless. Responses to the crisis were at first partial, stressing notions like 'acceleration' (*uskorenie*), 'openness' (*glasnost*) and 'restructuring' (*perestroika*), before more global approaches began to emerge examining the problems facing the Soviet Union in terms of 'systemic crisis' and problems of civilisational integration. Towering over this last period is the personality of the USSR's last leader, Mikhail Sergeevich Gorbachev, who was elected General Secretary of the party in March 1985.

Early Experiments

Zaslavskaya had condemned the way that the economy systematically undermined initiative and promoted alienation, arguing that middle-level functionaries were the most resistant to reform out of fear for their privileges. It was now time for Gorbachev to discover the route and possibilities of reform.

Document 10.1   Gorbachev's First Views

Although Gorbachev had already indicated dissatisfaction with the system, in particular in a speech of December 1984 when he had first raised the themes of *perestroika*, his early speeches as leader gave little indication of what would come later. The biggest change at first appeared to be one of style, with an active and obviously intelligent leader at the helm of the Soviet Union after so many years of rule by gerontocrats, rather than one of content. Elected General Secretary of the party at the Central Committee plenum of 11 March 1985, he had this to say.

The strategic line, developed at the Twenty-sixth Congress and later Central Committee plenums with the active involvement of Yu. V. Andropov and K. U. Chernenko, was and remains unchangeable. This line is for the acceleration of the socio-economic development of the country, for the improvement of all aspects of the life of society. We are speaking about the transformation of the material-technical bases of production. We are talking about improving the system of social relations, above all economic. We are speaking about the development of people themselves, of the qualitative improvement of the material conditions of their life and work, their spiritual well-being.

We have to achieve a decisive turn in transferring the economy on to the rails of intensive development. We must and are obliged in a very short time to achieve the most advanced scientific-technological positions, to the highest world levels of the productivity of social labour.

Source: Kommunist, *no. 5, 1985, pp. 8–9.*

Nowhere did Gorbachev state how this could realistically be achieved. While calling for the 'strengthening of socialist property' and for the 'undeviating fulfilment of the planned development of the economy', Gorbachev simultaneously called for 'increasing the independence and responsibility of enterprises'. These contradictory prescriptions were to become the hallmark of Gorbachev's policies. At his first full plenum (23 April 1985) as leader Gorbachev returned to the theme of 'acceleration' and outlined the general themes of *perestroika*. In setting ambitious but unrealistic targets Gorbachev actually disrupted the existing economy.

Document 10.2   The Anti-alcohol Campaign

The lack of foresight was nowhere more apparent than in the ill-conceived anti-alcohol campaign, launched by a Central Committee resolution on 7 May 1985. While alcohol abuse was a major drain on the Soviet economy and society, the authoritarian approach only increased the production of bootleg liquor and drove people to drink dangerous substitutes for vodka. Above all, an already unbalanced budget was deprived of one of its main sources of revenue. The decree was used to continue the crusade against private trade, described as 'speculation'.

Decree of the Supreme Soviet Presidium of 16 May 1985

2 The drinking of spirits during production (in the place of work, in buildings and on the premises of enterprises, institutions and organisations) or being drunk at work is liable to an administrative penalty in the form of a fine to the sum of 30 to 50 roubles . . .

7 The purchase and resale for the sake of gain of small amounts of vodka and other liquors, as well as mass consumption goods and agricultural products, till and sale receipts and bills, entertainment and other tickets, books, music notes, records, audio and video cassettes and other valuables, if the scale of profit does not exceed 30 roubles, is liable to an administrative penalty in the form of a fine of 50–100 roubles with the confiscation of the items being speculated.

Source: Spravochnik partiinogo rabotnika, *issue 26 (Moscow, Politizdat, 1986), pp. 617–23.*

Document 10.3 Gorbachev and the Need for *Perestroika*

Gorbachev's most considered analysis of perestroika in the early period of his rule came in his book of the same name. The work is imbued with an optimism over the reformability of the Soviet system. After the long blockage of substantive change in the Brezhnev years it appeared that it would take little more than a change of attitude on the part of the Soviet leadership to achieve a solution to the country's problems.

Perestroika is an urgent necessity arising from the profound processes of development in our socialist society . . . At some stage – this became particularly clear in the latter half of the seventies – something happened that was at first inexplicable. The country began to lose momentum. Economic failures became more frequent. Difficulties began to accumulate and deteriorate, and unresolved problems began to multiply. Elements of what we call stagnation and other phenomena alien to socialism began to appear in the life of society. A kind of 'braking mechanism' affecting social and economic development formed . . . Declining rates of growth and economic stagnation were bound to affect other aspects of the life of Soviet society. Negative trends seriously affected the social sphere. This led to the appearance of the so-called 'residual principle' in accordance with which social and cultural programs received what remained in the budget after allocations to production . . . This, unfortunately, is not all. A gradual erosion of the ideological and moral values of our people began . . . Propaganda of success – real or imagined – was gaining the upper hand. Eulogizing and servility were encouraged; the needs and opinions of ordinary working people, of the public at large, were ignored. In the social sciences scholastic theorization was encouraged and developed, but creative thinking was driven out from the social sciences, and superfluous and voluntarist assessments and judgements were declared indisputable truths . . . The presentation of a 'problem-free' reality backfired: a breach had formed in word and deed, which bred public passivity and disbelief in the slogans being proclaimed . . . Decay began in public morals; the great feeling of solidarity with each other that was forged during the heroic times of the Revolution, the first five-year plans, the Great Patriotic War and postwar rehabilitation was weakening . . . Party guidance was relaxed and initiative lost in some of the vital social processes . . . On the whole, society was becoming increasingly unmanageable . . . The need for change was brewing not only in the material sphere of life but also in public consciousness.

Source: Mikhail Gorbachev, Perestroika: New Thinking for our Country and the World *(London, Collins/Harvill, 1987), pp. 17, 18–19, 20, 21, 22, 23, 24.*

Some Fruits of *Glasnost*

The economic plans outlined in the 1961 Party Programme were a typical piece of Khrushchevite bombast. In practice, the impressive growth rates achieved in the 1950s gradually declined. If national income grew 7.2 per cent in 1966–70, in 1971–5 it fell to 5.1 per cent, 3.8 per cent in 1976–80 and down to 3.1 (if not lower) per cent in 1981–5. In the same period, the increase in labour productivity fell from 6.8 per cent per annum to 3.1 per cent (L. I. Abalkin, *Kursom uskorenie* (Moscow, Ekonomika, 1986), pp. 26–7; G. Khanin, 'Ekonomicheskii rost: al'ternativnaya otsenka', *Kommunist*, no. 17, 1988, p. 85).

Document 10.4   Soviet Economic Achievements: Alternative Views

There had long been doubts over the accuracy of Soviet statistics, and these came to a head over alternative evaluations of Soviet economic performance. In 1987 the economists G. Khanin and V. Selyunin were catapulted to fame when they argued that by 1985 Soviet income had not multiplied by 84.4 times the level of 1928, as claimed by the official statistics, but by only 6.6 times ('Lukavaya tsifra', *Novy mir*, no. 2, 1987). The scale of Soviet achievements had been radically inflated by the manipulation and falsification of data by officials. In the table below official Goskomstat (Central Statistical Agency) figures for the later period are compared with Khanin's (average annual rates in per cent). Note the dramatic deterioration in Soviet economic performance in 1990.

Average annual indices	*Source*	1971– 1975	1976– 1980	1981– 1985	1986	1987	1988	1989	1990
Growth in national income	Goskomstat	5.7	4.2	3.5	2.3	1.6	4.4	2.5	–4.0
	Khanin	3.2	1.0	0.6	1.3	0.7	0.3	–4.25	–9.0
Growth in labour productivity	Goskomstat	4.6	3.4	3.0	2.1	1.6	4.8	2.2	–3.0
	Khanin	1.9	0.2	0.0	1.2	0.8	1.3	–3.95	–8.0

Source: G. I. Khanin, Dinamika ekonomicheskogo razvitiya SSSR *(Novosibirsk, Nauka, 1991).*

Document 10.5   The USSR Compared to the Seven Most Developed Countries (1991, per cent)

Not only was the Soviet performance in comparison with its own past declining (however accurate the figures for the earlier years might be), its position relative to other leading countries was increasingly less impressive.

Country	Volume			Per capita		
	GNP	Industry	Agriculture	GNP	Industry	Agriculture
USA	100	100	100	100	100	100
Japan	42	72	42	84	144	82
Germany (united)	25	41	24	80	133	63
France	19	22	32	84	96	115
UK	16	1	13	68	81	45
Italy	14	15	15	59	67	78
Canada	10	9	12	98	81	100
USSR	38	48	64	30	42	38

Source: Argumenty i fakty, *no. 26, 1991, p. 4.*

Document 10.6   Consumption of Goods and Services, and Productivity of Labour in 1991

Although there is no agreement on the figures, the data at least indicate the scale of Soviet economic backwardness. In terms of consumption and productivity, the USSR had fallen far behind the more developed societies. Indeed, the argument was often made in the last years of the Soviet Union (not least by Yeltsin himself) that in relative terms the USSR was further behind in the late 1980s than Russia had been in 1914.

Country	Consumption per capita	Annual production per employed person	
		Industry	Agriculture
USA	100	100	100
Japan	65	90	22
Germany (united)	70	85	45
France	80	85	56
UK	70	60	56
Italy	60	60	42
Canada	95	90	85
USSR	20	25	9

Source: Argumenty i fakty, *no. 26, 1991, p. 4.*

Reform of the Political System

The much-delayed January 1987 CC plenum outlined some proposals for democratisation; while modest in themselves, they represented a major break with the past. The year 1988 was the decisive one for reforms. The extracts below show the resistance to *perestroika*, and at the same time the radicalisation of reforms by Gorbachev and his entourage. It was in this year that the reform consensus of 1985 finally disintegrated. While Alexander Yakovlev and others sought a decisive radicalisation of reforms, Yegor Ligachev represented the views of those who favoured moderate reforms within the framework of the existing system, but resisted solutions that would transform the existing social and political relations.

Document 10.7   Reform of the Political System: First Steps

It was only with the thrice-postponed Central Committee plenum of 27 January 1987 that the first steps were taken towards the democratisation of the political system. At the heart of the political reforms was the introduction of greater electivity for party and state officials. Gorbachev's speech recognised that reform would not be as easy as first thought, that the source of the problems lay deep in Soviet history, and that the decisions of the Twenty-seventh Party Congress, held in February 1986, had not gone far enough. Gorbachev retained his belief in a renewed Leninism, in particular harking back to the Lenin of the early 1920s; for a growing number of critics, however, Lenin was part of the problem, not the solution. Gorbachev's argument that 'We must not retreat and do not have anywhere to retreat to' became his unofficial motto of *perestroika* and was truer than even he realised.

The plenary meeting has on its agenda a matter of paramount importance to the effective fulfilment of the political strategy drafted by the April 1985 plenary meeting of the Central Committee and the 27th CPSU Congress, the question of reorganisation and the Party's personnel policy. It is considered in a broad social and political context, with due regard for the lessons of the past, the nature of the present time and the tasks to come . . .

The first political conclusion is that major changes are taking place in the life of Soviet society and that positive tendencies are gaining momentum. The policy line of the 27th Congress, the practical efforts to fulfil it and reorganisation itself have been given broad support by workers, by the entire Soviet people. At the same time, change for the better is taking place slowly, the cause of reorganisation is more difficult and the problems which have accumulated in society are more deep-rooted than was first thought. That is why there is an urgent need to return to an analysis of those problems which confronted the Party and Soviet society in the few years preceding the April 1985 plenary meeting of the CPSU Central Committee, to understand the reasons for negative processes and to work out measures to speed up our progress, to keep us from repeating mistakes . . .

The report draws the conclusion that in the recent past, conservative sentiments, inertia, a tendency to brush aside anything which did not fit into conventional patterns prevailed in policy-making and practical work. The extent to which vital problems and contradictions and societal tendencies and prospects were understood depended in many ways on the condition and progress of theory. Lenin's dictum that the value of a theory consists in its providing an exact picture 'of all the contradictions that are present in reality' was often merely ignored. The theoretical concepts of socialism remained to a large extent at the level of the 1930s–1940s when society had been tackling entirely different tasks. Developing socialism, the dialectics of its motive forces and contradictions and the actual condition of society did not become the subject of in-depth scientific research.

Lenin's ideas of socialism were interpreted simplistically and their theoretical depth and significance were often left emaciated. This was true of such key problems as public property, relations between classes and nationalities, the measure of work and measure of consumption, co-operation, methods of economic management, people's rule and self-government and others. Spurious notions of communism and various prophecies and abstract views gained currency. Production and incentive were actually orientated to quantitative, extensive growth. Control over who managed socialist property and how had been slackened. It was often eroded by departmental and parochial attitudes and become 'no-one's', free, without any real master, and in many cases came to be used to derive unearned income. There was an incorrect attitude to co-operative property, which had grievous consequences for agrarian and social policies . . .

The economy as a whole became cumbersome and relatively unreceptive to innovation. The quality of a considerable part of output no longer met the current requirements, and imbalances in production became aggravated. Negative processes seriously affected the social sphere. Having successfully resolved the question of employment and having provided basic social guarantees, we at the same time failed to realise in full the potential of socialism to improve housing conditions, food supply, transport, health care and education and the solution of a number of other vital problems. There emerged violations of the most important principle of socialism, distribution according to work. Efforts to control unearned income were indecisive. Parasitic sentiments grew stronger and the mentality of 'wage levelling' [*uravnilovka*] began to take hold. Elements of social corrosion that emerged in the past few years had a negative effect on the society's morale and inconspicuously eroded the lofty moral values which have always been characteristic of our people and of which we are proud, namely, ideological dedication, labour enthusiasm and Soviet patriotism. As an inevitable consequence of all this, interest in the affairs of society slackened, manifestations of callousness and scepticism appeared and the role of moral incentive to work declined.

Serious shortcomings in ideological and political education were in many cases disguised with ostentatious activities and campaigns and celebrations of numerous jubilees in the centre and in the provinces. The world of day-to-day realities and that of make-believe well-being were increasingly parting ways. Disregard for laws, report-padding, bribe-taking and encouragement of toadyism and adulation had a deleterious influence on the moral atmosphere in society. The ideology and mentality of stagnation had their effect on culture, literature and the arts. Criteria in appraising artistic creative work were reduced. As a consequence, there appeared quite a few mediocre, faceless works, which did not give anything to the mind or the heart, along with works which raised serious social and moral problems and reflected true-to-life collisions. There appeared stereotypes from capitalist mass culture with its propagation of vulgarity, primitive tastes and spiritual callousness, which began to infiltrate Soviet society to a larger extent . . . The principles of collective leadership were being violated, the role of Party meetings and elective bodies were being weakened. Many Party members in senior executive positions were beyond control or criticism. The guarantees of the morality of Party ranks incorporated in the Party rules were not effective.

Everything said above shows how serious the situation was in different spheres of society and how bad the need for deep change. It was in that situation, comrades, that the question of speeding up the socio-economic development of the country and the question of reorganisation was raised. In essence, we are actually talking about a turning-point and measures of a revolutionary character. We simply don't have any other choice. We must not retreat and do not have anywhere to retreat to. We must steer the course charted by the April plenum of the Central Committee and the 27th Congress consistently and unswervingly, we must advance and take society to a qualitatively new level of development . . .

Of primary importance is the development of democracy at the point of production and the consistent introduction of truly self-governing principles. It is necessary to create such conditions and to introduce such forms of organisation of production and of the life of work collectives that would give every worker a sense of being the true master of his plant. The tasks of effective use of all forms of direct democracy will be defined in a law on the state enterprise (amalgamation) of which a draft is to be submitted for nation-wide discussion. Giving general meetings and councils of work collectives decisive powers on matters pertaining to production, social and personnel issues, which are envisaged by the draft, will lead to the qualitative perfection of social relations.

The collective farms and socialist co-operation as a whole have broad possibilities for democratising the processes of management of the economy and the social sphere. The promising steps already undertaken in many republics, territories and regions to broaden the co-operative forms of activities deserve support. The crucial issue of the development of democracy in production is the introduction of the system of electing heads of enterprises, shops and departments, heads of sections, farms and units, production team leaders and foremen. Transition to new methods of economic management, economic cost-accounting, self-repayment put that task on a practical plane.

The democratisation of the process of forming the managerial personnel on the basis of the application of the principle of electivity everywhere signals a new step forward and lends a fundamentally new character to the participation of the working people in production management. Party and public organisations and economic management organs are placed in new conditions. The electivity of senior executives in production far from undermining, on the contrary strengthens one–one management. An organic combination of one-man command and collegiality deepens and develops Lenin's principles of democratic centralism and centralised planned guidance with reliance on the collective of the masses.

The Political Bureau considers the perfection of the election system to be a fundamental trend in democratisation. Its existing mechanism ensures the democratic formation and representation of all sections of the population in the Soviets. But in common with all political, economic and social institutions, the election system cannot be left unchanged. It cannot stand aloof from the processes linked with reorganisation. The task is to give the elector the opportunity to express his or her attitude to a larger number of candidates, to rid the voting procedure of a number of elements of formalism. The broadening of inner-Party democracy, above all in forming the leading bodies of Party organisations at all levels, is becoming increasingly topical. The report contains specific proposals on that issue.

The democratisation of society poses afresh the question of control over how Party, Soviet and economic bodies and their cadres work. Of great significance is to raise the level and effectiveness of control 'from the grassroots' so that every leader, every executive should permanently feel his responsibility to and dependence on the electors, the work collectives, public organisations, the Party and the people as a whole. It is proposed to introduce systematic accountability of all executives who are elected and appointed, to strengthen the democratic principles of work of the sessions and standing commissions of the Soviets, to broaden public openness in the activities of government and public organisations, to streamline the system of various checks and inspections . . .

Serious attention is given to national aspects of personnel policy. The successes of this policy are undeniable, but we ought to look at the real picture and the prospects for developing national relations in the country. The more so since negative phenomena and deformations with which we have started to deal have emerged in this sphere too. Party organisations are obliged to handle in a more profound way questions of developing national and international relations, questions of internationalist education. Any nationalist and chauvinistic trends can be successfully opposed only by consistent, sustained internationalism.

Sources: Mikhail Gorbachev, 'On Reorganisation and the Party's Personnel Policy', 27 January 1997, Soviet News, no. 6360, 4 February 1987, pp. 37–9;

'O perestroike i kadrovoi politike partii', in M. S. Gorbachev, Izbrannye rechi i stat'i, *vol. 4 (Moscow, Izd-vo politicheskoi literatury, 1987), pp. 299–354.*

Document 10.8   Gorbachev Celebrates the Seventieth Anniversary of the October Revolution

The speech on 2 November 1987 on the seventieth anniversary marked an important point in the Soviet evaluation of the past. The speech is quoted at length here because it represents the most consistent attempt to come to terms with the USSR's past and its place in the world. Given the nature of the occasion there were limits to how far Gorbachev could go in his critique of the past, and although he made some trenchant criticisms, it is clear that by and large the speech reflected Gorbachev's own beliefs: it reveals both the strengths and weaknesses of his analysis of the situation in which the Soviet Union found itself. Above all, the speech provided the theoretical basis for the New Political Thinking (NPT) in foreign policy.

Dear Comrades, esteemed foreign guests,

It is 70 years since the unforgettable days of October 1917, those legendary days that started the new epoch of social progress, of the real history of humankind. The October Revolution is truly the shining hour of humanity, its radiant dawn. The October Revolution is a revolution of the people and for the people, for every individual, for his emancipation and development. Seventy years is not a long time in world civilisation's ascent over the centuries, but history has known no other period like it for the scale of the achievements that our country has accomplished since the victory of the October Revolution. There is no greater honour than to be pioneers, devoting one's strength, energy, knowledge, and ability to the triumph of the October Revolution's ideals and goals.

The jubilee is a moment of pride. Pride is what has been achieved. Arduous trials fell to our lot. And we withstood them honourably. We did not simply withstand them, we wrested the country out of its state of dislocation and backwardness and made it a mighty power, transforming life and changing man's inner world beyond recognition. In the cruellest battles of the 20th Century we safeguarded the right to our own way of life, and defended our future . . .

I The October Road: Road of Pioneers

Comrades, our pioneering road has been long and difficult. No brief analysis can encompass it. There was the burden of the material and moral heritage left over by the old world. The First World War, the Civil War, and intervention. There was the novelty of change and the related hopes of people, the rate and scale of the invasion of the new and unusual, leaving us no time to look back and think. There were subjective factors, which play a special part in revolutionary storms. There were notions of the future, often simplistic and straightforward, and shot through with the maximalism of revolutionary times. And there were the pure, ardent strivings of the fighters for a new life to accomplish things as quickly, as well and as fairly as possible. The past – its heroism and drama – cannot fail to thrill our contemporaries. Our history is one, and it is irreversible. Whatever emotions it may evoke, it is our history, and we cherish it . . .

The year 1917 showed that the choice between socialism and capitalism is the main social alternative of our epoch, that in the 20th Century there can be no progress without advance to socialism, a higher form of social organisation. This fundamental conclusion is no less relevant today than when it was first drawn by Lenin. Such is the logic of society's progressive development. The Revolution in Russia has become, as it were, the summit of liberative aspirations, the living embodiment of the dreams of the world's finest minds – from the great humanists of the past to the proletarian revolutionaries of the 19th and 20th centuries. The year 1917 absorbed the energy of the people's struggle for self-sustained development and independence, of progressive national movements, and the peasant risings and wars against serfdom which abounded in our history. It embodied the spirited search of the 18th-Century enlighteners, the heroes and martyrs of the Decembrist movement, the splendid champions of revolutionary democracy, and the moral dedication of the eminent men of our culture . . .

Trotsky and Trotskyites negated the possibility of building socialism in conditions of capitalist encirclement. In foreign policy they gave priority to the export of revolution, and in home policy to tightening the screws on the peasants, to the cities' exploiting of the countryside, and to administrative and military decree in running society. Trotskyism was a political current whose ideologists took cover behind leftist pseudo-revolutionary rhetoric, and in effect assumed a defeatist posture. It was essentially an attack on Leninism all down the line. The matter was of practical concern for the future of socialism in our country, the fate of the Revolution. In the circumstances, it was essential to disprove Trotskyism before the whole people, and to lay bare its anti-socialist essence. The situation was complicated by the fact that the Trotskyites were acting in common with the new opposition headed by Grigori Zinoviev and Lev Kamenev. Aware that they constituted a minority, the opposition leaders had again and again saddled the party with discussions, counting on a split in its ranks. But in the final analysis, the party spoke out for the line of the central committee and against the opposition, which was soon ideologically and organisationally crushed. In short, the party's leading nucleus, headed by Joseph Stalin, had safeguarded Leninism in an ideological struggle . . .

It is sometimes said that Stalin did not know of many instances of lawlessness. Documents at our disposal show that this is not so. The guilt of Stalin and his immediate entourage before the party and the people for the wholesale repressive measures and acts of lawlessness is enormous and unforgivable. This is a lesson for all generations. Contrary to the assertions of our ideological opponents, the Stalin personality cult was certainly not inevitable. It was alien to the nature of socialism, represented a departure from its fundamental principles and therefore has no justification. At its 20th and 22nd congresses the party severely condemned the cult itself and its consequences . . .

It is said that the decision taken by the Soviet Union in concluding a non-aggression pact with Germany was not the best one. This may be so, if one is guided not by harsh reality, but by abstract conjectures torn out of their time frame. In these circumstances, too, the issue was roughly the same as it had been at the time of the Brest peace: was our country to be or not to be independent, was socialism on Earth to be or not to be. The USSR made great efforts to build up a system of collective security and to avert a global slaughter. But the Soviet initiatives met no response from the Western political leaders and politicians, who were coolly scheming how best to involve socialism in the flames of war and bring about its head-on collision with fascism. Outcasts already by virtue of our socialist birth, we could under no circumstances be right from the imperialist point of view. As I said, the Western ruling circles, in an attempt to blot out their own sins, are trying to convince people that the Nazi attack on Poland, and thereby the start of the Second World War, was triggered by the Soviet–German non-aggression pact of 23 August 1939. As if there had been no Munich Agreement with Hitler signed by Britain and France back in 1938, with the active connivance of the USA, no Anschluss of Austria, no crucifixion of the Spanish Republic, no Nazi occupation of Czechoslovakia and Klaipeda, and no conclusion of non-aggression pacts with Germany by London and Paris in 1938. Such a pact was concluded by pre-war Poland too. All this, as you see, fitted neatly into the structure of imperialist policy and was – is – considered to be in the nature of things.

It is known from documents that the date of Germany's attack on Poland ('not later than 1 September') was fixed as early as 3 April 1939 – long before the Soviet–German pact. In London, Paris and Washington it was known in minute detail how the preparations for the Polish campaign were really proceeding, just as it was known that the only barrier capable of stopping the Hitlerites could be the conclusion of an Anglo-Franco-Soviet military alliance not later than August 1939. These plans were also known to the leadership of our country, and that was why it sought to convince Britain and France of the need for collective measures. It also urged the Polish government of the time to co-operate in curbing aggression. But the Western powers had different designs: to hold out the promise of an alliance to the USSR and thereby prevent the conclusion of the non-aggression pact we had been offered, thus depriving us of the chance to make better preparations for the inevitable attack by Hitler['s] Germany on the USSR.

Nor can we forget that in August 1939 the Soviet Union faced a very real threat of war on two fronts: in the west with Germany and in the east with Japan, which had started a costly conflict on the Khalkhin-Gol. But life and death, scorning myths, went into their real orbits. A new chapter was beginning in contemporary history, a most grim and complex one. At that stage, however, we managed to stave off the collision with the enemy – an enemy who had left himself and his opponent but one choice: to triumph or perish.

The aggression to which we were subjected was a merciless test of the viability of the socialist system, of the strength of the multinational Soviet state, of the patriotic spirit of Soviet men and women. We withstood this test by fire and sword, comrades! We withstood it because for our people this war became a Great Patriotic War: for in a struggle with such an enemy as German fascism the issue was one of life or death, of being free or enslaved . . .

II Socialism in Development and Perestroika

Comrades, we had been led to the conclusion on the necessity for perestroika by pressing needs that brooked no delay. But the more deeply we examined our problems and probed their meaning, the clearer it became that perestroika also has a broader socio-political and historical context. Perestroika implies not only eliminating the stagnation and conservatism of the preceding period and correcting the mistakes committed, but also overcoming historically limited, outdated features of social organisation and work methods. It implies imparting to socialism the most contemporary forms, corresponding to the conditions and needs of the scientific and technological revolution and to the intellectual progress of Soviet society. This is a relatively lengthy process of the revolutionary renewal of society, a process that has its logic and stages . . .

Two key problems of the development of society determine the fate of perestroika. These are the democratisation of all social life and a radical economic reform . . . The purpose of the radical economic reform begun in the country is to assure, over the next two or three years, a transition from an overly centralised command system of management to a democratic system based mainly on economic methods and on an optimal combination of centralism and self-management . . .

III The October Revolution and Today's World

. . . The new thinking with its regard for universal human values and emphasis on common sense and openness is forging ahead on the international scene, destroying the stereotypes of anti-Sovietism and dispelling distrust of our initiatives and actions . . .

The new way of thinking has helped us to generally prove that a comprehensive system of international security in the context of disarmament is needed and is possible. Now we must prove that the attainment of this goal is necessary and feasible. We must identify the laws governing the interaction of the forces which, through rivalry, contradictions and conflicting interests, can produce the desired effect. In this connection we should begin by posing some tough questions – of course, tackling them from Leninist positions and using Leninist methodology.

The first question relates to the nature of imperialism. We know that it is the major source of the war threat. It goes without saying that external factors cannot change the nature of a social system. But, given the current stage of the world's development and the new level of its interdependence and integration, is it possible to influence that nature and block its more dangerous manifestations? In other words, can one count on the laws operating in the integral world, in which universal human values have top priority, to restrict the scope of the destructive effects produced by the operation of the egocentric laws which benefit only the ruling classes and which are basic to the capitalist system?

The second question is connected with the first one: can capitalism get rid of militarism and function and develop in the economic sphere without it? Is it not a delusion on our part to invite the West to draw up and compare conversion programmes for switching the economy to civilian production?

The third question: can the capitalist system do without neo-colonialism, currently one of the factors essential to its survival? In other words, can this system function without the practice of inequitable trade with the Third World which is fraught with unforeseeable consequences? Another related question: how realistic is our hope that the awareness of the terrible threat the world is facing – and we know that this awareness is making its way even into the higher echelons of the Western ruling elite – will be translated into practical policies? After all, however forceful the arguments of common sense, however well-developed the sense of responsibility, however powerful the instinct of self-preservation, there are still things which must not be underrated and which are determined by an economic and, consequently, a class-based self-interest.

In other words, the question is whether capitalism can adapt itself to the conditions of a nuclear-free world without weapons, to the conditions of a new and equitable economic order, to the conditions in which the intellectual and moral values of the two world systems will be compared honestly. These are far from idle questions. The course history will take in the coming decades will depend on the way they are answered. But even posing these questions is enough to grasp the gravity of the task that lies ahead. We will see them answered in due time. Meanwhile, the viability of the programme for a nuclear-free and safe world will not only depend on its flawless scientific substantiation but will also be tested by the course of events – something that is influenced by a wide variety of factors, many of them new. It is, in fact, already being tested. Here, too, we are loyal to the Leninist tradition, to the very essence of Leninism – an organic blend of theory and practice, an approach to theory as a tool of practice and to practice as a mechanism verifying the viability of theory. That is how we are acting, projecting the new way of thinking into our foreign policy activities, adjusting it by political experience. To sum up, what do we count on in our awareness that a safe world will have to be built jointly with capitalist countries? . . .

The next point. Can a capitalist economy develop without militarisation? This brings to mind the 'economic miracle' in Japan, West Germany and Italy – although it is true that when the 'miracle' was over, they switched to militarism again. But here one should examine the degree to which this switch was rooted in the substantive laws governing the operation of contemporary monopoly capital and the role played by extraneous factors – the 'contagious example' of the US military-industrial complex, the cold war and its spirit, considerations of prestige, the desire to have one's own 'mailed fist' to be able to talk to one's competitors in a commonly understood language, and the intention to back one's economic invasion of the Third World with power politics. Whatever the actual reasons, there was a period when the modern capitalist economy developed rapidly in several countries whose arms spending was minimal. The relevant historical experience is available . . .

The time of the Communist International, the information bureau, even the time of binding international conferences is over. But the world communist movement lives on. All parties are completely and irreversibly independent. We declared that as early as the 20th Congress. True, the old habits were not discarded at once. But today this has become an unalterable reality. In this sense, too, the 27th Congress of the CPSU was a final and irrevocable turning-point. I think this has been actually proved by our relations with fraternal parties in the course of perestroika . . .

The accumulated experience has ensured a better possibility of building relations between socialist countries on the following universally recognised principles:

- Unconditional and full equality;
- The ruling party's responsibility for the state of affairs in the country; its patriotic service to the people;
- Concern for the common cause of socialism;
- Respect for one another; a serious attitude to what has been achieved and tested by one's friends; voluntary and diverse co-operation;
- A strict observance of the principles of peaceful coexistence by all. This is what the practice of socialist internationalism rests on.

Today the socialist world appears before us in all its national and social variety. This is good and useful. We have satisfied ourselves that unity does not mean identity and uniformity. We have also become convinced of there being no 'model' of socialism to be emulated by everyone . . .

We can see today that humanity is not really doomed to always live the way it did before 1917. Socialism has evolved into a powerful, growing and developing reality. It is the October Revolution and socialism that show humankind the road to the future and identify the new values of truly human relations:

- Collectivism instead of egoism;
- Freedom from exploitation and oppression;
- The true power of the people instead of the tyranny of the few;
- The growing role of reason and humanism instead of the spontaneous and cruel play of social forces;
- Humankind's unity and peace instead of discord, strife and war . . .

In October 1917 we parted with the old world, rejecting it once and for all. We are moving towards a new world, the world of communism. We shall never turn off that road.

Sources: Mikhail Gorbachev, 'October and Perestroika: The Revolution Continues', 2 November 1987, Soviet News, no. 6399, 4 November 1987, pp. 393–7, 399, 403, 405; 'Oktyabr' i perestroika: revolyutsiya prodolzhaetsya', in Gorbachev, Izbrannye rechi i stat'i, vol. 5 (Moscow, Izd-vo politicheskoi literatury, 1988), pp. 386–436.

Document 10.9 Gorbachev – 'Revolutionary Perestroika and the Ideology of Renewal'

This speech, delivered to the Central Committee plenum on 18 February 1988, presented an extended analysis of Gorbachev's aims. This was perestroika's golden year, when political and economic reform moved forward and everything still seemed possible. In foreign relations the USSR committed itself to retreat from Afghanistan (the last Soviet forces left in February 1989) and relations with the West blossomed. Gorbachev enjoyed unprecedented personal popularity at home and abroad, the economy appeared to be growing, democratisation was taking root, and relations between state and society were moving towards a position of mutual trust. Gorbachev's vision of a renewed socialism returned to the themes of the *Praxis* group and the proponents of 'socialism with a human face' exactly twenty years earlier in Czechoslovakia, a socialism concerned with overcoming human alienation and placing humanistic concerns above class war, one where the ideology overcame the dogmatism of the past and where the party was subordinate to the movement: in short, a socialism that differed in almost every respect from the one in existence in the Soviet Union.

Comrades,
Our plenum is taking place at an important period of perestroika, or restructuring. The democratisation of social life and radical economic reform demand from the party a clear perspective of things to be done . . .

It is precisely the party, equipped with scientific knowledge of the past and present and of the tendencies that have real prospects of development, that is obliged to assume the lead in the processes of shaping socialist consciousness in society. It is precisely the party that can and must theoretically elucidate the new stage of socialist construction, taking into account the novelty brought to it by perestroika . . .

The awareness has been established now that perestroika is an objectively necessary stage of development of Soviet society whose essence is a transition to its new qualitative state. We must ensure radical changes in the productive forces and relations of production, revolutionary renewal of the social and political structures, and the growth of the spiritual and intellectual potential of society. We are striving in the present conditions to revive the Leninist look of the new system to rid it of the accumulations and deformations, of everything that shackled society and prevented it from realising the potential of socialism in full measure. And, which is the main thing, we are striving to impart new quality to socialist society, taking into account all the realities of the world today.

The essence of socialism lies in asserting the power of the working people, the priority of the benefit of man, the working class and the entire people. In the final account, the task of socialism is to put an end to the social alienation of man, characteristic of the exploiter society, alienation from power, from the means of production, from the results of one's work and from spiritual values.

The October Revolution opened the way to resolving this historic task. The establishment of the power of the working people, abolition of private ownership of the means of production and elimination of the exploitation of man by man have been steps of pivotal importance. These are the fundamental gains of socialism. Over 70 years our party and people have been inspired by the ideas of socialism and have been building it. But because of external and internal causes we have been unable fully to realise the Leninist principles of the new social system. This was seriously hampered by the cult of personality; the system of management by command and administration that formed in the '30s; bureaucratic, dogmatic and voluntarist aberration and arbitrariness; and the late '70s early '80s lack of initiative, and hindrances, that have led to stagnation.

These phenomena, and what has remained of them and come down to the present, should become things of the past. In this lies the answer to those who express their doubt, that we are retreating from socialism, from its foundations laid down by generations of Soviet people. No, we do not retreat even a step from socialism, from Marxism-Leninism, from everything that has been gained and created by the people. But we decisively reject a dogmatic bureaucratic and voluntarist legacy, as it has nothing in common either with Marxism-Leninism or with genuine socialism. Creative Marxism-Leninism is always an objective, profound scientific analysis of developing reality. It is critical analysis which does not look away from anything, which does not conceal anything, which does not fear any truth. Only such analysis is conducive to socialism. There are no, nor can there be any, limits to truly scientific quest. Questions of theory cannot and must not be decided by decrees . . .

I will recall that we started perestroika under the pressure of urgent, vital problems. On more than one occasion I had to return to the appraisal of the situation which had emerged in our country by the early '80s. I would like to add to that some considerations. As is known, the economic development rates were declining in our country, to reach a critical point. But even those rates, as has become clear now, were achieved in considerable measure on an unhealthy basis, due to temporary factors. I am referring to trade in oil in the world market at the high prices which had formed then, and the totally unjustified intensification of the sale of alcoholic beverages. If we look at the economic indicators of growth separately from these factors, we will see that during four five-year plan periods we had no increase in the absolute growth of the national income; it even started to decline in the early '80s. This is the real picture, comrades.

Only now is economic growth on a healthy basis beginning. We continue to experience, very much, the consequences of the situation shaped in the past. Now that the situation in the world market has changed and the prices of fuel and energy resources have declined, now that we are forced to reduce the production and sale of wines and vodka in the name of preserving the population's social health, the country's economy is confronted with a most serious financial problem. Over the past three years public revenues declined by more than 37,000 million roubles, as a result of the reduced sale of alcoholic beverages.

Sources: 'Mikhail Gorbachev's Speech at the CPSU Central Committee Plenum', 18 February 1988, Soviet News, no. 6413, 24 February 1988, pp. 61, 62–3, 64, 65, 67; 'Revolyutsionnoi perestroika ideologiyu obnovleniya', in Gorbachev, Izbrannye rechi i stat'i, vol. 6 (Moscow, Politizdat, 1989), pp. 58–92.

Document 10.10   Nina Andreeva, 'I Cannot Forgo Principles'

Nina Andreeva was a chemistry teacher in Leningrad when her letter denouncing some of the main principles of perestroika became a cause célèbre. She condemned the period's obsession with Stalin's crimes, the weakening of the class approach, the role played by 'neoliberals', and defended the heroic version of Russia's past. The letter represented a stark repudiation of perestroika and its version of history. There is some evidence to suggest that Ligachev had a hand in encouraging its preparation and publication.

I Cannot Forgo Principles

I decided to write this letter after a great deal of thought. I am a chemist, and I teach at the Leningrad Soviet Technological Institute in Leningrad. Like many others, I am an adviser for a group of students. In our days, after a period of social apathy and intellectual dependence, students are gradually beginning to be charged with the energy of revolutionary changes. Naturally, debates arise – about the paths of restructuring and its economic and ideological aspects. Openness, candour and the disappearance of zones closed to criticism, as well as emotional fervour in the mass consciousness, especially among young people, are frequently manifested in the posing of problems that, to one extent or another, have been 'prompted' by Western radio voices or by those of our compatriots who are not firm in their notions about the essence of socialism. What a wide range of topics is being discussed! A multiparty system, freedom of religious propaganda, leaving the country to live abroad, the right to a broad discussion of sexual problems in the press, the need for the decentralisation of the management of culture, the abolition of compulsory military service – among students, a particularly large number of arguments are about the country's past . . .

So much has been written and said about the Great Patriotic War and the heroism of those who took part in it. But recently a meeting took place in one of our Technological Institute's student dormitories with Hero of the Soviet Union V. F. Molozev, a retired colonel. One of the things he was asked about was political repression in the Army. The veteran replied that he had not encountered any repression, and that many of those who had started off the war with him and seen it through to the end had become major military commanders. Some of the students were disappointed with his answer. The now commonplace subject of repression has become excessively magnified in the perception of some young people, pushing an objective comprehension of the past into the background. Examples of this sort are not rare . . .

In talking with students and pondering crucial problems with them, I automatically come to the conclusion that a good many distortions and one-sided views have piled up in our country, notions that obviously need to be corrected. I want to devote special attention to some of these things.

Take the question of the place of J. V. Stalin in our country's history. It is with his name that the entire obsession with critical attacks is associated, an obsession that, in my opinion, has to do not so much with the historical personality itself as with the whole extremely complex transitional era – an era linked with the unparalleled exploits of an entire generation of Soviet people who today are gradually retiring from active labour, political and public activity. Industrialisation, collectivisation and the cultural revolution, which brought our country into the ranks of the great world powers, are being forcibly squeezed into the 'personality cult' formula. All these things are being questioned. Things have reached a point at which insistent demands for 'repentance' are being made on 'Stalinists' (and one can assign to their number whomever one wishes). Praise is being lavished on novels and films that lynch the era of tempestuous changes, which is presented as a 'tragedy of peoples'.

Let me note at the outset that neither I nor the members of my family have any relationship to Stalin or his entourage, retainers or extollers. My father was a worker in the Leningrad port, and my mother was a mechanic at the Kirov Plant. My older brother worked there, too. He, my father and my sister were killed in battles against the Hitlerites. One of my relatives was repressed and was rehabilitated after the 20th Party Congress. Together with all Soviet people, I share the anger and indignation over the large-scale repressions that took place in the 1930s and 1940s through the fault of the Party and state leadership of that time. But common sense resolutely protests the monochromatic colouring of contradictory events that has now begun to prevail in certain press organs.

I support the Party's call to uphold the honour and dignity of the trailblazers of socialism. I think that it is from these Party and class positions that we should assess the historical role of all Party and state leaders, including Stalin. In this case, one must not reduce the matter to the 'court' aspect or to abstract moralising by people far removed from that stormy time and from the people who lived and worked then. Indeed, they worked in such a way that what they did is an inspirational example for us even today.

For me and for many other people, the decisive role in assessing Stalin is played by the firsthand testimony of contemporaries who came into direct contact with him, on both our side of the barricades and the other side. Those in the latter group are not without interest. For example, take Churchill, who in 1919 was proud of his personal contribution to organising the military intervention of 14 foreign states against the young Soviet Republic but who, exactly 40 years later, was forced to use the following words to characterise Stalin – one of his most formidable political opponents:

> He was a man of outstanding personality who left an impression on our harsh times, the period in which his life ran its course. Stalin was a man of extraordinary energy, erudition and inflexible will, blunt, tough and merciless in both action and conversation, whom even I, reared in the British Parliament, was at a loss to counter. His works resounded with gigantic strength. This strength was so great in Stalin that he seemed unique among leaders of all times and peoples . . . This was a man who used his enemies' hands to destroy his enemy, who made us, whom he openly called imperialists, do battle against imperialists. He found Russia with a wooden plough, but he left it equipped with atomic weapons.

This assessment and admission on the part of a faithful guardian of the British Empire cannot be attributed to dissimulation or political expediency . . .

From long and frank discussions with young people, we draw the conclusion that the attacks on the state of the dictatorship of the proletariat and on the leaders of our country at that time have not only political, ideological and moral causes but also their own social substratum. There are quite a few people who have a stake in broadening the staging area of these attacks, and not just on the other side of our borders. Along with the professional anticommunists in the West, who long ago chose the supposedly democratic slogan of 'anti-Stalinism', there live and thrive the descendants of the classes overthrown by the October Revolution, by no means all of whom have been able to forget the material and social losses of their forebears. One must include here the spiritual heirs of Dan, Martov and others in the category of Russian Social Democratism, the spiritual followers or Trotsky or Yagoda, and the descendants of the NEPmen, the Basmachi [those who resisted Bolshevik rule in Central Asia in the early years of Soviet power] and the kulaks, who bear a grudge against socialism . . .

I think that, no matter how contradictory and complex a given figure in Soviet history may be, his true role in the construction and defence of socialism will, sooner or later, receive an objective and unambiguous assessment. Needless to say, it will be unambiguous not in the sense of being one-sided, of whitewashing or eclectically summing up contradictory phenomena, of an assessment that makes it possible, with qualifications, to create any kind of subjectivism, to 'forgive or not forgive', to 'discard or keep' elements of history. An unambiguous assessment means above all a historically concrete, nonopportunistic assessment that manifests – in terms of historical result! – the dialectics of the conformity of a given individual's activity to the basic laws of the development of society. In our country, these laws were also connected with the resolution of the question 'Who will win?' in its domestic and international aspects. If we are to follow the Marxist-Leninist methodology of historical research, then we must first of all, in M. S. Gorbachev's words, vividly show how millions of people lived, how they worked and what they believed in, and how victories and setbacks, discoveries and mistakes, the radiant and the tragic, the revolutionary enthusiasm of the masses and violations of socialist legality, and sometimes even crimes, were combined . . .

Recently, one of my students startled me with the revelation that the class struggle is supposedly an obsolete concept, as is the leading role of the proletariat. It would be all right if she were the only one maintaining such a thing. But, for example, a furious argument broke out recently over a respected academician's assertion that the present relations between states of the two different social and economic systems are devoid of class content. I admit that the academician did not deem it necessary to explain why for several decades he had written the exact opposite – that peaceful coexistence is nothing other than a form of class struggle in the international arena. It turns out that the philosopher has now repudiated that notion. Well, views do change. However, it seems to me that the duty of a leading philosopher does enjoin him to explain, at least to those who have learned and are learning from his books: Why does the international working class today, in the form of its state and political organs, really no longer act as a countervailing force to world capital?

It seems to me that the same question – which class or stratum of society is the guiding and mobilising force of restructuring? – is at the centre of many current debates . . . The first, and deepest, ideological current that has already revealed itself in the course of restructuring claims to be a model of some kind of left-liberal dilettantish socialism, to be the exponent of a humanism that is very true and 'clean' from class incrustations . . . It is the champions of 'left-liberal socialism' who are shaping the tendency to falsify the history of socialism. They suggest to us that in the country's past only the mistakes and crimes are real, in doing so keeping quiet about the supreme achievements of the past and the present. Laying claim to complete historical truth, they substitute scholastic ethical categories for social and political criteria of the development of society. I would very much like to understand: Who needs, and why, to have every prominent leader of the Party Central Committee and the Soviet government compromised after he leaves office and discredited in connection with his actual or supposed mistakes and miscalculations, made while solving some very complex problems on roads uncharted by history? Where did we get this passion for squandering the prestige and dignity of the leaders of the world's first socialist country?

Another special feature of the views of the 'left-liberals' is an obvious or camouflaged cosmopolitan tendency, a sort of nationality-less 'internationalism'. I have read somewhere that when, after the Revolution, a delegation of merchants and factory owners came to the Petrograd Soviet to see Trotsky 'as a Jew', complaining of oppression by Red Guards, he declared that he was 'not a Jew but an internationalist', which thoroughly bewildered the supplicants.

For Trotsky, the concept of the 'national' meant a kind of inferiority and narrowness in comparison to the 'international'. That's why he emphasised the 'national tradition' of October, wrote about 'the national element in Lenin', maintained that the Russian people 'had received no cultural legacy', etc. For some reason, we are ashamed to say that it was the Russian proletariat, which the Trotskyists slighted as 'backward and uncultured', that carried out, in Lenin's words, 'the three Russian Revolutions', or that the Slavic peoples were in the vanguard of mankind's battle against fascism . . .

Whereas the 'neoliberals' are oriented toward the West, the other [current], . . . the 'guardians and traditionalists', seek to 'overcome socialism by moving backward' – in other words, to return to the social forms of presocialist Russia. The spokesmen for this unique 'peasant socialism' are fascinated with this image. In their opinion, a loss of the moral values that the peasant community had accumulated through the dim haze of centuries took place 100 years ago. The 'traditionalists' have rendered undoubted services in exposing corruption, in fairly solving ecological problems, in combating alcoholism, in protecting historical monuments and in countering the dominance of mass culture, which they rightly assess as a psychosis of consumerism.

At the same time, the views of the ideologists of 'peasant socialism' contain a misunderstanding of the historical significance of October for the fatherland's fate, a one-sided appraisal of collectivisation as 'frightful arbitrary treatment of the peasantry', uncritical views on religious-mystical Russian philosophy, old tsarist concepts in scholarship relating to our country's history, and an unwillingness to see the postrevolutionary stratification of the peasantry and the revolutionary role of the working class.

In the class struggle in the countryside, for example, there is frequently an overemphasis on 'village' commissars who 'shot middle peasants in the back'. There were, of course, all kinds of commissars in our enormous country, which had been stirred to new life by the Revolution. But the basic tenor of our life was determined by those commissars who were themselves shot. It was they who had stars cut into their backs or were burned alive. The 'attacking class' had to pay not only with the lives of commissars, Chekists, village Bolsheviks, members of poor peasants' committees and 'twenty-thousanders', but also those of the first tractor drivers, rural correspondents, girl-teachers and rural Young Communists, with the lives of tens of thousands of other unknown fighters for socialism.

The difficulties in the upbringing of young people are deepened still more by the fact that unofficial [*neformalny*] organisations and associations are being created on the pattern of the ideas of the 'neoliberals' and 'neo-Slavophiles'. In some cases, extremist elements capable of provocations are gaining the upper hand in the leadership of these groups. Recently, the politicisation of these grass-roots [*samodeyatelny*] organisations on the basis of a pluralism that is far from socialist has been noted. Frequently the leaders of these organisations talk about 'power-sharing' on the basis of a 'parliamentary regime', 'free trade unions', 'autonomous publishing houses', etc. In my opinion, all this makes it possible to draw the conclusion that the main and cardinal question in the debates now under way in the country is the question of recognising or not recognising the leading role of the Party and the working class in socialist construction, and hence in restructuring – needless to say, with all the theoretical and practical conclusions for politics, the economy and ideology of the role and place of socialist ideology has taken on a very acute form. Under the aegis of a moral and spiritual 'cleaning', the authors of opportunistic constructs are eroding the boundaries and criteria of scientific ideology, manipulating openness and propagating an extrasocialist pluralism, which objectively impedes restructuring in social consciousness. This is having an especially detrimental effect on young people, something that, I repeat, we higher-school instructors, schoolteachers and all those who deal with young people's problems are distinctly aware of. As M. S. Gorbachev said at the February [1988] plenary session of the CPSU Central Committee: 'In the spiritual sphere as well, and perhaps in this sphere first of all, we must be guided by our Marxist-Leninist principles. Comrades, we must not forgo these principles under any pretexts.'

We stand on this, and we will continue to do so. We have not received these principles as a gift: We have gained them through suffering at decisive turning points in the history of the fatherland.

Sources: Nina Andreeva, 'I Cannot Forgo Principles', Letter to the Editors from an Instructor at a Leningrad Higher School, Sovetskaya Rossiya, 23 March 1988, p. 3; Current Digest of the Soviet Press, vol. XL, no. 13 (27 April 1988), pp. 1, 3–6.

Document 10.11   The Official Response to Nina Andreeva

The response was slow in coming, and for three weeks the intelligentsia remained silent, fearing that a change of official course had taken place. The response, published in *Pravda*, was drafted by Alexander Yakovlev, who by this time had become the main ideologue of *perestroika*.

The fight for *perestroika* is being carried out both in the production and in the cultural fields. Albeit that fight does not assume the form of class antagonisms, it is an acute one . . . [Nina Andreeva's letter] is an ideological platform, a manifesto of the anti-perestroika forces . . . not all forces realise fully that the administrative-command methods have exhausted themselves. All who pin their hopes on those methods or their modifications would do well to wake up to the fact that we have had that and more than once, but that it did not bring about the desired results . . .

The personality of Stalin is extremely contradictory. From this arise bitter debates. Standing on the position of historical truth, we must take into account Stalin's undoubted contribution to the struggle for socialism, the defence of the achievements, as well as crude political mistakes and arbitrariness made by him and his circle, for which our people paid an enormous price and which had terrible consequences for the life of our society. Yet voices are still raised that Stalin did not know about the acts of lawlessness. Not only did he know, he organised them, conducted them. Today this is already a proven fact. And Stalin's guilt, like the guilt of his closest circle, for having allowed mass repression and illegality before the party and people is enormous and unforgivable.

Indeed, any historical figure is formed by concrete socio-economic and ideological-political conditions. But the cult was not inevitable. It is alien to the essence of socialism and is possible only because of a retreat from its basic principles.

We firmly and undeviatingly will follow the revolutionary principles of *perestroika*: more *glasnost*, more democracy, more socialism. The past is essential for the present, for resolving the tasks of *perestroika*. The objective demand of life is 'more socialism', and forces us to sort out what we did yesterday and how we did it. What we have to reject, and what we have to take with us. What principles and values should we consider genuinely socialist? And if today we look at our past with a critical gaze, then it is only because we want better and more fully to understand the path to the future.

To ignore the painful questions of our history means to scorn the truth, to treat with disrespect the memory of those who were innocent victims of illegality and arbitrary rule. There is only one truth. Full clarity, accuracy and consistency and a moral orientation to the future are required.

Source: 'Printsipy perestroiki: revolyutsionnoe myshelenie i deistviya' ('The Principles of Perestroika: Revolutionary Thinking and Actions'), Pravda, 5 April 1988.

Document 10.12   The Nineteenth Party Conference

The Nineteenth Party Conference (28 June–1 July 1988) marked the decisive turning point in *perestroika*. On the one hand, a radical programme for the renewal of society was outlined. On the other, the end point remained unclear and vital questions remained unanswered: would the Communist Party retain its leading role; to what extent would a genuinely democratic legislature emerge; would an impartial judicial system be created; and much more. Gorbachev's report took the whole of the first day and was a remarkable *tour d'horizon* of where the Soviet Union was and where it should go.

Comrades, delegates,
The basic question facing us, delegates to the 19th All-Union Party Conference, is how to further the revolutionary restructuring launched in our country on the initiative and under the leadership of the party, and to make it irreversible.

I.1 Assess Achievements Self-critically

Comrades, revolutionary renewal is reaching ever deeper into the economy, that decisive sphere of life . . . How serious the situation is may be judged, among other things, by the country's financial situation. For many years, state budget expenditures grew more rapidly than revenue. The budget deficit is pressing down upon the market, undermining the stability of the rouble and of monetary circulation as a whole, and giving rise to inflationary processes . . . Let me begin with the food problem, which is probably the most painful and the most acute problem in the life of our society . . .

I.4 *Democratising International Relations*

Comrades, perestroika in the USSR has become a matter of global signifi-cance. The cardinal changes in our own home have called for new approaches to international affairs as well . . . As we analyse the contemporary world, we realise more clearly that international relations, without losing their class character, are increasingly coming to be precisely relations between nations. We note the enhanced role in world affairs of peoples, nations and emerging new national entities. And this implies that there is no ignoring the diversity of interests in international affairs. Consideration for these interests is an important element of the new political thinking . . .

World socialism is going through a crucial period. The fact that the socialist countries have advanced to new frontiers, that their potentials have been revealed nationally and internationally, enhances the prestige and role of socialism in world developments. A key factor in the new thinking is the concept of freedom of choice. We are convinced that this is a universal principle for international relations at a time when the very survival of civilisation has become the principal problem of the world, its common denominator . . .

In this situation the imposition of a social system, way of life, or policies from outside by any means, let alone military, are dangerous trappings of past epochs. Sovereignty and independence, equal rights and non-interference are becoming universally recognised rules of international relations, which is in itself a major achievement of the 20th Century. To oppose freedom of choice is to come out against the objective tide of history itself. That is why power politics in all their forms and manifestations are historically obsolescent . . .

II.1 *Why a Reform of the Political System is Necessary*

. . . The existing political system proved incapable of protecting us from the growth of stagnation phenomena in economic and social life in the latter decades, and doomed the reforms undertaken at the time to failure. While functions of economic management became increasingly concentrated in the hands of the party-political leadership, the role of the executive apparatus at the same time increased out of all proportion. The number of people elected to various governmental and non-governmental bodies reached one third of the country's adult population, but at the same time the mass of them were removed from real participation in handling state and civic affairs.

In the period of stagnation the machinery of management, which had grown to almost 100 national ministries and government agencies, and 800 in the republics, began practically to dictate its will in both the economic and the political field. It was these agencies and other administrative structures that handled the execution of the decisions taken, and that by their action or inaction determined what would be and what would not be. The soviets – and, in many respects, the party bodies as well – proved unable to control this pressure from departmental interests. It became a universal rule that the body taking the decisions bore no economic responsibility for the implications of its actions.

Another serious shortcoming of the political system that had taken shape was the excessive governmentalisation of public life. To be sure, the tasks and functions of the state under socialism are much bigger in scope than under capitalism. But as conceived by the founders of Marxism-Leninism, management functions should be expanded not by strengthening power resting upon high-handed administration and compulsion, but above all by increasing the role of the democratic factor and involving broad sections of the people in administration . . . State regulation was extended to an inordinately broad sphere of public activities. The tendency to encompass every nook of life with detailed centralised planning and control literally straitjacketed society and became a serious brake on the initiative of people, civic organisations and collectives. This gave rise, among other things, to a 'shadow' economy and culture, which thrive as parasites on the inability of state bodies to provide timely and adequate satisfaction of the population's material and spiritual requirements . . .

II.3 *Perfecting the Organisation of Government*

Summing up these views, the CPSU central committee is submitting the following proposals for consideration by the conference:

First, that representation of the working people in the top echelon of government be extended considerably. With this end in view, direct representation of the civic organisations incorporated into our political system should be added to the currently existing territorial representation of the entire population on the Soviet of the Union and the representation of our nations and nationalities on the Soviet of Nationalities.

Thus 1,500 deputies would be elected, as they are now, from the territorial and national districts, and approximately another 750 deputies would be elected at the congresses or at plenary sessions of the governing bodies of party, trade union, co-operative, youth, women's, veterans', academic and artistic organisations. The list of these organisations and the quotas of their representation could be incorporated into the Constitution. All these deputies, elected for a five-year term, would comprise a new representative supreme government body – the USSR Congress of People's Deputies. It would be convened annually to decide on the country's more important constitutional, political and socio-economic issues.

The Congress of People's Deputies would elect from among its members a relatively small (say, 400- to 450-strong) bicameral USSR Supreme Soviet which would consider and decide all legislative, administrative and monitoring questions and direct the activities of the bodies accountable to it and of the lower-level soviets. It would be a standing supreme government body reporting to the Congress of People's Deputies. In this way, all legislative and monitoring work would be concentrated directly within the Supreme Soviet and its commissions. That would be a new step forward in the democratisation of the highest structures of government. We can also consider a periodic renewal of part of the USSR Supreme Soviet . . .

II.5 *Promoting Inter-ethnic Relations*

Comrades, the union of our country's nations and nationalities which enjoy equal rights is one of the greatest accomplishments of socialism. Today this enables us to state with profound conviction that in the future, too, consistent implementation of Lenin's ethnic policy will be the only sound basis of our development . . . You know that the central committee plans to devote a special plenary meeting to the promotion of inter-ethnic relations. But since this subject is extremely important and topical, we should discuss it right now, at this conference . . . It is natural for the development of our multi-ethnic state to be accompanied by a growth of ethnic self-awareness. That is a positive development, but since the new requirements arising in this connection were not always treated with the attention they deserved, some issues began to develop complications and acquire a nationalistic aspect in some cases – although in principle, they could have been settled normally, without providing a pretext for all sorts of speculations and emotionally charged outbursts . . .

In advocating further consolidation of inter-ethnic relations, we proceed from the premise that the development of the Soviet Union, the internationalist ties within the brotherhood of our peoples are vibrantly dynamic processes. Both republican and Union-level agencies should never lose sight of them. The problems related to them should be tackled in accordance with the will of our peoples, in the spirit of concord and in the interests of all Soviet society . . .

II.6 *Establishing the Socialist Rule of Law*

. . . Just as all citizens have obligations to our state of the whole people, the state has obligations to our state of the whole people, the state has obligations to its citizens. Their rights must be firmly protected against any abuse by the authorities. Perestroika has thrown into particularly bold relief the conservatism of our legal system which is so far largely directed not at democratic or economic but at command-style methods of administration and government with their numerous bans and petty regimentation. Many legal instruments currently in force in fact hinder social development . . .

III.1 *Democracy within the Party Should be Fully Revived*

. . . We have defined the functions of the CPSU as the political vanguard. But to perform these functions the party should remodel its activity, style, methods and forms of work – from the grass-roots level up to the central committee. Each communist should really be a fighter for implementing its policy, for the interests of the people . . . The matter is, in the first place, that the principle of democratic centralism, which underlies the structure and activity of the CPSU, was at a certain stage largely replaced by bureaucratic centralism. This occurred primarily because the primary party organisations and rank-and-file communists to a great extent lost real opportunities to influence the party's activities. Lenin's demand that all party bodies and their cadres should be under the constant control of the party masses was grossly violated. Many negative phenomena in the party had been caused also by the decrease in the role of elective bodies and excessive growth of the role played by the party apparatus at all levels . . .

The plenary meeting of the Central Committee in October 1964, it will be recalled, was held, in fact, under the slogan of restoring Lenin's principles and norms of party life. But the real processes took a different turn and in the years of stagnation they sometimes appeared to be badly deformed . . . For that purpose the task now is to fully restore in the party an atmosphere of fidelity to principle, openness, discussion, criticism and self-criticism, conscientious discipline, party comradeship, unconditional personal responsibility, and efficiency. The current processes in primary party organisations proceed in these directions, and it is the task of the conference to give them resolute support and open up unlimited opportunities for them to go on . . .

It is necessary for elections at all levels to be conducted in a democratic atmosphere, which ensures a broad discussion of candidates, competitiveness and, as a result, the election of talented and worthy people who are genuinely dedicated to our cause, enjoy unquestionable authority and are capable of pursuing the policy of perestroika . . . There is universal interest in the proposal to establish a uniform five-year term for all party committees, to limit the holding of elected office in the CPSU to two successive terms, and to permit election for a third term only in exceptional cases . . .

III.2 Demarcating the Functions of Party and State Bodies

A factor of tremendous importance in the functioning of the party as a political vanguard in present conditions is the correct solution of the problem of clearly demarcating the functions of party and state bodies . . . It must be said that the question of separating the functions of the party and the state was raised more than once at different stages in the history of our society, with recognition being given to the abnormal character of the existing situation and the need to modify it in line with Lenin's principle . . . In these matters, we should fully assert the Leninist principle under which the CPSU is to conduct its policies via the communists working on government bodies and in all spheres of the social fabric. All party organisations are to act in strict compliance with the USSR Constitution and Soviet laws. We should rule out the practice of party committees adopting resolutions with direct instructions to government or economic agencies or civic organisations . . .

III.3 *Revolutionary Perestroika for a New Image of Socialism*

. . . Perestroika has pushed glasnost to the forefront. Glasnost is being practised in the most diverse forms – in the work of governmental and civic organisations, at meetings, at scientific and other conferences and at gatherings of citizens . . . Glasnost presupposes a plurality of opinions on all questions of home and international policy, a free play of different points of view, and discussion. It cannot fulfil its social role, it cannot serve the interests of the people and socialism in the absence of this approach.

But like any other token of democracy, glasnost presupposes a high sense of responsibility. It is incompatible with any claim to monopoly of opinion, with imposition of dogmas in place of those that we have rejected. It is incompatible with group interests, and doubly so with any distortion of the facts and with any settling of personal scores . . . Our aims are more democracy, more socialism, a better life for the working people and greatness and well-being for the country. In these several days, we shall have to sum up the work accomplished in the drive for these aims and adopt documents of tremendous importance – documents that will give new momentum to perestroika, that will make it irreversible. This, indeed, determines the measure of responsibility to the party and the people of every delegate, and our conference as a whole.

Sources: Mikhail Gorbachev, 'On Progress in Implementing the Decisions of the 27th Party Congress and the Tasks for Promoting Perestroika', 28 June 1988, Soviet News, no. 6432, 6 July 1988, pp. 237, 238, 243, 244, 245, 248–9, 251, 252, 254–5, 256, 257, 258; 'O khode realizatsii reshenii XXVII s''ezda KPSS i zadachakh po uglubleniyu perestroiki', in Gorbachev, Izbrannye rechi i stat'i, vol. 6, pp. 323–98.

Document 10.13   Dismantling the Apparatus

On the basis of the Nineteenth Party Conference decisions, the CC plenum on 30 September 1988 reorganised the Central Committee's Secretariat, abolishing its many departments, and in their place established six broad commissions. The change marked the end of the apparatus's ability to monitor and control political processes in the country. A whole epoch of party power came to an end. Vadim Medvedev, responsible for ideology, summarised the changes as follows.

When examining the issues of reorganising the Party apparatus, the plenum passed a decision on Central Committee commissions on key aspects of home and foreign policies.

It found it expedient to have the following Central Committee commissions:

- A commission on Party building and personnel policy (Georgi Razumovsky was endorsed as its chairman).

- An ideological commission (with [Vadim] Medvedev endorsed as its chairman).
- A commission on agrarian policy (with Yegor Ligachev as chairman).
- A commission on international policy (with Alexander Yakovlev as chairman).
- And a commission on legal policy (with Viktor Chebrikov as chairman).

The plenum instructed the Politburo to effect practical measures to create a new structure for the apparatus of the CPSU Central Committee and local Party committees with account taken of the changed function of Party bodies in conditions where the perestroika (restructuring) drive is making further headway and the country's political system is being reformed . . .

Referring to the reorganisation of the CPSU Central Committee apparatus, Vadim Medvedev stressed that a substantial reduction in the number of departments and apparatus is to be effected. 'Maybe by half'. The measure will affect not only the central apparatus but also those of the central committees of the communist parties of the union republics and regional Party committees, albeit to a lesser extent, it is true, than the Central Committee apparatus. As to the primary Party committees, district and city ones, there will be practically no reductions there . . .

Some of the Central Committee departments will be enlarged and merged . . . The Central Committee's ideological commission and ideological department are being organised on the basis of three existing Central Committee departments, one for propaganda, another for culture and the other on science and institutions of learning. In other cases, existing departments will be abolished. This applies to the departments dealing each with a specific economic sector. Their functions are being handed over to the Council of Ministers and to the Supreme Soviet and its commissions . . . Naturally enough, the Central Committee apparatus will have political rather than administrative functions, just as suggested at the [nineteenth] Party conference.

Source: 'News Conference on Plenary Meeting', 30 September 1988, Soviet News, no. 6445, 5 October 1988, pp. 375, 382.

Document 10.14   The First USSR Congress of People's Deputies

One of the most important constitutional changes envisaged by the Nineteenth Party Conference was the election of a 2,250-strong Congress of People's Deputies (CPD), to meet on average twice a year for about ten days with the power to change the constitution, that would in turn elect a smaller Supreme Soviet with normal legislative powers. The necessary changes to the old Soviet constitution were adopted on 1 December 1988, and the first relatively free elections were held in March 1989. Many of the most illustrious communist leaders were defeated, while Gorbachev himself did not have to face the electorate since he was one of the 750 deputies nominated directly by social organisations. The first convocation of the CPD was televised live and enthralled the nation; for the first time a Soviet legislative assembly was the scene of uninhibited debate. Gorbachev's speech on 30 May set the guidelines for domestic and foreign policy. Some of his earlier buoyancy was beginning to wear off as the economic situation deteriorated further.

Our Congress is in its fifth day. For all this time this hall has witnessed the simmering of passions. I think that we all agree that the work of the Congress is riding the wave of democratic renewal and deep-going revolutionary processes in society. There is hardly any need now to prove that the Congress itself, everything that preceded it and the character of the debates that have been started, signify a convincing victory for perestroika and open a new page in our state's history . . .

By the beginning of the 1980s, as a result of many years of stagnation, the country found itself in a serious crisis that had embraced all spheres of life. The situation demanded that the Party make a sharp turn. That was a crucial choice, and the Party made it. Today, we all see the correctness of that choice. The wave of renewal has woken the country. The process of mastering new forms of public life, in economy, politics and culture, has become established . . .

What is the matter? Why don't we yet feel even the effects of what has been achieved? First of all, because the country's financial system was seriously distorted, and the consumer market unbalanced. Any kind of shortage of consumer items gives rise to strong and legitimate discontent among people, and adds to the social strain in society. The causes are various. These negative phenomena are the hard legacy of the past and the tremendous losses connected with the fall in world prices of fuel and raw materials, the Chernobyl accident [April 1986], and natural calamities. At the same time the economic situation is connected to a considerable extent with our own actions and sometimes inaction even during the years of perestroika.

To begin with, the state continues to live beyond its means. Budget expenditures in the current five-year plan period grow faster than national income. Hence, the growing budget deficit. This is simply inadmissible from the economic point of view and should not be regarded other than as a serious miscalculation in economic policy, for which responsibility is borne primarily by the USSR Ministry of Finance and its apparatus . . .

Tackling problems of the nation's social and economic development, we should consistently realise the principle of social justice. It is not enough to proclaim it, it is essential to stimulate social and economic mechanisms to make it possible to remove the principal brake on our progress – levelled wages and the deeply ingrained psychology of parasitism. I have already had occasion at this Congress to touch upon the problem of social benefits and privileges. I will add the following to what I said then. The system of privileges – be it differentiated pensions or vacations, medical services or housing, and the provision of material and cultural benefits to different social, age and professional groups, territories and agencies – has taken shape over many dozens of years. Apparently, these issues should be treated in such a way as, on the one hand, to stimulate talent and highly efficient work and on the other, to help those groups of the population that need it. Of course, any aberrations or abuses must be resolutely eradicated . . .

Reliable defences were and remain a vital issue for our people who have lived through a most arduous war, and the Soviet Army has always been given special care. But in the present world there are increasing possibilities to ensure security by political and diplomatic means. This makes it possible to reduce military expenditures through giving new quality to the Soviet Armed Forces without detriment to the country's defence capability. Over the past two years military spending has been frozen. This helped save 10 billion roubles.

Now I'd like to give the real figure for military spending in 1989: 77.3 billion roubles. You are invited to consider a proposal for slashing the military budget for 1990–1991 by another 10 billion roubles, or by 14 per cent, and working further on all aspects of this issue at the Supreme Soviet, taking into account domestic requirements and the tasks of ensuring a reliable defence potential for the country. Outlays on space programmes have already been partially scaled down. These outlays are not that big. You will see it when working on this issue later on . . .

We spend some 40 billion roubles a year on the upkeep of the administrative apparatus in this country. Significantly, 2.5 billion of this goes to maintain state management bodies, whereas the rest is absorbed by the administrative staff of conglomerates and factories. This issue must be made clear . . .

One more thing, comrades. Life has demonstrated graphically that economic reform is simply impossible without radically updated socialist property relations and developing and combining various forms of this property. We favour establishing flexible and effective relations to use public property so that each form of property may prove its vitality and right to exist in real and fair competition. The only condition that should be made is that there be no exploitation of workers and their alienation from the means of production. Another decisive aspect of economic reform – the creation of a full-blooded socialist market – is inextricably connected with this attitude to property. The market, of course, is not omnipotent. But mankind has not been able to devise a different, more effective and democratic mechanism of economic management. A socialist plan-based economy cannot do without it. We should recognise this. We believe that as reform makes headway, we shall see the formation of such a system of relations in the economy as can be called a legal economy. It will be based on law-regulated relations rather than administrative injunctions and orders. Government guidance over the economy management will be clearly separated . . .

We together can state with every foundation – and this has already been stated here – that the broad democratisation of state and public of our country is the most substantial accomplishment of perestroika. The elections of People's Deputies of the USSR, the work of our Congress and the atmosphere of its deliberations convincingly attest to this . . .

First of all this is the implementation of the historic slogan 'All Power to the Soviets' that we have advanced again. The reconstruction of representative bodies, all-round widening of their rights and powers in accordance with the constitution, the unconditional subjugation of the apparatus to them is the first prerequisite for the return of real levers of power and management of the Soviets. Many people here have already declared in favour of this, and we should register this in the final documents of our Congress. Another condition for this is a clear delimitation of the powers of Party and government bodies. The Party condemned decisively the state of things when its organisations were substituting government bodies and were actually performing the functions of direct management of the economy and all other areas of life. Assuming the tasks uncharacteristic of them, party committees lost the ability to appraise critically the developments of society and play the role of its vanguard . . . At issue are principled questions pertaining to the structure of the federal state, the rights and opportunities of the local Soviets, the broadening of the self-governing principles in the whole of our political system . . .

I must say that Party and Soviet bodies are receiving proposals to hold the regular elections within the time span stipulated by the constitution: next spring when the term of office of the present Soviets is to expire. Both the first stage of political reform and everything that has to be done at its successive stages progress along the road of creating a social rule-of-law state, it goes without saying, however, that this does not resolve the task of building such a state. The task is a much vaster one, encompassing a broad domain of democratic regulations of society's life. Legal protection of the individual and ensuring all the conditions enabling the citizen to exercise all his rights and, naturally, to discharge his obligations *vis-à-vis* the state moves to the forefront here. All our steps to build a rule-of-law state, and their effectiveness, must be measured by the main criterion – by what they give to the Soviet man . . . Democracy can exist only with strict compliance by all – the state, public organisations, every collective and every citizen – with the rights and duties. This is axiomatic . . .

Comrades, the first days of the Congress brought to light again the acuteness of the nationalities question, the complexity of inter-ethnic relations. Indeed, multi-ethnic character is a unique quality of our state and society. On the one hand, it is a source of its strength, but on the other, given the slightest distortions of the nationalities policy, it can become the cause of the weakening of the state, of instability in society with unpredictably heavy consequences . . . Democratisation and glasnost made it possible to see the whole truth and start rectifying distortions, eliminating injustice. But it should be admitted that at the beginning of the perestroika drive we have not realised in full measure the need to renew the nationalities policy. Probably there has been a delay about solving a number of burning problems. Meanwhile, natural dissatisfaction with the accumulated economic and social problems came to be viewed as an infringement of national interests. Speculating on these common difficulties, definite elements tried to aggravate the situation still more. This resulted in excesses in a number of republics and led to the generally known tragic consequences with the loss of life . . .

The principle of national self-determination advanced by Lenin has been and remains one of chief elements of the nationalities policy of the Communist Party. It was at the basis of socialist statehood when the Union of Soviet Socialist Republics was formed . . . The federal structure of the state should now be filled with real political and economic content so that this form should fully meet the requirements and aspirations of nations and be in keeping with the realities of the present. On the whole, we view the key aspects of the restructuring of nationalities policies in the following way. In the political area these are the substantial widening of the rights of union and autonomous republics, of other national formations, relegation of an ever broader range of managerial functions to local government, and the enhancement of independence and responsibility of republican and local government bodies. There is a need for a firm definition in a federal state as to what should be in the jurisdiction in the union and what is a sovereign right of a union or autonomous republic. There should be juridical mechanisms for settling conflicts that might arise in their relations . . .

The vesting of Supreme Soviet members with special functions should in no way mean belittling the role of the other People's Deputies. Each of them has the chance to be elected to the Supreme Soviet during the annual renewal of one-fifth of it. Many Deputies will be included in Supreme Soviet committees and commissions, making up half of their members and having the right to vote. It appears reasonable that they may be invited to fill leading positions in commissions and committees as, say, deputy chairmen, representing this half. As I see it, we all agreed that every People's Deputy of the USSR may participate in the work of this or that commission or committee and in sessions of the chambers of the Supreme Soviet if he so wishes. And each of them should get full information on the current work of the Supreme Soviet, the government or other bodies of power.

And finally, each of them has an opportunity to engage in active political work in his own region or public organisation, maintaining permanent contact with his constituents and sending this or that enquiry or suggestion to local and central authorities. Local bodies should see to it that the Deputies have the opportunity to receive citizens and meet constituents. All these issues must be tackled immediately. Thereby we shall succeed in maintaining the most valuable quality of the Soviet system – the permanent link between the people's representatives and their constituents or, quoting Lenin, to combine the benefits of parliamentarism with those of direct democracy.

Sources: Mikhail Gorbachev, 'On the Main Directions of Internal and Foreign Policy of the USSR', 30 May 1989, Soviet News, no. 6478, 7 June 1989, pp. 181, 182, 184, 185, 186, 187, 189; 'Obosnovnykh napravleniyakh vnutrennei i vneshnei politiki SSSR', in Gorbachev, Izbrannye rechi i stat'i, vol. 7 (Moscow, Izd-vo politicheskoi literatury, 1990), pp. 558–89.

Document 10.15   Can the Party Survive?

The Congress was followed by an upsurge of worker unrest, in particular strikes by miners, and many new civic associations were founded. In late 1989 Gorbachev penned an important article arguing that even under conditions of democratisation the Communist Party would continue to exert an important role. As political order began to disintegrate there was a certain logic to Gorbachev's argument, yet he failed to convert the party into a competitive organisation suitable for a pluralistic multi-party environment. Gorbachev's article was summarised as follows.

Some people try to reproach us that we have no clear-cut detailed plan to realise the concept of perestroika . . . A new quality of social being and a new aspect of socialism are crystallizing in the competition of various economic and social forms, institutions and ideological trends. The renewal of developing socialism is a process which goes beyond the turn of the century . . . There is a world experience of socialism on which we can rely in determining the goals of our development. We now take a wider, deeper and more realistic view of socialism than in the recent past. We view it as a world process in which, along with the socialist countries with different stages of socio-economic and political development, there are also various currents of socialist thought in the rest of the world and some social movements different in their composition and motivation . . . Of everlasting importance is the fact that Marxism, developing the idea of socialism, represented socialism as the natural product of the progress of civilisation and of the historical creative endeavour of the people . . .

A special role in the new social organism belongs to the Communist Party which is called upon to be the political vanguard of Soviet society. The destiny of perestroika and the attainment of a qualitatively new state of society and a new aspect of socialism depends on the Party's activities immensely if not decisively . . . Getting rid of day-to-day administrative and managerial functions, the Party is now turning into the centre for the elaboration of political and ideological platforms recommended to society and the state in the shape of its elective bodies. Such a change of the Party's functions determines anew its place in the political system as the ideological, political and ethical vanguard of the people . . .

At the present complex stage, the interests of the consolidation of society and the concentration of all its sound forces on the accomplishment of the difficult tasks of perestroika prompt the advisability of keeping the one-party system. And in this case the Party will promote the development of pluralism, the emulation of opinions in society and the broadening of glasnost in the interests of democracy and the people. In the efforts to renew socialism the Party may not concede the initiative to either populist demagoguery, nationalist or chauvinistic currents or to the spontaneity of group interests . . . The socialism to which we advance during perestroika means a society based on the effective economy, on the highest achievements of science, technology and culture, and on the humanised social structures.

It means a society which has democratised all aspects of social life and has produced conditions for the active creative life and work of people. At the same time many processes of renewing socialism are common to the entire civilisation and develop in this or that form on other social soil. Global problems common to everyone begin to occupy more and more room in mankind's life. All this gives ground to suppose that various social systems, while retaining their peculiarities, develop within the framework which to an increasing extent is limited by the priority of universal human values such as peace, security, freedom and the opportunity for every people to decide its future. The world of socialism advances to the goals common to the whole of mankind within the framework of a single civilisation, without abandoning its own values and priorities, but increasingly developing and refining them along the road of revolutionary perestroika and the building of a genuinely humane society on the principles of reason and humanism.

Sources: Gorbachev, 'The Socialist Idea and Revolutionary Perestroika', Pravda, *26 November 1989; summarised in* Soviet News, *no. 6503, 29 November 1989, pp. 401–2.*

Document 10.16 The Abolition of the Party's Leading Role

Despite Gorbachev's effort to salvage a 'leading role' for the party the tide of pluralism appeared inexorable. In late 1989 the communist regimes in Eastern Europe fell one after the other, while in the USSR hostility to the communist regime took ever stronger forms. Gorbachev's attempts to maintain a dominant role for the party, defended in his article of 26 November 1989, was no longer tenable. Even as the Central Committee met in early February 1990 a demonstration of over 250,000 carrying placards declaring 'seventy-three years on the road to nowhere' demanded the end of party rule. Gorbachev was forced to bow to the inevitable.

Comrades, I think you will agree that we have gathered for a very important plenary meeting, a meeting which communists and all society have been waiting for with immense interest and impatience . . . The Soviet Communist Party initiated perestroika and generated its concept and policy. Profound revolutionary changes encompassing all spheres of life and all sections of the population have been launched on this basis in the country.

Of no less importance is the understanding of the fact – which is the other aspect of the problem that also demands the bringing forward of the congress – that the Party will only be able to fulfil the mission of political vanguard if it drastically restructures itself, masters the art of political work in the present-day conditions and succeeds in co-operating with all forces committed to perestroika. The crux of the Party's renewal is the need to get rid of everything that tied it to the authoritarian-bureaucratic system, a system that left its mark not only on methods of work and interrelationships within the Party, but also on ideology, ways of thinking and notions of socialism . . .

The Party's renewal presupposes a fundamental change in its relation with state and economic bodies and the abandonment of the practice of commanding them and substituting for their functions. The Party in a renewing society can exist and play its role as vanguard only as a democratically recognised force. This means that its status should not be imposed through constitutional endorsement. The Soviet Communist Party, it goes without saying, intends to struggle for the status of the ruling party. But it will do so strictly within the framework of the democratic process by giving up any legal and political advantages, offering its programme and defending it in discussions, co-operating with other social and political forces, always working amidst the masses, living by their interests and their needs. The extensive democratisation currently under way in our society is being accompanied by mounting political pluralism. Various social and political organisations and movements emerge. This process may lead at a certain stage to the establishment of parties.

Source: 'Mikhail Gorbachev's Report at Party Plenum', 5 February 1990, Soviet News, no. 6512, 7 February 1990, p. 41.

Document 10.17 The Amendment of Article 6

On 14 March 1990 the Third Congress of People's Deputies finally amended article 6 (for the old version, see Document 9.5) to remove the party's 'leading role'. The new version read as follows:

Article 6. The Communist Party of the Soviet Union and other political parties, as well as trade union, youth and other public organisations and mass movements, shall take part in the elaboration of the policy of the Soviet state and in the running of state and public affairs through their representatives elected to the Soviets of People's Deputies and in other ways.

Source: Novosti Press Agency, London, July 1990, p. 6.

The very next day (15 March) Gorbachev was elected president of the USSR. Gorbachev ignored calls to use the opportunity to place himself and the party before the people's judgement, and instead he was elected by the Congress of People's Deputies alone. Gorbachev's claim to represent the best interests of the people was thereafter fatally undermined. Disquiet over this undemocratic procedure was reflected in the voting figures: of the 1,878 deputies who voted, 1,329 supported his candidature, 495 voted against and 54 ballot papers were spoilt. He received 59.2 per cent of votes of the total number (2,245) of people's deputies, 66.45 per cent of the votes of deputies (2,000) who received ballot papers and 70.76 per cent of the votes of those who took part in the election (1,878) (*Izvestiya*, 17 March 1990). Even within this limited 'selectorate' Gorbachev failed to win by a convincing margin. The lack of an alternative candidate imbued the whole exercise with a slightly farcical tone and undermined the democratic legitimacy of Gorbachev's leadership.

Transcending the Cold War

In foreign policy this was a time of great changes, some of which have been suggested in the speeches reported above (in particular, Document 10.8, where Gorbachev had noted that a capitalist economy could develop without militarisation). On 8 February 1988 Gorbachev announced the withdrawal of troops from Afghanistan, and the last troops left on 15 February 1989, having lost 14,453 dead and 50,000 wounded since the invasion of 25 December 1979. A total of 620,000 military conscripts and officers had served in Afghanistan, traumatising a generation. Relations with Europe were now conducted within the framework of what Gorbachev called 'the Common European Home', and the USSR now committed itself to closer relations with the European Community and the Council of Europe. In the Third World, Gorbachev advanced the thesis that development should precede socialist revolution, thus undermining the logic of the Bolshevik revolution itself. Contrary to Stalin's assertion (Document 7.14) that capitalism inevitably leads to war, Gorbachev argued (on the basis of post-war German and Japanese experience) that capitalism could develop without militarism. Above all, superpower relations underwent an unprecedented thaw, allowing the signing of an INF treaty in 1987, for the first time abolishing a whole category of weapons: intermediate nuclear forces with a range of some 600 kilometres.

Document 10.18   The New Political Thinking in Action

In a speech to the United Nations on 7 December 1988 Gorbachev dramatically announced heavy cuts in Russian military forces. Typically, he had not discussed the question with the Russian High Command itself. The speech reflected the belief of the time that with the end of the Cold War the United Nations could come into its own and that a new era of politics and international relations would dawn. Above all, Gorbachev advanced his argument that nuclear weapons were fundamentally illegitimate instruments of war. 'Freedom of choice', moreover, was now to be extended to the countries that made up the 'Soviet bloc' in Eastern Europe.

We have come here to show our respect for the United Nations, which increasingly has been manifesting its ability to act as a unique international centre in the service of peace and security . . .

What will mankind be like when it enters the 21st Century? People are already fascinated by this not-too-distant future. We are looking ahead to it with hopes for the best and yet with a feeling of concern. The world in which we live today is radically different from what it was at the beginning or even in the middle of this century. And it continues to change, as do all its components. The advent of nuclear weapons was just another tragic reminder of the fundamental nature of that change. A material symbol and expression of absolute military power, nuclear weapons at the same time revealed the absolute limits of that power . . .

Some of the past differences and disputes are losing their importance. But conflicts of a different kind are taking their place. Life is making us abandon established stereotypes and outdated views, it is making us discard illusions. The very concept of the nature and criteria of progress is changing. It would be naive to think that the problems plaguing mankind today can be solved with the means and methods which were applied or seemed to work in the past. Indeed, mankind has accumulated a wealth of experience in the process of political, economic and social development under highly diverse conditions. But that experience belongs to the practices and to the world that have become or are becoming part of the past. This is one of the signs of the crucial nature of the current phase in history . . .

It is also quite clear to us that the principle of freedom of choice is mandatory. Its non-recognition is fraught with extremely grave consequences for world peace. Denying that right to the peoples under whatever pretext or rhetorical guise means jeopardising even the fragile balance that has been attained. Freedom of choice is a universal principle that should allow for no exceptions. It was not simply out of good intentions that we came to the conclusion that this principle is absolute. We were driven to it by an unbiased analysis of the objective trends of today. More and more characteristic of them is the increasing multi-optional character of social development in different countries. This applies both to the capitalist and to the socialist system. The diversity of the socio-political structures that have grown over the past decades out of national liberation movements also attests to this. This objective fact calls for respect for the views and positions of others, tolerance, a willingness to perceive something different as not necessarily bad or hostile, and an ability to learn to live side-by-side with others, while remaining different and not always agreeing with each other. As the world asserts its diversity, attempts to look down on others and to teach them one's own brand of democracy become totally improper, to say nothing of the fact that democratic values intended for export often very quickly lose their worth. What we are talking about, therefore, is unity in diversity. If we assert this politically, if we reaffirm our adherence to freedom of choice, then there is no room for the view that some live on Earth by virtue of divine will while others are here quite by chance . . .

What are the practical implications of that? It would be natural and sensible not to abandon everything positive that has already been accomplished and to build on all the gains of the past few years, on all that we have created by working together. I am referring to the process of negotiations on nuclear arms, conventional weapons and chemical weapons, and to the search for political approaches to ending regional conflicts. Of course, I am referring above all to political dialogue – a more intense and open dialogue pointed at the very heart of the problems instead of confrontation, at an exchange of constructive ideas instead of recriminations. Without political dialogue the process of negotiations cannot advance . . .

In this specific historical situation we face the question of a new role for the United Nations. We feel that states must to some extent review their attitude to the United Nations, this unique instrument without which world politics would be inconceivable today. The recent reinvigoration of its peace-making role has again demonstrated the United Nations' ability to assist its members in coping with the daunting challenges of our time and working to humanise their relations . . .

Take, for example, the problem of development, which is a truly universal human problem. The conditions in which tens of millions of people live in a number of Third World regions are becoming a real threat to all mankind. No closed entities or even regional communities of states, important as they are, are capable of untangling the main knots that tie up the principal avenues of world economic relations – North–South, East–West, South–South, South–East. What is needed here is joining the efforts and taking into account the interests of all groups of countries, something that only this organisation, the United Nations, can accomplish. External debt is one of the gravest problems . . .

We have immersed ourselves in constructing a socialist state based on the rule of law. A whole series of new laws have been elaborated or are nearing completion. Many will enter into force in 1989, and, we believe, comply fully with the highest standards in ensuring human rights. Soviet democracy will be placed on a solid normative base. I am referring, in particular, to laws on the freedom of conscience, glasnost, public associations and organisations, and many others. In places of confinement there are no persons convicted for their political and religious beliefs. Additional guarantees are to be included in the new draft laws that rule out any form of persecution on these grounds . . . The problem of exit from and entry to our country, including the question of leaving it for family reunification, is being dealt with in a humane spirit. As you know, one of the reasons for refusal to leave is a person's knowledge of secrets. Strictly warranted time limitations on the secrecy rule will now be applied. Every person seeking employment at certain agencies or enterprises will be informed of the rule. In case of disputes there is a right to appeal under the law. This removes from the agenda the problem of the so-called 'refuseniks' . . .

We are present at the birth of a new model of ensuring security – not through the build-up of arms, as was almost always the case in the past, but on the contrary, through their reduction on the basis of compromise. The Soviet leadership has decided to demonstrate once again its readiness to reinforce this healthy process not only by words but also by deeds. Today, I can report to you that the Soviet Union has taken a decision to reduce its armed forces. Within the next two years their numerical strength will be reduced by 500,000 men. The number of conventional armaments will also be substantially reduced. This will be done unilaterally, without relation to the talks on the mandate of the Vienna meeting. By agreement with our Warsaw Treaty allies, we have decided to withdraw by 1991 six tank divisions from the GDR, Czechoslovakia and Hungary, and to disband them. Assault landing troops and several other formations and units, including assault crossing units with their weapons and combat equipment, will also be withdrawn from the groups of Soviet forces stationed in those countries. Soviet forces stationed in those countries will be reduced by 50,000 men and their armaments by 5,000 tanks. All Soviet divisions remaining, for the time being, in the territory of our allies are being reorganised. Their structure will be different from what it is now: after a major cutback of their tanks it will become clearly defensive. At the same time, we shall reduce the numerical strength of the armed forces and the numbers of armaments stationed in the European part of the USSR. In total, Soviet armed forces in this part of our country and in the territories of our European allies will be reduced by 10,000 tanks, 8,500 artillery systems and 800 combat aircraft.

Source: 'Mikhail Gorbachev's Address to the UN General Assembly',
7 December 1988, Soviet News, no. 6455, 14 December 1988, pp. 459, 460,
461, 462.

Beyond *Perestroika* – Yeltsin Resurgent

The plan to introduce socialist democracy from above soon gave way to radical democratisation from below. Boris Yeltsin (*b.* 1 February 1931) trained as a construction engineer and had been party boss in Sverdlovsk region from 1976 until Gorbachev called him to Moscow in April 1985 to make him head of the construction department of the Central Committee Secretariat. In late 1985 he was appointed head of the Moscow party organisation, the largest in the country. Untainted by corruption, Yeltsin became increasingly disillusioned by the slow pace of change. In late summer 1987 he voiced his discontent to Gorbachev, indicating his wish to resign. Gorbachev hoped to delay the issue until after the seventieth anniversary celebrations, but this was beyond Yeltsin's patience. The conflict came out into the open, and Yeltsin was dismissed as Moscow party head and humiliated. Thereafter he became the symbol of the struggle against the regime.

Document 10.19   Sakharov on Political Reform and his 'Decree on Power'

In his speech to the First Congress of People's Deputies on 9 June 1989, Andrei Sakharov, in language remarkably reminiscent of some of the speeches at the First Congress of Soviets in June 1917 although with a diametrically opposed purpose, proposed a radical change to the Soviet system. The aim was to separate state functions from the interference of the CPSU, while at the same time limiting the powers of the KGB, above all depriving it of the right to interfere in domestic politics.

Comrade deputies, on you now – precisely now – lies an enormous historical responsibility. Political decisions are required, without which it will be impossible to strengthen the power of soviet authorities in the localities and to resolve economic, social, ecological and national problems. If the Congess of People's Deputies cannot take power into its own hands here, then there is not the slightest hope that soviets in the republics, *oblasts, raions* [districts] and villages can do so. But without strong soviets in the localities agrarian reform will be impossible or any reasonably effective agrarian policy differing from the senseless transfusion of resources into loss-making collective farms. Without a strong Congress and strong soviets it will be impossible to over-come the diktats of departments, the working out and implementation of laws about enterprises, the struggle against ecological folly. The Congress is called upon to defend democratic principles of popular power and, by the same token, the irreversibility of perestroika and the harmonious develop-ment of the country. I once again appeal to the Congress to adopt the 'Decree on Power'.

Decree on Power

Proceeding from the principles of democracy, the Congress of People's Deputies declares:
1 Article 6 of the USSR Constitution is annulled.
2 The adoption of USSR laws are the exclusive right of the USSR Congress of People's Deputies. On the territory of a union republic USSR laws gain juridical force only after they have been ratified by the highest legislative body of the union republic.
3 The Supreme Soviet is the working body of the Congress.
4 Commissions and Committees are created by the Congress and Supreme Soviet on principles of parity and are accountable to the Congress. They

prepare laws and the state budget, other laws and offer permanent supervision over the activity of state bodies, over the economic, social and
ecological situation in the country.

5 The election and recall of the highest USSR officials, namely:

   (a) The chairman of the USSR Supreme Soviet . . .

   And also:

   (a) The chairman of the USSR KGB,
   (b) The chairman of the state committee for television and radio,
   (c) The chief editor of the newspaper *Izvestiya*,

is the exclusive right of the Congress. The officials named above are subordinate
to the Congress and independent of decisions made by the CPSU . . .

7 The functions of the KGB are limited to the task of defending the international security of the USSR.

Note: In future direct elections for the chairman of the USSR Supreme
Soviet and his deputy on a competitive basis should be held.

Sources: A. D. Sakharov, Trevoga i nadezhda *(Moscow, Inter-Verso, 1990),
pp. 262–3; 'All Power to the Soviets',* XX Century and Peace, *no. 8, 1989,
pp. 9–12.*

Document 10.20 Russia's Declaration of State Sovereignty

In spring 1990 elections had been held to the RSFSR CPD on a rather more open
basis than the USSR elections held a year earlier. At its first convocation in May–
June 1990 the features of a distinctively *Russian* policy in opposition to that of the
USSR emerged. The figurehead of the reborn Russia was Yeltsin, who on 29 May
was elected chairman of the RSFSR Supreme Soviet after a bitter struggle in which
Gorbachev tried to dissuade deputies from voting for Yeltsin. On 12 June 1990
the First Russian Congress of People's Deputies adopted a declaration on 'state
sovereignty' that in effect declared Russia's laws superior to those of the USSR,
provoking a 'war of the laws' that ended only with the disintegration of the USSR in
late 1991. This was in effect the first step towards Russia's independence. An
accompanying 'Decree on Power' declared the separation of the party from the
state and the intention to govern on the basis of the separation of powers.

The First Congress of People's Deputies of the RSFSR,

- recognising its historical responsibility for the fate of Russia,
- respecting the sovereign rights of all the peoples making up the Union
  of Soviet Socialist Republics,
- expressing the will of the peoples of the RSFSR,

triumphantly declares the state sovereignty of the Russian Soviet Federated

Socialist Republic on its territory and declares its firm intention to create a democratic law-governed state within the framework of a renewed USSR.

1 The Russian Soviet Federated Socialist Republic is a sovereign state, created by the peoples historically united in it.

2 The sovereignty of the RSFSR is the natural and necessary condition for Russian statehood, having a centuries-long history, culture and tradition.

3 The bearer of sovereignty and the source of state power in the RSFSR is its multinational people. The people expresses its state power directly and through representative bodies on the basis of the RSFSR constitution.

4 The state sovereignty of the RSFSR is declared for a higher purpose, to ensure for every person the inalienable right for a worthy life, free development and the use of their native language, and for every people the right to self-determination in national-state and national-cultural forms chosen by them.

5 To secure political, economic and legal guarantees for the sovereignty of the RSFSR it is resolved that:

• the RSFSR should have full power in deciding all questions of state life, except for those voluntarily granted to the management of the USSR;

• the RSFSR constitution and RSFSR laws should be supreme throughout the territory of the RSFSR; USSR acts that contradict the sovereign rights of the RSFSR are abrogated by the republic on its territory. Disagreements between the republic and the Union are to be settled within the framework established by the Union Treaty;

• the people should have the exclusive right to own, use and dispose of the national wealth of Russia; there should be plenipotentiary representation of the RSFSR in other Union republics and foreign countries;

• the republic has the right to participate in the fulfilment of powers transferred to it from the USSR.

6 The Russian Soviet Federated Socialist Republic unites with other republics in a Union on the basis of a treaty. The RSFSR recognises and respects the sovereign rights of the union republics in the USSR.

7 The RSFSR reserves the right freely to secede from the USSR according to the terms established by the Union Treaty and laws based thereon.

8 The territory of the RSFSR cannot be changed without popular approval, expressed through a referendum.

9 The RSFSR Congress of People's Deputies recognises the necessity of substantially extending the rights of autonomous republics, autonomous *oblasts* and autonomous *okrugs*, as well as of *krais* and *oblasts* of the RSFSR. The concrete means of securing these rights are to be defined by RSFSR laws on the national-state and administrative-territorial structure of the Federation.

10 All citizens and those without citizenship living on the territory of the RSFSR are guaranteed rights and freedoms envisioned by the RSFSR constitution, the USSR constitution and the norms of international law . . .

11 RSFSR citizenship is established throughout the territory of the RSFSR. Every RSFSR citizen retains citizenship of the USSR.

A citizen of the RSFSR outside the republic is defended and protected by the RSFSR.

12 The RSFSR guarantees all citizens, political parties, social organisations, mass movements and religious organisations, acting within the RSFSR constitution, equal legal rights to participate in the management of state and social affairs.

13 The separation of legislative, executive and judicial powers is the central principle of the functioning of the RSFSR as a legal state.

Sources: 'Deklaratsiya o gosudarstvennom suverenitete RSFSR', Argumenty i fakty, *no. 24, 16–22 June 1990, p. 1;* Rodina, *no. 6, 1990, p. 26.*

Document 10.21   Yeltsin's Resignation from the Party

Elected chairman of the Russian parliament, Yeltsin used this position to continue his assault on the rule of the Communist Party. On 12 July 1990, at the Twenty-eighth (and last) Congress of the CPSU Yeltsin resigned from the party.

In connection with my election as chairman of the RSFSR Supreme Soviet and the enormous responsibility before the people of Russia, taking into account the transition of society towards a multi-party system, I cannot fulfil only decisions of the CPSU. As head of the highest legislative power of the republic I must subordinate myself to the will of the people and its plenipotentiaries. Therefore, I, in accordance with my promises made in the electoral campaign, declare my departure from the CPSU to be able more effectively to influence the activity of soviets. I am ready to cooperate with all parties and socio-political organisations in the republic.

Source: Izvestiya, *13 July 1990.*

Document 10.22 Yeltsin Becomes Russian President

Yeltsin had become the symbol of the sovereignty of the republics and of the democratic opposition to Gorbachev's attempts to reform socialism. Those associated wiith Yeltsin were no longer concerned with modernising socialism but now sought to make Russia a 'normal' country, as it was put at the time. In March 1991 Yeltsin managed to convince the Third Congress of People's Deputies to create a Russian executive presidency, and the necessary constitutional amendments were adopted by the Fourth Congress in May of that year. The first popular national elections for the Russian presidency were held on 12 June with six candidates; with Yeltsin receiving over 50 per cent of the vote, there was no need for a second round.

Candidate	Votes cast	Percentage
1 Yeltsin, Boris	45,552,041	57.30
2 Ryzhkov, Nikolai	13,395,335	16.85
3 Zhirinovskii, Vladimir	6,211,007	7.81
4 Tuleev, Aman	5,417,464	6.81
5 Makashov, Al'bert	2,969,511	3.74
6 Bakatin, Vadim	2,719,757	3.42
Invalid votes	3,242,167	4.10
Total votes cast	79,507,282	100.00

Sources: 'Soobshchenie tsentral'noi izbiratel'noi komissii po vyboram Prezidenta RSFSR', Izvestiya, 20 June 1991; Pravda, 20 June 1991.

Document 10.23 The Revised Party Programme

At the Twenty-eighth Congress the party adopted the draft of a new programme which in effect returned to the themes of traditional *evolutionary* social democracy. The draft was subtitled 'Towards a Humane, Democratic Socialism', and its final version was issued a year later.

The CPSU is a party with a socialist option and a communist outlook. We regard this prospect as the natural, historical thrust of the development of civilisation. Its social ideal absorbs the humanist principles of human culture, the age-old striving for a better life and social justice.

In our understanding, humane democratic socialism means a society in which: humankind is the aim of social development; living and working conditions for people are worthy of contemporary civilisation; man's alienation from political power and the material and spiritual values created by him are overcome and his active involvement in social processes is assured; the transformation of working people into the masters of production, the strong motivation of highly productive labour, and the best conditions for the progress of production forces and the rational use of nature are ensured on the basis of diverse forms of ownership and economic management; social justice and the social protection of working people are guaranteed – the sovereign will of the working people is the sole source of power; the state, which is subordinate to society, guarantees the protection of the rights, freedoms, honour and dignity of people regardless of social position, sex, age, national affiliation or religion; there is free competition and cooperation between all socio-political forces operating within the framework of law. This is a society which constantly advocates peaceful and equitable cooperation among the peoples and respect for the rights of every people to determine their own fate.

Source: Pravda, 8 August 1991.

The leading role of the party had gone, as had all mention of Marxism, the aim of building communism, class struggle, consciousness and the like. This was a new model of participatory and popular socialism, using elements of the market and based on genuine popular sovereignty, religious tolerance and social welfare. In short, a liberal agenda was bolted on to socialism. The regime was making peace with its own people, and by the same token this signalled the end of confrontation with the West.

Attempts to Save the Union

National relations were worsening. The final years of the USSR were accompanied by a number of bloody incidents. In Tbilisi on 9 April 1989 attempts to clear the Government House on Rustaveli Prospect of demonstrators demanding harsh measures against Abkhaz separatism led to the immediate deaths of sixteen demonstrators, with three more dying soon afterwards in hospital. After many delays the Central Committee in September 1989 held its long-promised plenum devoted to the renewal of the Union. Its outcome was disappointing, yet the process began to draft a new Union Treaty.

Document 10.24 The Union Treaty Process

A draft was published in late 1990 but already by then its provisions, enormously tolerant with respect for the past, had been superseded by events.

The sovereign republics which are parties to the treaty

Expressing the will of the peoples for the renewal of their Union, proceeding from the similarity of their previous development, determined to live in friendship and concord, and ensuring equitable cooperation,

Mindful of the interests of the material, cultural and emotional welfare of the peoples, mutual enrichment of national cultures, and common security,

Drawing lessons from the past and taking into account the changes taking place in the country and in the world,

Have decided to develop their relationships within the Union of Sovereign Soviet Republics on new principles.

I Basic Principles

First. Each republic which is party to the treaty shall be a sovereign state with full political power on its territory.

The USSR shall be a sovereign federative state formed as a result of voluntary unification of the republics and exercising the degree of political power given to it by the parties to the treaty.

Second. The republics forming the Union of Sovereign Soviet Republics shall recognise the inalienable right of each nation to self-determination and self-government, and independent action on all issues of its development.

They will strongly oppose racism, chauvinism and other extreme forms of nationalism, and any attempt to restrict the rights of the peoples. The parties to the treaty will seek a combination of common human and national values.

Third. The republics shall recognise the primacy of human rights set out in the UN Universal Declaration and international covenants as the most important principle of their union. The citizens of the USSR shall have guaranteed acces to the learning and use of their mother tongue, unrestricted access to information, freedom of religion, and other political and individual liberties.

Fourth. The republics see the formation and further development of civil society as crucial to the freedom and well-being of the peoples. They will seek to supply the needs of the people through the free choice of patterns of ownership and economic management and efforts to translate the principles of social justice and security into practice.

Fifth. It will be up to the republics themselves to determine their political system, administrative and territorial division, and the system of government and public administration. They recognise a democracy based on elected representation to be a common fundamental principle and seek to establish a law-governed state that would be a sure safeguard against any authoritarian practices and arbitrary rule.

Sixth. The republics regard the preservation and development of national traditions and state support for education, science and culture as their major task. They will work to promote intensive exchanges of humanitarian cultural values within the country and throughout the world for mutual benefit.

Seventh. The republics declare that their international priorities shall be lasting peace, abolition of nuclear and other weapons of mass annihilation, cooperation between nations, and solidarity of peoples in dealing with all other global challenges facing mankind.

Source: Pravda, *24 November 1990, p. 3.*

Document 10.25 The March 1991 Referendum

In early autumn 1990 the '500-days' plan for rapid economic reform was rejected, and over the winter of 1990–1 Gorbachev appeared to ally himself with the hardliners. In January 1991 troops were used to seize objects in Lithuania and Latvia, with some loss of life. The leaders of the republics became increasingly alarmed, fearing that as long as authority resided in Moscow their declarations of sovereignty remained fragile. The Union Treaty process appeared to be going nowhere. Gorbachev tried to strengthen his position by holding a referendum on the preservation of the Union. It was on this matter, in which he detailed how the question would be framed, that Gorbachev addressed the nation on 6 February 1991.

I would like to talk to you on a matter of crucial importance for the whole country – the forthcoming referendum on the future of our Union. The referendum is to be held in accordance with a decision of the Fourth Congress of People's Deputies of the USSR. The order of holding the referendum and its date have been set by the Supreme Soviet of the USSR. The Soviet people are to answer one question on 17 March. This is how this question has been worded by the Supreme Soviet:

> Do you think that it is necessary to preserve the Union of Soviet Socialist Republics as a renewed federation of equal and sovereign republics in which the rights and freedoms of each citizen, regardless of ethnic origin, will be fully guaranteed?

The answer should be either yes or no. Each and all of us should make a choice . . .

Although debates on this issue go on, we can pretty surely state right now that the Soviet people are for the preservation of the Union as a common asset of our peoples, and their reliable support. They favour, just as resolutely, the renewal of the Union so that all the people living in it can develop freely and feel that they are the masters of their own fate. A general outline of a renewed federal state, as it should be, is given in the draft Treaty of Union. This draft has been published in the press. What is the most important thing in the concept of renewing the Union? It is first and foremost the sovereignty of the republics, the subjects of the federation, which ensures the right of each people to self-determination and self-government. It is also the joint participation of the republics in the exercise of the federal terms of reference, i.e., all the powers they are delegating to the federal bodies of power and management. Sovereign republics need a viable federation which can really uphold common interests . . .

By virtue of history, a great many peoples, big and small, living on the vast expanse of Siberia, the flatlands and steppes of the Far East and Central Asia, in the valleys of the Caucasus and the Pamirs and on the Baltic, Caspian and Black Sea shores, have united around Russia. A huge Eurasian state with the world's largest territory and a large multilingual population has taken shape over centuries. To a large extent this is the result of complex processes that have taken shape over centuries, arising from the assimilation of new territories and from population shifts. Some of these territories were acquired by conquest, as has happened throughout the world, on all continents. Many peoples voluntarily allied themselves with Russia, seeking protection from outside aggression, or to gain access to a vast market and to one of the world's centres of science and culture. This was largely facilitated by the openness of the Russian nation, its willingness to cooperate on equal terms with various other peoples, its benevolent attitude towards their traditions, and willingness to share its own . . .

There is every justification to say that in this country a unique civilisation has taken shape, the outcome of many centuries of joint effort by all our peoples. And this also is vital in order to understand what we are now going through. First and foremost, we must take account of the fact that virtually all of our republics are multinational. Millions of people are descended from mixed marriages; 75 million, that is, one in four, live outside of, let us say, 'their own' republics. It would be madness to attempt to destroy this natural result of the flow of history. Yet in a number of republics attempts are being made to turn members of non-indigenous nationalities into second-class citizens, into outcasts, and in the long run to force them to leave. Think, comrades, about this: in peacetime, refugees have appeared in our country. And not in their tens or hundreds, but thousands, blameless victims of ethnic strife, political hot-headedness and uncontrolled emotion. Separatism threatens to tear millions of people away from their historical homelands, from the land where their ancestors are buried, and to disrupt the existing pattern of life . . .

Let us take the economy. It is glaringly obvious that all republics and regions of the country are economically dependent upon each other. This is the result of decades, perhaps even centuries, of sharing and cooperation in labour. It only takes one link within this integral system to break down, a few enterprises to cease work, and in the wake of this tens and hundreds of others also stop and then the entire country comes to a standstill. The Soviet Union possesses a vast scientific and cultural potential. This spiritual achievement is also the result of joint creativity. Those who decide to renounce this cultural power-house, clearly, stand to lose a great deal.

One of the advantages of a large federal state is the ability to ensure full and reliable security for one's country. And in any case, who is going to divide up the nuclear-missile, strategic potential of the Soviet Armed Forces? By virtue of its political weight and prestige, the Soviet Union is now a powerful player on the international stage, justifiably called a superpower. Its policies influence all the processes taking place in the world. Enormous effort was needed to acquire such influence and this can be so quickly squandered, thrown to the winds. Let me add that, with the exception of unreconstructed reactionaries and militarists, nobody in the world wants to weaken the role of the Soviet Union in international affairs.

These conclusions, dear comrades, form the basis of my firm conviction that our Union must be retained and profoundly reinvigorated. A renewed federal state, a federation of sovereign republics, means guaranteed security, a vast market, powerful science and culture. The Soviet Union is a world power, playing one of the key roles in the establishment of a new international order that is being built upon justice and solidarity. The Soviet Union represents a reliable future for all our peoples, for me and you, for our children and grandchildren.

Source: Pravda, *7 February 1991.*

In the referendum on 17 March 147 million people took part, of whom 112 million or 76 per cent voted in favour. Yet the fact that six republics refused to take part (Estonia, Latvia, Lithuania, Moldova, Georgia and Armenia) indicated how divided the Union had become. In Russia the result was ambiguous; while 71.3 per cent of Russia's 79.4 million turnout (75.1 per cent of the total electorate) voted 'yes' to the proposition, almost exactly the same number (69.6 per cent) voted in favour of a second question added to the ballot in Russia, about the creation of a Russian presidency, which implicitly challenged the postulates of the first. It was on the basis of this vote that the Russian presidency was created and Yeltsin elected in June 1991. From April 1991 Gorbachev brought together the leaders of the Union republics at his dacha at Novo-Ogarevo and together they hammered out a revised version of the Union Treaty that was to have been signed by three of the republics (Russia, Kazakhstan and Kyrgyzstan) on 20 August, with the others in principle signing later. The new version granted a significant devolution of powers and would in effect have converted the USSR into a confederation.

The August 1991 Coup

After months of living in the shadow of a coup, the plotters finally struck on the eve of the signing of the Union Treaty. The plotters had travelled to see Gorbachev in his vacation dacha at Foros in the Crimea on 18 August 1991, hoping at least to receive his tacit acquiescence, but Gorbachev ostensibly refused to be implicated in what he insisted was their adventurism. Despite this setback, they struck in the early hours of 19 August, declaring that the vice-president Gennadii Yanaev was taking over as president from Gorbachev 'due to the state of his health' (which they knew to be a blatant lie). They issued a *statement* announcing the creation of a State Committee for the State of Emergency (SCSE), a *resolution* establishing the administrative regulations governing the emergency, and an *appeal* to the Soviet people outlining the reasons for their action. Armoured columns moved into Moscow but no orders had been issued detailing their specific tasks. It was this sort of farcical incompetence that pervaded the whole coup. The White House, the seat of the Russian parliament, became the symbol of resistance. As the coup unravelled after three days, Yeltsin launched a counter-offensive against the party. Gorbachev himself never recovered his earlier prestige or authority.

Document 10.26   Statement by the Soviet Leadership

A state of emergency was announced for six months in some parts of the country, the priority of Soviet laws over the various 'declarations of state sovereignty' in the republics was asserted, and the membership of the coup committee was announced.

In connection with the inability of Mikhail Sergeevich Gorbachev to perform his duties of president of the USSR on account of the state of his health, and the transfer of the powers of the president of the USSR to Gennadii Ivanovich Yanaev, vice-president of the USSR, in accordance with Article 127.7 of the USSR Constitution;

with the aim of overcoming the profound and comprehensive crisis, political and civil conflict, the confrontation between nationalities, and the chaos and anarchy that threaten the lives and security of the citizens of the Soviet Union and the sovereignty, territorial integrity, freedom and independence of our fatherland;

proceeding from the results of the nationwide referendum on the preservation of the Union of Soviet Socialist Republics;

guided by the vitally important interests of the peoples of our homeland and of all Soviet people,

We declare:

1 That, in accordance with Article 127.3 of the USSR Constitution and Article 2 of the USSR law 'On the Legal Conditions Applying in a State of Emergency', and striving to fulfil the demands of broad strata of the population concerning the need to take very decisive measures to prevent society from sliding towards a national catastrophe and to safeguard legality and order, a state of emergency is introduced in certain localities of the USSR for a period of six months, beginning at 4 a.m. Moscow time on 19 August 1991.

2 That it is established that the USSR Constitution and USSR laws have unconditional supremacy throughout the USSR.

3 That, to administer the country and provide effective implementation of the conditions applying in a state of emergency, a State Committee for the State of Emergency in the USSR (USSR SCSE) is formed, with the following members: O. D. Baklanov, First Vice-Chairman of the USSR Defence Council; V. A. Kryuchkov, Chairman of the USSR Committee for State Security (KGB); V. S. Pavlov, Prime Minister of the USSR; B. K. Pugo, USSR Minister of Internal Affairs; V. A. Starodubtsev, Chairman of the USSR Peasants' Union; A. I. Tizyakov, President of the Association of State Enterprises and Industrial, Construction, Transportation and Communications Facilities; D. T. Yazov, USSR Minister of Defence; and G. I. Yanaev, acting President of the USSR.

4 That unswerving fulfilment of decisions of the USSR State Committee for the State of Emergency is mandatory for all bodies of power and adminis-tration, officials and citizens throughout the USSR.

G. Yanaev, V. Pavlov, and O. Baklanov
18 August 1991

Sources: Pravda, Izvestiya, *20 August 1991, p. 1;* Current Digest of the Soviet Press, *vol. XLIII, no. 33 (18 September 1991), pp. 1–2.*

Document 10.27 Resolution No. 1 of the USSR State Committee for the State of Emergency

The ban on parties and other organisations, the controls on the media, and the prohibition on rallies and strikes were balanced by a raft of populist measures that the putschists hoped would neutralise opposition to their seizure of power. The resolution sought to ground the acts of the putschists on the Soviet constitution, even as they comprehensively repudiated the changes that Gorbachev had introduced. The very tone of the resolution indicated just how little they understood of the profound processes that had transformed Soviet society, especially during the years of *perestroika*.

For the purpose of protecting the vitally important interests of the peoples and citizens of the USSR and the independence and territorial integrity of the country, restoring legality and law and order, stabilising the situation, overcoming the grave crisis and preventing chaos, anarchy and fratricidal civil war, the USSR State Committee for the State of Emergency resolves that:

1 All bodies of power and administration of the USSR, the Union and the autonomous republics, territories, provinces, cities, districts, settlements and villages are to ensure unswerving observance of the conditions applying in a state of emergency in accordance with the USSR law 'On the Legal Conditions Applying in a State of Emergency' and the resolutions of the USSR State Committee for the State of Emergency. In cases of inability to ensure fulfilment of these conditions, the powers of the relevant bodies of power and administration are to be suspended, and the performance of their functions is to be assigned to individuals specially empowered by the USSR State Committee for the State of Emergency.

2 Structures of power and administration and paramilitary formations acting in defiance of the USSR Constitution and USSR laws are to be immediately disbanded.

3 Laws and decisions of bodies of power and administration that are at variance with the USSR Constitution and USSR laws are henceforth to be considered invalid.

4 Activity by political parties, public organisations and mass movements that impedes the normalisation of the situation is to be suspended.

5 In connection with the fact that the State Committee for the State of Emergency in the USSR is temporarily assuming the functions of the USSR Security Council, the activity of the latter is suspended.

6 Citizens, institutions and organisations are immediately to surrender all types of firearms, ammunition, explosives and military equipment that are in their possession illegally . . . In cases of refusal, the firearms, etc., are to be taken by force and strict criminal and administrative charges are to be brought against the violators.

7 . . . The holding of rallies, street processions and demonstrations, as well as strikes, is not permitted.

When necessary, a curfew may be introduced, patrolling may be instituted, inspections may be conducted, and measures may be taken to reinforce border and customs regulations.

The most important state and economic facilities, as well as systems providing vital services, are to be taken under control, and, when necessary, put under guard.

The dissemination of inflammatory rumours, actions that provoke violations of law and order and the stirring up of discord between nationalities, and failure to obey officials who are ensuring the observance of the conditions applying in the state of emergency are to be resolutely curbed.

8 Control is to be established over the news media, with the implementation of this control assigned to a specially created agency under the USSR State Committee for the State of Emergency.

9 Organs of power and administration and executives of institutions and enterprises are to take measures to enhance the level of organisation and to establish order and discipline in all spheres of the life of society. The normal functioning of enterprises in all branches of the national economy, the strict fulfilment of measures to preserve and restore – during a period of stabilisation – vertical and horizontal ties among economic-management entities throughout the USSR, and the unswerving fulfilment of established volumes of production and of deliveries of raw and other materials and components are to be ensured.

A policy of strict economising with respect to materials, equipment and currency is to be established and maintained, and concrete measures are to be worked out and implemented to combat the mismanagement and squandering of public property.

A decisive struggle is to be waged against the shadow economy, and inescapable measures of criminal and administrative liability are to be applied in instances of corruption, embezzlement, speculation, the concealment of goods from sale, mismanagement and other law violations in the sphere of the economy.

Favourable conditions are to be created for increasing the real contribution of all types of entrepreneurial activity, carried out in accordance with USSR laws, to the country's economic potential and for providing for the urgent requirements of the population.

10 The holding of a permanent position in the structures of power and administration is to be considered incompatible with participation in entrepreneurial activity.

11 Within one week, the USSR Cabinet of Ministers is to conduct an inventory of all available resources of prime-necessity foodstuffs and industrial commodities, report to the people on what the country has at its

disposal, and put the safekeeping and distribution of these resources under the strictest possible control.

All restrictions impeding the shifting of food and consumer goods from one place to another in the USSR, as well as of material resources for their production, are to be lifted, and observance of this directive is to be strictly monitored.

Special attention is to be given to the top-priority supplying of children's preschool institutions, children's homes, schools, specialised secondary and higher educational institutions and hospitals, as well as of pensioners and disabled persons.

Within one week, proposals are to be submitted on putting in order, freezing and reducing prices for certain types of manufactured goods and foodstuffs, first of all goods for children, services to the population and public catering, and also on increasing wages, pensions, allowances and compensation payments for various categories of citizens.

Within two weeks, measures are to be worked out to put in order the size of salaries for executives at all levels of state, public, co-operative and other institutions, organisations and enterprises.

12 In view of the critical situation regarding harvest operations and the threat of hunger, emergency measures are to be taken to organise the procurement, storage and processing of agricultural output. Rural toilers are to be provided with the greatest possible assistance in the form of equipment, spare parts, fuel and lubricants, etc. The sending of workers and office employees from enterprises and organisations, students and servicemen to the countryside in the numbers needed to save the harvest is to be organised immediately.

13 Within one week, the USSR Cabinet of Ministers is to work out a resolution stipulating the provision, in 1991–1992, of plots of land up to 0.15 hectares in size to all urban residents who wish to use this land to grow fruit and vegetables.

14 Within two weeks, the USSR Cabinet of Ministers is to complete the planning of urgent measures to bring the country's fuel and energy complex out of crisis and to prepare for winter.

15 Within one month, real measures for 1992 aimed at fundamentally improving housing construction and providing housing to the population are to be prepared and reported to the people.

During a six-month period, a concrete five-year programme for accelerated development of state, co-operative and individual housing construction is to be worked out.

16 Central and local bodies of power and administration must devote top priority attention to the social needs of the population. Possibilities for a substantial improvement in free medical services and public education are to be sought out.

Sources: Pravda, Izvestiya, *20 August 1991, p. 1;* Current Digest of the Soviet Press, *vol. XLIII, no. 33 (18 September 1991), pp. 2–4.*

Document 10.28   Appeal to the Soviet People

The appeal even more underestimated the changes in public opinion. While there was indeed much concern that *perestroika* had undermined public order and labour discipline, nothing that the putschists stated here offered serious policies to tackle the mounting problems facing the country.

Fellow countrymen! Citizens of the Soviet Union!
At this grave, critical hour for the fate of the fatherland and of our peoples, we appeal to you! A mortal danger threatens our great homeland! For a number of reasons, the policy of reforms begun at the initiative of M. S. Gorbachev and conceived of as a means of ensuring the dynamic development of the country and the democratisation of the life of society has reached an impasse. The initial enthusiasm and hopes have given way to unbelief, apathy and despair. The authorities at all levels have lost the trust of the population. In the life of society, political intrigue has supplanted concern for the fate of the fatherland and the citizen. Malicious mocking of all state institutions is being propagated. In essence, the country has become ungovernable.

Taking advantage of the liberties that have been granted and trampling the shoots of democracy, which have just emerged, extremist forces have come into being and embarked on a course aimed at the liquidation of the Soviet Union, the break-up of the state and the seizure of power at any cost. The results of the nationwide referendum on the unity of the fatherland have been trampled. The cynical exploitation of national feelings is only a screen for satisfying ambitions. These political adventurists are troubled neither by the current misfortunes of their people nor by their future troubles. In creating an atmosphere of psychological and political terror and trying to hide behind the shield of the people's trust, they forget that the ties they are condemning and breaking were established on a basis of far broader popular support – support that, moreover, has undergone the test of history for many centuries. Today those who are essentially working toward the overthrow of the constitutional system should have to answer to mothers and fathers for the deaths of the many hundreds of victims in conflicts between nationalities. The crippled lives of more than half a million refugees are on their conscience. Because of them, tens of millions of Soviet people who only yesterday were living in a united family but today find themselves outcasts in their own homes have lost tranquillity and the joy of life.

The people should decide what the social system should be like, but they are being deprived of this right.

Instead of showing concern for the security and well-being of every citizen and of society as a whole, the people who have acquired power frequently use it for interests that are alien to the people, as a means of unscrupulous self-assertion. The streams of words and mountains of statements and promises only underscore the scanty and wretched nature of their practical deeds. The inflation of power, more frightening than any other kind of inflation, is destroying our state and society. Every citizen feels growing uncertainty about tomorrow and deep concern for the future of his or her children.

The crisis of power has had a catastrophic effect on the economy. The chaotic, ungoverned slide toward a market has caused an explosion of selfishness – regional, departmental, group and personal. The war of laws and the encouragement of centrifugal tendencies have brought about the destruction of a unified national-economic mechanism that took shape over decades. The result is a sharp fall off in the standard of living for the over-whelming majority of Soviet people and the flourishing of speculation and the shadow economy. It is high time to tell the people the truth: unless urgent and resolute measures are taken to stabilise the economy, hunger and a new round of impoverishment are inevitable in the very near future, from which it is only one step to large-scale manifestations of spontaneous discontent, with destructive consequences. Only irresponsible people can set their hopes on some kind of help from abroad. No hand-outs are going to solve our problems; salvation is in our own hands. The time has come to measure the authority of every person or organisation in terms of actual contributions to the restoration and development of the national economy.

For many years, we have heard from all sides incantations about commitment to the interests of the individual, to concern for his rights and social safeguards. But in fact people have been humiliated, their real rights and possibilities have been infringed, and they have been driven to despair. All the democratic institutions created through the expression of the people's will are losing their authority and effectiveness before our very eyes. This is the result of purposeful actions by those who, blatantly flouting the USSR Basic Law, are staging an unconstitutional coup, to all intents and purposes, and longing for unbridled personal dictatorship. Prefectures, mayoralties and other unlawful structures are increasingly supplanting, in an unauthorised way, the Soviets that have been elected by the people.

An offensive against the rights of the working people is under way. The rights to work, education, health care, housing and recreation have been called in question.

Even people's basic personal safety is increasingly under threat. Crime is growing at a rapid rate and is becoming organised and politicised. The country is sinking into an abyss of violence and lawlessness. Never before in the country's history has the propaganda of sex and violence gained such wide scope, jeopardising the health and lives of future generations. Millions of people are demanding that measures be taken against the octopus of crime and glaring immorality.

The deepening destabilisation of the political and economic situation in the Soviet Union is undermining our position in the world. Revanchist tones have been heard in some places, and demands for the revision of our borders are being put forward. Voices are even being heard calling for the dismemberment of the Soviet Union and for the possible establishment of international trusteeship over certain facilities in regions of the country. Such is the bitter reality. Only yesterday, a Soviet person who found himself abroad felt that he was a worthy citizen of an influential and respected state. Now he is often a second-class foreigner whose treatment bears the imprint of scorn or sympathy.

The pride and honour of Soviet people must be restored in full.

The State Committee for the State of Emergency in the USSR is fully aware of the depth of the crisis that has struck our country; it is assuming responsibility for the fate of the homeland, and it is fully resolved to take very serious measures to bring the state and society out of crisis as quickly as possible.

We promise to conduct a wide-ranging, nationwide discussion of the draft of a new Union Treaty. Everyone will have the right and opportunity to think about this highly important act in a calm atmosphere and to make up his mind about it, for the fate of the numerous peoples of our great homeland will depend on what the Union will be like.

We intend immediately to restore legality and law and order to put an end to bloodshed, to declare a merciless war against the criminal world, and to eradicate shameful phenomena that discredit our society and degrade Soviet citizens. We will clean the criminal elements from the streets of our cities and put an end to the high-handedness of the plunderers of public property.

We favour truly democratic processes and a consistent policy of reforms leading to the renewal of our homeland and to its economic and social prosperity, which will enable it to take a worthy place in the world community of nations.

The country's development should not be built on a fall-off in the population's living standard. In a healthy society, continual improvement in the well-being of all citizens will become the norm.

Without relaxing concern for strengthening and protecting the rights of the individual, we will focus attention on protecting the interests of the broadest strata of the population, of those who have been hit the hardest by inflation, the disorganisation of production, corruption and crime.

In the process of developing a mixed national economy, we will support private enterprise, providing it with the necessary possibilities for developing production and the service sphere.

Our primary concern will be solving the food and housing problems. All available forces will be mobilised for the satisfaction of these very urgent requirements of the people.

We call on workers, peasants, the working intelligentsia and all Soviet people to restore labour discipline and order in the shortest possible time and to raise the level of production, so as then to move resolutely forward. Our life, the future of our children and grandchildren and the fate of the fatherland will depend on this.

We are a peace-loving country and will unswervingly observe all the commitments we have made. We have no claims against anyone. We want to live in peace and friendship with everyone, but we firmly state that no one will ever be allowed to encroach on our sovereignty, independence and territorial integrity. Any attempts to talk to our country in the language of diktat, no matter where they come from, will be resolutely curbed.

For centuries, our multinational people have been filled with pride in their homeland; we have not been ashamed of our patriotic feelings, and we consider it natural and legitimate to raise present and future generations of citizens of our great power in this spirit.

To do nothing in this critical hour for the fate of the fatherland is to assume a grave responsibility for the tragic, truly unpredictable consequences. Everyone who cherishes our homeland, who wants to live and work in an atmosphere of tranquillity and confidence, who does not accept a continuation of bloody conflicts between nationalities and who sees his fatherland as independent and prosperous in the future must make the only correct choice. We call on all true patriots and people of goodwill to put an end to this time of troubles.

We call on all citizens of the Soviet Union to recognise their duty to the homeland and provide every kind of support to the State Committee for the State of Emergency in the USSR and to efforts to bring the country out of crisis.

Constructive proposals from public-political organisations, labour collectives and citizens will be gratefully accepted as a manifestation of their patriotic readiness to participate actively in the restoration of a centuries-old friendship in the single family of fraternal peoples and in the revival of the fatherland.

The State Committee for the State of Emergency in the USSR

Sources: Pravda, Izvestiya, *20 August 1991, p. 1;* Current Digest of the Soviet Press, *vol. XLIII, no. 33 (18 September 1991), pp. 4–5.*

Document 10.29 Yeltsin's Call for Resistance to the Coup

Yeltsin's response to the attempted coup was swift and unequivocal. The following statement was drafted by Ruslan Khasbulatov, the acting speaker of the Russian parliament, and Anatoly Sobchak, the mayor of Leningrad (soon to be renamed St Petersburg), who happened to be visiting at the time, in the morning of 19 August, at Yeltsin's dacha outside Moscow. Yeltsin then raced into the centre of Moscow and entered the White House without hindrance. There he issued this statement, and organised resistance to the coup. Soon the White House was surrounded by thousands of volunteers, willing to lay down their lives to ensure the continuation of democratic reforms.

To the Citizens of Russia

19 August 1991

On the night of 18 to 19 August 1991 the legally elected president of the country was removed from power. Whatever reasons might be given to justify this removal, we are dealing with a right-wing, reactionary and anti-constitutional coup.

Notwithstanding all the trials and difficulties the people of our country are experiencing, the democratic process in the country is becoming ever deeper and is becoming irreversible. The peoples of Russia are becoming masters of their own fate. The uncontrolled rights of the party and other unconstitutional bodies have been severely curtailed. The Russian leadership has assumed a decisive role in accordance with the Union Treaty, striving to maintain the unity of the Soviet Union and of Russia. Our stand on this question has made it possible substantially to speed up the preparation of the Union Treaty, coordinate it with all the republics, and set the date for its signing – 20 August.

Such a development aroused the animosity of reactionary forces and provoked them to try to solve the most complicated political and economic problems by the use of force. Such actions can only be described as irresponsible and adventuristic. Earlier attempts at a coup had already been made.

We have always considered that the use of force to solve political and economic problems is unacceptable. It discredits the USSR in the eyes of the world and undermines our prestige in the international community, returning us to the Cold War era and the isolation of the Soviet Union from the international community.

We are forced to declare unlawful this so-called committee together with all its decisions and resolutions.

We are convinced that local authorities will unswervingly follow constitutional law and the decrees of the president of the RSFSR.

We call upon the citizens of Russia to give fitting reply to the putschists and to demand that they immediately return the country to a normal path of constitutional development.

It is of vital importance that President Gorbachev be given the opportunity to address the people. We demand the immediate convocation of an extraordinary session of the Congress of People's Deputies of the USSR.

We are absolutely convinced that our compatriots will not allow the arbitrary rule and lawlessness of these putschists, men with neither shame nor conscience, to become firmly established. We appeal to the troops to demonstrate a sense of civic duty and not to take part in this reactionary coup.

We call for a general strike until such time as these demands are met. We do not doubt that the international community will correctly evaluate this cynical attempt at a rightist coup.

The President of the RSFSR	B. N. Yeltsin
The Chairman of the Council of Ministers of the RSFSR	I. S. Silaev
Acting Chair of the Supreme Soviet of the RSFSR	R. I. Khasbulatov

19 August 1991, 09.00

Read and pass on to others.

Sources: Rossiya, *newspaper of the Presidium of the RSFSR Supreme Soviet (special issue), 19 August 1991;* Current Digest of the Soviet Press, *vol. XLIII, no. 33 (18 September 1991), pp. 6–7; a truncated version is reported, with some direct quotations, on p. 2 of* Izvestiya, *20 August 1991.*

Document 10.30   Yeltsin Decrees the Acts of the SCSE Void

This decree was important because it placed the burden of illegality on to those carrying out the orders of the SCSE, making them liable to prosecution. In another decree issued at the same time, Yeltsin decreed Russia's takeover of all security and military agencies on Russian territory, placing himself temporarily at their head.

In connection with the activities of a group of people, declaring themselves a so-called State Committee for the State of Emergency, decree:

1 The declaration forming the Committee is unconstitutional, the actions of its organisers constitute a coup d'état, being nothing other than an act of treason.
2 All decisions made in the name of the so-called Committee for the State of Emergency to be considered illegal and without force on the territory of the RSFSR. On the territory of the Russian Federation the legally elected authorities in the form of the president, chairman of the Supreme Soviet and

chairman of the Council of Ministers, all state and local organs of power retain their jurisdictions.

3 The activity of responsible persons who fulfil the decisions of the said committee will be judged under the terms of the RSFSR Criminal Code and will be judged according to the law.

The present decree comes into force from the moment of its signing.
President of the RSFSR, B. Yeltsin

Sources: Rossiya, *newspaper of the Presidium of the RSFSR Supreme Soviet (emergency issue), 19 August 1991;* Kuranty, *19 August 1991 (special edition), p. 1;* Current Digest of the Soviet Press, *vol. XLIII, no. 33 (18 September 1991), p. 7.*

Document 10.31　Yeltsin's Address to the People of 20 August 1991

Only a limited number of republics had agreed to attend the signing ceremony for the Union Treaty on 20 August, yet it would undoubtedly have marked a decisive step in the transformation of the Soviet state into a genuine federal system. It represented not so much social as 'republican' pluralisation of the Soviet Union, enshrining the rights of the republics to conduct their own affairs with only relatively limited rights for the 'centre' in Moscow. Anatoly Lukyanov, Gorbachev's replacement as chairman of the USSR Supreme Soviet, was not formally a member of the coup committee yet acted as its *éminence grise.* In an article published in *Pravda* on 20 August, he condemned the text of the treaty that was to have been signed that day as failing to establish a single economic space and a unified banking system, and for not having unequivocally asserted the priority of the centre's laws. Yeltsin's view was very different.

The coup took place on 19 August. The date – this is absolutely clear – was chosen not at random: the last day before the signing of the new Union Treaty. The treaty, which, despite all the compromises, would have put an end to the absolute power of the CPSU and the military-industrial complex.

I listen to the speeches of the organisers of the coup and am amazed: what a degree of moral decline. Yesterday they stigmatised the Russian leadership for allegedly not wanting to sign the Union Treaty. Today they try to convince the people that our desire to sign it is directed towards the destruction of the renewal of the Union.

Objectively the new Union Treaty deprived practically every single member of the coup of possibilities. This is the secret of the coup. This is the main motive for the actions of its participants. Their lofty phrases about the fate of the motherland is no more than a game to cover their personal mercenary interests.

I mentioned the CPSU on purpose. We will not close our eyes – it was precisely this party that became the 'organiser and inspirer' of the coup. The committee dissolved all parties by decree, except the Communist. All newspapers were banned, except communist ones. Is that not so? I am convinced that the time will come and the leading group in the CPSU will disown any participation in this evil act against the people. But it is unlikely that demagogy will be able to cover the main essence of its activity – the struggle against the people to preserve its privileges.

I want once again forcefully to declare: all that has passed in the last few days is nothing other than a coup d'état. Its leaders are nothing other than state criminals.

> 20 August 1991
> Boris Yeltsin
> President of the Russian Federation

Source: Obshchaya gazeta, *21 August 1991.*

Document 10.32   The Suspension of the Russian Communist Party

The CPSU had not been directly involved in the coup, yet many of its central bodies were, at the least, acquiescent, and had done nothing to defend their own General Secretary, Gorbachev. The party in Russia was suspended on 23 August, its property was sequestered, and the party was then banned by a presidential decree on 6 November.

Acting on the territory of the RSFSR and not registered in the required way, the Communist Party of the RSFSR supported the so-called USSR State Committee for the State of Emergency, carrying out a coup d'état and forcefully removing from power the president of the USSR. In a number of regions of the RSFSR, with the direct participation of republican, *krai* and *oblast* organs of the RSFSR Communist Party, emergency committees (commissions) were established, which was a crude violation of the USSR law 'On Social Organisations'.

Organs of the RSFSR Communist Party in republics, *krais* and *oblasts* frequently and against the RSFSR Constitution interfered in the judicial process, and obstructed the fulfilment of the decree of the RSFSR president of 20 July 1991 'On the ending of the activity of the organisational structures of political parties and mass social movements in state organs, institutions and organisations of the RSFSR'.

On the basis of the above I resolve:

1 The Ministry of Internal Affairs of the RSFSR and the RSFSR Procuracy are to investigate the facts of the anti-constitutional activity of organs of the

Communist Party of the RSFSR. The relevant material is to be sent for examination by judicial organs.

2 To suspend the activity of the organs and organisations of the Communist Party of the RSFSR until the conclusive resolution of the issue of the anti-constitutional activity of the RSFSR Communist Party by the courts.

3 The Ministry of Internal Affairs of the RSFSR is to protect the property and financial resources of the organs and organisations of the Communist Party of the RSFSR up to the adoption of final decisions by the courts . . .

President of RSFSR B. N. Yeltsin
23 August 1991

Source: Rossiiskaya gazeta, *27 August 1991.*

The End of the USSR

Following the coup the USSR Congress of People's Deputies dissolved itself, and the highest body of power became the State Council, composed of the leaders of the republics and chaired by Gorbachev. At its first meeting on 6 September 1991 the USSR State Council recognised the independence of Estonia, Latvia and Lithuania. Despite the results of the March referendum, the unity of the Union never recovered from the blow delivered by the coup, and by the end of the year Russia had taken over many of the functions hitherto fulfilled by the centre. The overwhelming vote in favour of Ukrainian independence on 1 December sounded the death knell for the USSR. By the end of the year the country no longer existed.

Document 10.33   Declaration Establishing the Commonwealth of Independent States (CIS)

On 7–8 December the leaders of Russia, Ukraine and Belarus met at a hunting lodge in Belovezhskaya Pushcha in Belarus; an agreement was signed in Minsk on 8 December. They had gathered in the knowledge that with Ukrainian independence the chances of maintaining even a slimmed down USSR no longer appeared viable.

We, leaders of the Republics of Belarus, RSFSR, Ukraine,

- noting that negotiations to prepare a new Union Treaty have entered a dead end, the objective process of republics leaving the USSR and the formation of independent states has become a real fact;
- ascertaining that the short-sighted policies of the centre led to a profound economic and political crisis, to the destruction of output, the catastrophic fall in the standards of living of practically all strata of society;

- taking into account the growing social tensions in many regions of the former USSR, which have led to inter-ethnic conflicts and numerous human casualties;
- recognising responsibility before our people and world society and the desperate need to conduct political and economic reforms, we announce the creation of the Commonwealth of Independent States, to which the parties on 8 December 1991 signed an agreement.

The Commonwealth of Independent States comprising the Republic of Belarus, the RSFSR and Ukraine is open for all states, members of the USSR, to join, as well as other states, sharing the aims and principles of the present agreement.

The member states of the Commonwealth intend to conduct a course for the strengthening of international peace and security. They guarantee the implementation of international commitments arising for them from treaties and agreements of the former USSR, ensuring a single control over nuclear weapons and their non-proliferation.

Chairman of the Supreme Soviet of the Republic of Belarus S. Shushkevich
President of the RSFSR B. Yeltsin
President of Ukraine L. Kravchuk
8 December 1991, Minsk

Source: Rossiiskaya gazeta, *10 December 1991.*

Document 10.34   Declaration on the Creation of the CIS

The leaders drafted a basic outline for a successor to the USSR. The CIS was not intended to be a successor state to the USSR but a way of retaining residual links and of 'managing the divorce', as the Ukrainian leadership was to reiterate later.

We, the Republic of Belarus, the Russian Federation (RSFSR), and Ukraine, as founder states of the USSR who signed the Union Treaty of 1922, designated below as the High Contracting Parties, state that the USSR, as a subject of international law and a geopolitical reality, is ceasing to exist.

Basing ourselves on the historical community of our peoples and the ties that have formed between them, taking into consideration the bilateral treaties concluded between the High Contracting Parties, seeking to build democratic law-based states, intending to develop their relations on the basis of mutual recognition of and respect for state sovereignty, the inalienable right to self-determination, the principles of equality and noninterference in internal affairs, a rejection of the use of force, economic or any other methods of pressure, the settlement of disputes by means of conciliation, and other generally recognised principles and norms of international law, considering that the further development and strengthening of relations of friendship, good-neighbourliness and mutually advantageous cooperation between our states answers the fundamental national interests of their peoples and serves the cause of peace and security, confirming their adherence to the goals and principles of the United Nations Charter, the Helsinki Final Act, and other documents of the Conference on Security and Cooperation in Europe, pledging to observe the generally recognised international norms on the rights of man and of peoples, we have agreed on the following:

Article 1

The High Contracting Parties are forming the Commonwealth of Independent States.

Article 2

The High Contracting Parties guarantee their citizens, regardless of their nationality or other differences, equal rights and freedoms. Each of the High Contracting Parties guarantees the citizens of the other parties, and also stateless persons living on their territory, regardless of their national affiliation or other differences, civil, political, social, economic, and cultural rights and freedoms in accordance with the generally recognised international norms of human rights.

Article 3

The High Contracting Parties, wishing to promote the expression, preservation, and development of the ethnic, cultural, linguistic, and religious distinctiveness of the national minorities living on their territory and of the unique ethno-cultural groups that have formed there, take them under their protection.

Article 4

The High Contracting Parties will develop equal and mutually beneficial cooperation between their peoples and states in the spheres of politics, the economy, culture, education, health care, environmental protection, science, trade, and in the humanitarian and other spheres, promote a wide-scale exchange of information, and strictly observe mutual obligations.

The parties consider that it is necessary to conclude agreements on cooperation in these spheres.

Article 5

The High Contracting Parties recognise and respect each other's territorial integrity and the inviolability of existing frontiers within the framework of the commonwealth.

They guarantee the openness of frontiers and freedom of movement of citizens and the transfer of information within the framework of the commonwealth.

Article 6

The member states of the commonwealth will cooperate in ensuring international peace and security and the realisation of effective measures to reduce armaments and military expenditures. They will strive for the elimination of all nuclear weapons and for general and complete disarmament under strict international control.

The Parties will respect each other's desire to attain the status of nuclear-free zones and neutral states.

The member states of the commonwealth will preserve and maintain under joint command a common military-strategic space, including single control over nuclear weapons, the manner of implementing which will be regulated by a special agreement.

They also jointly guarantee the requisite conditions for the stationing, functioning, and material and social well-being of the Strategic Armed Forces. The parties undertake to conduct a coordinated policy as regards the social protection and pension arrangements for military personnel and their families.

Article 7

The High Contracting Parties acknowledge that the sphere of their joint activity, realised on an equal basis through common coordinating institutions, includes:

- coordination of foreign-policy activity;
- cooperation in the formation and development of a common economic space, of all-European and Eurasian markets, and in the sphere of customs policy;
- cooperation in the development of transport and communications systems;
- cooperation in the sphere of environmental protection, participation in the creation of an all-embracing international system of ecological safety;
- cooperation in questions of migration policy;
- cooperation in the fight against organised crime.

Article 8

The parties recognise the global nature of the Chernobyl' catastrophe and undertake to unite and coordinate their efforts to minimise and overcome its consequences.

For these purposes they have agreed to conclude special agreements that take account of the seriousness of the consequences of the catastrophe.

Article 9

Disputes regarding the interpretation of the norms of the present agreement are subject to solution by means of talks between the appropriate bodies, and, when necessary, at the level of heads of government and state.

Article 10

Each of the High Contracting Parties reserves the right to suspend the operation of the present agreement or its individual articles having notified the participants in the agreement a year in advance.

The provisions of the present agreement can be supplemented or changed by mutual agreement of the High Contracting Parties.

Article 11

The application of the norms of third states, including those of the former USSR, is not permitted on the territory of the states signing this agreement from the moment of its signing.

Article 12

The High Contracting Parties guarantee the fulfillment of the international obligations ensuing for them from the treaties and agreements of the former USSR.

Article 13

The present agreement does not affect the obligations of the High Contracting Parties as regards third states.

The present agreement is open to accession by all member states of the former USSR, and also by other states sharing the goals and principles of the present agreement.

Article 14

The official residence of the coordinating bodies of the commonwealth is the city of Minsk.

The activity of agencies of the former USSR on the territory of the commonwealth ceases.

Accomplished in the city of Minsk on 8 December 1991 in three copies, each in Belarussian, Russian, and Ukrainian, the three texts having identical force.

For the Republic of Belarus	S. Shushkevich, V. Kebich
For the RSFSR	B. Yeltsin, G. Burbulis
For Ukraine	L. Kravchuk, V. Fokin

Source: RFE/RL Research Report, *10 January 1992, pp. 4–5.*

Document 10.35 Gorbachev's Response to the Establishment of the CIS

Gorbachev had not been forewarned of what was afoot, and when he heard that the state of which he was leader had been abolished he was furious. He later admitted that he had thought of using military force at the time, but it is by no means clear that the armed forces would have obeyed him, even though he was formally commander-in-chief, nor is it clear against what precise object he would have moved. By then Russia had already gained significant sovereignty over its own territory and control over most federal institutions, including finances.

On 8 December 1991 in Minsk the leaders of Belarus, RSFSR and Ukraine reached an agreement on the creation of the Commonwealth of Independent States.

For me, as the country's president, the main criterion for evaluating this document is the degree to which it meets the interests of the security of citizens, the tasks of overcoming the present crisis, the preservation of statehood and the continuation of democratic reforms.

This agreement has its positive side.

The Ukrainian leadership participated in it, which in recent times did not show any interest in the treaty process.

The document stresses the need to create a single economic space, functioning on agreed principles with a single currency and financial-banking system. A readiness for cooperation is expressed in the fields of science, education, culture and other spheres. A defined formula for cooperation in the military-strategic sphere is proposed.

However, a document of such significance, which so profoundly affects the peoples of our country, the whole international community, demands an all-round political and legal evaluation.

In any case the following is clear to me. The agreement directly announces the end of the existence of the USSR. Undoubtedly, every republic has the right to leave the Union, but the fate of a multinational state cannot be decided by the will of the leaders of three republics. This question must be decided only by constitutional means with the participation of all sovereign states taking into account the will of their peoples.

The declaration on the end of the activity of all-Union legal norms is equally illegal and dangerous, which can only increase chaos and anarchy in society.

The hastiness of the appearance of the document also evokes amazement. It was discussed neither by the populations, nor by the Supreme Soviets of the republics, in whose name it was signed. Moreover, this took place just at the time when in the parliaments of the republics the draft of the Treaty on the Union of Sovereign States, devised by the USSR State Council, was being discussed.

In this situation, I am profoundly convinced, it is necessary that all the Supreme Soviets of the republics and the USSR Supreme Soviet should discuss both the draft Treaty on the Union of Sovereign States as well as the agreement signed in Minsk. Insofar as the agreement proposes a new form of statehood, a matter for the USSR Congress of People's Deputies, such a congress should be convened. Moreover, I would not exclude the carrying out of a popular referendum (plebiscite) on this question.

Source: Izvestiya, *10 December 1991.*

Document 10.36 The Alma Ata Declaration

On 21 December the three states which had met in Belarus were joined by another eight as founder members. Georgia joined the CIS in 1993, while the three Baltic republics at the time and later wanted nothing to do with organisation. Kazakhstan's leaders had been particularly upset that they had not participated at the 7–8 December meeting, and to avoid the impression that the new body was not much more than a 'Slavic Commonwealth', the enlarged meeting was held in the Kazakhstani capital.

The independent states:

Republic of Azerbaijan, Republic of Armenia, Republic of Belarus, Republic of Kazakhstan, Republic of Kyrgyzstan, Republic of Moldova, Russian Federation (RSFSR), Republic of Tajikistan, Turkmenistan, Republic of Uzbekistan, and Ukraine,

striving to build democratic legal states, relations between whom will develop on the basis of mutual recognition and respect for state sovereignty and sovereign equality, the inalienable right to self-determination, the principles of equality and non-interference in internal affairs, the rejection of the use of force or the threat of force, economic or other methods of exerting pressure, the peaceful regulation of conflicts, respect for human rights and freedoms including the rights of national minorities, the conscientious fulfilment of obligations and other generally recognised principles and norms of international law;

recognising and respecting each other's territorial integrity and the inviolability of the existing borders;

considering that the strengthening of the existing historical roots of relations of friendship, good-neighbourliness and mutually beneficial co-operation reflects the profound interests of the peoples and promotes the cause of peace and security;

recognising their responsibility for the preservation of civic peace and inter-ethnic concord;

being committed to the aims and principles of the agreement establishing the Commonwealth of Independent States,

declare the following:

Relations between members of the Commonwealth will be conducted on the principles of equality through coordinating institutions, formed on a parity basis and operating in a manner defined by agreements between the members of the Commonwealth, which is neither a state nor a suprastate body.

To ensure international strategic stability and security a single united command over military-strategic forces will be preserved and a single control over nuclear weapons; the parties will respect their mutual aim to achieve the status of non-nuclear and (or) neutral states.

The Commonwealth of Independent States is open with the agreement of all of its members for other members of the former USSR to join, as well as other states sharing the aims and principles of the Commonwealth.

The commitment to cooperation in the formation and development of a common economic space is affirmed, of the general European and Eurasian markets.

With the creation of the Commonwealth of Independent States the Union of Soviet Socialist Republics ceases to exist.

The member states of the Commonwealth guarantee in accordance with their constitutions procedures for the fulfilment of international commitments arising from treaties and agreements of the former USSR.

The member states of the Commonwealth commit themselves to the undeviating observance of the principles of this declaration.

For the Republic of Azerbaijan	A. Mutalibov
For the Republic of Armenia	L. Ter-Petrosyan
For the Republic of Belarus	S. Shushkevich
For the Republic of Kazakhstan	N. Nazarbaev
For the Republic of Kyrgyzstan	A. Akaev
For the Republic of Moldova	M. Snegur
For the Russian Federation (RSFSR)	B. Yeltsin
For the Republic of Tajikistan	R. Nabiev
For Turkmenistan	S. Niyazov
For the Republic of Uzbekistan	I. Karimov
For Ukraine	L. Kravchuk

Sources: Pravda, Izvestiya, *23 December 1991;* Rossiiskaya gazeta, *24 December 1991.*

Document 10.37 Gorbachev's Resignation, 25 December 1991

After six years at the helm Gorbachev had seen the whole mighty power of the Communist Party and the Soviet state evaporate, and now the country itself had disappeared. His evaluation of what he had achieved in those years was fair. This was his last broadcast as leader; on 31 December 1991 the USSR was formally dissolved. His final words are a fitting epitaph for the USSR.

Dear Compatriots, Citizens,

Arising from the developing situation with the formation of the Commonwealth of Independent States, my work in the post of president of the USSR has come to an end. I am taking this decision on the grounds of principle. I strongly spoke out in favour of the autonomy and independence of peoples, for the sovereignty of republics. But at the same time I defended the preservation of the Union state, for the integrity of the country. Events took a different path. The line favouring the dismemberment of the country and the separation of states, with which I cannot agree, triumphed.

After the Alma Ata meeting and the adoption there of decisions my position on this has not changed. Moreover, I am convinced that decisions of such a scale should be adopted on the basis of a popular plebiscite. Nevertheless, I will do all that I can so that the agreements signed there will lead to real consensus in society, ease the resolution of the crisis and the reform process. Appearing before you for the last time as president of the USSR, I consider it essential to state my evaluation of the path taken since 1985 . . .

- The totalitarian system has been liquidated, which deprived the country of becoming successful and flourishing.
- A breakthrough on the path of democratic transformation has been achieved. Free elections, freedom of the press, religious freedom, representative bodies of power, multi-partyism, have all become real. Human rights have been accepted as the highest principle.
- The movement towards a multi-layered economy has begun, the equality of all forms of property has been affirmed . . .

We are living in a different world:

- We have put an end to the 'Cold War', the arms race has been ended and so too the senseless militarisation of the country, which deformed our economy, popular consciousness and morality. The threat of world war has been lifted . . .
- We have opened the world, rejecting interference in the affairs of others, the use of troops outside the country . . .
- We have become one of the main bulwarks for the restructuring of contemporary civilisation on a peaceful, democratic basis.
- Nations and peoples have gained the real freedom to choose their own path of self-determination . . .

All these changes demanded enormous work and took place in sharp struggle, with growing resistance of the old, redundant and reactionary forces, including the former party-state structures, and the economic apparatus, and indeed our habits, ideological prejudices, levelling and dependency psychology. They played on our lack of tolerance, low level of political culture, fear of changes . . .

It seems to me vital to preserve the democratic gains of recent years. They have been achieved through the suffering of our entire history, our tragic experience . . .

I am leaving my post worried. But also with hope, with faith in you, in your wisdom and spiritual strength. We are the legatees of a great civilisation, and it now depends on each and every one for it to be reborn to the new contemporary and worthy life.

Source: Rossiiskaya gazeta, *27 December 1991.*

Guide to further reading

Carr, E. H., *The Russian Revolution from Lenin to Stalin, 1917–1929* (London, Macmillan, 1979).

Christian, David, *Imperial and Soviet Russia: Power, Privilege and the Challenge of Modernity* (Basingstoke, Macmillan, 1997).

Cohen, Stephen F., *Rethinking the Soviet Experience: Politics and History since 1917* (Oxford, Oxford University Press, 1985).

Crummey, R. O. (ed.), *Reform in Russia and the USSR: Past and Prospects* (Urbana, University of Illinois Press, 1989).

Daniels, Robert V., *The End of the Communist Revolution* (London, Routledge, 1993).

Gooding, John, *Rulers and Subjects: Government and People in Russia 1801–1991* (London, Arnold, 1996).

Heller, Mikhail and Nekrich, Aleksandr, *Utopia in Power, the History of the Soviet Union from 1917 to the Present*, trans. P. B. Carlos (New York, Summit Books, 1986).

Hosking, Geoffrey, *A History of the Soviet Union*, 2nd edn (London, Fontana, 1990).

——, *The Awakening of the Soviet Union*, enlarged edn (London, Harvard University Press, 1991).

Keep, John, *Last of the Empires: A History of the Soviet Union, 1945–1991* (Oxford, Oxford University Press, 1996).

Kochan, Lionel and Keep, John, *The Making of Modern Russia* (Harmondsworth, Penguin, 1997).

Kort, Michael, *The Soviet Colossus: The Rise and Fall of the USSR*, 4th edn (London, M. E. Sharpe, 1996).

Lane, David, *The Rise and Fall of State Socialism* (Cambridge, Polity, 1996).

Malia, Martin, *The Soviet Tragedy: A History of Socialism in Russia* (New York, The Free Press, 1994).

McAuley, Mary, *Soviet Politics: 1917–1991* (Oxford, Oxford University Press, 1992).

McCauley, Martin, *The Soviet Union, 1917–1991*, 2nd edn (Harlow, Longman, 1993).

Medish, Vadim, *The Soviet Union*, revised 4th edn (Englewood Cliffs, NJ, Prentice Hall, 1991).

Reshetar, John S. Jr., *The Soviet Polity* (New York and Toronto, Dodd, Mead, 1971).

Riasanovsky, Nicholas V., *A History of Russia*, 5th edn (Oxford, Oxford University Press, 1993).

Sakwa, Richard, *Soviet Politics in Perspective*, 2nd edn (London, Routledge, 1998).

Service, Robert, *A History of Twentieth-century Russia* (Harmondsworth, Penguin, 1997).

Shipler, D. K., *Russia: Broken Idols, Solemn Dreams* (London, MacDonald, 1983).

Thompson, John M., *Russia and the Soviet Union: An Historical Introduction from the Kievan State to the Present*, 3rd edn (Boulder, CO, Westview Press, 1994).

Treadgold, Donald W., *Twentieth Century Russia*, 8th edn (Boulder, Westview Press, 1995).

Von Laue, Theodore H., *Why Lenin? Why Stalin?*, 2nd edn (Philadelphia, Lippincott, 1971).

Ward, Chris (ed.), *The Stalinist Dictatorship* (London, Arnold, 1998).

Westwood, John, *Endurance and Endeavour: Russian History, 1812–1992*, 4th edn (Oxford, Oxford University Press, 1993).

Bibliography

The Action Programme of the Czechoslovak Communist Party (Nottingham, Spokesman Books, 1972).

Akhmatova, Anna, *Poems*, selected and translated by Lyn Coffin, Introduction by Joseph Brodsky (New York, W. W. Norton & Co., 1983).

Amalrik, Andrei, *Will the Soviet Union Survive until 1984?*, edited by Hilary Sternberg, revised and expanded edn (London, Harper Colophon Books, 1981).

Andreyev, Catherine, *Vlasov and the Russian Liberation Movement: Soviet Reality and Emigré Theories* (Cambridge, Cambridge University Press, 1987).

Andropov, Yu. V., *Speeches and Writings*, 2nd edn (Oxford, Pergamon Press, 1983).

Avrich, Paul, *Kronstadt 1921* (Princeton, Princeton University Press, 1970).

Bakunin, Michael, *Statism and Anarchy*, translated and edited by Marshall S. Shatz (Cambridge, Cambridge University Press, 1990).

Berdyaev, Nicholas, *The Russian Revolution* (London, Sheed & Ward, 1931).

——, *The Origin of Russian Communism* (Michigan, Ann Arbor Paperback, 1960).

Berkman, Alexander, *The Bolshevik Myth* (London, Pluto Press, 1989).

Bernshtam, M. S. (ed.), *Nezavisimoe rabochee dvizhenie v 1918 godu: dokumenty i materialy* (Paris, YMCA-Press, 1981).

Bethell, N., *The Last Secret: Forcible Repatriation to Russia* (Sevenoaks, Coronet, 1974).

Bogdanov, Alexander A., *Empiriomonism* (St Petersburg, 1905–6).

——, *Voprosy sotsializma* (Moscow, Politicheskaya literatura, 1990).

The Bolsheviks and the October Revolution: Minutes of the Central Committee of the Russian Social-Democratic Labour Party (bolsheviks), August 1917–February 1918, translated by Ann Bone (London, Pluto Press, 1974).

Brezhnev, L. I., *Aktual'nye voprosy ideologicheskoi raboty KPSS*, vol. 1 (Moscow, Politizdat, 1978).

British and Foreign State Papers, 1947, Part II, vol. 148 (London, Her Majesty's Stationery Office, 1955).

Browder, Robert Paul and Kerensky, Alexander F. (eds), *The Russian Provisional Government 1917: Documents*, vol. III (Stanford, Stanford University Press, 1961).

Brown, John, *I Saw for Myself* (London, Selwyn and Blount, n.d.).

Bukharin, N. I. *Put' k sotsializmu* (Novosibirsk, Nauka, 1990).

——, *Revolyutsiya orava: sbornik pervi* (Moscow, 1925).

——, *Pervyi vserossiiskii s''ezd Sovetov rabochikh I soldatskikh deputatov; stenografischeskii otchet* (Moscow and Leningrad, 1930).

Bukharin, N. and Preobrazhensky, E., *The ABC of Communism*, Introduction by E. H. Carr (Harmondsworth, Penguin, 1969).

Bukovsky, Vladimir, *To Build a Castle: My Life as a Dissenter*, translated by Michael Scammell (London, André Deutsch, 1978).

Bunyan, James and Fisher, H. H., *The Bolshevik Revolution, 1917–1818: Documents and Materials* (Stanford, Stanford University Press, 1934).

Burlatsky, Fyodor, *The Modern State and Politics* (Moscow, Progress, 1978).

Carr, E. H., *The Interregnum* (London, Macmillan, 1954).

Churchill, Winston, *The Second World War: The Gathering Storm* (London, Cassell/The Reprint Society, 1948).

——, *The Second World War: Triumph and Tragedy* (Boston, Houghton Mifflin, 1953).

Cohen, Stephen F. (ed.), *An End to Silence: Uncensored Opinion in the Soviet Union* (New York, W. W. Norton, 1982).

Crossman, Richard, (ed.), *The God That Failed: Six Studies in Communism* (London, Hamish Hamilton, 1950).

Daniels, R. V. (ed.), *A Documentary History of Communism*: vol. 1, *Communism in Russia*; vol. 2, *Communism and the World* (London, I. B. Tauris, 1987).

Dashichev, V. I., *Bankrotstvo strategii germanskogo fashizma: istoricheskie ocherki, dokumenty i materialy*, vol. 2 (Moscow, 1973).

Davies, Joseph E., *Mission to Moscow* (London, Victor Gollancz, 1942).

Deutscher, Isaac, *The Unfinished Revolution: Russia 1917–1967* (Oxford, Oxford University Press, 1967).

Djilas, Milovan, *The New Class* (New York, Praeger, 1957).

——, *Conversations with Stalin* (Harmondsworth, Pelican, 1969).

Documents of the 1923 Opposition (London, New Park Publications, 1975).

Drugaya voina 1939–1945 (Moscow, RGGU, 1996).

Dukes, Paul, *Red Dusk and the Morrow: Adventures and Investigations in Red Russia* (London, Williams and Norgate, 1923).

Dzyuba, Ivan, *Internationalism or Russification? A Study in the Soviet Nationalities Problem* (New York, Monad Press, 1974).

Elliot, M., *Pawns of Yalta: Soviet Refugees and America's Role in Their Repatriation* (Urbana, University of Illinois Press, 1982).

Elwood, Ralph Carter (ed.), *Resolutions and Decisions of the Communist*

Party of the Soviet Union, vol. 1, *The Russian Social Democratic Labour Party 1898–October 1917* (Toronto, University of Toronto Press, 1974).

Fel'tshtinskii, Yu. G., *Razgovory s Bukharinym* (Moscow, Izd-vo gumanitarnoi literatury, 1993).

Frank, S. L., 'Religiozno-istoricheskii smysl russkoi revolyutsii', in M. A. Maslin (ed.), *Russkaya ideya* (Moscow, Respublika, 1992).

Freeze, Gregory L. (ed.), *From Supplication to Revolution: A Documentary Social History of Imperial Russia* (Oxford, Oxford University Press, 1988).

Gorbachev, M., *Izbrannye rechi i stat'i*, vol. 4 (Moscow, Izd-vo politicheskoi literatury, 1987).

——, *Perestroika: New Thinking for our Country and the World* (London, Collins/Harvill, 1987).

——, *Izbrannye rechi i stat'i*, vol. 5 (Moscow, Izd-vo politicheskoi literatury, 1988).

——, *Izbrannye rechi i stat'i*, vol. 6 (Moscow, Politizdat, 1989).

Grossman, Vasily, *Life and Fate* (London, The Harvill Press, 1995).

Harrison, Mark, 'Soviet Economic Growth Since 1928: The Alternative Statistics of G. I. Khanin', *Europe-Asia Studies*, vol. 45, no. 1 (1993), pp. 141–67.

Istoriya otechestva v dokumentakh, 1917–1993gg: khrestomatiya dlya uchashchikhsya starshikh klassov srednei shkoly, vol. 1, 1917–20, edited by G. V. Klokova; vol. 2, 1921–39, edited by L. I. Larina; vol. 3, 1939–45, edited by A. G. Koloskov and E. A. Gevurkova; vol. 4, 1945–93, edited by A. G. Koloskov, E. A. Gevurkova and G. A. Tsvetkova (Moscow, Ilbi, 1994).

Istoriya sovetskoi politicheskoi tsenzury: dokumenty i kommentarii (Moscow, Rosspen, 1997).

IX konferentsiya RKP(b), sentyabr' 1920g: protokoly (Moscow, 1972).

Jacobs, Dan J., *From Marx to Mao and Marchais* (London, Longman, 1979).

Kataev, Valentine, *Forward, Oh Time!*, translated by Charles Malamuth (London, Victor Gollancz, 1934).

Kautsky, Karl, *The Dictatorship of the Proletariat* (Michigan, Ann Arbor Paperback, 1964).

Kennan, George F., *Memoirs 1950–63* (New York, Bantam, 1969).

—— [Mr X], 'The Sources of Soviet Conduct', *Foreign Affairs*, vol. 25, no. 4 (July 1947), pp. 566–82.

Khanin, G. I., *Dinamika ekonomicheskogo razvitiya SSSR* (Novosibirsk, Nauka, 1991).

Khrestomatiya po istorii Rossii, 1917–1940, edited by M. E. Glavatskii, 2nd edn (Moscow, Aspekt Press, 1995).

Khrushchev, N. S., *Khrushchev Remembers*, Introduction by Edward Crankshaw, translated by Strobe Talbott (London, Book Club Associates, 1971).

——, *The Secret Speech*, Introduction by Zhores Medvedev and Roy Medvedev (Nottingham, Spokesman Books, 1976).

Kollontai, Alexandra, *The Workers' Opposition in Russia* (London, Dreadnought Publishers, 1923).

Konstitutsiya (osnovnoi zakon) RSFSR (Moscow, Politizdat, 1980).

Kowalski, Ronald I. (ed.), *Kommunist: A Weekly Journal of Economic, Political and Social Opinion* (Millwood, NY, Kraus International Publications, 1990).

——, *The Russian Revolution, 1917–1921* (London, Routledge, 1997).

KPSS v rezolyutsiyakh s''ezdov, konferentsii i plenumov TsK (Moscow, Politizdat, 1983).

Kravchenko, Victor, *I Chose Freedom: The Personal and Political Life of a Soviet Official* (London, Robert Hale, 1947).

Kuznetsov, Anatoly, *Babi Yar: A Documentary Novel* (London, Sphere Books, 1969).

Lenin, V. I., *Polnoe sobranie sochinenii*, 5th edn (Moscow, 1975–9).

——, *Selected Works* (London, Lawrence & Wishart, 1969).

Ligachev, Yegor, *Inside Gorbachev's Kremlin* (Boulder, Westview Press, 1996).

Lukács, Georg, *History and Class Consciousness* (London, Merlin Press, 1971).

Luxemburg, Rosa, *Leninism or Marxism?* (Ann Arbor, University of Michigan Press, 1961).

——, *The Russian Revolution* (Ann Arbor, University of Michigan Press, 1961).

Machajski, Jan Wacław, *Burzhuaznaia revolyutsiia irabochee delo* (*The Bourgeois Revolution and the Workers' Cause*) (St Petersburg, 1906).

——, *Umstvennyi rabochii* (*The Intellectual Worker*) (Geneva, 1904).

Mandelshtam, Nadezhda, *Hope Abandoned*, translated by Max Hayward (Harmondsworth, Penguin Books, 1974).

Markovic, Mihailo, and Cohen, Robert S., *The Rise and Fall of Socialist Humanism* (Nottingham, Spokesman Books, 1975).

Marx, Karl, and Engels, Frederick, *The Communist Manifesto*, edited by David McLellan (Oxford, Oxford University Press, 1992).

Mif o zastoe (Leningrad, Lenizdat, 1991).

Mattick, Paul, *Anti-Bolshevik Communism* (London, Merlin Press, 1978).

McCauley, Martin, *The Origins of the Cold War* (London, Longman, 1983).

—— (ed.), *The Russian Revolution and the Soviet State, Documents, 1917–21* (London, Macmillan, 1975).

McDermott, Kevin, and Agnew, Jeremy, *The Comintern: A History of International Communism from Lenin to Stalin* (Basingstoke and London, Macmillan, 1996).

McNeal, R. H., (ed.), *Resolutions and Decisions of the CPSU* (Toronto, University of Toronto Press, 1974).

——— (ed.), I. V. Stalin, *Works*, vol. 3 (16) (Stanford, The Hoover Institution, 1967).

Medvedev, Roy A., *On Socialist Democracy*, translated and edited by Ellen de Kadt (Nottingham, Spokesman Books, 1977).

Mif o zastoe (Leningrad, Lenizdat, 1991).

Nicolaevsky, Boris, *Power and the Soviet Elite* (New York, Praeger, 1965).

O partiinoi i sovetskoi pechati, radioveshchanii i televidenii: sbornik dokumentov i materialov (Moscow, 1972).

Osinskii, V. V. 'Minority Report on Building the Economy', Ninth Party Congress, March 1920, *Devyati s"ezd RKP(b) (mart-aprel' 1920g): protokoly* (Moscow, Politizdat, 1960).

Pashukanis, Evgeny B., *Law and Marxism: A General Theory: Towards a Critique of the Fundamental Juridical Concepts* (London, Pluto Press, 1989).

Plyushch, Leonid, *History's Carnival: A Dissident's Autobiography* (London, Collins/Harvill Press, 1979).

Preobrazhenskii, E. A., 'Osnovnoi zakon sotsialisticheskogo nakopleniya', *Put' razvitiya: diskussi 20-x godov* (Leningrad, Lenizdat, 1990).

Programme of the Communist Party of the Soviet Union (Moscow, Foreign Languages Publishing House, 1916).

Protokoly TsK RSDRP(b): avgust 1917–fevral' 1918 (Moscow, Politizdat, 1958).

Rakovsky, Christian, *Selected Writings on Opposition in the USSR* (London, Allison & Busby, 1980).

Reed, John, *Ten Days That Shook the World* (Harmondsworth, Penguin Books, 1966).

Rossiya, kotoruyu my ne znali 1939–1993: khrestomatiya, edited by M. E. Glavatskii (Chelyabinsk, Yuzhno-ural'skoe knizhnoe izdatel'stvo, 1995).

Russell, Bertrand, *The Practice and Theory of Bolshevism* (London, George Allen & Unwin, 1920).

Sakharov, Andrei, 'All Power to the Soviets', *XX Century and Peace*, no. 8 (1991), pp. 9–12.

———, 'On Alexander Solzhenitsyn's "A Letter to the Soviet Leaders"', *Kontinent* (New York, Anchor Press/Doubleday, 1976).

———, *Trevoga i nadezhda* (Moscow, Inter-Verso, 1990).

Saunders, George (ed.), *Samizdat: Voices of the Soviet Opposition* (New York, Monad Press, 1974).

Shanin, Teodor (ed.), *Late Marx and the Russian Road: Marx and 'the Peripheries of Capitalism'* (London, Routledge & Kegan Paul, 1983).

Shatz, Marshall S., *Jan Waclaw Machajski: A Radical Critic of the Russian Intelligentsia and Socialism* (Pittsburgh, University of Pittsburgh Press, 1989).

Shevardnadze, Eduard, *The Future Belongs to Freedom* (London, Sinclair-Stevenson, 1991).

Soloukhin, Vladimir, *Chitaya Lenina* (*Reading Lenin*) (Moscow, samizdat mimeo).

Solzhenitsyn, Alexander, *Letter to Soviet Leaders*, translated by Hilary Sternberg (London, Collins/Harvill, 1974).

——, *One Day in the Life of Ivan Denisovich* (Harmondsworth, Penguin, 1963).

—— (ed.), *From under the Rubble* (London, Fontana/ Collins, 1974).

Spravochnik partiinogo rabotnika, issue 26 (Moscow, Politizdat, 1986).

Stalin, J., *Voprosy Leninizma* (*Problems of Leninism*), 3rd edn (Moscow, Gosizdat, 1931).

——, *Problems of Leninism* (Moscow, Foreign Languages Publishing House, 1947).

——, *Ekonomicheskie problemy sotsializma v SSSR* (*Economic Problems of Socialism in the USSR*) (Moscow, Gospolitizdat, 1952).

——, *War Speeches* (London, Hutchinson, n.d.).

Stojanovic, Svetozar, 'The Epochal Dilemma', *Between Ideals and Reality* (New York, Oxford University Press, 1973).

Struve, Petr, *Vekhi: sbornik statei o russkoi intelligentsii* (Moscow, 1909).

Tolstoy, N., *Victims of Yalta* (London, Hodder & Stoughton, 1979).

Trotsky, Leon, *The History of the Russian Revolution*, translated by Max Eastman (London, Victor Gollancz, 1934).

——, *The New Course*, annotated and translated by Max Shachtman (London, New Park Publications, 1956).

——, *The Revolution Betrayed* (London, New Park Publications, 1973).

——, *Terrorism and Communism: A Reply to Karl Kautsky* (London, New Park Publications, 1975).

Vneshyaya politika SSSR: sbornik dokumentov, vol. IV (Moscow, 1946).

Vozvrahchenie k pravde: reabilitirovan posmertno (Moscow, Yuridicheskaya literatura, 1988).

Webb, Sidney and Beatrice, *The Truth about Soviet Russia* (London, Longman, Green & Co., 1942).

Yevtushenko, Yevgeny, 'Babii Yar', *Yevgeny Yevtushenko: Early Poems*, translated by George Reavey (London, Marion Boyars, 1989).

Zajdłerowa, Zoë, *The Dark Side of the Moon*, edited by John Coutouvidis and Thomas Lane (London, Harvester Wheatsheaf, 1989).

Zaslavskaya, Tatyana, 'The Novosibirsk Report', *Survey*, vol. 28, no. 1 (spring 1984), pp. 83–108.

Index